Frommer's

Tokyo
8th Edition

by Beth Reiber

Here's what the critics say about Frommer's:

"Amazingly easy to use. Very portable, very complete."
—*Booklist*

"Detailed, accurate, and easy-to-read information for all price ranges."
—*Glamour Magazine*

"Hotel information is close to encyclopedic."
—*Des Moines Sunday Register*

"Frommer's Guides have a way of giving you a real feel for a place."
—*Knight Ridder Newspapers*

WILEY
Wiley Publishing, Inc.

About the Author

Beth Reiber worked for several years in Tokyo as editor of the *Far East Traveler*. Now a freelance writer residing in Lawrence, Kansas, with her husband and two sons, she is the author of several Frommer's guides including *Frommer's Japan* and *Frommer's Hong Kong*. She is a contributor to *Frommer's Europe from $70 a Day*, *Frommer's USA*, and *Frommer's Southeast Asia*.

Published by:

Wiley Publishing, Inc.

111 River St.
Hoboken, NJ 07030-5774

ISBN 0-7645-4322-9

Editor: Caroline Sieg
Production Editor: Ian Skinnari
Cartographer: Roberta Stockwell
Photo Editor: Richard Fox
Production by Wiley Indianapolis Composition Services

Front cover photo: Woman in kimono standing on subway platform
Back cover photo: Low angle of businessmen in traditional bow of greeting

For information on our other products and services or to obtain technical support, please contact our Customer Care Department within the U.S. at 800/762-2974, outside the U.S. at 317/572-3993 or fax 317/572-4002.

Wiley also publishes its books in a variety of electronic formats. Some content that appears in print may not be available in electronic formats.

Manufactured in the United States of America

5 4 3 2 1

Contents

6   What to See & Do in Tokyo   155

7   Tokyo Strolls   183

8   Shopping   203

9   Tokyo After Dark   222

10   Side Trips from Tokyo   242

List of Maps

An Invitation to the Reader

In researching this book, we discovered many wonderful places—hotels, restaurants, shops, and more. We're sure you'll find others. Please tell us about them, so we can share the information with your fellow travelers in upcoming editions. If you were disappointed with a recommendation, we'd love to know that, too. Please write to:

Frommer's Tokyo, 8th Edition
Wiley Publishing, Inc. • 111 River St. • Hoboken, NJ 07030-5774

An Additional Note

Please be advised that travel information is subject to change at any time—and this is especially true of prices. We therefore suggest that you write or call ahead for confirmation when making your travel plans. The authors, editors, and publisher cannot be held responsible for the experiences of readers while traveling. Your safety is important to us, however, so we encourage you to stay alert and be aware of your surroundings. Keep a close eye on cameras, purses, and wallets, all favorite targets of thieves and pickpockets.

Other Great Guides for Your Trip:

Frommer's Japan

Frommer's Star Ratings, Icons & Abbreviations

Every hotel, restaurant, and attraction listing in this guide has been ranked for quality, value, service, amenities, and special features using a **star-rating system.** In country, state, and regional guides, we also rate towns and regions to help you narrow down your choices and budget your time accordingly. Hotels and restaurants are rated on a scale of zero (recommended) to three stars (exceptional). Attractions, shopping, nightlife, towns, and regions are rated according to the following scale: zero stars (recommended), one star (highly recommended), two stars (very highly recommended), and three stars (must-see).

In addition to the star-rating system, we also use **seven feature icons** that point you to the great deals, in-the-know advice, and unique experiences that separate travelers from tourists. Throughout the book, look for:

Finds	Special finds—those places only insiders know about
Fun Fact	Fun facts—details that make travelers more informed and their trips more fun
Kids	Best bets for kids and advice for the whole family
Moments	Special moments—those experiences that memories are made of
Overrated	Places or experiences not worth your time or money
Tips	Insider tips—great ways to save time and money
Value	Great values—where to get the best deals

The following **abbreviations** are used for credit cards:

AE	American Express	DISC	Discover	V	Visa
DC	Diners Club	MC	MasterCard		

Frommers.com

Now that you have the guidebook to a great trip, visit our website at **www.frommers.com** for travel information on more than 3,000 destinations. With features updated regularly, we give you instant access to the most current trip-planning information available. At Frommers.com, you'll also find the best prices on airfares, accommodations, and car rentals—and you can even book travel online through our travel booking partners. At Frommers.com, you'll also find the following:

- Online updates to our most popular guidebooks
- Vacation sweepstakes and contest giveaways
- Newsletter highlighting the hottest travel trends
- Online travel message boards with featured travel discussions

What's New in Tokyo

Here are the latest openings, offerings, and events in Tokyo.

PLANNING YOUR TRIP TO TOKYO Visitor Information The Japan National Tourist Organization has closed its Chicago office but maintains offices in New York, Los Angeles, San Francisco, Toronto, and other locations around the world.

Health & Safety Although nine cases of **mad cow disease** have been confirmed in Japan since its first outbreak in 2001, fears of the disease have receded since regulations went into effect stipulating that all slaughtered cows must be tested for the disease. Most restaurants specializing in beef that switched to other dishes following the initial scare have now resumed serving beef.

Getting from Narita Airport to Tokyo Train reservations for the Narita Express (which travels between Narita Airport and Tokyo Station) can be booked online at www.world.eki-net.com up to 1 month in advance. See p. 33.

GETTING TO KNOW TOKYO Visitor Information Both the **Tourist Information Center (TIC,** managed by the Japan National Tourist Organization) and the **Tokyo Tourist Information Center** (operated by the Tokyo Metropolitan Government) have moved out of their expensive digs in the Tokyo International Forum to opposite ends of town. The TIC moved just a short distance away to rather cramped quarters on the 10th floor of the Tokyo Kotsu Kaikan Building at 2–10–1 Yuraku-cho (🕿 **03/3201-3331**), while the Tokyo Tourist Information Center is now ensconced in Shinjuku on the first floor of the Tokyo Metropolitan Government Building No. 1 (which also has a great, free observatory on the 45th floor).

Neighborhoods in Brief Several Tokyo neighborhoods have undergone wide-scale makeovers, most notably Roppongi with its 11-hectare (28-acre) **Roppongi Hills** filled with offices, shops, restaurants, apartments, hotel, sophisticated cinema complex, and art museum. Other construction projects are under way or have been completed on land auctioned off by Japan National Railways; all are located near major train stations, including Shinagawa, Shiodome (near Tokyo Bay), and Tokyo stations.

Getting Around Odaiba, a man-made island in Tokyo Bay and home to hotels, shopping complexes, several museums, and other attractions, can now be reached not only by the Yurikamome Line monorail but also by the **JR Saikyo Line** (18 min. from Shibuya) and the **Rinkai Line** from Osaki Station. See p. 48.

WHERE TO STAY Although the local tax was abolished a couple of years ago, Tokyo has since reinstated a **hotel tax** of ¥100 (85¢) per person per night for rates between ¥10,000 and ¥14,999 ($83–$125); and ¥200 ($1.65) for rates ¥15,000 and up.

Several long-time, moderately priced hotels have closed in Tokyo, victims of the recession and unable to compete with more up-to-date additions. The list includes Hotel Alcyone in the Ginza, the Holiday Inn Tokyo near Nihombashi, and the Fairmont Hotel with its enviable location on the palace moat.

On the other hand, several upper-end hotels have come on the scene in the past 2 years, including the exclusive **Four Seasons Hotel Tokyo at Marunouchi,** 1–11–1 Marunouchi (✆ **03/5222-7222**), with its great location next to Tokyo Station; The **Strings Hotel Tokyo,** 2–16–1 Konan in Shinagawa (✆ **03/4562-1111**); and the **Grand Hyatt Tokyo** in Roppongi Hills (✆ **03/4333-1234**). See chapter 4.

WHERE TO DINE Two fast-growing chains you're likely to hear more about are those belonging to **Wolfgang Puck** who, in addition to his Wolfgang Puck Bar and Grill in Roppongi Hills (✆ **03/5786-9630**), plans to open 100 more outlets in Japan over the next 10 years; and Global Dining, which has outlets for **Gonpachi** (Japanese cuisine), **Zest Cantina** (Tex-Mex), **La Boheme** (Italian), and **Monsoon** (Southeast Asian) at many hot spots around town. All

four outlets are open daily 11:30am to 5am. See chapter 5.

WHAT TO SEE & DO IN TOKYO With drills deep beneath the earth's crust releasing thermal waters right in the heart of Tokyo, Tokyoites no longer have to travel out of town to soak away their cares in hot-spring spas. **Oedo-Onsen Monogatari** on Odaiba (✆ **03/5500-1126**) is designed like bathhouses of yore and features shops, restaurants, massage rooms, sand baths, indoor/outdoor baths, and saunas. See p. 165. **Spa LaQua,** 1–1–1 Kasuga (✆ **03/3817-4173**), is a modern bathing facility next to Korakuen's Tokyo Dome City Complex and an adjoining amusement park. See p. 165.

TOKYO AFTER DARK Films Nonexistent in Japan just a decade ago, cinema complexes have revived the film industry and now account for more than half the country's screens. One of the newest and plushest is **Virgin Cinemas** in Roppongi Hills (✆ **03/5775-6090**), offering seven screens, plus a Premier Zone with armchair seating and a bar. Best of all: Movies are shown till midnight Sunday to Wednesday and till 5am the rest of the week. See p. 241.

The Best of Tokyo

Describing Tokyo to someone who has never been here is a formidable task. After all, how do you describe a city that—as one of my friends visiting Tokyo for the first time put it—seems like part of another planet?

To be sure, Tokyo is very different from Western capitals, but what really sets it apart is its people. Approximately 12 million people reside within Tokyo's 1,288 sq. km (800 sq. miles), and almost one-fourth of Japan's total population lives within commuting distance of the city. This translates into a crush of humanity that packs the subways, crowds the sidewalks, and fills the department stores beyond belief. In some parts of the city, the streets are as crowded at 3am as they are at 3pm. With its high-energy, visual overload, Tokyo makes even New York seem like a sleepy, laid-back town.

And yet, despite its limited space for harmonious living, Tokyo remains one of the safest cities in the world, with remarkably little crime or violence. No matter how lost I may become, I know that people will go out of their way to help me. Hardworking, honest, and helpful to strangers, the Japanese are their country's greatest asset.

With Tokyo so densely packed, it comes as no shock to learn that land here is more valuable than gold, and that buildings are built practically on top of each other, shaped like pieces in a jigsaw puzzle to fit the existing plots of real estate. More than perhaps any other city in the world, Japan's capital is a concrete jungle, with a few parks but not many trees to break the monotony, and it stretches on and on as far as the eye can see. Fires, earthquakes, wars, the zeal for modernization, and the price of land have taken their tolls on the city, eradicating almost all evidence of previous centuries. It's as though Tokyo was born only this morning, with all the messy aftermath of a city conceived without plan and interested only in the future.

Thus, first-time visitors to Tokyo are almost invariably disappointed. They come expecting an exotic Asian city, but instead find a megalopolis Westernized to the point of drabness. Used to the grand edifices and monuments of Western cities, they look in vain for Tokyo's own monuments to its past—ancient temples, exquisite gardens, imperial palaces, or whatever else they've imagined. Instead they find what may be, quite arguably, one of the ugliest cities in the world.

So, while Tokyo is one of my favorite cities, my appreciation came only with time. When I first moved here, I was tormented by the unsettling feeling that I was somehow missing out on the "real" Tokyo. Even though I was living and working here, Tokyo seemed beyond my grasp: elusive, vague, and undefined. I felt that the meaning of the city was out there, if only I knew where to look.

With time, I finally learned that I needn't look farther than my own front window. Tokyo has no center, but rather is made up of a series of small towns and neighborhoods clustered together, each with its own history, flavor, and atmosphere. There are narrow residential streets, ma-and-pa shops, fruit stands, and stores. There's the neighborhood tofu factory, the lunch-box stand, the grocery shop, and the tiny police station, where the cops know the residents by name and patrol the area by bicycle. There are carefully pruned bonsai trees gracing sidewalks, women in kimono bowing and shuffling down streets, and wooden homes on impossibly narrow streets. Walk in the old downtown neighborhoods of Asakusa or Yanaka and you're worlds apart from the trendy quarters of Harajuku or the high-rises of Shinjuku. Neighborhoods like these make Tokyo lovable and livable.

What's more, once visitors get to know Tokyo better, they learn that you can't judge Tokyo by what it looks like on the outside, for this is a city of interiors. Even those concrete monsters may house interiors that are fascinating in design and innovation. In the basement of that drab building could well be a restaurant with wooden beams, mud walls, and thatched ceiling, imported intact from a farmhouse in the Japan Alps; on its roof could be a small Shinto shrine, while the top floor could house a high-tech bar or a sophisticated French restaurant.

And beneath Tokyo's concrete shell is a thriving cultural life left very much intact. In fact, if you're interested in Japan's performing arts as well as such diverse activities as the tea ceremony or sumo, Tokyo is your best bet for offering the most at any one time. It is rich in museums and claims the largest repository of Japanese art in the world. It also gets my vote as the pop-art capital of the world, so if you're into kitsch, you'll be in high heaven. I can't imagine being bored here for even a minute.

1 Frommer's Favorite Tokyo Experiences

- **Strolling Through Asakusa.** No place better conveys the atmosphere of old Tokyo than Asakusa. Sensoji Temple is the city's oldest and most popular temple, and Nakamise Dori, the pedestrian lane leading to the temple, is lined with shops selling souvenirs and traditional Japanese goods. As in days of yore, arrive by boat via the Sumida River. See "Walking Tour: Asakusa" on p. 183.

- **Catching the Action at Tsukiji Fish Market.** Get up early your first morning in Japan (you'll probably be wide awake with jet lag, anyway) and head straight for the country's largest fish market, where you can watch the tuna auctions, browse through stalls of seafood, and sample the freshest sushi you'll ever have. See "The Top Attractions" in chapter 6.

- **Viewing Treasures at the Tokyo National Museum.** It's a feast for the eyes at the largest museum of Japanese art in the world, where you can see everything from samurai armor and lacquerware to kimono and woodblock prints. If you visit only one museum in Tokyo, this should be it. See "The Top Attractions" in chapter 6.

- **Sitting Pretty in Shinjuku.** On the 45th floor of the Tokyo Metropolitan Government Office (TMG), designed by well-known architect Kenzo Tange, an observatory offers a bird's-eye view of Shinjuku's cluster of skyscrapers, the never-ending metropolis and, on fine winter days, Mount Fuji. Best of all, it's free. See "Spectacular City Views" in chapter 6.

- **Time Traveling in the Edo-Tokyo Museum.** Housed in a high-tech modern building, this ambitious museum chronicles the fascinating and somewhat tumultuous history of Tokyo (known as Edo during the Feudal Period), with models, replicas, artifacts, and dioramas. Guided tours in English are available for free. See "The Top Attractions" in chapter 6.

Japan

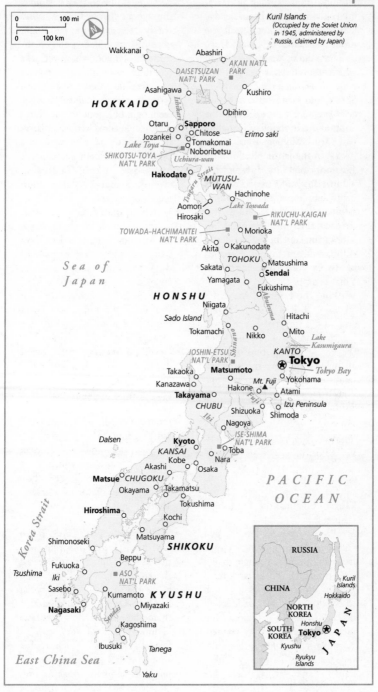

0 100 mi
0 100 km

Wakkanai

Abashiri

Kuril Islands
(Occupied by the Soviet Union
in 1945, administered by
Russia, claimed by Japan)

AKAN NAT'L
PARK

DAISETSUZAN
NAT'L PARK

Asahigawa

Kushiro

HOKKAIDO

Obihiro

Otaru **Sapporo**

Jozankei Chitose Erimo saki
Lake Toya Tomakomai
SHIKOTSU-TOYA Noboribetsu
NAT'L PARK Uchiura-wan

Hakodate

Ishikari

Tsugaru Strait

MUTUSU-
WAN

Hachinohe

Aomori Lake Towada
Hirosaki

RIKUCHU-KAIGAN
NAT'L PARK

TOWADA–HACHIMANTEI
NAT'L PARK Morioka

Akita Kakunodate

TOHOKU

Sakata Matsushima
Yamagata **Sendai**

Sea of
Japan

HONSHU

Fukushima

Niigata

Sado Island

Abukuma

Hitachi

Tokamachi Nikko Mito Lake
Kasumigaura

Shinano

JOSHIN-ÉTSU
NAT'L PARK

KANTO
⊛ **Tokyo**
Tokyo Bay

Takaoka

Kanazawa **Matsumoto**

Takayama Hakone Mt. Fuji ▲ Yokohama
Atami

CHUBU Shizuoka Izu Peninsula
Shimoda

Ibi Fuji

Nagoya

Dalsen ISE-SHIMA
NAT'L PARK

Kyoto
KANSAI Toba
Kobe Nara

Akashi Osaka

Matsue CHUGOKU

Okayama Takamatsu

PACIFIC
OCEAN

Korea Strait

Hiroshima

Tokushima

Kochi

Shimonoseki Matsuyama

SHIKOKU

Fukuoka Beppu

Tsushima Iki ASO
NAT'L PARK

Sasebo Kumamoto **KYUSHU**

Nagasaki Miyazaki

Sendai

Kagoshima

Ibusuki Tanega

East China Sea

Yaku

RUSSIA

CHINA Kuril
Islands

Hokkaido

NORTH
KOREA

SOUTH Honshu
KOREA ⊛ **Tokyo**

Kyushu Ryukyu
Islands

JAPAN

- **Hanging Out in Harajuku.** Nothing beats Sunday in Harajuku, where you can begin the day leisurely with brunch, stroll the promenade of Omotesando Dori, shop the area's many boutiques, take in a museum or two and perhaps a flea market, visit Meiji Shrine, and then relax over drinks at a sidewalk cafe watching the hordes of teenyboppers parading past. See "Walking Tour: Harajuku & Aoyama" on p. 188.

- **Escaping Big-City Life in the Temple Town of Yanaka.** With its many temples, offbeat attractions, sloping hills, and peaceful narrow streets, the neighborhood of Yanaka makes for a wonderful half-day escape from the crowds of Tokyo. See "Walking Tour: Yanaka" on p. 196.

- **Walking the Imperial Moat.** It's an easy, 4.8km (3-mile) walk around the Imperial Palace moat, especially beautiful in spring when the many cherry blossoms are aflame. Don't miss the attached (and free) East Garden. See "The Top Attractions" in chapter 6.

- **Taking Part in a Festival.** Tokyo offers a myriad of annual festivals, ranging from processions of portable shrines to ladder-top acrobatics. Be ready to battle good-natured crowds, as festivals can be unbelievably packed. See "Tokyo Calendar of Events" in chapter 2.

- **Strolling a Japanese Landscaped Garden.** There's no better escape from Tokyo's urban jungle than a stroll through one of its landscaped gardens, especially in spring, when irises, wisteria, peonies, azaleas, and other flowers are in bloom. Top picks are Hama Rikyu Garden, Koishikawa Korakuen, Shinjuku Gyoen and—in nearby Yokohama—Sankei-en Garden. See "Parks & Gardens" in chapter 6.

- **Viewing Cherry Blossoms at Ueno Park.** Ueno Park is famous throughout Japan for its 1,000 cherry trees, attracting multitudes of company employees and organizations. It's not, however, the communing with nature you might think, as everyone drinks, eats, dances, and sings karaoke, seemingly oblivious to the shimmering blossoms above. Observing Tokyoites at play here is a cultural experience you won't forget. See "Parks & Gardens" in chapter 6 and "Walking Tour: Ueno" on p. 192.

- **Watching the Fat Guys Wrestle.** Nothing beats watching huge, almost-nude sumo wrestlers, most weighing well over 300 pounds, throw each other around. Matches are held in Tokyo in January, May, and September; catch one on TV if you can't make it in person. Great fun and not to be missed. See "Spectator Sports" in chapter 6.

- **Getting a Massage.** After a hard day of work or sightseeing, nothing beats a relaxing massage. *Shiatsu*, or pressure-point massage, is available in the privacy of your room at virtually all first-class and most medium-range Tokyo hotels, as well as at a number of clinics in the city, many of which offer acupuncture as well. See "Five Unforgettable Ways to Immerse Yourself in Japanese Culture" in chapter 6.

- **Soaking Away your Cares.** Tokyo now has its own hot-spring spas, thanks to drilling that released therapeutic waters from deep below the surface. Top on my list is **Oedo-Onsen Monogatari,** a theme-based spa that emulates bathing houses of yore with its Feudal Period replica architecture, shops, restaurants, indoor and outdoor baths, massage rooms, and more. See "Five Unforgettable

Ways to Immerse Yourself in Japanese Culture" on p. 165.

- **Appreciating the Beauty of Ikebana.** After seeing how flowers, branches, and vases can be combined into works of art, you'll never be able to simply throw flowers into a vase again. You can learn the basics of *ikebana,* Japanese flower arranging, at several schools in Tokyo. Exhibitions of ikebana are held regularly at Yasukuni Shrine and department stores. See "Five Unforgettable Ways to Immerse Yourself in Japanese Culture" in chapter 6.

- **Experiencing the Serenity of the Tea Ceremony.** Developed in the 16th century as a means to achieve inner harmony with nature, the tea ceremony is a highly ritualized process that takes years to learn. You can experience a shortened version at several Tokyo hotels. See "Five Unforgettable Ways to Immerse Yourself in Japanese Culture" in chapter 6.

- **Browsing the Electronics Shops of Akihabara Electric Town.** Even if you don't buy anything, it's great fun—and very educational— to see the latest in electronic gadgets in Japan's largest electronics district, which offers many products unknown in Western markets. See "Shopping A to Z" in chapter 8.

- **Hunting for Bargains at Flea Markets.** You never know what treasure you might find at one of Tokyo's monthly outdoor flea markets, where vendors sell everything from used kimono to antiques and curios. Go early, and be sure to bargain. See "Shopping A to Z" in chapter 8.

- **Getting the Royal Treatment at Department Stores.** Tokyo's department stores are huge, spotless, and filled with merchandise you never knew existed; many also have first-rate art galleries. Shibuya and Ginza boast the greatest concentration of department stores. Tobu, in Ikebukuro, is the city's largest—a virtual city in itself. Service in a Japanese department store is an unparalleled experience: Be there when it opens, and you'll see employees lined up at the front door, bowing to incoming customers. See "Shopping A to Z" in chapter 8.

- **Shopping for Japanese Designer Clothes.** Japanese designer clothing is often outrageous, occasionally practical, but always fun. Department stores, designer boutiques in Aoyama, and secondhand shops in Ebisu are the places to try on the digs—assuming you've got both the money and the figure. See "Shopping A to Z" in chapter 8.

- **Feasting on a Kaiseki Meal.** Although expensive, a *kaiseki* feast, consisting of dish after dish of artfully displayed delectables, may well be the most beautiful and memorable meal you'll ever have. Splurge at least once on the most expensive kaiseki meal you can afford, and you'll feel like royalty. See "Tips on Dining, Japanese Style," in chapter 5.

- **Rubbing Elbows in a Yakitoriya.** There's no better place to observe Tokyo's army of office workers at play than at a *yakitoriya,* a drinking man's pub that also sells skewered grilled chicken and bar snacks. It's fun, noisy, and boisterous. See "Tips on Dining, Japanese Style," in chapter 5.

- **Attending a Kabuki Play at the Kabukiza Theater.** Kabuki has served as the most popular form of entertainment for the masses since the Edo Period. Watch the audience as they yell their approval; watch the stage for its gorgeous costumes, stunning settings, and easy-to-understand dramas of love, duty, and revenge. See "The Performing Arts" in chapter 9.

- **Taking a Spin Through Kabuki-cho.** Shinjuku's Kabuki-cho has the craziest nightlife in all of Tokyo, with countless strip joints, porn shops, restaurants, bars, and the greatest concentration of neon (and drunks) you're likely to see anywhere. It's a fascinating place for an evening stroll. See "The Club & Music Scene" in chapter 9.

- **Clubbing in Roppongi.** You can dance the night away in the madness that is Roppongi; most revelers party till dawn. See "The Club & Music Scene" in chapter 9.

2 Best Bets for Accommodations

- **Best Historic Hotel:** Established in 1937, the **Hilltop Hotel,** 1–1 Surugadai, in Kanda (ⓒ **03/ 3293-2311**), boasts an Art Deco facade and was once a favorite haunt of writers. It's changed little over the decades. Endearing touches include fringed lampshades, doilies, cherrywood furniture, velvet curtains, old-fashioned heaters, and washlet toilets (combination toilets and spray bidets). A unique, old-fashioned hotel at reasonable prices. See p. 95.

- **Best Historic Japanese-Style Inn: Homeikan,** 5–10–5 Hongo (ⓒ **03/3811-1181**), consists of three historic buildings, one with a Japanese garden and very nice tatami rooms. A great choice for those who don't mind roughing it a bit (there are no private bathrooms), this is traditional Japanese living at inexpensive rates. See p. 98.

- **Best Modern Japanese-Style Inn:** With a great location in historic Asakusa, just a stone's throw from famous Sensoji Temple, **Ryokan Shigetsu,** 1–31–11 Asakusa (ⓒ **03/3843-2345**), is a modern, moderately priced Japanese-style inn that combines the best of the old and the new with simple yet elegant interiors that utilize natural woods and artwork throughout. If you want to experience a Japanese inn but don't want to sleep on a futon, stay in one of Shigetsu's Western-style rooms, but don't pass up the public bath with views of the five-story pagoda. See p. 96.

- **Best Hotel if Money is No Object: Park Hyatt Tokyo,** 3–7–1–2 Nishi-Shinjuku, in Shinjuku (ⓒ **800/233-1234** in the U.S. and Canada, or 03/5322-1234), is among the most gorgeous and sophisticated hotels in Japan, with rooms to die for, stunning views, and one of Tokyo's best restaurants. See p. 74.

- **Best Location: Four Seasons Hotel Tokyo at Marunouchi,** 1–11–1 Marunouchi, next to Tokyo Station (ⓒ **800/332-3442** in the U.S., or 03/5222-7222), provides easy access to Narita International Airport, the Shinkansen bullet train, and local commuter and subway lines, and is also within easy walking distance of financial districts and the Ginza. Yet with only 57 rooms, it cocoons guests from the mad swirl of central Tokyo with the best money can buy. See p. 71.

- **Best for Business Travelers: Imperial Hotel,** 1–1–1 Uchi-saiwai-cho, across from Hibiya Park (ⓒ **800/223-6800** in the U.S. and Canada, or 03/3504-1111), wins my vote as the best for business travelers, with its central location close to the Ginza and financial districts, excellent service, 17 restaurants and bars, 24-hour room service, an extensively equipped business center, comfortable rooms complete with three phones, a fax machine, free high-speed Internet access (and a private e-mail address for each guest), and a safe large enough for a briefcase. See p. 79.

- **Best for a Romantic Getaway:** Nothing beats a weekend getaway to the historic **Fujiya Hotel,** in Hakone (© **0460/2-2211**). Established in 1878, it is one of Japan's finest, most majestic hotels, boasting great views, Japanese- and Western-style architecture, a wonderful 1930s dining hall, and a large landscaped garden perfect for moonlit walks. See p. 270.
- **Best Trendy Hotel: Hotel Sofitel,** 2–1–48 Ikenohata, in Ueno (© **800/221-4542** in the U.S. and Canada, or 03/5685-7111), is not only Tokyo's most uniquely shaped hotel—five trapezoids stacked on top of each other—but it's also Tokyo's best-kept secret. A sophisticated boutique hotel with only four rooms on each floor, it offers great views of Shinobazu Pond and a fine French restaurant. See p. 81.
- **Best for Internet Buffs: Royal Park Hotel,** 2–1–1 Nihombashi-Kakigara-cho (© **800/457-4000** in the U.S., or 03/3667-1111), offers a sophisticated TV center that provides high-speed Internet access, computer games, and e-mail capability in all its rooms. See p. 81.
- **Best Lobby for Pretending You're Rich:** With its high rates, tons of marble, neoclassical columns, statuary, huge floral bouquets, palm trees, and attentive doormen, the **Westin Tokyo,** 1–4–1 Mita, in Ebisu (© **800/WESTIN-1** in the U.S. and Canada, or 03/5423-7000), is a favorite among wealthy Japanese. See p. 75.
- **Best for Families: National Children's Castle Hotel,** 5–53–1

Jingumae, in Aoyama (© **03/3797-5677**), is located in the same complex as Tokyo's best and most sophisticated indoor/outdoor playground, and even offers some Japanese-style rooms where families can experience tatami living. See p. 99.

- **Best Moderately Priced Hotel:** Occupying the top floors of a Shinjuku skyscraper just a couple minutes' walk from Shinjuku Station, the **Hotel Century Southern Tower,** 2–2–1 Yoyogi (© **03/5354-0111**), offers great views, a convenient location, and comfortable rooms at reasonable prices. See p. 90.
- **Best Budget Accommodations:** Although the building is rather nondescript, **Ryokan Sawanoya,** 2–3–11 Yanaka, in Ueno (© **03/3822-2251**), is nestled in a delightful neighborhood of traditional shops and old wooden houses; the English-speaking owner goes out of his way to introduce the neighborhood and make guests feel at home with such extras as complimentary tea and instant coffee, and free laundry detergent. An added bonus is the free weekly lion dances performed by his son. See p. 98.
- **Best Health Club: Four Seasons Hotel Tokyo at Chinzan-So,** 2–10–8 Sekiguchi, in northwest Tokyo (© **800/332-3442** in the U.S., or 03/3943-2222), wins hands-down with its health spa boasting a gorgeous glass-enclosed indoor swimming pool with a retractable ceiling, sunning terrace, indoor and outdoor Jacuzzis, sauna, steam room, 24-hour fitness gym with personal-size TVs at most workstations, complimentary continental breakfast, and hot-spring baths with thermal water shipped in from Izu Peninsula—all absolutely free for

hotel guests, a rarity in Japan. See p. 79.

- **Best Hotel Pool for Serious Workouts: Park Hyatt Tokyo** in Shinjuku wins kudos for free entry for hotel guests to its dramatic, sunlit, 20m (66-ft.) indoor pool, on the 47th floor with great views over Tokyo. See p. 74.
- **Best Views:** If it's winter, when Mount Fuji is most likely to be visible, the **Park Hyatt Tokyo** in Shinjuku affords great views of Japan's tallest mountain. Otherwise, I love the views from the **Hotel Inter-Continental Tokyo Bay,** 1–16–2 Kaigan (© **800/ 327-0200** in the U.S. and Canada, or 03/5404-2222), located right on the waterfront with great views of Tokyo Bay and the chameleon Rainbow Bridge, even from the bathrooms. See p. 74 and 85.
- **Best Hotel for Spotting VIPs:** Located across from the American Embassy, the dignified **Hotel Okura,** 2–10–4 Toranomon, in Minato-ku (© **800/223-6800** in the U.S., or 03/3582-0111), provides discreet refuge for visiting U.S. dignitaries and a wide range of celebrities, including the Rolling Stones, the late Vladimir Horowitz, Yo-Yo Ma, Henry

Kissinger, and David Bowie. See p. 78.

- **Best Hotel Restaurant: New York Grill** in the Park Hyatt Tokyo has long been Tokyo's dining hot spot, boasting great food, excellent service, knockout views, live jazz, and tables booked weeks in advance. See p. 128.
- **Best Hotel Garden: Hotel New Otani,** 4–1 Kioi-cho, in Akasaka (© **800/421-8795** in the U.S. and Canada, or 03/3265-1111), has a beautiful 400-year-old Japanese garden that once belonged to a feudal lord. Its sprawling 4 hectares (10 acres) contain ponds, waterfalls, bridges, bamboo groves, and manicured bushes. See p. 84.
- **Best Hotel for Pretending You're Not in Tokyo:** Located on the man-made island of Odaiba, the **Hotel Nikko Tokyo,** 1–9–1 Daiba (© **800/645-5687** in the U.S. and Canada, or 03/5500-5500), has a resortlike atmosphere, is surrounded by parks and gardens, and is just a short walk away from a sandy swimming beach. A glance outside your hotel room, however, serves as a reminder—the city skyline crowds the edge of Tokyo Bay. See p. 86.

3 Best Bets for Dining

- **Best Spot for a Romantic Dinner:** Great Pacific Rim fusion cuisine, attentive but unobtrusive service, dim lighting in an airy, tropical setting, a year-round open deck for after-dinner drinks, and a row of massage chairs make **Casita,** 54–10–25 Roppongi (© **03/5414-3190**), a perfect rendezvous for a romantic evening. See p. 144.
- **Best Spot for a Business Lunch:** The convenient Akasaka location and varied, international menu of **Trader Vic's,** 4–1 Kioi-cho

(© **03/3265-4707**), make playing host or hostess here a cinch. See p. 151.

- **Best Spot for a Celebration: New York Grill,** 3–7–1–2 Nishi-Shinjuku (© **03/5322-1234**), has all the makings of a joyous occasion: great food, excellent service, breathtaking views, and superb live jazz. See p. 128.
- **Best Decor:** In a city where presentation counts as much as the food itself, it's difficult to choose the best decor. For traditional surroundings, nothing beats the

Japanese-style rooms of **Takamura** in Roppongi (℃ 03/3585-6600), **Komagata Dojo** in Asakusa (℃ 03/3842-4001), or **Kandagawa** in Kanda (℃ 03/3251-5031). For offbeat decor, one of my favorites is **Tableaux** in Daikanyama (℃ 03/5489-2201), with its whimsical, Russian-tearoom atmosphere. See p. 142, 124, and 153.

- **Best View: New York Grill,** located on the 52nd floor and surrounded by glass, offers breathtaking views of an endless city and, on clear days, Mount Fuji, making this the closest you can get to dining on a cloud. See p. 128.
- **Best Wine List: New York Grill** wins here, too, with 1,600 bottles in its cellar, featuring mostly California wines. **La Tour d'Argent,** New Otani Hotel, 4–1 Kioi-cho (℃ 03/3239-3111), has an excellent choice of French wines. See p. 128 and 150.
- **Best for Kids:** Loud music, rock 'n' roll memorabilia, and familiar fare like burgers, chicken, and sandwiches make the **Hard Rock Cafe,** with two locations at 5–4–20 Roppongi (℃ 03/3408-7018) and 7–1–1 Ueno (℃ 03/5826-5821), a sure winner with children and baby boomers alike. See p. 147.
- **Best American Cuisine:** Steaks and seafood are the mainstays of the classy **New York Grill** (see above), with high prices to match. Easier on the budget is the U.S. chain **Tony Roma's,** with several locations in Tokyo. See p. 128 and 152.
- **Best French Cuisine: La Tour d'Argent,** Hotel New Otani, 4–1 Kioi-cho, in Akasaka (℃ 03/3239-3111), is the Tokyo branch of this very famous Parisian restaurant, serving excellent classic French cuisine, including duckling

flown in from Brittany. A beautiful, dramatic setting and superb service round out the experience. See p. 150.

- **Best Kaiseki:** Perched on a wooded hill in a 50-year-old traditional house, **Takamura,** 3–4–27 Roppongi (℃ 03/3585-6600), offers eight private tatami rooms and exquisitely prepared kaiseki meals. Expensive but worth it. See p. 142.
- **Best Sushi:** If money is no object, head for **Sushiko,** 6–3–8 Ginza (℃ 03/3571-1968), a fourth-generation restaurant with room for only 11 privileged diners. Otherwise, for sushi on a budget, try **Sushi Dai,** located in the Tsukiji Fish Market (℃ 03/3542-1111), where the fish couldn't be any fresher. See p. 115 and 123.
- **Best Fusion/Crossover Cuisine: Nobu,** 6–10–17 Minami Aoyama (℃ 03/5467-0022), is Tokyo's hottest restaurant for fusion food, serving its own beautiful creations of East-meets-West cuisine with a unique blend of Pacific Rim ingredients. Also good: **Wolfgang Puck Bar & Grill** in Roppongi Hills (℃ 03/5786-9630) and **Casita** (see above). See p. 131, 145, and 144.
- **Best Burgers:** Hawaiian import **Kua' Aina,** 5–10–21 Minami Aoyama (℃ 03/3407-8001), hits the spot with the best burgers in town, a real lifesaver when nothing else will do. See p. 137.
- **Best Pizza:** Italian-owned **Trattoria-Pizzeria Sabatini,** 2–13–5 Kita-Aoyama (℃ 03/3402-2027), offers the closest thing to real pizza in Tokyo, with many ingredients actually flown in from Italy. See p. 139.
- **Best Late-Night Dining: La Boheme,** with several convenient locations around Tokyo, has made a name for itself by offering

inexpensive Italian food daily until 5am; ditto for **Zest Cantina,** which serves Mexican food, and **Gonpachi,** which specializes in Japanese fare, all under the same ownership and open daily until 5am. See p. 120 and 141.

- **Best People-Watching: Aux Bacchanales,** 1–6–1 Jingumae, in Harajuku (℗ **03/5474-0076**), with sidewalk seating, is a very civilized place from which to watch the hordes of teenyboppers throng past as you dine on good bistro fare and cheap wine, thankful that your own adolescent days are over. See p. 132.

- **Best for Japanese Desserts: Tatsutano,** 7–8–7 Ginza (℗ **03/ 3571-1850**), has been popular with Japanese housewives for more than a century, especially for its *anmitsu,* a dessert made from beans, molasses, sweet-bean paste, and gelatin. See p. 121.

- **Best Weekend Brunch:** The weekend brunch at **New York Grill** (see above) is so popular there's practically a waiting list. See p. 128.

- **Best Theatrics:** There's never a dull moment at **Inakaya,** 4–10–11 Roppongi (℗ **03/5775-1012**), with waiters shouting out orders, U-shaped counter seating, mountains of food, and kneeling cooks laboring over charcoal grills. Great fun. See p. 141.

- **Best Buffets: Imperial Viking,** on the 17th floor of the Imperial Hotel, 1–1–1 Uchisaiwai-cho (℗ **03/3504-1111**), with views of the Ginza and Hibiya, was a pioneer of all-you-can-eat buffets in Japan. After 40-some years, it still offers great lunch and dinner buffets with international selections. See p. 116.

- **Best Place to Chill Out:** When the crowds get you down, escape to **Selan,** 2–1–19 Kita-Aoyama (℗ **03/3478-2200**), with its glorious setting on a gingko-lined street, complete with sidewalk seating and an airy dining room with lots of windows. It's a good place to relax and do absolutely nothing. Another good choice: **Sunset Beach Brewing Company** on the man-made island of Odaiba (℗ **03/3599-6655**), with mediocre buffet meals but great views of the Tokyo skyline from its outdoor deck. See p. 134 and 154.

Planning Your Trip to Tokyo

This chapter will guide you through the what, when, where, and how of travel to Tokyo—from what documents you should take with you to how to get around easily and economically, despite the language barrier.

1 Visitor Information

The **Japan National Tourist Organization (JNTO)** publishes a wealth of free, colorful brochures and maps covering Tokyo and other cities. These include a tourist map of Tokyo; "Fuji-Hakone-Kamakura-Nikko," a brochure of popular destinations in the vicinity of Tokyo; "The Tourist's Language Handbook," a phrase booklet to help foreign visitors communicate with the Japanese; and "Your Traveling Companion, with Tips for Budget Travel," with money-saving advice on traveling, lodging, and dining in the Tokyo area.

JAPAN ONLINE You can reach JNTO via the Internet at **www.jnto. go.jp** (and at **www.japantravelinfo. com** for North American travelers; at **www.seejapan.co.uk** for British travelers), where you can read up on what's new, view maps, get the latest weather report, find links to online hotel reservation companies, and browse through information ranging from hints on budget travel to regional events, museums, and attractions.

The Tokyo Metropolitan Government also maintains a website at www.tourism.metro.tokyo.jp.

THE JNTO OVERSEAS If you'd like information on Japan before leaving home, contact one of these JNTO offices. In the **United States:** One Rockefeller Plaza, Suite 1250, New York, NY 10020 (℃ **212/757-5640;** info@jntonyc.org); 515 S. Figueroa, Suite 1470, Los Angeles, CA 90071 (℃ **213/623-1952;** info@jnto-lax. org); and 1 Daniel Burnham Court, Suite 250C, San Francisco, CA 94109 (℃ **415/292-5686;** info@jntosf.org).

In **Canada:** 165 University Ave., Toronto, ON M5H 3B8, Canada (℃ **416/366-7140;** info@jntoyyz. com). In the **United Kingdom:** Heathcoat House, 20 Savile Row, London W1X 1AE, England (℃ **020/ 7734-9638;** info@jnto.co.uk). In **Australia:** Room 1813, Australia Square Tower, 264 George St., Sydney, NSW 2000, Australia (℃ **02/9251-3034;** jntosyd@tokyonet.com.au).

2 Entry Requirements & Customs

ENTRY REQUIREMENTS

Americans traveling to Japan as tourists with the intention of staying 90 days or less need only a valid passport to gain entry into the country. *Note:* Only American *tourists* don't

need a visa—that is, those in the country for sightseeing, sports activities, family visits, inspection tours, business meetings, or short study courses. In other words, as a tourist, you cannot work in Japan or engage in any remunerative activity, including the teaching of English (though many young people ignore the law). No extensions of stay are granted, which means American tourists must absolutely leave the country after 90 days. If you're going to Japan to work or study and plan to stay longer, you'll need a visa; contact the Japanese embassy or consulate nearest you.

Australians and **New Zealanders** don't need a visa for stays of up to 90 days, **Canadians** don't need a visa for stays of up to 3 months, and **United Kingdom** and **Irish citizens** can stay for up to 6 months without a visa.

CUSTOMS
ENTERING JAPAN If you're 20 or older, you can bring duty-free into Japan up to 400 non-Japanese cigarettes or 500 grams of tobacco or 100 cigars; three bottles (760cc each) of alcohol; and 2 ounces of perfume. You can also bring in gifts and souvenirs whose total market value is less than ¥200,000 ($1,667).

GOING HOME Returning **U.S. citizens** who have been away for 48 hours or more are allowed to bring back, once every 30 days, $800 worth of merchandise duty-free including (for those 21 and older) 1 liter of wine

or spirits. Duty-free tobacco is limited to 200 cigarettes or 100 cigars. Beyond that, the next $1,000 worth of goods is assessed at a flat rate of 4% duty. Be sure to have your receipts handy. On mailed gifts, the duty-free limit is $200. You can't bring fresh foodstuffs into the U.S.; tinned foods, however, are allowed. For specifics on what you can bring back, download the invaluable free pamphlet *Know Before You Go* online at **www.customs.gov**. (Click on "Travel," and then click on "Know Before You Go Online Brochure.") Or contact the **U.S. Customs Service,** 1300 Pennsylvania Ave. NW, Washington, DC 20229 (© **877/287-8867**), and request the pamphlet.

For a clear summary of **Canadian** rules, write for the booklet *I Declare,* issued by the **Canada Customs and Revenue Agency** (© **800/461-9999** in Canada, or 204/983-3500; www.ccra-adrc.gc.ca). Canada allows its citizens a C$750 exemption, and you're allowed to bring back duty-free one carton of cigarettes, one can of tobacco, 40 imperial ounces of liquor, and 50 cigars. In addition, you're allowed to mail gifts to Canada valued at less than C$60 a day, provided they're unsolicited and don't contain

---

Tips Passport Savvy

Safeguard your passport in an inconspicuous, inaccessible place like a money belt and keep a photocopy of your passport's information page in your luggage. If you lose your passport, visit your nearest consulate as soon as possible for a replacement. *Note:* Foreigners are required to carry with them at all times either their passports or, for those who have been granted longer stays, their alien registration cards. Police generally do not stop foreigners, but if you're caught without the proper ID, you'll be taken to local police headquarters. It happened to me once and, believe me, I can think of better ways to spend an hour and a half than explaining in detail who I am, what I am doing in Japan, where I live, and what I plan to do for the rest of my life. I even had to write a statement explaining why I rushed out that day without my passport, apologizing and promising never to do such a thoughtless thing again. The policemen were polite, but they were simply doing their duty.

alcohol or tobacco (write on the package "Unsolicited gift, under $60 value"). *Note:* The $750 exemption can only be used once a year and only after an absence of 7 days.

U.K. citizens returning from Japan have a Customs allowance of 200 cigarettes; 50 cigars; 250 grams of smoking tobacco; 2 liters of still table wine; 1 liter of spirits or strong liqueurs (over 22% volume); 2 liters of fortified wine, sparkling wine or other liqueurs; 60cc (ml) perfume; 250cc (ml) of toilet water; and £145 worth of all other goods, including gifts and souvenirs. People under 17 cannot have the tobacco or alcohol allowance. For more information, contact **HM Customs & Excise** at ℂ **0845/010-9000** (from outside the U.K., ℂ **020/ 8929-0152**), or consult their website at www.hmce.gov.uk.

The duty-free allowance in **Australia** is A$400 or, for those under 18, A$200. Citizens can bring in 250 cigarettes or 250 grams of loose tobacco, and 1,125 milliliters of alcohol. For more information, call the **Australian Customs Service** at ℂ **1300/363-263,** or log onto www.customs.gov.au.

The duty-free allowance for **New Zealand** is NZ$700. Citizens over 17 can bring in 200 cigarettes, 50 cigars, or 250 grams of tobacco (or a mixture of all three if their combined weight doesn't exceed 250g); plus 4.5 liters of wine and beer, or 1.125 liters of liquor. New Zealand currency does not carry import or export restrictions. For more information, contact **New Zealand Customs,** The Customhouse, 17–21 Whitmore St., Box 2218, Wellington (ℂ **04/473-6099** or 0800/428-786; www.customs.govt.nz).

3 Money

CURRENCY The currency in Japan is called the *yen,* denoted by ¥. Coins come in denominations of ¥1, ¥5, ¥10, ¥50, ¥100, and ¥500. Bills come in denominations of ¥1,000, ¥2,000, ¥5,000, and ¥10,000. All coins get used (though you may find it hard getting rid of ¥1 coins); keep plenty of change handy for riding local transportation, especially buses. Change machines are virtually everywhere, even on buses where you can change larger coins and ¥1,000 bills, but it's faster to have the exact amount on hand. Although the **conversion rate** varies daily and can fluctuate dramatically, the prices in this book are based on the rate of US$1 to ¥120, or ¥100 to US83¢.

Personal checks are not used in Japan. Most Japanese pay with credit cards or cash—the country's overall crime rate is so low, you can feel safe walking around with money (but always exercise caution). The only exception is on a crowded subway during rush hour or in heavily touristed

areas such as Tsukiji or Asakusa. Although the bulk of your expenses—hotels, major purchases, meals in classier restaurants—can be paid for with credit cards, bring traveler's checks for those times when you might not have convenient access to an ATM for cash withdrawals, especially outside Tokyo in more rural areas.

CURRENCY EXCHANGE Some people like to arrive in a foreign country with that country's currency already on hand, but I do not find it necessary for Japan. **Narita Airport** has several exchange counters for all incoming international flights that offer better exchange rates than what you'd get abroad. In addition, all banks displaying an AUTHORIZED FOREIGN EXCHANGE sign can exchange currency, with exchange rates usually displayed at the appropriate foreign-exchange counter. **Banks** are generally open Monday through Friday from 9am to 3pm, though business hours for exchanging foreign currency usually don't begin until 10:30 or 11am (be

The Japanese Yen

For American Readers   At this writing $1 = approximately ¥120, or ¥100 = 83¢. This was the rate of exchange used to calculate the dollar values given in this guide (rounded off to the nearest nickel for prices less than $10 and to the nearest dollar for prices more than $10). To roughly figure the price of something in dollars, calculate $8 for every ¥1,000 or multiply the yen amount by .008. For example, ¥2,000 is about $16, close to the actual $16.65.

For British Readers   At this writing £1 = approximately ¥180, or ¥100 = 55p; this was the rate of exchange used to calculate the pound values in the table below. The euro is worth approximately ¥126.

¥	US$	UK£	¥	US$	UK£
10	.08	.06	1,500	12.50	8.35
25	.21	.14	2,000	16.65	11.10
50	.42	.28	2,500	20.85	13.90
75	.62	.42	3,000	25.00	16.65
100	.83	.56	4,000	33.35	22.20
200	1.65	1.10	5,000	41.65	27.80
300	2.50	1.65	6,000	50.00	33.35
400	3.35	2.20	7,000	58.35	38.90
500	4.15	2.80	8,000	66.65	44.45
600	5.00	3.35	9,000	75.00	50.00
700	5.85	3.90	10,000	83.35	55.55
800	6.65	4.45	15,000	125.00	83.35
900	7.50	5.00	20,000	166.65	111.10
1,000	8.35	5.55	25,000	208.35	138.90

A note on exchange rates: The most difficult task of writing a guide is to set the rate of exchange, especially for Japan; if I could advise you accurately on the future exchange rate, I'd be too rich to be a guidebook writer. Since these rates will surely fluctuate, check the rate again when you travel to Japan and use this table only as an approximate guide.

prepared for a long wait; you'll be asked to sit down as your order is processed). If you need to exchange money outside of banking hours, inquire at your **hotel.** Likewise, large **department stores** also offer exchange services and are often open until 7:30 or 8pm. Note, however, that hotels and department stores may charge a handling fee, offer a slightly less favorable exchange rate, and require a passport for all transactions.

TRAVELER'S CHECKS   Traveler's checks in U.S. and other denominations can be exchanged for yen at most banks with exchange services and at major hotels and department stores in Tokyo, but note that you'll need your passport every time you cash a check. Traveler's checks have a slight advantage in that they generally fetch a better exchange rate than cash; they also offer protection in case of theft and are useful for obtaining cash if ATMs are

What Things Cost in Tokyo	US$
Narita Express Train from airport to city center	$26
Subway ride from Akasaka to Roppongi	$1.35
Local telephone call (per minute)	$.10
Double room at the Park Hyatt Tokyo (deluxe)	$433
Double room at the Asakusa View Hotel (moderate)	$192
Double room at the Ryokan Sawanoya (inexpensive)	$73
Lunch for one at Zipangu (moderate)	$23
Lunch for one at Gonpachi (inexpensive)	$5
Dinner for one, without drinks, at Inakaya (deluxe)	$100
Dinner for one, without drinks, at Komagata Dojo (moderate)	$40
Dinner for one, without drinks, at Ganchan (inexpensive)	$21
Glass of beer	$4.15–6
Coca-Cola	$3.40–4.15
Cup of coffee	$2–4.15
Roll of ASA 100 Fujicolor film (36 exposures)	$3.80
Admission to the Tokyo National Museum	$3.50
Movie ticket	$15
Theater ticket to Kabuki	$5–20

not easily accessible. Note, however, that in some very remote areas, even banks won't cash them. Before taking off for small towns, be sure you have enough cash.

You can get traveler's checks before you leave home at almost any bank. **American Express** offers denominations of $20, $50, $100, $500, and (for cardholders only) $1,000. You'll pay a service charge ranging from 1% to 4%. You can also get American Express traveler's checks over the phone by calling ✆ **800/221-7282;** Amex gold and platinum cardholders who use this number are exempt from the 1% fee.

Visa offers traveler's checks at Citibank locations nationwide, as well as at several other banks. The service charge ranges between 1.5% and 2%; checks come in denominations of $20, $50, $100, $500, and $1,000. Call ✆ **800/ 732-1322** for information. American Automobile Association members can obtain Visa checks without a fee at most AAA offices or by calling ✆ **866/ 339-3378. MasterCard** also offers traveler's checks. Call ✆ **800/223-9920** for a location near you.

CREDIT CARDS Credit cards are convenient for obtaining cash and for paying for accommodations, meals at expensive restaurants, and major purchases, with the exchange rate better than what you can get for either cash or traveler's checks at a bank. (However, fees charged by your bank or credit card company may cancel any real savings; before going abroad, ask your card issuer how it calculates the exchange rate and about applicable fees.) They are a safe way to carry money and provide a convenient record of all your expenses.

The most readily accepted cards are **MasterCard** (also called Eurocard), **Visa,** and the Japanese credit card **JCB** (Japan Credit Bank); many touristoriented facilities also accept **American Express** and **Diners Club.** Shops

---

Tips   Dear Visa: I'm Off to Tokyo!

Some credit card companies recommend that you notify them of any impending trip abroad so that they don't become suspicious when the card is used numerous times in a foreign destination and your charges are blocked. Even if you don't call your credit card company in advance, you can always call the card's toll-free emergency number (see "Fast Facts" in chapter 3) if a charge is refused—a good reason to carry the phone number with you. But perhaps the most important lesson here is to carry more than one card with you on your trip; a card might not work for any number of reasons, so having a backup is the smart way to go. My Visa debit card was accepted at one ATM but not another—I have no idea why.

---

and restaurants accepting credit and charge cards will usually post which cards they accept at the door or near the cash register. However, some establishments may be reluctant to accept cards for small purchases and inexpensive meals; inquire beforehand. In addition, note that the vast majority of Tokyo's smaller and least-expensive businesses, including many restaurants, noodle shops, fast-food joints, ma-and-pa establishments, and the cheapest accommodations, do not accept credit cards.

GETTING CASH USING YOUR CREDIT OR BANK ATM CARD

You can also use bank-issued credit cards and ATM cards to get cash. Because most ATM machines in Japan accept only cards issued by Japanese banks, your best bet for obtaining cash is a **post office,** all of which have ATMs that accept foreign bank cards operating on the Cirrus (MasterCard) or PLUS (Visa) systems. The catch is that even though the ATM may be located outside the main postal transaction area, machines are operable

only limited hours (depending on the bank, that may be until 6 or 7pm weekdays and until 5pm on weekends). Besides post offices, other places with ATMs that might accept foreign-issued cards include Citibank (which usually accepts both Visa and MasterCard and sometimes American Express as well), large department stores, and Narita Airport. Note that there is no public American Express office in Japan.

To obtain cash from an ATM or credit card, you must have a personal identification number (PIN). If you've forgotten your PIN or didn't know you have one, call the phone number on the back of your card and ask the bank to send it to you. If you already have a PIN, it's a good idea to check with your card issuer to be certain your PIN will work in Japan. Ask, too, for a list of banks that will honor your card and what your daily withdrawal limit is. Or check websites: MasterCard (© **800/424-7787;** www.mastercard.com); Visa (© **800/843-7587;** www.visa.com).

---

4 When to Go

Although Tokyo's busiest foreign-tourist season is summer, the city lends itself to visiting year-round. In fact, when the rest of Japan is besieged with vacationing Japanese during Golden Week (Apr 29–May 5) and

summer vacation (mid-July through Aug), Tokyo is usually blissfully empty, as Tokyoites pour out of the city to the countryside. Keep in mind, however, that in mid-February, hotel rooms may be in short supply as high-school students from around the nation converge on Tokyo to compete in entrance exams for the city's prestigious universities. In addition, popular tourist destinations outside Tokyo, such as Nikko, Kamakura, and Hakone, will be jam-packed on major holidays. And from the end of December through the first 3 or 4 days of January, it seems as though the entire nation shuts down, including most restaurants and museums.

CLIMATE The Japanese are very proud of the fact that Japan has four distinct seasons; they place much more emphasis on the seasons than people do in the West. Kimono, dishes and bowls used for *kaiseki* (Japanese cuisine obeying strict etiquette rules for each detail of the meal and the dining surroundings), and even Noh plays change with the seasons, and most festivals are tied to seasonal rites. Even Tokyoites note the seasons; almost as though on cue, businessmen will change virtually overnight from their winter to summer business attire.

Summer, which begins in June, is heralded by the rainy season, which lasts from about mid-June to mid-July in Tokyo. July has, on the average, 10 rainy days, but even though it doesn't rain every day, umbrellas are imperative. When the rain stops, it gets unbearably hot and humid through August—you might want to head for Hakone for a bit of fresh air. Otherwise, you'll be most comfortable in light cottons, but be sure to pack a lightweight jacket for unexpected cool evenings and air-conditioned rooms. The period from the end of August through September is typhoon season, though most storms stay out at sea and vent their fury on land only as thunderstorms.

Autumn, which lasts September through November, is one of the best times to visit Tokyo. The days are pleasant and slightly cool, the skies are a brilliant blue, and the maple trees turn scarlet. Bring a warm jacket.

Winter lasts from about December to March in Tokyo, with days that are generally clear and cold with extremely low humidity. Tokyo doesn't get much snow, but it can, so be prepared. I remember one winter when snow fell in a slushy mush through March and into the cherry-blossom season. In any case, the temperature is usually above freezing.

Spring is ushered in by a magnificent fanfare of plum and cherry blossoms in March and April, an exquisite time of year when all of Japan is set ablaze in whites and pinks. The blossoms last only a few days, symbolizing to the Japanese the fragile nature of beauty and of life itself. Tokyo may still have cool, rainy weather until May, so be sure to bring a light jacket or sweater.

Tokyo's Average Daytime Temperatures & Rainfall

	Jan	Feb	Mar	Apr	May	June	July	Aug	Sept	Oct	Nov	Dec
Temp. (°F)	37	43	45	54	66	71	77	81	73	62	55	41
Temp. (°C)	3	6	7	13	19	22	25	27	23	17	13	5
Days of Rain	4.3	6.1	8.9	10	9.6	12.1	10	8.2	10.9	8.9	6.4	3.8

HOLIDAYS National holidays are January 1 (New Year's Day), second Monday in January (Coming-of-Age Day), February 11 (National Foundation Day), March 20 or 21 (Vernal Equinox Day), April 29 (Greenery Day), May 3 (Constitution Memorial Day), May 5 (Children's Day), third Monday in July (Maritime Day), third Monday in September (Respect-for-the-Aged Day), September 23 or 24 (Autumn Equinox Day); second Monday in October (Health Sports Day); November 3 (Culture Day),

November 23 (Labor Thanksgiving Day); and December 23 (Emperor's Birthday). For more information on holidays, see the "Tokyo Calendar of Events," below.

When a national holiday falls on a Sunday, the following Monday becomes a holiday. The most important holidays for the Japanese are **New Year's, Golden Week** (Apr 29–May 5), and the **Obon Festival** (about a week in mid-Aug). Avoid traveling on these dates at all costs, since long-distance trains and most accommodations are booked solid (and are also often more expensive), including most of those listed in chapter 10, "Side Trips from Tokyo." The weekends before and after these holidays are also likely to be very crowded. Luckily, Tokyo is an exception—since the major exodus is back to hometowns or the countryside, holidays such as Golden Week can be almost blissful in the metropolis. Another busy travel time is during summer school holidays, July 19 through August, when the Japanese take their vacations en masse.

Although government offices (including JNTO's Tourist Information Centers) and some businesses are closed on public holidays, restaurants and most stores remain open. The exception is during the New Year's celebration, the end of December through January 3, when almost all restaurants, public and private offices, and stores close up shop; during that time you'll have to dine in hotels.

All **museums** close for New Year's for 1 to 4 days, but most major museums remain open for the other holidays. If a public holiday falls on a Monday (when most museums are closed), many museums will remain open but will close instead the following day, on Tuesday. Note that privately owned museums, however, such as art museums or special-interest museums, generally close on public holidays. To avoid disappointment, be sure to phone ahead if you plan to visit a museum on or the day following a holiday.

FESTIVALS   Because Japan has two major religions, Shintoism and Buddhism, it celebrates festivals throughout the year. Every major shrine and temple observes at least one annual festival with events that might include traditional dances, colorful processions, and booths selling souvenirs and food.

Listed below in the "Tokyo Calendar of Events" are major festivals and events held in Tokyo and cities close by. In Tokyo alone, however, there are so many small, neighborhood festivals that you could probably visit one almost every week of the year. More information on events taking place in Tokyo and its vicinity is available by visiting JNTO's website at www.jnto.go.jp and clicking on "Events & Festivals." Or stop by the **Tourist Information Center** in Tokyo for a monthly leaflet called "Calendar Events."

TOKYO CALENDAR OF EVENTS
January

New Year's Day, nationwide. The most important national holiday in Japan, this is a time of family reunions and gatherings with friends to drink sake and eat special New Year's dishes. Because the Japanese spend this day with families, and because almost all businesses, restaurants, shops, and museums close down, it's not a particularly rewarding time of the year for foreign visitors. Best bets are shrines and temples, where Japanese come in their best kimono or dress to pray for good health and happiness in the coming year. January 1.

Dezomeshiki (New Year's Parade of Firemen), Odaiba, Tokyo. This annual event features agile firemen in traditional costumes who prove their worth with acrobatic stunts atop tall bamboo ladders. January 6.

Coming-of-Age Day, a national holiday. This day honors young people who have reached the age of 20, when they are allowed to vote, drink alcohol, and assume other responsibilities. They visit shrines to pray for their futures; in Tokyo, the most popular shrine is Meiji Shrine. Many women wear traditional kimono. Second Monday in January.

February

Setsubun (Bean-Throwing Festival), at leading temples throughout Japan. This festival celebrates the last day of winter according to the lunar calendar. People throng to temples to participate in the traditional ceremony of throwing beans to drive away imaginary devils. In Tokyo, popular sites include Kanda Myojin Shrine, Hie Shrine, and Sensoji Temple. February 3 or 4.

Hari-kuyo, Awashimado, near Sensoji Temple in Asakusa. To show respect for the needles that have done them great service, women bring broken pins and needles to Awashimado and stick them into squares of tofu, a custom since the Edo Period. February 8.

National Foundation Day (Kigensetsu), a national holiday. February 11.

March

Hinamatsuri (Doll Festival), observed throughout Japan. This festival is held in honor of young girls to wish them a future of happiness. In homes where there are girls, dolls dressed in ancient costumes representing the emperor, empress, and dignitaries are set up on a tier of shelves, along with miniature household articles. Many hotels also showcase doll displays in their lobbies. March 3.

Daruma Ichi Doll Festival, Jindaiji Temple (take the Keio Line to Tsutsujigaoka Station). A *daruma* is a legless, pear-shaped doll modeled after Bodhidharma, who founded the Zen sect in the 6th century and is said to have lost the use of his limbs from sitting 9 years in the lotus position on the way to enlightenment. Stalls here sell daruma with blank spots for eyes—according to custom, you're supposed to paint in one eye while making a wish; when your wish is fulfilled, you paint in the other eye. March 3 and 4.

Vernal Equinox Day, a national holiday. Throughout the week, Buddhist temples hold ceremonies to pray for the souls of the departed. March 19, 20, or 21.

April

Sakura Matsuri (Cherry-blossom Season). The bursting forth of cherry blossoms represents the birth of spring for Tokyoites, who gather en masse under the trees to drink sake, eat, and be merry. Popular cherry-viewing spots in Tokyo include Ueno Park, Yasukuni Shrine, Shinjuku Gyoen, Aoyama Bochi Cemetery, Sumida Koen Park in Asakusa, and the moat encircling the Imperial Palace, especially Chidorigafuchi Park. Early to mid-April.

Kanamara Matsuri, Kanayama Shrine, Kawasaki (just outside Tokyo). This festival extols the joys of sex and fertility (and, more recently, raised awareness about AIDS), featuring a parade of giant phalluses, some carried by transvestites. Needless to say, it's not your average festival, and you can get some unusual photographs here. First Sunday in April.

Buddha's Birthday (also called Hana Matsuri, or Floral Festival), nationwide. Ceremonies are held at all Buddhist temples, where a small image of Buddha is displayed and doused with a sweet tea called *amacha* in an act of devotion. April 8.

Kamakura Matsuri, Tsurugaoka Hachimangu Shrine in Kamakura. The festival honors heroes from the past, including Yoritomo Minamoto, who made Kamakura his shogunate capital back in 1192; highlights include horseback archery (truly spectacular to watch), a parade of portable shrines, and sacred dances. Second to third Sunday in April.

Yayoi Matsuri, Futarasan Shrine in Nikko. Featured is a parade of gaily decorated floats. April 16 and 17.

Greenery Day, a national holiday. This is the birthday of the former emperor Hirohito, who died in January 1989 and was known for his love of nature. April 29.

Golden Week, a major holiday period throughout Japan. It's a crowded time to travel, making reservations a must. Because so many factories and businesses close during the week, this is said to be the best time of year for a clear view of the city and beyond from atop Tokyo Tower. April 29 to May 5.

May

Constitution Memorial Day, a national holiday. May 3.

Children's Day, a national holiday. This festival is for all children but especially honors young boys. Throughout Japan colorful streamers of carp are flown from poles to symbolize perseverance and strength, considered desirable attributes for young boys. May 5.

Kanda Myojin Festival, Kanda Myojin Shrine. This festival, which commemorates Tokugawa Ieyasu's famous victory at Sekigahara in 1600, began during the Feudal Era as the only time townspeople could enter the shogun's castle and parade before him. Today it features a parade of dozens of portable shrines carried through the district, plus geisha dances and a tea ceremony. Held in odd-numbered years on the Saturday and Sunday before May 15.

Grand Festival of Toshogu Shrine, in Nikko. Commemorating the day in 1617 when Tokugawa Ieyasu's remains were brought to his mausoleum in Nikko, this festival re-creates that drama, with more than 1,000 armor-clad men escorting three palanquins through the streets. May 17 and 18.

Sanja Matsuri, Asakusa Shrine. This is one of Tokyo's best-known and most colorful festivals, featuring a parade of 100 portable shrines carried through the streets of Asakusa on the shoulders of men and women dressed in traditional garb. Friday, Saturday, and Sunday closest to May 18.

June

Sanno Festival, Hie Shrine. This festival first began in the Edo Period and features the usual portable shrines transported through the busy streets of the Akasaka district. Held in even years, June 10 to 16.

July

Ueki Ichi (Potted Plant Fair), on the streets around Fuji Sengen Shrine near Asakusa on the Ginza subway line. On display are different kinds of potted plants and bonsai (miniature trees), as well as a miniature Mount Fuji symbolizing the opening of the official climbing season. July 1.

Tanabata (Star Festival), celebrated throughout Japan. According to myth, the two stars Vega and Altair, representing a weaver and a shepherd, are allowed to meet only once a year on this day. If the skies are cloudy, however, the celestial pair cannot meet and must wait another year. July 7.

Hozuki Ichi (Ground Cherry Pod Fair), on the grounds of Asakusa's Sensoji Temple. Hundreds of street stalls sell ground cherry pods and colorful wind bells. July 9 and 10.

Obon Festival, nationwide. This festival is held in memory of dead ancestors who, according to Buddhist belief, revisit the world during this period. Obon Odori folk dances are held in neighborhoods everywhere. Many Japanese return to their hometowns for the event, especially if a member of the family has died recently. As one Japanese, whose grandmother had died a few months before, told me, "I have to go back to my hometown—it's my grandmother's first Obon." Mid-July or mid-August.

Maritime Day, a national holiday. The holiday commemorates the vital role of the sea in Japan's livelihood and honors those involved in the marine industry. Third Monday in July.

Hanabi Taikai (Fireworks Display). Tokyo's largest summer celebration features a spectacular fireworks display over the Sumida River in Asakusa. Get there early and spread a blanket on the bank of the river or in Sumida Koen Park (near Kototoibashi and Komagatabashi bridges). Last Saturday of July.

August
Waraku Odori, in Nikko. This is one of the most popular events for folk dances, with thousands of people dancing to music. August 5 and 6.

September
Respect-for-the-Aged Day, a national holiday. Third Monday in September.

Yabusame (Horseback Archery), Tsurugaoka Hachimangu Shrine in Kamakura. The archery performances by riders on horseback recall the days of the samurai. September 16.

Autumnal Equinox Day, a national holiday. September 23 or 24.

October
Health and Sports Day, a national holiday, established in commemoration of the Tokyo Olympic Games. Second Monday in October.

Oeshiki Festival, Hommonji Temple. This is the largest of Tokyo's commemorative services held for Nichiren (1222–82), a Buddhist leader who was exiled for his beliefs. Followers march to the temple carrying large lanterns decorated with paper flowers. October 11 to 13.

Autumn Festival of Toshogu Shrine, Toshogu Shrine in Nikko. A parade of warriors in early-17th-century dress are accompanied by spear-carriers, gun-carriers, flag-bearers, Shinto priests, pages, court musicians, and dancers as they escort a sacred portable shrine. October 17.

November
Culture Day, a national holiday. November 3.

Daimyo Gyoretsu, in Hakone. On this day the old Tokaido Highway that used to link Kyoto and Tokyo comes alive again with a faithful reproduction of a feudal lord's procession in the olden days. November 3.

Shichi-go-san (Children's Shrine-Visiting Day), held throughout Japan. *Shichi-go-san* literally means "seven-five-three"; it refers to children of these ages who are dressed in their best kimono and taken to shrines by their elders to express thanks and pray for their future. In Tokyo the most popular sites are the Meiji, Yasukuni, Kanda Myojin, Asakusa, and Hie shrines. November 15.

Tori-no-Ichi (Rake Fair), Otori Shrine in Asakusa. This fair features stalls selling rakes lavishly decorated with paper and cloth, which are thought to bring good luck and fortune. The date, based on the lunar calendar, changes each year. Mid-November.

Labor Thanksgiving Day, a national holiday. November 23.

December

Gishi-sai, Sengakuji Station. This memorial service honors 47 masterless samurai *(ronin),* who avenged their master's death by killing his rival and parading his head; for their act, all were ordered to commit suicide. Forty-seven men dressed as the ronin travel to Sengakuji Temple (site of their master's burial) with the enemy's head to place on their master's grave. December 14.

Hagoita-Ichi (Battledore Fair), Sensoji Temple. Popular since Japan's feudal days, this fair features decorated paddles of all types and sizes. Most have designs of Kabuki actors—images made by pasting together silk and brocade—and make great souvenirs and gifts. December 17 to 19.

Emperor's Birthday, celebrated nationwide. The birthday of Akihito, Japan's 125th emperor, is a national holiday. December 23.

New Year's Eve, celebrated nationwide. At midnight many temples ring huge bells 108 times to signal the end of the old year and the beginning of the new (each peal represents a sin). Many families visit temples and shrines to pray for good luck and prosperity and to usher in the coming year. In Tokyo, Meiji Shrine is the place to be for this popular family celebration; many coffee shops and restaurants in nearby Harajuku stay open all night to serve the revelers. Other popular sites are Kanda Myojin Shrine, Sensoji Temple, and Sanno Hie Shrine.

5 Travel Insurance

Check your existing insurance policies and credit card coverage before you buy travel insurance. You may already be covered for lost luggage, canceled tickets, or medical expenses. The cost of travel insurance varies widely, depending on the cost and length of your trip, your age, your health, and the type of trip you're taking.

TRIP-CANCELLATION INSURANCE Trip-cancellation insurance helps you get your money back if you have to back out of a trip, if you have to go home early, or if your travel supplier goes bankrupt. Allowed reasons for cancellation can range from sickness to natural disasters to the State Department declaring your destination unsafe for travel. (Insurers usually won't cover vague fears, though, as many travelers discovered who tried to cancel their trips in Oct 2001 because they were wary of flying.) In this unstable world, trip-cancellation insurance is a good buy if you're getting tickets well in advance—who knows what the state of the world, or of your airline, will be in 9 months? Insurance policy details vary, so read the fine print—and especially make sure that your airline or cruise line is on the list of carriers covered in case of bankruptcy. For information, contact one of the following insurers: **Access America** (✆ 866/807-3982; www.accessamerica.com); **Travel Guard International** (✆ 800/826-4919; www.travelguard.com); or **Travel Insured International** (✆ 800/243-3174; www.travelinsured.com).

MEDICAL INSURANCE Most health insurance policies cover you if

The Masterless Samurai

Every Japanese schoolchild knows the story of the 47 *ronin* (masterless samurai), a story also immortalized in a popular Kabuki play. In 1701, a feudal lord *(daimyo)* named Kira was ordered by the Tokugawa shogun to instruct another daimyo, Asano, in the etiquette of court ritual in preparation for a visit from an imperial entourage from Kyoto. The two quarreled, and the quick-tempered Asano, angered at the insults hurled by the older daimyo, drew his sword. Since the drawing of a sword in Edo Castle was strictly forbidden, Asano was ordered to commit ritual suicide, his family was disinherited and turned out of their home, his estate and castle were confiscated by the shogun, and his retainers *(samurai)* became masterless. Kira, on the other hand, was found innocent and went unpunished.

In those days, masterless samurai were men without a future. Their loyalty in question, they were unlikely to find daimyo willing to retain them, so many turned to a life of crime, hiring themselves out as mercenaries or becoming highway robbers. The 47 ronin, however, decided to avenge their master's death by killing Kira. Knowing that Kira was on the lookout for revenge, they bided their time until one snowy December night in 1702, when they attacked Kira's mansion, cut off his head, and paraded it through the streets of Edo on the way to their master's grave at **Sengakuji Temple.** Although the public was sympathetic toward the ronin for the steadfast loyalty they had shown their dead master, the shogun ordered all of them to commit ritual suicide through disembowelment.

In Tokyo today, all that remains of Kira's mansion, located near the Kokugikan sumo stadium at 3–13–9 Ryogoku, is a white-and-black wall crowned by a weeping willow and a small inner courtyard. The 47 ronin and their master, on the other hand, are memorialized by tombs at **Sengakuji Temple,** 2–11–1 Takanawa (© **03/3441-5560;** subway: Sengakuji, exit A2, a 2-min. walk), and by a small museum (open daily 9am–4pm; closed Mar 31 and Sept 30) containing clothing, armor, and personal items belonging to the ronin (a 15-min. video about the ronin and their era is shown in Japanese; if there are no other visitors, however, you can request to see it in English). Admission to the temple and tombs is free; admission to the museum is ¥500 ($4.15) for adults, ¥400 ($3.35) for students, and ¥250 ($2.10) for children. Every December 14, in a reenactment of the parade, 47 men dressed as ronin deliver a replica of Kira's head to Sengakuji Temple.

you get sick away from home—but check, particularly if you're insured by an HMO. With the exception of certain HMOs and Medicare/Medicaid, your medical insurance should cover medical treatment—even hospital care—overseas, which in Japan can be quite expensive. However, most out-of-country hospitals make you pay your bills up front, and send you a refund after you've returned home and filed the necessary paperwork. And in a worst-case scenario, there's the high cost of emergency evacuation. If you require additional medical insurance, try **MEDEX International** (✆ 800/527-0218 or 410/453-6300; www.medexassist.com) or **Travel Assistance International** (✆ 800/821-2828; www.travelassistance.com); for general information on services, call TAI's **Worldwide Assistance Services, Inc.,** at ✆ 800/777-8710.

LOST-LUGGAGE INSURANCE
On domestic flights, checked baggage is covered up to $2,500 per ticketed passenger. On international flights (including U.S. portions of international trips), baggage is limited to approximately $9.07 per pound, up to approximately $635 per checked bag. If you plan to check items more valuable than the standard liability, see if your valuables are covered by your homeowner's policy, get baggage insurance as part of your comprehensive travel-insurance package, or buy Travel Guard's "BagTrak" product. Don't buy insurance at the airport, as it's usually overpriced. Be sure to take any valuables or irreplaceable items with you in your carry-on luggage, as many valuables (including books, money, and electronics) aren't covered by airline policies.

If your luggage is lost, immediately file a lost-luggage claim at the airport, detailing the luggage contents. For most airlines, you must report delayed, damaged, or lost baggage within 4 hours of arrival. The airlines are required to deliver luggage, once found, directly to your house, hotel, or destination free of charge.

6 Health & Safety

STAYING HEALTHY
It's safe to drink tap water and eat to your heart's content everywhere in Japan (pregnant women, however, are advised to avoid eating raw fish or taking hot baths). Although Japan has had nine cases of mad cow disease since the first confirmed case in 2001, all slaughtered cows must be checked for the disease before the meat is authorized for consumption.

You don't need any inoculations to enter Japan. **Prescriptions** can be filled at Japanese pharmacies *only if they're issued by a Japanese doctor.* To avoid hassle, bring more prescription medications than you think you'll need, clearly labeled in their original vials, and be sure to pack them in your carry-on luggage. But to be safe, bring copies of your prescriptions with you, including generic names of medicines in case a local pharmacist is unfamiliar with the brand name. Over-the-counter items are easy to obtain, though name brands are likely to be different from back home, some ingredients allowed elsewhere may be forbidden in Japan, and prices are likely to be higher.

If you suffer from a chronic illness, consult your doctor before your departure. For conditions like epilepsy, diabetes, or heart problems, wear a **Medic Alert Identification Tag** (✆ 800/825-3785; www.medicalert.org), which will immediately alert doctors to your condition and give them access to your records through Medic Alert's 24-hour hot line.

Contact the **International Association for Medical Assistance to Travelers (IAMAT;** ✆ 716/754-4883 in the U.S., or 416/652-0137 in Canada; www.iamat.org) for information regarding local English-speaking doctors. In Japan, the local consulate and sometimes even the local tourist office can provide a list of area doctors who speak English. If you do get sick, you may want to ask the concierge at your hotel about medical assistance—some hotels even have in-house doctors or clinics. If you can't find a doctor who can help you right away, try the emergency room at the local hospital.

Many emergency rooms have walk-in-clinics for emergency cases that are not life-threatening, though there are usually set hours of operation and you'll have to pay out of pocket (and then try to get reimbursed from your insurance company later).

STAYING SAFE

One of the greatest delights of traveling in Japan is that the country is safe and the people are honest. When a friend forgot her purse in a public rest-room in Osaka in 2003, someone turned it in to the police station complete with money, digital camera, and passport. That said, petty crime is on the increase and you should stay alert for pickpockets in congested areas like subways in big cities like Tokyo. Women should avoid public parks at night. Otherwise, I feel safe walking anywhere in Japan day or night.

7 Tips for Travelers with Special Needs

TRAVELERS WITH DISABILITIES

Tokyo can be a nightmare for travelers with disabilities. City sidewalks can be so jam-packed that getting around on crutches or in a wheelchair is exceedingly difficult. Most subways are accessible only by stairs, and although the trains have seating for passengers with disabilities—located in the first and last compartments of the train and indicated by a white circle with a blue seat—subways can be so crowded that there's barely room to move. Moreover, the seats for travelers with disabilities are almost always occupied by commuters—so unless you look visibly handicapped, no one is likely to offer you a seat. Even Japanese homes are not very accessible, since the main floor is always raised about a foot above the entrance-hall floor.

When it comes to **facilities for the blind,** however, Japan has a very advanced system. At subway stations and on many major sidewalks in Tokyo, raised dots and lines on the ground guide blind people at intersections and to subway platforms. In some cities, streetlights chime a theme when the signal turns green east–west, and chime another for north–south. Even Japanese yen notes are identified by a slightly raised circle—the ¥1,000 note has one circle in a corner, while the ¥10,000 note has two. And finally, many elevators have floors indicated in Braille, and some hotels identify rooms in Braille.

In any case, a disability shouldn't stop anyone from traveling. There are more resources out there than ever before. You can join the **Society for Accessible Travel and Hospitality** (© 212/447-7284; www.sath.org) for $45 annually, $30 for seniors and students, to gain access to its vast network of connections in the travel industry. They provide information sheets on travel destinations and referrals to tour operators that specialize in travel for those with disabilities.

GAY & LESBIAN TRAVELERS

While there are many gay and lesbian establishments in Tokyo, the gay community in Japan is not a vocal one, and in any case, information in English is hard to come by. The **International Gay & Lesbian Travel Association** (IGLTA; © 800/448-8550 or 954/776-2626; www.iglta.org) is the trade association for the gay and lesbian travel industry and offers an online directory of gay- and lesbian-friendly travel businesses; go to their website and click on "Members."

Many agencies offer tours and travel itineraries specifically for gay and lesbian travelers. **Above and Beyond Tours** (© 800/397-2681; www.abovebeyondtours.com) is the exclusive gay and lesbian tour operator for United Airlines. **Now, Voyager**

(© **800/255-6951;** www.nowvoyager. com) is a well-known San Francisco–based gay-owned and operated travel service.

The following travel guides are available at most travel bookstores and gay and lesbian bookstores, or you can order them from **Giovanni's Room** bookstore, 1145 Pine St., Philadelphia, PA 19107 (© **215/923-2960;** www.giovannisroom.com): *Out and About* (© **800/929-2268** or 415/644-8044; www.outandabout.com), which offers guidebooks and a newsletter 10 times a year packed with solid information on the global gay and lesbian scene; *Spartacus International Gay Guide* (Bruno Gmunder Verlag) and *Odysseus: The International Gay Travel Planner* (Odysseus Enterprises Ltd.), both good, annual English-language guidebooks focused on gay men; the *Damron* guides (Damron Company), with separate, annual books for gay men and lesbians; and *Gay Travel A to Z: The World of Gay & Lesbian Travel Options at Your Fingertips* by Marianne Ferrari (Ferrari Publications; Box 35575, Phoenix, AZ 85069), a very good gay and lesbian guidebook series.

SENIOR TRAVEL

A few museums in Tokyo offer **free admission** to seniors over 65 (be sure to have your passport handy), including the **Tokyo National Museum;** others in Tokyo and elsewhere offer discounts. Discounts may not be posted, so be sure to ask. In addition, visitors to Japan should be aware that there are many stairs to navigate in metropolitan areas, particularly in subway and train stations and even on pedestrian overpasses.

Before leaving home, consider becoming a member of **AARP** (formerly known as the American Association of Retired Persons), 601 E St. NW, Washington, DC 20049 (© **800/424-3410** or 202/434-2277;

www.aarp.org), for $13, which brings you a wide range of special benefits, including *AARP: The Magazine* and a monthly newsletter.

If you want something more than the average vacation or guided tour, try **Elderhostel,** 11 Avenue de Lafayette, Boston, MA 02110-1746 (© **877/426-8056;** www.elderhostel. org), which arranges study programs for those 55 and over (and a spouse or companion of any age) in the United States and in 77 countries around the world, including Japan. On these escorted tours, the days are packed with seminars, lectures, and field trips, and academic experts guide the sightseeing. Most courses last about 3 weeks and many include airfare, accommodations in student dormitories or modest inns, meals, and tuition.

FAMILY TRAVEL

The Japanese are very fond of children, which makes traveling in Japan with kids a delight. All social reserve seems to be waived for children. While the average Japanese will not approach foreign adults, if you bring a child with you the Japanese will not only talk to you but they may even invite you home. Taking along some small and easy-to-carry gifts (such as colorful stickers) for your kids to give to other children is a great icebreaker.

While children may not like such foreign customs as eating raw fish, they will find many other Japanese customs to their taste. What child could resist taking baths *en famille* and actually getting to splash? If you go to a *ryokan,* chances are your kids will love wearing *yukata* (cotton kimono) and clattering around in *geta* (wooden sandals). Your children will be pampered and played with and receive presents and lots of attention.

As for the food, the transition from kid-favorite spaghetti to udon noodles is easy, and udon and soba shops are inexpensive and ubiquitous. In addition, most family-style restaurants, especially those in department stores, offer a special children's meal that often includes a small toy or souvenir. For those real emergencies, Western fast-food places such as McDonald's and Kentucky Fried Chicken are everywhere in Tokyo.

Tourist spots in Japan almost always have a table or counter with a stamp and ink pad so that visitors can commemorate their trip; you might wish to give your children a small notebook so that they can collect imprints of every attraction they visit.

Children 6 to 11 years old are generally charged half-price for everything from temple admission to train tickets, while children under 6 are often admitted free. If your child under 6 sleeps with you, you generally won't even have to pay for him or her in most hotels and ryokans. However, it's always advisable to ask in advance.

Safety also makes Japan a good destination for families. Still, plan your itinerary with care. To avoid crowds, visit tourist sights on weekdays. Never travel on city transportation during rush hour or on trains during popular public holidays. And remember that with all the stairways and crowded sidewalks, strollers are less practical than baby backpacks. Many of Tokyo's major hotels provide babysitting services, although they are almost prohibitively expensive. Expect to fork over a minimum of ¥5,000 ($42) for 2 hours of babysitting.

You can find good family-oriented vacation advice on the Internet from **Traveling Internationally with Your Kids** (www.travelwithyourkids.com), a comprehensive site offering sound advice for long-distance and international travel with children.

STUDENT TRAVEL

Students sometimes receive discounts at museums, though occasionally discounts are available only to students enrolled in Japanese schools. Furthermore, discounted prices are often not displayed in English. Your best bet is to bring along an International Student Identity Card (ISIC; see below) with your university student ID and show them both at museum ticket windows.

Before you leave home, arm yourself with the **International Student Identity Card (ISIC),** which offers substantial savings on entrance fees. It also provides you with basic health and life insurance and a 24-hour help line. The card is available for $22 from **STA Travel** (© **800/781-4040** [if you're not in North America there's probably a local number in your country]; www.statravel.com), the biggest student travel agency in the world.

SINGLE TRAVELERS

Traveling alone poses no difficulty, even for women. The main obstacle is expense, since the price of accommodations is usually cheaper for couples and groups. Single travelers, therefore, should do what traveling businessmen do: Stay at so-called business hotels. With their large number of single rooms, they cater almost exclusively to solo businessmen.

An alternative is to register with **Travel Companion Exchange (TCE)** (© **631/454-0880;** www.travel companions.com), one of the nation's oldest roommate finders for single travelers. Register with them to find a travel mate who will split the cost of the room with you and be around as little, or as often, as you like during the day.

Because of its physical isolation and the fact that it was never successfully invaded before World War II, Japan is one of the most homogeneous nations in the world. Almost 99% of Japan's population is Japanese, with hardly any influx of other genes into the country since the 8th century. The Japanese feel they belong to one huge tribe different from any other people on earth. A Japanese will often preface a statement or opinion with the words "We Japanese," implying that all Japanese think alike and that all people in the world can be divided into two groups, Japanese and non-Japanese.

While in the West the recipe for a full and rewarding life seems to be that elusive attainment of "happiness," in Japan it's the satisfactory performance of duty and obligation. Individuality in Japan is equated with selfishness and a complete disregard for the feelings and consideration of others. The Japanese are instilled with a sense of duty toward the group—whether it be family, friends, coworkers, or Japanese society as a whole. In a nation as crowded as Japan, such consideration of others is essential, especially in Tokyo, where space is particularly scarce.

MEETING THE JAPANESE

If you've been invited to Japan by some organization or business, you will receive the royal treatment and most likely be wined and dined so wonderfully and thoroughly that you'll never want to return home. If you've come to Tokyo on your own as an ordinary tourist, however, your experiences will depend largely on you. Although the Japanese will sometimes approach you to ask whether they might practice their English with you, for the most part you are left on your own unless you make the first move.

The best way to meet the Japanese is to participate in a super program launched by the Japan National Tourist Organization called the **Home Visit System,** which offers overseas visitors the opportunity to visit an English-speaking Japanese family in their home. Upon request, you might even be paired with a family with the same occupation as yours. It doesn't cost anything, and the visit usually takes place for 2 hours in the evening beginning at 7pm (dinner is not served). It's a good idea to bring a small gift, such as flowers, fruit, or something from your hometown. Unfortunately, Tokyo does not participate in the Home Visit System, but two nearby cities that do are **Narita** (✆ **0476/34-6251** or 0476/24-3198) and **Yokohama** (✆ **045-441-7300**). Reservations must be made at least 24 hours to 2 days in advance.

Another way to meet the Japanese is to go where they play, namely Tokyo's countless bars and eateries. There, you'll often find people who know some English and will want to practice it on you, as well as more inebriated people who want to talk to you whether they know English or not. If you're open to them, such chance encounters may prove to be highlights of your trip.

Alternatively, check ads in *Tokyo Notice Board* for English-conversation schools. Designed to help Japanese improve their English, the schools often offer social hours and events, admitting English-speaking foreigners for free or at a discount. One such school is **Com'Inn,** 1–3–9 Ebisu Minami (✆ **03/3710-7063;** www.cominn-jp.com; station: Ebisu), open daily from 3 to 10pm. Foreigners are welcome to join conversations for ¥500 ($4.15), which includes coffee or tea. Parties are staged two evenings a month with all you can eat and drink for ¥2,000 ($17). To find the school, take the west exit of JR Ebisu Station and follow the road alongside Doutour coffee shop; it will be in the next block on the corner to the left.

Finally, you can request the services of a volunteer **Goodwill Guide** for free guided tours of Nikko (✆ **0288/54-2027**), Yokohama (✆ **03/3201-3331**), Kamakura (✆ **090/9845-1290**) and other cities in Japan. Reservations for a guide should be made 1 week in advance; all you need pay is the guide's travel expenses, admission fees to sights, and meals.

MINDING YOUR P'S & Q'S

When European merchants and missionaries began arriving in Japan almost 400 years ago, the Japanese took one look at them and immediately labeled them barbarians. After all, these hairy and boisterous outsiders rarely bathed and didn't know the first thing about proper etiquette and behavior.

The Japanese, on the other hand, had a strict social hierarchy that dictated exactly how a person should speak, sit, bow, eat, walk, dress, and live. Failure to comply with the rules could bring swift punishment and sometimes even death. More than one Japanese literally lost his head for committing a social blunder.

Of course, things have changed since then, and the Japanese have even adopted some of the Western barbarians' customs. However, what hasn't changed is that the Japanese still attach much importance to proper behavior and etiquette, which developed to allow relationships to be as frictionless as possible—important in a country as crowded as Japan. The Japanese don't like confrontations, and although I'm told they do occur, I've never seen a fight in Japan.

One aspect of Japanese behavior that sometimes causes difficulty for foreigners is that the Japanese find it very hard to say no. They're much more apt to say that your request is very difficult to fulfill; or else they'll beat around the bush without giving a definite answer. At this point you're expected to let the subject drop. Showing impatience, anger, or aggressiveness rarely gets you anywhere in Japan. Apologizing sometimes does. And if someone does give in to your request, you can't say thank you often enough.

BOWING The main form of greeting in Japan is the bow rather than the handshake. Although at first glance it may seem simple enough, the bow—together with its implications—is actually quite complicated. The depth of the bow and the number of seconds devoted to performing it, as well as the total number of bows, depend on who you are and to whom you're bowing. In addition to bowing in greeting, the Japanese also bow upon departing and to express gratitude. The proper form for a bow is to bend from the waist with a straight back and to keep your arms at your sides, but as a foreigner you'll probably feel foolish and look pretty stupid if you try to imitate what the Japanese have spent years learning. A simple nod of the head is enough. Knowing that foreigners shake hands, a Japanese may extend a hand but probably won't be able to stop from giving a little bow as well. The Japanese will bow even when speaking to an invisible someone on the telephone.

VISITING CARDS You're a nonentity in Japan if you don't have a business or visiting card, called a *meishi*. Everyone from housewives to plumbers to secretaries to bank presidents carries meishi with them to give out upon introduction. If you're trying to conduct business in Japan, you'll be regarded suspiciously if you don't have business cards. As a tourist you don't have to have business cards, but it certainly doesn't hurt, and the Japanese will be greatly impressed by your preparedness. The card should have your address and occupation on it. As a nice souvenir, you might consider having your meishi made in Japan with the Japanese syllabic script (*katakana*) written on the reverse side.

The proper way to present a meishi depends on the status of the two people involved. If you are both of equal status, you exchange meishi simultaneously; otherwise, the lower person on the totem pole presents the meishi first and delivers it underneath the card being received, to show deference. Turn it so that the other person can read it (that is, upside down to you) and present it with both hands and a slight bow. Afterward, don't simply put the meishi away. Rather, it's customary for both of you to study the meishi for a moment and, if possible, to comment on it (such as "You're from Kyoto? My brother lived in Kyoto!" or "Sony! What a famous company!").

SHOES   Nothing is so distasteful to the Japanese as the bottoms of shoes, and therefore shoes are taken off before entering a home, a Japanese-style inn, a temple, and even some museums and restaurants. Usually, there will be plastic slippers at the entranceway for you to slip on, but whenever you encounter tatami floors you should remove even these slippers—only bare feet or socks are allowed to tread upon tatami.

Restrooms present another whole set of slippers. If you're in a home or Japanese inn, you'll notice a second pair of slippers—again plastic or rubber—sitting just inside the restroom door. Step out of the hallway plastic shoes and into the bathroom slippers and wear these the whole time you're in the bathroom. When you're finished, change back into the hallway slippers. If you forget this last changeover, you'll regret it—nothing is as embarrassing as walking into a room wearing toilet slippers and not realizing what you've done until you see the mixed looks of horror and mirth on the faces of the Japanese.

GUEST ETIQUETTE   If you are invited to a Japanese home, you should know it is both a rarity and an honor. Most Japanese consider their homes too small and humble for entertaining guests, which is why there are so many restaurants, coffee shops, and bars. If you are lucky enough to get an invitation, don't show up empty-handed. Bring a small gift, such as candy, fruit, flowers, or a

souvenir of your hometown. Alcohol is also appreciated.

Instead of being invited to a private home, you may be invited out for dinner and drinks, especially if you're in Japan on business, in which case your hosts may have an expense account. In any event, it's nice to reciprocate by taking them out later to your own territory, say, to a French or other Western-style restaurant, where you'll feel comfortable playing host.

If you're with friends, the general practice is to divide the check equally among everyone, no matter how much or little each person consumed.

In any case, no matter what favor a Japanese has done for you—whether it was giving you a small gift, buying you a drink, or making a telephone call for you—be sure to give your thanks profusely the next time you meet. The Japanese think it odd and rude not to be remembered and thanked upon your next meeting, even if a year has elapsed.

OTHER CUSTOMS   When the Japanese give back change, they **hand it to you in a lump sum** rather than counting it out. Trust them. It's considered insulting for you to stay there and count it in front of them because you are insinuating that they will cheat you. The Japanese are honest. It's one of the great pleasures of being in their country.

Don't **blow your nose in public** if you can help it, and never at the dinner table. It's considered disgusting. On the other hand, even though the Japanese are very hygienic, they are not averse to spitting on the sidewalk. And even more peculiar, men often urinate when and where they want, usually against a tree or a wall and most often after a night of carousing in the bars.

This being a **man's society,** men will walk in and out of doors and elevators before women, and in subways will often sit down while their wives stand. Some Japanese men, however, who have had contact with the Western world, will make a gallant show of allowing a Western woman to step out of the elevator or door first.

THE JAPANESE BATH

On my very first trip to Japan, I was certain that I would never get into a Japanese bath. I was under the misconception that men and women bathed together, and I couldn't imagine getting into a tub with a group of smiling and bowing Japanese men. I needn't have worried. In almost all circumstances, bathing is gender-segregated. There are some exceptions, primarily at outdoor hot-spring spas in the countryside, but the women who go to these are usually grandmothers who couldn't care less. Young Japanese women wouldn't dream of jumping into a tub with a group of male strangers.

Japanese baths are delightful—and I, for one, am addicted to them. You'll find them at Japanese-style inns, at hot-spring spas, and at neighborhood baths (not everyone has his or her own bath in Japan). Sometimes they're elaborate affairs with many tubs, plants, and statues, and sometimes they're nothing more than a tiny tub. Public baths have long been regarded as social centers for the Japanese—friends and co-workers visit hot-spring resorts together; neighbors exchange gossip at the neighborhood bath. Sadly, however, the neighborhood bath has been in great decline over the past decades, as more and more Japanese acquire private baths. In 1968, Tokyo alone had 2,687 neighborhood baths; today that number has dropped to less than 1,150.

In any case, whether large or small, the procedure at all Japanese baths is the same. After you completely disrobe in the changing room and put your clothes in either a locker or a basket, hold a washcloth in front of your vital parts and walk into the bath area. There you'll find plastic basins and stools (they used to be made of wood), and faucets along the wall. Sit on a stool in front of the faucet and repeatedly fill your basin with water, splashing it all over you. If there's no hot water from the faucet, it's acceptable to dip your plastic basin into the hot bath. Soap yourself completely—and I mean completely—and then rinse away all traces of soap. I have never seen a group of people wash themselves so thoroughly as the Japanese, from their eyes to their toes. Only after you're squeaky-clean are you ready to get into the bath. When you've finished bathing, do not pull the plug. The same bathwater is used by everyone, which is why it's so important to soap down and rinse before entering the tub.

Your first attempt at a Japanese bath may be painful—simply too scalding for comfort. It helps if you ease in gently and then sit perfectly still. You'll notice all tension and muscle stiffness ebbing away, a decidedly relaxing way to end the day. The Japanese are so fond of baths that many take them nightly, especially in winter, when a hot bath keeps you toasty warm for hours afterward. With time, you'll probably become addicted, too.

9 Flying to Japan

Most visitors to Tokyo arrive by air, at **Narita International Airport** 66km (40 miles) outside Tokyo in **Narita.**

THE AIRLINES

Since the flying time to Tokyo is about 12 hours from Los Angeles and 13½ hours from Chicago or New York, you'll want to consider on-board services and even mileage programs (you'll earn lots of miles on this round-trip) as well as ticket price when choosing your carrier. Airlines flying to Tokyo from North America, England, Australia, and New Zealand include:

Air Canada (© 888/247-2262; www.aircanada.com) offers flights from Vancouver to Tokyo daily.

Air New Zealand (© 0800/737-000 in New Zealand, or 800/262-1234 in the U.S.; www.airnewzealand.com) flies from Auckland to Tokyo.

All Nippon Airways (© 800/235-9262; www.fly-ana.com) is Japan's largest domestic carrier. It offers daily nonstop service from New York, Washington, D.C., Los Angeles, and San Francisco to Tokyo. It also flies from London and Sydney to Tokyo. ANA has a code-share alliance with United Airlines (meaning that both airlines can sell each other's tickets; you can also earn United frequent-flier miles with ANA). ANA passengers can also receive discounts at ANA hotels in Japan with free baggage transfers. Another great perk is that passengers flying round-trip from Canada or the United States can receive complimentary domestic-use cellphone hours for up to 2 weeks, with passengers paying only the calling charges; you can reserve phones online and pick them up at Narita Airport upon your arrival.

American Airlines (© 800/433-7300; www.aa.com) offers flights daily from Dallas and Chicago to Tokyo and code-shares with Japan Airlines.

British Airways (© 0870 850 9850 in Britain; www.ba.com) flies from London to Tokyo.

Continental Airlines (© 800/523-3273; www.continental.com) offers flights daily from Newark and Houston to Tokyo.

Delta Airlines (© 800/241-4141; www.delta.com) offers daily flights from Atlanta to Tokyo.

Japan Airlines (© 800/525-3663; www.japanair.com), Japan's flagship carrier, offers more international flights to Japan than any other carrier

and is noted for its excellent service. JAL flies to Tokyo from New York, Chicago, San Francisco, Los Angeles, Las Vegas, and Vancouver. It also connects Japan with England, New Zealand, and Australia.

Northwest Airlines (© 800/447-4747; www.nwa.com), operating across the Pacific for more than 50 years (longer than any other airline), offers more nonstop service between North America and Japan than any other American carrier. North American gateways to Japan are Los Angeles, San Francisco, Seattle, Detroit, New York, Minneapolis–St. Paul, and Honolulu. Japan-bound flights also offer connecting service to 10 cities in Asia, making it easy to coordinate onward travel plans to, say, Hong Kong or Bangkok. The airline's stellar service has even attracted the hard-to-please Japanese, who regularly fly Northwest.

Qantas (© 800/227-4500, or 13-13-13 in Australia; www.qantas.com) flies from Sydney, Melbourne, and Brisbane to Tokyo.

United Airlines (© 800/538-2929; www.united.com) has daily flights from San Francisco, Los Angeles, Seattle, Chicago, and New York to Tokyo. It code-shares with ANA.

AIRFARES

Because the flight to Tokyo is such a long one, you may wish to splurge on upgraded service and a roomier seat. But we're talking about a serious splurge: Japan Airlines' round-trip first-class fare from New York to Tokyo averages about $14,180, plus tax, while business class will cost about $7,694. Even full-fare economy-class tickets run about $5,655, but I doubt many people end up paying full fare.

Japan Airlines' lowest economy fares average $840, but you can save even more money by buying an APEX (Advance Purchase Excursion) ticket. It's usually loaded with restrictions and is based on the seasons. There are three fare seasons: peak season (summer) is the most expensive, basic season (winter) is the least expensive, and shoulder season is between the other two in time and in price. During all three seasons, APEX fares are a little higher on weekends. Japan Airlines' APEX fare in October 2003, requiring a 7-day advance purchase and with minimum- and maximum-stay restrictions, was $660 for round-trip travel between New York and Tokyo on a weekday during the shoulder season.

FLYING FOR LESS: TIPS FOR GETTING THE BEST AIRFARE

Passengers sharing the same airplane cabin rarely pay the same fare. Travelers who need to purchase tickets at the last minute, change their itinerary at a moment's notice, or fly one-way often get stuck paying the premium rate. Here are some ways to keep your airfare costs down.

- Passengers who can book their ticket **long in advance** or who **fly midweek** or **at less-trafficked hours** will pay a fraction of the full fare. If your schedule is flexible, say so, and ask if you can secure a cheaper fare by changing your flight plans by staying an extra day or flying midweek.

- You can also save on airfares by checking local newspapers or the travel sections of major West Coast newspapers for **promotional specials** or **fare wars,** when airlines lower prices on their most popular routes. You rarely see fare wars offered during peak travel times, but if you can travel in the off season, you may snag a bargain.

- Search **the Internet** for cheap fares. The "big three" online travel agencies, **Expedia.com, Travelocity. com,** and **Orbitz.com** sell most of the air tickets bought on the Internet. (Canadian travelers should try Expedia.ca and Travelocity.ca; U.K. residents can go for Expedia. co.uk and Opodo.co.uk.) Each

has different business deals with the airlines and may offer different fares on the same flights, so it's wise to shop around. Expedia and Travelocity will also send you **e-mail notification** when a cheap fare becomes available to your favorite destination. Another place to look for discounted fares is **www.cheaptickets.com**.

Also remember to check airline websites. Even with major airlines you can often shave a few bucks from a fare by booking directly through the airline and avoiding a travel agency's transaction fee. But you'll get these discounts only by booking online: Most airlines now offer online-only fares that even their phone agents know nothing about. For the websites of airlines that fly to Tokyo, see "The Airlines," above.

- **Consolidators,** also known as bucket shops, are great sources of international tickets, although they usually can't beat the Internet on fares within North America. Start by looking in Sunday newspaper travel sections; U.S. travelers should focus on the *New York Times, Los Angeles Times,* and *Miami Herald.* For less-developed destinations, small travel agents who cater to immigrant communities in large cities often have the best deals. *Beware:* Bucket shop tickets are usually nonrefundable or rigged with stiff cancellation penalties, often as high as 50% to 75% of the ticket price, and some put you on charter airlines with questionable safety records. Your best bet may be to deal with a company specializing in Japan. One that does is **Nippon Travel** (© **800/445-2332;** www.nta. co.jp/english), which offers discounted tickets on ANA.

- Join **frequent-flier clubs.** Accrue enough miles, and you'll be rewarded with free flights and elite status. It's free, and you'll get the best choice of seats, faster response to phone inquiries, and prompter service if your luggage is stolen, if your flight is canceled or delayed, or if you want to change your seat. You don't need to fly to build frequent-flier miles—**frequent-flier credit cards** can provide thousands of miles in exchange for doing your everyday shopping.

LONG-HAUL FLIGHTS: HOW TO STAY COMFORTABLE

Long flights can be trying, but with a little advance planning, you can make an otherwise unpleasant experience almost bearable.

- Your choice of airline and airplane will definitely affect your legroom. Find details on seat pitch (the distance between a seat and the row in front of it) and more at www.seatguru.com, which has extensive details about almost every seat on six major U.S. airlines. For international airlines, research firm Skytrax has posted a list of average seat pitches at www.airlinequality.com.
- Emergency-exit seats and bulkhead seats typically have the most legroom. Emergency-exit seats are usually held back to be assigned the day of a flight (to ensure that the seat is filled by someone able-bodied); it's worth getting to the ticket counter early to snag one of these spots for a long flight. Keep in mind that bulkheads are where airlines often put baby bassinets, so you may be sitting next to an infant. In addition, you have to stow hand-carried items in overhead bins.
- To have two seats to yourself, try for an aisle seat in a center section toward the back of coach. If you're traveling with a companion, book an aisle and a window seat. Middle seats are usually booked last, so chances are good you'll end up

with three seats to yourselves. And in the event that a third passenger is assigned the middle seat, he or she will probably be more than happy to trade for a window or an aisle.
- Ask about entertainment options. Many airlines offer seatback video systems that allow you to choose movies or play video games—but only on some of their planes. (Boeing 777s are your best bet.)
- To sleep, avoid the last row of any section or a row in front of an emergency exit, as these seats are the least likely to recline. Avoid seats near highly trafficked toilet areas. You may want to reserve a window seat so that you can rest your head and avoid being bumped in the aisle.
- Get up, walk around, and stretch every 60 to 90 minutes to keep your blood flowing. This helps you avoid deep-vein thrombosis, or "economy-class syndrome," a rare and deadly condition that can be caused by sitting in cramped conditions for too long.
- Drink water before, during, and after your flight to combat the lack of humidity in airplane cabins—which can be drier than the Sahara. Bring a bottle of water on board. Avoid alcohol, which will dehydrate you.
- If you're flying with kids, don't forget to carry on toys, books, pacifiers, and chewing gum to help them relieve ear pressure buildup during ascent and descent. Let each child pack his or her own backpack with favorite toys.

ARRIVING AT NARITA AIRPORT

Tokyo has two airports. International flights land at **Narita International Airport** in Narita about 66km (40 miles) outside Tokyo. (If you're arriving in Tokyo from elsewhere in Japan, your flight will probably land at

Haneda Airport, used primarily for domestic flights; see below.)

Narita International Airport (© 0476/34-5000) consists of two terminals, Terminal 1 and 2. Arrival lobbies in both terminals have banks for money exchange open daily 6am to 11pm as well as ATMs (change money here, as facilities in town are limited) and are connected to all ground transportation into Tokyo.

A Tourist Information Center (TIC), managed by the Japan National Tourist Organization, is located in the arrival lobbies of both Terminal 1 (© 0476/30-3383) and Terminal 2 (© 0476/34-6251). The TIC offers free maps and pamphlets and can direct you to your hotel or inn. Both are open daily 9am to 8pm; if you don't yet have a hotel room and want one at a modest price, you can make reservations here free of charge Monday through Friday until 7:30pm.

Other facilities at both terminals include post offices, medical clinics and, in their departure lounges, shower rooms and day rooms for napping as well as children's playrooms. Departure lounges of both terminals also have coin-operated computers with Internet capabilities (¥100/85¢ for 10 min.).

GETTING FROM NARITA AIRPORT TO TOKYO

Everyone grumbles about Narita Airport because it's so far away from Tokyo. In fact, Narita is a different town altogether, with miles of paddies, bamboo groves, pine forests, and urban sprawl between it and Tokyo.

BY TAXI   Obviously, jumping into a taxi is the easiest way to get to Tokyo, but it's also prohibitively expensive—and may not even be the quickest method during rush hours. Expect to spend around ¥25,000 ($208) or more for a 1½- to 2-hour taxi ride from Narita.

BY AIRPORT BUS   The most popular and stress-free way to get from Narita to Tokyo is via the Airport Limousine Bus (© 03/3665-7220; www.limousinebus.co.jp), which picks up passengers and their luggage from just outside the arrival lobbies of terminals 1 and 2 and delivers them to downtown hotels. This is the best mode of transportation if you have heavy baggage or are staying at one of the many hotels served by the bus. Buses operate most frequently to the Tokyo City Air Terminal (TCAT), located in downtown Tokyo and reached in about 70 minutes. Buses also depart frequently—up to four or five times an hour during peak times—for Tokyo Station and Shinjuku Station. They also serve more than 40 major hotels on a slightly less frequent schedule—generally once an hour—and it can take almost 2 hours to reach a hotel in Shinjuku. Check with the staff at the Airport Limousine Bus counter in the arrival lobbies to inquire which bus stops nearest your hotel and the time of departure. Fares for the limousine bus average ¥2,700 to ¥3,000 ($23–$25), based on distance traveled. Children 6 to 12 are charged half-fare; those under 6 ride free.

If you take a limousine bus into Tokyo, plenty of taxis are available at the end of the line. TCAT, Shinjuku Station, and Tokyo Station are also served by public transportation; TCAT is connected to the Hanzomon subway line via moving walkways and escalators; Shinjuku and Tokyo stations are hubs for subway lines and commuter trains.

BY TRAIN   The quickest way to reach Tokyo is by train. Trains depart directly from the airport's two underground stations, called Narita Airport Station (in Terminal 1) and Airport Terminal 2. The JR Narita Express (NEX; © 03/3423-0111; www.japan rail.com) is the fastest way to reach Tokyo Station, Shinagawa, Shinjuku, Ikebukuro, and Yokohama, with departures approximately once an hour, or twice an hour during peak hours. The 53-minute trip to Tokyo Station costs ¥3,140 ($26) one-way. The trip to Shinagawa, Shinjuku, or Ikebukuro costs ¥3,310 ($28). *Note:* Seats are sometimes sold out in advance, especially during peak travel times. If you plan to journey to Tokyo during a travel crunch (say, the end of Golden Week), consider purchasing a reserved seat before your arrival in Japan at **www.world.eki-net.com**. You'll have to sign up for free membership and provide a credit card (American Express, Diners Club, MasterCard, or Visa). You can view timetables and select the train you'd like to take, and you will receive a confirmation via e-mail. Print it out and take with you to the JR Reservation Ticket Office or View Plaza at the airport, and then pay for your ticket using the credit card you used to make the reservation (if you fail to show up, you will still be charged). Reservations can be made 1 month to 2 days in advance. Otherwise, if you wish to purchase your return ticket to Narita Airport—and I strongly urge you to—you can do so here at the NEX counter, at a JR Reservation Ticket Office, at a View Plaza at major JR stations in Tokyo, or at a travel agency; try to arrive at the airport at least 2 hours before your plane's departure.

If the NEX is sold out, take the slower JR **Airport Liner,** which will get you to Tokyo Station in 80 minutes and costs ¥1,280 ($11). An alternative is the privately owned **Keisei Skyliner** train (© **03/3831-0131;** www.keisei. co.jp), which departs directly from both Narita Airport Station (Terminal 1) and Airport Terminal 2 and travels to Ueno Station in Tokyo in about 1 hour, with a stop at Nippori Station on the way. You'll find Keisei Skyliner counters in the arrival lobbies of both terminals. Trains depart approximately 40 minutes between 7:49am and 9:58pm. The fare from Narita Airport to Ueno Station in Tokyo is ¥1,920 ($17) one-way; early morning and evening fares are cheaper. If you're on a strict budget, you can take one of Keisei's slower limited express trains to Ueno Station; fares start at ¥1,000 ($8.70) for the 75-minute trip. At Ueno Station you can take either the subway or the JR Yamanote Line to other parts of Tokyo. There are also plenty of taxis available.

GETTING FROM HANEDA AIRPORT TO CENTRAL TOKYO

If you're arriving at **Haneda Airport** (© **03/5757-8111**), located closer to the center of Tokyo and used mainly for domestic flights, you can take the **Airport Limousine Bus** to Shinjuku Station, Tokyo Station, the Tokyo City Air Terminal (TCAT) in downtown Tokyo, and hotels in Shinjuku, Ikebukuro, and Akasaka. Fares run from ¥900 to ¥1,200 ($7.50–$10). Locals, however, are more likely to take the **monorail** from Haneda Airport 15 minutes to Hamamatsucho Station (fare: ¥470/$3.90), or the **Keikyu Line** 19 minutes to Shinagawa (fare: ¥400/$3.35). Both Hamamatsucho and Shinagawa connect to the very useful Yamanote Line, which travels to major stations, including Tokyo Station and Shinjuku Station. Be sure to stop by the **Tokyo Tourist Information Center** (© **03/5757-9345**) in Haneda Airport, open daily 9am to 10pm.

10 Escorted & Package Tours

ESCORTED TOURS

If you're the kind of traveler who doesn't like leaving such arrangements as accommodations, transportation, and itinerary to chance, consider joining an escorted tour of Japan.

Escorted tours are structured group tours, with a guide. The price usually includes everything from airfare to hotels, meals, tours, admission costs, and local transportation. Many people derive a certain ease and security from escorted trips; whether made by bus, motor coach, train, or boat, they let travelers sit back and enjoy their trip without having to spend lots of time behind the wheel. All the little details are taken care of; you know your costs up front; and there are few surprises. Escorted tours can take you to the maximum number of sights in the minimum amount of time with the least amount of hassle—you don't have to sweat over the plotting and planning of a vacation schedule. They are particularly convenient for people with limited mobility. On the downside, an escorted tour often requires a big deposit up front, and lodging and dining choices are predetermined. As part of a crowd of tourists, you'll get fewer opportunities for serendipitous interaction with locals. Tours can be jam-packed with activities, leaving little room for individual sightseeing, whim, or adventure—plus they often focus on heavily touristed sites, so you miss out on the lesser-known gems.

Other companies offer escorted group tours as well. **General Tours** (© 800/221-2216; www.generaltours. com) offers tours to major tourist destinations in Japan. **Elite Orient Tours** (© 800/668-8100; www.japanstory san.com) offers tours to less-visited regions, including Shikoku, Kyushu, and Tohoku. **Esprit Travel** (© 800/ 377-7481; www.esprittravel.com) specializes in small-group walking trips, hiking trips, and special trips that cover such interests as textile arts, Japanese gardens, and the old Tokaido Road.

PACKAGE TOURS

Package tours are not the same as escorted tours. They are simply ways to buy the airfare, accommodations, and other elements of your trip (such as airport transfers and day tours) at the same time and often at discounted prices—kind of like one-stop shopping. For destinations like Japan, they are a smart way to go because they may save you a lot of money (packages are sold in bulk to tour operators, who then resell them to the public at a cost that drastically undercuts standard rates).

Packages vary widely. Some offer a better class of hotels than others, or offer the same hotels for lower prices or a range of hotel choices at different prices. Flights may be on scheduled airlines; others book charters. Some allow you to add on excursions or day trips (at lower prices than you could find yourself) without booking an entirely escorted tour. If you shop around, you'll save in the long run. The best places to start your search are the travel section of your local Sunday newspaper, and the ads at the backs of national travel magazines like *Travel & Leisure, National Geographic Traveler,* and *Condé Nast Traveler.* One such company offering independent packages to Japan is **Isramworld** (© 800/ 223-7460; www.orientflexipax.com). But the best resource is the airlines themselves, which often package their flights with accommodations. **All Nippon Airways** (© 800/235-9262; www.fly-ana.com), Japan's largest domestic carrier, offers discounts at ANA hotels. **Japan Airlines,** Japan's flagship carrier, operates JALPAK (© 800/221-1081; www.jalpak.com), with airfare and hotel packages to Japan, plus optional escorted day trips. **Northwest Airlines World Vacations** (© 800/800-1504; www. nwaworldvacations.com) also offers flight-and-hotel packages to Tokyo.

3

Getting to Know Tokyo

Tokyo's sheer size and the language barrier provide the greatest challenges facing newcomers. This chapter will help you orient yourself in the city and answer some essential questions, from how to get around using public transportation to what numbers to call in an emergency.

1 Orientation

VISITOR INFORMATION

The **Japan National Tourist Organization (JNTO)** maintains three tourist offices, known as **Tourist Information Centers (TIC),** in the vicinity of Tokyo to handle inquiries from foreigners and the general public about Tokyo and the rest of Japan and to provide free maps and sightseeing materials. You can even make reservations here for inexpensive accommodations throughout Japan at no extra charge.

If you arrive by plane at **Narita Airport,** you'll find TICs in the arrivals lobbies of Terminal 1 (© **0476/30-3383**) and Terminal 2 (© **0476/34-6251**), both open daily from 9am to 8pm.

Otherwise, there's another TIC in the heart of Tokyo at 2–10–1 Yurakucho (© **03/3201-3331**), within walking distance of the Ginza. It's located on the 10th floor of a rather obscure office building next to Yurakucho Station called the **Kotsu Kaikan Building** (look for the building's circular top). Assuming you're able to find them, the TIC staff is courteous and efficient; I cannot recommend them highly enough. In addition to city maps and sightseeing materials, the office has more information on the rest of Japan than any other tourist office, including pamphlets and brochures on major cities and attractions such as Nikko and Kamakura. Hours are Monday through Friday from 9am to 5pm and Saturday from 9am to noon; closed Sunday and national holidays. Note that the hotel reservations service is available only on weekdays and is closed from 11:30am to 1pm.

Another great source of information on Tokyo is the **Tokyo Tourist Information Center,** operated by the Tokyo Metropolitan Government and located on the first floor of the Tokyo Metropolitan Government (TMG) Building No. 1, 2–8–1 Nishi-Shinjuku (© **03/5321-3077;** www.tourism.metro.tokyo.jp and www.tcvb.or.jp); you'll probably want to come here anyway for the TMG's great observation floor. The center dispenses advice, pamphlets, and its own city map (which I consider better than the one issued by JNTO's TICs) and is open daily 10am to 6:30pm. Other city-run information counters are located at Keisei Ueno Station (© **03/3836-3471**), open daily 9:30am to 6:30pm; and at Haneda Airport (© **03/5757-9345**), open daily 9am to 10pm.

TOURIST PUBLICATIONS   Be sure to pick up *Calendar Events* at the TIC, a monthly leaflet listing festivals, antiques and crafts fairs, and other events throughout the metropolitan area. English-language newspapers such as the

Japan Times and the ***Daily Yomiuri*** carry information on theater, films, and special events. Of the many free giveaways available at TIC, restaurants, bars, bookstores, hotels, and other establishments visitors and expats are likely to frequent, best is the weekly ***Metropolis,*** with features on Tokyo, club listings, and restaurant and movie reviews. ***Tokyo Weekender*** also carries a section on what's going on in and around the city, including outdoor recreation and activities. Look also for the free *JapanZine.*

CITY LAYOUT

Tokyo is located on the mid-eastern part of **Honshu,** Japan's largest and most historically important island, and sprawls westward onto the **Kanto Plain** (the largest plain in all Japan). It is bounded on the southeast by **Tokyo Bay** which, in turn, opens into the Pacific Ocean.

If you look at a map, you'll see that Tokyo retains some of its Edo-Period features, most notably a large green oasis in the middle of the city, site of the former Edo Castle and today home of the Imperial Palace and its grounds. Surrounding it is the castle moat; a bit farther out are remnants of another circular moat built by the Tokugawa shogun. The **JR Yamanote Line** forms another loop around the inner city; most of Tokyo's major hotels, nightlife districts, and attractions are near or inside this oblong loop.

For administrative purposes, Tokyo is broken down into 23 wards, known as *ku.* Its business districts of Marunouchi and Hibiya, for example, are in Chiyoda-ku, while Ginza is part of Chuo-ku (Central Ward). These two ku are the historic hearts of Tokyo, for it was here that the city had its humble beginnings.

MAIN STREETS & ARTERIES   One difficulty in finding your way around Tokyo is that hardly any streets are named. Think about what that means—12 million people living in a huge metropolis of nameless streets. Granted, major thoroughfares and some well-known streets in areas like Ginza and Shinjuku received names after World War II at the insistence of American occupation forces, and a few more have been labeled or given nicknames only the locals know. But for the most part, Tokyo's address system is based on a complicated number scheme that must make the postal worker's job here a nightmare. To make matters worse, most streets in Tokyo zigzag—an arrangement apparently left over from olden days, to confuse potential attacking enemies. Today they confuse Tokyoites and visitors alike.

Among Tokyo's most important named streets are **Meiji Dori,** which follows the loop of the Yamanote Line and runs from Ebisu in the south through Shibuya, Harajuku, Shinjuku, and Ikebukuro in the north; **Yasukuni Dori** and **Shinjuku Dori,** which cut across the heart of the city from Shinjuku to Chiyoda-ku; and **Sotobori Dori, Chuo Dori, Harumi Dori,** and **Showa Dori,** which pass through Ginza. (*Dori* means avenue or street, as does *michi.*)

An intersection in Tokyo is called a crossing; it seems every district has a famous crossing. Ginza 4–chome Crossing is the intersection of Chuo Dori and Harumi Dori. Roppongi Crossing is the intersection of Roppongi Dori and Gaien-Higashi Dori.

FINDING AN ADDRESS   Because streets did not have names when Japan's postal system was established, the country has a unique address system. A typical Tokyo address might read 1–9–1 Marunouchi, Chiyoda-ku, which is the address of the Tokyo Station Hotel. Chiyoda-ku is the name of the ward. Wards are further divided into districts, in this case Marunouchi. Marunouchi itself is broken down into chome (numbered subsections), here 1–chome. Number 9

Tokyo at a Glance

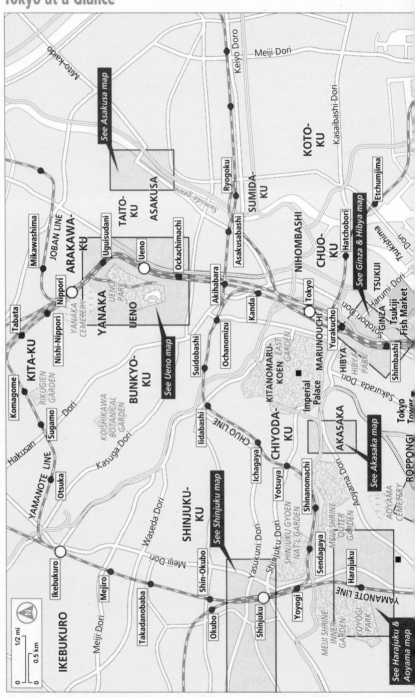

See Asakusa map

See Ginza & Hibya map

See Ueno map

See Shinjuku map

See Akasaka map

See Harajuku & Aoyama map

Mito-kaido

Keiyo Doro

Meiji Dori

Kasaibashi-Dori

KOTO-KU

Etchujima

Tsukishima Dori

Sumida-gawa

Ryogoku

SUMIDA-KU

Asakusabashi

TAITO-KU

ASAKUSA

NIHOMBASHI

CHUO-KU

Hatchobori

Harumi-Dori

Mikawashima

JOBAN LINE

ARAKAWA-KU

Uguisudani

Ueno

Ockachimachi

TSUKIJI

GINZA

Tsukiji Fish Market

Sotobori Dori

Nippori

YANAKA

UENO PARK

YANAKA CEMETERY

UENO

Akihabara

Kanda

Tokyo

Yurakucho

MARUNOUCHI

HIBYA

Shimbashi

Nishi-Nippori

Tabata

KITA-KU

RIKUGIEN GARDEN

Komagome

Sugamo

Dori

KOISHIKAWA BOTANICAL GARDEN

BUNKYO-KU

Suidobashi

Ochanomizu

KITANOMARU-KOEN EAST GARDEN

Imperial Palace

HIBYA PARK

Sakurada-Dori

Hakusan

Otsuka

YAMANOTE LINE

Kasuga-Dori

CHUO LINE

Iidabashi

CHIYODA-KU

AKASAKA

Tokyo Tower

Tokyo

Ichagaya

AOYAMA CEMETERY

ROPPONGI

Ikebukuro

IKEBUKURO

Mejiro

Waseda-Dori

Meiji-Dori

SHINJUKU-KU

Yotsuya

Shinanomachi

Yasukuni-Dori

Shinjuku-Dori

SHINJUKU GYOEN NAT'L GARDEN

MEIJI SHRINE OUTER GARDEN

Aoyama-Dori

Takadanobaba

Shin-Okubo

Okubo

Shinjuku

Yoyogi

Sendagaya

Harajuku

MEIJI SHRINE INNER GARDEN

YOYOGI PARK

YAMANOTE LINE

See Harajuku & Aoyama map

1/2 mi

0.5 km

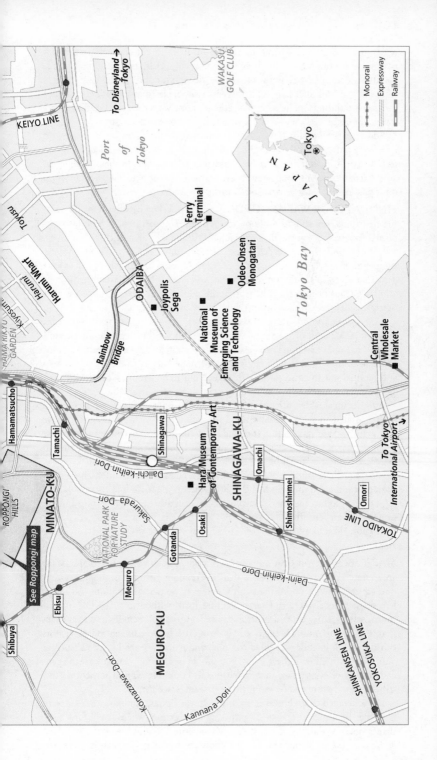

refers to a smaller area within the chome—usually an entire block, sometimes larger. Thus, houses on one side of the street will usually have a different middle number from houses on the other side. The last number, in this case 1, refers to the actual building. Although it seems reasonable to assume that next to a number 1 building will be a number 2, that's not always the case; buildings were assigned numbers as they were constructed, not according to location.

Addresses are usually, but not always, posted on buildings beside doors, on telephone poles, and by streetlights, but often they are written in kanji only. In recent years Roman letters have been added to addresses posted below stoplights at major intersections. But one frustrating trend is that new, modern buildings omit posting any address whatsoever on their facades.

FINDING YOUR WAY AROUND   If you're traveling by subway or JR train, the first thing you should do upon exiting your compartment is look for signs posted on every platform that tell which exit to take for particular buildings, attractions, and chome. At Roppongi Station, for example, you'll find yellow signboards that tell you which exit to take for Roppongi Hills, which will at least get you pointed in the right direction once you emerge from the station. Stations also have maps of the area either inside the station or at the exit; these are your best plans of attack when you're trying to find a particular address.

As you walk around Tokyo, you will also notice maps posted beside sidewalks giving a breakdown of the postal number system for the area. The first time I tried to use one, I stopped one Japanese, then another, and asked each to point to the location of a particular address on the map. Each person studied the map and pointed out the direction. Both turned out to be wrong. Not very encouraging, but if you learn how to read these maps, they're invaluable.

Another invaluable source of information is the numerous police boxes, called *koban,* located in every neighborhood throughout the city. Police officers have area maps and are very helpful (helping lost souls seems to occupy much of their time). You should also never hesitate to ask a Japanese the way, but be sure to ask more than one. You'll be amazed at the conflicting directions you'll receive. Apparently, the Japanese would rather hazard a guess than impolitely shrug their shoulders and leave you standing there. The best thing to do is ask several Japanese and then follow the majority opinion. You can also duck into a shop and ask someone where a nearby address is, although in my experience employees do not even know the address of their own store. They may, however, have a map of the area.

MAPS   Before setting out on your own, arm yourself with a few maps. Maps are so much a part of life in Tokyo that they're often included in shop or restaurant advertisements, on business cards, and even on party invitations. Although I've spent years in Tokyo, I rarely venture forth without a map. The Tourist Information Center issues a *Tourist Map of Tokyo,* which includes a subway map. Better, in my opinion, are the free maps from the Tokyo Convention & Visitors Bureau, which include a detailed city map and maps of several districts (such as Shinjuku). Armed with these maps, you should be able to locate at least the general vicinity of every place mentioned in this book. Hotels also sometimes distribute their own maps. In short, never pass up a free map.

For a detailed map, however, head for Tower Books, Kinokuniya, or one of the other bookstores with an English-language section, where you'll find more than a dozen variations of city maps. My favorite is Nippon Kokuseisha's *Map of Central Tokyo,* listing chome and chome subsections for major areas; the compact folded map can be carried in a purse or backpack. Another useful publication is Shobunsa's *Tokyo Metropolitan Atlas,* which covers all 23 of Tokyo's wards with specific postal maps, as well as greater Tokyo and its vicinity, along with expressway and Tokyo-area road maps. If you plan to write a guidebook, consider Kodansha International's heftier *Tokyo City Atlas,* which has both Japanese and English-language place names, along with rail and subway maps, district maps, and an index to important buildings, museums, and other places of interest.

NEIGHBORHOODS IN BRIEF

Taken as a whole, Tokyo seems formidable, so the smart strategy is to divide and conquer. It's best to think of Tokyo as a variety of neighborhoods scrunched together, much like the pieces of a jigsaw puzzle. Holding the pieces together, so to speak, is the **Yamanote Line,** a commuter train loop around central Tokyo, passing through such important stations as Yurakucho, Tokyo, Ueno, Ikebukuro, Shinjuku, Harajuku, Shibuya, and Shinagawa. Since 2001, several districts have witnessed massive redevelopment, including Shinagawa, both sides of Tokyo Station, and Roppongi.

Hibiya This is not only the business heart of Tokyo, but its spiritual heart as well. Hibiya is where the Tokugawa shogun built his magnificent castle, and was thus the center of old Edo. Today, Hibiya, in Chiyoda-ku, is no less important as the home of the **Imperial Palace,** built on the ruins of Edo Castle and today the residence of Japan's 125th emperor. Bordering the palace is the wonderful **East Garden,** open free to the public.

Nihombashi Back when Edo became Tokugawa's shogunate capital, Nihombashi was where merchants set up shop, making it the commercial center of the city and therefore of all Japan. Nihombashi, which stretches east of Tokyo Station, still serves as Tokyo's financial center, home of the computerized

Tokyo Stock Exchange and headquarters for major banks and companies. The area takes its name from an actual **bridge,** Nihombashi, which means "Bridge of Japan" and served as the focal point for all main highways leading out of the city to the provinces during the Edo Period.

Marunouchi To the west and south of Tokyo Station is Marunouchi, one of Tokyo's oldest business districts, with tree-lined avenues and office buildings. The historic landmark Marunouchi Building, originally constructed in 1923, was recently replaced with a 36-story complex of restaurants, shops, and offices. South of Tokyo Station is the Four Seasons Hotel Tokyo at Marunouchi, Japan's most expensive and exclusive hotel.

Ginza Ginza is the swankiest and most expensive shopping area in all Japan. When the country opened to foreign trade in the 1860s following 2 centuries of self-imposed seclusion, it was here that Western imports and adopted Western architecture were first displayed. Today, Ginza is where you'll find a multitude of department stores, boutiques, exclusive restaurants, hotels, art galleries, hostess clubs, and drinking establishments. Although Tokyo's younger generation favors less staid districts like Harajuku, Shibuya, and Shinjuku, the Ginza is still a good place to window-shop and dine, especially on Sundays, when several major thoroughfares are closed to vehicular traffic, giving it a festive atmosphere. On the edge of Ginza is **Kabukiza,** the nation's main venue for Kabuki productions.

Tsukiji Located only two subway stops from Ginza, Tsukiji was born from reclaimed land during the Tokugawa shogunate; its name, in fact, means "reclaimed land." During the Meiji Period, it housed a large foreign settlement. Today it's famous for the **Tsukiji Fish Market,** one of the largest wholesale fish markets in the world. Nearby are **Shiodome,** an urban development project with skyscrapers; and **Hama Rikyu Garden,** considered by some to be the best garden in Tokyo. From Hama Rikyu Garden, sightseeing boats depart for Asakusa in the north.

Asakusa Located in the northeastern part of central Tokyo, Asakusa and areas to its north served as the pleasure quarters for old Edo. Even older, however, is the famous **Sensoji Temple,** one of Tokyo's top and oldest attractions. Asakusa also has a wealth of tiny shops selling traditional Japanese crafts, most clustered along a pedestrian street called **Nakamise Dori** that leads straight to Sensoji Temple; the street's atmosphere alone makes it one of the most enjoyable places to shop for Japanese souvenirs. When Tokyoites talk about *shitamachi* (old downtown), they are referring to the traditional homes and tiny narrow streets of the Asakusa and Ueno areas.

Ueno Located just west of Asakusa, on the northern edge of the JR Yamanote Line loop, Ueno retains some of the city's old *shitamachi* atmosphere, especially at its spirited **Ameya Yokocho** food and flea market, which is spread underneath the Yamanote train tracks. Ueno is

most famous, however, for **Ueno Park,** a huge green space comprising a zoo, a concert hall, a temple, a shrine, and several acclaimed museums, including the **Tokyo National Museum,** which houses the largest collection of Japanese art and antiquities in the world. North of Ueno is **Yanaka,** a delightful residential area of traditional old homes, neighborhood shops, and temples; several of Tokyo's most affordable Japanese-style inns are located here.

Shinjuku Originating as a post town in 1698 to serve the needs of feudal lords and their retainers traveling between Edo and the provinces, Shinjuku was hardly touched by the 1923 Great Kanto Earthquake, making it an attractive alternative for businesses wishing to relocate following the widespread destruction. In 1971, Japan's first skyscraper was erected here with the opening of the Keio Plaza Hotel in western Shinjuku, setting a dramatic precedent for things to come. Today more than a dozen skyscrapers, including several hotels, dot the Shinjuku skyline, and with the opening of the **Tokyo Metropolitan Government Office (TMG)** in 1991 (with a tourist office and a great observation floor), Shinjuku's transformation into the capital's upstart business district was complete. Eastern Shinjuku is known for its shopping, particularly the huge **Takashimaya Times Square** complex. It's also known for its nightlife, especially in **Kabuki-cho,** one of Japan's most famous—as well as naughtiest—amusement centers, and in **Shinjuku 2–chome,** Tokyo's premier gay nightlife district. Separating eastern and western Shinjuku is **Shinjuku Station,** the nation's busiest commuter station, located on the western end of the Yamanote Line loop. An oasis in the middle of

Shinjuku madness is **Shinjuku Gyoen Park,** a beautiful garden for strolling.

Harajuku The mecca of Tokyo's younger generation, Harajuku swarms throughout the week with teenagers in search of fashion and fun. At its center is **Omotesando Dori,** a fashionable tree-lined avenue flanked by trendy shops, restaurants, and sidewalk cafes, making it a premier promenade for people-watching. Nearby is **Takeshita Dori,** a narrow pedestrian lane packed with young people looking for the latest in inexpensive clothing. Harajuku is also home to one of Japan's major attractions, the **Meiji Jingu Shrine,** built in 1920 to deify Emperor and Empress Meiji; and the small but delightful **Ota Memorial Museum of Art,** with its woodblock prints. Another drawing card is the **Oriental Bazaar,** Tokyo's best shop for products and souvenirs of Japan; two Sundays a month, nearby **Togo Shrine** holds an antiques flea market.

Aoyama While Harajuku is for teenyboppers, nearby chic Aoyama serves as playground for Tokyo's trend-setting yuppies, boasting sophisticated restaurants, expensive boutiques, and more designer-fashion outlets than anywhere else in the city. It's located on the eastern end of **Omotesando Dori** (and an easy walk from Harajuku), centered on Aoyama Dori.

Ikebukuro Located north of Shinjuku on the Yamanote Line loop, Ikebukuro is the working person's Tokyo, less refined and a bit rougher around the edges. Ikebukuro is where you'll find **Seibu** and **Tobu,** two of the country's largest department stores, as well as the **Japan Traditional Craft Center,** with its beautifully crafted traditional items. The **Sunshine City Building,** one of Japan's tallest skyscrapers, is home to a huge indoor shopping center and aquarium.

Akihabara Japan's foremost center for electronic and electrical appliances contains more than 600 shops offering a look at the latest in gadgets and gizmos. A stop on the Yamanote Line, this is a fascinating place for a stroll, even if you aren't interested in buying anything.

Shibuya Located on the southwestern edge of the Yamanote Line loop, Shibuya serves as an important commuter nucleus. More subdued than Shinjuku, more down-to-earth than Harajuku, and less cosmopolitan than Roppongi, it caters to students and young office workers with its many shops and thriving nightlife, including more than a dozen department stores specializing in everything from designer clothing to housewares. Don't miss the light change at Shibuya Crossing, reportedly Japan's busiest intersection, with its hordes of pedestrians, neon, and five video billboards that have earned it the nickname "the Times Square of Tokyo."

Ebisu One station south of Shibuya on the JR Yamanote Line, Ebisu was a minor player in Tokyo's shopping and nightlife league until the 1995 debut of **Yebisu Garden Place,** a smart-looking planned community of apartments, concert halls, two museums (one highlighting Sapporo Beer, the other Japanese photography), restaurants, a department store, and a first-class hotel, all connected to Ebisu Station via moving walkway. The vicinity east of Ebisu Station, once a sleepy residential and low-key shopping district, has blossomed into a small but thriving nightlife mecca, popular with expats who find Roppongi too crass or commercial.

Roppongi Tokyo's best-known nightlife district for young Japanese and foreigners, Roppongi has more bars and nightclubs than any other district outside Shinjuku, as well as a multitude of restaurants serving international cuisine. The action continues until dawn. Nearby **Nishi Azabu,** once a residential neighborhood (many foreigners live here), offers a quieter and saner dining alternative to frenetic Roppongi. In between Roppongi and Nishi Azabu is the newest kid on the block, the eye-popping, 11-hectare (28-acre) **Roppongi Hills,** Tokyo's largest urban development with 210 shops and restaurants, a first-class hotel, a garden, apartments, offices, a cinema complex, and an art museum.

Akasaka With its several large hotels and a small nightlife district, Akasaka caters mostly to businessmen, making it of little interest to tourists. It does, however, boast some good restaurants; in recent years, so many Koreans have opened restaurants and other establishments here that it has been dubbed "Little Korea."

Shinagawa Once an important post station on the old Tokaido Highway, Shinagawa remains an important crossroads in large part because of **Shinagawa Station,** a stop on the Shinkansen bullet train and on the southern end of the Yamanote Line loop. Home to several hotels, it has also witnessed a major blossoming of office construction in recent years, making it a serious rival of Shinjuku's business district. Other than the **Hara Museum of Contemporary Art,** however, there's little here to attract sightseers.

Ryogoku Located outside the Yamanote Line loop east of the Sumida River, Ryogoku has served as Tokyo's sumo town since the 17th century. Today it's home not only to Tokyo's large **sumo stadium and museum,** but also to about a dozen sumo stables, where wrestlers live and train. You can often see the giants as they stroll the district in their characteristic *yukata* robes. In 1993, Ryogoku became a tourist destination with the opening of the **Edo-Tokyo Museum,** which outlines the history of this fascinating city.

Odaiba This is Tokyo's newest district, quite literally—it was constructed from reclaimed land in Tokyo Bay. Connected to the mainland by the **Rainbow Bridge** (famous for its chameleon colors after nightfall), the Yurikamome Line monorail, the Rinkai Line, and a vehicular harbor tunnel, Odaiba is home to hotels, Japan's largest convention space, several shopping complexes (including the very fancy Venus Fort), futuristic buildings (including the Kenzo Tange–designed Fuji TV building), several museums (like the Museum of Maritime Science and the National Museum of Emerging Science and Innovation), a hot-spring public bath that harkens back to the Edo era, a monolithic Ferris wheel, and Megaweb (a huge multimedia car amusement and exhibition center sponsored by Toyota). For young Japanese, Odaiba is one of Tokyo's hottest dating spots; it's also a good escape from city life, with a seaside park and a sandy beach that capitalize on the city's bayside location.

2 Getting Around

Your most frustrating moments in Tokyo will probably occur when you find you're totally lost. Maybe it will be in a subway or train station, when all you see are signs in Japanese, or on a street somewhere as you search for a museum, restaurant, or bar. At any rate, accept here and now that you will get lost if you are at all adventurous and eager to strike out on your own. It's inevitable. But take comfort in the fact that Japanese get lost, too—even taxi drivers!

The second rule of getting around Tokyo: It will always take longer than you think. For short-term visitors, calculating travel times in Tokyo is tricky business. Taking a taxi is expensive and involves the probability of getting stuck interminably in traffic, with the meter ticking away. Taking the subway is usually more efficient, even though it's more complicated and harder on your feet: Choosing which route to take isn't always clear, and transfers between lines are sometimes quite a hike in themselves. If I'm going from one end of Tokyo to the other by subway, I usually allow myself anywhere from 30 to 60 minutes, depending on the number of transfers and the walking distance to my final destination. The journey from Roppongi or Shibuya to Ueno, for example, takes approximately a half-hour because it's a straight shot on the subway, but a trip requiring transfers can take much longer. Traveling times to destinations along each line are posted on platform pillars.

Your best bet for getting around Tokyo is to take the subway or Japan Railways (JR) commuter train to the station nearest your destination. From there you can either walk, using a map and asking directions along the way, or take a taxi.

For all hotels, ryokan, restaurants, sights, shops, and nightlife venues listed in this book, I've included both the nearest station and, in parentheses, the number of minutes' walk required to get from the station to the destination.

BY TAXI

Taxis are shamefully expensive in Tokyo. Fares start at ¥660 ($5.50) for the first 2km (1¼ miles) and increase ¥80 (65¢) for each additional 274m (904 ft.) or 40 seconds of waiting time. Smaller, more compact taxis start out at slightly less—¥640 ($5.35) for the first 2km (1¼ miles)—but their fare increases ¥80 (60¢) for each additional 290m (957 ft.). In 1997, when controls regulating taxi fares became less restrictive, some taxis began offering fares cheaper than the standard rates for short distances. Fares are posted on the back of the front passenger seat. If you're like me, however, you probably won't shop around—you'll gratefully jump into the first taxi that stops. Note that from 11pm to 5am, an extra 30% is added to your fare.

With the exception of some major thoroughfares in the downtown area, you can hail a taxi from any street or go to a taxi stand or a major hotel. A red light above the dashboard shows if a taxi is free to pick up a passenger; a green light indicates that the taxi is occupied. Be sure to stand clear of the back door—it swings open automatically. Likewise, it shuts automatically once you're in. Taxi drivers are quite perturbed if you try to maneuver the door yourself.

Unless you're going to a well-known landmark or hotel, it's best to have your destination written out in Japanese, since most taxi drivers don't speak English. But even that may not help. Tokyo is so complicated that even taxi drivers may not know a certain area, although they do have detailed maps. If a driver doesn't understand where you're going, he may refuse to take you. Otherwise, don't be surprised if he jumps out of the cab to inquire about directions at a nearby shop—with the meter ticking.

There are so many taxis cruising Tokyo that it seems you can always hail one easily on most thoroughfares—except when you need it most. That is, when it's raining and sometimes just after 1am on weekends, after all subways and trains have stopped. However, one surprising effect of the recession has been an increase in the number of taxis available late at night; now that companies no longer pay for employees' expensive after-the-last-train taxi fares, nighttime revelers no longer have to stay out until 3am just to find a taxi.

Call one of the following major taxi companies for a pickup: **Nihon Kotsu** (*℃* **03/3586-2151**), **Kokusai** (*℃* **03/3491-6001**), **Daiwa** (*℃* **03/3563-5151**), or **Hinomaru** (*℃* **03/3814-1111**). Note, however, that Japanese is spoken, and you'll be required to pay extra (usually not more than ¥500/$4.35) for the pickup. I have rarely telephoned for a taxi—just like in the movies, one usually cruises by just when you raise your hand.

BY PUBLIC TRANSPORTATION

If you think you'll be using a combination of public transportation systems in 1 day—subway, JR train, and Toei bus (except double-decker buses)—consider purchasing a **Tokyo Free Kippu** which, despite its name, costs ¥1,580 ($13) but does allow unlimited travel for 1 day. It's available at all JR stations, JR View Plazas, and most subway stations.

There's a four-color **Tokyo Metro map,** with subway and train lines, on the inside back cover of this book.

BY SUBWAY

To get around Tokyo on your own, it's imperative that you learn how to ride its subways. Fortunately, the subway system is efficient, modern, clean, and easy to use, and all station names are written in English. Some cars also post the next station in English on digital signs above their doors or even announce stops in English. Altogether, there are 13 underground subway lines crisscrossing the city, and each line is color-coded. The Ginza Line, for example, is orange, which means that all its trains and signs are orange. If you're transferring to the Ginza Line from another line, just follow the orange signs and circles to the Ginza Line platform. Before boarding, however, make sure the train is going in the right direction; otherwise, you'll end up at the opposite end of the city. Tokyo's newest line, the Oedo Line, makes a zigzag loop around the city and is useful for traveling between Roppongi and Shinjuku; be aware, however, that it's buried deep underground and that platforms take a while to reach, despite escalators.

TICKETS   **Vending machines** at all subway stations sell tickets, which begin at ¥160 ($1.35) for the shortest distance and increase according to how far you're traveling, with ¥300 ($2.50) charged for the longest distance. Children under 6 ride free; children 6 to 11 pay half-fare. Vending machines give change, and most accept ¥1,000, ¥5,000, and ¥10,000 notes. To purchase your ticket, insert money into the vending machine until the fare buttons light up, then push the amount for the ticket you want. Your ticket and change will drop onto a little platform at the bottom of the machine.

Fares are posted on a large subway map above the vending machines, but they're generally in Japanese only; major stations also post a smaller map listing fares in English, but you may have to search for one. An alternative is to look at your Tourist Information Center subway map—it lists stations in both Japanese and English. Once you know what the Japanese characters look like, you may be able to locate your station and the corresponding fare. If you still don't know the fare, just buy a basic-fare ticket for ¥160 ($1.35). When you exit at your destination, look for the **fare adjustment machine;** insert your ticket to find out how much more you owe, or look for a fare adjustment window where a subway employee will tell you how much you owe.

In any case, be sure to hang onto your ticket, since you must give it up at the exit wicket at the end of your journey

If you think you'll be using Tokyo's subway system a lot or if you wish to avoid having to purchase an individual ticket for each ride, invest in a **Passnet Metro Card,** a prepaid card also sold at vending machines for rides worth ¥1,000 ($8.35), ¥3,000 ($25), and ¥5,000 ($42). Insert the card into the automatic ticket gates upon entering and exiting the subway wickets; the charge for your ride will be electronically deducted from the card. You can also use your Metro Card in the vending machine to purchase regular single tickets for someone traveling with you. Since rides on the subway can really add up, you'll find the ¥1,000 Metro Card useful even if you're staying in Tokyo only a few days (five rides alone will probably end up costing more than ¥1,000). Alternatively, **a One-day Economy Pass (Echinichi Josha Ken)** for unlimited rides on all subway lines costs ¥1,000 ($8.35). Although other types of tickets and passes are available, I find them too complicated for short-time visitors.

HOURS   Most subways run from about 5am to midnight, although the times of the first and last trains depend on the line, the station, and whether it's a weekday or weekend. Schedules are posted in the stations, and through most of the day trains arrive every 3 to 5 minutes.

Avoid taking the subway during the weekday morning **rush hour,** from 8 to 9am—the stories you've heard about commuters packed into trains like sardines are all true. There are even "platform pushers," men who push people into compartments so that the doors can close. If you want to witness Tokyo at its craziest, go to Shinjuku Station at 8:30am—but go by taxi unless you want to experience the crowding firsthand.

Transfers on the Subway & Train

You can transfer between most subway lines without buying another ticket, and you can transfer between JR train lines on one ticket. However, your ticket or prepaid card does not allow a transfer between subway lines, JR train lines, and private train lines connecting Tokyo with outlying destinations such as Nikko. You usually don't have to worry about this, though, because if you exit through a wicket and have to give up your ticket, you'll know you have to buy another one.

There are a few instances, however, when you pass through a ticket wicket to transfer between subway lines, in which case your ticket will be returned to you if your destination is farther along. The general rule is that if your final destination and fare are posted above the ticket vending machines, you can travel all the way to your destination with only one ticket. But don't worry about this too much—the ticket collector will set you straight if you've miscalculated. Note, however, that if you pay too much for your ticket, the portion of the fare that's left unused is not refundable—so, again, the easiest thing to do if in doubt is to buy the cheapest fare.

Another thing you'll want to keep in mind are **station exits,** which are always numbered. Once you reach your destination, look for the yellow signs designating which exit to take for major buildings, museums, and addresses. If you're confused about which exit to take from the station, ask someone at the window near the ticket gate. Taking the right exit can make a world of difference, especially in Shinjuku, where there are more than 60 station exits.

For more information on tickets, passes, and lines for the subway, stop by **information desks** located at Ginza, Shinjuku, Nihombashi, and Otemachi stations.

BY JR TRAIN

As an alternative to subways, electric commuter trains operated by the East Japan Railways Company (JR) run aboveground. These trains are also color-coded, with fares beginning at ¥130 ($1.10). Buy your ticket from vending machines the same as you would for the subway.

The **Yamanote Line** (green-colored coaches) is the best-known and most convenient JR line. It makes an oblong loop around the city, stopping at 29 stations along the way. In fact, you may want to take the Yamanote Line and stay on it for a roundup view of Tokyo; the entire trip takes about an hour, passing stations like Shinjuku, Tokyo, Harajuku, Akihabara, and Ueno on the way.

Another convenient JR line is the orange-colored **Chuo Line;** it cuts across Tokyo between Shinjuku and Tokyo stations. The yellow-colored **Sobu Line** runs between Shinjuku and Akihabara and beyond to Chiba. Other JR lines serve outlying districts for the metropolis's commuting public. Since the Yamanote, Chuo, and Sobu lines are rarely identified by their specific names at major stations, look for signs that say JR LINES.

If you think you'll be traveling by JR lines quite a bit, consider purchasing an **IO Card,** a prepaid transit card similar to the NYC Metro Card; it allows you to pass through automatic fare gates without having to purchase a separate JR ticket each time. These cards come in values of ¥1,000 ($8.35), ¥3,000 ($25), and ¥5,000 ($42). There's also a JR **1-Day Tokyo Rail Pass (Tokunai Free Kippu),** which allows unlimited travel on JR trains for 1 day for ¥730 ($6.10).

For more information on JR lines and tickets, stop by one of JR's **Information Centers** at Tokyo Station (Central Passage; open daily 9am–7pm) or Shinjuku Station (the east side; open daily 10am–6:30pm). You can also call JR's English-language telephone service at ℂ **03/3423-0111,** available Monday through Friday from 10am to 6pm.

BY BUS

Buses are difficult to use in Tokyo because destinations are sometimes written in Japanese only (who knows where the heck you might end up?) and most bus drivers don't speak English. Buses are sometimes convenient for short distances, however. If you're feeling adventurous, board the bus at the front and drop the exact fare into the box by the driver. If you don't have the exact fare (usually ¥200/$1.65), a slot located next to the driver will accept coins only; your change will come out below, minus the fare. Another slot will accept ¥1,000 bills; the change, minus the fare, comes out in the same place it does if you insert a coin. A signboard at the front of the bus displays the next stop, sometimes in English. When you wish to get off, press one of the buttons on the railing near the door or the seats. You can pick up an excellent Toei bus map showing all major routes at one of the Tokyo Tourist Information Centers operated by the Tokyo Convention and Visitors Bureau (see "Visitor Information," earlier).

BY BOAT

Although all tourist destinations are accessible by land transportation, some sights in Tokyo Bay or on the Sumida River are served by sightseeing boat, an enjoyable way to travel and see the Tokyo skyline. Boats depart from **Hinode Pier** near Hamamatsucho and Hinoda stations and travel to **Asakusa** via the Sumida River, as well as to Tokyo Sea Life Park and the Museum of Maritime Science on **Odaiba.** The trip from Hinode Pier to Asakusa takes approximately 40 minutes and costs ¥660 ($5.50). You can also reach Asakusa by boat from Hama Rikyu Garden. Pick up a brochure at the TIC or call the **Tokyo Cruise Ship Co.** at ℂ **03/3457-7830.**

FAST FACTS: Tokyo

If you can't find answers to your questions here, call the **Tourist Information Center** (ℂ 03/3201-3331) Monday through Friday from 9am to 5pm and Saturday from 9am to noon; or call the city-run **Tokyo Tourist Information Center** (ℂ 03/5321-3077) daily from 10am to 6:30pm. If you're staying in a first-class hotel, another valuable resource is the concierge or guest-relations desk; the staff there can tell you how to reach your destination, answer general questions, and even make restaurant reservations for you.

Airport See "Flying to Japan" in chapter 2.

American Express There are no American Express customer service offices in Japan.

Area Code If you're calling a Tokyo number from outside Tokyo but within Japan, the area code for Tokyo is **03**. For details on calling Tokyo from outside Japan, see "Telephones," below.

Babysitters Most major hotels can arrange babysitting services, but expect to pay about ¥5,000 ($42) for 2 hours. A very few also provide in-house day-care centers. **Tokyo Domestic Service** (ℂ 03/3584-4769) can provide bilingual sitters. There's a 3-hour minimum charge of ¥5,500 ($46), then ¥1,500 ($12) per hour after that. Parents are also required to pay transportation (¥1,000/$8.35 during the day, ¥1,500/$12 9–11pm, and ¥3,000/$25 after 11pm) and to provide meals.

Business Hours **Government offices and private companies** are generally open Monday through Friday 9am to 5pm. **Banks** are open Monday through Friday 9am to 3pm, while neighborhood **post offices** are open Monday through Friday 9am to 5pm. Some major post offices (located in each ward), however, are open Monday through Friday from 9am to 7pm.

Department stores are open from about 10am to 7:30 or 8pm. Some are open every day, while others have irregular closing days one to four times a month (but always the same day of the week). **Smaller stores** are generally open from about 10am to 8pm, closed 1 day a week. Convenience stores such as 7-Eleven are open 24 hours.

Keep in mind that **museums, gardens,** and **attractions** stop selling admission tickets at least 30 minutes before the actual closing time. Similarly, **restaurants** take their last orders at least 30 minutes before the posted closing time (even earlier for kaiseki restaurants).

Currency See "Money" in chapter 2 for an explanation of the yen and its dollar and British-pound equivalents.

Currency Exchange You can exchange money in major banks throughout Tokyo; this service is often indicated by a sign in English near the front door. Banks give a slightly better exchange rate for traveler's checks than for cash; *you'll need your passport to exchange traveler's checks.* If you need to exchange money outside banking hours, your best bet is your hotel or a large department store, though exchange rates won't be as favorable (note that you'll need your passport). At Narita Airport (which also has ATMs for major credit cards), exchange counters are open from 6am to 11pm.

Otherwise, the most convenient ATMs are located in post offices, available for Visa, MasterCard, and PLUS and Cirrus cards during regular post office hours. The ATM at the Central Post Office near Tokyo Station (see "Mail," below) is open Monday to Friday from 7am to 11:55pm, Saturday from 5am to 11:55pm, and Sunday and holidays from 5am to 8pm; note, however, that it did not accept my Visa debit card. You can also get cash advances using Visa credit cards at any Sumitomo Bank and from Master-Card at Union Credit (UC) banks and some Sumitomo banks, Citibanks, Mitsubishi-Tokyo banks, and affiliated banks, with branches all over town; you'll have to show your passport for cash advances.

Dentists & Doctors Many first-class hotels offer medical facilities or an in-house doctor. Otherwise, your embassy can refer you to English-speaking doctors, specialists, and dentists. In addition, the **AMDA International Medical Information Center** (✆ 03/5285-8088), available Monday through Friday 9am to 5pm, can provide information on English-speaking staff. The following clinics have some English-speaking staff and are popular with foreigners living in Tokyo: **The International Clinic,** 1–5–9 Azabudai, Minato-ku, within walking distance of Roppongi or Azabu Juban stations (✆ 03/3582-2646; open Mon–Fri 9am–noon and 2–5pm, Sat 9am–noon; walk-ins only); the **Ishikawa Clinic,** Azabu Sakurada Heights, Room 201, 3–2–7 Nishi Azabu, Minato-ku, near Roppongi Station (✆ 03/3401-6340; open Mon–Fri 9am–12:30pm, as well as Mon 3:15– 4:30pm and Tues and Thurs 3:15–6:30pm; appointments are preferred); **Tokyo Medical & Surgical Clinic,** 32 Mori Building, 3–4–30 Shiba-koen, Minato-ku, near Kamiya-cho, Onarimon, or Shiba-koen stations and across from Tokyo Tower (✆ 03/3436-3028; open Mon–Fri 9am–pm and 2–5pm, Sat 9am–noon; appointments only). At the Tokyo Medical & Surgical Clinic, above, is also the **Tokyo Clinic Dental Office** (✆ 03/3431-4225), open Monday, Wednesday, Thursday, and Friday from 9am to 6pm and Saturday from 9am to 5pm. You can also make appointments to visit doctors at the hospitals listed below.

Drugstores There is no 24-hour drugstore in Tokyo, but ubiquitous 24-hour convenience stores such as 7-Eleven, Lawson, and FamilyMart carry things like aspirin. If you're looking for specific pharmaceuticals, a good bet is the **American Pharmacy,** in the basement of the Marunouchi Building, 2–4–1 Marunouchi, Chiyoda-ku (✆ 03/5220-7716; open Mon–Fri 9am–9pm, Sat 10am–9pm, and Sun and holidays 10am–8pm), which has many of the same over-the-counter drugs you can find at home (many of them imported from the United States) and can fill American prescriptions—but note that you *must first visit a doctor in Japan* before foreign prescriptions can be filled, so it's best to bring an ample supply of any prescription medication with you.

Earthquakes   Kobe's tragic 1995 earthquake brought attention to the fact that Japan is earthquake-prone, but in reality, most earthquakes are too small to detect. However, in the event of an earthquake you can feel, there are a few precautions you should take. If you're indoors, take cover under a doorway or against a wall and do not go outdoors. If you're outdoors, stay away from trees, power lines, and the sides of buildings; if you're surrounded by tall buildings, seek cover in a doorway. Never use elevators during a quake. You should be sure to note emergency exits wherever you stay. All hotels supply flashlights, usually found attached to your bedside table.

Electricity   The electricity throughout Japan is 100 volts AC, but there are two different cycles in use: In Tokyo and in regions northeast of the capital, it's 50 cycles, while in Nagoya, Kyoto, Osaka, and all points to the southwest, it's 60 cycles. Leading hotels in Tokyo often have two outlets, one for 110 volts and one for 220 volts; almost all hotels also have hair dryers in the rooms. You can use many American appliances, such as radios and hair dryers, because the American standard is 110 volts and 60 cycles, but they may run a little more slowly; note, too, that the flat, two-legged electrical plugs used in Japan are the same size and fit as those in North America, but three-pronged appliances are not accepted. For sensitive equipment, either have it adjusted or use batteries if it's also battery-operated.

Embassies & Consulates   The visa or passport sections of most embassies are open only at certain times during the day, so it's best to call in advance.

- **U.S. Embassy:** 1–10–5 Akasaka, Minato-ku, near Toranomon subway station (© **03/3224-5000**; consular section open Mon–Fri 8:30am–12:30pm and 2–4pm; telephone inquiries accepted Mon–Fri 8:30am–1pm and 2–5:30pm).

- **Canadian Embassy:** 7–3–38 Akasaka, Minato-ku, near Aoyama-Itchome Station (© **03/5412-6200**; consular section open Mon–Fri 9am–noon and 1:30–5pm).

- **British Embassy:** 1 Ichibancho, Chiyoda-ku, near Hanzomon Station (© **03/3265-5511**; consular section open Mon–Fri 9am–noon and 2–4pm).

- **Embassy of Ireland:** 5th floor, 2–10–7 Kojimachi, Chiyoda-ku, near Hanzomon Station, exit 4 (© **03/3263-0695**; open Mon–Fri 10am–12:30pm and 2–4pm; telephone inquiries accepted Mon–Fri 9:30am–5:30pm).

- **Australian Embassy:** 2–1–14 Mita, Minato-ku (© **03/5232-4111**; open Mon–Fri 9am–12:30pm and 1:30–4:30pm; make an appointment for the consular section). A 15-minute walk from Shiba-koen Station; or take a taxi from Kamyacho, Mita, Hamamatsucho, or Tamachi.

- **New Zealand Embassy:** 20–40 Kamiyama-cho, Shibuya-ku, a 15-minute walk from Shibuya Station (© **03/3467-2271**; consular section open Mon–Fri 9am–12:30pm and 1:30–5pm).

Emergencies The national emergency numbers are ⓒ **110** for **police** and ⓒ **119** for **ambulance** and **fire.** You do not need to insert any money into public telephones to call these numbers, but you must push a red button before dialing. Be sure to speak slowly and precisely.

Holidays See "When to Go," in chapter 2.

Hospitals In addition to going to these hospitals for an emergency, you can also make appointments at their clinics to see a doctor: **The International Catholic Hospital (Seibo Byoin),** 2–5–1 Naka-Ochiai, Shinjuku-ku, near Meijiro Station on the Yamanote Line (ⓒ 03/3951-1111; clinic hours Mon–Sat 8–11am; closed 3rd Sat of each month; appointments required); **St. Luke's International Hospital (Seiroka Byoin),** 9–1 Akashi-cho, Chuo-ku, near Tsukiji Station on the Hibiya Line (ⓒ 03/3541-5151; Mon–Fri 8:30–11am; appointments necessary for some treatments); and the **Japan Red Cross Medical Center (Nihon Sekijujisha Iryo Center),** 4–1–22 Hiroo, Shibuya-ku (ⓒ 03/3400-1311; Mon–Fri 8:30–11am; walk-ins only), whose closest subway stations are Roppongi, Hiroo, and Shibuya—from there, you should take a taxi.

Hot Lines In addition to the Tourist Information Centers (see "Visitor Information," earlier in this chapter), the Tokyo Metropolitan Government maintains a **Foreign Residents' Advisory Center** (ⓒ 03/5320-7744) that can answer questions on topics ranging from problems of daily life to Japanese customs and culture, Monday to Friday from 9:30am to noon and 1 to 4pm. The **Japan Helpline** (ⓒ 0120/46-1997) is a crisis hot line that can also answer questions about life in Japan, For criminal matters or concerns, the Metropolitan Police Department has a telephone counseling service for foreigners (ⓒ 03/3503-8484), available Monday to Friday 8:30am to 5pm.

Information See "Visitor Information," earlier in this chapter.

Internet Access Most upper-range hotels in Tokyo are used to catering to international business travelers and therefore offer in-room dataports for laptop modems and adapters; some even offer high-speed broadband and adapters to let you access the Internet or have TVs that double as computers. Although a few hotels provide Internet access free of charge, the majority charge anywhere from ¥500 to ¥1,500 ($4.15–$13) a day.

If your hotel doesn't provide Internet access, Kinko's has more than 25 locations throughout Tokyo, including one at Tokyo Station at the Yaesu north exit (ⓒ 03/3213-1811); one at 1–2–12 Yurakucho (ⓒ 03/5251-4808; new Hibiya Station and opposite the Imperial Hotel); and one in the Odakyu Southern Tower Building, 2–2–1 Yoyogi (ⓒ 03/3377-5711; near Shinjuku Station's south exit). Most Kinko's are open 24 hours and charge ¥200 ($1.65) per 10 minutes of computer time. Cheaper are cybercafes. I like Yahoo Café, 5–11–2 Jingumae, above Starbucks, on a side street off Omotesando Dori behind Oriental Bazaar and Kiddy Land (ⓒ 03/3797-6821; station: Meiji-Jingumae or Harajuku). Its 31 computers are free, which means you might have to wait; open daily 8am to 10pm. Alternatively, there's Internet Café Geragera, 6–1–26 Roppongi (station: Roppongi), on the fifth floor above Almond Coffee Shop on Roppongi Crossing. Open 24 hours, it charges ¥100 (85¢) per 15 minutes.

Finally, another option—albeit a fairly awkward one if you're trying to balance a laptop on your knees—is telephone. Nippon Telegraph &

Telephone (NTT) operates newer public telephone models equipped with a modular jack for portable computer hookups, making it possible to scan websites and receive e-mail. Look for gray ISDN telephones—readily available in lobbies of major hotels, airports, and train stations—which have English-language explanations on how to use them and which accept prepaid telephone cards.

Laundry/Dry Cleaning All upper- and most medium-range hotels offer laundry and dry-cleaning services. Note that for same-day service, it's usually necessary to hand over your laundry by 10am; many hotels do not offer laundry service on Sundays and holidays. Several Japanese-style accommodations in the budget category have coin-operated washers. Otherwise, launderettes are abundant.

Liquor Laws The legal drinking age is 20. If you intend to drive in Japan, you are not allowed even one drink.

Lost Property If you've forgotten something on a subway, in a taxi, or on a park bench, don't assume it's gone forever—if you're willing to trace it, you'll probably get it back. If you can remember where you last saw it, the first thing to do is telephone the establishment or return to where you left it; there's a good chance it will still be sitting there. If you've lost something on the street, go to the nearest police box *(koban);* items found in the neighborhood will stay there for 3 days or longer.

If you've lost something in a taxi, have someone who speaks Japanese contact the **Taxi Kindaika Center,** 7–3–3 Minamisuma, Koto-ku (✆ 03/3648-0300). For JR trains, have someone who speaks Japanese call or go to the **Lost and Found Sections** at JR Tokyo Station (✆ 03/3231-1880) or at JR Ueno Station (✆ 03/3841-8069); or you can call the **JR East Infoline** at (✆ 03/3423-0111). If you've lost something on a Tokyo Metropolitan subway or bus, immediately contact the nearest station where you think you lost it. After 3 days, contact the lost-and-found section of the **Tokyo Metropolitan Government,** 2–40–8 Hongo, Bunkyo-ku (✆ 03/3812-2011).

Eventually, every unclaimed item in Tokyo ends up at the Central Lost and Found Office of the **Metropolitan Police Board,** 1–9–11 Koraku, Bunkyo-ku (✆ 03/3814-4151; Mon–Fri 8:30am–5:15pm; station: Iidabashi).

Be sure to notify all your credit card companies the minute you discover your wallet has been lost or stolen, and file a report at the nearest police precinct. Your credit card company or insurer may require a police report number or record of the loss. Most credit card companies have an emergency toll-free number to call if your card is lost or stolen; they may be able to wire you a cash advance immediately or deliver an emergency credit card in a day or two. **Visa**'s U.S. emergency number is ✆ 800/847-2911; in Japan it's 00531/11-1555. **American Express** cardholders can call ✆ 800/233-5432, while Amex traveler's check holders should call ✆ 800/221-7282. In Japan, the emergency number for American Express is 6565/35-1561. MasterCard holders should call ✆ 800/MC-Assist in the U.S. or 00531/11-3886 in Japan. For other credit cards, call the toll-free number directory at ✆ 800/555-1212.

Luggage & Lockers At Narita International Airport, delivery service counters will send luggage to your hotel the next day (or from your hotel to the airport) for about ¥2,000 ($17) for bags up to 20 kilograms (44 lb.).

Coin-operated lockers are located at all major JR stations, such as Tokyo, Shinjuku, and Ueno, as well as at most subway stations. Lockers cost ¥300 to ¥700 ($2.50–$5.85), depending on the size.

Mail If your hotel cannot mail letters for you, ask the concierge where the nearest post office is. Post offices are easily recognizable by the red logo of a capital T with a horizontal line over it. Mailboxes are bright orange-red. It costs ¥110 (90¢) to airmail letters weighing up to 25 grams and ¥70 (60¢) to mail postcards to North America and Europe. Domestic mail costs ¥80 (65¢) for letters weighing up to 25 grams and ¥50 (40¢) for postcards. Post offices throughout Japan are also convenient for their ATMs, which accept international bank cards operating on the PLUS and Cirrus systems, as well as MasterCard and Visa.

Although all post offices are open Monday through Friday from 9am to 5pm, the **Central Post Office,** just southwest of Tokyo Station at 2-7-2 Marunouchi, Chiyoda-ku (✆ **03/3284-9527**), has longer business hours than most: Monday through Friday 9am to 9pm, and Saturday, Sunday, and holidays 9am to 7pm. An after-hours counter remains open throughout the night for mail and packages, making this the only 24-hour service facility in town. If you don't know where you'll be staying in Tokyo, you can have your mail sent here c/o **Poste Restante,** Central Post Office, Tokyo, Japan.

As for mailing packages, your hotel may have a shipping service. Otherwise, it's only at larger post offices that you can mail packages abroad. Conveniently, they sell cardboard boxes in four sizes with the necessary tape and string. Packages mailed abroad cannot weigh more than 20 kilograms (about 44 lb.). A package weighing 10 kilograms (about 22 lb.) will cost ¥6,750 ($56) to North America via surface mail and will take about a month. Express packages, which take 3 days to North America and can weigh up to 30 kilograms (66 lb.), cost ¥12,900 ($108) for 10 kilograms (22 lb.). For English-language postal information, call ✆ **03/5472-5851** Monday through Friday between 9:30am and 4:30pm.

Maps Unless you're living in Japan or plan on doing extensive sightseeing, the free maps offered by the **Tourist Information Center** and the **Tokyo Metropolitan Government** are adequate for most sightseeing purposes. Otherwise, see "City Layout," earlier in this chapter, for information on more detailed maps.

Measurement Before the metric system came into use in Japan, the country had its own standards for measuring length and weight. One of these old standards is still common—rooms are still measured by the number of **tatami** straw mats that will fit in them. A six-tatami room, for example, is the size of six tatami mats, with a tatami roughly 3 feet wide and 6 feet long.

Newspapers & Magazines Three English-language newspapers are published daily in Japan: the *Japan Times,* the *Daily Yomiuri* (with weekly supplements from the *Los Angeles Times, Washington Post,* and *Chicago Tribune*), and the *International Herald Tribune/Asahi Shimbun.* Hotels and major bookstores carry the international editions of such news magazines as *Time* and *Newsweek.* You can also read the *Japan Times* online at www.japantimes.co.jp.

Police The national emergency telephone number is ℂ **110.** For non-emergency criminal matters or concerns, the **Metropolitan Police Department** also maintains a telephone counseling service for foreigners at ℂ **03/3503-8484** Monday through Friday from 8:30am to 5pm.

Radio For English-language radio programs, **AFN Eagle 810** (at 810 kHz), is the English-language radio station operated by the U.S. military, with news updates on the hour, music, talk shows, and sports events from the United States as well as Tokyo sumo matches. Tokyo's **J-Wave** (81.3 mHz) broadcasts programs in English with a wide range of music. **InterFM** (76.1 mHz) in Tokyo specializes in foreign-language broadcasts including adult contemporary music and information, mostly in English but also in French, Chinese, Korean, Spanish, and other languages.

Restrooms If you're in need of a restroom in Tokyo, your best bets are train and subway stations (though these tend to be dirty), big hotels, department stores, and fast-food chains like McDonald's. Use of restrooms is free in Japan, but since public facilities often do not supply toilet paper, it's a good idea to carry a packet of tissues.

To find out whether a stall is empty, knock on the door. If it's occupied, someone will knock back. Similarly, if you're inside a stall and someone knocks, answer with a knock or else the person will keep on knocking and try to get in. And don't be surprised if you go into some restrooms and find men's urinals and private stalls in the same room. Women are supposed to walk right past the urinals without noticing them.

Many toilets in Japan, especially those at train stations, are **Japanese-style toilets:** They're holes in the ground over which you squat facing the end that has a raised hood. Men stand and aim for the hole. Although Japanese lavatories may seem uncomfortable at first, they're actually much more sanitary because no part of your body touches anything.

Across Japan, the rage nowadays is **washlets,** combination toilet/bidets with heated toilet seats and buttons and knobs directing sprays of water of various intensities to various body parts. But alas, instructions are usually in Japanese only. The voice of experience: Don't stand up until you've figured out how to turn the darn spray off.

Safety Tokyo is one of the safest cities in the world. However, crime—especially pickpocketing—is on the increase, and there are precautions you should always take when traveling: Stay alert and be aware of your immediate surroundings. Be especially careful with cameras, purses, and wallets, particularly in crowded subways, department stores, or tourist attractions (such as the retail district around Tsukiji Market). Some Japanese also caution women against walking through parks alone at night.

Smoking Tokyo is a smoker's paradise. Most restaurants in Tokyo are smoking-friendly, and few have nonsmoking sections. A few wards (city districts) have no-smoking ordinances that ban smoking on sidewalks and in public places, but metropolitan police rarely enforce them.

Taxes A 5% consumption tax is imposed on goods and services in Japan, including hotel rates and restaurant meals. Some budget accommodations include the tax in their tariff, while others don't; be sure to ask whether rates include tax (rates given in my book do not include tax unless stated otherwise). In Tokyo, hotels also levy a separate tax of ¥100 (85¢) per person per night on rooms costing ¥10,000 to ¥14,999 ($125); rates ¥15,000 and up are taxed at ¥200 ($1.65) per night per person.

In addition to these taxes, a 10% to 15% **service charge** will be added to your bill in lieu of tipping at most of the fancier restaurants and at moderately priced and upper-end hotels. Thus, the 15% to 20% in tax and service charge that will be added to your bill in the more expensive locales can really add up. Most *ryokan,* or Japanese-style inns, include a service charge but not a consumption tax in their rates. If you're not sure, ask. Business hotels, *minshuku,* youth hostels, and inexpensive restaurants do not impose a service charge.

As for **shopping,** a 5% consumption tax is also levied on most goods. (Some of the smaller vendors are not required to levy tax.) Travelers from abroad, however, are eligible for an exemption on goods taken out of the country, although only the larger department stores and specialty shops seem equipped to deal with the procedures. In any case, most department stores grant a refund on the consumption tax only when the total amount of purchases for the day exceeds ¥10,000 ($83). You can obtain a refund immediately by having a sales clerk fill out a list of your purchases and then presenting the list to the tax-exemption counter of the department store; you will need to show your passport. Note that no refunds for consumption tax are given for food, drinks, tobacco, cosmetics, film, and batteries.

Telephones **To call Japan:** For dialing Japan, the country code is **81.** If you're calling a Tokyo telephone number from outside Tokyo but within Japan, the **area code** for Tokyo is **03.** If you're calling Tokyo from abroad, drop the zero and dial only **3.** If you have questions, call the international operator in the country from which you are placing your call.

Domestic calls: If you're staying in a medium- or upper-range hotel, you can make local, domestic, and international calls from your room. It's cheaper, however, to use a **public telephone.** You can find public telephones virtually everywhere—in telephone booths on the sidewalk, on stands outside shops, on train platforms, in restaurants and coffee shops, even on bullet trains (but these require a magnetic telephone card; see below). A local call costs ¥10 (8¢) for each minute; a warning chime will ring to tell you to insert more coins or you'll be disconnected. I usually insert two or three coins at the start so I won't have to worry about being disconnected; ¥10 coins that aren't used are always returned at the end of the call. Some older, red models available for public use outside ma-and-pa shops accept only ¥10 coins, but most public phones accept both ¥10 and ¥100 coins. The latter is convenient for long-distance calls. All gray, ISDN telephones are equipped for international calls and have dataports for Internet access.

Toll-free numbers in Japan begin with **0120** or **0088.** However, calling a 1-800 number in the U.S. from Japan is not toll-free but costs the same as an international call.

If you think you'll be making a lot of domestic calls from public telephones and don't want to deal with coins, purchase a magnetic, **prepaid telephone card.** These are available in values of ¥500 ($4.15) and ¥1,000 ($8.35) and are sold at vending machines (many of which are located right beside telephones), station kiosks, and even tourist attractions, where cards are imprinted with photos of temples, castles, and other sights (but are also often more expensive than regular telephone cards since they double as collectors' items). Green and gray telephones accept telephone cards. In fact, many nowadays accept only telephone cards; insert the card into the slot. On the gray ISDN telephones, there's a second slot for a second telephone card, which is convenient if the first one is almost used up or if you think you'll be talking a long time. Domestic long-distance calls are 20% to 40% cheaper at night, on weekends, and on national holidays for calls of distances more than 60km (37 miles).

Mobile Phones: Of course, you can also avoid public telephones altogether by joining what seems like the rest of the population and using a **mobile phone**, a *keitai denwa* (more than 80 million Japanese have cellphones). Unfortunately, Japan uses a system that is incompatible with GSM or the U.S. system. Your best bet may be to rent a cellphone before you leave home. That way you can give loved ones your new number and make sure the phone works. One well-known wireless rental company is **InTouch USA** (© **800/872-7626**; www.intouchglobal.com), which charges $49 per week for telephone rental, plus a short-term activation fee of $29 and 99¢ per minute for local calls (incoming calls are free). Or, if you're flying All Nippon Airways from North America, you might qualify for complimentary cellphone usage during your stay (contact ANA).

Cellphones can also be rented from stores at Narita International Airport. Otherwise, if you're in Japan for only a few days and are staying in an upper-class hotel, it's probably most convenient to rent a mobile phone from your hotel. A quick check of several hotels in Tokyo turned up an average rental fee of ¥2,000 ($17) per day, with placed calls costing an extra ¥330 ($2.75) per minute (there is no charge for incoming calls).

If your hotel does not offer such services, contact **Mova Rental Center** (a division of NTT's DoCoMo mobile phone division), on the first floor of the Shin-Otemachi Building, near Tokyo Station, at 2–2–21 Otemachi (© **0120-68-0100**; open Mon–Fri 10am–7pm and Sat 10am–5pm), which charges ¥10,500 ($88) for a week's rental, plus ¥60 (50¢) per minute of domestic calls (international calls require an additional ¥4,000/$33 fee). Or call **DoCoMo's Customer Service Center** at © **0120-005-250**. In addition, **Sony Finance International** (© **03/3475-8711**) has commercial outlets at Narita Airport, Ueno Station, the New Otani Hotel, and the Shinagawa Prince Hotel. It charges a base rate of ¥1,000 ($8.35) per week, plus ¥1,000 ($8.35) per day and ¥90 (75¢) per domestic call or ¥330 ($2.75) for the ability to make both domestic and international calls.

For extended stays, you're better off purchasing a mobile phone. **Tu-Ka** and **Au** are two major cellphone companies, with outlets seemingly on every corner. Basic phones cost ¥4,800 to ¥5,800 ($40–$48), plus you'll have to purchase special prepaid cards (available at convenience stores) that are good for a limited number of calls within 3 months or so. Many plans are available.

To make international calls: There are several ways to make international calls. For a collect call or to place an operator-assisted call through KDDI, dial the international telephone operator at © **0051.** From a public telephone, look for a specially marked INTERNATIONAL AND DOMESTIC CARD/COIN TELEPHONE. Although many of the specially marked green or gray telephones, the most common public telephone, accept both coins and magnetic telephone cards for domestic calls, most do not accept magnetic cards for international calls (due to illegal usage of telephone cards), especially in big cities. You'll have to purchase a pre-paid international telephone card, often sold from a vending machine next to telephone booths in hotels or in convenience stores like 7-Eleven or Lawson. There are numerous such cards (with instructions in English), such as the **Brastel Smart Phonecard** (℗ 0120/659-543), **Telecom's Moshi Moshi Card** (℗ 0088/223-133), the **KDDI Superworld Card** (℗ 0057), and **NTT's World Prepaid Card** (℗ 0120/535-603). Essentially, they work like telephone cards issued by U.S. telephone companies. An access number must first be dialed, followed by a secret telephone number and then the number you wish to dial. NTT also has its own IC Card Payphones (found mostly in hotel lobbies) with its own card (sold in adjacent vending machines) which you insert into the phone. Some hotels also have special phones equipped to accept credit cards.

International rates vary according to when you call, which telephone company you use, and what type of service you use. Direct-dial service is cheaper than operator-assisted calls and is offered by both international public telephones and by hotels that advertise the service (though remember to ask about the surcharge). You can also save money by calling between 11pm and 8am Japan time, when rates are up to 40% cheaper than during a weekday. From 7 to 11pm, rates are 20% cheaper than daytime rates on weekdays. Weekend day rates are also 20% cheaper than weekday rates. KDDI's weekday prime-time rates are ¥450 ($3.75) for 3 minutes; after 11pm, it drops to ¥350 ($2.90) for 3 minutes.

If you're not using a prepaid card (which has its own set of instructions and access numbers), to make a direct-dial international call you must first dial one of the international access codes—**001** (KDDI), **0041** (Japan Telecom), **0033** (NTT-Com), or **0061** (IDC)—followed by **010** and then the country code. The country code for the United States and Canada is **1**; for the United Kingdom, it's **44**; for Australia, it's **61**; and for New Zealand, it's **64**. To call the United States, for example, dial an access code such as 001, followed by 010, the country code 1, the area code, and the telephone number. If you're dialing from your hotel room, you must first dial for an outside line, usually 0.

If you wish to be connected with an operator in your home country, you can do so from green international telephones by dialing ℗ **0039** followed by the country code. (For the United States, dial **0039-111**.) These calls can be used for collect calls or credit card calls. Some hotels and other public places are equipped with special phones that will link you to your home operator with the push of a button, and there are instructions in English.

If you have a U.S. calling card, ask your phone company for the direct access number from Japan that will link you directly to the United States. If you have AT&T, for example, dial **00539-111** (you can also pay by credit card at this number for calls made to the United States); if you're using

MCI, however, it depends on which Japanese company you're using (for KDD, it's **0053-121**).

Television If you enjoy watching television, you've come to the wrong country. Almost nothing is broadcast in English; even foreign films are dubbed in Japanese. However, if you have what's called a **bilingual television,** you can switch from Japanese to the original language to hear programs and movies in English. Most of the upper-range hotels offer bilingual TVs, though note that very few English movies and sitcoms are broadcast each week (and most of these are fairly old). In my opinion, a major plus of bilingual TVs is that they allow you to listen to the nightly national news broadcast by NHK at 7 and 10pm. Otherwise, major hotels in Tokyo also have cable TV with English-language programs including CNN broadcasts and BBC World as well as in-house pay movies. Note, however, that CNN is sometimes broadcast in Japanese only. On the other hand, even if you don't understand Japanese, I suggest that you watch TV at least once; maybe you'll catch a samurai series or a sumo match. Commercials are also worth watching.

A word on those **pay video programs** offered by hotels and many resort ryokan: Upper-range hotels usually have a few choices in English, and these are charged automatically to your bill. Most business hotels usually offer only one kind of pay movie; since the descriptions are usually in Japanese only, I'll clear up the mystery—they're generally "adult entertainment" programs. If you're traveling with children, you'll want to be extremely careful about selecting your TV programs. Many adult video pay channels appear with a simple push of the channel-selector button, and they can be difficult to get rid of.

In budget accommodations, you may come across televisions with coin boxes attached to their sides. Occasionally this means that the TVs can be activated only by inserting coins into the box; I call these coin-operated TVs. But if the TV functions without having to insert coins, the coin box is for those special adult entertainment videos. Now you know.

Time Zone Japan is 9 hours ahead of Greenwich mean time, 14 hours ahead of New York, 15 hours ahead of Chicago, and 17 hours ahead of Los Angeles. Since Japan does not go on daylight savings time, subtract 1 hour from the above times if you're calling the United States in the summer.

Because Japan is on the other side of the International Date Line, you lose a day when traveling from the United States to Asia (if you depart the U.S. on Tues, you'll arrive on Wed). Returning to North America, however, you gain a day, which means that you arrive on the same day you leave. (In fact, it often happens that you arrive in the U.S. at an earlier time than when you departed from Japan.)

Tipping One of the delights of being in Japan is that there is no tipping—not even to waitresses, taxi drivers, or bellhops. If you try to tip them, they'll probably be confused or embarrassed. Instead, you'll have a 10% to 15% service charge added to your bill at higher-priced accommodations and restaurants.

Water The water is safe to drink anywhere in Japan, although some people claim it's too highly chlorinated. Bottled water is readily available.

4

Where to Stay

Tokyo has no old, grand hotels in the tradition of the Peninsula in Hong Kong or the Raffles in Singapore; it has hardly any old hotels, period. But what the city's hotels may lack in quaintness or old grandeur is more than made up for by excellent service—for which the Japanese are legendary—as well as cleanliness and efficiency. Be prepared, however, for small rooms. Space is at a premium in Tokyo, so with the exception of some rooms in very expensive hotels, rooms seem to come in three sizes: minuscule, small, and barely adequate.

Unfortunately, Tokyo also doesn't have many first-class *ryokan,* or Japanese-style inns. I suggest, therefore, that you wait for your travels outside Tokyo (see chapter 10, "Side Trips from Tokyo," for recommended excursions) to experience a first-rate ryokan. Alternatively, most of Tokyo's upper-bracket hotels offer at least a few Japanese-style rooms, with tatami mats, a Japanese bathtub (deeper and narrower than the Western version), and a futon. Although these rooms tend to be expensive, they're usually large enough for four people. There are also moderate and inexpensive Japanese-style inns in Tokyo. In fact, if you're traveling on a tight budget, a simple Japanese-style inn is often the cheapest way to go.

PRICE CATEGORIES The hotel recommendations below are arranged first according to price, then by geographical location. Since Tokyo's attractions, restaurants, and nightlife are widely scattered, and since the public transportation system is fast and efficient (I've provided the nearest subway or train stations for each listing), there's no one location within Tokyo that is more convenient than another—and because this is one of the most expensive hotel cities in the world, the overriding factor in selecting accommodations will likely be cost. I've divided Tokyo's hotels into price categories based upon two people per night, excluding tax and service charge: **Very Expensive** hotels charge ¥37,000 ($308) and above, **Expensive** hotels charge ¥26,000 to ¥36,000 ($216–$300), **Moderate** hotels offer rooms for ¥14,100 to ¥25,000 ($117–$208), and **Inexpensive** accommodations offer rooms for ¥14,000 ($116) and less. Unless otherwise indicated, units have private bathrooms.

TAXES & SERVICE CHARGES In addition to quoted prices, upper-class hotels and most medium-range hotels will add a **service charge** of 10% to 15% (cheaper establishments do not charge service, because no service is provided). Furthermore, all hotels add an additional 5% **tax.** An additional local hotel tax applies to rooms that cost more than ¥10,000 ($83) per person per night. ¥100 (85¢) is levied per person per night for rates between ¥10,000 and ¥14,999 ($83–$125); rates of ¥15,000 ($125) and up are taxed at ¥200 ($1.65). *Unless otherwise stated, the prices given in this chapter do not include tax or service.*

BUSY TIMES Although Tokyo doesn't suffer from a lack of hotel rooms during peak holidays (when most Japanese head for the hills and beaches), rooms may be in short supply because of **conventions** and other events. If possible, avoid coming to Tokyo in **mid-February** unless you book well in advance—that's when university entrance exams bring multitudes of aspiring high-school students and their parents to the capital for a shot at entering one of the most prestigious universities in the country. And in **summer,** when there are many foreign tourists in Japan, the cheaper accommodations are often the first to fill up.

It's always best, therefore, to **make your hotel reservations in advance,** especially if you're arriving in Tokyo after a long transoceanic flight and don't want the hassle of searching for a hotel room.

WELCOME INN RESERVATION CENTER   If you're looking for help in booking moderately priced and budget accommodations, at the top of my list is the Welcome Inn Reservation Center, operated in cooperation with the Japan National Tourist Organization. Some 100 modestly priced accommodations in Tokyo, mostly business hotels but also some tourist hotels and Japanese-style inns, are members of Welcome Inn; another 600 are spread throughout Japan. Room rates are ¥8,000 ($67) or less for a single and ¥13,000 ($108) or less for a double. No fee is charged for the service, but you are asked to guarantee your reservation with a credit card.

You can book a reservation at Welcome Inn online at **www.itcj.or.jp** (reservations should be made at least 1 week prior to your departure; proof of a confirmed flight is required). Otherwise, contact the nearest **Japan National Tourist Organization** office,

known as the **Tourist Information Center (TIC)** (p. 37 and 40) and request the *Directory of Welcome Inns,* which not only lists all the properties but contains a reservation request form that you should then fax to the Tokyo TIC 1 week prior to your departure or mail to the TIC 2 weeks prior to your departure; you'll then receive a confirmation slip and detailed information and access maps for your selected accommodations.

If you're already in Japan, you can apply by mailing, faxing, or e-mailing your reservation request form (telephone reservations are not accepted) or by appearing in person at one of the two TIC offices in Tokyo—at Narita Airport (in the arrivals lobbies of Terminals 1 and 2) or near Yurakucho Station in the heart of the city (see p. 37 and 40). Reservations are accepted at the Narita TIC daily from 9am to 7:30pm; and at the Tokyo TIC Monday through Friday from 9 to 11:30am and 1 to 4:45pm. The Tokyo TIC is closed on public holidays.

SURFING FOR ROOMS   Government-approved moderate and higher-priced hotels that are members of the Japan Hotel Association are listed at **www.j-hotel.or.jp/welcome-e.html**. Likewise, high-priced, government-registered members of the Japan Ryokan Association can be found at **www.ryokan.or.jp**. Budget-priced Japanese inns—which do not offer the service or the class of high-priced inns but do offer the experience of sleeping Japanese-style—who are members of the Japanese Inn Group (details provided below) are listed at **www.jpinn.com**. But Japan's largest online hotel reservations company for budget and moderately priced accommodations is **www.mytrip.net/en/index.html**.

1 Japanese & Western-Style Accommodations

JAPANESE-STYLE ACCOMMODATIONS

RYOKAN   Although it can be very expensive, spending the night in a traditional Japanese inn *(ryokan)* is worth the splurge at least once during your trip.

Unfortunately, you won't find many first-class ryokan in Tokyo itself. Unable to compete with the more profitable high-rise hotels, many have closed. If you want to stay in a deluxe Japanese inn, therefore, your best bet is a resort or a hot-spring spa, such as Hakone (chapter 10). Alternatively, most of Tokyo's upper-class hotels offer Japanese-style rooms as well. If you don't have time for a side trip from Tokyo, however, you can still find some decent ryokan in the city, though they won't provide the full experience.

And the full ryokan experience is unforgettable. Nothing conveys the simplicity and beauty—indeed, the very atmosphere—of old Japan like these inns, with their gleaming polished wood, tatami floors, rice-paper sliding doors, and meticulously pruned gardens. Exquisitely prepared kaiseki meals and personalized service by kimono-clad hostesses are the trademarks of such inns, and staying in one is like taking a trip back in time.

Traditionally, ryokan are small—only one or two stories high and containing about 10 to 30 rooms—and are made of wood with a tile roof. Most guests arrive at their ryokan around 3 or 4pm. The entrance is often through a gate and small garden, where you're met by a bowing woman in a kimono. Remove your shoes, slide on the proffered plastic slippers, and follow the hostess down long wooden corridors until you reach the sliding door of your room. After taking off the slippers, step into your tatami room, almost void of furniture except for a low table in the middle of the room, floor cushions, an antique scroll hanging in an alcove, and a simple flower arrangement. Best of all is the view past rice-paper sliding screens of a Japanese landscaped garden with bonsai, stone lanterns, and a meandering pond filled with carp. Notice that the room has no bed.

Almost immediately your hostess welcomes you with hot tea and a sweet, served at your low table so that you can sit there for a while and appreciate the view, the peace, and the solitude. Next comes a hot bath, either in your own room (if you have one), or in the communal bath. (Be sure to follow the procedure outlined in "Social Skills 101" in chapter 2—soap and rinse yourself before you get into the tub.) After bathing and soaking away tension, aches, and pains, change into your *yukata,* a cotton kimono provided by the ryokan.

When you return to your room, you'll find the maid ready to serve your kaiseki dinner, an elaborate spread that is the highlight of a ryokan stay. It generally consists of locally grown vegetables, sashimi (raw fish), grilled or baked fish or another meat dish, and various regional specialties, served in many tiny plates; the menu is determined by the chef. Admire how each dish is in itself a delicate piece of art-work; it all looks too wonderful to eat, but finally hunger takes over. If you want, you can order sake or beer to accompany your meal (you'll pay extra for drinks).

After you've finished eating, the maid will return to clear away the dishes and to lay out your bed. The bed is really a futon, a kind of mattress with quilts, and is laid out on the tatami floor. The next morning the maid will wake you up, put away the futon, and serve a breakfast of fish, pickled vegetables, soup, dried sea-weed, rice, and a raw egg to be mixed with the rice. Feeling rested, well fed, and pampered, you're then ready to pack your bags and pay your bill. Your hostess sees you to the front gate, smiling and bowing as you set off for the rest of your travels.

Such is life at a good ryokan. Sadly, however, the number of upper-class ryokan diminishes each year. And, although ideally a ryokan is an old wooden structure that once served traveling feudal lords or was perhaps the home of a wealthy merchant, many are actually modern concrete affairs with as many as 100 or more rooms. Meals are served in dining rooms. What they lack in intimacy and

Love Hotels

In addition to Japanese-style inns, Japan has another unique form of accommodations—so-called love hotels. Usually found close to entertainment districts such as Shinjuku and Shibuya, such hotels do not, as their name might suggest, provide sexual services; rather, they offer rooms for rent by the hour to lovers. Even married couples use love hotels, particularly if they share small quarters with in-laws.

Altogether, there are an estimated 35,000 such love hotels in Japan, usually gaudy affairs shaped like ocean liners or castles and offering such extras as rotating beds, mirrored walls, video cameras, and fantasy-provoking decor. Love hotels are often clustered together. You'll know you've wandered into a love-hotel district when you notice discreet entryways and—a dead giveaway—hourly rates posted near the front door. Many have reasonable overnight rates as well. I have friends who, finding themselves out too late and too far from home, have checked into love hotels, solo.

personal service, however, they make up for with slightly cheaper prices and such amenities as modern bathing facilities and perhaps a bar and outdoor recreational facilities. Most guest rooms are fitted with a color TV, telephone, safe for locking up valuables, and yukata, as well as amenities like soap, shampoo, razor, toothbrush, and toothpaste.

Rates are based on a per-person charge rather than a straight room charge, and include breakfast, dinner, and often service; tax is extra. Thus, while ryokan rates may seem high, they're actually competitive compared to what you'd pay for a hotel room and comparable meals in a restaurant. Although rates can vary from ¥9,000 to an astonishing ¥150,000 ($75–$1,250) per person, the average cost is generally ¥12,000 to ¥20,000 ($100–$167). Even within a single ryokan the rates can vary greatly, depending on the room you choose, the dinner courses you select, and the number of people in your room. If you're paying the highest rate, you can be certain you're getting the best room, the best view of the garden, or perhaps even your own private garden, as well as a much more elaborate meal than that given to lower-paying guests. All the rates for ryokan in this book are based on double occupancy; if there are more than two of you in one room, you can generally count on a slightly lower per-person rate.

Although I heartily recommend spending at least 1 night in a ryokan, there are a number of **disadvantages** to these accommodations. The most obvious problem is that you may find it uncomfortable sitting on the floor. And because the futon is put away during the day, there's no place to lie down for an afternoon nap or rest, except on the hard, tatami-covered floor. In addition, some of the older ryokan, though quaint, are bitterly cold in the winter and may have only Japanese-style toilets ("Fast Facts: Tokyo," p. 53). As for breakfast, you might find it difficult to swallow raw egg, rice, and seaweed in the morning (I've even been served grilled grasshopper—quite crunchy). Sometimes you can get a Western-style breakfast if you order it the night before, but more often than not the fried or scrambled eggs arrive cold, leading you to suspect that they were cooked right after you ordered them.

A ryokan is also quite rigid in its **schedule.** You're expected to arrive sometime between 3 and 5pm, take your bath, and then eat at around 6 or 7pm. Breakfast is served early, usually by 8am, and checkout is by 10am. That means you can't sleep in, and because the maid is continually coming in and out, you have a lot less privacy than you would in a hotel. You should always make a reservation if you want to stay in a first-class or medium-priced ryokan, since the chef has to shop for and prepare your meals. You can make reservations through any travel agency in Japan or by calling or faxing a ryokan directly. You may be required to pay a deposit. The Japan National Tourist Organization offers free publications: the *Japan Ryokan Guide* lists members of the Japan Ryokan Association (© **03/3231-5310;** www.ryokan.or.jp), while *The Tourist's Handbook* describes the rules of etiquette for staying in a ryokan, along with handy translations for common situations that may arise.

JAPANESE INN GROUP   If you want the experience of staying in a Japanese-style room but cannot afford the extravagance of a ryokan, you might consider staying in one of the participating members of the Japanese Inn Group—a special organization of more than 80 Japanese-style inns and hotels throughout Japan offering inexpensive lodging and catering largely to foreigners. Although you may balk at the idea of staying at a place filled mainly with foreigners, keep in mind that many inexpensive Japanese-style inns are not accustomed to guests from abroad and may be quite reluctant to take you in. I have covered many of the Japanese Inn Group members in this book over the years and have found the owners for the most part to be an exceptional group of friendly people eager to offer foreigners the chance to experience life on tatami and futons. In many cases, these are good places in which to exchange information with other world travelers, and they are popular with both young people and families.

Although many of the group members call themselves ryokan, they are not ryokan in the true sense of the word, because they do not offer the trademark personalized service nor the beautiful setting common to ryokan. However, they do offer simple tatami rooms that generally come with TVs and air-conditioners (occasionally both coin-operated); most have towels and cotton yukata. Some offer Western-style rooms as well, and/or rooms with private bathrooms. Facilities generally include a coin-operated washer and dryer and a public bath. The average cost of a 1-night stay is about ¥4,500 to ¥7,500 ($38–$63) per person, without meals. Breakfast is usually available if you pay extra; dinner is also sometimes available.

You can view member inns at **www.jpinn.com**. Or, upon your arrival in Tokyo, head to the Tourist Information Center for the free pamphlet called *Japanese Inn Group,* which lists the members and is available at the Tourist Information Center in Tokyo. Make reservations directly with the ryokan in which you wish to stay (most have faxes and many have e-mail). In some cases, you'll be asked to pay a deposit (equal to 1 night's stay), which can be in the form of a personal check, traveler's check, money order, or bank check, but it's easiest to pay through American Express. For more information, contact the Inn Group's headquarters at Ryokan Asakusa Shigetsu, 1–31–11 Nishi-Asakusa, Taito-ku, Tokyo 111-0032 (© **03/3843-2345**). Some member inns belong to the Welcome Inn Group as well, which means you can also make reservations through one of the methods described earlier.

MINSHUKU   Technically, a *minshuku* is inexpensive Japanese-style lodging in a private home—the Japanese version of a bed-and-breakfast—usually located in resort areas or smaller towns. Because minshuku are family-run affairs, there's no personal service, which means that you're expected to lay out your own futon at night, stow it away in the morning, and tidy up your room. Most also do not supply towels or yukata, nor do they have units with private bathrooms. Meals are served in a communal dining room.

Officially, what differentiates a ryokan from a minshuku is that the ryokan is more expensive and provides more services, but the difference is sometimes very slight. I've stayed in cheap ryokan providing almost no service and in minshuku too large and modern to be considered private homes. The average per-person cost for 1 night in a minshuku is generally ¥7,000 to ¥9,000 ($58–$75), including two meals.

WESTERN-STYLE ACCOMMODATIONS

Western-style lodgings range from large first-class hotels to inexpensive ones catering primarily to Japanese businessmen.

When you book a hotel room, contact the hotel directly to inquire about rates, even if a toll-free 800 number is provided; sometimes there are special packages, such as weekend or honeymoon packages, that central reservations desks do not know about. Special, cheaper rates may also be offered on the hotel's website. In addition, always ask what kinds of rooms are available. Many hotels, especially those in the upper and medium range, offer a variety of rooms at various prices, with room size the overwhelming factor in pricing. Other aspects that often have a bearing on rates include bed size, floor height (higher floors are more expensive), and in-room amenities. Views are generally not a factor in Tokyo (though some hotels near Tokyo Bay charge more for harbor views; Mt. Fuji in the far distance is generally visible only in the winter or on rare, clear days). In Japan, a **twin room** usually refers to a room with two twin beds, while a **double room** refers to a room with one double bed. Most hotels charge more for a twin room, but sometimes the opposite is the case. When making your reservation, therefore, inquire about the differences in rates and what they entail.

Once you decide on the type of room you want, ask for the best in that category. For example, if you want a standard room, and deluxe rooms start on the 14th floor, ask for a standard on the 13th floor. In addition, be specific about the kind of room you want, whether it's a nonsmoking room, a room with a view of Mount Fuji, a room with a dataport for your computer, or a room away from traffic noise. If possible, give the hotel your approximate time of arrival, especially if you'll be arriving after 6pm, when untaken rooms are sometimes given away.

PRICE CATEGORIES

VERY EXPENSIVE & EXPENSIVE   Tokyo's top hotels can rival upper-range hotels anywhere in the world. Although many of the city's best hotels may not show much character from the outside, inside they're oases of subdued simplicity where hospitality reigns supreme. In addition to fine Japanese- and Western-style restaurants, they may also offer a travel agency, a business center, a guest relations officer to help with any problems or requests you may have (from making a restaurant reservation to finding an address), shopping arcades, cocktail lounges with live music, and a health club with swimming pool. Unfortunately, health clubs and swimming pools usually cost extra—anywhere from ¥2,000 to an outrageous ¥5,000 ($17–$42) per single use. In addition, outdoor pools are generally open only in July and August.

Rooms in upper-range hotels come with such standard features as a minibar, cable TV with CNN and pay movies, dataport, clock, radio, yukata, hot-water pot and tea (and sometimes coffee, but you usually pay extra for it), hair dryer, and private bathroom with tub-and-shower combination. Many also have **washlet toilets: combination toilets and spray bidets.** Because they're accustomed to foreigners, most upper-range hotels employ an English-speaking staff and offer nonsmoking floors. Services provided include room service, same-day laundry and dry-cleaning service, and complimentary English-language newspapers such as the *Japan Times* delivered to your room. Many hotels also offer executive floors, which are generally on the highest floors and offer such perks as a private lounge with separate check-in, more in-room amenities, free continental breakfast and cocktails, extended checkout time, and privileges that can include free use of the health club; at just a few thousand yen more than regular rates, these can be quite economical.

MODERATE   Moderately priced accommodations vary from tourist hotels to business hotels, with business hotels making up the majority in this category. Catering primarily to traveling Japanese businessmen, a business hotel is a no-frills establishment with tiny, sparsely furnished rooms, most of them singles, with barely enough space to unpack your bags. If you're a large person, you may have trouble sleeping in a place like this. Primarily just a place to crash for the night, these rooms usually have everything you need—minuscule private bathroom, TV, telephone, radio, clock, hair dryer, hot-water pot with tea, and often a minibar. There's no room service, and sometimes not even a lobby or coffee shop, although there may be vending machines that dispense beer and soda. There may be same-day laundry service as well, if you give up your laundry by 10am (no laundry service is available Sun and holidays). Business hotels rarely have nonsmoking rooms. On the plus side, they're usually situated in convenient locations near train or subway stations. If you're interested simply in a clean and functional place to sleep rather than in roomy comfort, a nondescript business hotel may be the way to go.

INEXPENSIVE   It's difficult to find inexpensive lodgings in Tokyo; the price of land is simply prohibitive. You can, however, find rooms—tiny though they may be—for less than $90 a night for two people, which is pretty good considering that you're in one of the most expensive cities in the world. Inexpensive accommodations include a bed or futon and (usually) phone, TV, heating, and air-conditioning. Unless otherwise indicated, units also have private bathrooms. Facilities are generally spotless, and prices sometimes include tax. Inexpensive Japanese-style rooms make up the majority in this category; they're described in more detail above.

Many foreigners find Japan so expensive that they end up becoming **youth hostel** regulars, even though they may never consider staying in one in other countries. There's no age limit at hostels in Japan (though children younger than 4 may not be accepted), and although most require a youth-hostel membership card, they often let foreigners stay without one for about ¥600 ($5) extra per night. However, there are usually quite a few restrictions, such as a 9 or 10pm curfew, a lights-out policy shortly thereafter, an early breakfast time, and closed times through the day, generally from about 10am to 3pm. In addition, rooms usually hold many bunk beds or futons, affording little privacy. On the other hand, these are certainly the cheapest accommodations in Tokyo.

2 Very Expensive

GINZA

Hotel Seiyo Ginza ★★★   Conveniently located between the Ginza and Nihombashi financial center, this small luxury hotel targets famous personalities, royalty, and top executives. A member of The Leading Hotels of the World, it maintains a low profile to protect its guests' privacy (in fact, you can easily overlook it when passing by) and strives to create an environment similar to that of a posh residential building. Check-in is conducted at individual-size desks fitted with comfortable chairs, and the atmosphere is one of hushed tranquillity. The hotel's snob appeal is enhanced by Japan's first 24-hour personalized butler service, a plus for those who don't like to unpack their bags or draw their own bath water. The large rooms—one-third of which are suites and no two of which are alike—are comfortable homes-away-from-home, decorated in English countryside style and offering everything you'd expect, including service buttons for immediate maid or butler response, and large bathrooms with mini-TVs and separate tub and shower areas. In short, this elegant hotel is a refuge from the sensory overload that is Tokyo.

1–11–2 Ginza, Chuo-ku, Tokyo 104-0061. ℂ 800/447-3496 in the U.S. or 03/3535-1111. Fax 03/3535-1110. www.seiyo-ginza.com. 77 units. ¥42,000 – ¥57,000 ($350–$475) single or double; from ¥60,000 ($500) suite. AE, DC, MC, V. Station: Ginza-Itchome or Kyobashi (2 min.). **Amenities:** 4 restaurants (French, Italian, kaiseki, sushi); 2 bars; small fitness room (free); use of a nearby fitness center (fee: ¥3,000/$25); concierge; business center; 24-hr. room service; in-room massage; same-day laundry/dry-cleaning service. *In room:* A/C, TV w/cable and on-demand pay movies and CD/DVD/MD players, high-speed dataport, minibar, hot-water pot with tea, hair dryer, safe.

NEAR TOKYO STATION

Four Seasons Hotel Tokyo at Marunouchi ★★★   If it's your dream to stay in Japan's most expensive hotel, this is for you. With only 57 rooms, it offers the ultimate in service, privacy, and exclusivity, with a well-trained staff that goes out of its way to make guests feel welcome. Next to Tokyo Station and within walking distance of the Ginza, it boasts the most convenient location in town. For first-timers leery of traveling between Narita Airport and Tokyo Station, the hotel offers a unique "greeting" service at the airport to assure a seamless transition all the way to the hotel (cost: ¥5,000/$42). Despite its bustling location, the hotel is buffered from the outside world with triple-glazed glass and a soothing, ultra-contemporary design that employs natural woods and color schemes of ecru and charcoal or off-white and black.

Guests are escorted to rooms by guest-relations officers, and with good reason, as rooms are so high-tech it's almost impossible to figure out even such mundane tasks as double-locking the doors or engaging the bathtub stopper. At 44 sq. m (474 sq. ft.) and larger, the attractive rooms are among the largest in

---

Tips **A Note on Prices**

The prices quoted in this book were figured at ¥120 = US$1. Because of fluctuations in the exchange rate of the yen, however, the U.S. dollar equivalents given will probably vary during the lifetime of this edition. Be sure to check current exchange rates when planning your trip. In addition, the rates given below may increase, so be sure to ask for the current rate when making your reservation.

Nightlife & Where to Stay & Dine in Ginza & Hibiya

ACCOMMODATIONS ■

Four Seasons Hotel Tokyo
  at Marunouchi **32**
Ginza Nikko Hotel **4**
Hotel Monterey La Soeur **26**
Hotel Seiyo Ginza **27**
Imperial Hotel **1**
Mitsui Urban Hotel Ginza **5**
Renaissance Tokyo Hotel Ginza
  Tobu **22**

DINING ◆

Atariya **29**
Donto **33**
Farm Grill **7**
Fukusuke **15**
Gonpachi **30**
Ginza Daimasu **20**
Imperial Viking **1**
Kamon **1**
Kazan **23**
Kihachi **31**
Kushi Colza **13**
La Boheme **14** & **30**
L'Osier **2**
Munakata **5**
Ohmatsuya **16**
Rangetsu **28**
Shabusen **21**
Shiseido Parlour **8**
Sushi Sei **3**
Sushiko **12**
Tatsutano **10**
Ten-ichi **17**
To the Herbs **24**
Yakitori Under the Tracks **10**
Zest Cantina **30**
Zipangu **6**

NIGHTLIFE ●

Ginza Sapporo Lion **9**
Kabukiza **25**
Lupin **18**
Nanbatei **19**
Old Imperial **1**
Takarazuka Gekijo **11**

| Railway |
| Subway |
| Tourist Info (i) |

HIBIYA PARK

HIBIYA LINE

**Imperial
Tower**

KEIHIN-TOHOKU LINE

Sotobori Dori

Soni Dori

Namiki Dori

Metropolitan (Shuto) Expressway

Nishi-Go-Bangai

Azuma Dori

| 0 | | 1/10 mile |
| 0 | 100 meters | |

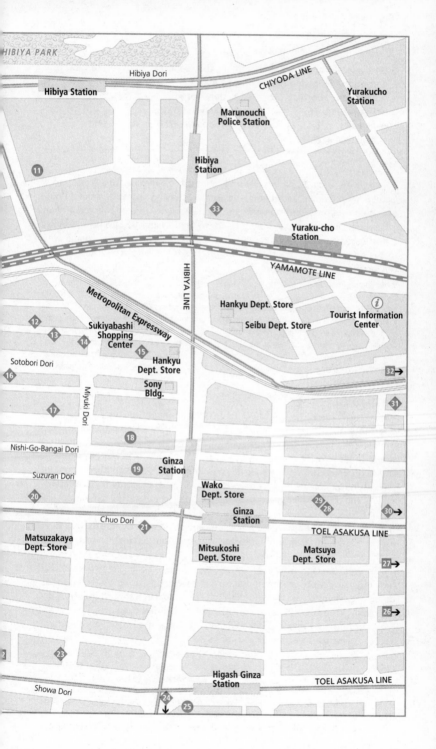

HIBIYA PARK

Hibiya Dori

CHIYODA LINE

Hibiya Station

Yurakucho Station

Marunouchi Police Station

Hibiya Station

⑪

㉝

Yuraku-cho Station

YAMAMOTE LINE

HIBIYA LINE

Metropolitan Expressway

Hankyu Dept. Store

Seibu Dept. Store

Tourist Information Center

ⓘ

⑫

⑬

⑭

Sukiyabashi Shopping Center

㉜→

⑮

Hankyu Dept. Store

Sotobori Dori

⑯

Sony Bldg.

㉛

⑰

Miyuki Dori

⑱

Nishi-Go-Bangai Dori

⑲

Ginza Station

Suzuran Dori

⑳

Wako Dept. Store

㉙ ㉘

㉚→

Chuo Dori

㉑

Ginza Station

TOEL ASAKUSA LINE

Matsuzakaya Dept. Store

Mitsukoshi Dept. Store

Matsuya Dept. Store

㉗→

㉖→

2

㉓

Higash Ginza Station

TOEL ASAKUSA LINE

Showa Dori

㉔

㉕

Tips **A Guide to Tokyo Maps**

Once you've chosen accommodations that appeal to you, you can locate
it using the following neighborhood maps:

- **Ginza** and **Hibiya,** p. 72.
- **Shinjuku,** p. 76.
- **Akasaka,** p. 83.
- **Asakusa,** p. 89.
- **Ueno,** p. 91.
- **Harajuku,** p. 133.
- **Roppongi,** p. 143.

Tokyo, with such standouts as wall-mounted 42-inch plasma-screen TVs,
leather-covered desks, bathrooms with separate tub and shower areas, and floor-
to-ceiling windows. Unfortunately, the hotel's location on the lower levels of an
office high-rise affords views only of Tokyo Station and its Shinkansen bullet
trains or surrounding buildings, and at these prices, you have to wonder why
there's no mini-TV in the bathroom. Still, this is a great place to stay—if you
can get someone else to pay for it.

Pacific Century Place, 1–11–1 Marunouchi, Chiyoda-ku, Tokyo 100-6277. ℭ **800/332-3442** in the U.S. or
03/5222-7222. Fax 03/5222-1255. www.fourseasons.com/marunouchi. 57 units. ¥55,000 – ¥65,000
($485–$542) single; ¥60,000 – ¥70,000 ($500–$583) double or twin; from ¥85,000 ($708) suite. AE, DC, MC,
V. Station: Tokyo (2 min.). **Amenities:** Restaurant (Modern French); bar; lounge; 24-hr. exercise room (free);
public bath with imported hot-springs mineral water and steam room (free); spa; concierge; 24-hr. small business center; 24-hr. room service; in-room massage; babysitting; same-day laundry/dry-cleaning service; nonsmoking room; complimentary shoeshine. *In room:* A/C, TV w/cable and CD/DVD players (free rentals),
fax/printer/scanner/copier, dataport, minibar, hot-water pot with tea and coffee, hair dryer, safe, bathroom
scale, washlet toilet.

SHINJUKU

Park Hyatt Tokyo ✦✦✦   Located in West Shinjuku on the 39th to 52nd
floors of Kenzo Tange's granite-and-glass Shinjuku Park Tower, the Park Hyatt
is among the most gorgeous and sophisticated hotels in Japan, a perfect reflection of high-tech, avant-garde Tokyo in the 21st century. If you can afford it,
stay here. Check-in, on the 41st floor, is comfortably accomplished at one of
three sit-down desks. Elevators reserved only for the guest-room floors offer privacy; if you do see other guests, they're likely to be personalities, fashion designers, or CEOs. In contrast to Shinjuku's other hotels, there's no off-the-street foot
traffic here; rather, a hushed, soothing atmosphere prevails. Be sure to book early
for the 52nd-floor New York Grill, one of Tokyo's best restaurants, which offers
a spectacular setting (p. 128).

All rooms average at least 45 sq. m (484 sq. ft.—the largest in Tokyo) and
have original artwork, stunning and expansive views (including Mt. Fuji on clear
days), bathrooms to die for with deep tub (plus separate shower), walk-in closets, remote-control curtains, and even Japanese/English dictionaries. Despite the
recent opening of Roppongi Hill's Grand Hyatt (p. 77), this hotel isn't worried,
as it considers itself in a higher class of its own.

3–7–1–2 Nishi-Shinjuku, Shinjuku-ku, Tokyo 163-1055. ℭ **800/233-1234** in the U.S. and Canada, or
03/5322-1234. Fax 03/5322-1288. www.parkhyatttokyo.com. 178 units. ¥52,000 – ¥63,000 ($433–$525) single or double; from ¥100,000 ($833) suite. AE, DC, MC, V. Station: Shinjuku (a 13-min. walk or 5-min. free
shuttle ride), Hatsudai on the Keio Line (7 min.), or Tochomae (8 min.). **Amenities:** 3 restaurants (French, contemporary Japanese, American); 2 bars; lounge; dramatic 20m (66-ft.) indoor swimming pool with great views
(free for hotel guests); health club and spa (fee: ¥4,000/$33); concierge; business center; salon; 24-hr. room
service; in-room massage; babysitting; same-day laundry/dry-cleaning service; nonsmoking rooms; CD and

book libraries; free shuttle service to Shinjuku Station 1–3 times an hour; complimentary shoeshine. *In room:* A/C, wide-screen plasma TV w/cable and pay movies, CD player (with free rentals), fax/printer, high-speed dataport, minibar, hot-water pot with tea and coffee, hair dryer, safe, bathroom scale, washlet toilet.

EBISU

Westin Tokyo ★★ *Value*   A black marble floor, neoclassical columns and statuary, huge floral bouquets, and palm trees set this smart-looking hotel apart from other Tokyo hotels—it would fit right into Hong Kong. Opened in 1994 and set in the attractive Yebisu Garden Place (Tokyo's first planned community), it's still a hike from Ebisu Station, even with the aid of the elevated moving walkways. It's also far from Tokyo's business center. But the largely Japanese clientele (though North Americans account for 25% of the guests) favors it for its European ambience, relaxed atmosphere, Westin name, Yebisu Garden Place with its restaurants and shopping, and reasonable rates compared to those of Tokyo's other deluxe hotels.

The spacious, high-ceilinged rooms blend 19th-century Biedermeier styles with contemporary furnishings and Westin's trademark "Heavenly Beds" that are either king-size (in double rooms) or two double beds (in twins), oversize desks, separate lighted vanities, and large bathrooms with separate shower and tub areas. Guest Office rooms provide such additional features as laser printers, fax machines, and office supplies. Rooms on higher floors cost more, with the best views considered those facing Tokyo Tower, though on clear days those facing west treat you to views of Mount Fuji.

Kids Family-Friendly Hotels

Hotel New Otani (p. 84)   This huge hotel has both indoor and outdoor swimming pools, but best for parents is the babysitting room for children ages 1 month to 5 years. For a small fortune, you can even leave the darlings overnight.

Imperial Hotel (p. 79)   Although oriented toward business travelers, this famous hotel makes it easier to bring the family along, with its day-care center for children ages 2 weeks to 6 years, its babysitting service, and an indoor pool.

Keio Plaza Inter-Continental Tokyo (p. 82)   A children's day-care center for children 2 months and older and free admission to an outdoor pool with children's pool are family pleasers, but if that's not enough, maybe the kids will find it cool to stay in one of Tokyo's tallest hotels.

National Children's Castle Hotel (p. 99)   This is the absolutely top place to stay with kids, since the same building contains Tokyo's best indoor/outdoor playground and activity rooms for all ages, offering everything from building blocks to computer games.

Sakura Ryokan (p. 96)   This modern Japanese-style inn offers a large family room that sleeps up to eight people in traditional Japanese style, on futons laid out on tatami mats.

Shinagawa Prince (p. 95)   Japan's largest hotel boasts a children's day-care center, an IMAX theater, an amusement arcade, indoor and outdoor pools, a sports center, and more.

Nightlife & Where to Stay & Dine in Shinjuku

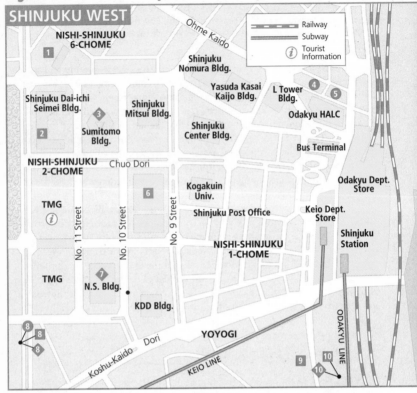

SHINJUKU WEST

Railway
Subway
ⓘ Tourist Information

NISHI-SHINJUKU 6-CHOME
1

Ohme Kaido

Shinjuku Nomura Bldg.

Yasuda Kasai Kaijo Bldg.

L Tower Bldg.
4
5

Odakyu HALC

Shinjuku Dai-ichi Seimei Bldg.
3
Shinjuku Mitsui Bldg.

Sumitomo Bldg.
2

Shinjuku Center Bldg.

Bus Terminal

NISHI-SHINJUKU 2-CHOME   Chuo Dori

Kogakuin Univ.

Odakyu Dept. Store

TMG ⓘ

No. 11 Street
No. 10 Street
No. 9 Street

6

Shinjuku Post Office

Keio Dept. Store

Shinjuku Station

NISHI-SHINJUKU 1-CHOME

TMG

7
N.S. Bldg.

KDD Bldg.

Koshu-Kaido   Dori   YOYOGI

ODAKYU LINE

8
8
8

KEIO LINE

9   10
10

1–4–1 Mita, Meguro-ku, Tokyo 153-8580. ⓒ 800/WESTIN-1 in the U.S. and Canada, or 03/5423-7000. Fax 03/5423-7600. www.westin.co.jp. 445 units. ¥34,000 – ¥44,000 ($283–$367) single; ¥39,000 – ¥49,000 ($325–$408) double or twin; from ¥105,000 ($875) suite. Guest Office or Executive Club ¥51,000 ($425) single; ¥56,000 ($467) double or twin. AE, DC, MC, V. Station: Ebisu (7 min. via Yebisu Sky Walk). **Amenities:** 6 restaurants; 3 bars and lounges; access to nearby health club with heated indoor pool and gym (fee: ¥4,000/$33); concierge; business center; 24-hr. room service; in-room massage; babysitting; same-day laundry/dry-cleaning service; nonsmoking rooms; executive-level rooms. *In room:* A/C, TV w/cable and on-demand pay movies, dataport, minibar, hot-water pot with tea, hair dryer, iron, bathroom scale, washlet toilet.

ROPPONGI & AKASAKA

Capitol Tokyu Hotel ★★ *Finds*   This Tokyo old-timer is a popular choice for knowledgeable travelers seeking up-to-date accommodations with traditional touches. Built just before the 1964 Olympics, it's nestled against the wooded hillside leading to Hie Shrine, one of the city's most important Edo Period shrines, yet it is centrally located in Akasaka convenient to the city's many sights. A member of the Tokyu hotel chain, it has the unique ability to make foreign guests feel as if they're in Asia and at home at the same time, making it a longtime local favorite. Fantastically large floral bouquets are the trademark of the dark, subdued lobby, which overlooks a small Japanese garden with a carp pond. The level of service is extraordinary. While double and twin rooms are comfortably large, the 50 single rooms are fairly small. All come with traditional shoji screens, as well as light-blocking sliding panels; the best ones overlook the greenery of Hie Shrine. Some of the more expensive rooms also have high-speed Internet connections.

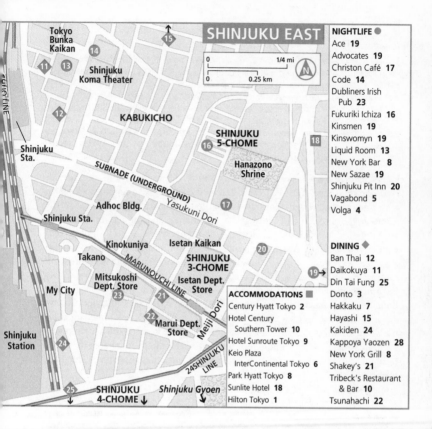

SHINJUKU EAST

0 —— 1/4 mi
0 —— 0.25 km
N

Tokyo Bunka Kaikan

Shinjuku Koma Theater

KABUKICHO

SHINJUKU 5-CHOME

Hanazono Shrine

SUBNADE (UNDERGROUND)

Yasukuni Dori

Shinjuku Sta.

Shinjuku Sta.

Adhoc Bldg.

Kinokuniya

Takano

MARUNOUCHI LINE

Isetan Kaikan

SHINJUKU 3-CHOME

Mitsukoshi Dept. Store

Isetan Dept. Store

My City

Marui Dept. Store

Meiji Dori

Shinjuku Station

SHINJUKU LINE

SHINJUKU 4-CHOME

Shinjuku Gyoen

2–10–3 Nagata-cho, Chiyoda-ku, Tokyo 100-0014. ℂ **800/888-4747** in the U.S. and Canada, or 03/3581-4511. Fax 03/3581-5822. www.capitoltokyu.com. 454 units. ¥26,000 – ¥29,000 ($217–$242) single; ¥38,000 – ¥55,000 ($312–$458) double or twin; from ¥100,000 ($833) suite. AE, DC, MC, V. **Station:** Kokkai Gijido-mae (1 min.) or Tameikesanno (3 min.). **Amenities:** 5 restaurants; cafe; bar; lounge; outdoor pool (free); small fitness room (free); concierge; travel agency; business center; shopping arcade; salon; barbershop; 24-hr. room service; in-room massage; babysitting; same-day laundry/dry-cleaning service; nonsmoking rooms; executive-level rooms; in-house dentist. *In room:* A/C, TV w/cable and on-demand pay movies, dataport, minibar, hot-water pot with tea, hair dryer, washlet toilet.

Grand Hyatt Tokyo ✰✰✰ Opened in 2003 and counting on the surrounding Roppongi Hills development with its 200-some shops and restaurants to act as a major draw, this ambitious hotel wows with a wide range of recreational and dining facilities of its own, as well as technically advanced rooms older hotels can only dream about. In contrast to sister Park Hyatt's subdued, sophisticated atmosphere that attracts bigwigs hoping to escape the limelight, the Grand Hyatt strives for a livelier clientele who relish being in the center of things. Still, key cards inserted into elevators block public access to guest floors, and those seeking pampering can opt for the Grand Club floor. Rooms, at 42 sq. m (452 sq. ft.) among Tokyo's largest, feature Italian furnishings, large mahogany desks, the fastest high-speed Internet connection currently available (free of charge), blackout blinds, 30-inch flat-screen TVs, safes designed for laptops with plug-ins for recharging, and a 24-hour in-house technology concierge to correct guests' computer woes. One-quarter of each unit's space is taken up by a huge bathroom equipped with separate shower and tub areas and a 13-inch flat-screen TV.

6–10–3 Roppongi, Minato-ku, Tokyo 106-0032. © **800/233-1234** in the U.S. and Canada, or 03/4333-1234. Fax 03/4333-8123. www.tokyo.grand.hyatt.com. 389 units. ¥46,000 – ¥53,000 ($383–$442) single or double; ¥54,000 ($450) Grand Club; from ¥66,000 ($550) suite. AE, DC, MC, V. Station: Roppongi (exit 1, 3 min.) or Azabu Juban (exit A3, 5 min.). **Amenities:** 7 restaurants; bar; 20m (66-ft.) indoor pool with Jacuzzi and sauna (fee: ¥4,000/$33); fitness room (free); spa; concierge; business center; shopping arcade; salon; barbershop; 24-hr. room service; in-room massage; babysitting; same-day laundry/dry-cleaning service; nonsmoking rooms; executive-level rooms; complimentary shoeshine. *In room:* A/C, TV w/cable and on-demand pay movies and CD/DVD player (free DVD rentals), high-speed dataport, minibar, hot-water pot with tea and coffee, hair dryer, safe, bathroom scale, washlet toilet.

Hotel Okura ✦✦✦   Located across from the U.S. embassy and long considered one of Tokyo's most venerable hotels, the Okura is struggling to keep up with pricier—and newer—top-rated hotels in the city. Still, it remains a favorite home-away-from-home of visiting U.S. dignitaries, and the service is gracious and impeccable. Rich decor elegantly combines ikebana and shoji screens with an old-fashioned Western spaciousness. The atmosphere is low-key, almost Zen-like, with none of the flashiness inherent in some of the newer hotels. All rooms are comfortable, with clean, crisp furnishings of maple and chrome. My favorite rooms are in the main building facing the garden; some on the fifth floor here have balconies overlooking the garden and pool. Other rooms have views of a rooftop garden or Tokyo Tower. *Tip:* Although fees are charged for use of the health club and pools, hotel guests can use facilities for free simply by becoming members of Okura Club International—there's no charge for membership, which starts immediately upon filling out an application at the guest relations desk.

2–10–4 Toranomon, Minato-ku, Tokyo 105-0001. © **800/223-6800** in the U.S., or 03/3582-0111. Fax 03/3582-3707. www.okura.com. 858 units. ¥29,000 – ¥42,000 ($242–$350) single; ¥37,500 – ¥57,000 ($312–$475) double; ¥40,000 – ¥57,000 ($333–$475) twin; from ¥79,000 ($658) suite. AE, DC, MC, V. Station: Toranomon or Kamiyacho (5 min.). **Amenities:** 9 restaurants; 2 bars; nicely landscaped outdoor pool (fee: ¥2,000/$17); health club (fee: ¥3,500/$29 to use everything; ¥2,000/$17 for indoor pool only); concierge; tour desk; comprehensive business center; shopping arcade; salon; barbershop; 24-hr. room service; in-room massage; same-day laundry/dry-cleaning service; nonsmoking rooms; free shuttle service to the nearest subway (weekends only); tea-ceremony room; private museum showcasing Japanese art (free for hotel guests); pharmacy; in-house doctor and dentist; post office; packing and shipping service. *In room:* A/C, satellite TV w/on-demand pay movies which doubles as a computer with Internet access, high-speed dataport, minibar, hot-water pot with tea, hair dryer, bathroom scale, washlet toilet.

SHINAGAWA

The Strings Hotel Tokyo ✦✦✦   One of several deluxe hotels to debut in 2003, the Strings seems destined to be a winner, both for its affiliation with ANA (All Nippon Airways) and for its location just a short walk from Shinagawa Station surrounded by a sea of office buildings. Guests—corporate CEOs during the week and well-heeled tourists on weekends—are beamed up via express elevators to the 26th floor of an office high-rise, where the lobby soars seven stories in a light-filled atrium featuring slatted wood and a reflecting pond. In fact, natural sunlight, stone, wood, and water are dominant themes throughout public areas, in almost defiant rejection of the marble so favored by hotels in the past. Brown is the color of choice for contemporary, high-ceilinged rooms occupying the top six floors, with low-slung sofas and walnut furnishings designed so as not to obstruct city views; even the beds are higher than normal, so that guests can see outside while resting. Rooms have everything you'd expect, as well as unexpected surprises like free high-speed Internet access, LCD flat-screen TVs, and roomy bathrooms with separate tub and shower areas.

Shinagawa East One Tower, 2–16–1 Konan, Minato-ku, Tokyo 108-8282. ⓒ **800/262-1030** in the U.S. and Canada, or 03/4562-1111. Fax 03/4562-1112. www.stringshotel.com. 206 units. ¥33,000–¥38,000 ($275–$317) single; ¥42,000–¥44,000 ($350–$367) double or twin; from ¥120,000 ($1,000) suite. Club Room ¥42,000–¥48,000 ($350–$400) single; ¥48,000–¥54,000 ($400–$450) twin or double. AE, DC, MC, V. Station: Shinagawa (Konan exit, 1 min.). **Amenities:** 2 restaurants (French Fusion, Chinese); bar; lounge; 24-hr. gym with steam room (free for hotel guests); concierge; small 24-hr. business center (free for hotel guests); 24-hr. room service; in-room massage; babysitting; same-day laundry/dry-cleaning service; nonsmoking rooms; executive-level rooms; complimentary shoeshine. *In room:* A/C, TV w/cable, high-speed dataport, mini-bar, hot-water pot with tea and coffee, hair dryer, iron, safe, bathroom scale, washlet toilet.

ELSEWHERE IN THE CITY

Four Seasons Hotel Tokyo at Chinzan-So ★★★ *Finds*   Although inconveniently located in northwest Tokyo (about a 15-min. taxi ride from Ikebukuro), the Four Seasons, built in 1992, is a superb hotel set in the luscious 6.8-hectare (17-acre), 100-year-old Chinzan-So Garden, making it extremely inviting after a bustling day in Tokyo. It also has one of Tokyo's best health clubs and spas, including a gorgeous glass-enclosed indoor pool surrounded by greenery with a glass ceiling that opens in summer, indoor and outdoor Jacuzzis (the outdoor one overlooks a small Japanese garden), and a Japanese hot-springs bath (the water is shipped in from Izu Peninsula)—all free for hotel guests. The health club, with personal-size TVs at most workstations, even offers free continental breakfasts. In contrast to the starkly modern Four Seasons at Marunouchi, the luxurious interiors here make this one of the most beautiful European-style hotels in Japan. Since the hotel embraces the park, most rooms have peaceful garden views from their V-shaped bay windows. Even the smallest rooms, which occupy the lower floors, boast king-size beds and are twice the size of most Japanese hotel rooms. Bathrooms have mini-TVs and separate shower and tub areas. Don't miss a stroll through the garden.

2–10–8 Sekiguchi, Bunkyo-ku, Tokyo 112-8667. ⓒ **800/332-3442** in the U.S., 800/268-6282 in Canada, or 03/3943-2222. Fax 03/3943-2300. www.fourseasons-tokyo.com. 283 units. ¥43,000–¥50,000 ($358–$417) single; ¥48,000–¥55,000 ($400–$458) double or twin; from ¥68,000 ($567) suite. Club Floor ¥48,000–¥55,000 ($400–$458) single; ¥55,000–¥62,000 ($458–$517) twin or double. AE, DC, MC, V. Station: Edogawabashi (exit 1a, a 10-min. walk or a 2-min. ride). **Amenities:** 4 restaurants (Italian, Chinese, Japanese, French); bar; lounge; indoor pool and health club (free for hotel guests); concierge; business center; 24-hr. room service; in-room massage; same-day laundry/dry-cleaning service; nonsmoking rooms; executive-level rooms; complimentary shoeshine. *In room:* A/C, TV w/satellite and on-demand pay movies, CD/MD player, high-speed dataport, minibar, hot-water pot with tea, hair dryer, safe, bathroom scale, washlet toilet.

3 Expensive

GINZA & HIBIYA

Imperial Hotel ★★ *Kids*   Located across from Hibiya Park, within walking distance of the Ginza and Imperial Palace, this is one of Tokyo's best-known and most popular hotels, with foreigners (mostly business executives) making up about 40% of the guests. The Imperial's trademark is impeccable service: Guests are treated like royalty. Although the Imperial's history goes back to 1890, when it opened at the request of the imperial family to house the many foreigners coming to Japan; and although it was rebuilt in 1922 by Frank Lloyd Wright, the present hotel dates from 1970, with a 31-story tower added in 1983. Unfortunately, Wright's legacy lives on only in the hotel's Art Deco Old Imperial Bar. (Part of Wright's original structure survives at Meiji-Mura, an architectural museum outside Nagoya.) On the plus side, the Imperial is one of the few hotels with a children's day-care center.

Rooms in the main building are quite large for Tokyo. Tower rooms, while slightly smaller but pricier, are higher up, have floor-to-ceiling bay windows, and offer fantastic views of either Imperial Palace grounds or, my preference, the Ginza and Tokyo Bay. All come with the amenities you'd expect from a first-class hotel, as well as such appreciated extras as hands-free phone, bedside controls for the curtains, and free high-speed Internet access, with a private e-mail address for each guest. *Tip:* Become a member of the Imperial Club (membership is free), and you can use the small pool and gym free of charge.

1–1–1 Uchisaiwaicho, Chiyoda-ku, Tokyo 100-8558. © **800/223-6800** in the U.S. and Canada, or 03/3504-1111. Fax 03/3581-9146. www.imperialhotel.co.jp. 1,059 units. ¥30,000 –¥56,000 ($250–$467) single; ¥35,000 –¥61,000 ($292–$508) double or twin; from ¥110,000 ($917) suite. AE, DC, MC, V. Station: Hibiya (1 min.). **Amenities:** 13 restaurants; 4 bars; 20th-floor indoor pool (fee: ¥1,000/$8.35; free for Imperial Club members); fitness room (fee: ¥1,000/$8.35; free for Imperial Club members); sauna; day-care center for children ages 2 weeks to 6 years (fee: ¥5,000/$42 for 2 hr.); concierge; limousine and car-rental services; business center; impressive shopping arcade; salon; barbershop; 24-hr. room service; in-room massage; babysitting; same-day laundry/dry-cleaning service; nonsmoking rooms; in-house doctor and dentist; tea-ceremony room; post office. *In room:* A/C, TV w/cable and pay movies, fax, high-speed dataport, minibar, hot-water pot with tea and coffee, hair dryer, large safe, bathroom scale, washlet toilet.

Renaissance Tokyo Hotel Ginza Tobu ⭐ This small, classy, and personable hotel, located on Showa Dori behind the Ginza Matsuzakaya department store and within easy walking distance of shopping and the Kabuki theater, attracts a foreign clientele as high as 60%, due mainly to its association with Marriott. Primarily a business hotel (a whopping 90% of its guests are business travelers), it has limited facilities; you clearly pay for location here. Interestingly, the cheapest singles (which have single-size beds) are not offered to foreigners—they're considered too small—but if you insist, they'll let you have one (contact the hotel directly); though indeed small, I find them more nicely appointed than those offered by most business hotels. Be sure to pick up the hotel's sightseeing leaflets at the concierge's desk, with advice on what to see and how to get there.

6–14–10 Ginza, Chuo-ku, Tokyo 104-0061. © **888/236-2427** in the U.S. and Canada, or 03/3546-0111. Fax 03/3546-8990. www.marriott.com. 206 units. ¥17,000 – ¥23,000 ($142–$192) single; ¥28,000 ($233) double or twin. Renaissance Floor ¥24,000 –¥30,000 ($200–$250) single; ¥35,000 ($292) double or twin. AE, DC, MC, V. Station: Ginza (5 min.) or Higashi-Ginza (1 min.). **Amenities:** 2 restaurants (Japanese, coffee shop); bar; concierge; 24-hr. business center; salon; room service (6:30am–midnight); in-room massage; same-day laundry/dry-cleaning service; nonsmoking rooms; executive-level rooms. *In room:* A/C, TV w/cable and on-demand pay videos, fax, dataport, minibar, hot-water pot with tea, hair dryer.

NIHOMBASHI & AROUND TOKYO STATION

Palace Hotel ⭐ This 10-story hotel has an enviable location across the street from the Imperial Palace and its lovely gardens, but it's also close to Tokyo's business district, making it a longtime favorite with foreign business travelers. However, built in the 1960s, the brown-brick structure shows its age; the lobby, the signature Crown Restaurant, and the guest rooms are so passé that in a decade or two they might be camp. If you can afford it, spring for a deluxe twin—it's large, it offers high-speed Internet access and a spacious bathroom with separate shower and tub areas, but best of all, it faces the gardens with glass-sliding doors that open onto a balcony. Singles face another building. For added security and prompt service, attendants are on call at service stations on each floor.

1–1–1 Marunouchi, Chiyoda-ku, Tokyo 100-0005. © **800/457-4000** in the U.S. and Canada, or 03/3211-5211. Fax 03/3211-6987. www.palacehotel.co.jp. 389 units. ¥24,000 – ¥29,000 ($200–$242) single; ¥33,000 – ¥45,000 ($275–$375) double; ¥32,000 –¥60,000 ($267–$500) twin; from ¥100,000 ($833) suite. AE, DC,

MC, V. Station: Otemachi (2 min.) or Tokyo (7 min.). **Amenities:** 7 restaurants; bar; 2 lounges; access to nearby health club (free for hotel guests); concierge; business center; shopping arcade; salon; 24-hr. room service; in-room massage; babysitting; same-day laundry/dry-cleaning service; nonsmoking rooms. *In room:* A/C, satellite TV w/on-demand pay movies, dataport, minibar, hot-water pot with tea and coffee, hair dryer, safe, bathroom scale, washlet toilet.

Royal Park Hotel ★★★   Opened in 1989, the Royal Park is located east of Tokyo Station (about a 10-min. ride by taxi), not far from the Tokyo Stock Exchange and Suitengu Shrine (popular with expectant mothers hoping for safe deliveries). One of its greatest assets, aside from the friendly and superbly efficient staff, is that it's connected via enclosed walkway to the Tokyo City Air Terminal, the main terminus of the Airport Limousine Bus (which shuttles passengers to and from Narita Airport), making this a convenient place for visitors with only a night or two to spend in Tokyo. It's also the first hotel I've seen with a Woman's Traveler Desk, offering check-in and other special services. But what makes it particularly attractive to business travelers (including many Americans) are its up-to-date guest rooms with a sophisticated computerized TV system that allows guests to access the Internet, send e-mail, check airline schedules, watch videos on demand, play computer games, and more. The best views are from twins facing the Sumida River or upper-floor rooms facing the city skyline to the north.

2–1–1 Nihombashi-Kakigara-cho, Chuo-ku, Tokyo 103-8520. © 800/457-4000 in the U.S., or 03/3667-1111. Fax 03/3667-1115. http://rph.co.jp/english. 449 units. ¥22,000–¥26,000 ($183–$217) single; ¥30,000–¥43,000 ($250–$358) double or twin. Executive floor from ¥28,000 ($233) single; ¥36,000 ($300) double. AE, DC, MC, V. Station: Suitengu-mae (underneath the hotel). **Amenities:** 7 restaurants; bar; 2 lounges; health club with 20m (66-ft.) indoor pool (fee: ¥3,000/$25; ¥1,500/$12 for pool alone); concierge; tour desk; small 24-hr. business center; small shopping arcade; convenience store; salon; 24-hr. room service; in-room massage; babysitting; same-day laundry/dry-cleaning service; nonsmoking rooms; executive-level rooms. *In room:* A/C, TV w/cable and pay movies and Internet access, fax, high-speed dataport, minibar, hot-water pot with tea, hair dryer, safe, bathroom scale, washlet toilet.

UENO

Hotel Sofitel ★★★ *Finds*   Located across from Shinobazu Pond in the heart of Ueno, this French-owned hotel is easily recognizable by its unique architecture: five pyramid-shaped trapeziums, stacked on top of each other. Inside, it's an oasis of refined beauty, excellent service, and great views. And with only a handful of rooms on each floor, it has the atmosphere of an intimate, luxury boutique hotel. Its restaurant, Provence, with a French chef, draws rave reviews. Chic rooms, with rates based on size, boast inlaid wood furniture, original artwork, and TVs that double as computers for Internet access (but no e-mail capabilities). Nothing beats the view over Shinobazu Pond with its bird refuge and the adjoining zoo (some rooms facing the opposite side have occasional views of Mt. Fuji). I'm partial to the superior rooms on the 25th floor. Easy accessibility to Ueno Park and its museums make this unique hotel a natural for joggers and art lovers alike.

2–1–48 Ikenohata, Taito-ku, Tokyo 110-0008. © 800/221-4542 in the U.S. and Canada, or 03/5685-7111. Fax 03/5685-6171. www.sofiteltokyo.com. 83 units. ¥24,000–¥29,000 ($200–$242) single; ¥30,000–¥35,000 ($250–$292) double or twin; from ¥50,000 ($417) suite. AE, DC, MC, V. Station: Yushima (7 min.) or Ueno (10 min.). **Amenities:** Restaurant (French); bar; lounge; exercise room (free); 24-hr. room service; in-room massage; same-day laundry/dry-cleaning service; nonsmoking rooms. *In room:* A/C, TV w/cable and pay movies and Internet access, high-speed dataport, minibar, hot-water pot with tea and coffee, hair dryer, safe, washlet toilet.

SHINJUKU

Century Hyatt Tokyo ★★   Located on Shinjuku's west side next to Shinjuku Central Park (popular with joggers), this 28-story hotel features an impressive seven-story atrium lobby with three of the most massive chandeliers you're likely to see anywhere. Many foreigners (mostly American) pass through the hotel's doors, ably assisted by the excellent staff with the Hyatt's usual high standards. Rates are based on size; even the cheapest units are adequate, but they do face another building and don't receive much sunshine. If you can afford it, spring for a more expensive room on a high floor with bay windows overlooking the park (in winter, you might also have a view of Mt. Fuji). Only a quarter of the rooms cater to business travelers with fax machines, high-speed Internet connections, and two-line, hands-free speakerphones—a reflection of the fact that the hotel attracts leisure travelers as well, including tour groups.

2–7–2 Nishi-Shinjuku, Shinjuku-ku, Tokyo 160-0023. ℂ **800/233-1234** in the U.S. and Canada, or 03/3349-0111. Fax 03/3344-5575. www.centuryhyatt.co.jp. 766 units. ¥23,000 – ¥32,000 ($192–$267) single; ¥32,000 – ¥34,000 ($267–$283) double or twin. Regency Club from ¥36,000 ($300) single or double. AE, DC, MC, V. Station: Tochomae (1 min.), Nishi-Shinjuku (3 min.), or Shinjuku (a 10-min. walk, or a free 3-min. shuttle ride). **Amenities:** 6 restaurants; bar; lounge; health club with indoor pool (fee: ¥1,500/$13); concierge; tour desk; shopping arcade; salon; 24-hr. room service; in-room massage; same-day laundry/dry-cleaning service; nonsmoking rooms; executive-level rooms; free shuttle service to Shinjuku Station every 20 min. *In room:* A/C, TV w/cable and pay movies, minibar, hot-water pot with tea, hair dryer, safe, washlet toilet.

Hilton Tokyo ★★ Located on Shinjuku's west side, the 38-story Tokyo Hilton with its sensually curving facade opened in 1984 as the largest Hilton in the Asia/Pacific area. Today it keeps a lower profile than most of the other Shinjuku hotels, with a quiet, subdued lobby, and it remains popular with business and leisure travelers alike. Rooms are up-to-date and adequate in size. As with all Hiltons, the room decor here reflects traditional native style, with shoji screens instead of curtains and simple yet elegant furnishings that include queen-size beds or larger in all rooms. Deluxe-floor rooms come with the extras of free high-speed Internet access, fax, and safe.

6–6–2 Nishi-Shinjuku, Shinjuku-ku, Tokyo 160-0023. ℂ **800/HILTONS** in the U.S. or Canada, or 03/3344-5111. Fax 03/3342-6094. www.hilton.com. 806 units. ¥29,000 – ¥40,000 ($242–$333) single; ¥35,000 – ¥46,000 ($292–$383) twin or double. Executive floor ¥36,000 – ¥44,000 ($300–$367) single; ¥42,000 – ¥50,000 ($350–$417) twin or double; from ¥70,000 ($583) suite. Children stay free in parent's room. AE, DC, MC, V. Station: Nishi-Shinjuku (2 min.), Tochomae (3 min.), or Shinjuku (10-min walk or free shuttle bus). **Amenities:** 5 restaurants; bar; lounge; 2 outdoor tennis courts; health club with indoor pool (fee: ¥1,500/$12 for either pool or gym alone, ¥2,500/$21 for sauna, ¥2,000/$17 for pool and gym, or ¥4,000 ($33) for everything); concierge; tour desk; small shopping arcade; convenience store; salon; 24-hr. room service; in-room massage; same-day laundry/dry-cleaning service; nonsmoking rooms; executive-level rooms; Kinko's (open 24 hr.); complimentary shuttle service to Shinjuku Station 3–6 times an hour. *In room:* A/C, satellite TV w/pay movies, dataport, minibar, hot-water pot with tea, hair dryer.

Keio Plaza Inter-Continental Tokyo ★ *Kids* The closest hotel to Shinjuku Station's west side, the Keio Plaza is also West Shinjuku's oldest and biggest hotel, built in 1971. It has the distinction of being not only Japan's first skyscraper but also, at 47 stories high, still one of Tokyo's tallest and largest hotels. It's popular with both Japanese and foreign travelers, including group tours, and the lobby bustles with activity—sometimes too much, making it difficult to get personalized service. But the hotel does boast a number of first-class facilities and services, including several that appeal to families such as day care for children 2 months and older, and free access to an outdoor pool and children's pool. And with almost 20 restaurants and bars, choices seem limitless. Rooms are small but comfortably furnished, with views of the surrounding Shinjuku area.

2–2–1 Nishi-Shinjuku, Shinjuku-ku, Tokyo 160-8330. ℂ **800/222-KEIO** in the U.S., or 03/3344-0111. Fax 03/3345-8269. www.keioplaza.co.jp. 1,485 units. ¥22,000 – ¥37,000 ($183–$308) single; ¥26,000 – ¥40,000 ($217–$333) twin or double; from ¥80,000 ($667) suite. AE, DC, MC, V. Station: Tocho-mae (1 min.) or

Nightlife & Where to Stay & Dine in Akasaka

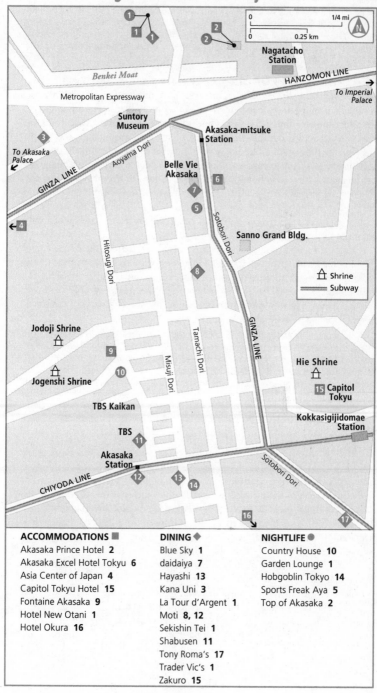

0   1/4 mi
0   0.25 km

Benkei Moat

HANZOMON LINE

Nagatacho
Station

Metropolitan Expressway

To Imperial
Palace

Suntory
Museum

Akasaka-mitsuke
Station

To Akasaka
Palace

Aoyama Dori

GINZA LINE

Belle Vie
Akasaka

Sanno Grand Bldg.

Sotobori Dori

⌂ Shrine

Subway

Hitosugi Dori

GINZA LINE

Jodoji Shrine
⌂

Tamachi Dori

Hie Shrine
⌂

Jogenshi Shrine
⌂

Misuji Dori

Capitol
Tokyu

TBS Kaikan

Kokkasigijidomae
Station

TBS

Akasaka
Station

Sotobori Dori

CHIYODA LINE

ACCOMMODATIONS ■
Akasaka Prince Hotel **2**
Akasaka Excel Hotel Tokyu **6**
Asia Center of Japan **4**
Capitol Tokyu Hotel **15**
Fontaine Akasaka **9**
Hotel New Otani **1**
Hotel Okura **16**

DINING ◆
Blue Sky **1**
daidaiya **7**
Hayashi **13**
Kana Uni **3**
La Tour d'Argent **1**
Moti **8, 12**
Sekishin Tei **1**
Shabusen **11**
Tony Roma's **17**
Trader Vic's **1**
Zakuro **15**

NIGHTLIFE ●
Country House **10**
Garden Lounge **1**
Hobgoblin Tokyo **14**
Sports Freak Aya **5**
Top of Akasaka **2**

Shinjuku (5 min.). **Amenities:** 10 restaurants; 8 bars; outdoor pool with wading pool (free); children's day-care center (open daily 10am–6pm; evenings by reservation only); concierge; business center; shopping arcade; salon; 24-hr. room service; in-room massage; same-day laundry/dry-cleaning service; nonsmoking rooms; in-house doctor and dentist. *In room:* A/C, TV w/cable and pay movies, dataport, minibar, hot-water pot with tea, hair dryer, washlet toilet.

AKASAKA & ROPPONGI

Akasaka Prince Hotel ⊙⊙   This 40-story white skyscraper—an Akasaka landmark with a facade that reminds me of an unfolding fan—caused quite a stir when it opened in 1983, with some Tokyoites complaining that it was too cold and sterile. I think that the Prince, designed by Kenzo Tange, was simply ahead of its time, with a blindingly white marble lobby intentionally spacious and empty, so as not to compete with brilliant Japanese kimono (weddings are big business in Japanese hotels). It set the pace for a flurry of hotels that followed, though nowadays marble is out while wood, stone, and hues of brown are the current hotel-fashion statement. Never out of fashion is the hotel's signature restaurant, Le Trianon, housed in a stately 80-year-old mansion that once belonged to the imperial family.

Average-size guest rooms are set at a 45-degree angle from the center axis of the building's core, giving each one a corner view with expansive windows overlooking the city and letting in lots of sunshine; request one overlooking the Akasaka side, and you'll have a view of neon lights down below and Tokyo Tower in the distance. The single rooms are among the nicest in Tokyo, with three windows forming a pleasant alcove around a sofa.

1–2 Kioi-cho, Chiyoda-ku, Tokyo 102-8585. ⊙ **800/542-8686** in the U.S. and Canada, or 03/3234-1111. Fax 03/3262-5163. www.princehotels.co.jp/english. 761 units. ¥25,000–¥37,000 ($208–$308) single; ¥37,000–¥45,000 ($308–$375) double; ¥33,000–¥42,000 ($275–$350) twin; from ¥90,000 ($667) suite. AE, DC, MC, V. Station: Akasaka-mitsuke or Nagatacho (2 min.). **Amenities:** 8 restaurants; 2 bars; 2 lounges; outdoor heated pool open May–Sept (fee: ¥1,000/$8.35); small exercise room (fee: ¥500/$4.15); concierge; tour desk; excellent business center with a spectacular 20th-floor view; convenience store; salon; 24-hr. room service; in-room massage; babysitting; same-day laundry/dry-cleaning service; nonsmoking rooms. *In room:* A/C, TV w/cable and pay movies, high-speed dataport, minibar, hot-water pot with tea, hair dryer, small safe, washlet toilet.

Hotel New Otani ⊙⊙ *Kids*   If you like small, quiet hotels, this monolith is not for you. Like a city unto itself, the New Otani is so big that two information desks are needed to assist lost souls searching for a particular restaurant or one of the shops in the meandering arcade; there are even two check-in desks. The hotel's most splendid feature is its garden, the best of any Tokyo hotel—a 400-year-old Japanese garden that once belonged to a feudal lord, with 4 hectares (10 acres) of ponds, waterfalls, bridges, bamboo groves, and manicured bushes. The outdoor pool, flanked by greenery, is also nice.

A variety of rooms, in a main building and a newer tower, are available. Those in the main building are comfortable, with shoji-like screens on the windows, bedside controls for the curtains, air-conditioning, and even the DO NOT DISTURB signs; more expensive rooms have such extras as bathroom scales, walk-in closets, and fax machines (otherwise, fax machines are available free of charge). Tower rooms range from chic ones done in jade, black, and chrome to "*fusui* healing" rooms with such extras as in-room humidifier, foot bath, and compact CD/MD player. The tower offers the best views—of the garden, the skyscrapers of Shinjuku and, on clear days, Mount Fuji in the distance. Since rates are the same no matter which way you face, be sure to request a room overlooking the garden. Parents appreciate the 24-hour Baby Room and the fact that the pool is free for those who become Hotel Club members (membership is free).

4–1 Kioi-cho, Chiyoda-ku, Tokyo 102-8578. ⓒ **800/421-8795** in the U.S. and Canada, or 03/3265-1111. Fax 03/3221-2619. www.newotani.co.jp/en. 1,600 units. ¥29,000–¥36,000 ($242–$300) single; ¥34,000–¥57,000 ($283–$475) double; ¥41,000–¥57,000 ($342–$475) twin; from ¥80,000 ($667) suite. AE, DC, MC, V. Station: Akasaka-mitsuke or Nagatacho (3 min.). **Amenities:** 28 restaurants; 5 bars and lounges; outdoor pool (fee: ¥2,000/$17; free for Hotel Club members); small exercise room (free for hotel guests); health club with lighted outdoor tennis courts (fee: ¥5,000/$42); day-care center for children from 1 month to 5 years old (fee: ¥6,000/$50 for 2 hr.); concierge; tour desk; business center; shopping arcade with 120 stores; convenience store; salon; room service (6am–1am); in-room massage; same-day laundry/dry-cleaning service; medical and dental clinics; post office; tea-ceremony room; chapel with daily services; art museum (free for hotel guests); nonsmoking rooms. *In room:* A/C, TV w/cable and pay movies, high-speed dataport, minibar, hot-water pot with tea, hair dryer, safe, washlet toilet.

SHINAGAWA

Miyako Hotel Tokyo ★ *Value*   A Radisson affiliate, this hotel is one of my favorites in Tokyo, for its calm peacefulness as well as its small-luxury-hotel service. Because it's a bit off the beaten path, it has a quieter, more relaxed atmosphere than those found at more centrally located hotels, evident the moment you step into its lobby lounge with its gas-flame fireplace on one end and the greenery of a garden on its other. Attracting mostly Japanese guests, it offers average-size rooms, the best of which are renovated rooms on higher floors (with an unfortunate choice of psychedelic carpet) with beds so comfortable you'd sneak them into your luggage if you could, pinpoint reading lights, and huge floor-to-ceiling windows overlooking the hotel's own lush garden, a famed garden next door, or Tokyo Tower.

1–1–50 Shirokanedai, Minato-ku, Tokyo 108-8640. ⓒ **800/333-3333** in the U.S. and Canada, or 03/3447-3111. Fax 03/3447-3133. www.radisson.com/tokyojp_miyako. 498 units. ¥27,000–¥42,000 ($225–$350) single; ¥30,000–¥45,000 ($250–$375) double or twin; from ¥100,000 ($833) suite. AE, DC, MC, V. Station: Shirokanedai (4 min.), Shirokane-Takanawa (5 min.), or free shuttle from Meguro or Shinagawa stations. **Amenities:** 5 restaurants; bar; lounge; health club with 25m (82-ft.) indoor heated pool and sauna (fee: ¥700/$5.85); concierge; tour desk; shopping arcade; convenience store; salon; 24-hr. room service; in-room massage; same-day laundry/dry-cleaning service; nonsmoking rooms; free shuttle service to Meguro Station every 15 min. and to Shinagawa Station mornings only; dental/medical clinics. *In room:* A/C, TV w/cable and pay movies, minibar, hot-water pot with tea, hair dryer, safe, washlet toilet, trouser press.

ON OR NEAR ODAIBA/TOKYO BAY

Hotel Inter-Continental Tokyo Bay ★★   Located on Tokyo Bay and offering the city's best views of Rainbow Bridge and Odaiba, this fairly small hotel has a cozy, comfortable lobby, which some guests find a welcome relief from the expansive lobbies favored in Tokyo proper. Counting on international recognition of its name to compensate for its somewhat isolated location, it caters to business travelers (of which 45% are foreign, mostly American) during the week, with leisure guests filling rooms on weekends. Though convenient to Haneda Airport, the international convention center (Tokyo Big Sight), and the Ginza (a 5-min. taxi ride), the hotel's closest station, Takeshiba, is served only by the monorail Yurikamome Line (connecting Shimbashi with Odaiba), which can be quite crowded on weekends. Takeshiba also serves as a passenger terminal for boats to outlying islands. All the handsomely decorated, good-sized rooms feature well-appointed bathrooms with separate tub and shower areas. Most face the water, but it's worth paying extra for the bay view of Rainbow Bridge and Odaiba, which is spectacular at night. The highest-priced rooms afford harbor views even from the bathrooms.

1–16–2 Kaigan, Minato-ku, Tokyo 105-8576. ⓒ **800/327-0200** in the U.S. and Canada, or 03/5404-2222. Fax 03/5404-2111. www.interconti.com. 336 units. ¥36,000–¥52,000 ($300–$433) single or double; from ¥100,000 ($833) suite. Club Inter-Continental Floor from ¥43,000 ($358). AE, DC, MC, V. Station: Takeshiba

(1 min.), Hamamatsucho (6 min.), or Daimon (12 min.). **Amenities:** 5 restaurants; bar; lounge; access to nearby health club (¥2,000/$17); concierge; 24-hr. business center; salon; 24-hr. room service; in-room massage; same-day laundry/dry-cleaning service; nonsmoking rooms; executive-level rooms. *In room:* A/C, TV w/cable and on-demand pay movies, high-speed dataport, minibar, hot-water pot with tea, hair dryer, safe, bathroom scale, washlet toilet.

Hotel Nikko Tokyo ★★   This is by far the most un-Tokyo-like hotel in the city. Opened in 1996 as the first hotel on Odaiba, this grand, elegant lodging is now somewhat dwarfed by the Meridien Grand Pacific across the street. Although its claim on the best views of the Tokyo skyline has been usurped by its competitor, it exudes a more relaxed, resortlike atmosphere and has a more inspiring view from its airy lobby. It bills itself as an "urban resort," offering incentives for both the business and leisure traveler, and is especially popular with young well-to-do Japanese in search of an exotic weekend getaway. Closer to the waterfront than the Meridien, it is surrounded by parks and gardens, with a wooden walkway linking it to the Tokyo Decks shopping mall. A curved facade assures waterfront views from most rooms, which have the added benefit of private balconies with two chairs. The most expensive rooms offer commanding views of Tokyo Bay, Rainbow Bridge, and the city skyline (impressive at night); the least expensive rooms, smaller in size, face the Meridien hotel or the Maritime Museum and Haneda Airport across the bay.

1–9–1 Daiba, Minato-ku, Tokyo 135-8625. © **800/645-5687** in the U.S. and Canada, or 03/5500-5500. Fax 03/5500-2525. www.hnt.co.jp/english. 453 units. ¥28,000 – ¥40,000 ($233–$333) single; ¥33,000 – ¥45,000 ($275–$375) double or twin; from ¥80,000 ($667) suite. AE, DC, MC, V. Station: Daiba (1 min.) or Tokyo Teleport Station (10 min.). **Amenities:** 8 restaurants; bar; lounge; spa with indoor pool connected to outdoor heated tub, Jacuzzi and sun terrace overlooking Rainbow Bridge (fee: ¥3,000/$25 the 1st day; thereafter ¥1,000/$8.35); concierge; business center; room service (6am–11am and 6pm–2am); in-room massage; same-day laundry/dry-cleaning service; nonsmoking rooms. *In room:* A/C, TV w/cable and pay movies, dataport, minibar, hot-water pot with tea, hair dryer, safe, washlet toilet.

Le Meridien Grand Pacific Tokyo ★   Opened in 1998, this soaring, 30-story hotel offers great views of the Tokyo skyline and Rainbow Bridge from its location on Odaiba, an island of reclaimed land with the Tokyo Big Sight convention center, shopping malls, and sightseeing attractions. Although the marbled lobby's imitation Louis XIV furniture and large chandeliers seem rather stuffy and out of place in this leisure destination, it nonetheless attracts many visiting Japanese, especially on weekends, and boasts an efficient, accommodating staff. Wide corridors lead to fairly small rooms that repeat the French decor and offer views of either the Port of Tokyo in the distance or, even better, Rainbow Bridge and the Tokyo skyline (but only from rooms above the 20th floor). Odaiba is a great choice if you want to get away from the bustle of Tokyo, but the location can be a disadvantage; it's served only by the monorail Yurikamome Line, the JR Saikyo Line from Shibuya, and the inconvenient Rinkai Line, which can be quite crowded on weekends, as can bus and taxi travel via the Rainbow Bridge or harbor tunnel.

2–6–1 Daiba, Minato-ku, Tokyo 135-8701. © **800/543-4300** in the U.S,. or 03/5500-6711. Fax 03/5500-4507. www.htl-pacific.co.jp. 884 units. ¥26,000 – ¥33,000 ($217–$275) single; ¥31,000 – ¥41,000 ($258–$342) double or twin; from ¥80,000 ($667) suite. Executive floor from ¥39,000 ($325) double; ¥42,000 ($350) twin. AE, DC, MC, V. Station: Daiba (1 min.) or Tokyo Teleport Station (9 min.). **Amenities:** 7 restaurants; 2 bars; 2 lounges; outdoor pool (fee: ¥2,000/$17); fitness club with indoor swimming pool (fee: ¥1,000 ($8.35); concierge; business center; room service (6am–noon and 5pm–1am); in-room massage; same-day laundry/dry-cleaning service; nonsmoking rooms; executive-level rooms; art gallery. *In room:* A/C, TV w/cable and pay movies, minibar, hot-water pot with tea and coffee, hair dryer, safe, washlet toilet.

4 Moderate

GINZA

Ginza Nikko Hotel   There's nothing fancy or out of the ordinary about this small business hotel, an affiliate of Japan Airlines, but it's personable and clean and has an unbeatable location in southern Ginza. Built more than 40 years ago, it's one of the oldest hotels in the area. Rates are based on room size, with the cheapest rooms very tiny indeed; even the largest tend to be cramped and dark because of surrounding taller buildings.

Sotobori Dori, 8–4–21 Ginza, Chuo-ku, Tokyo 104-0061. ℂ 03/3571-4911. Fax 03/3571-8379. http://wwd.jalhotels.co.jp/english. 112 units. ¥12,000–¥16,000 ($100–$133) single; ¥25,000 ($208) double; ¥24,000–¥28,000 ($200–$233) twin. AE, DC, MC, V. Station: Shimbashi, Ginza, or Hibiya (5 min.). **Amenities:** Restaurant (Western); in-room massage; same-day laundry/dry-cleaning service; nonsmoking rooms. *In room:* A/C, TV w/cable and pay movies, minibar, hot-water pot with tea, hair dryer, washlet toilet.

Hotel Monterey La Soeur ★★ *Finds*   The Monterey chain targets female travelers with its feminine decor, and this hotel—designed by a woman—is no exception. A small, boutiquelike hotel with a slight European ambience (note the display of Art Deco perfume bottles in the tiny lobby), it rises above the ordinary business hotel with small but comfortable rooms that show a woman's touch without being fussy. Specially designated ladies' rooms contain amenities geared toward women. If rooms here are full, try the nearby sister **Hotel Monterey Ginza** (ℂ **03/3544-7111**), with the same boutique-hotel concept and similar prices.

1–10–18 Ginza, Chuo-ku, Tokyo 104-0061. ℂ **03/3562-7111.** Fax 03/3544-1600. 141 units. ¥13,500–¥14,000 ($113–$117) single; ¥18,000 ($150) double; ¥24,000–¥26,000 ($200–$217) twin. AE, DC, MC, V. Station: Ginza Itchome (2 min.) or Ginza (4 min.). **Amenities:** Restaurant (French/Italian); same-day laundry/dry-cleaning service; nonsmoking rooms. *In room:* A/C, TV w/pay movies, minibar, hot-water pot with tea, hair dryer, washlet toilet.

Mitsui Urban Hotel Ginza ★   Because of its great location, convenient to the Ginza, Shimbashi, and Hibiya shopping and business centers, this attractive hotel caters mostly to business travelers but appeals to tourists as well. The lobby, on the second floor, has a friendly staff. The bright and snazzy guest rooms are tiny but feature a few amenities usually found at more expensive hotels, including decent-size bathrooms with no-fog mirrors. Note, however, that the cheapest rooms have no closets and no space to unpack, a good example of what $175 buys in Tokyo. I suggest asking for a room away from the highway overpass beside the hotel.

8–6–15 Ginza, Chuo-ku, Tokyo 104-0061. ℂ **03/3572-4131.** Fax 03/3572-4254. www.mitsuikanko.co.jp. 265 units. ¥14,000–¥17,500 ($117–$146) single; ¥21,000–¥24,500 ($175–$204) double; ¥21,000–¥30,000 ($175–$250) twin. AE, DC, MC, V. Station: Shimbashi (2 min.). **Amenities:** 3 restaurants (Western, Japanese, Chinese); 2 lounges; room service (Mon–Fri 10pm–1am); same-day laundry service. *In room:* A/C, TV w/cable and pay movies, dataport, hot-water pot with tea, hair dryer, trouser press, washlet toilet.

AROUND TOKYO STATION

Tokyo Station Hotel ★   If you want quick access to the Shinkansen bullet train or Narita Airport (1 hour by train), the Tokyo Station Hotel is the most convenient, mid-priced choice. Opened in 1915, this historic hotel occupies the Marunouchi (west) side of the original, handsome, redbrick Tokyo Station, one of Tokyo's few pre-war landmarks. Its unpretentious interior has changed little over the decades, from the old-fashioned dark and crowded lobby to the wood staircases leading to what are probably the widest corridors in Tokyo. Its rooms are large for Tokyo and offer views that could only excite a train buff. The most expensive twins are spacious, with high ceilings, floor-to-ceiling windows facing the front, and modern decor—but the red velvet furniture is a bit much. The cheaper rooms feature outdated floral wallpaper and face the interior of the station. In short, the hotel's quirky, eccentric interior amuses—it's so different from high-tech Tokyo that it's almost refreshing, if not endearing. Still, I advise asking to see a room before taking it, as rooms do vary. Astonishingly, the 59-room hotel has 11 restaurants and bars serving French, Italian, Chinese, and Japanese food; their business depends largely on travelers passing through.

1–9–1 Marunouchi, Chiyoda-ku, Tokyo 100-0005. ℂ 03/3231-2511. Fax 03/3231-3513. www.tshl.co.jp. 59 units. ¥10,000–¥15,000 ($83–$125) single; ¥23,000 ($192) double; ¥17,000–¥26,000 ($142–$217) twin. AE, DC, MC, V. Station: Tokyo (1 min.). In Tokyo Station. **Amenities:** 8 restaurants; 3 bars; room service (weekdays 2–10pm; weekends/holidays (2–8pm); same-day laundry service. *In room:* A/C, TV, hot-water pot with tea, hair dryer.

ASAKUSA

Asakusa View Hotel   This is the only upper-bracket and modern hotel in the Asakusa area, and it looks almost out of place rising 28 stories above this famous district's older buildings. It's a good place to stay if you want to be in Tokyo's old downtown but don't want to sacrifice any creature comforts. The medium-size guest rooms are very pleasant, with sleek, contemporary furnishings and bay windows that let in plenty of sunshine (and smaller windows that can be opened, a rarity in Tokyo); rooms facing the front have views over the famous Sensoji Temple. Eight Japanese-style rooms are also available, sleeping up to five people; on the same floor are a small, rooftop Japanese garden and Japanese-style public baths featuring tubs made of 2,000-year-old cypress.

Kokusai Dori, 3–17–1 Nishi-Asakusa, Taito-ku, Tokyo 111-8765. ℂ 03/3847-1111. Fax 03/3842-2117. www. viewhotels.co.jp/Asakusa/. 337 units. ¥13,000–¥18,000 ($108–$150) single; ¥23,000–¥31,000 ($192–$258) double; [¥34,000 ($283) triple; Yen]26,000–¥31,000 ($217–$258) twin. Japanese-style rooms from ¥40,000 ($333) for 2. Executive floor ¥32,000 ($267) single or double. AE, DC, MC, V. Station: Tawaramachi (8 min.). **Amenities:** 5 restaurants; bar; lounge; 20m (66-ft.) indoor pool with retractable roof (fee: ¥3,000/$25, but request a 50% discount coupon at the front desk); shopping arcade; salon; Japanese-style public baths (fee: ¥1,050/$8.75); room service (7am–2am); same-day laundry/dry-cleaning service; nonsmoking rooms; executive-level rooms. *In room:* A/C, TV w/cable and pay movies, minibar, hot-water pot with tea, hair dryer.

Hotel Sunroute Asakusa ⭐   Located on Kokusai Dori, this modern, pleasant hotel opened in 1998 as a business hotel but is a good choice for leisure travelers as well. Not only does it boast a good location near the sightseeing attractions of Asakusa, but it is classier than most business hotels, with Miró reprints in the lobby and modern artwork in each guest room. Though small, the (mostly single) rooms come with all the comforts, with slightly larger beds and bathrooms than those found at most business hotels. The hotel's one coffee shop, a chain called Jonathan's serving both Japanese and Western food, is open daily 24 hours.

1–8–5 Kaminarimon, Taito-ku, Tokyo 111-0034. ℂ 03/3847-1511. Fax 03/3847-1509. www.sunroute-asakusa.jp. 120 units. ¥8,500–¥10,500 ($71–$87) single; ¥14,500 ($121) double; ¥16,500–¥19,000 ($137–$158) twin. AE, DC, MC, V. Station: Tawaramachi (1 min.) or Asakusa (8 min.). **Amenities:** Restaurant; same-day laundry service; nonsmoking rooms (singles only). *In room:* A/C, TV, hot-water pot with tea, hair dryer, washlet toilet.

Sukeroku-no-yado-Sadachiyo ⭐⭐   Located in the heart of Asakusa's traditional neighborhood, this 50-year-old ryokan entices with its whitewashed walls, stone lanterns, paper lanterns, bamboo screens, and rickshaw beside the front

Nightlife & Where to Stay & Dine in Asakusa

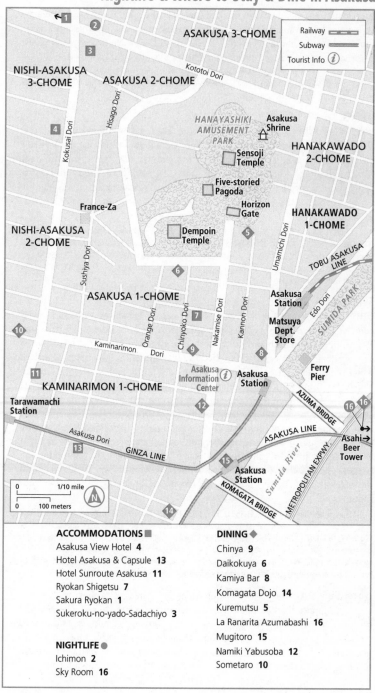

ASAKUSA 3-CHOME

Railway
Subway
Tourist Info ⓘ

NISHI-ASAKUSA 3-CHOME

ASAKUSA 2-CHOME

Kototoi Dori

Hisago Dori

Kokusai Dori

HANAYASHIKI AMUSEMENT PARK

Asakusa Shrine

Sensoji Temple

HANAKAWADO 2-CHOME

Five-storied Pagoda

France-Za

Horizon Gate

HANAKAWADO 1-CHOME

NISHI-ASAKUSA 2-CHOME

Dempoin Temple

Umamichi Dori

TOBU ASAKUSA LINE

Sushiya Dori

ASAKUSA 1-CHOME

Orange Dori

Chinyoko Dori

Nakamise Dori

Kannon Dori

Asakusa Station

Edo Dori

SUMIDA PARK

Matsuya Dept. Store

Kaminarimon Dori

Asakusa Information ⓘ Center

Asakusa Station

Ferry Pier

KAMINARIMON 1-CHOME

Tarawamachi Station

Asakusa Dori

GINZA LINE

AZUMA BRIDGE

ASAKUSA LINE

Asahi Beer Tower

Asakusa Station

Sumida River

METROPOLITAN EXPWY.

KOMAGATA BRIDGE

0   1/10 mile
0   100 meters

N

ACCOMMODATIONS ■

Asakusa View Hotel **4**
Hotel Asakusa & Capsule **13**
Hotel Sunroute Asakusa **11**
Ryokan Shigetsu **7**
Sakura Ryokan **1**
Sukeroku-no-yado-Sadachiyo **3**

NIGHTLIFE ●

Ichimon **2**
Sky Room **16**

DINING ◆

Chinya **9**
Daikokuya **6**
Kamiya Bar **8**
Komagata Dojo **14**
Kuremutsu **5**
La Ranarita Azumabashi **16**
Mugitoro **15**
Namiki Yabusoba **12**
Sometaro **10**

door. Inside, antiques line hallways that lead to tatami guest rooms. Even the public lounge, lobby, and public baths are Japanese style, making this inn a great choice for those wishing to experience a bit of old Edo in the modern metropolis.

2–20–1 Asakusa, Taito-ku, Tokyo 111-0032. ✆ **03/3842-6431.** Fax 03/3842-6433. www.sadachiyo.co.jp. 20 units. ¥12,000 ($100) single; ¥17,600 ($145) twin. Off-season discounts available. AE, MC, V. Station: Tawaramachi (8 min.) or Asakusa (15 min.). **Amenities:** Restaurant (Japanese); in-room massage. *In room:* A/C, TV, hot-water pot with tea, hair dryer.

UENO

Hotel Park Side Located across from the south end of Shinobazu Pond, this 1980s hotel has a good location near Ueno Park's many attractions and views of the park. Otherwise, it's rather ordinary and worn around the edges, with dark corridors leading to uninspiring small rooms. Be sure to ask for a room on an upper floor facing the park, since that's this hotel's best feature. I also like the sky lounge on the top (10th) floor for its panoramic views, inexpensive lunches, and cocktails.

2–11–18 Ueno, Taito-ku, Tokyo 110-0005. ✆ **03/3836-5711.** Fax 03/3831-6641. 128 units. ¥9,200–¥11,500 ($77–$96) single; ¥16,100–¥17,500 ($134–$146) double or twin. AE, MC, V. Station: Yushima (1 min.), Ueno Okachimachi or Ueno Hirokoji (4 min.), or Ueno (6 min.). **Amenities:** 3 restaurants (Italian, Chinese, shabu-shabu); lounge; room service (3–10:30pm); same-day laundry service. *In room:* A/C, TV, dataport, minibar, hot-water pot with tea, hair dryer.

SHINJUKU

Hotel Century Southern Tower ★★★ *Finds* Opened in 1998 and a welcome addition to the Shinjuku hotel scene, this sleek, modern hotel is located just south of the station and just a footbridge away from the huge Takashimaya Times Square shopping complex. Because it occupies the top floors of a sleek white building, it seems far removed from the hustle and bustle of Shinjuku below. Its 20th-floor lobby is simple and uncluttered and boasts almost surreal views of Tokyo stretching in the distance. Also on the 20th floor is Tribecks, a contemporary restaurant offering Asian- and European-influenced American food and great views of Shinjuku. Ask for a room on a high floor. Rooms facing east are considered best (and are therefore more expensive), especially at night when neon is in full regalia. Rooms facing west have views of Shinjuku's skyscrapers and, on clear days (mostly in winter), of Mount Fuji. A playful touch: the maps in each room outlining the important buildings visible from your room.

2–2–1 Yoyogi, Shibuya-ku, Tokyo 151-8583. ✆ **03/5354-0111.** Fax 03/5354-0100. www.southerntower. co.jp. 375 units. ¥16,000–¥18,000 ($133–$150) single; ¥22,000–¥28,000 ($183–$233) double; ¥22,000–¥24,000 ($183–$200) twin. AE, DC, MC, V. Station: Shinjuku (south exit, 3 min.). **Amenities:** 3 restaurants (Japanese, Chinese, contemporary American); lounge; exercise room (free); convenience store; 24-hr. Kinko's; same-day laundry/dry-cleaning service; nonsmoking rooms. *In room:* A/C, TV w/cable and pay movies, dataport, fridge, hot-water pot with tea, hair dryer, safe, washlet toilet.

Hotel Sunroute Tokyo *Value* Conveniently located just a short walk southwest of Shinjuku Station, this no-frills hotel attracts a large foreign clientele and calls itself a "city hotel." While it does boast a couple of restaurants and limited services, its guest rooms—mostly singles and twins—resemble those in a business hotel rather than tourist accommodations, with just the basics. Essentially, this is a place to sleep in a convenient location without spending a fortune.

2–3–1 Yoyogi, Shibuya-ku, Tokyo 151-0053. ✆ **03/3375-3211.** Fax 03/3379-3040. http://sunroutetokyo.hsr-hq.co.jp. 546 units. ¥12,500–¥15,500 ($104–$129) single; ¥17,500 ($146) double; ¥18,000–¥25,000 ($150–$208) twin. Rates include service charge. AE, DC, MC, V. Station: Shinjuku (3 min.). **Amenities:**

Nightlife & Where to Stay & Dine in Ueno

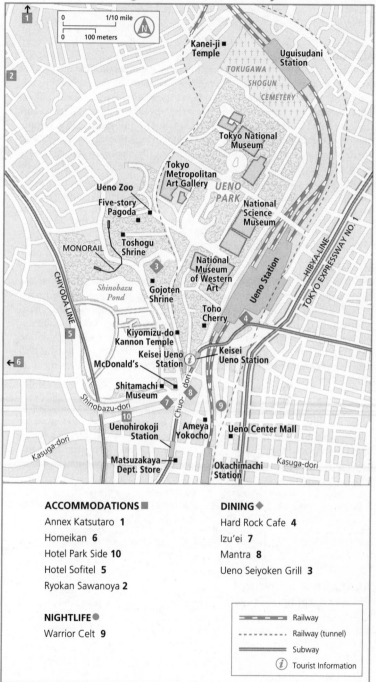

0   1/10 mile
0   100 meters

Kanei-ji Temple
Uguisudani Station
TOKUGAWA SHOGUN CEMETERY
Tokyo National Museum
Tokyo Metropolitan Art Gallery
UENO PARK
Ueno Zoo
Five-story Pagoda
National Science Museum
MONORAIL
Toshogu Shrine
3
National Museum of Western Art
Ueno Station
HIBIYA LINE
TOKYO EXPRESSWAY NO. 1
CHIYODA LINE
Shinobazu Pond
Gojoten Shrine
Toho Cherry
4
Kiyomizu-do Kannon Temple
5
6
Keisei Ueno Station
Keisei Ueno Station
McDonald's
Shitamachi Museum
7
8
Chuo-dori
9
Shinobazu-dori
10
Uenohirokoji Station
Ameya Yokocho
Ueno Center Mall
Kasuga-dori
Matsuzakaya Dept. Store
Okachimachi Station
Kasuga-dori

ACCOMMODATIONS ■
Annex Katsutaro **1**
Homeikan **6**
Hotel Park Side **10**
Hotel Sofitel **5**
Ryokan Sawanoya **2**

NIGHTLIFE ●
Warrior Celt **9**

DINING ◆
Hard Rock Cafe **4**
Izu'ei **7**
Mantra **8**
Ueno Seiyoken Grill **3**

	Railway
	Railway (tunnel)
	Subway
(i)	Tourist Information

3 restaurants (Japanese, Chinese, Italian); bar; convenience store; salon; room service (11am–10:30pm); same-day laundry/dry-cleaning service; nonsmoking rooms. *In room:* A/C, TV, minibar, hot-water pot with tea, hair dryer.

AOYAMA

President Hotel ★ *Value*   This small hotel is a good choice for the budget-conscious business traveler, not only because it's a respected address in Tokyo but also thanks to its reasonable prices and great location, between Akasaka, Shinjuku, Aoyama, and Roppongi. It also offers some of the same conveniences and services offered by larger, more expensive hotels. The unpretentious lobby has a comfortable European atmosphere—you don't have to be embarrassed about meeting business clients here. Units, which are mostly singles, are tiny but cheerful. You'll take your life in your own hands trying to shave in the dark bathrooms. Ask for a unit on a high floor facing the front.

Aoyama Dori, 2–2–3 Minami Aoyama, Minato-ku, Tokyo 107-8545. ② **03/3497-0111.** Fax 03/3401-4816. www.president-hotel.co.jp. 210 units. ¥12,000–¥13,000 ($100–$108) single; ¥17,000 ($142) double; ¥17,000–¥21,000 ($142–$175) twin. AE, DC, MC, V. Station: Aoyama-Itchome (1 min.). **Amenities:** 3 restaurants (Japanese, French, coffee shop); room service (5–9pm); same-day laundry/dry-cleaning service, nonsmoking rooms. *In room:* A/C, TV w/cable, dataport, minibar, hot-water pot with tea, hair dryer.

SHIBUYA

Shibuya Excel Hotel Tokyu ★★   Across from bustling Shibuya Station and connected by a footbridge and underground passage, this busy, modern hotel opened in 2000, the first new hotel to debut in Shibuya in many years. It's been so successful (I don't know why no one thought of locating hotels in Shibuya before), Tokyu promptly built another one farther from the station. With an excellent location above Mark City shopping mall (reception is on the fifth floor), the Excel tries hard to appeal to everyone: For business travelers, there are "Excel" twin rooms that feature a fax/copier machine and high-speed dataports. For women, there are two floors reserved only for females and accessed by a special key, with in-room amenities, such as face cream, also geared toward women. There are also handicapped-accessible rooms, and almost half the rooms are for nonsmokers. Rooms, on the 7th to 24th floors, are comfortable. Ask for an upper-floor room facing Shinjuku; the night view is great. In-room refrigerators are empty so that you can stock them yourself from hotel vending machines which, by the way, management claims are the largest in Japan.

1–12–2 Dogenzaka, Shibuya-ku 150-0043. ② **800/428-6598** in the U.S., or 03/5457-0109. Fax 03/5457-0309. www.tokyuhotels.co.jp. 408 units. ¥18,000–¥19,000 ($150–$158) single; ¥23,000–¥25,000 ($192–$208) double; ¥25,000–¥36,000 ($208–$300) twin. AE, DC, MC, V. Station: Shibuya (1 min. by footbridge). **Amenities:** 2 restaurants (Japanese, French) plus many more in Mark City mall; shopping mall beneath hotel; room service (7–9am and 9pm–midnight); same-day laundry/dry-cleaning service; nonsmoking rooms; public fax and copy machine. *In room:* A/C, satellite TV w/pay movies, dataport, fridge, hot-water pot with tea, hair dryer, trouser press, washlet toilet.

AKASAKA & ROPPONGI

Akasaka Excel Hotel Tokyu ★   This classy but simple business hotel boasts a high occupancy rate thanks to its ideal location in the middle of Akasaka and its reasonable rates. Built in 1969 and undergoing a much-needed renovation in 2002, it's easily recognizable by its candy-striped exterior (it's called the "Pajama Building" by the locals). Rooms feature shoji screens and window panels that slide shut for complete darkness (even in the middle of the day), as well as windows that can be opened (a rarity in Tokyo). There are 200 single rooms, but the lower-priced ones are pretty small. There are also specialty rooms: 92 with free high-speed Internet access, 10 "Comfort Rooms" with massage chairs and specially designed pillows, and 17 "Ladies Rooms" with corridor camera surveillance and such extras as music jewelry boxes and herbal tea. Front-facing rooms look upon the whirl and neon of Akasaka; those in the back are quieter and face a steep slope of greenery.

2–14–3 Nagata-cho, Chiyoda-ku, Tokyo 100. ⓒ **800/428-6598** in the U.S., or 03/3580-2311. Fax 03/3580-6066. www.tokyuhotels.co.jp. 535 units. ¥18,000 –¥23,000 ($150–$192) single; ¥26,000 ($217) double; ¥25,000 –¥30,000 ($208–$250) twin. AE, DC, MC, V. Station: Akasaka-mitsuke (1 min.). **Amenities:** 3 restaurants (Japanese, French, coffee shop); lounge; business center; shopping arcade; convenience store; salon; room service (7am–11:30pm); same-day laundry/dry-cleaning service; nonsmoking rooms, free shuttle service to Tokyo Disneyland. *In room:* A/C, TV w/cable and pay movies, minibar, hot-water pot with tea, hair dryer, washlet toilet.

Hotel Ibis   The Ibis is about as close as you can get to the night action of Roppongi, just a minute's walk away from Roppongi Crossing. It caters to both businessmen and couples who come to Roppongi's discos and don't make (or want to make) the last subway home. The lobby, with public computers available for accessing the Internet (and costing ¥500/$4.15 for 25 min.), is on the fifth floor, with the guest rooms above. Small but comfortable, the rooms feature modern furniture and windows that you can open—though with a freeway nearby, I'm not sure you'd want to. The cheapest doubles come with semi-double–size beds, just slightly wider than a single. On the 13th floor is a branch of the well-known Italian restaurant Sabatini, with views of the city.

7–14–4 Roppongi, Minato-ku, Tokyo 106-0032. ⓒ **03/3403-4411.** Fax 03/3479-0609. www.ibis-hotel.com. 182 units. ¥11,500 –¥14,100 ($96–$118) single; ¥14,100 –¥23,000 ($117–$192) double; ¥19,000 –¥23,000 ($158–$192) twin; ¥24,000 ($200) triple. AE, DC, MC, V. Station: Roppongi (1 min.). **Amenities:** 3 restaurants (Italian, pizza/pasta, coffee shop); room service (Mon–Fri 11:30am–9pm); same-day laundry/dry-cleaning service; nonsmoking rooms. *In room:* A/C, TV w/cable and pay movies, minibar, hot-water pot with tea, hair dryer.

Roppongi Prince Hotel   This is a good choice if you want to be close (about a 6-min. walk) to Roppongi's night action yet somewhat removed. Opened in 1984, the hotel attracts Japanese businessmen on weekdays and vacationers ages 20 to 25 on weekends, and caters to them with a young and cheerful staff, modern designs with bold colors, and a resortlike atmosphere. The hotel wraps around an inner courtyard, which features a pool with a Jacuzzi and heated deck—a solar mirror on the roof directs sun rays toward the sunbathers below, making it Tokyo's only outdoor heated pool open year-round. Unfortunately for the shy, sides of the raised pool are see-through acrylic, giving diners at the adjacent outdoor patio unique ringside views. Rooms are small but bright and modern, with either black or white decor.

3–2–7 Roppongi, Minato-ku, Tokyo 106-0032. ⓒ **800/542-8686** in the U.S. and Canada, or 03/3587-1111. Fax 03/3587-0770. www.princehotels.co.jp/Roppongi-e. 216 units. ¥18,500 ($154) single; ¥23,000 –¥24,500 ($192–$204) double; ¥21,500 –¥24,500 ($179–$204) twin. AE, DC, MC, V. Station: Roppongi (8 min.). **Amenities:** 4 restaurants (Italian, tempura, sushi, teppanyaki); bar; outdoor heated pool and Jacuzzi open year-round (fee: ¥1,000/$8); sauna; room service (11am–2am); same-day laundry/dry-cleaning service; nonsmoking rooms. *In room:* A/C, TV w/cable and pay movies and video games, fridge, hot-water pot with tea, hair dryer.

Shiba Park Hotel ⭐ *Finds*   This small, older hotel in an out-of-the-way location offers enthusiastic, personalized service, a boon to those who don't like getting lost in the shuffle of larger hotels. Popular with budget-conscious overseas business travelers, it's a bit far from Roppongi nightlife (the walk home is sobering), near Shiba Park, Tokyo Tower, and Zozoji Temple. The mostly single rooms are in the main building and an annex across the street, but all are very small with just the basics. Higher-priced rooms are slightly larger and offer free high-speed Internet access, minibars, and washlet toilets. If you plan on being gone most of the day and aren't claustrophobic, this place will be just fine.

1–5–10 Shiba Koen, Minato-ku, Tokyo 105-0011. ☎ 03/3433-4141. Fax 03/3433-4142. www.shibapark hotel.com. 391 units. ¥13,500 – ¥19,000 ($113–$158) single; ¥20,500 ($171) double; ¥20,500 – ¥30,500 ($171–$254) twin. AE, DC, MC, V. Station: Onarimon (2 min.), Daimon (4 min.), or Hammamatsucho (8 min.). **Amenities:** 4 restaurants (Japanese, French, Chinese, coffee shop); bar; small business center; room service (6:45am–11pm); coin-op laundry room w/free detergent and iron/ironing board; same-day laundry/dry-cleaning service; nonsmoking rooms. In room: A/C, TV w/pay movies, hot-water pot with tea and coffee, hair dryer.

Tokyo Prince Hotel (Overrated)   Set in Shiba Park near Zozoji Temple and Tokyo Tower, this is the Prince Hotel chain's oldest Tokyo property, built in 1964 for the Olympic Games and now passed over as visitors flock to the city's newer, glitzier hotels. While it offers facilities rivaling those of much more expensive choices, parts of the hotel show its age (particularly in corridors and some of the lowest-priced rooms). In 2005, a new tower will open with an additional 700 rooms that should bring the property up to par. In the meantime, guests have to put up with rather mediocre rooms dressed in pastels and reproduction French furniture. The most expensive rooms are larger and face the front of the hotel and a parking lot; opt for a cheaper, smaller room on a top floor with a view of the park and Tokyo Tower. Nonsmokers will like the fact that there's a nonsmoking lounge on the 11th floor with an up-close view of the Tower.

3–3–1 Shiba Koen, Minato-ku, Tokyo 105-8560. ☎ 800/542-8686 or 03/3432-1111. Fax 03/3434-5551. www.princehotels.co.jp/english. ¥24,000 ($200) single; ¥25,000 – ¥32,000 ($208–$267) double or twin. AE, DC, MC, V. Station: Onarimon (1 min.), Daimon or Akabanebashi (both 7 min.), or Kamiyacho or Hammamatsucho (both 10 min.). **Amenities:** 10 restaurants (including an all-weather beer garden); 2 bars; nonsmoking lounge; outdoor pool (fee: ¥1,000/$8.35); concierge; tour desk; business center; small shopping arcade; convenience store; salon; 24-hr. room service; in-room massage; same-day laundry/dry-cleaning service; nonsmoking rooms. In room: A/C, TV w/cable and pay movies and games, high-speed dataport, fridge, hot-water pot with tea, hair dryer, washlet toilet.

SHINAGAWA

Le Meridien Pacific Tokyo ★★   This graceful and dignified hotel across the street from Shinagawa Station occupies grounds that once belonged to Japan's imperial family, a reminder of which remains in the peaceful, tranquil garden with pond and waterfall that serves as a dramatic backdrop for the lobby lounge. Approximately 50% of the hotel's guests are foreigners, mostly French, German, and American. Its location on the Yamanote Line makes it convenient for travel in the city, while trains to Kamakura and other points west and south, as well as the Shinkansen bullet train, make it convenient for travel farther afield. I also like its glass-enclosed coffee shop serving buffet meals. Room rates are based mostly on room size, with those facing the front slightly larger and offering partial views of Tokyo Bay between buildings. Smaller rooms at the back are a bargain, as they face the garden and are quieter. In any case, rooms offer nothing out of the ordinary, and most bathrooms are surprisingly small, with almost no counter space to speak of. *Tip:* The outdoor pool's fee is for use of a locker; forgo that, and you can use the pool free of charge.

3–13–3 Takanawa, Minato-ku, Tokyo 108-8567. ☎ 800/543-4300 in the U.S., or 03/3445-6711. Fax 03/3445-5733. www.htl-pacific.co.jp. 954 units. ¥21,000 – ¥25,500 ($175–$213) single; ¥25,000 – ¥38,000 ($208–$317) twin or double; from ¥50,000 ($412) suite. AE, DC, MC, V. Station: Shinagawa (1 min.). **Amenities:** 6 restaurants; 2 bars; lounge; outdoor pool (fee: ¥1,000/$8); access to fitness center at Le Meridien Grand Pacific in Odaiba (fee: ¥1,050/$8.75); concierge; business center; small shopping arcade; salon; room service (6am–midnight); in-room massage; babysitting; same-day laundry/dry-cleaning service; nonsmoking rooms; free shuttle bus to Le Meridien Grand Pacific Tokyo Hotel in Odaiba and Tokyo Disneyland. *In room:* A/C, TV w/cable and pay movies, high-speed dataport (not in all rooms), minibar, hot-water pot with tea, hair dryer, washlet toilet.

Shinagawa Prince Hotel *(Kids)*   With four gleaming white buildings added at various stages (each with its own check-in), the Shinagawa Prince is the largest sleep factory in Japan. It's a virtual city within a city, with more than a dozen food and beverage outlets, a 10-screen cinema complex, a large sports center with nine indoor tennis courts, an 80-lane bowling center, an indoor golf practice center, a SEGA amusement/arcade-game center, indoor and outdoor pools, and a fitness center. It caters to Japanese businessmen on weekdays and to students and family vacationers on weekends and holidays. Rooms vary widely depending on which building you select: The Main Tower has only very small singles, at the cheapest rates; the Annex has singles, twins, and doubles in a medium price range; the 39-story New Tower, with its outdated pastel colors and mostly twins, is no longer very new; the upscale Executive Tower, with only doubles, has the smartest-looking rooms and the highest prices. Assuming you can find it, be sure to have a drink or meal at the 39th-floor Top of Shinagawa; its views of Tokyo Bay and the city are among the best in town. With its many diversions, this hotel is like a resort getaway but is too big and busy for my taste.

4–10–30 Takanawa, Minato-ku, Tokyo 108-8611. (C) **800/542-8686** or in the U.S. or Canada, or 03/3440-1111. Fax 03/3441-7092. 3,680 units. ¥9,800–¥18,000 ($82–$150) single; ¥14,600–¥31,000 ($122–$258) double; ¥14,100–¥27,500 ($117–$229) twin. AE, DC, MC, V. Station: Shinagawa (2 min.). **Amenities:** 14 restaurants; bar; 24-hr. Internet cafe; sports center (various fees charged, ¥1,000/$8.35 for indoor pool); tour desk; business center; shopping arcade; convenience store; salon; same-day laundry/dry-cleaning service; nonsmoking rooms; cinema complex; IMAX; amusement arcade; children's day-care center. *In room:* A/C, TV, fridge, hot-water pot with tea, hair dryer.

OTHER NEIGHBORHOODS
The Hilltop Hotel (Yama-no-Ue Hotel) *★★ (Finds)*   This is a delightfully old-fashioned, unpretentious (some might say dowdy) hotel with character. Opened in 1937 and boasting an Art Deco facade, it was once the favorite haunt of writers, including novelist Mishima Yukio. Avoid the cheaper, more boring rooms in the annex; rooms in the main building have such endearing, homey touches as fringed lampshades, doilies, cherrywood furniture (and mahogany desks), velvet curtains, vanity tables, and old-fashioned heaters with intricate grillwork. Some twins even combine a tatami area and shoji with beds; the most expensive twin overlooks its own terraced Japanese garden. Don't be surprised if the reception desk remembers you by name. Although the Hilltop is not as centrally located or up-to-date as other hotels, nearby Meiji University brings lots of young people to the area.

1–1 Surugadai, Kanda, Chiyoda-ku, Tokyo 101-0062. (C) **03/3293-2311.** Fax 03/3233-4567. www.yamanoue-hotel.co.jp. 75 units. ¥17,000–¥20,000 ($142–$167) single; ¥24,000–¥25,000 ($200–$208) double; ¥26,000–¥32,000 ($217–$267) twin. AE, DC, MC, V. Station: Ochanomizu or Shin-Ochanomizu (8 min.) or Jimbocho (5 min.). **Amenities:** 7 restaurants; 3 bars; room service (7am–2am); same-day laundry/dry-cleaning service. *In room:* A/C, TV w/cable, minibar, hot-water pot with tea, hair dryer, washlet toilet.

5 Inexpensive
AROUND TOKYO STATION
Hotel Yaesu Ryumeikan *★ (Value)*   This 40-year-old, nondescript hotel is your best bet for reasonably priced lodging just minutes away from Tokyo Station. From the north Yaesu exit, turn left onto Sotobori Dori; it will be on your

right, just before Eitai Dori. Surprising for this location, it offers both Japanese-style tatami rooms and Western-style rooms with beds. I personally prefer the Japanese-style rooms, especially the most expensive tatami rooms, which have a nice, traditional feel and come with sitting alcove and Japanese-style deep tub. Only Japanese breakfasts are available; if you can't stomach rice and fish in the morning, opt for a room without breakfast and subtract ¥1,000 ($8.35) per person from the rates below.

1–3–22 Yaesu, Chuo-ku 103-0028. ℂ 03/3271-0971. Fax 03/3271-0977. www.ryumeikan.co.jp/yaesu.html. 30 units (23 with bathroom, 5 with toilet only, 2 without bathroom). ¥8,000 ($67) single without bathroom, ¥10,000 – ¥13,000 ($83–$108) single with bathroom; ¥9,500 ($79) single with toilet only; ¥14,000 ($117) double with toilet only; ¥17,000 – ¥18,000 ($142–$150) double with bathroom. Rates include Japanese breakfast. AE, DC, MC, V. Station: Tokyo (3 min. from the north Yaesu exit) or Nihombashi (exit A3, 1 min.). On the corner of Eitai Dori and Sotobori Dori. **Amenities:** 2 restaurants (Italian, coffee shop). *In room:* A/C, TV, dataport, hot-water pot with tea, hair dryer.

ASAKUSA

Sakura Ryokan *Kids*   A member of the Japanese Inn and Welcome Inn groups, this family-run establishment is a combination business-tourist hotel and caters to both Japanese and foreign guests. It's located in Asakusa just northwest of the Kappabashi Dori and Kototoi Dori intersection, about a 12-minute walk from Sensoji Temple. The reception area is on the second floor, and the friendly owner speaks some English. Each spotless room comes with a sink and an alarm clock. Both Western- and Japanese-style units are available with or without private bathroom. The single rooms are quite spacious compared to those in business hotels. There's one Japanese-style room, complete with a terrace, large enough for a family of six or seven.

2–6–2 Iriya, Taito-ku, Tokyo 110-0013. ℂ 03/3876-8118. Fax 03/3873-9456. www.sakura-ryokan.com. 20 units (9 with bathroom). ¥5,300 – ¥5,500 ($44–$46) single without bathroom, ¥6,300 ($52) single with bathroom; ¥9,600 ($80) double without bathroom, ¥10,600 ($88) double with bathroom; ¥12,600 – ¥13,500 ($105–$112) triple without bathroom, ¥13,800 – ¥15,600 ($115–$130) triple with bathroom. Japanese or Western breakfast ¥800 ($6.65) extra, Japanese dinner ¥1,600 ($13) extra (reservations required). AE, MC, V. Station: Iriya (6 min., exit 1 or 2). **Amenities:** Computer with Internet access free for guest use; coin-op washer and dryer. *In room:* A/C, TV, hot-water pot with tea.

Ryokan Shigetsu ★★ *Finds*   Whenever a foreigner living in Tokyo, soon to play host to first-time visitors to Japan, asks me to recommend a moderately priced ryokan in Tokyo, this is the one I most often suggest. It has a great location in Asakusa just off Nakamise Dori, a colorful, shop-lined pedestrian street leading to the famous Sensoji Temple—an area that gives you a feel for the older Japan. A member of the Japanese Inn Group, it represents the best of modern yet traditional Japanese design—simple yet elegant, with shoji, unadorned

---

Tips   **A Note on Japanese Symbols**

Many hotels, restaurants, and other establishments in Japan do not have signs giving their names in Roman (English-language) letters. As an aid to the reader, appendix C lists the Japanese symbols for all such places described in this guide. Each set of characters representing an establishment name has a number, which corresponds to the number that appears inside the box before the establishment's name in the text. Thus, to find the Japanese symbols for, say, the **Hotel Asakusa & Capsule,** below, refer to no.1 in appendix C.

Fun Fact **Capsule Hotels**

There's another inexpensive lodging option in Tokyo, but it's not for the claustrophobic. So-called capsule hotels, which became popular in the early 1980s, are used primarily by Japanese businessmen who have spent an evening out drinking with fellow workers and missed the last train—a capsule hotel is cheaper than a taxi ride home. They're located mostly near nightlife districts or major train stations. Sleeping units are small (no larger than a coffin) and contain a bed, private color TV, alarm clock, and radio; the units are usually stacked two deep in rows down a corridor, and the only thing separating you from your probably inebriated neighbor is a curtain. A cotton kimono and locker are provided, and facilities usually include public baths, sauna, and vending machines selling everything from beer to instant noodles to toothbrushes.

Most capsule hotels do not accept women. Two that do, with separate facilities for men and women, are ① **Hotel Asakusa & Capsule,** 4–14–9 Kotobuki, Taito-ku (✆ **03/3847-4477**; station: Tawaramachi, 3 min.), which accepts only drop-ins and is located about a 6-minute walk south of Asakusa's Sensoji Temple; and **Fontaine Akasaka,** 4–3–5 Akasaka, Minato-ku (✆ **03/3583-6554**; station: Akasaka, 2 min., or Akasaka-mitsuke, 5 min.). Prices average about ¥4,500 to ¥4,800 ($38–$40) per night; credit cards are usually not accepted. Check-in is generally 4 or 5pm, and checkout is about 9:30 or 10am. Since everyone has to pack up and vacate cubicles during the day (coin lockers are generally available but may not be large enough for a big suitcase), curious foreigners may wish to experience a capsule hotel only as a 1-night stand.

---

wood, and artwork throughout. Traditional Japanese music or the recorded chirping of birds play softly in the public spaces. Two public Japanese baths have views of the nearby five-storied pagoda. A Japanese restaurant serves excellent Japanese breakfasts, as well as mini-kaiseki dinners (discounts given to hotel guests; reserve 1 week in advance; closed Sun–Mon) and lunches. There are 11 Western-style rooms, but I prefer the 12 slightly more expensive Japanese-style tatami rooms, which include Japanese-style mirrors and comfortable chairs for those who don't like relaxing on the floor. In short, this establishment costs no more than a regular business hotel but has much more class.

1–31–11 Asakusa, Taito-ku 111-0032. ✆ **03/3843-2345**. Fax 03/3843-2348. www.shigetsu.com. 23 units. ¥7,300–¥9,000 ($61–$75) single; ¥14,000–¥16,000 ($117–$133) twin. Japanese or Western breakfast ¥1,200 ($10) extra, Japanese dinner ¥3,500 ($29) extra. AE, MC, V. Station: Asakusa (4 min.). **Amenities:** Restaurant (Japanese); Apple laptop in lobby providing free Internet access; nonsmoking rooms. *In room:* A/C, TV, minibar, hot-water pot with tea, hair dryer.

UENO

Annex Katsutaro ★★ *Finds* Opened in 2001, this thoroughly modern concrete ryokan is a standout for its simple yet chic designs, spotless Japanese-style rooms (all with bathroom), and location—right in the heart of Yanaka with its old-fashioned neighborhood and about a 20-minute walk northwest of Ueno Park. The Keisei Skyliner from Narita Airport stops at nearby Nippori Station. If you have your own laptop and LAN card, you can tap into the Internet free of charge from your room; or you can use a public computer for free. If the ryokan is full, don't let management talk you into taking a room in its much older main Ryokan Katsutaro; it's not nearly as nice as the annex.

3–8–4 Yanaka, Taito-ku, Tokyo 110-0001. 🕾 **03/3828-2500.** Fax 03/3821-5400. www.katsutaro.com. 17 units. ¥6,000 ($50) single; ¥10,000 – ¥12,000 ($83–$100) twin; ¥14,000 – ¥16,000 ($117–$133) triple. Continental breakfast ¥800 ($6.65) extra. AE, MC, V. Station: Sendagi (2 min.) or Nippori (7 min.). **Amenities:** Computer with Internet access free for guest use; coin-op washers and dryers; free coffee service. *In room:* A/C, TV w/cable, fridge, hot-water pot with tea and coffee, hair dryer.

Homeikan ⭐⭐⭐ *(Finds)* Although a bit of a hike from Ueno Park (about 30 min.) and not as conveniently located as the other ryokan, this lovely place is my number-one choice if you want to experience an authentic, traditional ryokan in a traditional neighborhood. It consists of three separate buildings acquired over the last century by the present owner's grandfather. Homeikan, the main building (Honkan), was purchased almost 100 years ago; today it is listed as a "Tangible Cultural Property" and is used mainly by groups of students and seniors. Across the street is Daimachi Bekkan, built after World War II to serve as the family home. A beautiful, 31-room property, it boasts a private Japanese garden with a pond, public baths (including one open 24 hr.), and wood-inlaid and pebbled hallways leading to nicely detailed tatami rooms adorned with such features as gnarled wood trim and sitting alcoves, as well as simpler tatami rooms for budget travelers. This is where most foreigners stay, and if you opt for meals, they will be served in your room in true ryokan fashion. The third building, Morikawa Bekkan, about a 5-minute walk away, was built as an inn about 45 years ago and, with 35 rooms, is the largest. Owner Koike-san, who speaks excellent English, points out that travelers who need the latest in creature comforts (including private bathrooms) should go elsewhere; those seeking a traditional ryokan experience, however, will not be disappointed.

5–10–5 Hongo, Bunkyo-ku, Tokyo 113-0033. 🕾 **03/3811-1181** or 03/3811-1187. Fax 03/3811-1764. www1. odn.ne.jp/homeikan. 91 units (none with bathroom). ¥6,500 – ¥7,000 ($54–$58) single; ¥11,000 – ¥12,000 ($92–$100) double; ¥13,500 – ¥15,000 ($112–$125) triple. ¥500 more per person in peak season; ¥500 less per person in off season. Western- or Japanese-style breakfast ¥1,000 ($8.35); Japanese dinner ¥2,000 ($17; not available 1st night of stay). AE, DC, MC, V. Station: Hongo Sanchome (8 min.) or Kasuga (5 min.). *In room:* A/C, TV, minibar, hot-water pot with tea, safe.

Ryokan Sawanoya ⭐ Although this family-run ryokan is relatively modern looking and unexciting, it's delightfully located in a wonderful residential area of old Tokyo, northwest of Ueno Park and within walking distance of the park's many attractions and Nezu Shrine. Upon your arrival, the owner, English-speaking Sawa-san, will give you a short tour of the establishment before taking you to your tatami room; throughout the ryokan are written explanations to help the novice. The owner also gives you a map outlining places of interest in the vicinity. Once a week or so, Sawa-san's son provides guests with a special treat—a traditional Japanese lion dance, free of charge. His daughter-in-law sometimes gives demonstrations of the tea ceremony. In short, this is a great place to stay thanks to Sawa-san's enthusiastic devotion to his neighborhood, which he readily imparts to his guests. Highly recommended.

2–3–11 Yanaka, Taito-ku, Tokyo 110-0001. 🕾 **03/3822-2251.** Fax 03/3822-2252. www.sawanoya.com. 12 units (2 with bathroom). ¥4,700 – ¥5,000 ($39–$42) single without bathroom; ¥8,800 ($73) double without bathroom; ¥9,400 ($78) double with bathroom; ¥12,000 ($100) triple without bathroom; ¥13,500 ($113) triple with bathroom. Breakfast of toast and fried eggs ¥300 ($2.50) extra, Japanese breakfast ¥900 ($7.80) extra. AE, MC, V. Closed Dec 29–Jan 3. Station: Nezu (exit 1, 7 min.). **Amenities:** Computer with Internet access free for guest use; coin-op washers and dryers (free laundry detergent); ironing board, iron, and trouser press (on 3rd floor); free coffee/tea service; public fridge. *In room:* A/C, TV, hot-water pot with tea, hair dryer.

SHINJUKU

Sunlite Hotel   In 1985 this business hotel moved across the street from its old location into a new building, turning the older building into the Hotel Sunlite Annex (the cheaper rates below are for rooms in the older annex). A plus to staying here: the weekly antiques flea markets held at nearby Hanazono Shrine. Rooms are cheerful and clean, although annex rooms are small (its singles are minuscule). Feelings of claustrophobia are somewhat mitigated by windows that can be opened. The main (new) building's corner twins with windows on two sides are the best. *Note:* If you're a night prowler, beware: Doors close at 2am and don't reopen until 5:30am.

5–15–8 Shinjuku, Shinjuku-ku, Tokyo 160-0022. ℂ 03/3356-0391. Fax 03/3356-1223. 197 units. ¥8,300 – ¥8,900 ($69–$74) single; ¥14,000 ($117) double; ¥13,500 – ¥15,000 ($113–$125) twin. AE, DC, MC, V. Station: Shinjuku (12 min.) or Shinjuku Sanchome (5 min.). The hotel is on the east side of Shinjuku Station, on Meiji Dori. **Amenities:** 2 restaurants (Western, coffee shop); same-day laundry service. *In room:* A/C, TV, hot-water pot with tea, hair dryer.

Tokyo International Youth Hostel *(Value)*   This spotless hostel, operated by the Tokyo Metropolitan Government and situated in a high-rise, is definitely the best place to stay in its price range—it offers fantastic Tokyo views. Even the public baths boast good views (especially at night). All beds are dormitory style, with two, four, or five bunk beds to a room. Rooms are very pleasant, with big windows, and each bed has its own curtain for privacy. There are also accessible rooms for travelers with disabilities, and two Japanese-style tatami rooms for families that sleep up to six persons. If there are vacancies, you can stay longer than the normal 3-day maximum. In summer, it's a good idea to reserve about 3 months in advance. The hostel is closed from 10am to 3pm and locked at 10:30pm (lights out at 11pm).

1–1 Kagura-kashi, Shinjuku-ku, Tokyo 162-0823. ℂ 03/3235-1107. Fax 03/3264-4000. www.tokyo-yh.jp. 158 beds. ¥3,500 ($29) adult, ¥2,000 ($17) child. Breakfast ¥400 ($3.35); dinner ¥900 ($7.50). No youth-hostel card required; no age limit. No credit cards. Closed Dec 29–Jan 3. Station: Iidabashi (2 min.). Reception is on the 18th floor of the Central Plaza Building. **Amenities:** Shopping mall on 1st and 2nd floors of same building; washer and dryer free of charge. *In room:* A/C, no phone.

SHIBUYA

National Children's Castle Hotel (Kodomo-no-Shiro Hotel) *(Kids)*   The National Children's Castle, located on Aoyama Dori about halfway between Aoyama and Shibuya (and a bit of a trek from either station), is a great place to stay if you're traveling with children. Located on the sixth and seventh floors, the hotel is plain rather than playful, but the complex boasts Tokyo's best and most sophisticated indoor/outdoor playground for children. Guests range from businesspeople on weekdays to families and young college students on weekends. The rooms—mainly twins—are simple and of adequate size, with large windows. The most expensive twins, which face Shinjuku, have the best views and are a great value. Note that the hotel's three singles do not have windows, but you can pay extra to stay in a twin. The three Japanese-style rooms, available for three or more people, are a good way for families to experience the traditional Japanese lifestyle. Make reservations at least 2 months in advance, especially if you plan on being in Tokyo in the summer. Note that there's an 11pm curfew, check-in isn't until 3pm, and not much English is spoken.

5–53–1 Jingumae, Shibuya-ku, Tokyo 150-0001. ℂ 03/3797-5677. Fax 03/3406-7805. 27 units. ¥6,400 ($53) single; ¥14,000 – ¥15,400 ($117–$128) twin; ¥6,800 ($57) per person Japanese-style room. AE, DC, MC, V. Station: Omotesando (8 min.) or Shibuya (10 min.). Front desk on the 7th floor. **Amenities:** Restaurant (Japanese/Western); National Children's Castle. *In room:* A/C, TV, hot-water pot with tea, washlet toilet.

AKASAKA & ROPPONGI

Arca Torre *(Value)*   This smart-looking, 10-story property looks expensive from the outside but is actually a business hotel. Opened in 2002, it has a great location on Roppongi Dori, between Roppongi Crossing and Roppongi Hills, making it popular with both business types and tourists on a budget. Its (mostly single) rooms are small but cheerful, with flat-panel TVs and complimentary bottled water in the otherwise empty fridge. Rooms facing the back are quiet but face another building. If you opt for a room facing the front, ask for a high floor above the freeway; otherwise, your view will be of cars and, at certain times of the day, traffic jams.

6–1–23 Roppongi, Minato-ku, Tokyo 106-0032. ℂ **03/3404-5111.** Fax 03/3404-5115. 77 units. ¥11,000 – ¥13,000 ($92–$108) single; ¥14,000 – ¥17,000 ($117–$142) double; ¥21,000 ($175) twin. AE, DC, MC, V. Station: Roppongi (1 min.) **Amenities:** Restaurant (coffee shop); same-day laundry/dry-cleaning service; non-smoking rooms. *In room:* A/C, TV w/cable, fridge, hot-water pot with tea, hair dryer, washlet toilet.

Asia Center of Japan *(star) (Value)*   Great rates make this a top choice if you're looking for inexpensive Western-style accommodations in the center of town. It's so popular that it's often fully booked, prompting management to add an addition in 2003 that more than doubled the number of rooms (even so, it's wise to reserve months in advance). Everyone—from businessmen to students to travelers to foreigners teaching English—stays here; I know one teacher who lived here for years. Resembling a college dormitory, the Asia Center is popular with area office workers for its inexpensive cafeteria with outdoor seating. Accommodations are basic, with few frills, and in the singles you can almost reach out and touch all four walls. The cheapest doubles are actually single rooms with small, semi-double-size beds (not quite full size but larger than single/twin size). Avoid rooms on the ground floor—windows can open and in Japan there are no screens. Tucked on a side street off Gaien-Higashi Dori not far from Aoyama Dori, the center is a 15-minute walk to the nightlife of Roppongi or Akasaka, one station away by subway.

8–10–32 Akasaka, Minato-ku, Tokyo 107-0052. ℂ **03/3402-6111.** Fax 03/3402-0738. www.asiacenter.or.jp. 171 units. ¥7,800 – ¥9,800 ($65–$82) single; ¥11,800 – ¥13,800 ($98–$115) double; ¥15,800 ($132) twin; ¥17,800 – ¥19,800 ($146–$165) triple. AE, MC, V. Station: Aoyama-Itchome (exit 4, 5 min.) or Nogizaka (exit 3, 5 min.). **Amenities:** Restaurant; coin-op washers and dryers. *In room:* A/C, TV w/cable and pay movies, high-speed dataport (not all rooms), fridge, hair dryer.

SHINAGAWA

Family Inn Fifty's   Despite its catchy name, little English is spoken at this wannabe American 1950s-style motel. Opened in 2000, it sports red bar stools in its lobby and photos of Marilyn Monroe and other American icons in the rooms. Otherwise, these are no-nonsense, cheerful accommodations, offering identical small rooms with one double bed, a sofa bed, and a tiled bathroom but no closet. A machine handles check-in (you'll need a credit card; the front desk staff will guide you through the process). And you'll save ¥1,000 ($8.35) per night on the rates below if you book your reservation online. If you want a smoking room, you'll pay ¥1,000 ($8.35) more than the quoted rates; you even pay extra for slippers here. Still, there aren't many places this cheap, this straightforward, and this streamlined in Japan. A motel chain in the making?

1–3–25 Osaki, Shinagawa-ku, Tokyo 141-0032. ℂ **03/3490-0050.** www.fiftys.com. 50 units. ¥6,000 ($50) single; ¥9,000 ($75) twin; ¥10,000 ($83) triple. Rates include continental breakfast. MC, V. Station: Osaki (2 min.). From the east exit, turn left and take the stairs or elevator to ground level, cross under the highway, and then turn left. **Amenities:** Internet computer in the lobby (fee: ¥500/$4.15) for 2 hr.); nonsmoking rooms. *In room:* A/C, TV.

Keihin Hotel   Established in 1871, the Keihin is the oldest hotel in Shina-gawa, and with the opening of much fancier luxury hotels, is about a century away from being the best hotel in the neighborhood. Although the present brick building, dating from the 1930s and updated in the 1960s, doesn't have any of the graceful ambience you might wish for in a hotel this age, it does possess a certain charm, and the staff is friendly and accommodating, happy to see the occasional foreign guest. Rooms tend to be dark and gloomy—especially the single rooms, which are tiny and may face another building. The three Japanese-style rooms, in contrast, are simple but nice. Rooms facing the front are plagued by traffic noise. Still, the hotel's location across from Shinagawa Station, served by the Yamanote Line, by commuter trains to Kamakura, and by Shinkansen bullet train, makes it convenient for sightseeing.

4–10–20 Takanawa, Minato-ku, Tokyo 108-0074. ℂ 03/3449-5711. Fax 03/3441-7230. www.keihin-hotel. co.jp. 52 units. ¥8,000 – ¥8,500 ($67–$71) single; ¥13,500 – ¥14,000 ($112–$117) double; ¥13,000 ($108) twin. Japanese-style room ¥12,000 ($100) single; ¥16,500 ($138) double. AE, DC, MC, V. Station: Shinagawa (1 min.). Across the street from the Takanawa (west) exit. **Amenities:** 5 restaurants; same-day laundry/dry-cleaning service. In room: A/C, TV, fridge, hot-water pot with tea.

Toyoko Inn Shinagawa-Eki Takanawaguchi ⭐ *Value*   I like this hotel chain for its clean functional rooms, complimentary breakfast of coffee and pastries served in the lobby, free use of dataports (and for those who don't have their own laptop, free use of a computer in the lobby), and complimentary movies (unfortunately in Japanese only). Rooms are mostly singles and doubles, but the 25 twin rooms feature beds perpendicular to one another rather than crowded side-by-side, a plus for people who like traveling together but don't necessarily want to be *that* close.

4–23–2 Takanawa, Minato-ku, Tokyo 108-0074. ℂ 03/3280-1045. Fax 03/3280-1046. www.toyoko-inn. co.jp. 181 units. ¥6,800 ($57) single; ¥8,800 ($73) double; ¥9,800 ($82) twin. Rates include continental break-fast. AE, DC, MC, V. Station: Shinagawa (3 min.). From JR Station's Takanawa (west) exit, turn left. **Amenities:** Computer with Internet access free for hotel guests; laundry/dry-cleaning service; nonsmoking rooms. In room: A/C, TV w/free movies, dataport, fridge, hot-water pot with tea, hair dryer.

IKEBUKURO

Kimi Ryokan ⭐   This has long been a Tokyo favorite for inexpensive Japanese-style lodging. Spotlessly clean and with such Japanese touches as sliding screens, flower arrangements in public spaces, and traditional Japanese music playing softly in the hallways, it caters almost exclusively to foreigners (mostly 20-somethings) and is so popular there's sometimes a waiting list. A bulletin board lists rental apartments and job opportunities (primarily teaching English); a lounge with cable TV is a favorite hangout and a good place to network with other travelers. Rooms are Japanese style, with singles and the cheapest doubles the size of 4½ tatami mats, and the larger doubles the size of six tatami mats (a single tatami measures 1m by 1.8m/3 ft. by 6 ft.). Note that there's a 1am curfew.

2–36–8 Ikebukuro, Toshima-ku, Tokyo 171-0014. ℂ 03/3971-3766. Fax: 03/3987-1326. www.kimi-ryokan. jp. 38 units (none with bathroom). ¥4,500 ($37) single; ¥6,500 – ¥7,500 ($54–$62) double. Rates include tax. No credit cards. Station: Ikebukuro (west exit, 5 min.). The police station (take the west exit from Ikebukuro Station and turn right) has maps that will guide you to Kimi. In room: A/C.

5

Where to Dine

From stand-up noodle shops and pizzerias to exclusive kaiseki restaurants and sushi bars, restaurants in Tokyo number at least 80,000—which gives you some idea of how fond the Japanese are of eating out. In a city where apartments are so small and cramped that entertaining at home is almost unheard of, restaurants serve as places for socializing, meeting friends, and wooing business associates—as well as great excuses for drinking a lot of beer, sake, and whiskey.

1 How to Dine in Tokyo Without Spending a Fortune

Even with Japan's economy today, Tokyo is still an extremely expensive city. During your first few days here, money will seem to flow out of your pockets like water. (Many people become convinced they must have lost some of it somehow.) Here are some invaluable dining tips on getting the most for your money.

SET LUNCHES I know people in Tokyo who claim they haven't cooked in years—and they're not millionaires. They simply take advantage of one of the best deals in Tokyo—the fixed-price lunch, usually available from 11am to 2pm. Called a *teishoku* in a Japanese restaurant, a fixed-price meal is likely to include a soup, a main dish such as tempura or whatever the restaurant specializes in, pickled vegetables, rice, and tea. In restaurants serving Western food, the fixed-price lunch is variously referred to as a set lunch, *seto coursu,* or simply *coursu,* and usually includes an appetizer, a main course with one or two side dishes, coffee or tea, and sometimes dessert. Even restaurants listed under **very expensive** (where you'd otherwise spend at least ¥12,000/$100 or more for dinner, excluding drinks) and **expensive** (where you can expect to pay ¥8,000–¥12,000/ $67–$100 for dinner) usually offer set-lunch menus, allowing you to dine in style at very reasonable prices. To keep costs down, therefore, try having your biggest meal at lunch, avoiding, if possible, the noon-to-1pm weekday crush when Tokyo's army of office workers floods area restaurants. Since the Japanese tend to order fixed-price meals rather than a la carte, set dinners are also usually available (though they're not as cheap as set lunches). All-you-can-eat buffets (called *viking* in Japanese; I suspect it derives from the Scandinavian "smorgasbord"), offered by many hotel restaurants, are also bargain meals for hearty appetites.

So many of Tokyo's good restaurants fall into the **moderate** category that it's tempting simply to eat your way through the city—and the range of cuisines is so great you could eat something different at each meal. A dinner in this category will average ¥4,000 to ¥8,000 ($33–$67). Lunch is likely to cost half as much.

Many of Tokyo's most colorful, noisy, and popular restaurants fall into the **inexpensive** category, where meals usually go for less than ¥4,000 ($33); many offer meals for less than ¥2,000 ($17) and lunches for ¥1,000 ($8.35) or less. The city's huge working population heads to these places to catch a quick lunch or socialize with friends after hours.

Notes on Dining

The restaurants listed below are organized first by neighborhood, then by price category.

- Note that a **5% consumption tax** will be added to restaurant bills. In addition, many first-class restaurants, as well as hotel restaurants, will add a **10% to 15% service charge.** Unless otherwise stated, the prices given do not include the extra tax and service charge.
- **Restaurants that have no signs in English letters are preceded by a numbered icon, which is keyed to a list of** *kanji* **(Japanese writing symbols) in appendix C. See p. 292.**
- Finally, keep in mind that the **last order** is taken at least 30 minutes before the restaurant's actual closing time, sometimes even an hour before closing at the more exclusive restaurants.

COFFEE & BREAKFAST   Since prices are markedly different here (steeper), a bit of readjustment in thinking and habits is necessary. Coffee, for example, is something of a luxury, and some Japanese are astonished at the thought of drinking four or five cups a day. Traditional coffee shops (as opposed to imports like Starbucks) offer what's called "morning service" until 10 or 11am; it generally consists of a cup of coffee, a small salad, a boiled egg, and the thickest slice of toast you've ever seen for about ¥600 ($5). That's a real bargain when you consider that just one cup of coffee can cost ¥250 to ¥500 ($2.10–$4.15), depending on where you order it (with the exception of some hotel breakfast buffets, there's no such thing as the bottomless cup in Japan). For a coffee break later in the day, look for an inexpensive chain such as Doutour, Excelsior, or Pronto. Starbucks has also conquered Japan, with more than 400 branches throughout the country (and probably a good deal more by the time you read this); it charges ¥280 ($2.35) for a short to ¥370 ($3.10) for a grande caffe latte (per company policy, smoking is banned).

If you're on a tight budget, avoid eating breakfast at your hotel—after a week of buffet breakfasts consisting of scrambled eggs, processed ham, and lettuce, you'll probably tire of them anyway.

CHEAP EATS   Inexpensive restaurants can be found in department stores (often one whole floor will be devoted to restaurants, most with plastic food displays), underground shopping arcades, and nightlife districts, and in and around train and subway stations. Look for **yakitori-ya** (evening drinking establishments that also sell skewered meats and vegetables), **noodle** and **ramen shops, coffee shops** (which often offer inexpensive Western snacks and sandwiches), and **conveyor-belt sushi bars** where you reach out and take the plates that interest you. Tokyo also has American fast-food chains, such as McDonald's (where Big Macs cost about ¥250/$2.10 and tofu sandwiches ¥230/$1.90), Wendy's, and KFC, as well as Japanese chains—Lotteria, Moos Burger, Freshness Burger, and First Kitchen among them—that sell hamburgers and french fries.

In the past few years, a number of excellent yet inexpensive **French bistros** and **Italian trattorie** have burst onto the culinary scene. **Ethnic restaurants,** particularly those serving Indian, Chinese, and other Asian cuisines, are also plentiful and usually inexpensive. **Hotel restaurants** are good bargains for inexpensive set lunches and buffets. Finally, remember to check the nightlife section in chapter 9 for suggestions on **inexpensive drinking places** that serve food.

PREPARED FOODS You can save even more money by avoiding restaurants altogether. There are all kinds of prepared foods you can buy; some are even complete meals, perfect for picnics in the park or right in your hotel room.

Perhaps the best known is the **obento,** or box lunch, commonly sold in major train stations and on train-station platforms, in food sections of department stores, and at counter windows of tiny shops throughout Tokyo. Costing usually between ¥800 and ¥1,500 ($6.65–$13), the basic obento contains a piece of meat (generally fish or chicken), various side dishes, rice, and pickled vegetables. Sushi box lunches are also available.

My favorite places to shop for prepared foods are **department stores.** Located in basements, these food and produce sections hark back to Japanese markets of yore, with vendors yelling out their wares and crowds of housewives deciding on the evening's dinner. Different counters specialize in different items—tempura, yakitori, eel, Japanese pickles, cooked fish, sushi, salads, vegetables, and desserts. Almost the entire spectrum of Japanese cuisine is available, and numerous samples are available (some travelers have been known to "dine" in department-store basements for free). What I love about buying my dinner in a department store is that I can compose my own meal exactly as I wish—perhaps some sushi, some mountain vegetables, boiled soybeans, maybe even Chinese food—in combinations never available in most restaurants. There are also counters selling obento box meals. In any case, you can eat for less than ¥1,200 ($10), and there's nothing like milling with Japanese housewives to make you feel like one of the locals. Though not as colorful, 24-hour convenience stores also sell packaged foods, including sandwiches and obento.

Street-side stalls, called **yatai,** are also good sources of inexpensive meals. These restaurants-on-wheels sell a variety of foods, including *oden* (fish cakes), *yakitori* (skewered barbecued chicken), and *yakisoba* (fried noodles), as well as sake and beer. They appear mostly at night, illuminated by a single lantern or a string of lights, and many have a counter with stools as well, protected in winter by a wall of tarp. These can be great places for rubbing elbows with the locals. Sadly, traditional pushcarts are slowly being replaced by motorized vans, which are not nearly as romantic and don't offer seating.

2 Tips on Dining, Japanese Style

Whenever I leave Japan, it's the food I miss the most. Sure, there are sushi bars and other Japanese specialty restaurants in major cities elsewhere, but they don't offer nearly the variety available in Japan (and they often aren't nearly as good). Just as America has more to offer than hamburgers and steaks, Japan has more than sushi and teppanyaki. For both the gourmet and the uninitiated, Tokyo is a treasure trove of culinary surprises.

JAPANESE CUISINE

Altogether, there are more than a dozen different and distinct types of Japanese cuisine, plus countless regional specialties. A good deal of what you eat may be completely new to you, as well as completely unidentifiable. No need to worry—often the Japanese themselves don't even know what they're eating, so varied and so wide is the range of available edibles. The rule is simply to enjoy, and enjoyment begins even before you raise your chopsticks to your mouth.

To the Japanese, presentation of food is as important as the food itself, and dishes are designed to appeal to the eye as well as to the palate. In contrast to the

American way of piling as much food as possible onto a single plate, the Japanese often use many small plates, each arranged artfully with bite-size morsels of food. After you've seen what can be done with maple leaves, flowers, bits of bamboo, and even pebbles to enhance the appearance of food, your relationship with what you eat may change forever.

Below are explanations of some of the most common types of Japanese cuisine. Generally, only one type of cuisine is served in a given restaurant—for example, only raw seafood is served in a sushi bar, while tempura is served at a tempura counter. There are some exceptions to this, especially in regards to raw fish, which is served as an appetizer in many restaurants. In addition, some of Japan's drinking establishments (called *izakaya* or *nomiya*) offer a wide range of foods, from soups to sushi to skewered pieces of chicken known as yakitori. Japanese restaurants in hotels may also offer great variety.

For a quick rundown of individual dishes, refer to the food terms in appendix B.

FUGU   Known as blowfish, puffer fish, or globefish in English, fugu is one of the most exotic and adventurous foods in Japan—if it's not prepared properly, it means almost certain death for the consumer! In the past decade or so, some 50 people in Japan have died from fugu poisoning, usually because they tried preparing it at home. The ovaries and intestines of the fugu are deadly and must be entirely removed without being punctured. So why eat fugu if it can kill you? Well, for one thing, it's delicious, and for another, fugu chefs are strictly licensed by the government and greatly skilled in preparing fugu dishes. You can order fugu raw *(fugu-sashi)*, sliced paper-thin and dipped into soy sauce with bitter orange and chives; in a stew *(fugu-chiri)* cooked with vegetables at your table; or in a rice porridge *(fugu-zosui)*. The season for fresh fugu is October or November through March, but some restaurants serve it throughout the year.

KAISEKI   The king of Japanese cuisine, kaiseki is the epitome of delicately and exquisitely arranged food, the ultimate in aesthetic appeal. It's also among the most expensive meals you'll ever find. A kaiseki dinner can cost ¥25,000 ($208) or more per person; some restaurants, however, do offer more affordable mini-kaiseki courses. In addition, the better *ryokan* (Japanese inns) serve kaiseki, a reason for their high cost. Kaiseki, which is not a specific dish but rather a complete meal, is expensive because much time and skill are involved in preparing each of the many dishes, with the ingredients cooked to preserve natural flavors. Even the plates are chosen with great care to enhance the color, texture, and shape of each piece of food.

Kaiseki cuisine, both in selection of food and presentation, is based on the four seasons. The kaiseki gourmet can tell what time of year it is just by looking at a meal.

A kaiseki meal is usually a lengthy affair, with various dishes appearing in set order. First come the appetizer, clear broth, and one uncooked dish. These are followed by boiled, broiled, fried, steamed, heated, and vinegared dishes, which are finally followed by another soup, rice, pickled vegetables, and fruit. Although

Impressions
There is a saying that the Chinese eat with their stomachs and the Japanese with their eyes.
—Bernard Leach, *A Potter In Japan* (1960)

meals vary greatly depending on what's fresh, common dishes include some type of sashimi, tempura, cooked seasonal fish, and an array of bite-size pieces of various vegetables. Since kaiseki is always a set meal, there's no problem in ordering; let your budget be your guide.

KUSHIAGE   Kushiage foods are breaded and deep-fried on skewers and include chicken, beef, seafood, and lots of seasonal vegetables (snow peas, green peppers, gingko nuts, lotus roots, and the like). They're served with a slice of lemon and usually a specialty sauce. The result is delicious, and I highly recommend trying it. Ordering the set meal is easiest, and what you get may be determined by both the chef and the season. A restaurant serving kushiage, called a *kushiage-ya,* is often open only for dinner.

OKONOMIYAKI   Okonomiyaki, which originated in Osaka after World War II and literally means "as you like it," is often referred to as Japanese pizza. To me, it's more like a pancake to which meat or fish, shredded cabbage, and vegetables are added, topped with a thick Worcestershire sauce. Since it's a popular offering of street vendors, restaurants specializing in this type of cuisine are very reasonably priced. At some places the cook makes it for you, but at other places it's do-it-yourself, which can be quite fun if you're with a group. *Yakisoba* (fried Chinese noodles and cabbage) are also usually on offer at okonomiyaki restaurants.

RICE   As in other Asian countries, rice has been a Japanese staple for about 2,000 years. In fact, rice is so important to the Japanese diet that *gohan* means both "rice" and "meal." It's eaten plain—no salt, no butter, no soy sauce (it's considered rather uncouth to dump a lot of sauces in your rice)—and is sticky, making it easier to pick up with chopsticks. In the old days, not everyone could afford the expensive white kind of rice, which was grown primarily to pay taxes or rent to the feudal lord; the peasants had to be satisfied with a mixture of brown rice, millet, and greens. Today, some Japanese still eat rice three times a day, although they're now just as apt to have bread and coffee for breakfast.

ROBATAYAKI   Robatayaki refers to restaurants in which seafood and vegetables are cooked over an open charcoal grill. In the olden days, an open fireplace *(robata)* in the middle of an old Japanese house was the center of activity for cooking, eating, socializing, and simply keeping warm. Therefore, today's robatayaki restaurants are like nostalgia trips into Japan's past and are often decorated in rustic farmhouse style, with staff dressed in traditional clothing. Robatayaki restaurants, usually open only in the evening, are popular among office workers for both eating and drinking.

There's no special menu in a robatayaki restaurant—rather, it includes just about everything eaten in Japan. The difference is that most of the food will be grilled. Favorites of mine include gingko nuts *(ginnan),* asparagus wrapped in bacon (asparagus bacon), green peppers *(piman),* mushrooms (various kinds), potatoes *(jagabataa),* and just about any kind of fish. You can also usually get skewers of beef or chicken as well as a stew of meat and potatoes *(nikujaga)*—delicious in cold winter months. Since ordering is generally a la carte, you'll just have to look and point.

SASHIMI & SUSHI   It's estimated that the average Japanese eats 38 kilograms (83½ lb.) of seafood a year—that's six times the average American consumption. Although this seafood may be served in any number of ways, from grilled to boiled, a great deal of it is eaten raw.

Sashimi is raw seafood, usually served as an appetizer and eaten alone (that is, without rice). If you've never tried it, a good choice to start out with is *maguro,* or lean tuna, which doesn't taste fishy at all and is so delicate in texture that it almost melts in your mouth. The way to eat sashimi is to first put *wasabi* (pungent green horseradish) into a small dish of soy sauce, and then dip the raw fish in the sauce using your chopsticks.

Sushi, which is raw fish with vinegared rice, comes in many varieties. The best known is *nigiri-zushi:* raw fish, seafood, or vegetables placed on top of vinegared rice with just a touch of wasabi. It's also dipped in soy sauce. Use chopsticks or your fingers to eat sushi; remember, you're supposed to eat each piece in one bite—quite a mouthful, but about the only way to keep it from falling apart. Another trick is to turn it upside down when you dip it in the sauce, to keep the rice from crumbling.

Also popular is *maki-zushi,* which consists of seafood, vegetables, or pickles rolled with rice inside a sheet of nori seaweed. *Inari-zushi* is vinegared rice and chopped vegetables inside a pouch of fried tofu bean curd.

Typical sushi includes tuna *(maguro),* flounder *(hirame),* sea bream *(tai),* squid *(ika),* octopus *(tako),* shrimp *(ebi),* sea eel *(anago),* and omelet *(tamago).* Ordering is easy because you usually sit at a counter, where you can see all the food in a refrigerated glass case in front of you. You also get to see the sushi chefs at work. The typical meal begins with sashimi and is followed by sushi, but if you don't want to order separately, there are always various set courses *(seto).*

By the way, the least expensive sushi is **chiraishi,** which is a selection of fish, seafood, and usually tamago on a large flat bowl of rice. Because you get more rice, those of you with bigger appetites may want to order chiraishi. Another way to enjoy sushi without spending a fortune is to eat at a **kaiten sushi** shop, in which plates of sushi circulate on a conveyor belt on the counter—customers reach for the dishes they want and pay for the number they take.

SHABU-SHABU & SUKIYAKI   Until about a hundred years ago, the Japanese could think of nothing so disgusting as eating the flesh of animals (fish was okay). Considered unclean by Buddhists, meat consumption was banned by the emperor in the 7th century. It wasn't until a little more than a century ago, when Emperor Meiji himself announced his intention to eat meat, that the Japanese accepted the idea. Today, the Japanese have become skilled in preparing a number of beef dishes.

Sukiyaki is among Japan's best-known beef dishes and is preferred by many Westerners. Sukiyaki is thinly sliced beef cooked at the table in a broth of soy sauce, stock, and sake, with scallions, spinach, mushrooms, tofu, bamboo shoots, and other vegetables. All diners serve themselves from the simmering pot and then dip their morsels into their own bowl of raw egg. You can skip the raw egg if you want (most Westerners do), but it adds to the taste and also cools the food down enough so that it doesn't burn your tongue.

Shabu-shabu is also prepared at your table and consists of thinly sliced beef cooked in a broth with vegetables, in a kind of Japanese fondue. (It's named for the swishing sound the beef supposedly makes when cooking.) The main difference between the two dishes is the broth: Whereas in sukiyaki it consists of stock flavored with soy sauce and sake and is slightly sweet, in shabu-shabu it's relatively clear and has little taste of its own. The pots used are also different.

Using their chopsticks, shabu-shabu diners hold pieces of meat in the watery broth until they're cooked. This usually takes only a few seconds. Vegetables are left in longer, to swim around until fished out. For dipping, there's either sesame sauce with diced green onions or a more bitter fish stock sauce. Restaurants serving sukiyaki usually serve shabu-shabu as well.

SOBA & UDON NOODLES   The Japanese love eating noodles, and I suspect at least part of the joy comes from the way they eat them—they slurp, sucking in the noodles with gravity-defying speed. What's more, slurping noodles is considered proper etiquette. Fearing that it would stick with me forever, however, I've neglected to learn the technique. Places serving noodles range from stand-up eateries—often found at train and subway stations and the ultimate in fast food—to more refined noodle restaurants with tatami seating. Regardless of where you eat them, noodles are among the least expensive dishes in Japan.

There are many different kinds of noodles—some are eaten plain, some are eaten in combination with other foods such as shrimp tempura; some are served hot, others are served cold. **Soba,** made from buckwheat flour, is eaten hot *(kake-soba)* or cold *(zaru-soba)*. **Udon** is a thick, white, wheat noodle originally from Osaka; it's usually served hot. **Somen** is a fine, white noodle eaten cold in the summer and dunked in a cold sauce.

TEMPURA   Today a well-known Japanese food, tempura was actually introduced by the Portuguese in the 16th century. Tempura is fish and vegetables delicately coated in a batter of egg, water, and wheat flour and then deep-fried; it's served piping hot. To eat tempura, you usually dip it in a sauce of soy, fish stock, radish *(daikon)*, and grated ginger; in some restaurants, only some salt, powdered green tea, and perhaps a lemon wedge are provided as accompaniments. Tempura specialties include eggplant *(nasu)*, mushroom *(shiitake)*, sweet potato *(satsumaimo)*, small green pepper *(shishito)*, sliced lotus root *(renkon)*, shrimp *(ebi)*, squid *(ika)*, lemon-mint leaf *(shiso)*, and many kinds of fish. Again, the easiest thing to do is to order the set meal, the teishoku.

TEPPANYAKI   A teppanyaki restaurant is a Japanese steakhouse. As in the well-known Benihana restaurants in many U.S. cities, the chef slices, dices, and cooks your meal of tenderloin or sirloin steak and vegetables on a smooth hot grill right in front of you—though with much less fanfare than in the U.S. Because beef is relatively new in Japanese cooking, some people categorize teppanyaki restaurants as "Western." However, I consider this style of cooking and presentation unique, and throughout this book I refer to such restaurants as Japanese. Teppanyaki restaurants tend to be expensive, simply because of the price of beef in Japan, with Kobe beef the most prized.

TONKATSU   Tonkatsu is the Japanese word for "pork cutlet," made by dredging pork in wheat flour, moistening it with egg and water, dipping it in breadcrumbs, and deep-frying it in vegetable oil. Since restaurants serving tonkatsu are generally inexpensive, they're popular with office workers and families. The easiest order is the teishoku, which usually features either pork filet *(hirekatsu)* or pork loin *(rosukatsu)*. In any case, your tonkatsu is served on a bed of shredded cabbage, and one or two sauces will be at your table—a Worcestershire sauce and perhaps a specialty sauce. If you order the teishoku, it will come with rice, miso soup, and shredded cabbage.

UNAGI   I'll bet that if you eat unagi without knowing what it is, you'll find it very tasty—and you'll probably be very surprised to learn you've just eaten eel. Popular as a health food because of its high vitamin A content, eel is supposed to help you fight fatigue during hot summer months but is eaten year-round. Broiled eel *(kabayaki)* is prepared by grilling filet strips over a charcoal fire; the eel is repeatedly dipped in a sweetened barbecue soy sauce while cooking. A favorite way to eat broiled eel is on top of rice, in which case it's called *unaju* or *unagi donburi*. Do yourself a favor and try it.

YAKITORI   Yakitori is chunks of chicken or chicken parts basted in a sweet soy sauce and grilled over a charcoal fire on thin skewers. Places that specialize in yakitori (*yakitori-ya,* often identifiable by a red paper lantern outside the front door) are technically not restaurants but drinking establishments; they usually don't open until 5 or 6pm. Most yakitori-ya are popular with workers as inexpensive places to drink, eat, and be merry.

The cheapest way to dine on yakitori is to order a set course, which will often include various parts of the chicken, including the skin, heart, and liver. If this is not to your taste, you may wish to order a la carte, which is more expensive but gets you exactly what you want. In addition to chicken, other skewered, charcoaled delicacies are usually offered (called *kushi-yaki*). If you're ordering by the stick, you might want to try chicken breast *(sasami),* chicken meatballs *(tsukune),* green peppers *(piman),* chicken and leeks *(negima),* mushrooms *(shiitake),* or gingko nuts *(ginnan).*

OTHER CUISINES   During your dining expeditions you might also run into these types of Japanese cuisine: **Kamameshi** is a rice casserole, served in individual-size cast-iron pots, with different kinds of toppings that might include seafood, meat, or vegetables. **Donburi** is also a rice dish, topped with tempura, eggs, and meat like chicken or pork. **Nabe,** a stew cooked in an earthenware pot at your table, consists of chicken, beef, pork, or seafood; noodles; and vegetables. **Oden** is a broth with fish cakes, tofu, eggs, and vegetables, served with hot mustard. If a restaurant advertises that it specializes in **Kyodo-Ryori,** it serves local specialties for which the region is famous and is often very rustic in decor. **Shojin Ryori** is a vegetarian meal, created centuries ago to serve the needs of Zen Buddhist priests and pilgrims. In recent years, the big Tokyo craze has been restaurants serving **crossover fusion cuisine**—creative dishes inspired by ingredients from both sides of the Pacific Rim.

Although technically Chinese fast-food restaurants, **ramen shops** are a big part of inexpensive dining in Japan. Serving what I consider to be generic Chinese noodles, soups, and other dishes, ramen shops can be found everywhere; they're easily recognizable by red signs, flashing lights, and quite often pictures of dishes displayed beside the front door. Many are stand-up affairs—just a high counter to rest your bowl on. In addition to ramen (noodle and vegetable soup), you can also get such items as **yakisoba** (fried noodles) or—my favorite—**gyoza** (fried pork dumplings). What these places lack in atmosphere is made up for by cost: Most dishes average about ¥600 ($5), making them one of the cheapest places in Japan for a quick meal.

JAPANESE DRINKS

All Japanese restaurants serve complimentary Japanese **green tea** with meals. If that's a little too weak for your taste, you may want to try **sake** (pronounced *sah-*kay), also called *Nihon-shu,* an alcoholic beverage made from rice and served either hot or cold. It goes well with most forms of Japanese cuisine. Produced since about the 3rd century, sake varies by region, production method, alcoholic content, color, aroma, and taste. Altogether, there are more than 1,800 sake brewers in Japan producing about 10,000 varieties of sake. Miyabi is a prized classic sake; other popular brands are Gekkeikan, Koshinokanbai, Hakutsuru (meaning "white crane"), and Ozeki.

Japanese **beer** is also very popular. The biggest sellers are Kirin, Sapporo, Asahi, and Suntory, each with its own bewildering variety of brews. There are also many microbreweries. Businessmen are fond of **whiskey,** which they usually drink with ice and water. Popular in recent years is **shochu,** an alcoholic beverage generally made from rice but sometimes from wheat, sweet potatoes, or sugar cane. It used to be considered a drink of the lower classes, but sales have increased so much that it's threatening the sake and whiskey businesses. A clear liquid, comparable, perhaps, to vodka, it can be consumed straight but is often combined with soda water in a drink called *chu-hai;* but watch out—the stuff can be deadly. **Wine,** usually available only at restaurants serving Western food, has gained in popularity in recent years, with both domestic and imported brands available. Although **cocktails** are available in discos, hotel lounges, and fancier bars at rather inflated prices, most Japanese stick with beer, sake, or whiskey.

RESTAURANT ESSENTIALS

ORDERING   The biggest problem facing the hungry foreigner in Tokyo is ordering a meal in a restaurant without an English-language menu. This book alleviates the problem to a large extent by giving sample dishes and prices for recommended restaurants. I've also noted which restaurants have English-language menus.

One aid to simplified ordering is the common use of **plastic food models** in glass display cases either outside or just inside the front door of many restaurants. Sushi, tempura, daily specials, spaghetti—they're all there in mouthwatering plastic replicas, along with the corresponding prices. Decide what you want and point it out to your waiter.

Unfortunately, not all restaurants in Japan have plastic display cases, especially the more exclusive or traditional ones. In fact, you'll miss a lot of Tokyo's best cuisine if you restrict yourself to eating only at those with displays. If there's no display from which to choose, look at what people around you are eating and order what looks best. An alternative is to order the *teishoku,* or daily special meal (also called "set course" or simply "course," especially in restaurants serving Western food); these are fixed-price meals that consist of a main dish and several side dishes, often including soup, rice, and Japanese pickles. Although most restaurants have special set courses for dinner as well, lunch is the usual time for the teishoku, generally from about 11 or 11:30am to about 2pm.

HOURS   Restaurants are usually open from about 11am to 10 or 11pm. Of course, some establishments close earlier, while others stay open past midnight; many close for a few hours in the afternoon as well. Try to avoid the lunchtime rush, which is from noon to 1pm.

Keep in mind that the closing time posted for most restaurants is exactly that—everyone is expected to pay his or her bill and leave. A general rule of thumb is that the last order is taken at least a half-hour before closing time, sometimes an hour or more for kaiseki restaurants. To be on the safe side, therefore, try to arrive at least an hour before closing time so that you have time to relax and enjoy your meal.

DINING PROCEDURE & ETIQUETTE

UPON ARRIVAL   As soon as you're seated in a Japanese restaurant (that is, a restaurant serving Japanese food), you'll be given a wet towel, which will be steaming hot in winter or pleasantly cool in summer. Called an **oshibori,** it's for wiping your hands. In all but the fanciest restaurants, men can get away with wiping their faces as well, but women are not supposed to (I ignore this if it's hot and humid outside). The oshibori is a great custom, one you'll wish would be adopted back home. Sadly, some cheaper Japanese restaurants now resort to a paper towel wrapped in plastic, which isn't nearly the same. Oshibori are generally not provided in Western restaurants.

CHOPSTICKS   The next thing you'll probably be confronted with is chopsticks. The proper way to use a pair is to place the first chopstick between the base of the thumb and the top of the ring finger (this chopstick remains stationary), and the second one between the top of the thumb and the middle and index fingers (this 2nd chopstick is the one you move to pick up food). The best way to learn to use chopsticks is to let a Japanese person show you. It's not difficult, but if you're having trouble, some restaurants might have forks as well. How proficiently foreigners handle chopsticks is a matter of great curiosity for the Japanese, and they're surprised if you know how to use them; even if you were to live in Japan for 20 years, you would never stop receiving compliments on how talented you are with chopsticks.

As for etiquette involving chopsticks, if you're taking something from a communal bowl or tray, you're supposed to turn your chopsticks upside down and use the part that hasn't been in your mouth. After transferring the food to your plate, you turn the chopsticks back to their proper position. The exceptions are shabu-shabu and sukiyaki. Never stick your chopsticks down vertically into your bowl of rice and leave them there—that is done only when a person has died. Also, don't pass anything from your chopsticks to another person's chopsticks, as that's done only to pass the bones of the cremated.

EATING SOUP   If you're eating soup, you won't use a spoon. Rather, you'll pick up the bowl and drink from it. Use your chopsticks to fish out larger morsels of food. It's considered in good taste to slurp with gusto, especially if you're eating noodles. Noodle shops in Japan are always well orchestrated with slurps and smacks.

DRINKING   If you're drinking in Japan, the main thing to remember is that you never pour your own glass. Bottles of beer are so large that people often share one. The rule is that, in turn, one person pours for everyone else in the group, so be sure to hold up your glass when someone is pouring for you. Only as the night progresses do the Japanese get sloppy about this rule. It took me a while to figure this out, but if no one notices your empty glass, the best thing to do is to pour everyone else a drink so that someone will pour yours. If someone wants to pour you a drink and your glass is full, the proper thing to do is to take a few gulps so that he or she can fill your glass. Because each person is continually filling everyone else's glass, you never know exactly how much you've had to drink, which (depending on how you look at it) is either very good or very bad.

PAYING THE BILL   If you go out with a group of friends (not as a visiting guest of honor and not with business associates), it's customary to split the dinner bill equally, even if you all ordered different things. This makes it difficult if you're trying to spend wisely, especially if others had a lot more to eat and drink. But even foreigners living in Japan adopt the practice of splitting the bill; it certainly makes figuring everyone's share easier, especially since there's no tipping in Japan.

OTHER ETIQUETTE TIPS   It's considered bad manners to walk down the street in Japan eating or drinking (except at a festival). You'll notice that if a Japanese buys a drink from a vending machine, he'll stand there, gulp it down, and throw away the container before moving on. To the chagrin of the elders, young Japanese sometimes ignore this rule.

3 Restaurants by Cuisine

AMERICAN

Anderson (Harajuku, $, p. 135)

Bamboo Sandwich House
(Harajuku, $, p. 135)

Farm Grill (Ginza, $, p. 119)

Hamburger Inn (Roppongi, $,
p. 147)

Hard Rock Cafe (Roppongi, $,
p. 147)

Kua' Aina ✪ (Aoyama, $, p. 137)

Lunchan (Aoyama, $$, p. 134)

New York Grill ✪✪✪ (Shinjuku,
$$$$, p. 128)

Sonoma (Shibuya, $, p. 139)

Spago ✪✪ (Roppongi, $$, p. 145)

Tony Roma's (Akasaka, Roppongi,
$, p. 152)

Tribecks Restaurant & Bar
(Shinjuku, $$, p. 129)

Wolfgang Puck Bar & Grill ✪✪
(Roppongi, $$, p. 145)

CHINESE

Blue Sky (Akasaka, $$, p. 151)

Chinese Restaurant AOI (Aoyama,
$, p. 135)

Daini's Table ✪✪ (Aoyama, $$,
p. 132)

Din Tai Fung (Shinjuku, $, p. 130)

Hong Kong Garden (Nishi Azabu,
$, p. 147)

Toriyoshi (Harajuku, $, p. 139)

COFFEE/TEA/DESSERTS

Aux Bacchanales (Harajuku, $$,
p. 132)

Tatsutano ✪ (Ginza, $, p. 121)

DOJO

Komagata Dojo ✪ (Asakusa, $$,
p. 124)

DOMBURI/KAMAMESHI
(RICE CASSEROLES)

Hayashi ✪✪✪ (Akasaka, $, p. 150)

Tatsutano ✪ (Ginza, $, p. 121)

Torigin (Roppongi, $, p. 150)

EEL

Izu'ei (Ueno, $$, p. 127)

Kandagawa ✪ (Kanda, $$, p. 153)

FRENCH

Aux Amis Tokyo ✪ (Around
Tokyo Station, $$$, p. 121)

Aux Bacchanales (Harajuku, $$,
p. 132)

Cafe Creperie Le Bretagne
(Aoyama, $, p. 135)

Cafe Francais ✪ (Ebisu, $$,
p. 140)

Chez Figaro (Nishi Azabu, $$,
p. 144)

Kana Uni ✪ (Akasaka, $$$,
p. 151)

La Tour d'Argent ✪✪ (Akasaka,
$$$$, p. 150)

Le Gaulois (Aoyama, $$, p. 134)

L'Osier ✪✪✪ (Ginza, $$$$,
p. 115)

Nagase ✪✪ (Harajuku, $, p. 138)

Ueno Seiyoken Grill ✪ (Ueno,
$$$, p. 127)

FUGU (BLOWFISH)

Tentake (Tsukiji, $$, p. 123)

GYOZA

Harajuku Gyoza Lou ✪
(Harajuku, $, p. 136)

INDIAN

Mantra (Ueno, $, p. 127)

Moti ✪ (Roppongi, Akasaka, $,
p. 149)

INTERNATIONAL

Central Mikuni's ✪ (Around
Tokyo Station, $$, p. 121)

Imperial Viking ✪, Hibiya, $$,
p. 116)

Kitchen Five ✪ (Roppongi, $,
p. 148)

Las Chicas ✪ (Aoyama, $, p. 137)

Pariya ✪ (Aoyama, $, p. 138)

Sunset Beach Brewing Company
(Odaiba, $, p. 154)

Tableaux ✪✪ (Daikanyama, $$$,
p. 153)

Taimeikan (Nihombashi, $,
p. 122)

The Terrace Restaurant at
  Hanezawa Garden ★★ (Ebisu,
  $$, p. 140)
Toriyoshi (Harajuku, $, p. 139)
Trader Vic's ★ (Akasaka, $$$,
  p. 151)

ITALIAN
La Boheme (Ginza, Harajuku,
  Meguro, Nishi Azabu, Odaiba,
  Shibuya, $, p. 120)
La Ranarita Azumabashi ★
  (Asakusa, $$, p. 124)
Ristorante Il Bianco (Roppongi, $,
  p. 149)
Sabatini ★ (Aoyama, $$$, p. 132)
Selan (Aoyama, $$, p. 134)
Trattoria-Pizzeria Sabatini
  (Aoyama, $, p. 139)

JAPANESE (VARIED)
Central Mikuni's ★ (Around
  Tokyo Station, $$, p. 121)
daidaiya ★ (Akasaka, $$, p. 152)
Doka Doka ★ (Nishi Azabu, $$,
  p. 144)
Donto ★★ (Hibiya, Shinjuku, $$,
  p. 116)
Gonpachi ★★ (Ginza, Nishi
  Azabu, Odaiba, $ p. 120)
Hakkaku ★ (Shinjuku, $, p. 130)
Honoji ★ (Roppongi, $, p. 148)
Ichioku ★ (Roppongi, $, p. 148)
Kamiya Bar (Asakusa, $, p. 126)
Mominoki House ★ (Harajuku, $,
  p. 137)
Pariya ★ (Aoyama, $, p. 138)
Tengu (Shibuya, $, p. 140)
The Terrace Restaurant at
  Hanezawa Garden ★★(Ebisu,
  $$, p. 140)
Toriyoshi (Harajuku, $, p. 139)
Zipangu (Shimbashi, $$, p. 154)

KAISEKI
Gesshinkyo ★★ (Harajuku, $$$$,
  p. 131)
Ginza Daimasu (Ginza, $$, p. 116)
Kakiden ★★ (Shinjuku, $$$,
  p. 128)
Kappoya Yaozen ★ (Shinjuku, $$,
  p. 129)

Kisso ★★ (Roppongi, $$$, p. 144)
Kuremutsu ★ (Asakusa, $$$,
  p. 124)
Mikura (Shibuya, $$, p. 139)
Mugitoro (Asakusa, $$, p. 125)
Munakata ★ (Ginza, $$, p. 117)
Rangetsu (Ginza, $$, p. 118)
Takamura ★★★ (Roppongi, $$$$,
  p. 142)
Tamura ★ (Tsukiji, $$$, p. 122)

KUSHIYAKI
Kushi Colza ★ (Ginza, $$, p. 117)

MEXICAN
Fonda de la Madrugada (Hara-
  juku, $, p. 135)
La Fiesta (Roppongi, $, p. 149)
Sonoma (Shibuya, $, p. 139)
Zest Cantina (Ebisu, Ginza,
  Harajuku, Odaiba, Shibuya, $,
  p. 141)

NOODLES
Kanda Yabusoba ★ (Kanda, $,
  p. 154)
Namiki Yabusoba ★ (Asakusa, $,
  p. 126)

OKONOMIYAKI
Sometaro ★ (Asakusa, $, p. 126)

PACIFIC RIM/ FUSION-CROSSOVER
Casita ★★★ (Roppongi, $$,
  p. 144)
daidaiya (Akasaka, $$, p. 152)
Doka Doka (Nishi Azabu, $$,
  p. 144)
Fujimamas (Harajuku, $$, p. 132)
Ichioku (Roppongi, $, p. 148)
Kazan (Ginza, $$, p. 117)
Kihachi ★ (Ginza, $$, p. 117)
Mominoki House (Harajuku, $,
  p. 137)
Nobu ★★★ (Aoyama, $$$, p. 131)
Sonoma (Shibuya, $, p. 139)
Tribecks Restaurant & Bar ★
  (Shinjuku, $$, p. 129)
Wolfgang Puck Bar & Grill ★★
  (Roppongi, $$, p. 145)
Zipangu (Shimbashi, $$, p. 154)

PIZZA

Bellini Trattoria (Roppongi, $,
p. 146)

Shakey's (Harajuku, Shinjuku, $,
p. 131)

To the Herbs (Ginza, Harajuku, $,
p. 138)

Trattoria-Pizzeria Sabatini
(Aoyama, $, p. 139)

ROBATAYAKI (JAPANESE GRILL)

Hakkaku ✿ (Shinjuku, $, p. 130)

Hayashi ✿✿✿ (Akasaka, $$$,
p. 150)

Hayashi ✿✿ (Shinjuku, $$, p. 129)

Inakaya ✿✿ (Roppongi, $$$$,
p. 141)

Kuremutsu ✿ (Asakusa, $$$,
p. 124)

Ohmatsuya ✿✿ (Ginza, $$,
p. 118)

SHABU-SHABU

Chinya ✿ (Asakusa, $, p. 125)

Daikokuya (Shinjuku, $, p. 130)

Genkaya Shabu-Shabu Kan
(Harajuku, $, p. 136)

Mimiu (Shibuya, $$, p. 139)

Rangetsu (Ginza, $$, p. 118)

Shabusen ✿ (Akasaka, Ginza, $,
p. 120)

Zakuro ✿ (Akasaka, $$$, p. 151)

SUKIYAKI

Botan ✿ (Kanda, $$, p. 153)

Chinya ✿ (Asakusa, $, p. 125)

Daikokuya (Shinjuku, $, p. 130)

Genkaya Shabu-Shabu Kan
(Harajuku, $, p. 136)

Rangetsu (Ginza, $$, p. 118)

Zakuro ✿ (Akasaka, $$$, p. 151)

SUSHI

Bikkuri Sushi (Roppongi, $,
p. 146)

Central Mikuni's ✿ (Around
Tokyo Station, $$, p. 121)

Edogin (Tsukiji, $, p. 123)

Fukusuke (Ginza, $, p. 119)

Fukuzushi ✿✿ (Roppongi, $$$,
p. 142)

Heirokuzushi (Harajuku, $, p. 136)

Kakiya Sushi (Harajuku, $, p. 137)

Sushi Dai ✿ (Tsukiji, $, p. 123)

Sushi Sei (Ginza, $, p. 121)

Sushiko ✿✿✿ (Ginza, $$$$,
p. 115)

TEMPURA

Daikokuya (Asakusa, $, p. 126)

Ten-ichi ✿ (Akasaka, Ginza,
Hibaya, Shinjuku, $$$, p. 116)

Tsunahachi (Akasaka, Ginza,
Shinjuku, $$, p. 130)

TEPPANYAKI

Kamon ✿✿✿ (Hibiya, $$$$,
p. 115)

Sekishin Tei ✿✿ (Akasaka, $$$$,
p. 150)

THAI

Ban-Thai (Shinjuku, $$, p. 129)

Erawan ✿✿ (Roppongi, $$,
p. 145)

TONKATSU (PORK CUTLET)

Tonki ✿ (Meguro, $, p. 141)

VEGETARIAN/HEALTH FOOD

Hiroba (Aoyama, $, p. 136)

Gesshinkyo ✿✿ (Harajuku, $$$$,
p. 131)

Mominoki House ✿ (Harajuku, $,
p. 137)

WESTERN (JAPANESE VERSION)

Kamiya Bar (Asakusa, $, p. 126)

Shiseido Parlour ✿ (Ginza, $$,
p. 118)

Taimeikan (Nihombashi, $, p. 122)

YAKITORI

Atariya ✿ (Ginza, $, p. 119)

Ganchan ✿ (Roppongi, $, p. 146)

Kamakura (Roppongi, $, p. 148)

Kushi Colza ✿ (Ginza, $$, p. 117)

Tengu (Shibuya, $, p. 140)

Torigin (Roppongi, $, p. 150)

Yakitori Under the Tracks
(Ginza/Hibiya, $, p. 121)

YAM

Mugitoro (Asakusa, $$, p. 125)

4 Ginza & Hibiya

Note: To locate these restaurants, see the map on p. 72.

VERY EXPENSIVE

Kamon ✦✦✦ TEPPANYAKI   Kamon, which means "Gate of Celebration," has an interior that could be a statement on Tokyo itself—traditionally Japanese yet ever so high-tech. Located on the 17th floor of the Imperial Hotel, the restaurant offers seating at one of several large counters (some with views over Hibiya) centered around grills where expert chefs prepare excellent teppanyaki before your eyes. Japanese sirloin steaks or filets, cooked to perfection, are available, as well as seafood ranging from fresh prawns and scallops to crabmeat and fish, and seasonal vegetables. The service is, of course, imperial.

On the 17th floor of the Imperial Hotel, 1–1–1 Uchisaiwai-cho. ✆ 03/3504-1111. Reservations recommended for dinner. Set dinners ¥12,000 – ¥18,000 ($100–$150); set lunches ¥3,500 – ¥7,000 ($29–$48). AE, DC, MC, V. Daily 11:30am–2:30pm and 5:30–9:30pm. Station: Hibiya (1 min.).

L'Osier ✦✦✦ FRENCH   Chef Jacques Borie, recipient of the prestigious Meilleur Ouvrier de France award, reigns at this elegant, modern restaurant decorated with an understated Art Deco motif. Serving only 40 lucky diners, Mr. Borie and his staff of 40 are able to coddle, pamper, amaze, and seduce with excellent service and superb cuisine. Set meals start with *amuse-bouche* (literally "mouth amusers") and end with *les petit fours and café* (small cakes and coffee); in between may be such dishes as the French classic *foie gras de canard* (duck's liver), imported French sea bass with braised fennel, or roast suckling lamb. An ample wine selection, a large variety of cheeses, and a dessert trolley overflowing with some 30 temptations round out the meal. To join the politicians and other movers and shakers who flock here, reserve well in advance.

7–5–5 Ginza. ✆ 03/3571-6050. Reservations required. Main dishes ¥6,200 – ¥9,800 ($52–$82); set lunches ¥5,000 – ¥8,000 ($42–$67); set dinners ¥16,000 – ¥20,000 ($133–$167). AE, DC, MC, V. Mon–Sat noon–1:45pm and 6–9pm (closed holidays). Subway: Ginza (2 min.). On Namiki Dori.

② **Sushiko** ✦✦✦ SUSHI   If you're in pursuit of top-quality sushi, your search will eventually bring you here, considered by some to be one of the best sushi bars in town. There's no written menu, and the counter seats 11 customers only. Owned by a fourth-generation restaurateur, this establishment doesn't display its fish as most sushi bars do, but keeps it freshly refrigerated until the moment it meets the swift blade of the expert chefs. Unless you know your sushi, you're best off telling the chef how much you want to spend and letting him take it from there.

6–3–8 Ginza. ✆ 03/3571-1968. Reservations required. Meals ¥10,000 – ¥15,000 ($83–$125). AE, MC, V. Daily 11:30am–10:30pm. Station: Ginza or Hibiya (4 min.). A block east of the elevated tracks of the JR Yamanote Line, on the Ginza side on Sukiyabashi Dori.

A Note on Japanese Symbols

Many restaurants, hotels, and other establishments in Japan do not have signs giving their names in Roman (English-language) letters. As an aid to the reader, appendix C lists the Japanese symbols for all such places described in this guide. Each set of characters representing an establishment name has a number, which corresponds to the number that appears inside the box preceding the establishment's name in the text. Thus, to find the Japanese symbols for, say, **Sushiko,** refer to number 2 p. 292 in appendix C.

EXPENSIVE

Ten-ichi ✿ TEMPURA   In this restaurant, located on Namiki Dori in the heart of Ginza's nightlife, you can sit at a counter and watch the chef prepare your meal. This is the main outlet of a 70-year-old restaurant chain that helped the tempura style of cooking gain worldwide recognition by serving important foreign customers. Today Ten-ichi still has one of the best reputations in town for serving the most delicately fried foods, along with its special sauce (or, if you prefer, you can dip the morsels in lemon juice with a pinch of salt).

There are 10 Ten-ichi restaurants in Tokyo. Locations include the Ginza Sony Building at the intersection of Harumi Dori and Sotobori Dori (✆ **03/3571-3837;** station: Hibiya or Ginza); the Imperial Hotel's Tower basement (✆ **03/3503-1001;** station: Hibiya); and Isetan department store, 3–14–1 Shinjuku (✆ **03/5379-3039;** station: Shinjuku Sanchome).

6–6–5 Ginzai. ✆ **03/3571-1949.** Reservations recommended for lunch, required for dinner. Set dinners ¥10,000 – ¥18,000 ($83–$150); set lunches ¥7,000 – ¥10,000 ($58–$83). AE, DC, MC, V. Daily 11:30am–9:30pm. Station: Ginza (3 min.). On Namiki Dori.

MODERATE

③ **Donto** ✿✿ *Finds* VARIED JAPANESE   Located in Hibiya on Harumi Dori in the basement of an unlikely looking office building, this is a great place for lunch. Popular with the local working crowd (and therefore best avoided noon–1pm), it's pleasantly decorated in a rustic style with shoji screens, wooden floors, and an open kitchen. Take off your shoes at the entryway and put them into one of the wooden lockers. Choose what you want from the plastic display case, which shows various teishoku and set meals. Everything from noodles, sashimi, tempura, and obento to kaiseki is available. Unfortunately, the best deals are daily specials written in Japanese only; ask about them or look around at what others are eating.

There's another Donto on the 49th floor of the Sumitomo Building in Shinjuku (✆ 03/3344-6269; station: Tochomae).

Yurakucho Denki Building basement, 1–7–1 Yurakucho, on Harumi Dori. ✆ **03/3201-3021.** Set dinners ¥3,500 – ¥7,500 ($29–$62); set lunches ¥830 – ¥1,000 ($6.90–$8.35). AE, DC, MC, V. Mon–Sat 11am–2pm and 5–11pm. Closed holidays. Station: Hibiya (1 min.).

④ **Ginza Daimasu** KAISEKI/OBENTO   This 65-year-old restaurant has a simple, modern decor with Japanese touches. Experienced, kimono-clad waitresses serve artfully arranged set meals from the English-language menu. The *Fukiyose-zen obento*—many delicate dishes served in three courses—includes beautiful tempura delicacies served in an edible basket, and a menu (in Japanese) explaining what you're eating. A plastic-food display in the front window will help you recognize the restaurant. Set lunches are served until 3pm.

6–9–6 Ginza. ✆ **03/3571-3584.** Reservations required for kaiseki. Kaiseki ¥5,000 – ¥12,000 ($42–$100); obento ¥2,300 – ¥3,800 ($19–$32); set lunches ¥2,000 – ¥2,500 ($17–$21). DC, MC, V. Daily 11:30am–9:30pm (last order 8:30pm). Station: Ginza (2 min.). Across from Matsuzakaya department store on Chuo Dori.

Imperial Viking ✿ INTERNATIONAL   No, this has nothing to do with Scandinavian invaders; rather, *viking* is the Japanese word for "all-you-can-eat buffet." Although lots of Tokyo hotels now offer such spreads, this 17th-floor restaurant has been serving buffets for more than 40 years. It offers more than 40 mostly European and some international dishes, which vary according to seasonal food promotions spotlighting a country's cuisine, from Indonesian to Swiss.

Views are of Ginza and Hibiya Park, and there's live jazz in the evenings. This restaurant has enjoyed great popularity for decades, making reservations a must.

Imperial Hotel, 17th floor, 1–1–1 Uchisaiwai-cho. © 03/3504-1111. Reservations recommended. Buffet dinner ¥7,500 ($63); buffet lunch ¥5,000 ($42). AE, DC, MC, V. Daily 11:30am–2:30pm and 5–9:30pm. Station: Hibiya (1 min.).

Kazan FUSION SEAFOOD   This stylish restaurant, with a glass-enclosed kitchen and jazz playing softly in the background, distinguishes itself from the tsunami of other fusion restaurants swamping Tokyo by specializing in seafood that blends Japanese, Chinese, Italian, and French cuisines and ingredients. Another gimmick: The floor is heated, supposedly to prevent circulating air from drying the fresh seafood. At any rate, the creative dishes are essentially whatever the chef dreams up, with past choices including stir-fried king crab, deep-fried lobster, oysters grilled in the shell in three sauces, prawns in chili sauce, grilled salmon in miso sauce, and—verboten for many—whale meat carpaccio.

6–14–2 Ginza. © 03/3524-8480. Main dishes ¥1,100 – ¥2,500 ($9.15–$21); set dinners ¥5,000 – ¥8,000 ($42–$67); set lunches ¥1,800 – ¥5,000 ($15–$42). AE, DC, V. Mon–Fri 11am–3pm and 5–10:30pm (last order); Sat–Sun and holidays 11am–10pm. Station: Higashi-Ginza (2 min.) or Ginza (4 min.). On the corner of Showa Dori and Miyuki Dori.

Kihachi ✿ FUSION-CROSSOVER   With a cool, crisp interior accented with Art Nouveau trimmings, this restaurant offers an interesting French menu that combines flavors of the West with Japanese and Asian ingredients, creations of its French-trained chef. Past choices have included starters like baked smoked salmon and asparagus with truffles, and Thai-style spicy king crab cocktail with jellyfish; mains have included Mexican-style chicken curry, duck grilled with Japanese vegetables, and Chinese-style roasted quail with blueberry sauce. The hardest part of dining here? Limiting yourself to one meal—you just might have to come back.

2–2–6 Ginza. © 03/3567-6281. Main dishes ¥2,400 – ¥3,200 ($20–$27); set dinners ¥5,000 – ¥10,000 ($42–$83); set lunches ¥2,500 – ¥5,000 ($21–$42). AE, DC, MC, V. Daily 11:30am–2:30pm and 6–9:30pm (last order). Station: Yurakucho (5 min.). Between JR Yurakucho Station and Printemps department store.

⑤ **Kushi Colza** ✿ YAKITORI/KUSHIYAKI   Kikkoman, the well-known producer of soy sauce, maintains a few restaurants, including this one. It serves yakitori and *kushiyaki* (grilled meats and vegetables on skewers), delicately seasoned with—what else?—Kikkoman soy sauce. Small, pleasant, and with an open counter where you can watch friendly chefs prepare your food, Kushi Colza has an English-language menu that lists three set dinners consisting of skewered filets of beef, fish, eel, or pork, along with an appetizer, salad, soup, and dessert. There's also a special weekend and holiday set dinner for ¥3,000 ($25). A la carte selections for skewered specialties average ¥350 to ¥800 ($2.90–$6.65) per skewer. My favorite accompaniment is the seasonal salad with soy sauce dressing. Lunch specials featuring beef or fish dishes are also available, though the menu is in Japanese only.

6–4–18 Ginza. © 03/3571-8228. Reservations recommended. Set dinners ¥3,300 – ¥4,500 ($27–$37); set lunches ¥850 – ¥1,500 ($7.10–$13). AE, DC, MC, V. Mon–Fri 11:30am–1:30pm and 5–10pm (last order); Sat 5–10pm. Closed holidays. Station: Hibiya (5 min.) or Ginza (10 min.). Located on a small side street between and paralleling Sotobori Dori and the elevated JR Yamanote Line tracks, behind Sukiyabashi Hankyu department store; look for its sign, which says KUSHI & WINE.

Munakata ✿ *Value* KAISEKI/OBENTO   Kaiseki is one of the most expensive meals you can have in Japan, but some lunch specials here (served until 2pm) make it quite reasonable. This basement restaurant is cozy, with slats of wood and low lighting that give customers a sense of privacy even in the middle of the day. In addition to mini-kaiseki meals, there are also tempura and various obento lunch boxes like the Shokado bento for ¥1,300 ($11). If you come before 9pm, you can take advantage of a special kaiseki meal for ¥5,000 ($42). This is a great place for lunch or for a dinner splurge. There's an English-language menu.

Mitsui Urban Hotel basement, 8–6–15 Ginza. © 03/3574-9356. Main dishes ¥1,200 – ¥4,000 ($10–$33); kaiseki set meals ¥7,000 – ¥15,000 ($58–$125); mini-kaiseki lunches ¥2,500 ($21). AE, DC, MC, V. Mon–Fri 11:30am–3pm and 5–10pm; Sat–Sun and holidays 11:30am–10pm. Station: Shimbashi (2 min.) or Hibiya (10 min.).

6 Ohmatsuya ★★ *Finds* JAPANESE GRILL   Enter this second-floor restaurant of a nondescript building and you're instantly back in time: After you're greeted by waitresses clad in traditional country clothing, you'll find yourself enveloped in an old farmhouse atmosphere. (Part of the decor is from a 17th-century samurai house in northern Japan.) Even the style of cooking is traditional, as customers grill their own food over a hibachi. Sake, served in a length of bamboo, is drunk from bamboo cups. Dinner menus include such delicacies as grilled fish, skewered meat, and vegetables. This true find—and easy to find at that—is located on Sony Street, the small side street behind the Sony Building.

6–5–8 Ginza. © 03/3571-7053. Reservations required. Set dinners ¥4,800 – ¥9,000 ($40–$75), plus a ¥500 ($4.15) table charge. AE, DC, MC, V. Mon–Fri 5–10pm; Sat 4:30–9pm (last order). Closed holidays. Station: Ginza (3 min.). On the 2nd floor of the modern Ail D'Or Building behind the Sony Building on Sony St.

7 Rangetsu SUKIYAKI/SHABU-SHABU/KAISEKI/OBENTO   This well-known Ginza restaurant has been dishing out sukiyaki, shabu-shabu, obento (traditional box meals), and steaks for 5 decades. It uses only Matsuzaka beef (bought whole and carved up by the chefs), which ranges from costlier fine-marbled beef to cheaper cuts with thick marbling. There are also crab dishes (including a crab sukiyaki), kaiseki, sirloin steaks, and eel dishes. Especially good deals are the obento box meals (available day and night and offering a variety of small dishes) and the set lunches served until 2:30pm. In the basement is a sake bar with more than 80 different kinds of sake from all over Japan, which you can also order with your meal.

3–5–8 Ginza. © 03/3567-1021. Reservations recommended. Beef sukiyaki or shabu-shabu set meals from ¥7,000 ($58) for dinner, ¥2,200 ($18) for lunch; obento meals and mini-kaiseki ¥2,200 – ¥5,500 ($18–$46); set lunches ¥1,200 – ¥3,800 ($10–$32). AE, DC, MC, V. Daily 11:30am–10pm. Station: Ginza (3 min.). On Chuo Dori across from the Matsuya department store.

Shiseido Parlour ★ WESTERN   Shiseido was founded in Ginza in 1872 as Japan's first Western-style pharmacy, later becoming one of the nation's most successful cosmetic companies. In 1902 Shiseido Parlour opened as a soda fountain. Today it's an upscale restaurant serving the classic Japanese version of Western food (there's even a name for it—*yoshoku*), with dishes ranging from scallop and shrimp gratin, to beef stroganoff served with buttered rice, to what would be considered plebeian fare in the West: hashed beef and rice, omelet rice, tomato macaroni gratin. And all this in a golden-hued venue of white tablecloths and with an army of waitresses dressed in black with white aprons. An "only in Japan" dining experience.

Tokyo Ginza Shiseido Building, 4th floor, 8–8–3 Ginza. © 03/5537-6241. Reservations recommended. Main dishes ¥1,800 – ¥3,600 ($15–$30); set dinners ¥7,000 – ¥15,000 ($58–$125); set lunches ¥3,800 – ¥6,000

($32–$50). AE, DC, MC, V. Daily 11:30am–9:30pm. Closed 1st and 3rd Mon of the month. Station: Shimbashi (3 min.) or Ginza (5 min.). On Chuo Dori.

INEXPENSIVE

In addition to the restaurants here, check out the chain **To the Herbs** next to Kabukiza at 4–13–11 Ginza (✆ **03/5565-9800**), open daily 11am to 9:50pm (last order) and serving inexpensive pizza and pasta (see review in "Harajuku & Aoyama," later in this chapter).

(8) **Atariya** ★ *Finds* YAKITORI   Because it's open mostly at night and serves yakitori, this is technically a drinking establishment, but it also is a good choice for inexpensive dining in Ginza, due in no small part to the welcoming, enthusiastic staff. You have your choice of table or counter seating on the first floor, while up on the second floor you take off your shoes and sit on split-reed mats. A set course will include most parts of the chicken, including the liver, gizzard, and skin, so you might wish to order your favorites a la carte. My set course included asparagus wrapped in grilled pork, *tskune* (ground chicken meatballs on a skewer), and *shoniku* (chicken breast yakitori). The shop's name means "to be right on target, to score a bull's-eye," implying that a meal here is certain to bring good luck.

3–5–17 Ginza. ✆ **03/3564-0045.** Yakitori set course ¥1,600 ($13); individual skewers ¥150–¥300 ($1.25–$2.50). Snack charge ¥300 ($2.50) per person. No credit cards. Tues–Sat 4:30–11pm. Station: Ginza (3 min.). Near Ginza 4-chome Crossing. Take the small side street that runs between Wako department store and Wako Annex; Atariya is on the 2nd block on the right.

Farm Grill *Kids* *Value* AMERICAN   After all of Tokyo's cramped, tiny restaurants, what impresses you immediately about this place is the space—enough for 260 widely placed tables. And with its simple wood decor and (for Tokyo) reasonable prices, the second thing that will come to mind is that it's just like millions of casual restaurants in the U.S., which is what makes this restaurant so unusual. Such a variety of American food in Japan is hard to come by, and at these prices, it's otherwise nonexistent outside hotels (sorry guys—you have to pay more than women do). Overflowing buffets, offering a variety of vegetables, casseroles, meats, and desserts, invite gluttony, but it's gluttony, thank goodness, with a time limit—90 minutes for lunch and 2 hours for dinner. Add ¥1,000 ($8.35) to your meal, and you can drink all you want of a variety of beverages including wine, cocktails, and beer. The food is rather ordinary, but for budgeters with hearty appetites, this may become a regular haunt.

Ginza Nine Building 3, 8–5 Ginza. ✆ **03/5568-6156.** Dinner buffet ¥2,500 ($21) men, ¥1,900 ($16) women, ¥1,200 ($10) children 6–12, ¥500 ($4.15) children 3–5; lunch buffet ¥1,000 ($8.35) weekdays, ¥1,200 ($10) Sat–Sun and holidays. AE, MC, V. Mon–Fri 11:30am–2pm and 5–11pm; Sat–Sun11:30am–4pm and 5–11pm. Station: Shimbashi (exit 1, 4 min.). On the 2nd floor of a building underneath the Shuto Expwy.

(9) **Fukusuke** SUSHI   In this basement full of cheap restaurants, called Ginza Palmy, walk all the way to the back (away from Harumi Dori) to this very inexpensive sushi bar, popular with area office workers. It has an exceptionally long counter, which makes it a good choice if you're looking for an empty seat during the noon-to-1pm rush (a branch of the same restaurant lies catty-corner). A counter outside displays set meals. The ¥800 ($6.65) set lunch includes soup, sushi, Japanese pickles, and tea.

Toshiba Building B2, 5–2–1 Ginza. ✆ **03/3573-0471.** Sushi a la carte ¥120–¥500 ($1–$4.15); set dinners ¥1,300–¥3,200 ($11–$27); set lunches ¥850–¥2,000 ($7.10–$17). AE, DC, MC, V. Daily 11am–10pm. Station: Ginza or Hibiya (4 min.). In the 2nd basement below the Sukiyabashi Hankyu department store on Sotobori Dori at Sukiyabashi Crossing.

Gonpachi ★★ *Finds* VARIED JAPANESE   Housed in a re-created *kura* (traditional Japanese warehouse) with exposed wooden beams, Gonpachi is a fun place to dine on a variety of dishes such as fish (like miso-glazed black cod), yakitori (like chicken or asparagus wrapped with bacon), sushi (evenings only), noodles, and more. It's actually one of four restaurants ensconced under a freeway in a nifty dining complex called **G-Zone,** all part of a chain belonging to the Global Dining group. Mexican food is offered in the rustic, cowboy-themed **Zest Cantina** (✆ **03/5524-3621;** see "Ebisu & Meguro," later in this chapter, for a review); pizza and pasta in Italian-themed **La Boheme** (✆ **03/5524-3616;** see below for a review); and Southeast Asian fare in **Monsoon** (✆ **03/5524-3631**). English-language menus, inexpensive food, friendly and polished staff, and late opening hours make all Global Dining restaurants winners whether you're a Tokyo novice or a pro.

You'll find other Gonpachi at 1–13–11 Nishi Azabu (✆ 03/5771-0170), and on the fourth floor of Mediage on Odaiba (✆ 03/3599-4807). Both are open daily from 11:30am to 5am.

1–2–3 Ginza. ✆ **03/5524-3641.** Main dishes ¥550–¥1,800 ($4.60–$15); set lunches ¥600–¥950 ($5–$7.90). AE, DC, MC, V. Daily 11:30am–5am. Station: Kyobashi (exit 3, 2 min.) or Ginza-Itchome (exit 7, 1 min.). On Chuo Dori, at the northern edge of Ginza.

La Boheme ITALIAN   The food is passable, but what sets La Boheme apart is that it's open every day until 5am, making it a good bet for a late-night meal. I also like its huge, open kitchen in the middle of the room, surrounded by a U-shaped counter that provides a ringside view of the action. The pasta ranges from lasagna to spaghetti Bolognese, along with Japanese-style versions that include steamed breast of chicken with Japanese baby leek, spinach, and sesame oil; and fresh shrimp and basil with garlic, olive oil, and shimeji mushrooms.

You'll find other La Boheme restaurants in the Ginza at 1–2–3 Ginza (✆ 03/5524-3616); in Harajuku at 6–7–18 Jinguma (✆ 03/3400-3406) and at 5–8–5 Jingumae (✆ 03/5467-5666); in Shibuya at 1–6–8 Jinnan (✆ 03/3477-0481); in Nishi Azabu at 2–25–18 Nishi Azabu (✆ 03/3407-1363); in Meguro at 4–19–17 Shirokanedai (✆ 03/3442-4488); and on the fourth floor of Mediage on Odaiba (✆ 03/3599-4801). All are open daily from 11:30am to 5am.

6–4–1 Ginza ✆ **03/3572-5005.** Pizza and pasta ¥500–¥1,300 ($4.15–$11); set lunches ¥800–¥1,300 ($6.65–$11). AE, DC, MC, V. Daily 11:30am–5am. Station: Hibiya (5 min.) or Ginza (10 min.). Behind Sukiyabashi Hankyu department store, on a corner.

(10) **Shabusen** ★ *Value* SHABU-SHABU   Located on the second floor of a fashion department store just a stone's throw from Ginza 4–chome Crossing (the Harumi Dori–Chuo Dori intersection), this is a fun restaurant where you can cook your own sukiyaki or shabu-shabu in a boiling pot as you sit at a round counter. It's also one of the few restaurants that caters to individual diners (shabu-shabu is usually shared by a group). Orders are shouted back and forth among the staff, service is rapid, and the place is lively. There's an English-language menu complete with cooking instructions, so it's user-friendly. The special shabu-shabu dinner for ¥3,950 ($32), with appetizer, tomato ("super dressing") salad, beef, vegetables, noodles or rice porridge, and dessert, is enough for most voracious appetites.

You'll find a branch of Shabusen in the basement of the TBS Building at 5–3–3 Akasaka (✆ 03/3582-8161).

Core Building 2F, 5–8–20 Ginza. ✆ **03/3571-1717.** Set dinners ¥2,200–¥5,600 ($18–$47); set lunches ¥930–¥3,000 ($7.75–$25). AE, DC, MC, V. Daily 11am–10pm. Station: Ginza (1 min.). On Chuo Dori next to the Nissan Building.

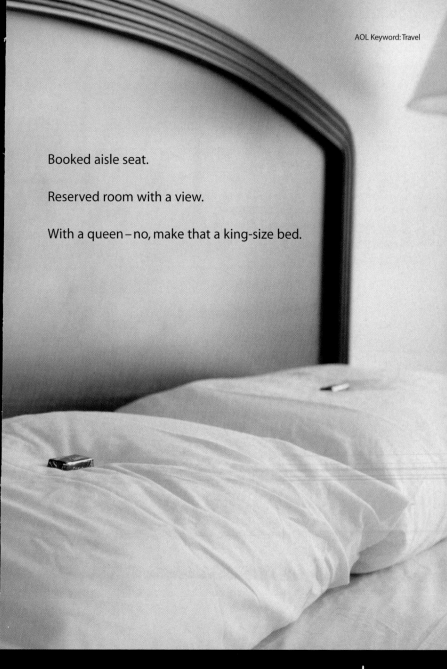

Booked aisle seat.

Reserved room with a view.

With a queen – no, make that a king-size bed.

With Travelocity, you can book your flights and hotels together, so you can get even better deals than if you booked them separately. You'll save time and money without compromising the quality of your trip. Choose your airline seat, search for alternate airports, pick your hotel room type, even choose the neighborhood you'd like to stay in.

Travelocity

Visit www.travelocity.com
or call 1-888-TRAVELOCITY

⑪ **Sushi Sei** SUSHI   One of a dependably good chain of reasonably priced sushi bars, this place is a natural for both novices and more experienced fans of raw fish. Order a la carte for your favorites, or stick to one of the set meals if you don't know much about sushi. The chef will prepare your food and place it on a raised platform on the counter in front of you, which serves as your plate.

8–2–13 Ginza. ℂ **03/3571-2772** or 03/3572-4770. Sushi a la carte ¥150–¥350 ($1.25–$2.90); set lunches ¥1,680–¥1,800 ($14–$15); set dinners ¥2,500–¥3,300 ($21–$28). AE, DC, MC, V. Mon–Sat 11:30am–2pm and 5–10:45pm. Closed holidays. Station: Shimbashi (1 min.) or Hibiya (5 min.). Across from the elevated tracks of the JR Yamanote Line.

⑫ **Tatsutano** ✿ DESSERTS/KAMAMESHI   If you'd like to try a traditional Japanese dessert, head to this 100-year-old shop, famous for its sweets. Most popular is *anmitsu,* a dessert made from beans, molasses, sweet-bean paste, and gelatin. Other traditional desserts are *oshiruko,* a hot sweet-bean porridge; and sweet-bean ice cream. If you crave something more substantial, you might wish to order a reasonably priced *kamameshi* (rice casserole) or *zosui* (rice porridge).

7–8–7 Ginza. ℂ **03/3571-1850.** Desserts ¥600–¥930 ($5–$7.75); kamameshi ¥1,150–¥1,380 ($9.60–$12). No credit cards. Daily 11am–8pm. Station: Ginza (3 min.). On Chuo Dori, across from Yamaha.

Yakitori Under the Tracks *Finds* YAKITORI   This is not a restaurant but a place—underneath an arch of the elevated Yamanote railway tracks. Although several fancier establishments occupy entire arches, look for the one arch located about halfway between Harumi Dori and the Imperial Hotel Tower; it has a handful of tiny yakitori stands, each with a few tables and chairs. They cater to a rather boisterous working-class clientele, mainly men. The atmosphere, unsophisticated and dingy, harks back to prewar Japan, somewhat of an anomaly in the otherwise chic Ginza. Dining here can be quite an experience, and on my last visit, several stall owners enthusiastically beckoned me to join them.

Under the Yamanote Line tracks separating Ginza from Hibiya. No phone. Skewers ¥180–¥400 ($1.50–$3.35). No credit cards. Mon–Sat 5pm–midnight. Station: Hibiya or Yurakucho (3 min.).

5 Nihombashi & Around Tokyo Station

EXPENSIVE

Aux Amis Tokyo ✿ FRENCH   This small, tony restaurant specializing in creative French cuisine is one of several on the top two floors of the newly remodeled Marunouchi Building (called *Maru Biru* by locals), located on the Marunouchi (west) side of Tokyo Station. Sweeping views make it a dining hot spot (reserve one of the few coveted window seats), as do an extensive wine list and a changing French/Japanese menu that might include such entrees as roast lamb with herbs of Provence, pork filet in a red-wine sauce, or fish of the day. It's also a great spot for lunch, but note that the rather bare dining room fails to absorb the constant chatter of this popular venue. Other restaurants on the two floors serve shabu-shabu, sushi, tempura, and kaiseki, as well as Italian, Thai, French, and Chinese cuisines. There are many more inexpensive eateries in the basement.

Marunouchi Building, 35th floor, 2–4–1 Marunouchi. ℂ **03/5220-4011.** Main dishes ¥3,200–¥4,000 ($27–$33); set dinners ¥6,000–¥8,500 ($50–$71); set lunches ¥2,800–¥5,000 ($23–$42). AE, DC, MC, V. Daily 11am–3:30pm and 5:30pm–midnight (last order). Station: Tokyo (Marunouchi exit, 2 min.).

MODERATE

Central Mikuni's ✿ VARIED JAPANESE/SUSHI/FUSION/INTERNATIONAL   This is my top pick for a reasonably priced Japanese meal in Tokyo Station. Owned by popular local chef Mikuni, it resembles an early-20th-century diner and is divided into themed sections flanking a central open kitchen. The conveyor-belt sushi counter, with dishes color-coded according to price, offers standards as well as original creations, including Mexican and Californian rolls. Diners help themselves to dishes that appeal to them. There are also so-called "compartment" lunches (obento) featuring Asian contemporary or Japanese/French fusion cuisine, as well as inexpensive noodle and rice dishes served cafeteria-style. Weekday Continental lunches start at ¥900 ($7.50), while dinner early birds should take advantage of a set French course for ¥5,500 ($46) available from 5 to 7pm. In short, this restaurant's offerings are so varied that you could dine here several days in a row, each time with a different dining experience.

Basement of Tokyo Station, 1–9–1 Marunouchi. ✆ 03/5218-5123. Main dishes ¥800 – ¥1,600 ($6.65–$13); sushi a la carte ¥150 – ¥650 ($1.25–$5.40) for lunch, ¥550 – ¥950 ($4.60–$7.90) for dinner; compartment lunches ¥2,000 – ¥3,500 ($17–$29). AE, DC, MC, V. No credit cards. Daily 11am–8pm (last order). Station: Nihombashi (3 min.). Off Eitai Dori, between Chuo Dori and Showa Dori.

INEXPENSIVE

⑬ **Taimeikan** INTERNATIONAL   This old-fashioned, Western-style restaurant, located in the same building as the Kite Museum and under the same management, has been in business since 1931. It's simple, inexpensive, and often crowded with mainly middle-aged and older Japanese; it's also one of the few nonsmoking restaurants I've seen in Japan. Its English-language menu lists such dishes as hamburger steak, ramen noodles, beef filet steak, omelet, spaghetti, curry rice, and an intriguing-sounding Dandylion a la Itami (a rice dish). To Western eyes, the food looks Japanese; to Japanese, it's Western fare. In other words, this restaurant serves the classic Japanese version of Western food (*yoshoku*), and in that respect has probably changed little since it opened. Diners are usually given both chopsticks and silverware, as though even the management isn't sure what it serves. However you classify it, it's a good place for a quick, cheap meal. For slightly fancier dining, there's another restaurant up on the second floor (closed Sun and holidays) serving pasta, roast chicken, steaks, and other Western fare, with most main courses ranging from ¥2,000 to ¥3,000 ($17–$25).

1–12–10 Nihombashi. ✆ 03/3271-2463. Main dishes ¥850 – ¥2,850 ($7.10–$24); set lunch (Mon–Fri only) ¥800 ($6.65). No credit cards. Daily 11am–8pm (last order). Station: Nihombashi (3 min.). Off Eitai Dori, between Chuo Dori and Showa Dori.

6 Tsukiji

Since Tsukiji is home to the nation's largest wholesale fish market, it's not surprising that this area abounds in sushi and seafood restaurants. In addition to the recommendations here, don't neglect the many stalls in and around the market, where you can eat everything from noodles to fresh sashimi.

EXPENSIVE

⑭ **Tamura** ⭐ KAISEKI   This modern kaiseki restaurant has a friendly staff of smiling and bowing kimono-clad waitresses and hostesses who make you feel as though they've been waiting all this time just for you. The menu is in Japanese only, so they can help you decide what to order, but since the meals are set ones, your budget will probably decide for you. Lunch is by far the most economical meal; many Japanese housewives come for the obento lunch boxes, served in a pleasant dining room with tables and chairs. If you order a kaiseki meal for ¥20,000 ($165) or more, you are ushered to a tatami room upstairs; frankly, I can't even imagine what a ¥50,000 ($417) meal looks like.

2–12–11 Tsukiji. ℂ **03/3541-2591.** Reservations required for dinner, recommended for lunch. Set meals ¥8,000 – ¥50,000 ($67–$417); lunch obento ¥3,500 ($29); set lunches ¥6,000 – ¥15,000 ($29–$125). AE, DC, MC, V. Daily 11:30am–3pm (last order 1pm) and 5:30–10pm. Station: Tsukiji (Honganji exit, 1 min.). Off Shinohashi Dori, catty-corner from Honganji Temple, down the street running between Doutour Coffee Shop and a schoolyard.

MODERATE

⑮ **Tentake** FUGU People who really know their *fugu*, or blowfish, will tell you that the only proper time to eat it is October through March, when it's fresh. You can eat fugu year-round, however, and a good place to try this Japanese delicacy is Tentake, popular with the Tsukiji working crowd. An English-language menu lists dishes such as tempura fugu; a complete fugu dinner with all the trimmings costs ¥9,000 ($75). You can wash it all down with fugu sake. Otherwise, if you want suggestions, try the *fugu-chiri* for ¥3,800 ($32), a do-it-yourself meal in which you cook raw blowfish, cabbage, dandelion leaves, and tofu in a pot of boiling water in front of you—this was more than I could eat, but you can make a complete meal of it by ordering the fugu-chiri course for ¥5,900 ($49), which adds tempura, yakitori, and other dishes. If someone in your party doesn't like fugu, I recommend the crab set menu for ¥3,900 ($32). And yes, that's fugu swimming in the fish tank.

Before you eat here, be sure you read about fugu in "Tips on Dining, Japanese Style," earlier in this chapter.

6–16–6 Tsukiji. ℂ **03/3541-3881.** Fugu dishes ¥1,000 – ¥3,900 ($8.35–$32); fugu set courses ¥5,900 – ¥13,500 ($49–$112); set lunches ¥800 – ¥1,000 ($6.65–$8.35). AE, MC, V. Daily 11:30am–9:30pm (last order). Station: Tsukiji (7 min.). From the Harumi Dori/Shinohashi intersection, walk on Harumi Dori in the opposite direction of Ginza; the restaurant is on the left just before the bridge in a modern building.

INEXPENSIVE

⑯ **Edogin** SUSHI There are four Edogin sushi restaurants in Tsukiji, all located within walking distance of one another. Since they're close to the famous fish market, you can be sure that the fish will be fresh. There's nothing aesthetic about the main Edogin, first established about 80 years ago—the lights are bright, it's packed with the locals, and it's noisy and busy. It's particularly crowded during lunch- and dinnertime because the food is dependably good and plentiful. The menu is in Japanese only, but a glass case outside displays some of the set meals, with prices for most ¥3,000 ($25) or less. As an alternative, look at what the people around you are eating or, if it's lunchtime, order the teishoku (served until 2pm). The *nigiri-zushi* teishoku for ¥1,000 ($8.35) offers a variety of sushi, along with soup and pickled vegetables; if you're really hungry, a more plentiful nigiri-zushi teishoku is available for ¥1,400 ($12).

4–5–1 Tsukiji. ℂ **03/3543-4401.** Set meals ¥1,000 – ¥3,500 ($8.35–$29); lunch teishoku ¥1,000 – ¥1,400 ($8.35–$12). AE, DC, MC, V. Mon–Sat 11am–9:30pm; Sun and holidays 11:30am–9pm. Station: Tsukiji (3 min.). Located near the Harumi and Shinohashi Dori intersection behind McDonald's; anyone in the neighborhood can point you in the right direction.

⑰ **Sushi Dai** ✦ SUSHI Located right in the Tsukiji Fish Market, this sushi bar boasts some of the freshest fish in town (and often a long line of people waiting to get in). The easiest thing to do is order the *seto*, a set sushi course that usually comes with tuna, eel, shrimp, and other morsels, plus six rolls of tuna and rice in seaweed *(onigiri)*. If you can't stomach sushi for breakfast, order *tamago* (a slice of layered fried omelet).

Tsukiji Fish Market. ℂ **03/3547-6797.** Sushi a la carte ¥200 – ¥1,000 ($1.65–$8.35); sushi seto ¥1,500 – ¥3,800 ($13–$32). No credit cards. Mon–Sat 5am–2pm. Closed Wed if the market is closed, and also on holidays. Station: Tsukiji (10 min.). Located in a row of barracks housing other restaurants and shops beside the covered market. Cross the bridge that leads to the market grounds, take a right, and then take the 1st left; to your right will be the barracks. Sushi Dai is in Building 6 in the 3rd alley (just past the mailbox); it's the 3rd shop on the right.

7 Asakusa

Note: To locate these restaurants, see the map on p. 89.

EXPENSIVE

(18) **Kuremutsu** ✯ KAISEKI   Just southeast of Sensoji Temple, Kuremutsu is actually a tiny, traditional house tucked behind a bamboo fence and an inviting courtyard with willow and maple trees, a millstone covered with moss, and an entrance invitingly lit with lanterns. Inside, it's like a farmhouse in the countryside filled with farm implements, old chests, masks, cast-iron teakettles, hibachi, and other odds and ends. Traditionally dressed to match the mood, waitresses serve one of three kaiseki meals.

2–2–13 Asakusa. ✆ 03/3842-0906. Reservations recommended. Kaiseki courses ¥5,000 ($42), ¥8,000 ($67), and ¥10,000 ($83). AE, DC, MC, V. Tues–Sun 4–9:15pm (last order). Station: Asakusa (5 min.). Walk on Nakamise Dori toward Sensoji Temple, turning right after the last shop; go past the 2 stone Buddhas and then turn right again at the tiny Benten-do Temple with the large bell; the restaurant is on the right side of the street across from the playground.

MODERATE

(19) **Komagata Dojo** ✯ *Finds* DOJO   This is a restaurant very much out of the Edo Period. Following a tradition spanning 200 years and now in its sixth generation of owners, this old-style dining hall specializes in *dojo,* a tiny sardine-like river fish that translates as "loach." It's served in a variety of styles, from grilled to stewed. Easiest is to order one of the set meals, which includes a popular *dojo nabe,* cooked on a charcoal burner at your table (dojo nabe ordered a la carte costs ¥1,400/$12). Otherwise, look around and order what someone else is eating. The dining area is a single large room of tatami mats, with ground-level boards serving as tables and waitresses in traditional dress moving quietly about.

1–7–12 Komagata, Taito-ku. ✆ 03/3842-4001. Reservations recommended for dinner. Dojo dishes ¥1,200–¥1,400 ($10–$12); set meals ¥2,000–¥6,300 ($17–$53). AE, DC, MC, V. Daily 11am–9pm. Station: Asakusa (3 min.). To reach the restaurant, walk south on Edo Dori (away from Kaminarimon Gate and Sensoji Temple); the restaurant—a large, old-fashioned wood house on a corner, with blue curtains at its door—is on the right side of the street, about a 5-min. walk from Kaminarimon Gate, past the UFJ Bank.

La Ranarita Azumabashi ✯ ITALIAN   The Asahi Beer Tower may not mean anything to you, but if I mention the building with the golden hops poised on top, you'll certainly know it when you see it (the building was designed by Philippe Starck). The Asahi Beer Tower is the high-rise beside the golden hops, looking like . . . a foaming beer mug? On the top floor (in the foam) is this Italian restaurant with soaring walls and great views of Asakusa. It's a perfect perch from which to watch barges on the river or the sun set over Asakusa as you dine on everything from pizza to pasta (available also in half sizes) to grilled scampi. The set lunches, which begin at ¥1,200 ($10) on weekdays and ¥1,500 ($13) on weekends and holidays, include an antipasto, salad, main dish, and coffee. If you want a ringside seat, make a reservation at least 3 days in advance or avoid the weekends.

Asahi Beer Tower (on the opposite side of the Sumida River from Sensoji Temple), 22nd floor, 1–23–1 Azumabashi. ✆ 03/5608-5277. Reservations recommended on weekends. Pizza ¥1,300–¥1,800 ($11–$15); pasta ¥650–¥1,900 ($5.40–$16); main dishes ¥1,900–¥2,800 ($16–$23). AE, DC, MC, V. Mon–Sat

Kids **Family-Friendly Restaurants**

Café Creperie Le Bretagne (p. 135)   If sweet bean paste is not your child's idea of dessert, then perhaps the crepes at this casual establishment will do the trick, filled with fruit, chocolate, and other yummy concoctions.

Farm Grill (p. 119)   A huge dining hall with all-you-can-eat American food might satisfy picky eaters. Children are given discounts, but any yen saved are likely to be spent at the nearby Hakuhinkan Toy Park toy store.

Hard Rock Cafe (p. 147)   This internationally known establishment should pacify grumbling teenagers. They can munch on hamburgers, gaze at famous guitars and other rock 'n' roll memorabilia and, most importantly, buy that Hard Rock Cafe T-shirt.

Kua' Aina (p. 137)   When your kids start asking for "real food," take them here for the best burgers in town.

Las Chicas (p. 137)   This cool hangout has an outdoor terrace (good for kids who can't talk quietly), an English-language menu, foreign staff, and dishes just for the little ones.

Shakey's (p. 131)   When nothing but pizza will satisfy the kids, head for one of these chain pizza parlors for an all-you-can-eat bargain lunch.

11:30am–2pm (last order) and 5–9pm (last order); Sun and holidays 11:30am–3pm and 4–8pm (last order). Station: Asakusa (4 min.).

20 Mugitoro YAM/KAISEKI   Founded about 60 years ago but now housed in a new building, this restaurant specializes in *tororo-imo* (yam) kaiseki and has a wide following among middle-aged Japanese women. Popular as a health food, the yams used here are imported from the mountains of Akita Prefecture and are featured in almost all the dishes. If you're on a budget or want a quick meal, come for the weekday lunch buffet offered until 1pm; it includes a main dish like fish or beef, yam in some form, vegetable, soup, and rice. Deposit ¥1,000 ($8.35) into the pot on the table and help yourself.

2-2-4 Kaminarimon. © 03/3842-1066. Reservations recommended. Set dinners ¥5,000 – ¥10,000 ($42–$83); set lunches ¥2,500 – ¥5,000 ($21–$42). AE, DC, MC, V. Mon–Sat 11:30am–9pm (last order); Sun and holidays 11am–9pm. Station: Asakusa (2 min.). From Sensoji Temple, walk south (with your back to Kaminarimon Gate) until you reach the 1st big intersection with the stoplight. Komagata-bashi Bridge will be to your left; Mugitoro is right beside the bridge on Edo Dori, next to a tiny temple and playground. Look for the big white lantern hanging outside.

INEXPENSIVE

21 Chinya **Value** SHABU-SHABU/SUKIYAKI   Established in 1880, Chinya is an old sukiyaki restaurant with a new home in a seven-story building to the left of Kaminarimon Gate. The entrance to this place is open-fronted; all you'll see is a man waiting to take your shoes and a hostess in a kimono ready to lead you to one of the tatami-floored dining areas above. Chinya offers very good shabu-shabu or sukiyaki set lunches for ¥2,300 ($19), available until 4pm and including soup and side dishes. Otherwise, dinner set meals of shabu-shabu or sukiyaki, including rice and soup, begin at ¥2,500 ($21). A display case out front shows a few options, but the very good English-language menu includes instructions, making this a good bet for the sukiyaki/shabu-shabu novice.

1–3–4 Asakusa. ✆ 03/3841-0010. Set meals ¥2,500–¥7,500 ($21–$63). AE, DC, MC, V. Mon–Sat 11:45am–9:15pm; Sun and holidays 11:30am–9pm. Station: Asakusa (1 min.). On Kaminarimon Dori; located to the left of the Kaminarimon Gate if you stand facing Asakusa Kannon Temple (look for the SUKIYAKI sign).

㉒ **Daikokuya** TEMPURA   This simple tempura restaurant has been popular with the locals since 1887, and though it does not offer the most refined tempura, it has atmosphere, and its huge portions are legendary. It specializes in Edo-style tempura and *tendon* (tempura on a bowl of rice, usually ebi, or prawn), prepared with sesame oil. Although there's no English-language menu, there are photos of many of the dishes. An annex around the corner (next to Shigetsu Ryokan) handles the overflow crowd (and is open when the main shop is closed); a map at the door shows the way.

1–38–10 Asakusa. ✆ 03/3844-1111. Set courses ¥3,000–¥4,300 ($25–$36). No credit cards. Daily 11:10am–8:30pm. Closed irregularly once or twice a month. Station: Asakusa (5 min.). Off Nakamise Dori to the west; take the small street that passes by the south side of Dempoin Temple (also spelled Demboin); the restaurant is at the 1st intersection on the left, a white corner building with a Japanese-style tiled roof and sliding front door.

Kamiya Bar VARIED JAPANESE/WESTERN   This inexpensive restaurant, established in 1880 as the first Western bar in Japan, serves both Japanese and Western fare on its three floors. The first floor is the bar, popular with older, tobacco-smoking Japanese men. The second floor offers Western food of a sort (that is, the Japanese version of Western food), including fried chicken, smoked salmon, spaghetti, fried shrimp, and hamburger steak; the third floor serves Japanese food ranging from udon noodles and yakitori to tempura and sashimi. I personally prefer the third floor for both its food and its atmosphere. Although the menus are in Japanese only, extensive plastic-food display cases show set meals costing ¥1,500 to ¥3,500 ($12–$29). This is a very casual restaurant, very much a place for older locals, and it can be quite noisy and crowded.

1–1–1 Asakusa. ✆ 03/3841-5400. Main dishes ¥610–¥1,300 ($5.10–$11). No credit cards. Wed–Mon 11:30am–9:30pm (last order). Station: Asakusa (1 min.). Located on Kaminarimon Dori in a plain, brown-tiled building between Kaminarimon Gate and the Sumida River.

㉓ **Namiki Yabusoba** NOODLES   Asakusa's best-known noodle shop, founded in 1913, offers plain buckwheat noodles in cold or hot broth as well as more substantial tempura with noodles, all listed on an English-language menu. Seating is at tables or on tatami mats, and it's a small place, so you won't be able to linger if people are waiting.

2–11–9 Kaminarimon. ✆ 03/3841-1340. Dishes ¥650–¥1,600 ($5.40–$13). No credit cards. Fri–Wed 11:30am–7:30pm. Station: Asakusa (2 min.). From Kaminarimon Gate, walk south (away from Sensoji Temple); Namiki is on the right side of the street in the 2nd block, a brown building with bamboo trees, a small maple, and a stone lantern by the front door.

㉔ **Sometaro** *Finds* OKONOMIYAKI/YAKISOBA   This very atmospheric neighborhood restaurant specializes in *okonomiyaki*, a working-class meal that is basically a Japanese pancake filled with beef, pork, and vegetables, and prepared by the diners themselves as they sit on tatami at low tables inset with griddles. Realizing that some foreigners may be intimidated by having to cook an unfamiliar meal, this restaurant makes the process easier with an English-language menu complete with instructions. The busy but friendly staff can also help you get started. In addition to okonomiyaki, *yakisoba* (fried noodles) with meat or vegetables and other do-it-yourself dishes are available. This is a fun, convivial way to enjoy a meal. Before entering the restaurant, be sure to deposit your shoes in the proffered plastic sacks by the door.

2–2–2 Nishi-Asakusa. ⓒ 03/3844-9502. Main dishes ¥560 – ¥700 ($4.65–$5.85); set courses ¥1,500 – ¥2,800 ($13–$23). No credit cards. Daily noon–10pm (last order). Station: Tawaramachi (2 min.) or Asakusa (5 min.). Just off Kokusai Dori, on the side street that runs between the Drum Museum and the police station, on the 2nd block on the right.

8 Ueno

Note: To locate these restaurants, see the map on p. 91.

EXPENSIVE

Ueno Seiyoken Grill ⭐ CLASSIC FRENCH   Seiyoken opened in 1876 as one of Japan's first restaurants serving Western food. Now a nondescript building dating from the 1950s, it nonetheless remains the best place to eat in Ueno Park, serving pricey but quite good classic French cuisine, with a relaxing view of greenery outside its large windows and classical music playing softly in the background. The English-language menu includes seafood such as sole stuffed with shrimp in white wine sauce, and meat dishes ranging from filet mignon in red wine sauce to roast duck in green pepper sauce. There's a varied selection of French wines as well as wines from Germany, California, and Australia. The Grill is located to the right as you enter the building and is not to be confused with the much cheaper utilitarian restaurant to the left.

In Ueno Park between Kiyomizu Temple and Toshogu Shrine. ⓒ 03/3821-2181. Main dishes ¥3,000 – ¥7,000 ($25–$58); set dinners ¥5,000 – ¥12,000 ($42–$100); set lunches ¥4,000 – ¥5,000 ($33–$42). AE, DC, MC, V. Daily 11am–8pm (last order). Station: JR Ueno (6 min.).

MODERATE

㉕ **Izu'ei** EEL   Put aside all your prejudices about eels and head for this modern yet traditionally decorated multistoried restaurant with a 260-year history dating back to the Edo Period and views of Shinobazu Pond. Since eels are grilled over charcoal, the Japanese place a lot of stock in the quality of the charcoal used, and this place boasts its own furnace in the mountains of Wakayama Prefecture, which is said to produce the best charcoal in Japan. *Unagi donburi* (rice topped with strips of eel), tempura, and sushi are available, as well as set meals. There's no English-language menu, but there is a display case outside, and the menu has some pictures.

2–12–22 Ueno. ⓒ 03/3831-0954. Reservations recommended. Main dishes ¥1,500 – ¥3,000 ($12–$25); set meals ¥2,000 – ¥8,000 ($17–$67). AE, DC, MC, V. Daily 11am–9:30pm (last order). Station: JR Ueno (3 min.). On Shinobazu Dori, across the street from Shinobazu Pond and the Shitamachi Museum, next to KFC Home Kitchen.

INEXPENSIVE

In addition to the restaurant below, try **Hard Rock Cafe Ueno,** 7–1–1 Ueno (ⓒ 03/5826-5821), located in JR Ueno Station; see "Roppongi & Nishi Azabu," later in this chapter, for a review.

Mantra INDIAN   Decorated in pink with etched mirrors and lots of brass, this tiny, spotless restaurant offers curries and tandoori at inexpensive prices. A good way for lone diners to try a variety of dishes is the all-you-can-eat lunch buffet served from 11am to 3pm; or try one of the meat or vegetarian set meals *(thali).*

Nagafuji Building Annex, 3rd floor, 4–9–6 Ueno. ⓒ 03/3835-0818. Main dishes ¥980 – ¥1,200 ($8.15–$10); set meals ¥2,400 – ¥2,500 ($20–$21); lunch buffet ¥950 ($7.90) weekdays, ¥1,270 ($11) weekends and holidays. AE, DC, MC, V. Daily 11am–9:30pm (last order). Station: JR Ueno (2 min.). From the south end of Ueno Park, look for the modern Nagafuji Building on Chuo Dori; the annex is in the back, facing the north end of Ameyokocho shopping street.

9 Shinjuku

In addition to the suggestions below, be sure to check out the restaurant floors of several buildings in Shinjuku, where you can find eateries in all price categories serving a variety of Japanese and international cuisines; some even have the bonus of great city views. These include the 29th and 30th floors of the **N. S. Building** where, in addition to Hakkaku (described below), other restaurants serve tempura, tonkatsu, teppanyaki, and sushi, as well as Italian, German, and French food; the top four floors of the **Sumitomo Building** where, in addition to Donto (see review under "Ginza & Hibiya," earlier in this chapter), you'll find more than 20 outlets offering everything from tempura to Chinese cuisine; and the 12th, 13th, and 14th floors of **Takashimaya Times Square** where, in addition to Kappoya Yaozen and Din Tai Fung (described below), there are restaurants serving sushi, tonkatsu, noodles, and more.

Note: To locate these restaurants, see the map on p. 76.

VERY EXPENSIVE

New York Grill ★★★ AMERICAN   On the 52nd floor of Tokyo's most exclusive hotel, the New York Grill has remained *the* place to dine ever since its 1994 opening; some swear it's the most sophisticated restaurant in all of Japan. Surrounded on four sides by glass, it features stunning views (especially at night), artwork by Valerio Adami, live jazz in the evenings, and a 1,600-bottle wine cellar (with an emphasis on California wines). The restaurant backs up its dramatic setting with generous portions of U.S. and Japanese steaks, seafood, and other fare ranging from delectable roast duck to rack of "certified organically raised" lamb, all prepared in an open kitchen. Both the set lunch and the weekend and holiday brunches are among the city's best and most sumptuous (reservations required)—and are great options for those who don't want to pawn their belongings to eat dinner here. I wouldn't miss it.

Park Hyatt Hotel, 3–7–1–2 Nishi-Shinjuku. ⓒ 03/5322-1234. Reservations required. Main dishes ¥4,000 – ¥7,800 ($33–$65); set lunch ¥4,600 ($38); set dinners ¥10,000 – ¥15,000 ($83–$125); Sat–Sun and holiday brunch ¥5,800 ($48). AE, DC, MC, V. Daily 11:30am–2:30pm and 5:30–10:30pm. Station: Shinjuku (west exit, a 13-min. walk or a 5-min. free shuttle ride), Hatsudai on the Keio Line (7 min.) or Tochomae on the Oedo Line (8 min.).

EXPENSIVE

㉖ **Kakiden** ★★ KAISEKI   Although it's located on the eighth floor of a rather uninspiring building, Kakiden has a relaxing teahouse atmosphere with low chairs, shoji screens, bamboo trees, and soothing traditional Japanese music playing softly in the background. Sibling restaurant to one in Kyoto founded more than 260 years ago as a catering service for the elite, this kaiseki restaurant serves set meals that change with the seasons according to what's fresh and available. An English-language menu lists the set meals, but it's probably best to simply pick a meal to fit your budget. The set lunch is available until 3pm. Set dinners include box kaiseki starting at ¥5,000 ($42), mini-kaiseki for ¥8,000 ($67), and kaiseki courses ranging from ¥8,000 to ¥15,000 ($67–$125). Some of the more common dishes here include fish, seasonal vegetables, eggs, sashimi, shrimp, and mushrooms, but don't worry if you can't identify everything—I've found that even the Japanese don't always know what they're eating.

3–37–11 Shinjuku, 8th floor. ☎ **03/3352-5121.** Reservations recommended for lunch. Set dinners ¥5,000 – ¥15,000 ($42–$125); set lunch ¥4,000 ($33). AE, DC, MC, V. Daily 11am–9pm (last order). Station: Shinjuku (east exit, 1 min.). On the east side of Shinjuku Station next to My City shopping complex.

MODERATE

Ban-Thai THAI   One of Tokyo's longest-running Thai restaurants and credited with introducing authentic Thai food to the Japanese, Ban-Thai still prepares excellent Thai fare, with 90 mouthwatering items listed on the menu. My favorites are the cold and spicy meat salad, the chicken soup with coconut and lemon grass, and the *pad Thai*. Note that set dinners are available only for parties of two or more; also, portions are not large, so if you order several portions and add beer, your tab can really climb.

1–23–14 Kabuki-cho, 3rd floor. ☎ **03/3207-0068.** Main dishes ¥1,200 – ¥1,800 ($10–$15); set dinners ¥2,500 – ¥6,000 ($21–$50); set lunches ¥600 – ¥1,300 ($5–$11) weekdays, ¥1,600 – ¥2,200 ($13–$18) weekends and holidays. AE, MC, V. Mon–Fri 11:30am–3pm and 5–11pm (last order); Sat–Sun and holidays 11:30am–11pm. Station: Shinjuku (east exit, 7 min.). In East Shinjuku in the seediest part of Kabuki-cho (don't worry, the interior is nicer than the exterior) on a neon-lit pedestrian street connecting the Koma Building with Yasukuni Dori (look for the red neon archway and Pronto coffee shop), about halfway down, next to a game arcade.

㉗ **Hayashi** ★★ *Finds* JAPANESE GRILL   This restaurant specializes in Japanese set meals cooked over your own hibachi grill. It's small and cozy, with only five grills and women in kimono overseeing the cooking operations, taking over if customers seem the least bit hesitant. The rustic interior was imported intact from the mountain region of Takayama. Four set meals are offered (vegetarian meals are available on request). My ¥5,000 ($42) meal came with sashimi, yakitori, tofu steak, scallops cooked in their shells, shrimp, and vegetables, all grilled one after the other. Watch your alcohol intake—drinks can really add to your bill.

Jojoen Daini Shinjuku Building, 2–22–5 Kabuki-cho. ☎ **03/3209-5672.** Reservations recommended. Set dinners ¥4,000 – ¥7,000 ($33–$58). AE, MC, V. Mon–Sat 5–11:30pm. Closed holidays. Station: Shinjuku (east exit, 10 min.). On the northern edge of Kabuki-cho; you'll know you're getting close when you see Godzilla hanging from a building; the restaurant is just a bit farther to the north, on a corner.

㉘ **Kappoya Yaozen** ★ *Value* KAISEKI   Established 280 years ago, this Shinjuku branch in a department store has a rather plain interior, but the hostesses in kimono are friendly and the view of surrounding Shinjuku is pleasant. It's also a very good choice for inexpensive kaiseki. A display case gives an approximation of some of the set meals available (they change with the seasons), and there's an English-language menu—or order according to your budget. This place is popular with older shoppers at the humongous Takashimaya Times Square who, probably exhausted, come here for a civilized break.

Takashimaya Times Sq., 14th floor, 5–24–2 Sendagaya. ☎ **03/5361-1872.** Set meals ¥1,800 – ¥15,000 ($15–$125); set lunches ¥1,500 ($13). AE, MC, V. Daily 11am–10pm (last order). Station: Shinjuku (south exit, 1 min.).

Tribecks Restaurant & Bar AMERICAN/FUSION-CROSSOVER   On the 20th floor of the sleek Hotel Century Southern Tower, this upbeat, contemporary restaurant with an open kitchen offers great city views and American food with a twist—heavily influenced by Asian and European cuisines. Although the dishes don't always live up to expectations, the service is great and the views sublime, making it popular with shoppers from nearby Takashimaya Times Square (make reservations or avoid peak hours). Dinner selections may include grilled spearfish with a white bean sauce or grilled rib loin steak with ginger sauce, while the very popular set lunches offer your choice of main dishes such as tuna, sautéed scallops with prawns, or grilled chicken, along with a salad bar, dessert, and coffee.

Hotel Century Southern Tower, 20th floor, 2–2–1 Yoyogi. ☎ **03/5354-2177**. Reservations recommended. Main dishes ¥1,200 – ¥3,200 ($10–$27); set dinner ¥5,000 ($42); set lunch ¥2,500 ($21). AE, DC, MC, V. Mon–Fri 11:30am–3pm; Sat–Sun and holidays 11:30am–4pm; Sun–Thurs and holidays 5:30–10pm; Fri–Sat 5:30–11pm (last order). Station: Shinjuku (south exit, 2 min.).

㉙ **Tsunahachi** TEMPURA   Inside a small, old-fashioned brown building in the heart of fashionable East Shinjuku is the main branch of a restaurant that has been serving tempura since 1923. Now there are more than 40 outlets in Japan, including three in Shinjuku Station alone, and others in Ginza and Akasaka. Hours may vary, but most shops are open daily from 11:30am to 10pm. This is the largest outlet, and though it has an English-language menu, the easiest option is to order the teishoku, the least expensive of which includes six pieces of tempura, including deep-fried shrimp, cuttlefish, white fish, green pepper, conger eel, and Japanese pickles. The most expensive teishoku offers 10 pieces of tempura.

3–31–8 Shinjuku. ☎ **03/3352-1012**. Reservations recommended. Tempura a la carte ¥450 – ¥1,200 ($3.75–$10); teishoku ¥1,100 – ¥1,800 ($9.15–$15). AE, V. Daily 11:15am–10pm. Station: Shinjuku San-chome (2 min.) or Shinjuku (east exit, 5 min.). Off Shinjuku Dori on the side street that runs along the east side of Mitsukoshi department store.

INEXPENSIVE

Donto, on the 49th floor of the Sumitomo Building, offers a Japanese lunch buffet for ¥980 ($8.15) and set meals for dinner (see review in "Ginza & Hibiya, earlier in this chapter").

Daikokuya *Value* SHABU-SHABU/SUKIYAKI/YAKINIKU   If you're a big eater traveling on a budget, you won't want to miss dining here. This place offers only three main dishes—shabu-shabu, sukiyaki, and yakiniku—and serves up as much of it as you can consume in a 2-hour period. If you want to drink beer, whiskey, or shochu with your meal, add ¥1,000 ($8.35) to the prices below, and you'll be able to drink to your heart's content as well. Popular with students and young office workers, Daikokuya is a rather strange place (its interior is kind of cavernous—maybe harking back to cave-age gluttony?) and, needless to say, it can be quite rowdy.

Naka-Dai Building, 4th floor, 1–27–5 Kabuki-cho. ☎ **03/3202-7272**. All-you-can-eat main dishes ¥1,750 – ¥2,250 ($15–$19). No credit cards. Mon–Thurs 5–11:30pm; Fri–Sun 3pm–midnight. Station: Shinjuku (east exit, 10 min.). In Kabuki-cho, 1 block west of Koma and across from Hotel Kent.

Din Tai Fung CHINESE   One of several dining options on the 10th floor of Takashimaya department store in the Takashimaya Times Square shopping complex, this is the Tokyo branch of one of Taipei's best-selling dim-sum spots; it's so popular that you may have to wait for a table. Photos at the entrance show the various dim sum and noodle and rice dishes available, most priced under ¥1,000 ($9), as well as several set meals from which to choose. A glass window lets you view the hectic action in the kitchen.

Takashimaya Times Sq., 10th floor, 5–24–2 Sendagaya. ☎ **03/5361-1381**. Dim sum ¥400 – ¥1,300 ($3.35–$11); set meals ¥1,000 – ¥1,300 ($8.35–$11). MC, V. Daily 10am–7:30pm (last order). Closed some Wed. Station: Shinjuku (south exit, 1 min.).

㉚ **Hakkaku** ★ *Finds* VARIED JAPANESE/ROBATAYAKI   This lively, crowded establishment has a lot going for it: a corner location in a skyscraper with expansive views over Yoyogi Park, inexpensive dishes and meals, and Kirin beer on tap. Although its decor and food resemble those of a bar, it's open for lunch, when only set meals are available; choose grilled fish, *hirekatsu* (breaded pork cutlet), or from the display case. Dinner offers a wider range of possibilities, including sashimi, grilled fish, *nikujaga* (a very tasty beef and potato stew), and salads. Yakitori, beginning at ¥300 ($2.50) per skewer, includes asparagus wrapped in bacon and tsukune (chicken meatballs), two of my favorites. Since the menu is in Japanese only, perhaps you'll want to sit at the robatayaki counter, where you can point at various dishes, watch them be prepared on the open grill, and then receive them from a wooden paddle passed in your direction.

N. S. Building, 29th floor, 2–4–1 Nishi-Shinjuku. ✆ 03/3345-1848. Main dishes ¥500 – ¥850 ($4.15–$7.10); set lunches ¥750 – ¥850 ($6.25–$7.10). AE, DC, MC, V. Daily 11am–3pm and 5–10pm. Station: Tochomae (3 min.) or Shinjuku (west exit, 8 min.).

Shakey's (Kids) PIZZA   If you want to gorge yourself on pizza, the best deal is at one of several Shakey's around town, offering all-you-can-eat pizza, spaghetti, and fried potatoes for lunch every day until 4pm. Although kids may be horrified by the thought of pizza with octopus, they're sure to find other slices more to their liking. There's another Shakey's in Harajuku on Omotesando Dori at 6–1–10 Jingumae (✆ 03/3409-2404), open for lunch Monday through Saturday from 11am to 3pm.

3–30–11 Shinjuku. ✆ 03/3341-0322. All-you-can-eat pizza lunch ¥750 ($6.25) Mon–Sat, ¥950 ($7.90) Sun and holidays. No credit cards. Daily 11am–10:30pm. Station: Shinjuku Sanchome (1 min.). In East Shinjuku on Shinjuku Dori, in the basement of a building across from the Isetan department store.

10 Harajuku & Aoyama

VERY EXPENSIVE

Gesshinkyo ★★ BUDDHIST VEGETARIAN   Developed centuries ago to serve the needs of priests and pilgrims visiting temples, Buddhist vegetarian cuisine *(shojin ryori)* is a veritable feast of vegetables and tofu dishes that change with the seasons, kind of like a vegetarian kaiseki. This restaurant, located in a house in a quiet residential neighborhood, is overseen by Toshio Tanahashi, a local expert on shojin ryori. Dining is on tatami mats or at a counter with leg wells for those who find it uncomfortable to sit on the ground. Although there are many shojin ryori restaurants in Kyoto, this is probably your best bet in Tokyo.

4–24–12 Jingumae. ✆ 03/3796-6575. Reservations required at least 1 day in advance. Set meal ¥12,000 ($100). No credit cards. Mon–Sat 6–8pm (last order). Closed holidays. Station: Meiji-Jingumae (5 min) or Omotesando or Harajuku (7 min). From the Meiji Dori, walk on the left side of Omotesando Dori (in the direction of Omotesando) to the police box and ask for directions from there.

EXPENSIVE

Nobu ★★★ NOUVELLE JAPANESE/PACIFIC RIM FUSION-CROSSOVER   Sister restaurant to New York's Nobu, this classy, modern establishment is the place to see and be seen—and you can count on being seen since the staff yells *"Irashaimase!"* ("Welcome!") the minute anyone is ushered into the dining room. Jazz plays softly in the background, flowers sit atop each table, and the efficient staff keeps everything running smoothly. The food, beautifully presented and served one dish at a time, is a unique blend of Pacific Rim ingredients (not quite Japanese) with decidedly American/Latin influences. Sushi and sashimi are served, as well as sushi rolls like California rolls (with avocado) and soft-shell-crab rolls. Other dishes include yellowtail sashimi with jalapeño, scallop sashimi with Peruvian red chili paste, and black cod with miso.

If ordering is too much of a chore, you can leave your meal to the discretion of Chef Matsuhisa by ordering the *omakase,* a complete chef's-choice dinner starting at ¥10,000 ($83). Prices are less expensive at lunch. In fine weather, you can dine on an outdoor patio with a retractable roof.

6–10–17 Minami Aoyama. ℂ 03/5467-0022. Reservations recommended. Sushi and sashimi (per piece) ¥500 – ¥1,000 ($4.15–$10); tempura a la carte (per piece) ¥300 – ¥1,200 ($2.50–$10); set dinners ¥4,000 – ¥20,000 ($33–$167); set lunches ¥2,800 – ¥8,500 ($23–$71). AE, DC, MC, V. Mon–Fri 11:30am–2pm; daily 6–10pm (last order). Station: Shibuya or Omotesando (15 min.). On Roppongi Dori near Komazawa Dori and Kotto Dori.

Sabatini ★ ITALIAN   This restaurant, with its Italian furniture and tableware and strolling musicians, seems as if it has been moved intact from the Old World. In fact, the only thing to remind you that you're in Tokyo is your Japanese waiter. The Italian family that owns Sabatini has had a restaurant in Rome for more than 40 years, and family members take turns overseeing the Tokyo restaurants, so one of them is always here. The menu includes seafood, veal, steak, lamb, and a variety of vegetables; many of the ingredients, like olive oil, ham, salami, tomato sauce, and Parmesan, are flown in fresh from Italy. Naturally, there's a wide selection of Italian wines.

Suncrest Building, 2–13–5 Kita-Aoyama. ℂ 03/3402-3812. Reservations recommended for dinner. Pasta ¥1,800 – ¥3,200 ($15–$27); main dishes ¥2,100 – ¥6,500 ($18–$54); set dinner ¥15,000 ($125); set lunch ¥3,500 – ¥5,000 ($29–$42). AE, DC, MC, V. Daily 11:30am–2:30pm and 5:30–11pm. Station: Gaienmae (2 min.). On Aoyama Dori near Gaien-Nishi Dori.

MODERATE

Aux Bacchanales FRENCH   This is a real French sidewalk cafe, right in Tokyo's favorite people-watching neighborhood of Harajuku. Actually, it consists of two sections, both of which are packed on weekends: a brasserie with sandwiches and omelets priced at less than ¥650 ($5.40), strong espresso, and good cheap wine (counter prices are slightly cheaper than at one of the sit-down tables, just like in France); and a restaurant with both outdoor and indoor seating offering such dishes as grilled lobster, steak tartare, *lapin à la moutarde,* and lamb with thyme. A perfect place for pretending you don't have a care in the world.

Palais France Building, 1–6–1 Jingumae (on Meiji Dori). ℂ 03/5474-0076. Main dishes ¥1,800 – ¥3,000 ($15–$25); set meal ¥ 3,800 ($32). AE, DC, MC, V. Cafe daily 9am–10:30pm (last order); restaurant daily 6–10:30pm (last order). Station: Meiji-Jingumae (2 min.) or Harajuku (7 min.). On Meiji Dori near Takeshita Dori.

Daini's Table ★★ NOUVELLE CHINESE   This elegant Chinese restaurant, located next to the Blue Note jazz club off Kotto Dori, serves intriguing dishes that are nicely presented one dish at a time rather than all at once as in most Chinese restaurants. It offers both traditional dishes (roast Peking duck, boiled prawns with red chili sauce, and hot-and-sour Peking-style soup) and more unusual combinations that change with the seasons. Everything I've had here has been delicious.

6–3–14 Minami Aoyama. ℂ 03/3407-0363. Reservations recommended. Main dishes ¥1,800 – ¥3,800 ($15–$32); set dinners ¥4,000 – ¥12,000 ($33–$100); set lunches ¥1,500 – ¥2,500 ($13–$21). AE, DC, MC, V. Mon–Fri 11:30am–2pm; daily 5:30–11pm (last order). Station: Omotesando (6 min.).

Fujimamas PACIFIC RIM/FUSION   This airy restaurant employs lots of wood to impart a beach-shack atmosphere, but naturally at Tokyo prices. The culinary crossroad of cuisines presented on the changing English-language menu may include salads like a Thai-style Caesar salad with crispy calamari croutons, or minced Asian chicken salad in a crispy shell. Main dishes may include such

Nightlife & Where to Stay & Dine in Harajuku & Aoyama

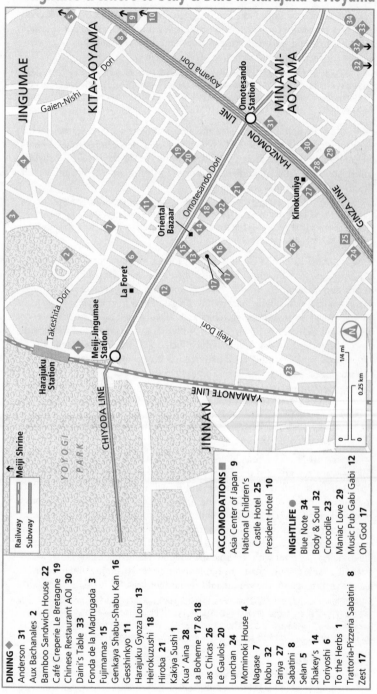

ACCOMODATIONS ■
Asia Center of Japan **9**
National Children's
    Castle Hotel **25**
President Hotel **10**

NIGHTLIFE ●
Blue Note **34**
Body & Soul **32**
Crocodile **23**
Maniac Love **29**
Music Pub Gabi Gabi **12**
Oh God **17**

DINING ◆
Anderson **31**
Aux Bachanales **2**
Bamboo Sandwich House **22**
Café Creperie Le Bretagne **19**
Chinese Restaurant AOI **30**
Daini's Table **33**
Fonda de la Madrugada **3**
Fujimamas **15**
Genkaya Shabu-Shabu Kan **16**
Gesshinkyo **11**
Harajuku Gyoza Lou **13**
Heirokuzushi **18**
Hiroba **21**
Kakiya Sushi **1**
Kua' Aina **28**
La Boheme **17 & 18**
Las Chicas **26**
Le Gaulois **20**
Lunchan **24**
Mominoki House **4**
Nagase **7**
Nobu **32**
Pariya **27**
Sabatini **8**
Selan **5**
Shakey's **14**
Toriyoshi **6**
To the Herbs **1**
Trattoria-Pizzeria Sabatini **8**
Zest **17**

tempting choices as grilled chicken on garlic mashed potatoes with bok choy and oyster barbecue sauce; New York strip steak with miso mashed potatoes and shiitake salad; and stir-fried roast duck with crispy vegetables. Lunch offers lighter fare, including sandwiches, stir-fries, and curries.

6–3–2 Jingumae. © 03/5485-2262. Reservations recommended. Main dishes ¥1,200 – ¥2,600 ($10–$22); set lunch ¥1,000 ($8.35). AE, DC, MC, V. Mon–Fri noon–3pm and 6–10pm; Sat–Sun and holidays noon–4pm and 6–10pm. Station: Meiji-Jingumae (2 min.) or Harajuku (5 min.). Off Omotesando Dori, on a side street near Kiddy Land.

Le Gaulois FRENCH   This pleasant, unpretentious bistro is so tiny there's room for only 18 at one table and a counter, where diners can watch the owner-chef prepare set meals that may include fresh fish of the day, beef in red wine, grilled lamb with basil, and other dishes from the open kitchen. You almost feel like an invited guest in a private home.

4–3–21 Jingumae. © 03/3404-0820. Reservations required. Set dinners ¥3,800 – ¥7,200 ($32–$60); set lunches ¥2,800 – ¥4,400 ($23–$37). AE, DC, MC, V. Tues–Sun noon–2pm and 6:30–9pm (last order). Station: Omotesando (4 min.). Off Omotesando Dori; take the side street opposite the Hanae Mori Building (between McDonald's and Ito Hospital) and turn left.

Lunchan AMERICAN   Good American food is the forte of this contemporary, open, and airy bistro, with a dinner menu that includes pasta, pizza, sandwiches, and meat entrees. Choose from among such dishes as pizza al forno with Italian smoked ham, fresh mushrooms, oregano, and hot peppers; meat loaf; grilled sea bass with sautéed vegetables and served with a caper berry sauce; or steak. A wide selection of lunch specials is offered, among them sandwiches with all the trimmings. Sunday brunch, which includes a glass of champagne and is served until 3pm, features breakfast treats like eggs Benedict and pancakes, ordered from a menu.

1–2–5 Shibuya. © 03/5466-1398. Reservations required for Sun brunch. Pizza ¥1,400 – ¥1,600 ($12–$13); main dishes ¥1,600 – ¥3,600 ($13–$30); set lunches ¥1,200 – ¥2,300 ($10–$19); Sun brunch ¥2,500 ($21). AE, DC, MC, V. Mon–Sat 11:30am–10pm; Sun 11am–9pm. Station: Omotesando or Shibuya (10 min.). Easy to find, halfway between Shibuya and Aoyama and just off Aoyama Dori on the side street south of the National Children's Castle.

Selan ITALIAN   This restaurant has one of the most envied spots in all of Tokyo—on a gingko-lined street that serves as the entrance to Meiji-Jingu-gaien Park. The food, Italian with Japanese and French influences, is sometimes hit-and-miss, with past offerings including roasted duck with black and green olive sauce and baked scampi with black chili sauce, plus an assortment of pizzas and pastas—but on a warm summer's day, there's nothing more sublime than sitting on the outdoor terrace and reveling in all that greenery. The hours below are for the upstairs restaurant with large picture windows; the ground-floor cafe, which offers the same menu, boasts an outdoor terrace open throughout the day—make that throughout the year, thanks to outdoor heaters.

2–1–19 Kita-Aoyama. © 03/3478-2200. Pasta and pizza ¥1,200 – ¥1,660 ($10–$14); main dishes ¥2,200 – ¥2,800 ($18–$23); set lunches ¥1,800 – ¥4,000 ($15–$33). AE, DC, MC, V. Mon–Fri 11:30am–2:30pm and 6–9:30pm; Sat 11am–2:30pm and 6–9:30pm; Sun 11am–2:30pm and 6–8:30pm. Station: Gaienmae or Aoyama-Itchome (5 min.). Off Aoyama Dori, at the entrance to Meiji-Jingu-gaien Park.

INEXPENSIVE

In addition to the choices below, also consider Tex-Mex restaurant **Zest Cantina,** 6–7–18 Jingumae (© **03/3409-6268**), open daily from 11:30am to 5pm (see "Ebisu & Meguro," later in this chapter, for a review). Here, too, is **La Boheme** (© **03/3400-3406**), which has a second location on Omotesando Dori at 5–8–5

Jingumae (© **03/5467-5666**); both serve pizza and pasta and are open daily from 11:30am to 5pm (see "Ginza & Hibiya," earlier in this chapter, for a review). **Shakey's,** on Omotesando Dori near Oriental Bazaar at 6–1–10 Jingumae (© **03/3409-2404**), offers an all-you-can eat pizza buffet Monday through Saturday from 11am to 3pm (see "Shinjuku," earlier in this chapter, for a review).

Anderson AMERICAN/SANDWICHES   This popular, nonsmoking bakery has a self-serve deli and sandwich bar in its basement, where you can choose from a variety of salads and cold and warm sandwiches, including ham and cheese, chicken salad, and lobster and avocado. On the second and third floors is a restaurant with waitress service, featuring more elaborate, open-faced sandwiches and stews and seating near big windows, good for people-watching.

5–1–26 Minami-Aoyama. © 03/3407-4833. Sandwiches ¥550 – ¥980 ($4.60–$8.15). No credit cards. Daily 9am–10pm; closed 3rd Mon each month. Station: Omotesando (1 min.). On Aoyama Dori.

Bamboo Sandwich House AMERICAN/SANDWICHES   Although its sandwiches aren't as good as Anderson's (see above), the setting here is much more hip; it even boasts an outdoor terrace. It offers 20 sandwich fillings on your choice of bread. The fillings can be a bit odd (unless you've been searching for shrimp and broccoli with anchovy sauce or a potato-and-meat-sauce gratin filling), but there are more mundane choices like tuna or roast pork, and with great outdoor seating, even a weird sandwich seems okay here.

5–8–8 Jingumae. © 03/3407-8427. Sandwiches ¥350 – ¥700 ($2.90–$5.85). No credit cards. Daily 11am–10pm. Station: Omotesando or Meiji-Jingumae (5 min.) or Harajuku (8 min.). Off Omotesando Dori on a side street that runs beside the Paul Stuart shop.

Cafe Creperie Le Bretagne *(Kids)* FRENCH/CREPES   With an inviting open-fronted shop, posters of Brittany, natural wood and brick, and a French staff, this is *the* place for authentic buckwheat galettes and crepes filled with yummy fruit or chocolate (or with such irresistible combinations as banana, chocolate, and rum). Kids will love this place, too.

4–9–8 Jingumae. © 03/3478-7855. Crepes ¥700 – ¥1,200 ($5.85–$10); set lunches ¥1,400 – ¥1,600 ($12–$13). No credit cards. Tues–Thurs 11:30am–11pm; Fri–Sat 11:30am–midnight; Sun 11:30am–10pm (last order). Station: Omotesando. Off Omotesando Dori; take the side street opposite the Hanae Mori Building (the one between McDonald's and Ito Hospital, with a HARAJUKU sign above it), walk to the end of the block, and turn left.

Chinese Restaurant AOI CHINESE   This popular, casual, noisy restaurant offers more than 100 items on its regular English-language menu, which has pictures. Two plate sizes are available for the chicken, pork, beef, shark's fin, tofu, seafood, vegetable, and casserole dishes. I especially like this place for dim sum; there are about 30 different varieties from which to choose.

5–9–1 Minami-Aoyama. © 03/3407-9727. Main dishes ¥1,200 – ¥2,500 ($10–$21); dim sum ¥600 – ¥1,200 ($5–$10). DC, MC, V. Daily 11:30am–3pm and 5:30–10pm. Station: Omotesando (B1 exit, 1 min.). Across Aoyama Dori from Kinokuniya, on a small side street.

Fonda de la Madrugada MEXICAN   Serving what is probably Tokyo's most authentic Mexican food, this dark basement restaurant has a cavernous main dining room, several small and cozy offshoots, and a strolling mariachi band, making it seem like you're dining in a Mexican villa. Shrimp marinated in tequila, chicken mole, and soft-tortilla tacos served with chicken, fish, beef, or pork are just some of the items on the trilingual (Japanese/Spanish/English) menu, along with the requisite Mexican beers; tequila shots and shooters; margaritas; rum and vodka cocktails; and wine from Mexico, Chile, and Argentina.

2–33–12 Jingumae. ☎ **03/5410-6288**. Main dishes ¥1,000 – ¥2,600 ($8.35–$22). AE, DC, MC, V. Sun–Thurs 5:30pm–2am; Fri–Sat 5:30pm–5am. Station: Meiji-Jingumae (10 min.). From the Meiji Dori/Omotesando intersection, walk north on Meiji Dori (toward Shinjuku); it will be on your right after the pedestrian overpass.

㉛ Genkaya Shabu-Shabu Kan *Value* SHABU-SHABU/SUKIYAKI   This casual restaurant with a rustic interior is one of the cheapest I've ever seen for shabu-shabu and sukiyaki. For ¥1,500 ($13) you can have all the shabu-shabu or sukiyaki you can eat; for ¥1,700 ($14) you can add vegetables. Thank goodness there's a 90-minute time limit; otherwise, you might have to be airlifted out.

6–7–8 Jingumae. ☎ **03/3406-6500**. All-you-can-eat shabu-shabu or sukiyaki ¥1,500 – ¥1,700 ($13–$14). No credit cards. Daily 5pm–2am. Station: Meiji-Jingumae (3 min.) or Harajuku (5 min.). From the Meiji/Omotesando Dori intersection, walk on Omotesando Dori toward Aoyama and take the 3rd right (just before Kiddy Land); it's at the end of this street, to the left.

㉜ Harajuku Gyoza Lou ★ GYOZA   If you like *gyoza* (pork dumplings), you owe yourself a meal here. Unlike most greasy spoons that specialize in fast-food Chinese (and tend to be on the dingy side), this restaurant in the heart of Harajuku is hip yet unpretentious and draws a young crowd with its straightforward menu posted on the wall. Only four types of gyoza are offered: boiled *(sui-gyoza)* or fried *(yaki-gyoza),* and with or without garlic *(ninniku).* A few side dishes, such as cucumber, boiled cabbage with vinegar, sprouts with a spicy meat sauce, and rice, are available, as are beer and sake. A U-shaped counter encloses the open kitchen, giving diners something to watch as they chow down on the very good gyoza.

6–2–4 Jingumae. ☎ **03/3406-4743**. Gyoza ¥290 ($2.40) for a plate of 6. No credit cards. Mon–Sat 11:30am–4:30am; Sun and holidays 11:30am–11:30pm. Station: Meiji-Jingumae (3 min.) or Harajuku (5 min.). From the Meiji/Omotesando Dori intersection, walk on Omotesando Dori toward Aoyama and take the 3rd right (just before Kiddy Land); it's at the end of this street, on the right.

㉝ Heirokuzushi SUSHI   Bright (a bit too bright), clean, and modern, this is one of those fast-food sushi bars where plates of food are conducted along a conveyor belt on the counter. Customers help themselves to whatever strikes their fancy. To figure your bill, the cashier counts the number of plates you took from the conveyor belt: pink plates cost ¥120 ($1), green ones ¥160 ($1.35), blue ones ¥240 ($2), black ones ¥350 ($2.90), and gold ones ¥500 ($4.15). There's a plastic display case of takeout sushi; you might want to eat in nearby Yoyogi Park.

5–8–5 Jingumae. ☎ **03/3498-3968**. Sushi ¥120 – ¥500 ($1–$4.15) each. No credit cards. Daily 11am–9pm. Station: Meiji-Jingumae (2 min.) or Omotesando (5 min.). On Omotesando Dori close to the Oriental Bazaar.

Hiroba JAPANESE HEALTH FOOD/VEGETARIAN   Located in the basement of the Crayon House, which specializes in Japanese children's books, this natural-food restaurant offers a buffet lunch of organic veggies, fish, brown rice, and other health foods. For dinner, only set meals are available. The dining hall is very simple (its atmosphere reminds me of a potluck supper in a church basement), and because of the upstairs bookstore, there are likely to be families here. Sharing the same phone, open hours, and cash register is **Home,** with waitress service and also offering wholesome meals using organic ingredients, including vegetarian choices. Set lunches here are ¥1,800 to ¥2,500 ($15–$21), with dinner entrees costing ¥1,800 to ¥2,200 ($15–$18).

Crayon House, 3–8–15 Kita Aoyama. ☎ **03/3406-6409**. Lunch buffet ¥1,200 ($10); set dinner ¥1,200 ($10). No credit cards. Daily 11am–2pm and 5–10pm. Station: Omotesando (2 min.). Off Omotesando Dori on the side street to the right of the Hanae Mori Building.

(34) **Kakiya Sushi** SUSHI   This conveyor-belt sushi bar is more hip than most, attracting a mostly youngish crowd with its contemporary interior, modern art on the walls, music that might include the Rolling Stones, and windows overlooking the greenery of Meiji Shrine. An English-language menu on each table describes the options, which include sushi rolls, salmon, conger eel, sea urchin roe, and the ubiquitous tuna, all delivered via color-coded plates of varying prices. Smoking is not allowed.

3rd floor, 1–14–27 Jingumae. © **03/3423-1400**. Plates of sushi ¥60 – ¥480 (50¢–$4). No credit cards. Daily 11am–11pm. Station: Harajuku (1 min.). Across from Harajuku Station; look for the sign SUSHI KAITEN.

Kua' Aina ★ (Kids) AMERICAN/HAMBURGERS/SANDWICHES   How far will you go for a great burger? Quite simply, the best burgers in town make this Hawaiian import a smashing success. In fact, if you come at mealtime you'll probably have to wait for a table in one of the tiny upstairs dining rooms. Burgers come as third- and (whopping) half-pounders. There are also sandwiches ranging from BLTs with avocado to roast beef to tuna. A good carnivore fix.

A branch at 1–10–4 Shibuya (© 03/3409-3200) is open daily 11am to 11pm.

5–10–21 Minami Aoyama. © **03/3407-8001**. Burgers and sandwiches ¥580 – ¥1,380 ($4.85–$12). No credit cards. Mon–Sat 11am–11pm; Sun 11am–10pm. Station: Omotesando (2 min.). On Aoyama Dori at its busy intersection with Kotto Dori, catty-corner from Kinokuniya grocery store.

Las Chicas ★ (Kids) INTERNATIONAL   Opened by fashion house Vision Network, Las Chicas is a trendy cafe/bar in a complex housing several alternative bars and shops, including a tattoo parlor and stores selling original clothing and imports. Popular as a hangout for young foreigners and those in the fashion/design business, Las Chicas has an English-language menu and foreign waiters and cooks. Its food is fun and eclectic, borrowing ingredients and recipes from around the world for its constantly changing menu that always includes vegetarian choices, salads, pizza, dishes for children, and homemade desserts and bread. Examples of past entrees include Gorgonzola risotto with spinach and sweet basil pesto, and Australian rack of lamb coated with macadamia nuts, garlic, and herbs. Its laid-back, outdoor terrace makes it a good spot also for espresso, fruit smoothies, herbal tea, wine, or beer. Be sure to explore the rest of the complex.

5–47–6 Jingumae. © **03/3407-6865**. Main dishes ¥1,350 – ¥2,400 ($11–$22). AE, DC, V. Daily 11am–11pm. Station: Omotesando (5 min.). Take the Kinokuniya exit and head down Aoyama Dori toward Shibuya, taking a right 2 blocks after Kinokuniya; Las Chicas is down this small street, near the end on the left.

Mominoki House ★ (Finds) NOUVELLE JAPANESE/HEALTH FOOD   Mominoki House dishes could be described as French, except they're the creations of a very busy chef (who is also the owner) who uses lots of soy sauce, ginger, Japanese vegetables, and macrobiotic foods (there's even organic wine and beer). This alternative restaurant, in a category by itself, features hanging plants and split-level dining, which allows for more privacy than you would think possible in such a tiny place. Its recorded jazz collection is extensive. Dinner features approximately 50 a la carte dishes and may include the likes of tofu steak, roasted organic chicken with rosemary, sole, eggplant gratin (delicious), salads, and homemade sorbet. Note that there's a dinner table charge of ¥300 ($2.50) per person. Especially good deals are the four daily lunch specials featuring brown rice, miso soup, seasonal vegetables, and fish or another main dish. There's an English-language menu, but daily specials are written on the blackboard in Japanese only. The chef, Mr. Yamada, speaks English, so if in doubt, ask him what he recommends.

2–18–5 Jingumae. ℂ **03/3405-9144.** Main dishes ¥1,000–¥2,000 ($8.35–$17); set dinners ¥1,800–¥3,500 ($15–$29); set lunches ¥1,000–¥1,800 ($8.35–$15). No credit cards. Mon–Sat 11am–10:30pm (last order). Closed Golden Week. Station: Meiji-Jingumae (10 min.) or Harajuku (15 min.). From the Meiji Dori/Omotesando intersection, walk north on Meiji Dori and turn right at the pedestrian overpass; it will be on the left at the 2nd street on the corner.

Nagase ✿✿ *Finds* FRENCH   This is another one of those casual neighborhood bistros offering great food at very reasonable prices that made its debut following the economic recession. Like most of the others, a cut in prices means a crowding of tables to accommodate as many diners as possible, but except for the most special of occasions, I'll gladly settle for cheaper prices over spaciousness. Set menus give a choice of a half-dozen main dishes, which might include the fish of the day, beef Burgundy, *confit de canard,* or *noisettes de lamb au thym,* along with a salad or side dish, bread, and coffee. My ¥1,000 ($9) lunch was one of the best Western meals I've ever had in Japan at that price—a salad with boiled egg, chicken, mushrooms, and tomato, followed by whitefish on mashed potatoes with an eggplant-tomato sauce subtly flavored with curry.

3–21–12 Jingumae. ℂ **03/3423-1925.** Reservations required on weekends. Set dinners ¥2,300 and ¥3,500 ($19–$29); set lunches ¥1,000–¥2,300 ($8.35–$19). No credit cards. Tues–Sat 11:30am–2pm and 5:30–9:30pm; Sun and holidays 11:30am–2pm and 5:30–8:30pm (last order). Station: Meiji-Jingumae (3 min.) or Harajuku (8 min.). On the opposite side of Meiji Dori from Takeshita Dori, on a side street nicknamed Harajuku Dori; it's on the left side of the street, up on the 2nd floor.

Pariya ✿ VARIED JAPANESE/INTERNATIONAL   What a clever concept: Design a chic, airy restaurant sure to draw in the fashionable Aoyama crowd, and then keep 'em coming with set lunches that change weekly. Diners compose their own meals from choices of a main course, one side dish, a salad, *genmai* (unpolished brown rice) or *hakumai* (polished white rice), soup, and coffee and tea. Ethnic-influenced offerings have included grilled chicken, salmon, and sukiyaki beef, while side dishes have ranged from sweet potatoes to pasta. At dinner, the establishment is a combination bar/restaurant, with an English-language menu listing salads (a standout is the Asian Caesar salad with oyster and poached egg, as well as the compose-your-own salads), noodle and rice dishes (recommended are the gyoza with leek or the pumpkin gnocchi with porcini cream sauce), pizza, and other fare that changes with the season. Sunday (11:30am–3pm) features a set meal for brunch with a choice of dishes for ¥1,300 ($11).

3–12–14 Kita Aoyama. ℂ **03/3486-1316.** Set lunches ¥1,100 ($9.15) with genmai, ¥1,000 ($8.35) with hakumai; dinner main courses ¥900–¥2,000 ($7.50–$17). AE, MC, V. Mon–Sat 11:30am–3pm and 6–10pm (last order). Station: Omotesando (4 min.). On a side street off Aoyama Dori, past Kinokuniya grocery store.

To the Herbs PIZZA/PASTA   This chain of pizza/pasta restaurants has sprouted like mushrooms throughout Tokyo and is so successful it must be doing something right. I find its choices more interesting than those of other chains of this ilk. With more than 50 pastas and 20 pizzas to choose from (including pizza with regular or crispy crust), there's something to please everyone. Spaghetti toppings run from the familiar (ground beef with tomato sauce) to the esoteric (cod roe and cuttlefish with Korean pickles and basil). Half portions of some pizzas are available.

There's another convenient To the Herbs next to Kabukiza at 4–13–11 Ginza (ℂ 03/5565-9800), open daily 11am to 11pm.

3rd floor, 1–14–27 Harajuku. ℂ **03/3423-2700.** Pizza and pasta ¥950–¥1,200 ($7.90–$10); set lunches ¥1,050 ($8.75). AE, DC, MC, V. Daily 11am–10:30pm. Station: Harakuju (1 min.). Across from the station.

(35) **Toriyoshi** VARIED JAPANESE/INTERNATIONAL   Open and airy
and decorated like a traditional warehouse *(kura)* with its gleaming woods, shoji
screens, and tatami seating (with leg wells for those errant legs), this chain has
an English-language menu listing a variety of Japanese and Asian pub fare,
including salads, yakitori, tofu (I love the black sesame tofu, called *kuroi gomad-
ofu*), chicken dishes, *kimchi* (spicy Korean cabbage), and more. A good place for
a convivial evening.

4–28–21 Jingumae. ✆ 03/3470-3901. Main dishes ¥580 – ¥1,500 ($4.85–$13). AE, DC, MC, V. Mon–Fri
5–11pm; Sat–Sun 4–11pm (last order). Station: Meiji-Jingumae (3 min.). From the Meiji Dori/Omotesando,
walk on Omotesando toward Aoyama and turn left at Wendy's; Toriyoshi is down this street, on the right side
beside a willow tree.

Trattoria-Pizzeria Sabatini ITALIAN/PIZZA   This basement restaurant,
opened in 1984 and owned by brothers from Rome who also operate Sabatini,
an expensive Italian restaurant in the same building (see review, earlier in this
chapter), offers the closest thing to real pizza in town. Many ingredients are
flown in from Italy, including olive oil and huge slabs of Parmesan and other
cheeses, as well as the restaurant's large wine selection; they've even shipped in a
pasta machine. In addition to pizzas, there's spaghetti, lasagna, fettuccine, and
meat and seafood dishes. All you need order, however, is pizza.

Suncrest Bldg., 2–13–5 Kita-Aoyama. ✆ 03/3402-2027. Pasta and pizza ¥1,300 – ¥1,800 ($11–$15); main
dishes ¥2,200 – ¥3,000 ($18–$25); set lunches ¥1,500 – ¥3,200 ($13–$27). AE, DC, MC, V. Mon–Sat
11:30am–2:30pm and 5:30pm–3am; Sun and holidays 11:30am–2:30pm and 5:30–11pm. Station: Gaienmae
(1 min.). At the intersection of Aoyama Dori and Gaien-Nishi Dori.

11 Shibuya

Serving as a major commuter nucleus, Shibuya caters primarily to students and
young office workers with its many fashion department stores and lively
nightlife scene. In addition to the suggestions below, consider the fourth floor
of **Mark City**, 1–12–5 Dogenzaka, across from Shibuya Station (and next to the
Shibuya Excel Hotel Tokyu), where you'll find a dozen or so restaurants specializing in Japanese, Italian, and Chinese food. Try (36) **Mikura** (✆ 03/5459-
4011), simply but elegantly decorated, for its obento and kaiseki; set lunches
cost ¥2,800 to ¥3,800 ($23–$32) and dinners cost ¥3,800 to ¥6,800
($32–$57). It's open daily 11am to 1:30pm and 5 to 9pm (last order). I also like
(37) **Mimiu** (✆ 03/5459-2620), which offers shabu-shabu for ¥3,800 ($32)
per person. It's open daily 11am to 9:30pm (last order).

   You'll also find branches of **La Boheme** (✆ 03/3477-0481) and **Zest Cantina**
(✆ 03/5489-3332), both at 1–6–8 Jinnan and open daily 11:30am to 5am (see
"Ginza & Hibiya," earlier in this chapter, for a review of the pizza/pasta restaurant La Boheme; and "Ebisu & Meguro," below, for a review of Zest Cantina).

INEXPENSIVE

Sonoma *Value* CALIFORNIAN   This unpretentious, small restaurant with an
open kitchen serves Californian/Mexican fusion cuisine (the chef is Mexican), at
very good prices. You might want to start with a California roll of spicy tuna and
Mexican cactus or the Cuban black bean soup, followed by roast chicken with
coriander and avocado paste, chicken enchiladas with bleu cheese and jalapeño
sauce, or spicy miso grilled swordfish with fried tofu and steamed veggies. It's all
yummy—so many choices, so little time.

2–25–17 Dogenzaka. ✆ 03/3462-7766. Main dishes ¥1,000 – ¥1,800 ($8.35–$15); set lunch ¥900 ($7.50).
AE, DC, MC, V. Daily 11:30am–11:30pm. Station: Shibuya (Hachiko exit, 3 min.). From the station, walk on

Dogenzaka to The Prime Building and MOS and take the 1st right. Sonoma is at the end of the diagonal street, on the right, surrounded by love hotels.

Tengu VARIED JAPANESE   Founded in 1969, this a great place for an inexpensive meal. Although a drinking establishment and located smack-dab in the middle of Shibuya's Center Gai nightlife district, it is more brightly lit than most Japanese pubs and is popular with young Japanese professionals. An English-language menu with photos makes ordering easy and includes all the typical bar food and snacks—yakitori, sashimi, sushi, tofu, salad, gyoza, pizza, fried noodles, and more. And there's plenty of beer, shochu, sake, wine, and cocktails to wash it all down.

15–3 Udagawacho. ⓒ **03/3496-7392.** Main dishes ¥380–¥500 ($3.15–$4.15). AE, DC, MC, V. Daily 5–11:30pm. Station: Shibuya (Hachiko exit, 4 min.). Off Center Gai just past HMV on the right; look for the Tengu logo—a red face with a long nose.

12 Ebisu & Meguro

MODERATE

Cafe Francais ✹ FRENCH   Housed in a reproduction 18th-century French château planted in the midst of swanky Yebisu Garden Place, this ground-floor brasserie offers nouveau French cuisine at a fraction of what meals cost at the more expensive and more formal Taillevent Robuchon upstairs (where entrees start at ¥7,000/$58 and set dinners cost ¥22,000/$183). The cafe allows you to compose your own set meals from a generous list of soups, appetizers, and main dishes. (Ravenous diners beware: Portions are small, so you might want to order one of the higher-priced set meals.) In any case, Cafe Francais is fancy enough for most tastes, with its Louis XV paneled dining room complete with portraits. On warm, sunny days, you can dine outdoors on the terrace. The wine list is extensive, with more than 300 vintages from throughout France, and at reasonable prices to boot.

Yebisu Garden Place, 1–13–1 Mita. ⓒ **03/5424-1338.** Reservations recommended. Set dinners ¥4,200–¥7,500 ($35–$63); set lunches ¥2,800–¥4,200 ($23–$35) Mon–Fri, ¥3,400–¥5,000 ($28–$42) Sat–Sun. AE, DC, MC, V. Mon–Fri 11:30am–2pm and 5:30–9pm; Sat–Sun 11:30am–2:30pm and 6–9pm (last order). Station: Ebisu (6 min.).

The Terrace Restaurant at Hanezawa Garden ✹✹ *Finds* VARIED JAPANESE/INTERNATIONAL   There's no finer place to enjoy balmy summer nights than this outdoor garden, spread under trees on a raised deck lit by Tiki torches. In inclement weather, diners are sheltered by a retractable awning and warmed by outdoor heaters (though I must admit that's not nearly as romantic as dining under the stars). In addition to Kirin beer, wine, and cocktails, the restaurant offers a limited English-language menu that includes Vietnamese tuna spring rolls, fried shrimp with mayonnaise, Korean lettuce salad, Caesar salad, *edamame* (steamed soy beans), kimchi, and do-it-yourself barbecues of seafood, beef, sausage, or vegetables. I usually order one of the set meals, which include various meats and vegetables for your table's own grill, plus side dishes.

3–21–15 Hiroo. ⓒ **03/3400-2013.** Main dishes ¥900–¥2,000 ($7.50–$17); set meals ¥3,500–¥5,000 ($29–$42). AE, DC, MC, V. Apr to mid-Oct 11:30am–1:30pm and 5:30–9:30pm (last order). Closed mid-Oct to Mar. Station: Ebisu, Omotesando, or Shibuya (then take a taxi).

INEXPENSIVE

In addition to the choices here, there's a **La Boheme** on Gaien-Nishi Dori, 4–19–17 Shirokanedai (ⓒ **03/3442-4488;** station: Shirokanedai, 4 min.), open daily 11:30am to 5am for pizza and pasta (see "Ginza & Hibiya," earlier in this chapter, for a review).

㊳ **Tonki** 🏮 TONKATSU   This is perhaps the best-known *tonkatsu* (pork cutlet) restaurant in town. You'll probably have to wait for a seat at the counter, but it's worth it. A man will ask whether you want the *hirekatsu* (a filet cut of lean pork) or the *rosukatsu* (a loin cut, with some fat on it). *Kushi-katsu* (skewered pork with onions) is also available. No matter what you choose, ask for the teishoku, the set meal featuring soup, rice, cabbage, pickled vegetable, and tea. The man will scribble your order on a piece of paper and put it with all the other scraps of paper, miraculously keeping track of not only which order belongs to whom but also which customers have been waiting for seats the longest. The open kitchen behind the counter takes up most of the space in the restaurant, and as you eat you can watch the half-dozen or so cooks scrambling to turn out orders—never a dull moment, and in my opinion one of the highlights of dining here. You can get free refills of tea, rice, and cabbage.

1–1–2 Shimo Meguro. ℂ **03/3491-9928.** Kushi-katsu teishoku ¥1,200 ($10); hirekatsu or rosukatsu teishoku ¥1,650 ($14). V. Wed–Mon 4–10:45pm (last order). Closed 3rd Mon each month. Station: Meguro (west exit, 1 min.). On the west side of JR station, catty-corner to the left behind a tall, nondescript bank building; look for blue curtains over sliding glass doors.

Zest Cantina TEX-MEX   You can probably find better Mexican restaurants at home, but this will do for a quick fix, especially once the margaritas kick in. A huge, multilevel restaurant decorated cantina-style with corrugated sheet metal on the outside and wood and brick on the inside, Zest offers chicken and cheese burritos, shrimp enchiladas, and other Tex-Mex fare, as well as steaks, hamburgers, and very good salads. If you're wearing stiletto heels, beware: I saw several lasses snared by the wide-planked flooring, which made for an interesting side show.

You'll find other Zest Cantinas, all open 11:30am to 5am, in the Ginza at 1–2–3 Ginza (ℂ 03/5524-3621); in Harajuku at 6–7–18 Jingumae (ℂ 03/3409-6268); in Shibuya at 1–6–8 Jinnan (ℂ 03/5489-3332); and in Odaiba on the fourth floor of Mediage (ℂ 03/3599-4803).

1–22–19 Ebisu. ℂ **03/5475-6291.** Main dishes ¥950 – ¥2,600 ($7.90–$22); set lunches ¥850 – ¥1,350 ($7.10–$11). AE, DC, MC, V. Daily 11:30am–5am. Station: Ebisu (east exit, 8 min.). On the right side of street that runs between the Sumitomo and Fuji banks.

13 Roppongi & Nishi Azabu

Because Roppongi is such a popular nighttime hangout for young Tokyoites and foreigners, it boasts a large number of both Japanese and Western restaurants. To find the location of any of the Roppongi addresses below, stop by the tiny police station on **Roppongi Crossing** (Roppongi's main intersection of Roppongi Dori and Gaien-Higashi Dori), where you'll find a map of the area. If you still don't know where to go, ask one of the policemen.

About a 10-minute walk west of Roppongi (via Roppongi Dori in the direction of Shibuya) is **Nishi Azabu.** Once primarily a residential neighborhood, Nishi Azabu has slowly changed over the years as it began absorbing the overflow of Roppongi. It has restaurants and a few bars, yet remains mellower and much less crowded than Roppongi.

Note: To locate these restaurants, see the map on p. 143.

VERY EXPENSIVE

㊴ **Inakaya** 🏮🏮 *Overrated* ROBATAYAKI   Whenever I'm playing hostess to foreign visitors in Tokyo, I always take them to this festive restaurant, and they've never been disappointed. Although tourist-oriented and over-priced, it's still great fun; the drama of the place alone is worth it. Customers sit at a long, U-shaped counter, on the other side of which are mountains of fresh vegetables, beef, and seafood. And in the middle of all that food, seated in front of a grill, are male chefs—ready to cook whatever you point to in the style of robatayaki. Orders are yelled out by your waiter and are repeated in unison by all the other waiters, resulting in ongoing, excited yelling. Sounds strange, I know, but actually it's a lot of fun. Food offerings may include yellowtail, red snapper, sole, king crab legs, giant shrimp, steak, meatballs, gingko nuts, potatoes, eggplant, and asparagus, all piled high in wicker baskets and ready for the grill. There's another nearby branch at 5–3–4 Roppongi (✆ 03/3408-5040), open daily 5pm to 5am.

4–10–11 Roppongi. ✆ **03/5775-1012.** Meals average ¥12,000 ($100). AE, DC, MC, V. Daily 5–11pm. Station: Roppongi (2 min.). Off Gaien-Higashi Dor on a side street opposite Ibis Hotel; from Roppongi Crossing, walk on Gaien-Higashi Dori in the direction of Aoyama and take the 2nd right.

(40) **Takamura** ★★★ *Finds* KAISEKI Takamura is a must for anyone who can afford it. Located at the edge of Roppongi, this wonderful 60-year-old house, perched on a hill and hidden by greenery, is a peaceful oasis that time forgot. You'll dine in one of eight private tatami rooms, each one different. Charcoal hearths in the rooms are built into the floors, and windows look out onto miniature gardens. Takamura has a very Japanese feeling, which intensifies proportionately with the arrival of your meal—seasonal kaiseki food arranged so artfully you almost hate to destroy it. Your pleasure increases, however, as you savor the various textures and flavors of the food. Specialties may include quail, sparrow, or duck, grilled on the hearth in your private tatami room. Seating is on the floor, as it is in most traditional Japanese restaurants, but with leg wells. The price of dinner here usually averages about ¥27,000 to ¥33,000 ($225–$275) by the time you add drinks, tax, service charge, and table charge (¥2,000/$17 per person). Dinner is for parties of two or more, while lunch is available only for parties of four or larger.

3–4–27 Roppongi. ✆ **03/3585-6600.** Reservations required (1 day in advance for lunch, a week in advance for dinner, at which time you must order your meal). Set dinners ¥17,000, ¥20,000, and ¥25,000 ($142, $165, and $208); set lunches ¥15,000, ¥17,000, and ¥20,000 ($125, $142, and $165). AE, DC, MC, V. Tues–Sat noon–3pm and Mon–Sat 5–10:30pm. Closed for lunch the day following a holiday, 1st week in Jan, and 1 week in mid-Aug. Station: Roppongi (4 min.). The restaurant has 2 entrances, each marked by a wooden gate with a little roof. The sign on the restaurant is in Japanese only, but look for the credit-card signs. From Roppongi Crossing, take Roppongi Dori in the direction of Kasumigaseki; turn right on Yosezaka (you'll have to ask, since it's not clearly marked).

EXPENSIVE

(41) **Fukuzushi** ★★ SUSHI This is one of Tokyo's classiest sushi bars, attracting a cosmopolitan crowd. Although it has a traditional entrance through a small courtyard with lighted lanterns and the sound of trickling water, the interior is slick and modern with bold colors of black and red. Some people swear it has the best sushi in Tokyo, although with 7,000 sushi bars in the city, I'd be hard-pressed to say which one is tops. Certainly, you can't go wrong here. Five different set lunches are available, which feature sushi, *chirashi-zushi* (assorted sashimi with rice), or eel as the main course. Dinners are more extensive, with the ¥8,000 ($72) set course consisting of salad, sashimi, steamed egg custard, grilled fish, sushi, miso soup, dessert, and coffee (set dinners require orders by a minimum of two people).

5–7–8 Roppongi. ✆ **03/3402-4116.** Reservations recommended, especially for dinner. Set dinners ¥6,000 – ¥8,000 ($50–$67); set lunches ¥2,500 – ¥4,500 ($21–$38). AE, DC, MC, V. Mon–Sat 11:30am–2pm and

Nightlife & Where to Stay & Dine in Roppongi

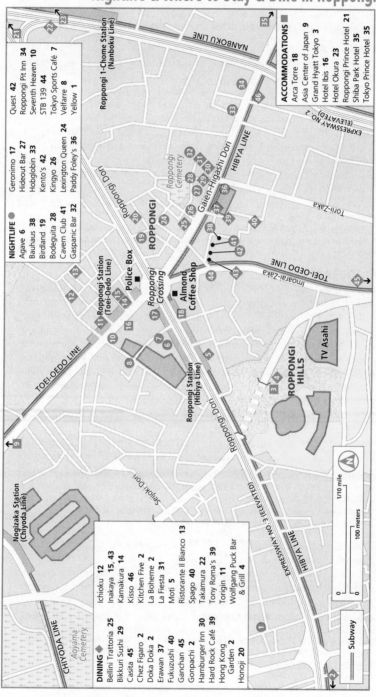

NIGHTLIFE ●
Agave **6**
Bauhaus **38**
Birdland **19**
Bodeguita **28**
Cavern Club **41**
Gaspanic Bar **32**
Geronimo **17**
Hideout Bar **27**
Hobglobin **33**
Kento's **42**
Kingyo **26**
Lexington Queen **24**
Paddy Foley's **36**
Quest **42**
Roppongi Pit Inn **34**
Seventh Heaven **10**
STB 139 **44**
Tokyo Sports Café **7**
Velfarre **8**
Yellow **1**

ACCOMMODATIONS ■
Arca Torre **18**
Asia Center of Japan **9**
Grand Hyatt Tokyo **3**
Hotel Ibis **16**
Hotel Okura **23**
Roppongi Prince Hotel **21**
Shiba Park Hotel **35**
Tokyo Prince Hotel **35**

DINING ◆
Bellini Trattoria **25**
Bikkuri Sushi **29**
Casita **45**
Chez Figaro **2**
Doka Doka **2**
Erawan **37**
Fukuzushi **40**
Ganchan **2**
Gonpachi **2**
Hamburger Inn **30**
Hard Rock Café **39**
Hong Kong
Garden **2**
Honoji **20**
Ichioku **12**
Inakaya **15, 43**
Kamakura **14**
Kisso **46**
Kitchen Five **2**
La Boheme **2**
La Fiesta **31**
Moti **5**
Ristorante Il Bianco **13**
Spago **40**
Takamura **22**
Tony Roma's **39**
Torigin **11**
Wolfgang Puck Bar
& Grill **4**

ROPPONGI

ROPPONGI HILLS

TV Asahi

Roppongi Crossing

Almond Coffee Shop

Police Box

Roppongi Station (Toei-Oedo Line)
Roppongi Station (Hibya Line)
Roppongi 1-Chome Station (Nanboku Line)
Nogizaka Station (Chiyoda Line)

Roppongi Cemetery
Aoyama Cemetery

Roppongi Dori
Gaien-Higashi Dori
Imoarai-Zaka
Torii-Zaka
Seijoki Dori

NANBOKU LINE
HIBYA LINE
TOEI-OEDO LINE
CHIYODA LINE
EXPRESSWAY NO. 2 (ELEVATED)
EXPRESSWAY NO. 3 (ELEVATED)

N

1/10 mile
100 meters
0
0

— Subway

5:30–11pm; holidays 5:30–10pm (last order). Station: Roppongi (4 min.). From Roppongi Crossing, walk toward Tokyo Tower on Gaien-Higashi Dori, turning right after McDonald's and left in front of Hard Rock Cafe.

Kisso ★★ KAISEKI   There should be more places like this in Tokyo. I love eating here because Kisso represents all that is best about modern Japan—understated elegance and a successful marriage between the contemporary and the traditional. This thoroughly modern establishment sells Japanese gourmet cookware, including expensive ceramics, utensils, and lacquerware of contemporary design, in its shop on the third floor. The restaurant, in the basement of this interesting building filled with shops dedicated to the best in interior design, is simple but elegant, with heavy tables, sprigs of flowers, and soft lighting. The food is kaiseki and comes only in set meals, served (as you might guess) on beautifully lacquered bowls and trays and ceramic plates. Before or after your meal, be sure to wander through the shops.

Axis Building, 5–17–1 Roppongi. ℂ 03/3582-4191. Reservations recommended for dinner. Set dinners ¥3,500 – ¥15,000 ($29–$125); set lunches ¥1,200 – ¥5,000 ($10–$42). AE, DC, MC, V. Mon–Sat 11:30am–2pm; Mon–Fri 5:30–9pm (last order); Sat 5:30–8pm (last order). Closed holidays. Station: Roppongi (5 min.). From Roppongi Crossing, walk toward Tokyo Tower on Gaien-Higashi Dori; the Axis Building will be on your right.

MODERATE

Casita ★★★ (Finds) PACIFIC RIM/FUSION-CROSSOVER   One of the reasons I'm a great fan of Casita's is that I feel truly pampered here. Who wouldn't, with a staff that proffers flashlights to the aged among us who have difficulty reading menus in dim lighting, stands ready to carry out every whim and, on chilly nights, tucks us in under electric blankets so we can enjoy after-dinner drinks on the deck before we head over to the massage chairs? Casita aims to please, carving its own niche in Tokyo's fiercely competitive market by creating a tropical, resortlike atmosphere bolstered by great service, an airy dining room with palm trees and orchids on every table, and a year-round outdoor deck that's heated in winter and covered when it rains. Of course, none of that matters if the food falls short, but Casita turns out dishes that border on awesome, whether it's the Caesar salad with serious shavings of Parmesan, the caramelized foie gras with sweet-and-spicy chutney, the Asian roasted lobster, or the tuna roast flavored with black truffle and port wine sauce. Who wouldn't be a fan?

54–10–25 Roppongi, 3rd floor. ℂ 03/5414-3190. Reservations highly recommended. Main dishes ¥2,000 – ¥3,600 ($17–$30). AE, DC, MC, V. Daily Sun–Thurs 6pm–2am; Fri–Sat 6pm–4am (to 4am daily in summer). Station: Roppongi (7 min.). From Roppongi Crossing, take the small side street going downhill to the left of the Almond Coffee Shop. Casita is at the bottom of the hill on the left.

Chez Figaro TRADITIONAL FRENCH   A small, cozy place that has changed little over the decades, this Tokyo old-timer has been serving the same authentic, traditional French cuisine since 1969. It's a good, dependable standby, offering such specialties as homemade pâté, escargot, sautéed sweetbreads, pepper steak, and young duckling with orange sauce.

4–4–1 Nishi Azabu. ℂ 03/3400-8718. Main dishes ¥1,500 – ¥4,500 ($13–$38); set dinners ¥4,900 ($41); set lunches ¥1,500 – ¥5,000 ($13–$42). AE, DC, MC, V. Daily noon–2:30pm and 6–9:30pm (last order). Station: Hiroo (7 min.) or Roppongi (15 min.). From Hiroo, take exit 3 and walk straight toward Nishi Azabu Crossing; the restaurant is on your left. From Roppongi, walk toward Shibuya on Roppongi, turning left onto Gaien-Nishi Dori; it will be on your right.

Doka Doka ★ NOUVELLE JAPANESE   Opened in 1996, this restaurant/ drinking establishment is a curious blend of the traditional and quirky, but it's done so well that the atmosphere intrigues rather than annoys. The traditional interior features mud-textured walls, heavy wood beams, and an open coal fire in the middle of the small first floor. Balcony seating upstairs rings a hand-carved balustrade and antique shoji dating from the early Showa Period (retrieved from a former geisha house in the Yoshiwara red-light district of yore). Soft jazz plays in the background, and seating is on an odd assortment of tiny chairs imported from Africa, Tibet, Bali, and other exotic lands. The food, on a handwritten Japanese-only menu (ask the manager for explanations), changes every 3 months according to what's fresh and available. Past dishes have included duck with miso salad, fish nabe, and an excellent chicken cassoulet. The bread is homemade. Expect to spend at least ¥5,000 ($42) per person.

4–2–14 Nishi Azabu. ✆ **03/3406-1681.** Reservations recommended on weekends. Main dishes ¥1,000 – ¥3,200 ($8.35–$27); set dinner ¥4,500 – ¥5,500 ($38–$46). AE, DC, MC, V. Mon–Thurs 6pm–2am; Fri–Sat 6pm–3am (last order). Closed holidays. Station: Hiroo (7 min.) or Roppongi (15 min.). On a small side street across Gaien-Nishi Dori from the gas station, next to Kitchen Five (see later in this chapter).

Erawan ★★ THAI   Perched 13 floors above the Roppongi madness and offer-ing cool, aloof views on three sides (ask for the Tokyo Tower side), this restau-rant is massive but does a good job of sectioning the floor space into intimate dining areas and re-creating its native homeland with dark gleaming woods, wood carvings, plants, bamboo screens, and a smiling Thai staff. The food lives up to its reputation, with plenty of seafood and curry selections, including deep-fried prawns with chili sauce, steamed whitefish with Thai sauce, and red curry with beef and eggplant.

Roi Building, 13th floor, 5–5–1 Roppongi. ✆ **03/3404-5741.** Main dishes ¥1,200 – ¥2,000 ($10–$17); set dinners ¥3,500 – ¥4,500 ($29–$38). AE, DC, MC, V. Daily 5–11:30pm. Station: Roppongi (3 min.). From Rop-pongi Crossing, Erawan is on the right side of Gaien-Higashi Dori (the road leading to Tokyo Tower), just past McDonald's.

Spago ★★ AMERICAN/CALIFORNIAN   Like its sister restaurant in Los Angeles, this franchise serves innovative California cuisine made famous by world-renowned Austrian-born chef Wolfgang Puck and now prepared by a Japanese chef who travels to the Beverly Hills Spago annually. The atmosphere here is bright, airy, and cheerful—very Californian—with huge bouquets of flowers, potted palms, and ferns. The menu changes every 3 months to reflect what's in season; expect the likes of angel-hair pasta with fresh thyme in goat cheese sauce and broccoli; grilled swordfish with jalapeno, cilantro, & cumin vinaigrette; and roasted baby lamb with Marsala wine sauce and mashed pota-toes. There are Japanese dishes as well. Needless to say, the main dishes are always imaginative, and the service is great. I especially like the nonsmoking ter-race. As you might expect, Spago has one of the largest selections of California wines in town.

5–7–8 Roppongi. ✆ **03/3423-4025.** Reservations required. Pizza and pasta ¥1,800 – ¥2,000 ($15–$17); main dishes ¥2,600 – ¥5,200 ($22–$43); set lunches ¥1,500 – ¥3,000 ($13–$25). AE, DC, MC, V. Mon–Fri 11:30am–2pm and 6–10pm; Sat–Sun 11:30am–2pm and 6–9:30pm; holidays 6–9:30pm. Station: Roppongi (4 min.). From Roppongi Crossing, walk toward Tokyo Tower on Gaien-Higashi Dori, turning right after McDonald's and left in front of Hard Rock Cafe.

Wolfgang Puck Bar & Grill ★★ AMERICAN/FUSION-CROSSOVER Whereas Spago (above) is a franchise, this restaurant, launched in 2003 in Rop-pongi Hills, is under the direct supervision of Puck himself, who plans to open a mind-boggling 100 more outlets in Japan over the next 10 years (including lower-priced cafes focusing on pizzas, sandwiches, and salads). Stylishly chic and more laid-back than Spago, it offers East-meets-West fusion cuisine created by

Puck, including original recipes designed for Japan. Dinner features such dishes as pan-seared swordfish with coconut curry and Basmati rice; or marinated honey soy lamb chop with stir-fried Californian vegetables in a mint sauce. Lunch is more casual, with everything from grilled hamburgers to barbecued chicken pizza with cilantro and red onion.

Hollywood Plaza 2nd floor, 6–4–1 Roppongi. © 03/5786-9630. Reservations recommended. Main dishes ¥2,500–¥3,200 ($21–$27). AE, DC, MC, V. Daily 11am–2:30pm and 5–10pm (last order). Station: Roppongi (Roppongi Hills exit, 1 min.).

INEXPENSIVE

In addition to the recommendations below, **Tony Roma's,** below the Hard Rock Cafe at 5–4–20 Roppongi (© **03/3408-7018**), is a U.S. chain specializing in barbecued ribs (see "Akasaka," below, for a review). In addition, **La Boheme,** 2–25–18 Nishi Azabu (© **03/3407-1363**), serving pizza and pasta; and **Gonpachi,** 1–13–11 Nishi Azabu (© **03/5771-0180**), serving Japanese food, are good places for inexpensive fare (see "Ginza & Hibiya," earlier in this chapter, for reviews of both).

Bellini Trattoria PIZZA/PASTA   With an open-fronted facade giving close-up views of Roppongi's never-ending parade of humanity, an open kitchen turning out inexpensive pizzas and pasta, and an easy-to-find location, this casual eatery is a no-brainer for an inexpensive meal in Roppongi. The best, front tables are reserved for smokers, while unfortunate nonsmokers are relegated to the back room. Good for smaller appetites: Half-size pizzas are available.

3–14–12 Roppongi. © 03/3470-5650. Pizza and pasta ¥1,100–¥1,800 ($9.15–$15); set lunches (Mon–Fri only) ¥1,000–¥1,800 ($8.35–$15). AE, MC, V. Mon–Thurs 11:30am–3:30pm and 6–10pm; Fri 11:30am–3:30pm and 6pm–3am; Sat 11:30am–3am; Sun 11:30am–10pm (last order). Station: Roppongi (2 min.). On the left-hand side of Gaien-Higashi Dori (the road leading to Tokyo Tower).

㊷ **Bikkuri Sushi** *Value* SUSHI   This is one of the cheapest places to eat in this popular nightlife district. Plates of sushi move along a conveyor belt past customers seated at the counter, who help themselves to whichever plates strike their fancy; this makes dining a cinch since it's not necessary to know the name of anything. The white plates of sushi are all priced at ¥130 ($1.10), while the colored dishes run ¥250 ($2.10) and ¥650 ($5.40). Your bill is tallied according to the number of plates you've taken.

3–14–9 Roppongi. © 03/3403-1489. Dishes ¥130–¥650 ($1.10–$5.40). No credit cards. Daily 11am–5am. Station: Roppongi (3 min.). On the left-hand side of Gaien-Higashi Dori (the road leading to Tokyo Tower), across the street from the Roi Building.

㊸ **Ganchan** ⭐ YAKITORI   This is one of my favorite yakitori-ya. Small and intimate, it's owned by a friendly and entertaining man who can't speak English worth a darn but keeps trying with the help of a worn-out Japanese-English dictionary he keeps behind the counter. His staff is young and fun-loving. There's an eclectic cassette collection—I never know whether to expect Japanese pop tunes or American oldies. Seating is along just one counter with room for only a dozen or so people. Though there's an English-language menu, it's easiest to order the yakitori *seto,* a set course that comes with salad and soup and eight skewers of such items as chicken, beef, meatballs, green peppers, and asparagus rolled with bacon. Be aware that there's a table charge of ¥600 ($5) per person, which includes an appetizer.

6–8–23 Roppongi. © 03/3478-0092. Yakitori skewers ¥200–¥400 ($1.65–$3.35); yakitori set course ¥2,500 ($21). AE, MC, V. Mon–Sat 5:30pm–1:30am; Sun and holidays 5:30pm–midnight. Station: Roppongi

---

A Note on Japanese Symbols

Many restaurants, hotels, and other establishments in Japan do not have signs giving their names in Roman (English-language) letters. As an aid to the reader, the second appendix to this book lists the Japanese symbols for all such places described in this guide. Each set of characters representing an establishment name has a number, which corresponds to the number that appears inside the box preceding the establishment's name in the text. Thus, to find the Japanese symbols for, say, **Ichioku,** refer to number 46 on p. 293 in appendix C.

(7 min.). From Roppongi Crossing, take the small street going downhill to the left of the Almond Coffee Shop; Ganchan is at the bottom of the hill on the right.

Hamburger Inn AMERICAN/HAMBURGERS   In a city that constantly re-invents itself, this totally uncool, 50-something hamburger joint is a surprise in trendy Roppongi. With its U-shaped counter and booth seating, it's the closest thing Roppongi has to an old-fashioned diner. The food—hamburgers, hot dogs, sandwiches, tacos, curry rice, spaghetti—is only for the desperate (I've tried the hamburger and couldn't identify the meat), but late hours and a great corner location make it a safe and convenient haven from which to observe Roppongi's parade of drunken revelry.

3–15–22 Roppongi. ✆ 03/3405-8980. Main dishes ¥350 – ¥1,080 ($2.90–$9). No credit cards. Mon–Sat 11:30am–5am. Station: Roppongi (3 min.). From Roppongi Crossing, walk on Gaien-Higashi Dori toward Tokyo Tower; Hamburger Inn will be on your left, on a corner across from the Roi Building.

Hard Rock Cafe *Kids* AMERICAN   Founded by two American expatriates in London in 1971, Hard Rock Cafe now has half a dozen locations in Japan; this was the first. If you have disgruntled teenagers in tow, bring them to this world-famous hamburger joint dedicated to rock 'n' roll to ogle the memorabilia on the walls, chow down on burgers, and look over the T-shirts for sale. In addition to hamburgers, the menu includes salads, sandwiches, steak, barbecued ribs, barbecued chicken, fish of the day, and fajitas. The music, by the way, is loud.

A branch is located in an old section of JR Ueno Station at 7–1–1 Ueno (✆ **03/5826-5821**), open daily 11am to 11pm.

5–4–20 Roppongi. ✆ 03/3408-7018. Main dishes ¥1,280 – ¥3,000 ($11–$25). AE, DC, MC, V. Mon–Thurs 11:30am–2am; Fri–Sat 11:30am–4am; Sun and holidays 11:30am–11:30pm. Station: Roppongi (3 min.). From Roppongi Crossing, walk on Gaien-Higashi Dori toward Tokyo Tower and take a right at McDonald's.

㊹ Hong Kong Garden Chinese Restaurant CHINESE   This huge, rather sterile restaurant with room for more than 500 lively diners is a no-non-sense kind of place, where dining is the main order of the day. In that respect, it does mirror the many spacious, family-oriented restaurants that dominate the former British colony. To dispel any doubt, a diorama of the Hong Kong sky-line takes up an entire wall. Rather than a menu, all-you-can-eat dim sum is available from pushcarts that weave throughout the dining room. Approximately 50 different dishes are offered, including spring rolls, fried dumplings (*gyoza*), steamed shrimp dumplings, braised bean curd with hot and spicy sauce, roast Peking duck, and sweet-and-sour vegetables. Look over the offerings, and take what looks good. Desserts are served from a buffet.

4–5–2 Nishi Azabu. ✆ 03/486-3711. All-you-can-eat dim sum dinner ¥4,000 ($33); lunch ¥3,000 ($25). AE, DC, MC, V. Mon–Fri 11:30am–3pm and 5:30–10:30pm; Sat–Sun and holidays 11:30am–4:30pm and

5:30–10pm. Station: Hiro (5 min.). On Gaien-Nishi Dori. From Hiroo, take exit 3 and walk straight toward Nishi Azabu Crossing; the restaurant is on your left. From Roppongi, walk toward Shibuya on Roppongi, turning left onto Gaien-Nishi Dori; it will be on your right.

45 Honoji ★ *Finds* VARIED JAPANESE   A plain wooden facade and a stark interior of concrete walls with wire-mesh screens set the mood for what this restaurant offers: good, home-style Japanese cooking, along with some Japanese interpretations of Western food. Although it looks small at first glance (an open kitchen takes up half the space), back-room nooks and crannies give diners a sense of privacy as they enjoy grilled fish, sashimi, yakitori, grilled eggplant with miso, deep-fried tofu, and a few Western dishes like creamed spinach and scallop gratin. Honoji serves the kinds of food offered by neighborhood *nomiya* (drinking establishments) all over Japan, which isn't exactly the kind of fare you'd expect to find in trendy Roppongi. Still, the crowds that wait at the door, especially on weekend nights, attest to its success. There's an English-language menu, but probably the best deal is the set dinner, which includes sashimi, a main dish such as grilled fish, seasonal vegetables, and several other side dishes. Otherwise, expect to spend ¥3,000 to ¥3,500 ($27–$32) per person; note that there's a dinner table charge of ¥450 ($3.75) per person at night. The lunch teishoku, available for ¥900 ($7.50) and the only item offered for lunch, draws Japanese from all walks of life.

3–4–33 Roppongi. ✆ **03/3588-1065.** Main dishes ¥400 – ¥680 ($3.35–$5.65); set dinner ¥3,000 ($25). AE, DC, MC, V. Mon–Fri 11:30am–1:30pm (last order); Mon–Sat 5:30–11pm (last order 10:15pm). Station: Roppongi (3 min.). On the right side of Roppongi Dori as you walk from Roppongi Crossing in the direction of Akasaka.

46 Ichioku ★ JAPANESE ORIGINALS   This is one of my favorite restaurants in Tokyo for casual dining. It's a tiny, cozy place with only eight tables, and you fill out your order yourself using the English-language menu—complete with pictures—which is glued underneath the clear glass tabletop. The food, featuring organically grown vegetables, can best be called Japanese nouvelle cooking, with original creations offered at very reasonable prices. There's tuna and ginger sauté, mushroom sauté, shrimp spring rolls, Thai curry, asparagus salad, fried potatoes, and a dish of crumbled radish and tiny fish. I recommend the tofu steak (fried tofu and flakes of dried fish) as well as the cheese gyoza (a fried pork dumpling with cheese melted on it).

4–4–5 Roppongi. ✆ **03/3405-9891.** Main dishes ¥350 – ¥2,950 ($2.90–$25). AE, DC, MC, V. Mon–Fri 11:30am–2pm and 5pm–midnight (last order); Sat 5pm–midnight; holidays 5–10:30pm. Station: Roppongi (4 min.). On a side street in the neighborhood behind the police station; look for the Rastafarian colors and a yin/yang sign.

Kamakura YAKITORI   Much more refined than most yakitori-ya, this basement establishment is decorated with paper lanterns and sprigs of fake but cheerful spring blossoms, with traditional koto music playing softly in the background. The English-language menu lists yakitori set courses, and a la carte sticks are skewered with shrimp, meatballs, gingko, squid, eggplant, or mushrooms.

4–10–11 Roppongi. ✆ **03/3405-4377.** Yakitori skewers ¥180 – ¥280 ($1.50–$2.35); set dinners ¥2,300 – ¥4,300 ($19–$36). AE, DC, MC, V. Mon–Sat 5pm–midnight. Station: Roppongi (2 min.). Off Gaien-Higashi Dori on a side street opposite Ibis Hotel; from Roppongi Crossing, walk on Gaien-Higashi Dori in the direction of Aoyama and take the 2nd right.

Kitchen Five ★ *Finds* MEDITERRANEAN/ETHNIC   If it's true that love is the best spice for cooking, then perhaps that's why Yuko Kobayashi's 15-year-old, 16-seat restaurant is so popular. She goes to market every morning to fetch ingredients for a dozen main dishes, which may include stuffed eggplant, moussaka, and other casseroles and curries. Every summer Kobayashi goes off to search for recipes in Sicily, South America, northern Africa, and other countries that feature garlic, tomatoes, and olive oil in their cuisine. The love for what she does shines in her eyes as she cooks, serves, and walks you through the menu of daily dishes displayed. *A word of warning:* The food is so delicious, it's tempting to over-order. Highly recommended.

4-2-15 Nishi Azabu. ✆ 03/3409-8835. Dishes ¥1,300 – ¥1,900 ($11–$16). MC, V. Tues–Sat 6–9:45pm (last order). Closed holidays, Golden Week, and late July to early Sept. Station: Hiroo (7 min.) or Roppongi (15 min.). Opposite Gaien-Nishi Dori from the gas station, down a side street.

La Fiesta MEXICAN   Although there is an ever-growing number of Mexican restaurants in Tokyo, the majority serve only passable food. This one is better than most, and even though its renditions may not be what you're used to, they're usually very tasty in their own right and are good for a spicy fix. Colorfully decorated with south-of-the-border memorabilia and set to the pace of lively Mexican music, it offers quesadillas, enchiladas, tacos, chimichangas, fajitas, and very good burritos. And, of course, everything goes down better with a margarita. Mexican beers and a good selection of tequilas are also available.

3-15-23 Roppongi. ✆ 03/3475-4412. Main dishes ¥800 – ¥2,280 ($7–$19); fixed-price meals ¥1,580 – ¥2,850 ($13–$24). AE, DC, MC, V. Sun–Thurs 5pm–1am; Fri–Sat 5pm–4am. Station: Roppongi (4 min.). From Roppongi Crossing, walk down Gaien-Higashi Dori in the direction of Tokyo Tower, turning left after passing McDonald's on your right.

Moti ✿ INDIAN   This is my favorite Indian restaurant in town. Dishes include vegetable curries, chicken and mutton curries (I usually opt for the *sag* mutton—lamb with spinach), and tandoori chicken. Set lunches, served until 2:30pm, offer a choice of vegetable, chicken, or mutton curry along with Indian bread *(naan)* and tea or coffee.

There are two branches of **Moti** in Akasaka: on the second floor of the Akasaka Floral Plaza, 3-8-8 Akasaka (✆ 03/3582-3620); and on the third floor of the Kinpa Building, 2-14-31 Akasaka (✆ 03/3584-6640).

6-2-35 Roppongi. ✆ 03/3479-1939. Main dishes ¥1,350 – ¥1,500 ($11–$13); set dinners ¥2,600 – ¥3,000 ($22–$25); set lunches ¥950 – ¥1,350 ($7.90–$11) Mon–Sat, ¥1,250 – ¥1,650 ($10–$14) Sun and holidays. AE, DC, MC, V. Mon–Sat 11:30am–10pm (last order); Sun and holidays noon–10pm. Station: Roppongi (3 min.). From Roppongi Crossing, walk toward Shibuya on Roppongi Dori; Moti will be on the left.

Ristorante Il Bianco ITALIAN   My friends and I don't know how they do it (or why, considering they probably lose money on us), but this very tiny Italian restaurant offers inexpensive wines (mostly from Chile) beginning at ¥1,000 ($8.35) for a bottle. More amazing, you can bring your own favorite bottle without paying a corkage fee. (There's a limit of one bottle per person, but truly, who should drink more?) Pasta comes in three sizes, with the smallest size perfect as a starter for one person. Main courses include sautéed red snapper with a red pimento sauce, and sautéed lamb chops with an herb-flavored caper sauce. The only problem is finding the place—stop at the police station at Roppongi Crossing to look at the map or ask for directions. And once you get there, be sure to take the stairs to the second-floor restaurant unless you want a cheap thrill—the elevator deposits you directly into the kitchen.

4-5-2 Roppongi. ✆ 03/3470-5678. Reservations a must for dinner. Pasta ¥1,200 – ¥1,600 ($10–$13); main dishes ¥1,600 – ¥2,600 ($13–$22); set dinners ¥3,800 – ¥5,000 ($33–$67); set lunches ¥1,000 – ¥2,800 ($8.35–$23). AE, DC, MC, V. Mon–Fri 11:30am–2pm and 5–10pm (last order); Sat 5–10pm. Station: Roppongi (3 min.). From Roppongi Crossing, take Roppongi Dori in the direction of Akasaka, turning left at the stoplight with a small park and water fountain; the restaurant is down this street, on the left.

47 **Torigin** YAKITORI/RICE CASSEROLES   Part of a chain of yakitori establishments, this no-frills place is typical of the smaller Japanese restaurants all over the country patronized by the country's salarymen, who stop off for a drink and a bite to eat before boarding the commuter trains for home. An English-language menu includes skewers of grilled chicken, gingko nuts, green peppers, quail eggs, and asparagus with rolled bacon, as well as various *kamameshi* (rice casseroles cooked and served in little pots and topped with chicken, bamboo shoots, mushrooms, crab, salmon, or shrimp).

4–12–6 Roppongi. ℂ 03/3403-5829. Yakitori skewers ¥140–¥250 ($1.15–$2.10); kamameshi ¥800–¥1,200 ($6.65–$10). No credit cards. Daily 11:30am–2pm and 5–10:30pm. Station: Roppongi (2 min.). From Roppongi Crossing, follow Gaien-Higashi Dori in the direction of Akasaka and take the 3rd right.

14 Akasaka

Note: To locate these restaurants, see the map on p. 83.

VERY EXPENSIVE

La Tour d'Argent ★★ CLASSIC FRENCH   Here's the place to dine if you're celebrating a very special occasion, are on a hefty expense account, or fancy yourself a jet-setter. Opened in 1984, La Tour d'Argent is the authentic sister to the one in Paris, which opened back in 1582 and was visited twice by Japan's former emperor, Hirohito. Entrance to the Tokyo restaurant is through an impressive hallway with a plush interior and displays of tableware used in the Paris establishment throughout the centuries. The dining hall looks like an elegant Parisian drawing room. The service is superb, and the food is excellent. The specialty here is roast duckling—it meets its untimely end at the age of 3 weeks and is flown to Japan from Brittany. Other dishes on the menu, which changes seasonally, may include lobster, roasted quail, or Kobe beef sirloin.

Hotel New Otani, 4–1 Kioi-cho. ℂ 03/3239-3111. Reservations required. Main dishes ¥6,500–¥13,000 ($54–$108). AE, DC, MC, V. Tues–Sun 5:30–10:30pm (last reservation accepted for 8:30pm). Station: Akasaka-mitsuke or Nagatacho (3 min.).

Sekishin Tei ★★ TEPPANYAKI   Nestled in the New Otani's 400-year-old garden (which is the reason this is the hotel's most popular restaurant), this glass-enclosed teppanyaki pavilion has an English-language menu for Kobe beef, fish, lobster, and vegetables, cooked on a grill right in front of you. If you order a salad, try the soy sauce dressing; it's delicious. You'll eat surrounded by peaceful views, making this place a good lunchtime choice.

Hotel New Otani, 4–1 Kioi-cho, Chiyoda-ku. ℂ 03/3238-0024. Reservations required. Set dinners ¥13,000–¥18,000 ($108–$150); set lunches ¥3,500–¥6,000 ($29–$50). AE, DC, MC, V. Mon–Fri 11:30am–2pm and 6–9pm; Sat–Sun and holidays 11:30am–3pm and 6–9pm. Station: Nagatacho or Akasaka-mitsuke (3 min.).

EXPENSIVE

48 **Hayashi** ★★★ *Finds* JAPANESE GRILL/RICE CASSEROLES   One of the most delightful old-time restaurants I've been to in Tokyo, this cozy, rustic-looking place serves home-style country cooking and specializes in grilled food that you prepare over your own square hibachi. Altogether, there are eight grills in this small restaurant, some of them surrounded by tatami mats and some by wooden stools or chairs. As the evening wears on, the one-room main dining areas can get quite smoky, but that just adds to the ambience. Other nice touches are the big gourds and memorabilia hanging about and the waiters in traditional baggy pants. Hayashi serves four set menus, which change with the seasons. The ¥6,000 ($50) meal—which will probably end up being closer to

¥8,000 ($67) by the time you add drinks, tax, and service charge—may include such items as sashimi and vegetables, chicken, scallops, and gingko nuts, which you grill yourself. At lunch, only *oyakodonburi* is served: literally, "parent and child," a simple rice dish topped with egg and chicken.

Sanno Kaikan Building, 4th floor, 2–14–1 Akasaka. ✆ 03/3582-4078. Reservations required for dinner. Set dinners ¥4,000, ¥6,000, ¥8,000, and ¥10,000 ($33, $50, $67, and $83); set lunches ¥900 ($7.50). AE, DC, MC, V. Mon–Fri 11:30am–2pm and 5:30–11pm; Sat 5:30–11pm. Closed holidays. Station: Akasaka (exit 2, 1 min.). Just south of Misuji Dori on the 3rd and 4th floors of a nondescript, improbable-looking building.

Kana Uni ⭐ FRENCH   This cozy and intimate restaurant/bar is owned and managed by a man who speaks excellent English and loves to have foreign guests. In fact, because the place is a little hard to find, they'll even come and fetch you if you call from Akasaka-mitsuke Station. Open since 1966 and claiming to have introduced sangria and espresso to Japan, Kana Uni features such main dishes as sliced raw tenderloin, steaks, beef stew, grilled fish, sautéed scallops, and poached filet of sole with sea-urchin sauce. But the real treat is the soft live jazz nightly from 8pm to 1:30am (music charge ¥1,500/$12 per person), so after dinner, relax with cocktails and enjoy the ambience. The red rose on each table, by the way, symbolizes the owner's favorite song, which is also the nightly closing number. Guesses, anyone?

1–1–16 Moto-Akasaka. ✆ 03/3404-4776. Reservations recommended. Main dishes ¥1,600–¥5,200 ($13–$43). AE, DC, MC, V. Mon–Fri 6pm–2:30am; Sat 6–11pm. Closed holidays. Station: Akasaka-mitsuke (3 min.). In the block behind the Suntory Building (look for the key-shaped logo).

Trader Vic's ⭐ SEAFOOD/STEAKS/INTERNATIONAL   The decor of this offshoot of an American chain operating out of California is Hollywood-set Polynesian. The extensive menu offers salads, seafood, Chinese dishes, curries, steak, and chicken. At lunch, lighter fare such as sandwiches is also available. A few tables boast views of the hotel's famous gardens (reserve in advance). For a major feast, come for the all-you-can-eat-and-drink sparkling-wine brunch on Sundays and holidays. Otherwise, a limited, less expensive menu is served at the bar, including weekday set lunches starting at ¥1,400 ($12), and a very popular U.S. rib-eye steak set dinner for ¥5,000 ($42). Try one of its 150 cocktails.

Hotel New Otani, 4–1 Kioi-cho. ✆ 03/3265-4707. Reservations recommended. Main dishes ¥3,500–¥6,300 ($29–$53); set dinners ¥9,500–¥14,000 ($79–$117); set lunches ¥3,700–¥3,900 ($31–$33); Sun and holidays brunch (including tax and service charge) ¥6,000 ($50). AE, DC, MC, V. Daily 11:30am–2:30pm and 5–10pm. Station: Akasaka-mitsuke (3 min.) or Yotsuya (5 min.).

㊾ **Zakuro** ⭐ SHABU-SHABU/SUKIYAKI   Zakuro, a local chain, is one of several restaurants claiming to have introduced shabu-shabu in Japan. It serves Kobe beef and is decorated with folk art (including works by famous Japanese artists Shiko Munakata and Shoji Hamada). Friendly, kimono-clad hostesses serve shabu-shabu, sukiyaki, tempura, and teriyaki beef, all available as set dinners with various side dishes. At lunch there are set meals of tempura, sashimi, sukiyaki, and teriyaki beef. Since Zakuro (which means "pomegranate") has an English-language menu, ordering is no problem. It's a popular place to bring visiting foreign clients.

TBS Kaikan Building basement, 5–3–3 Akasaka. ✆ 03/3582-6841. Reservations recommended. Set dinners ¥6,800–¥16,000 ($57–$133); set lunches ¥1,500–¥3,800 ($13–$32). AE, DC, MC, V. Daily 11am–10pm (last order). Station: Akasaka (TBS exit, 1 min.).

MODERATE

Blue Sky CHINESE   Located on the 17th floor of the New Otani's main building with great views of the city, this revolving restaurant provides panoramic views and all-you-can eat buffets, primarily Chinese. The food, tasty and varied, consists of approximately 40 different items for lunch and 50 for dinner, and includes spicy Szechuan cuisine, dim sum, Japanese food, and freshly baked pizza. My only complaint is that the restaurant revolves at such breakneck speed—making a complete turn every 45 minutes—that it almost matches fast-paced Tokyo. If the thought makes you dizzy, another buffet-style restaurant called **Top of the Tower,** on the 40th floor of the New Otani's tower, also has spectacular views of the city and offers Continental buffet lunches for ¥4,800 ($40) and dinners for ¥7,500 ($63).

Hotel New Otani, 4–1 Kioi-cho, Chiyoda-ku. ℭ **03/3238-0028.** Dinner buffet ¥6,300 ($53); lunch buffet ¥3,500 ($29). AE, DC, MC, V. Daily 11:30am–2pm and 5–9pm. Station: Akasaka-mitsuke or Nagatacho (3 min.).

daidaiya ★ *Finds* VARIED JAPANESE/NOUVELLE JAPANESE Upon exiting the elevator, you'll be forgiven for confusedly thinking you've landed in a nightclub rather than a restaurant—daidaiya's dark, theatrical entrance is the first clue that this is not your ordinary Japanese restaurant. The dining room, a juxtaposition of modern and traditional with a slate stone floor, shoji screens, warm woods, and black furniture, is rather like the cuisine—a curious mix of traditional Japanese food and original nouvelle creations, all mouthwateringly good. Pop music or jazz plays in the background. Tatami seating is also available, with views over Akasaka. An English-language menu lists such intriguing entrees as oven-baked Spanish mackerel wrapped in rice paper and then grilled over charcoal with a soybean paste; and beef loin slices baked on hot pebbles with lettuce and sesame leaf and served with a soy-sauce-flavored dip. Lunch sets, including obento, are equally satisfying. I love this place.

Bellevie Akasaka Building, 9th floor, 3–1–6 Akasaka. ℭ **03/3588-5087.** Reservations recommended for dinner. Main dishes ¥1,200 – ¥2,500 ($10–$21); set dinners ¥6,000 – ¥8,000 ($50–$58); set lunches ¥780 – ¥3,500 ($6.50–$29). AE, DC, MC, V. Mon–Fri 11:30am–2pm and 5pm–midnight (last order); Sat–Sun 11:30am–3pm and 5–11pm. Station: Akasaka-mitsuke (1 min., underneath the Bellevie Akasaka Building).

INEXPENSIVE

Don't forget to consider **Hayashi,** on the fourth floor of the Sanno Kaikan Building, 2–14–1 Akasaka, described above as an expensive restaurant. I mention it again here simply because I don't want those of you on a budget to miss it. This is one of the coziest and most delightful restaurants in town. Although dinner is costly, you can enjoy the same atmosphere for much, much less at lunch, when only one dish, *oyakodonburi* (rice topped with chunks of chicken and omelet), is served, with pickled vegetables, clear soup, and tea for ¥900 ($7.50). Open for lunch Monday through Friday from 11:30am to 2pm.

Akasaka is also home to two branches of **Moti,** my favorite Indian restaurant: on the second floor of the Akasaka Floral Plaza, 3–8–8 Akasaka (ℭ **03/3582-3620**); and on the third floor of the Kinpa Building, 2–14–31 Akasaka (ℭ **03/3584-6640**). See "Roppongi & Nishi Azabu," above, for a complete review.

Tony Roma's *Value* AMERICAN/BARBECUED RIBS This well-known U.S. chain dishes out large portions of the same barbecued baby-back ribs served back home, in a similar setting. It's popular with staff from the nearby American embassy, as well as area office workers. You can order ribs alone or in combination with barbecued chicken, grilled swordfish, steamed lobster, or other entrees, all of which include coleslaw and a choice of side dish such as baked potato or french fries. Steaks, seafood, and hamburgers are also available.

Other Tokyo locations include 3–1–30 Minami-Aoyama (ℭ 03/3479-5214) and 5–4–20 Roppongi (ℭ 03/3408-2748), below the Hard Rock Cafe.

2–3–4 Akasaka. ℂ **03/3585-4478.** Main dishes ¥1,280 – ¥3,580 ($11–$30); set lunch ¥955 ($7.95). AE, DC, MC, V. Mon–Fri 11:30am–2:30pm and 5:30–10:30pm (last order); Sat noon–10:30pm; Sun and holidays noon–10pm. Station: Tameike-Sanno (1 min.), Akasaka (7 min.), or Kokkai Gijido-mae (4 min.). On Sotobori Dori, near Roppongi Dori.

15 Other Neighborhoods

EXPENSIVE

Tableaux 🌟🌟 INTERNATIONAL   This place is just too cool. Designer Margaret O'Brien must have had fun here—it's a medieval Russian tearoom gone slightly mad, with bead-fringed curtains, mosaics of cracked mirrors, chandeliers, stars and moons, animal skins, and red velvet upholstery. There's even a subterranean courtyard for alfresco dining. The effect is fantastical and a bit surreal; eating here is like playing a two-bit part in your own murky dreams. Luckily, the professional staff and excellent, beautifully presented food live up to the setting. You might wish to start with the spicy Thai soup with shimp and lemon grass served in a coconut shell, or with the chicken tortilla roll, and follow the starter with the rare grilled tuna with sautéed foie-gras, scallops, shallots, noisette butter and balsamic sauce; or the roasted chicken breast stuffed with sautéed foie-gras and mushroom duxelle, served with mashed potatoes enhanced with a sauce of lentil puree and smoked mushrooms. An adjoining cigar lounge offers live jazz (avoid the cover charge by sitting at the bar).

Sunroser Daikanyama Building, 11–6 Sarugaku-cho. ℂ **03/5489-2201.** Reservations required. Main dishes ¥1,900 – ¥4,100 ($16–$34). AE, DC, MC, V. Daily 5:30–11pm (last order). Station: Daikanyama (5 min.).

MODERATE

㊿ **Botan** 🌟 *Finds* CHICKEN SUKIYAKI   Whereas most sukiyaki consists of beef, this famous restaurant, housed in a traditional Japanese-style house with a maple tree gracing its entrance, has been serving only one dish—tori (chicken) sukiyaki—for more than a century. Take your shoes off at the entrance, where the friendly staff will guide you past a huge rock and stone lantern to a tatami room. If there are two of you, you'll share a room with others; if your party is larger, you'll probably have a private room (make reservations for parties of more than four persons). You'll cook your chicken sukiyaki yourself over the tableside charcoal grill, making for a fun, convivial evening.

1–15 Kanda Sudacho. ℂ **03/3251-0577.** Tori sukiyaki ¥6,700 ($56). No credit cards. Mon–Sat 11:30am–8pm (last order). Closed holidays. Station: Ogawamachi or Awajicho (exit A3, 3 min.) or Akihabara (10 min.). Down the street from Kanda Yabusoba (see below).

51 **Kandagawa** 🌟 *Finds* EEL   Dining in this beautiful, old-fashioned, traditional Japanese restaurant, famous for its eel dishes since the Edo Period, is unforgettable. A Japanese-style wooden house, hidden behind a wooden gate, it offers seven private tatami rooms, as well as a larger tatami dining room. The menu, in Japanese only, offers side dishes of soup, rice, and Japanese pickles, and such main dishes as *kabayaki* (broiled and basted eel), *unaju* (broiled eel on rice with a sweet sauce), *shiroyaki* ("white" eel, broiled without soy sauce or oil), and *umaki* (eel wrapped in an omelet). If you've never eaten eel, I can think of no finer place to first try it. Expect to spend a minimum of ¥7,500 ($63) per person, including drinks, appetizers, tax, and service. No one here speaks English, so it's best to have a Japanese-speaking person make your reservation, at which time you must order the dishes you'd like to be served.

2–5–11 Soto-Kanda. © **03/3251-5031.** Reservations required. Main dishes ¥2,400–¥3,800 ($20–$32). MC, V. Mon–Sat 11:30am–2pm and 5–8pm. Closed holidays and 2nd Sat of the month Sept–May. Station: Akihabara (5 min.). On Sotobori Dori.

Zipangu VARIED JAPANESE   Located high in the sky—on the 47th floor of the new Caretta Shiodome building with shimmering views over Hama Rikyu Garden, Tokyo Bay, the Rainbow Bridge, and Odaiba—this contemporary Japanese restaurant offers set meals for lunch that are difficult to describe—the constantly changing presentations border on nouvelle Japanese cuisine, with international influences. In the evenings, the stone-and-wood venue is more of a drinking bar, with an a la carte menu offering charcoal-grilled steak, yakitori, dim sum, and dishes that go well with wine. In any case, this is a great choice if you're visiting nearby Hama Rikyu Garden..

Caretta Shiodome, 1–8–1 Higashi-Shimbashi. © **03/6215-8111.** Reservations required. Main dishes (dinner only) ¥800–¥3,000 ($6.65–$25); set lunches ¥2,800–¥3,000 ($23–$25) Mon–Fri, ¥3,500–¥7,000 ($29–$58) weekends and holidays. AE, DC, MC, V. Daily 11:30am–2:30pm and 5–10pm (last order). Station: Shiodome (2 min.) or Shimbashi (5 min.).

INEXPENSIVE

In addition to the choices here, there's a **La Boheme** serving pizza and pasta (© **03/3599-4801**), **Gonpachi** serving Japanese food (© **03/3599-4807**), and **Zest Cantina** serving Tex-Mex (© **03/3599-4803**) on the fourth-floor Mediage on the island of Odaiba, all open daily 11:30am to 5am. For reviews, see "Ginza & Hibiya" for La Boheme and Gonpachi; and "Ebisu & Meguro" for Zest Cantina.

52 **Kanda Yabusoba** ★ (Finds) NOODLES   *Soba* (noodle) shops are among the least expensive restaurants in Japan, and this is one of Tokyo's most famous, established in 1880 and rebuilt after the 1923 Great Kanto Earthquake. The house, which is surrounded by a wooden gate with an entryway through a small grove of bamboo, features shoji screens, a wooden ceiling, and a dining area with tatami mats and tables. It's often filled with middle-aged businessmen and housewives, so you'll probably have to wait for a seat if you come during lunchtime. There's a menu in English. The specialties are hot and cold wheat noodles, which you can order with shredded yam, grilled eel, or crispy shrimp tempura. Listen to the woman sitting at a small counter by the kitchen—she sings out orders to the chef, as well as hellos and good-byes to customers.

2–10 Awajicho, Kanda. © **03/3251-0287.** ¥600–¥1,700 ($5–$14). No credit cards. Daily 11:30am–7:30pm (last order). Station: Awajicho or Ogawamachi (exit A3, 3 min.) or Akihabara (10 min.). Northeast of the Soto-bori Dori and Yasukuni Dori intersection; from Sotobori Dori, take the side street that runs between the Tokyo Green Hotel and the New Kanda Hotel on this block and look toward the left.

Sunset Beach Brewing Company INTERNATIONAL   Located in Tokyo Decks Beach, a shopping/dining complex on the man-made island of Odaiba, this microbrewery is one of my favorites for outdoor dining, with great views of the beach, the bay, and Rainbow Bridge. Although the food—which runs the gamut from lasagna and pizza to salads and vegetables—is mediocre at best, the price is right, the beer is good, and the location is a great summertime escape from the concrete jungle.

Tokyo Decks Beach, 5th floor, 1–6–1 Daiba. © **03/3599-6655.** Lunch buffet Mon–Fri ¥1,200 ($10), Sat–Sun ¥1,500 ($13); dinner buffet ¥1,980 ($17). AE, DC, MC, V. Daily 11am–3:30pm and 5–10pm (last order). Station: Odaiba Kaihin Koen (2 min.).

What to See & Do in Tokyo

Many Westerners grow up with a highly romanticized view of Japan, picturing it as a woodblock print—exquisite, mysterious, and ancient.

What a shock, then, to come to Tokyo. In a country known around the world for its appreciation of the aesthetic, Tokyo is disappointingly unimpressive. Some foreigners, unable to reconcile unrealistic expectations with the cold facts of reality, summarily dismiss Tokyo as a monstrosity of the 21st century and go off in search of the "real" Japan. What they don't realize is that beneath Tokyo's concrete shell is a cultural life left very much intact. In fact, Tokyo is the best place in the world to experience Japanese performing arts, like Kabuki, as well as participate in such diverse activities as the tea ceremony and flower arranging. It's also the nation's foremost repository of Japanese arts and crafts and boasts a wide range of both first-class and unique museums.

SEEING THE CITY BY GUIDED TOUR With the help of this book and a good map, you should be able to visit Tokyo's major attractions easily on your own. Should you be pressed for time, however, consider taking one of several group tours of Tokyo and its environs offered by the **Japan Travel Bureau (JTB; ℂ 03/5796-5454;** www.jtb.co.jp/sunrisetour) or **Japan Gray Line (ℂ 03/3433-5745;** www. jgl.co.jp/inbound/index.htm). Day tours may include Tokyo Tower, the Imperial Palace district, Asakusa Sensoji Temple, Meiji Jingu Shrine, a harbor or river cruise, and the Ginza. A

number of organized evening tours take in such activities as Kabuki or entertainment by geisha. Be warned, however, that tours are very tourist-oriented and are more expensive than touring Tokyo on your own. Prices range from about ¥4,000 ($33) for a morning tour to about ¥9,800 ($82) for a night tour with dinner and Kabuki. You can easily book tours through most tourist hotels and travel agencies.

One tour I especially like is a **boat trip on the Sumida River** between Hama Rikyu Garden and Asakusa. Commentary on the 40-minute trip is in both Japanese and English (be sure to pick up the English leaflet, too). You'll get descriptions of the 12 bridges you pass along the way and views of Tokyo you'd otherwise miss. Boats depart Hama Rikyu Garden hourly or more frequently between 10:20am and 3:50pm, with the fare to Asakusa costing ¥620 ($5.15) one-way. Other cruises are available from Hinode Pier (closest station: Hinode, about a 1-min. walk) to Asakusa (fare: ¥660/$5.50), Tokyo Sea Life Park (fare: ¥800/$6.65), and Odaiba (fare: ¥500/$4.15). For more information, contact the **Tourist Information Center (ℂ 03-3201-3331)** or the **Tokyo Cruise Ship Co. (ℂ 03/3457-7830;** www.suijobus.co.jp).

For personalized, one-on-one tours of Tokyo, contact **Jun's Tokyo Discovery Tours,** managed by Tokyoite Junko Matsuda, which offers tailored sightseeing trips to Tsukiji, Asakusa, Yanaka, Harajuku, Aoyama, Shibuya,

Did You Know?

- Tokyo has been the capital of Japan only since 1868; before that, Kyoto served as capital for more than 1,000 years.
- Ten percent of Japan's total population lives in Tokyo—more than 12 million residents. Almost a quarter of Japan's total population lives within commuting distance.
- Tokyo's workers commute to work an average of 90 minutes one-way. Shinjuku Station handles the most train and subway passengers in all of Japan, more than one million people a day; more than 60 exits lead out of the station.
- Tokyo has suffered widespread destruction twice in the past century—in the 1923 Great Kanto Earthquake and from World War II firebombs. In both instances, more than 100,000 people lost their lives.
- During the Edo Period (1603–1867), Edo (former Tokyo) witnessed almost 100 major fires, not to mention countless smaller fires.
- Tokyo sprawls over 1,288 sq. km (800 sq. miles), yet most streets are not named.
- Rickshaws originated in Tokyo in 1869; 4 years later, there were 34,000 of the people-propelled vehicles in the capital city.
- Park space in Tokyo is woefully inadequate—just 4.52 sq. m (5.40 sq. yd.) per capita, compared to 45.7 sq. m (54.7 sq. yd.) in Washington, D.C.
- According to city government 2003 estimates, approximately 6,000 homeless were living in Tokyo, mainly in city parks and along riverbanks. There are 25,000 homeless nationwide.

and Shinjuku, as well as shopping trips and special trips tailored to fit your interests. Tours, which are especially useful if you wish to communicate with shopkeepers and the locals, want to learn more about what you're seeing, or are timid about finding your way on public transportation (if you wish, you'll be met at your hotel), cost ¥12,000 ($100) for 1 day (8 hr.) and are available for up to four adults or a family. Reserve tours at least 3 days in advance (1 week preferred) by fax (03/3749-0445) or e-mail (me2@gb3.so-net.ne.jp), stating the desired tour date and what you'd like to see; messages can also be left at ℅ **03/3749-0445.**

SUGGESTED ITINERARIES

There are two things to remember in planning your sightseeing itinerary: The city is huge, and it takes time to get from one end to the other. Plan your days so you cover Tokyo neighborhood by neighborhood, coordinating sightseeing with dinner and evening plans. To help you get the most out of your stay, the suggested itineraries below will guide you to the most important attractions. Note, however, that some attractions are closed 1 day of the week, so plan your days accordingly.

If You Have 1 Day Start by getting up in the wee hours of the morning (if you've just flown in from North America, you'll suffer from jet lag anyway and will be wide awake by 5am) and head for the **Tsukiji Fish Market,** Japan's largest wholesale fish market (closed Sun, holidays, and some Wed). Be brave and try a breakfast of the freshest sushi you'll ever have. By 9am you should be on the Hibiya Line on your way to Ueno, where you'll head to the **Tokyo National Museum,** the country's largest and most important museum (closed Mon). From there, move on to **Asakusa** for lunch in one of the area's traditional Japanese restaurants, and follow it by a walk on Nakamise Dori (good for souvenirs) to **Sensoji Temple.** In the late afternoon you might want to head to **Ginza** for some shopping, followed by dinner in a restaurant of your choice. Drop by a yakitori-ya, a typical Japanese watering hole, for a beer and a snack. You might be exhausted by the end of the day, but you'll have seen some of the city's highlights.

If You Have 2 Days On the first day, get up early and go to **Tsukiji Fish Market.** Next, head for the nearby **Hama Rikyu Garden,** which opens at 9am; it's about a 20-minute walk from Tsukiji, or a short taxi ride away. After touring the garden, one of the city's best, board the ferry that departs from inside the grounds for a trip up the Sumida River to **Asakusa,** where you can visit **Sensoji Temple** and shop along Nakamise Dori, following that with lunch in a traditional Japanese restaurant. You might even wish to take the recommended walking tour of Asakusa covered in chapter 7. Next, ride the bus to Ueno, where you should walk through Ueno Park to the **Tokyo**

National Museum. Afterwards, head to **Ginza's** many department stores. If there's a performance, drop by the **Kabukiza Theater** for part of a Kabuki play. Have dinner at a Ginza restaurant.

On your second day, go early in the morning to the **Edo-Tokyo Museum** (located next to the sumo stadium), a great museum that illuminates the city's tumultuous history. From there, head to colorful **Harajuku,** where you can visit **Meiji Jingu Shrine,** Tokyo's most famous Shinto shrine; the **Ota Memorial Museum of Art,** with its collection of woodblock prints; and the **Oriental Bazaar,** a great place to shop for souvenirs. Spend the evening in one of Tokyo's famous nightlife districts, such as **Shinjuku** or **Roppongi.**

If You Have 3 Days Spend the first 2 days as outlined above, and on the third day head for **Kamakura,** one of Japan's most important historical sites. Located an hour south of Tokyo by train, Kamakura served as the capital back in the 1100s and is packed with temples and shrines, one of which features the Great Buddha outdoor bronze statue.

If You Have 4 Days or More Consider yourself lucky. Spend the first 3 days as outlined above; devote the fourth day to pursuing your own interests, such as taking a trip to one of Tokyo's numerous art or specialty museums, shopping, soaking in a hot spring, or following one of the recommended walking tours in chapter 7. This may be the evening to party wildly, staying out until the first subways start running at 5am.

If you have a fifth day, you might visit **Nikko,** approximately 2 hours north of Tokyo, to see the sumptuous **mausoleum of Toku-gawa Ieyasu,** the shogun who succeeded in unifying Japan in the 1600s. Or you might consider a 2-day trip to **Hakone,** famous for its fantastic open-air sculpture

museum and home to some of the best old-fashioned Japanese inns near Tokyo. It also offers unparalleled views of Mount Fuji, if the weather is clear. See chapter 10 for more ideas on side trips from Tokyo.

1 The Top Attractions

The Imperial Palace (Kyokyo) ⓐ   The Imperial Palace, home of the imperial family, is the heart and soul of Tokyo. Built on the very spot where Edo Castle used to stand during the days of the Tokugawa shogunate, it became the imperial home upon its completion in 1888 and is now the residence of Emperor Akihito, 125th emperor of Japan. Destroyed during air raids in 1945, the palace was rebuilt in 1968 using the principles of traditional Japanese architecture. But don't expect to get a good look at it; most of the palace grounds' 114 hectares (284 acres) are off-limits to the public, with the exception of 2 days a year when the royal family makes an appearance before the throngs: New Year's Day and the emperor's birthday (Dec 23). Or you can visit imperial grounds on free **guided tours** Monday through Friday at 10am and 1:30pm, but you must register at least 1 day in advance (reservations are accepted up to 1 month in advance) by calling Ⓒ **03/3213-111,** ext. 485 or 486, and then stopping by the Imperial Household (located at the Sakashita-mon Gate, on the east side of palace grounds) to provide your passport number, nationality, name, age, occupation, and address in Tokyo. Tours, conducted in Japanese only, last about 75 minutes and lead past official buildings, the inner moat and historic fortifications, and Nijubashi Bridge. I recommend this tour only if you have time to spare and have already seen Tokyo's other top attractions.

Otherwise, you'll have to console yourself with a camera shot of the palace from the southeast side of **Nijubashi Bridge,** where the moat and the palace turrets show above the trees. Most Japanese tourists make brief stops here to pay their respects. The wide moat, lined with cherry trees, is especially beautiful in the spring. You might even want to spend an hour strolling the 4.8km (3 miles) around the palace and moat. But the most important thing to do in the vicinity of the palace is to visit its **Higashi Gyoen (East Garden),** where you'll find what's left of the central keep of old Edo Castle, the stone foundation; see "Parks & Gardens," later in this chapter.

Hibiya Dori Ave. Station: Nijubashi-mae (1 min.) or Hibiya (5 min.).

Sensoji Temple ⓐⓐⓐ   This is Tokyo's oldest and most popular temple, with a history dating back to 628. That was when, according to popular lore, two brothers fishing in the nearby Sumida River netted the catch of their lives—a tiny golden statue of Kannon, the Buddhist goddess of mercy and happiness who is empowered with the ability to release humans from all suffering. Sensoji Temple (also popularly known as Asakusa Kannon) was erected in her honor, and although the statue is housed here, it's never shown to the public. Still, through the centuries, worshippers have flocked here seeking favors of Kannon; and when Sensoji Temple burned down during a 1945 bombing raid, the present structure was rebuilt with donations by the Japanese people.

Colorful **Nakamise Dori,** a pedestrian lane leading to the shrine, is lined with traditional shops and souvenir stands, while nearby **Demboin Garden** remains an insider's favorite as a peaceful oasis away from the bustling crowds. Asakusa is one of my favorite neighborhoods, and you can easily spend half a day here; see the walking tour in chapter 7 for more on this fascinating part of old Tokyo.

2–3–1 Asakusa, Taito-ku. ✆ 03/3842-0181. Free admission. Daily 6am–5pm. Station: Asakusa (2 min.).

Meiji Jingu Shrine ★★ This is Tokyo's most venerable Shinto shrine, opened in 1920 in honor of Emperor and Empress Meiji, who were instrumental in opening Japan to the outside world more than 120 years ago. Japan's two largest *torii* (the traditional entry gate of a shrine), built of cypress more than 1,700 years old, give dramatic entrance to the grounds, once the estate of a *daimyo* (feudal lord). The shaded pathway is lined with trees, shrubs, and dense woods. In late May/June, the **Iris Garden** is in spectacular bloom (separate admission fee charged). About a 10-minute walk from the first torii, the shrine is a fine example of dignified and refined Shinto architecture. It's made of plain Japanese cypress and topped with green-copper roofs. Meiji Jingu Shrine is the place to be on New Year's Eve, when more than two million people crowd onto the grounds to usher in the New Year.

Meiji Shrine Inner Garden, 1–1 Kamizono-cho, Yoyogi, Shibuya-ku. ✆ 03/3379-5511. Free admission. Daily sunrise–sunset (until 4:30pm in winter). Station: Harajuku (2 min.).

Tokyo National Museum (Tokyo Kokuritsu Hakubutsukan) ★★★ The National Museum not only is the largest and oldest museum in Japan, it also boasts the largest collection of Japanese art in the world. This is where you go to see antiques from Japan's past—old kimono, samurai armor, priceless swords, lacquerware, metalwork, pottery, scrolls, screens, *ukiyo-e* (woodblock prints), calligraphy, ceramics, archaeological finds, and more. Items are shown on a rotating basis with about 4,000 on display at any one time—so no matter how many times you visit the museum, you'll always see something new. Schedule at least 2 hours to do the museum justice.

The museum is composed of five buildings. The **Main Gallery (Honkan),** straight ahead as you enter the main gate, is the most important one, devoted to Japanese art. Here you'll view Japanese ceramics; Buddhist sculptures dating from about A.D. 538 to 1192; samurai armor, helmets, and decorative sword mountings; swords, which throughout Japanese history were considered to embody spirits all their own; textiles and kimono; lacquerware; and paintings, calligraphy, ukiyo-e, and scrolls. Be sure to check out the museum shop in the basement; it sells reproductions from the museum's collections as well as traditional crafts by contemporary artists.

The **Gallery of Eastern Antiquities (Toyokan)** houses art and archaeological artifacts from everywhere in Asia outside Japan. There are Buddhas from China and Gandhara, stone reliefs from Cambodia, embroidered wall hangings and cloth from India, Iranian and Turkish carpets, Thai and Vietnamese ceramics, and more. Chinese art—including jade, paintings, calligraphy, and ceramics—makes up the largest part of the collection, illustrating China's tremendous influence on Japanese art, architecture, and religion. You'll also find Egyptian relics, including a mummy dating from around 751 to 656 B.C. and wooden objects from the 20th century B.C.

The **Heiseikan Gallery,** opened in 1999, is where you'll find archaeological relics of ancient Japan, including pottery and Haniwa clay burial figurines of the Jomon Period (10,000 B.C.–1,000 B.C.) and ornamental, keyhole-shaped tombs from the Yayoi Period (400 B.C.–A.D. 200). The **Gallery of Horyuji Treasures**

Tokyo Attractions

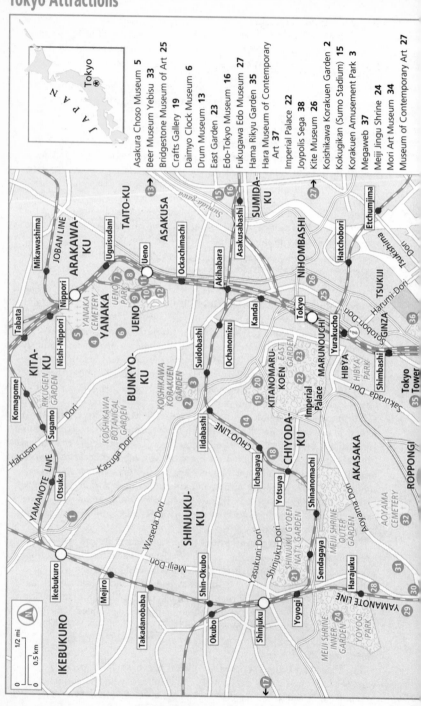

Asakura Choso Museum **5**
Beer Museum Yebisu **33**
Bridgestone Museum of Art **25**
Crafts Gallery **19**
Daimyo Clock Museum **6**
Drum Museum **13**
East Garden **23**
Edo-Tokyo Museum **16**
Fukugawa Edo Museum **27**
Hama Rikyu Garden **35**
Hara Museum of Contemporary Art **37**
Imperial Palace **22**
Joypolis Sega **38**
Kite Museum **26**
Koishikawa Korakuen Garden **2**
Kokugikan (Sumo Stadium) **15**
Korakuen Amusement Park **3**
Megaweb **37**
Meiji Jingu Shrine **24**
Mori Art Museum **34**
Museum of Contemporary Art **27**

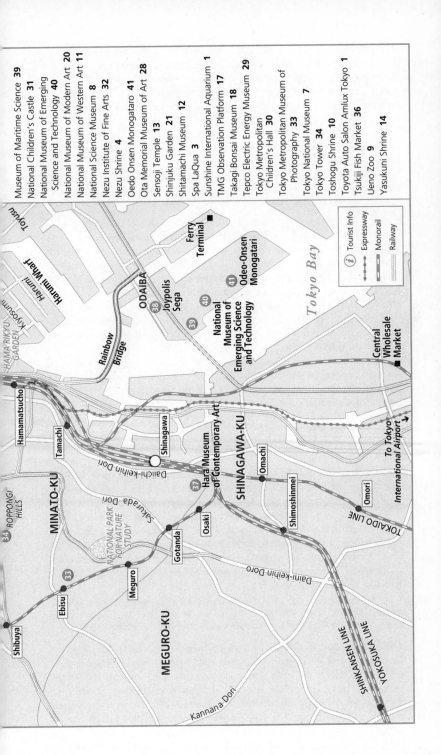

Museum of Maritime Science **39**
National Children's Castle **31**
National Museum of Emerging
  Science and Technology **40**
National Museum of Modern Art **20**
National Museum of Western Art **11**
National Science Museum **8**
Nezu Institute of Fine Arts **32**
Nezu Shrine **4**
Oedo Onsen Monogatari **41**
Ota Memorial Museum of Art **28**
Sensoji Temple **13**
Shinjuku Garden **21**
Shitamachi Museum **12**
Spa LaQua **3**
Sunshine International Aquarium **1**
TMG Observation Platform **17**
Takagi Bonsai Museum **18**
Tepco Electric Energy Museum **29**
Tokyo Metropolitan
  Children's Hall **30**
Tokyo Metropolitan Museum of
  Photography **33**
Tokyo National Museum **7**
Tokyo Tower **34**
Toshogu Shrine **10**
Toyota Auto Salon Amlux Tokyo **1**
Tsukiji Fish Market **36**
Ueno Zoo **9**
Yasukuni Shrine **14**

ⓘ Tourist Info
┅┅ Expressway
▬▬ Monorail
═══ Railway

Toyosu
HAMA RIKYU
Kiyosumi
Harumi Wharf
Ferry Terminal
ODAIBA
Joypolis Sega
38
Odeo-Onsen Monogatari 41
40
39
National Museum of
Emerging Science
and Technology

Tokyo Bay

Central Wholesale Market

Rainbow Bridge

Hamamatsucho

Tamachi

Shinagawa

Daiichi-keihin Dori

ROPPONGI HILLS
34

MINATO-KU

Sakurada Dori

NATIONAL PARK
FOR NATURE STUDY

Hara Museum
of Contemporary Art
37

SHINAGAWA-KU

Omachi

Shimoshinmei

Omori

TOKAIDO LINE

To Tokyo
International Airport

Osaki

Gotanda

Daini-keihin Doro

33
Ebisu

Meguro

Shibuya

MEGURO-KU

SHINKANSEN LINE

YOKOSUKA LINE

Kannana Dori

(Horyuji Homotsukan) displays priceless Buddhist treasures from the Horyuji Temple in Nara, founded by Prince Shotoku in 607. Although the building's stark modernity (designed by Taniguchi Yoshio, who also designed the expansion of the New York Museum of Modern Art) seems odd for an exhibition of antiquities, the gallery's low lighting and simple architecture lend dramatic effect to the museum's priceless collection of bronze Buddhist statues, ceremonial Gigaku masks used in ritual dances, lacquerware, and paintings. The **Hyokeikan,** built in 1909 to commemorate the marriage of Emperor Taisho, holds special exhibitions.

Ueno Park, Taito-ku. © 03/3822-1111. www.tnm.jp. Admission ¥420 ($3.50) adults, ¥130 ($1.10) students, ¥70 (60¢) children, free for seniors (except during special exhibitions). Oct–Mar Tues–Sun 9:30am–5pm (enter by 4:30pm); Apr–Sept Tues–Thurs and Sat–Sun 9:30am–5pm, Fri 9:30am–8pm. Closed Dec 26–Jan 3. Station: Ueno (10 min.).

Edo-Tokyo Museum (Edo-Tokyo Hakubutsukan) ★★★ *Kids* The building housing this impressive museum is said to resemble a rice granary when viewed from afar, but to me it looks like a modern *torii,* the entrance gate to a shrine. This is the metropolitan government's ambitious attempt to present the history, art, disasters, science, culture, and architecture of Tokyo from its humble beginnings in 1590—when the first shogun, Tokugawa Ieyasu, made Edo (old Tokyo) the seat of his domain—to 1964, when Tokyo hosted the Olympics. All in all, the museum's great visual displays create a vivid portrayal of Tokyo through the centuries. I wouldn't miss it.

After purchasing your tickets and taking the escalator to the sixth floor, you'll enter the museum by walking over a replica of Nihombashi Bridge, the starting point for all roads leading out of old Edo. Exhibits covering the Edo Period portray the lives of the shoguns, merchants, craftsmen, and townspeople. The explanations are mostly in Japanese only, but there's plenty to look at, including a replica of an old Kabuki theater, a model of a daimyo's mansion, portable floats used during festivals, maps and photographs of old Edo, and—perhaps most interesting—a rowhouse tenement where Edo commoners lived in cramped quarters measuring only 10 sq. m (107.6 sq. ft.). Other displays cover the Meiji Restoration, the Great Kanto Earthquake of 1923, and the bombing raids of World War II (Japan's own role as aggressor is disappointingly glossed over).

If you wish, take advantage of a free museum tour offered by volunteers daily 10am to 3pm (last tour). Most tours last 1 to 2 hours, depending on the level of visitor interest, and are insightful for their explanations of the Japanese-only displays. However, tours are necessarily rushed and focus on particular displays; you may wish to tour the museum afterward on your own. At any rate, plan on spending about 2 hours here.

1–4–1 Yokoami, Sumida-ku. © 03/3626-9974. www.edo-tokyo-museum.or.jp/museum-e/guide.htm. Admission ¥600 ($5) adults, ¥300 ($2.50) students through high school. Tues–Wed and Sat–Sun 9:30am–5:30pm; Thurs–Fri 9:30am–8pm. Station: Ryogoku on the JR Sobu and Oedo lines (2 min.).

Tsukiji Fish Market ★★★ This huge wholesale fish market—the largest in Japan and one of the largest in the world—is a must for anyone who has never seen such a market in action. And the action here starts early: At about 3am, boats begin arriving from the seas around Japan, from Africa, and even from America, with enough fish to satisfy the demands of a nation where seafood reigns supreme. To give you some idea of its enormity, this market handles almost all the seafood consumed in Tokyo. The king is tuna, huge and frozen, unloaded from the docks, laid out on the ground, and numbered. Wholesalers walk up and down the rows, jotting down the numbers of the best-looking tuna, and by 5:30am, the tuna auctions are well under way (the entire auction of sea products takes place about 5–7am). The wholesalers then transfer what they've bought to their own stalls in the market, subsequently selling the fish to their regular customers, usually retail stores and restaurants.

The market is held in a cavernous, hangarlike building, which means you can visit it even on a dismal rainy morning. There's a lot going on—men in black rubber boots rushing wheelbarrows and carts through the aisles, hawkers shouting, knives chopping and slicing. Wander the aisles and you'll see things you never dreamed were edible. This is a good place to bring your camera: The people working here burst with pride if you single them out for a photograph. The floors are wet, so leave your fancy shoes at the hotel.

Tsukiji is also a good place to come if you want sushi for breakfast. Alongside the covered market are rows of barracklike buildings divided into sushi restaurants and shops related to the fish trade. In addition, as you walk the distance between the Tsukiji subway station and the fish market, you'll find yourself in a delightful district of tiny retail shops and stalls where you can buy the freshest seafood in town, plus dried fish and fish products, seaweed, vegetables, knives, and other cooking utensils. There are also a lot of pottery shops and stores that sell plastic and lacquered trays, bowls, and cups. Although they sell in great quantities to restaurant owners, shopkeepers will usually sell to the casual tourist as well. *Warning:* While walking through the retail district on our way from Tsukiji Market, my Japanese friend and I were warned several times by local shopkeepers to keep watch over our purses, advice we didn't take lightly. Apparently, pickpockets have been at work here on unsuspecting tourists.

5–2–1 Tsukiji, Chuo-ku. © 03/3542-1111. Free admission. Mon–Sat 5–11am (best time 5:30–9am). Closed some Wed, holidays, Dec, New Year's, and Aug 15–16. Station: Tsukijishijo (exit A2, 2 min.) or Tsukiji (Honganji Temple exit, 10 min.).

2 Five Unforgettable Ways to Immerse Yourself in Japanese Culture

Just walking down the street could be considered a cultural experience in Japan. But there are a few more concrete ways to learn about this country's cultural life: The best is by participating in some of its time-honored rituals and traditions.

IKEBANA   Instruction in *ikebana,* or Japanese flower arranging, is available at several schools in Tokyo, a few of which offer classes in English on a regular basis. (Note that you should call beforehand to enroll.) **Sogetsu Ikebana School,** 7–2–21 Akasaka (© **03/3408-1151;** station: Aoyama-Itchome, a 5-min. walk from exit 4), offers instruction in English on Monday from 10am to noon (closed in Aug). The cost of one lesson for first-time participants is ¥4,850 ($41), including the flowers and materials. The **Ohara Ikebana School,** 5–7–17 Minami Aoyama (© **03/5774-5097;** www.ohararyu.or.jp; station: Omotesando, 3-min. walk from exit B1), offers 2-hour instruction in English at 10am on Wednesday and 10am and 1:30pm on Thursday, charging ¥4,000 ($33) for instruction and materials.

If you wish to see ikebana, ask at the **Tourist Information Office** whether there are any special exhibitions. Department stores sometimes have special ikebana exhibitions in their galleries. Another place to look is **Yasukuni Shrine,** located on Yasukuni Dori northwest of the Imperial Palace (closest station: Ichigaya or Kudanshita). Dedicated to Japanese war dead, the shrine is also famous for ongoing ikebana exhibitions on its grounds.

Pachinko Parlors

Brightly lit and garish, pachinko parlors are packed with upright pin-ball-like machines, at which row upon row of Japanese businessmen, housewives, and students sit intently immobile. Originating in Nagoya and popular since the 1950s, pachinko is a game in which ball bearings are flung into a kind of vertical pinball machine, one after the other. Humans control the strength with which the ball is released, but otherwise there's very little to do. Some players even wedge a matchstick under the control and just watch the machine with folded arms. Points are amassed according to which holes the ball bearings fall into. If you're good at it, you win ball bearings back, which you can subsequently trade in for food, cigarettes, watches, calculators, and the like.

It's illegal to win money in Japan, but outside many pachinko parlors and along back alleyways, there are slots where you can trade in the watches, calculators, and other prizes for cash. The slots are so small that the person handing over the goods never sees the person who hands back money. Police, meanwhile, look the other way.

Pachinko parlors compete in an ever-escalating war of themes, lights, and noise. Step inside, and you'll wonder how anyone could possibly think; the noise level of thousands of ball bearings clanking is awesome. Perhaps that's the answer to its popularity: You can't think, making it a getaway pastime. Some people seem to be addicted to the mesmerizing game, newspaper articles talk of errant husbands who never come home anymore, and psychologists analyze its popularity. At any rate, every hamlet seems to have a pachinko parlor, and major cities like Tokyo are inundated with them. You'll find them in nightlife districts and clustered around train stations, but with their unmistakable clanging and clanking, you'll hear them long before you notice their brightly lit, gaudy facades.

TEA CEREMONY   Several first-class hotels hold tea-ceremony demonstrations in special tea-ceremony rooms. Reservations are usually required, and since the ceremonies are often booked by groups, you'll want to call in advance to see whether you can participate. **Seisei-an,** on the seventh floor of the Hotel New Otani, 4–1 Kioi-cho, Chiyoda-ku (© **03/3265-1111,** ext. 2443; station: Nagatacho or Akasaka-mitsuke, a 3-min. walk from both), holds 20-minute demonstrations Thursday through Saturday from 11am to 4pm. The cost is ¥1,050 ($8.75), including tea and sweets. **Chosho-an,** on the seventh floor of the Hotel Okura, 2–10–4 Toranomon, Minato-ku (© **03/3582-0111;** station: Toranomon or Kamiyacho, a 10-min. walk from both), gives 30-minute demonstrations anytime between 11am and noon and between 1 and 4pm Monday through Saturday except holidays. Appointments are required; the cost is ¥1,050 ($8.75) for tea and sweets. At **Toko-an,** on the fourth floor of the Imperial Hotel, 1–1–1 Uchisaiwaicho, Chiyoda-ku (© **03/3504-1111;** station: Hibiya, 1 min.), demonstrations are given from 10am to noon and 1 to 4pm Monday through Saturday except holidays. Reservations are required. The fee is ¥1,500 ($13) for tea and sweets.

Lessons in the tea ceremony conducted in English are held several times weekly at the **Waraku-an,** located just behind the Canadian Embassy in Minato Ward. A one-time membership fee is ¥5,000 ($42), while monthly fees are ¥5,000 ($42) for two lessons and ¥8,000 ($67) for three lessons. For more information, contact the **International Chado Culture Foundation** at © 03/3512-2566.

ACUPUNCTURE & SHIATSU   Although most Westerners have heard of acupuncture, they may not be familiar with *shiatsu* (Japanese pressure-point massage). Most first-class hotels in Japan offer shiatsu in the privacy of your room. There are acupuncture clinics everywhere in Tokyo, and the staff of your hotel may be able to tell you of one nearby. As it's not likely the clinic's staff will speak English, it might be a good idea to have the guest relations officer at your hotel not only make the reservation but specify the treatment you want. Otherwise, English is spoken at **Yamate Acupuncture Clinic,** second floor of the ULS Nakameguro Building, 1–3–3 Higashiyama, Meguro-ku (© 03-3792-8989; station: Nakameguro, 6 min.), open Monday to Friday 9am to 8pm and Saturday 9am to 2pm and charging ¥3,000 ($25) for a specific treatment or ¥5,000 ($42) for the whole body, plus a ¥1,000 ($8.35) initial fee. English is also spoken at **Tani Clinic,** third floor of the Taishoseimei Hibiya Building, 1–9–1 Yurakucho, Chiyoda-ku (© 03/3201-5675; station: Hibiya, 1 min.), open Monday, Tuesday, Wednesday, Friday, and Saturday 9am to noon and 2 to 5pm and charging ¥10,500 ($88) for the first visit, ¥6,300 ($53) for each subsequent visit.

PUBLIC BATHS   Tokyo has an estimated 1,145 *sento* (public baths)—which may sound like a lot but is nothing compared to the 2,687 the city used to have just 30-some years ago. Easily recognizable by a tall chimney and shoe lockers just inside the door, a sento sells just about anything you might need at the bathhouse—soap, shampoo, towels, even underwear.

For a unique bathing experience, nothing beats a 3- or 4-hour respite at the **Oedo-Onsen Monogatari,** 2–57 Aomi on Odaiba (© 03/5500-1126; station: Telecom Center Station, 2 min.), which tapped mineral-rich hot-spring waters 1,380m (4,600 ft.) below ground to supply this re-created Edo-era bathhouse village. After changing into *yukata* (cotton kimono) and depositing your belongings in a locker (your key is bar-coded so there's no need to carry any money), you'll stroll past souvenir shops and restaurants on your way to massage rooms, sand baths (extra fee charged), and *onsen* (hot-spring baths) complete with outdoor baths, Jacuzzi, steam baths, and saunas. Since as many as 6,500 bathers pour into this facility on weekends, try to come on a weekday, and since signs in English are virtually nonexistent, observe gender before entering bathing areas (a hint: women's baths usually have pink or red curtains, men's blue). Open daily 11am to 9am the next day. Admission is ¥2,700 ($23) for adults and ¥1,500 ($13) for children.

Not quite as colorful is **Spa LaQua,** 1–1–1 Kasuga (© 03/3817-4173; station: Kasuga, 2 min.), located in the heart of Tokyo at Korakuen's Tokyo Dome City Complex. It, too, has hot-spring indoor/outdoor baths, saunas, and massage options, but an adjoining amusement park with roller coasters (and screaming passengers) make this a less relaxing alternative. It's open daily 11am to 9am the next day, with admission priced at ¥2,300 ($19) for adults and ¥1,700 ($14) for children. Note that no children under 7 are allowed and no minors under 18 are allowed after 6pm.

ZAZEN   A few temples in the Tokyo vicinity occasionally offer sitting meditation with instruction in English. Approximately 30 minutes east of Akihabara on the Sobu Line is **Ida Ryogoku-do Zazen Dojo** of the Sotoshu Sect, 5–11–20 Minami Yawata, Ichikawa City (℡ **0473/79-1596;** station: Moto-Yawata, 5 min.). Zazen is held daily at 5:30 and 10am and 3 and 8:30pm, generally for 45 minutes (call to confirm times). A Dogen-Sangha meeting is held the fourth Saturday of the month from 1 to 2:30pm, consisting of 30 minutes for Zazen followed by a 1-hour lecture. Participation is free, and if you call from Moto-Yawata Station, someone will come for you. You can also stay here for longer periods to practice Zen; call Mr. Nishijima at ℡ **03/3435-0701** for more information.

In addition, the **Young Men Buddhist Association of Tokyo University,** of the Sotoshu Sect, second floor of the Nippon Shimpan Building, 3–33–5 Hongo (℡ **03/3235-0701;** station: Hongo-Sanchome, 3 min.) holds a Dogen-Sangha meeting the first, third, and fifth Saturday of each month from 1 to 2:30pm, which includes 30 minutes of Zazen and a 1-hour lecture in English. There's a ¥400 ($2.50) fee. This one, too, allows long-term stays.

3 Parks & Gardens

Although Japan's most famous gardens are not in Tokyo, most of the places listed below use principles of Japanese landscaping and give visitors at least an idea of the scope and style of these gardens.

Hama Rikyu Garden ★★   Considered by some to be the best garden in Tokyo (but marred, in my opinion, by nearby buildings that detract from its charm), this peaceful oasis has origins stretching back 300 years, when it served as a retreat for a former feudal lord and as duck-hunting grounds for the Tokugawa shoguns. In 1871, possession of the garden passed to the imperial family, who used it to entertain such visiting dignitaries as Gen. Ulysses S. Grant. Come here to see how the upper classes enjoyed themselves during the Edo Period. Located on Tokyo Bay and surrounded by water on three sides, the garden contains an inner tidal pool, spanned by three bridges draped with wisteria. There are also other ponds; a refuge for ducks, herons, and migratory birds; a promenade along the bay lined with pine trees and offering views of Rainbow Bridge; a 300-year-old pine; moon-viewing pavilions; and teahouses. Plan on at least an hour's stroll to see everything. From a boarding pier on the garden's grounds, ferries depart for Asakusa every hour (or more often) between 10:15am and 4:05pm; the fare is ¥620 ($5.15) one-way.

1–1 Hamarikyuteien, Chuo-ku. ℡ 03/3541-0200. Admission ¥300 ($2.50). Daily 9am–5pm. Station: Shiodome (exit 5, 5 min.) or Shimbashi (12 min.).

East Garden (Higashi Gyoen) ★★   The 21 hectares (53 acres) of the formal Higashi Gyoen—once the main grounds of Edo Castle and located next to the Imperial Palace—are a wonderful respite in the middle of the city. Yet surprisingly, this garden is hardly ever crowded. **Ninomaru** ★★★, my favorite part, is laid out in Japanese style with a pond, stepping stones, and winding paths; it's particularly beautiful when the wisteria, azaleas, irises, and other flowers are in bloom. Near Ninomaru is the **Sannomaru Shozokan,** which displays changing exhibitions of art treasures belonging to the imperial family free of charge.

On the highest spot of Higashi Gyoen is the **Honmaru** (inner citadel), where Tokugawa's main castle once stood. Built in the first half of the 1600s, the castle was massive, surrounded by a series of whirling moats and guarded by 23 watchtowers and 99 gates around its 16km (10-mile) perimeter. At its center was Japan's tallest building at the time, the five-story castle keep, soaring 50m (168 ft.) above its foundations and offering an expansive view over Edo. This is where

Tokugawa Ieyasu would have taken refuge, had his empire ever been seriously threatened. Although most of the castle was a glimmering white, the keep was black with a gold roof, which must have been quite a sight in old Edo as it towered above the rest of the city. Today all that remains of Tokugawa's castle are a few towers, gates, stone walls, and moats, and the stone foundations of the keep.

1–1 Chiyoda, Chiyoda-ku. *C* 03/3213-1111. Free admission. Mar–Oct Tues–Thurs and Sat–Sun 9am–4:30pm (enter by 4pm); Nov–Feb Tues–Thurs and Sat–Sun 9am–4pm (enter by 3:30pm). Closed Dec 23 and Dec 28–Jan 3; open other national holidays. Station: Otemachi, Takebashi, or Nijubashi-mae.

Koishikawa Korakuen Garden (identified as Korakuen Garden on the TIC map) ★★ *Finds*   Constructed in the 17th century by a member of the Tokugawa clan with the assistance of a Chinese scholar refugee, this lovely, circular-pathed garden once spread over 25 hectares (63 acres) but has been whittled away by urbanization to only 6 hectares (16 acres). Surrounding buildings (especially Tokyo Dome) are an eyesore. Still, this remains Tokyo's oldest and one of its most celebrated stroll gardens, known for its miniature replicas of famous scenic spots in Japan and China. With its bridges, maple and pine groves, wisteria, ponds, flowering shrubs and trees, and other feasts for the eyes, little wonder it's been designated an Outstanding Scenic Place of Historical Importance. Indeed, the name Korakuen translates as "a pleasure afterward," reference to a Chinese poem with the verse "Be the first to take the world's trouble to heart, be the last to enjoy the world's pleasure." Not as well known as Hama Rikyu, it's also generally less crowded; a stroll should take about 30 minutes.

1–6–6 Koraku, Bunkyo-ku. *C* 03/3811-3015. Admission ¥300 ($2.50) adults, ¥150 ($1.25) seniors, free for children under 12. Daily 9am–5pm (enter by 4:30pm). Station: Iidabashi or Korakuen (8 min.). Entrance is at the southwestern edge of the garden.

Shinjuku Gyoen ★★ *Kids*   Formerly the private estate of a feudal lord and then of the imperial family, this is considered one of the most important parks of the Meiji Era. It's wonderful for strolling because of the variety of its planted gardens; styles range from French and English to Japanese traditional. This place amazes me every time I come here. The park's 58 hectares (144 acres) make it one of the city's largest, and each bend in the pathway brings something completely different: Ponds and sculpted bushes give way to a promenade lined with sycamores that opens onto a rose garden. Cherry blossoms, azaleas, chrysanthemums, and other flowers provide splashes of color from spring through autumn. There are also wide grassy expanses, popular for picnics and playing, and a greenhouse filled with tropical plants. You could easily spend a half-day of leisure here, but for a quick fix of rejuvenation, 1½ hours will do.

11 Naitocho, Shinjuku-ku. *C* 03/3350-0151. Admission ¥200 ($1.65). Tues–Sun 9am–4:30pm (enter by 4pm). Station: Shinjuku Gyoen-mae (2 min.).

Ueno Park *Kids*   Ueno Park—on the northeast edge of the Yamanote Line—is one of the largest parks in Tokyo and one of the most popular places in the city for Japanese families on a day's outing. It's a cultural mecca with a number of attractions, including the prestigious Tokyo National Museum, the National Museum of Western Art, the delightful Shitamachi Museum with its displays of old Tokyo, Ueno Zoo, and Shinobazu Pond (a bird sanctuary). The busiest time of the year at Ueno Park is in April, during the cherry-blossom season.

Other well-known landmarks in Ueno Park are **Toshogu Shrine,** erected in 1651 and dedicated to Tokugawa Ieyasu, founder of the Tokugawa shogunate; and **Kiyomizu-do Kannon Temple,** completed in 1631 as a copy of the famous Kiyomizu-do Kannon Temple in Kyoto (see "Shrines & Temples," below).

For more information on Ueno Park, see the walking tour of Ueno in chapter 7.

Taito-ku. Free admission to the park; separate admissions to each of its attractions. Open daily 24 hr. Station: Ueno (1 min.).

4 Shrines & Temples

In addition to the temples and shrines listed here, don't forget **Sensoji Temple** and **Meiji Jingu Shrine** (see "The Top Attractions," earlier).

Kiyomizu Kannon-do Temple   Established in 1631 and moved to its present site overlooking Shinobazu Pond in 1698, this small but important structure is a copy of the famous Kiyomizu Temple in Kyoto (but on a much less grander scale). It was once part of the Kan'eiji Temple precincts that covered Ueno Hill during the Edo Period. Remarkably, the temple survived both the 1868 battle between imperial and shogunate forces and bombings during World War II. Today, it's one of Tokyo's oldest temples. It enshrines Kosodate Kannon, protectress of childbearing and child-raising; women hoping to become pregnant come here to ask for the goddess's mercy, and those whose wishes have been fulfilled return to pray for their child's good health and protection. Many leave behind dolls as symbols of their children—if you take your shoes off and walk to the door to the right of the main altar, you'll see some of them. Once a year, on September 25, a requiem service is held for all the dolls at the temple, after which they are cremated.

Ueno Park, Taito-ku. ☎ 03/3821-4749. Free admission. Daily 7am–5pm. Station: Ueno (3 min.).

Toshogu Shrine ★   Come here to pay respects to the man who made Edo (present-day Tokyo) the seat of his government and thus elevated the small village to the most important city in the country. The only shrine in Tokyo that's been designated a National Treasure, Toshogu Shrine was erected in 1651 and is dedicated to Tokugawa Ieyasu, founder of the Tokugawa shogunate. Like Toshogu Shrine in Nikko, it was built by Ieyasu's grandson, Iemitsu, and boasts some of the same richly carved, ornate design favored by the Tokugawas. Remarkably, it survived the civil war of 1868, the Great Kanto Earthquake of 1923, and even World War II. The pathway to the shrine is lined with massive stone lanterns, as well as 50 copper lanterns donated by *daimyo* (feudal lords) from all over Japan. Inside the shrine, you'll see some exquisite art, including murals by a famous Edo artist, Kano Tan-yu, and samurai armor worn by Ieyasu. On a more somber note, a display on the grounds appeals for world peace, with graphic photos of Hiroshima following its destruction by the atom bomb and of victims dead and alive.

Ueno Park, Taito-ku. ☎ 03/3822-3455. Admission ¥200 ($1.65) adults, ¥100 (85¢) children. Summer daily 9am–6pm; winter daily 9am–4:30pm. Station: Ueno (4 min.).

Yasukuni Shrine ★   Built in 1869 to commemorate Japanese war dead, Yasukuni Shrine is constructed in classic Shinto style, with a huge steel *torii* gate at its entrance. During times of war, soldiers were told that if they died fighting for their country, their spirits would find glory here; even today, it's believed that the spirits of some 2.5 million Japanese war dead are at home here, where they are worshipped as deities. During any day of the week, you're likely to encounter older Japanese paying their respects to friends and families who perished in World War II. But every August 15 the shrine is thrust into the national spotlight when World War II memorials are held. Visits by prime ministers cause

Cherry-Blossom Viewing in Ueno Park

If you happen to come to Ueno Park during that brief single week in April when the cherry blossoms burst forth in glorious pink, consider yourself lucky. Cherry blossoms have always been dear to the Japanese heart as a symbol of beauty, fragility, and the transitory nature of life. Ueno Park, with its 1,000 cherry trees, has been popular as a viewing spot since the Edo Period. Today, Tokyoites throng here en masse to celebrate the birth of the new season. It's not, however, the spiritual communion with nature you might think. In the daytime on a weekday, Ueno Park may be peaceful and sane enough, but on the weekends and in the evenings during cherry-blossom season, havoc prevails as office workers break out of their winter shells.

Sending underlings to stake out territory early in the day, whole companies of workers later converge on Ueno Park to sit under the cherry trees on plastic or cardboard, their shoes neatly lined up along the perimeter. They eat obento box lunches and drink sake and beer; many get drunk and can be quite rowdy. The worst offenders are those singing karaoke. Still, visiting Ueno Park during cherry-blossom season is a cultural experience no one should miss. More than likely, you'll be invited to join one of the large groups—and by all means do so. You'll all sit there drinking and making merry, seemingly oblivious to the fragile pink blossoms shimmering above.

national uproars and outrage among Japan's Asian neighbors, who think it improper for a prime minister to visit—and thereby condone—a shrine so closely tied to Japan's nationalistic and militaristic past.

On the shrine's grounds is a war memorial museum, the **Yushukan** ★★. It chronicles the rise and fall of the samurai, the Sino-Japanese War, the Russo-Japanese War, and World Wars I and II, though explanations in English are rather vague and Japan's military aggression in Asia is glossed over. Still, a fascinating 90 minutes can be spent here gazing on samurai armor, uniforms, tanks, guns, and artillery, as well as such thought-provoking displays as a human torpedo (a tiny submarine guided by one occupant and loaded with explosives) and a suicide attack plane. But the most chilling displays are the seemingly endless photographs of war dead, some of them very young teenagers. In stark contrast to the somberness of the museum, temporary exhibits of beautiful ikebana (Japanese flower arrangements) and bonsai are often held on the shrine grounds in rows of glass cases. Yasukuni Shrine is also famous for its cherry blossoms.

3–1–1 Kudan-kita, Chiyoda-ku. (℃) 03/3261-8326. www.yasukuni.or.jp. Free admission to shrine; Yushukan ¥800 ($6.65) adults, ¥500 ($4.15) high-school and college students, ¥300 ($2.50) children. Shrine, daily 24 hr.; Yushukan, daily 9am–5:30pm (to 5pm Nov–Feb). Station: Kudanshita (3 min.) or Ichigaya or Iidabashi (7 min.). On Yasukuni Dori.

5 More Museums

For details on the **Tokyo National Museum** and the **Edo-Tokyo Museum,** see "The Top Attractions," earlier.

ART MUSEUMS

Bridgestone Museum of Art (Bridgestone Bijutsukan) ⭐   This privately owned museum contains a small but impressive collection of French Impressionist art, as well as Japanese paintings in the Western style dating from the Meiji Period onward. This is one of the best of Tokyo's private art museums, and since there are only five rooms of displays, it makes a quick and worthwhile 1-hour detour if you're in the vicinity. The permanent collection includes works by Monet, Manet, Degas, Sisley, Cézanne, Pissarro, Renoir, Corot, Gauguin, van Gogh, Matisse, Picasso, Modigliani, and Rousseau, as well as Japanese painters Asai Chu, Kuroda Seiki, Aoki Shigeru, Kuniyoshi Wasuo, and Saeki Yuzo. Special exhibitions are mounted three or four times a year.

Bridgestone Building, 1–10–1 Kyobashi, Chuo-ku. ⓒ 03/3563-0241. www.bridgestone-museum.gr.jp. Admission ¥700 ($5.85) adults, ¥600 seniors, ¥500 ($4.15) students, free for children under 15 (except during special exhibits). Special exhibits cost more. Tues–Fri 10am–8pm; Sat–Sun 10am–6pm. Closed during exhibit changes. Station: Tokyo (Yaesu Central exit, 5 min.), Kyobashi (Meidi-ya exit, 5 min.), or Nihombashi (Takashimaya exit, 5 min.). On Chuo Dori (with an entrance around the corner on Yaesu Dori), a short walk directly east of Tokyo Station.

Hara Museum of Contemporary Art (Hara Bijutsukan) ⭐⭐   Japan's oldest museum devoted to contemporary international and Japanese art is housed in a 1930s tiled, Bauhaus-style Art Deco home that once belonged to the current director's grandfather; the building alone is worth the trip. The museum stages three or four exhibitions annually; some are on the cutting edge of international art, but at least one features works from its own collection, which focuses on paintings and sculptures mainly from the 1950s and 1960s by Japanese and foreign artists and includes works by Andy Warhol, Roy Lichtenstein, Claes Oldenburg, Jackson Pollock, Karel Appel, Robert Rauschenberg, and Frank Stella. Be sure to check out the downstairs toilet by Morimura Yasumasu. Afterward, relax at the lovely greenhouselike cafe with outdoor seating. You should plan on spending at least an hour at this great museum.

4–7–25 Kita-Shinagawa, Shinagawa-ku. ⓒ 03/3445-0651. www.haramuseum.or.jp. Admission ¥1,000 ($8.35) adults, ¥700 ($5.85) students 16 and older, ¥500 ($4.15) children, free for seniors. Tues, Thurs–Sun, and holidays 11am–5pm; Wed 11am–8pm. Closed during exhibition changes. Station: Shinagawa (Takanawa exit, 15 min.).

Mori Art Museum (Mori Bijutsukan)   This is Tokyo's highest museum, on the 52nd floor of the Roppongi Hills Mori Tower. Opened in 2003, it features state-of-the art galleries with 6m (20-ft.) tall ceilings, controlled natural lighting,

---

Tips **Museum Tips**

Note that most museums in Tokyo are closed on Mondays and for New Year's—generally the last few days in December and the first 3 days of January. If Monday happens to be a national holiday, most museums will remain open but will close Tuesday instead. Some of the privately owned museums, however, may be closed on national holidays or the day following every national holiday, as well as for exhibition changes. Call beforehand to avoid disappointment. Remember, too, that you must enter museums at least 30 minutes before closing time. For a listing of current special exhibitions, including those being held at major department stores, consult *Metropolis*, published weekly.

and bird's-eye views of Tokyo. Exhibitions of emerging and established artists from around the world are shown four times a year, with past shows centering on contemporary Asian, African, and Japanese art.

Roppongi Hills Mori Tower, 6–10–1 Roppongi, Minato-ku. (✆ **03/6406-6100**. www.mori.art.museum/english/index.html. Admission varies according to the exhibit. Sun–Thurs 10am–10pm; Fri–Sat 10am–midnight. Station: Roppongi (2 min.).

Museum of Contemporary Art, Tokyo (MOT; Tokyo-to Gendai Bijutsukan) ✿

The MOT is inconveniently located but is well worth the trek if you're a fan of the avant-garde (you'll pass the Fukagawa Edo Museum, described below, on the way, so you may wish to visit both). This modern structure of glass and steel, with a long corridor entrance that reminds me of railroad trestles, houses both permanent and temporary exhibits of Japanese and international postwar art in large rooms that lend themselves to large installations. Although temporary exhibits, which occupy most of the museum space, have ranged from Southeast Asian art to a retrospective of Jasper Johns, the smaller permanent collection presents a chronological study of 50 years of contemporary art, beginning with Japanese postwar avant-garde and continuing with anti-artistic trends and pop art in the 1960s, Minimalism, and art after the 1980s, with about 100 works displayed on a rotating basis. Included may be works by Andy Warhol, Gerhard Richter, Roy Lichtenstein, David Hockney, Frank Stella, Sandro Chia, and Julian Schnabel. Depending on the number of exhibits you visit, you'll spend anywhere from 1 to 2 hours here. Bonus: A computer room lets you surf the Internet for free.

4–1–1 Miyoshi, Koto-ku. (✆ **03/5245-4111**. Admission to permanent collection ¥500 ($4.15) adults, ¥400 ($3.35) students, ¥250 ($2.10) children; special exhibits ¥1,000 ($8.35) or more. Tues–Sun 10am–6pm. Station: Kiyosumi-Shirakawa (exit A3, 13 min.). On Fukagawa Shiroyokan-dori Street, just off Mitsume Dori.

National Museum of Modern Art (Tokyo Kokuritsu Kindai Bijutsukan) ✿✿

This newly renovated museum houses the largest collection of modern Japanese art under one roof, including both Japanese- and Western-style paintings, prints, watercolors, drawings, and sculpture, all dating from the Meiji Period to World War II. Names to look for include Munakata Shiko, Kuroda Seiki, and Yokoyama Taikan. To provide a wider context, a few Western artists are also represented, among them Klee and Kandinsky. Expect to spend about 1½ hours here.

3 Kitanomaru Koen Park, Chiyoda-ku. (✆ **03/3214-2561**. www.momat.go.jp. Admission ¥420 ($3.50) adults, ¥130 ($1.10) students, free for children; special exhibits cost more. Tues–Thurs and Sat–Sun 10am–5pm; Fri 10am–8pm. Station: Takebashi (5 min.).

National Museum of Western Art (Kokuritsu Seiyo Bijutsukan) ✿

Japan's only national museum dedicated to Western art is housed in a main building designed by Le Corbusier and in two more recent additions. It presents a chronological study of sculpture and art from the end of the Middle Ages through the 20th century, beginning with works by old masters, including Lucas Cranach the Elder, Rubens, El Greco, Murillo, and Tiepolo. French painters and Impressionists of the 19th and 20th centuries are well represented, including Delacroix, Monet (with a whole room devoted to his work), Manet, Renoir, Pissarro, Sisley, Courbet, Cezanne, and Gauguin. The museum's 20th-century collection includes works by Picasso, Max Ernst, Miró, Dubuffet, and Pollock. The museum is also famous for its 50-odd sculptures by Rodin, one of the largest collections in the world, encompassing most of his major works including *The Kiss, The Thinker, Balzac,* and *The Gates of Hell.* Plan on spending at least an hour here.

Ueno Park, Taito-ku. Ⓒ **03/3828-5131**. www.nmwa.go.jp. Admission ¥420 ($3.50) adults, ¥130 ($1.10) students, ¥70 (60¢) high-school students, free for children and seniors; special exhibits require separate admission fee. Free admission to permanent collection 2nd and 4th Sat of the month. Tues–Thurs and Sat–Sun 9:30am–5pm; Fri 9:30am–8pm. Station: Ueno (4 min.).

Nezu Institute of Fine Arts (Nezu Bijutsukan)   This is one of Tokyo's best-known private museums. It houses a fine collection of Asian art, including Chinese bronzes, Japanese calligraphy, Korean ceramics, and other artwork ranging from paintings and sculpture to lacquerware, Buddhist and Shinto art, and items used in tea ceremonies, displayed in rotating exhibitions. In addition, temporary exhibits may highlight antique Imari ware, Noh masks and costumes, or decorative Chinese clocks. Admission includes entrance to a delightful small garden with a pond. You'll want to spend about 45 minutes here.

6–5–1 Minami Aoyama, Minato-ku. Ⓒ **03/3400-2536**. Admission ¥1,000 ($8.35) adults, ¥700 ($5.85) students and children. Tues–Sun 9:30am–4:30pm. Closed days following holidays and during exhibit changes. Station: Omotesando (8 min.).

Ota Memorial Museum of Art (Ota Kinen Bijutsukan) ★ _Finds_   This great museum features the private _ukiyo-e_ (woodblock print) collection of the late Ota Seizo, who early in life recognized the importance of ukiyo-e as an art form and dedicated himself to its preservation. Although the collection contains 12,000 prints, only 80 to 100 are displayed at any given time, in thematic exhibitions that change monthly and include English descriptions. The museum itself is small but delightful, with such traditional touches as bamboo screens and stone pathways. You can tour the museum in about 30 minutes.

1–10–10 Jingumae, Shibuya-ku. Ⓒ **03/3403-0880**. www.ukiyoe-ota-muse.jp. Admission ¥700 – ¥1,000 ($5.85–$8.35) adults, ¥500 – ¥700 ($4.15–$5.85) high-school and college students, ¥200 – ¥500 ($1.65–$4.15) junior high students, free – ¥200 ($1.65) children; price depends on the exhibit. Tues–Sun 10:30am–5:30pm (enter by 5pm). Closed from the 27th to end of each month. Station: Harajuku (2 min.) or Meiji-Jingumae (1 min.). Near the Omotesando Dori and Meiji Dori intersection, behind La Forêt.

SPECIALTY MUSEUMS & EXHIBITION HALLS

Asakura Choso Museum ★★ _Finds_   This unique museum is one of my favorites and is well worth a visit if you haven't been to a Japanese home. It served as the residence and studio of sculptor Asakura Fumio (1883–1964), famous for his statues of statesmen, women, and cats, many of which are on display here. The house, which combines modern and traditional architecture, wraps around an inner courtyard pond fed by a natural spring, and contains some furniture and antiques in its many tatami rooms, including a beautiful library, a tearoom, and a room for enjoying the morning sun. There's even a rooftop garden. Since you won't want to rush, plan on spending 30 to 45 minutes here. See the recommended stroll of Yanaka in chapter 7 for more information.

7–18–10 Yanaka, Taito-ku. Ⓒ **03/3821-4549**. Admission ¥400 ($3.35) adults, ¥150 ($1.25) children. Tues–Thurs and Sat–Sun 9:30am–4:30pm. Station: Nippori (west exit, 3 min.).

Beer Museum Yebisu   If you find yourself in Yebisu Garden Place (perhaps to see the Museum of Photography), you may wish to take a 30-minute spin through this showcase of Sapporo breweries. Named after Yebisu Beer, which made its debut in 1890 and to which both Ebisu Station and the surrounding neighborhood owe their names, it presents a high-tech explanation (in Japanese only) of an age-old process, including a "virtual brewery" which lets viewers observe the brewing process through 3D glasses, with such startling close-ups that it's almost like swimming in the brew. I especially like the gallery of old beer advertisements. Alas, there are no free samples; visitors must purchase tickets from vending machines at the tasting lounge.

Yebisu Garden Place, 4–20–1 Ebisu, Shibuya-ku. ☎ **03/5423-7255**. Free admission. Tues–Sun 10am–6pm (enter by 5pm). Station: Ebisu (8 min.). Behind Mitsukoshi department store (take the B1 exit from the store).

Crafts Gallery (Bijutsukan Kogeikan)   Housed in a handsome Gothic-style brick building constructed in 1910 as headquarters of the Imperial Guard, this gallery exhibits contemporary crafts, including pottery, ceramics, kimono, metalwork, glassware, lacquerware, bambooware, and more; objects are changed approximately four times a year to reflect the seasons. Most exhibitions concentrate on a specific theme such as bambooware or the works of a single artist, usually one noted for skill in traditional arts. Unfortunately, the exhibition space is very limited; you can tour the place in 45 minutes or less.

Kitanomaru Koen Park, Chiyoda-ku. ☎ **03/3211-7781**. Admission ¥420 – ¥800 ($3.50–$6.65) adults, ¥130 – ¥450 ($1.10–$3.75) students, free – ¥330 (60¢–$2.75) children; price depends on the exhibit. Tues–Sun 10am–5pm. Station: Takebashi (7 min.).

Drum Museum (Taikokan) *Kids*   This fourth-floor museum, which you can tour in about 20 minutes, is a collection of more than 600 instruments, displayed on a rotating basis and including traditional Japanese drums as well as a variety of drums from all over the world. With the exception of some of the rare, older pieces (distinguished by a red marking), many of the 200 or so drums always on display can be touched and played, making this a good spot for children. There are also videos of drumming from Japan and around the world. On the ground floor is a shop specializing in Japanese percussion instruments and items used in Japanese festivals, including decorative Japanese drums, lion heads for the lion dance, Japanese flutes, and masks.

Miyamoto Japanese Percussion and Festival Store, 2–1–1 Nishi-Asakusa, Taito-ku. ☎ **03/3842-5622**. Admission ¥300 ($2.70) adults, ¥150 ($1.35) children. Wed–Sun 10am–5pm. Closed holidays. Station: Tawaramachi (2 min.) or Asakusa (5 min.). On Kokusai Dori, north of Kaminarimon Dori.

Edo-Tokyo Open Air Architectural Museum (Edo-Tokyo Tatemono-en) *Finds*   Although located on the far western outskirts of Tokyo, this branch of the Edo-Tokyo Museum is a must for architecture buffs. Spread on 6.8 hectares (17 acres) in the middle of an expansive park, it showcases some two dozen buildings from the late Edo Period to the 1950s, arranged along streets in a village setting. Included are 200-year-old thatch-roofed farmhouses, traditional Japanese and Western-style residences, a teahouse, soy-sauce shop, bathhouse, police box, flower shop, and more, filled with related objects and furniture. You'll need a minimum of 2 hours to see everything here.

3–7–1 Sakura-cho, Koganei-shi. ☎ **042/388-3300**. Admission ¥500 ($4.15) adults, ¥300 ($2.50) children, free for seniors. Apr–Sept Tues–Sun 9:30am–5:30pm; Oct–Mar Tues–Sun 9:30am–4:30pm. Directions: From Shinjuku Station, take the rapid Chuo Line about 30 min. to Musashi-Koganei Station. Take the north exit and board bus no. 21 for a 5-min. ride to Koganei Koen Nishi Guchi stop, from which it's a 5-min. walk; or board bus no. 14 to Edo-Tokyo Tatemono-en-mae stop, from which it's a 3-min. walk.

Fukagawa Edo Museum (Fukagawa Edo Shiryokan) *Kids*   This is the Tokyo of your dreams, the way it appears in all those samurai flicks on Japanese TV: a reproduction of a 19th-century neighborhood in Fukagawa, a prosperous community on the east bank of the Sumida River during the Edo Period. This delightful museum is located off Kiyosumi Dori on a pleasant tree-lined, shop-filled street called Fukagawa Shiryokan Dori. The museum's hangarlike interior contains 11 full-scale replicas of traditional houses, vegetable and rice shops, a fish store, two inns, a fire watchtower, and tenement homes, all arranged to resemble an actual neighborhood. There are lots of small touches and flourishes to make the community seem real and believable—a cat sleeping on a roof, a snail crawling up a fence, a dog relieving itself on a pole, sounds of birds, and a vendor shouting his wares. The village even changes with the seasons (with trees sprouting cherry blossoms in spring and threatened by thunderstorms in summer) and, every 45 minutes or so, undergoes a day's cycle from morning (rooster crow, lights brighten) to night (the sun sets, the retractable roof closes to make everything dark). Of Tokyo's museums, this one is probably the best for children; plan on spending about an hour here. Don't confuse this museum with the much larger Edo-Tokyo Museum, which traces the history of Tokyo.

1–3–28 Shirakawa, Koto-ku. ✆ 03/3630-8625. Admission ¥300 ($2.50) adults, ¥50 (40¢) children 6–14. Daily 9:30am–5pm. Closed 2nd and 4th Mon of each month. Station: Kiyosumi-Shirakawa (3 min.).

John Lennon Museum ★ Opened on October 9, 2000, the day John Lennon would have turned 60, this museum chronicles the former Beatles musician from his childhood through his early years in Liverpool, the various stages of the Beatles' fame, his relationship with Yoko Ono and their commitment to the peace movement, the breakup of the Beatles, and his years as a house husband caring for their son Sean. It's worth noting that only Japanese captions mention Lennon's son Julian from his first marriage or the fact that Yoko had been married twice before meeting Lennon and had a daughter. Otherwise, the museum does an excellent job with displays of Lennon's handwritten lyrics, trademark wire-rim glasses, leather jacket, U.K. passport, guitars, white Steinway, and other memorabilia, with concert videos and personal footage throughout. Few Lennon fans will probably escape dry-eyed, especially in the Imagine room, adorned only with the powerful lyrics of his song "Imagine." You can easily spend an hour here.

Saitama Super Arena, 2–27 Kamiochiai, Yono-city, Saitama. ✆ 048/601-0009. www.taisei.co.jp/museum. Admission ¥1,500 ($13) adults, ¥1,000 ($8.35) students, ¥500 ($4.15) children. Wed–Mon 11am–6pm. Directions: From Shinagawa or Tokyo Station, take the JR Keihin-Tohoku Line 30 to 40 min. to Saitama Shin-toshin Station, from which it's a 2-min. walk from the west exit.

Kite Museum (Tako-no-Hakubutsukan) This private collection consists of more than 3,000 kites, mainly Japanese, all jam-packed in a few small rooms you can tour in about 30 minutes. They range from miniature kites the size of postage stamps to kites dating from the Taisho Period, some ornately decorated with Kabuki stars, samurai, and animals. There are even hand-painted kites by ukiyo-e master Hiroshige.

Taimeiken Building, 5th floor, 1–12–10 Nihombashi, Chuo-ku. ✆ 03/3275-2704. Admission ¥200 ($1.65) adults, ¥100 (85¢) children. Mon–Sat 11am–5pm. Closed holidays. Station: Nihombashi (3 min.). Off Eitai Dori, near Showa Dori, behind Merrill Lynch.

Megaweb (Kids) This huge technology playground and amusement spot on Odaiba is a Toyota showroom in disguise. For the kids there are several virtual thrill rides, including driving simulators, a 3-D roller-coaster ride through a city of the future, a 3-D motion theater with seats that move to the action, and driverless electric commuter cars (some rides have passenger height restrictions). The History Garage displays models from around the world, mostly from the 1950s through the 1970s. But the complex's main raison d'être is its Toyota City Showcase, with 140-odd Toyota models, including racing cars. Car buffs and families can probably kill an hour or two here, but serious Toyota fans may want to skip this in favor of the adult-oriented Toyota Auto Salon Amlux, described below. Beside Megaweb is a 113m (377-ft.) tall Ferris wheel that takes 16 minutes to make a complete turn and costs ¥900 ($7.50) to ride.

Palette Town, 1 Aomi, Koto-ku. ✆ 03/3599-0808. www.megaweb.gr.jp. Admission free to Megaweb; thrill rides cost ¥200–¥800 ($1.65–$6.65) each. Daily 11am–9pm for most attractions. Station: Aomi, on the Yurikamome Line from Shimbashi (1 min.) or Tokyo Teleport, on the Rinkai Line (3 min.). Located on Odaiba.

Museum of Maritime Science (Fune-no-Kagakukan)   The building housing the Museum of Maritime Science is a perfect match for a passenger liner, complete with an observation tower atop its bridge. Appropriately enough, it's located on Odaiba, reclaimed land in Tokyo Bay, and offers a good view of Tokyo's container port nearby. The museum, which you can tour in about an hour, contains an excellent collection of model boats, including warships like the 1898 battleship *Shikishima*, submarines, ferries, supertankers, container ships, and wooden ships used during the Edo Period. Technical explanations, unfortunately, are mostly in Japanese. Children love the radio-controlled boats they can direct in a pond. Moored nearby is the *Soya*, constructed in 1938 as a cargo icebreaker; it served as Japan's first Antarctic observation ship. Those with a lot of time on their hands can also visit the *Yotei Maru*, which once ferried the waters between Aomori and Hokkaido before the opening of an underwater tunnel made its job obsolete; today, oddly enough, it serves as a floating amusement center of sorts. Beside the museum is a public swimming pool open July and August, and the National Museum of Emerging Science and Innovation (see below) is nearby, making this area of Odaiba a good destination for families.

3-1 Higashi-Yashio, Shinagawa-ku. ✆ 03/5500-1111. Combination ticket to everything ¥1,000 ($8.35) adults, ¥600 ($5) children; main museum and the Soya, ¥700 ($5.85) adults, ¥400 ($3.35) children. Daily 10am–5pm. Station: Fune-no-Kagakukan, on the Yurikamome Line from Shimbashi (1 min.). On Odaiba.

National Museum of Emerging Science and Innovation (Nippon Kagaku Miraikan) *Kids*   Opened in 2001 on Odaiba, this fascinating, educational museum provides hands-on exploration of the latest developments in cutting-edge science and technology, including interactions with robots, virtual-reality rides, and displays that suggest future applications such as noninvasive medical procedures and an environmentally friendly home. Everything from nanotechnology to genomes are explained in detail; touch-screens in English and a volunteer staff eager to assist in demonstrations and answer questions catapult this to one of the most user-friendly technology museums I've ever seen. A great place to get your brain cells up and running whether you're 4 years old or 80, this museum deserves at least 3 or 4 hours.

2-41 Aomi, Koto-ku. ✆ 03/3570-9151. www.miraikan.jst.go.jp. Admission ¥500 ($4.15) adults, ¥200 ($1.65) children. Wed–Mon 10am–5pm. Station: Telecom Center or Fune-no-Kagakukan (5 min.). On Odaiba.

National Science Museum (Kokuritsu Kahaku Hakubutsukan) *Kids*   This is a sprawling complex, comprising three buildings and covering everything from the evolution of life to electronics in Japan. Unfortunately, most displays are in Japanese (be sure to pick up the museum's English pamphlet), but the museum is worth visiting for its exhibits relating to Japan. There are also plenty of exhibits geared toward children. Dinosaurs greet visitors on the ground floor of the main hall, while up on the third floor plants and animals of Japan are featured, including the Japanese brown bear, the Japanese crested ibis, the Japanese monkey, and marine life such as huge king crabs. Other highlights include a display on the origin, development, and history of the Japanese people; a hands-on discovery room for children exploring sound, light, magnetism, and other scientific phenomena; a map of Japan showing the location of all its active volcanoes; re-created wood and marine habitats; and an amazing room of stuffed and preserved animals, including a gorilla and other primates, bears, alligators, and a giant squid. You'll want to spend about 2 hours here, more if you have children in tow.

Ueno Park, Taito-ku. ℂ 03/3822-0111. www.kahaku.go.jp/english. Admission ¥420 ($3.50) adults, ¥70 (60¢) children; more for special exhibits. Tues–Sun 9am–4:30pm. Station: Ueno (5 min.).

Open-Air Folk House Museum (Nihon Minka-en) ★★ *Finds*   Whereas the Edo-Tokyo Tatemono-en (above) is an open-air museum of traditional and modern Tokyo homes and buildings mostly dating from the late 1800s to the 1950s, this architectural museum concentrates on rural Japan from centuries past. Located in the neighboring city of Kawasaki, 30 minutes by express train from Shinjuku, it features 23 traditional houses and other historical buildings, in a lovely setting along wooded hillsides. Most buildings are heavy-beamed thatched houses (the oldest are 300 years old), but there are also warehouses, a samurai's residential gate, a water wheel, and a Kabuki stage from a small fishing village, all originally from other parts of Honshu and reconstructed here. An English pamphlet and numerous signs explain each of the buildings, all open to the public so you can wander in and inspect the various rooms, gaining insight into rural Japanese life in centuries past. Plan on spending a half-day here, including transportation back and forth.

7–1–1 Masugata, Tama-ku, Kawasaki. ℂ 044/922-2181. Admission ¥500 ($4.15) adults, ¥300 ($2.50) students and children. Tues–Sun 9:30am–4pm. From Shinjuku Station, take the express Odakyu Line 30 min. to Mukogaoka Yuen Station, from which it's a 15-min. walk.

Shitamachi Museum (Shitamachi Fuzoku Shiryokan)   Shitamachi means "downtown" and refers to the area of Tokyo in which commoners used to live, mainly around Ueno and Asakusa. Today there's very little left of old downtown Tokyo, and with that in mind, the Shitamachi Museum seeks to preserve for future generations a way of life that was virtually wiped out by the great earthquake of 1923 and World War II. Shops are set up as they may have looked back then, including a merchant's shop and a candy shop, as well as one of the Shitamachi tenements common at the turn of the 20th century. These tenements—long, narrow buildings with one roof over a series of dwelling units separated by thin wooden walls—were the homes of the poorer people. Everyone knew everyone else's business; few secrets could be kept in such crowded conditions. The narrow back alleyways where they were located served as communal living rooms. The museum also displays relics relating to the lives of these people, including utensils, toys, costumes, and tools, most of which you can pick up and examine more closely. Individuals, many living in Shitamachi, donated all the museum's holdings. This museum is small (you can see everything in about 30 min.) and is recommended only if you don't have time to see the better Edo-Tokyo Museum or Fukagawa Edo Museum (described above).

Ueno Park, Taito-ku. ℂ 03/3823-7451. Admission ¥300 ($2.50) adults, ¥100 (85¢) children. Tues–Sun 9:30am–4:30pm. Station: Ueno (3 min.).

Sony Building   A popular place to kill an hour or so of free time in the Ginza, the Sony Building offers six floors of showrooms and amusements, as well as restaurants and shops. The latest in Sony video and digital cameras, high-definition TVs, CD and other portable players, laptops, and computers are all on display for public inspection. A PlayStation on the sixth floor has Sony games you can interact with for free.

5–3–1 Ginza, Chuo-ku. ℂ 03/3573-2371. Free admission. Daily 11am–7pm. Station: Ginza (B9 exit, 1 min.). At the intersection of Harumi Dori and Sotobori Dori.

Takagi Bonsai Museum *(Finds)*   If you've ever admired Japanese bonsai, you owe yourself a visit to this unique museum, housed in an unlikely commercial building on the eighth and ninth floors. Out of a collection of 500 miniature trees and bushes, 30 are on display each week (keeping them inside longer would be damaging), along with a changing display of bonsai pots from the Edo through Meiji periods and ukiyo-e (woodblock prints) by Utagawa and Hiroshige that include bonsai. There's also a rooftop garden with a pond and the pride of the museum—a 500-year-old bonsai pine—as well as an outdoor nursery where the rest of the museum's bonsai are cultivated, and an English-language video on bonsai. At the end of your visit (which should take no longer than 20–30 min.), you're invited to have a cup of coffee or tea.

1–1 Gobancho, Chiyoda-ku. ℂ 03/3221-0006. Admission ¥800 ($6.65) adults, ¥500 ($4.15) students and children. Tues–Sun 10am–5pm. Station: Ichigaya (1 min.).

Tepco Electric Energy Museum (Den Ryoku-kan) *(Kids)*   If you have children with you, or are interested in electricity, drop by the Tokyo Electric Power Company's (TEPCO) public-service facility. TEPCO operates thermal electric, nuclear, and hydroelectric power plants that supply Tokyo and its vicinity with electricity. This showroom, which was established to teach urban dwellers how electricity is generated, supplied to homes, and consumed, doubles as a much-needed public relations outlet since the firm was caught falsifying safety reports in 2002, causing the temporary shutdown of all its nuclear reactors for inspection. But things hum along happily here, with five floors of displays that include a 19-minute video in English describing nuclear energy, a model of a nuclear reactor, and a children's play area with computers and games. Although displays are in Japanese only, English-language pamphlets on each floor answer all the technological questions you may have. Plan on 45 to 60 minutes here.

1–12–10 Jinnan, Shibuya-ku. ℂ 03/3477-1191. Free admission. Thurs–Tues 10am–6pm. Station: Shibuya (5 min.).

Tokyo Metropolitan Museum of Photography (Tokyo-to Shashin Bijut-sukan) ★   This museum has an impressive 18,000 works in its collection of photographs, ranging from the historical to the contemporary, with about 70% by Japanese photographers. Exhibitions from Japan and abroad, many on the cutting edge of contemporary photography, are shown in one gallery, while another features a rotating exhibit of the museum's holdings (occasionally the permanent collection is usurped by a special exhibition). In the basement is the Images & Technology Gallery, which displays materials and equipment from the earliest days of filming to the latest technological advances. I can easily spend an hour here, lost in another world.

Yebisu Garden Place, 1–13–3 Mita, Meguro-ku. ℂ 03/3280-0099. Admission to permanent collection ¥500 ($4.15) adults, ¥400 ($3.35) students, ¥250 ($2.10) children and seniors; more for special exhibits. Sun, Tues, Wed, and Sat 10am–6pm; Thurs–Fri 10am–8pm. Station: Ebisu (8 min.).

Toyota Auto Salon Amlux Tokyo   I'm not a big car fan, but even I have fun at Amlux. Japan's largest automobile showroom when it opened 20-some years ago, this sophisticated facility holds its own with four floors of exhibition space containing more than 70 vehicles (be sure to stop by the information desk on the first floor for an English-language pamphlet). Everything from sports and racing cars to family and luxury cars is on view, all open so that potential customers can climb inside and play with the dials. There are also exhibits relating to Toyota's plans for the future. As opposed to Megaweb on Odaiba (see above), which is mainly for entertainment, this is for serious automobile fans.

3–3–5 Higashi Ikebukuro, Toshima-ku. © **03/5391-5900.** www.amlux.jp. Free admission. Tues–Sun 11am–7pm. Station: Higashi Ikebukuro (2 min.) or Ikebukuro (5 min.).

6 Spectacular City Views

Tokyo Metropolitan Government Office (TMG) ★★★ *Kids* Tokyo's city hall—designed by one of Japan's best-known architects, Kenzo Tange—is an impressive addition to the skyscrapers of west Shinjuku. Three buildings comprise the complex—TMG No. 1, TMG No. 2, and the Metropolitan Assembly Building—and together they contain everything from Tokyo's Disaster Prevention Center to the governor's office. Most important for visitors is TMG No. 1, the tall building to the north that offers one of the best views of Tokyo. This 48-story, 240m (800-ft.) structure, the tallest building in Shinjuku, boasts two observatories located on the 45th floors of both its North and South towers, with access from the first floor. Both observatories offer the same spectacular views—on clear winter days you can even see Mount Fuji—as well as a small souvenir shop and coffee shop. In expensive Tokyo, this is one of the city's best bargains, and kids love it. On the first floor is a Tokyo Tourist Information Center, open daily 10am to 6:30pm.

2–8–1 Nishi-Shinjuku. © **03/5321-1111.** Free admission. Daily 9:30am–10pm. Closed Dec 29–Jan 3. Station: Tochomae (1 min.), Shinjuku (10 min.), or Nishi-Shinjuku (4 min.).

Tokyo Tower ★ *Overrated* Japan's most famous observation tower was built in 1958 and was modeled after the Eiffel Tower in Paris. Lit up at night, this 330m (1,099-ft.) tower, a relay station for TV and radio stations, is a familiar and beloved landmark in the city's landscape; but with the construction of skyscrapers over the past few decades (including the TMG, above, with its free observatory), it has lost some of its appeal as an observation platform and seems more like a relic from the 1950s. With its tacky souvenir shops and assorted small-time attractions, this place is as about as kitsch as kitsch can be.

The tower has two observatories: the main one at 149m (495 ft.) and the top observatory at 248m (825 ft.). The best time of year for viewing is said to be during Golden Week at the beginning of May. With many Tokyoites gone from the city and most factories and businesses closed down, the air at this time is thought to be the cleanest and clearest. There are several off-beat tourist attractions in the tower's base building, including a wax museum (where you can see the Beatles, a wax rendition of Leonardo's *Last Supper*, Hollywood stars, and a medieval torture chamber), a small aquarium, a museum of holography, and a trick art gallery, all with separate admission fees and appealing mainly to children.

4–2 Shiba Koen, Minato-ku. © **03/3433-5111.** www.tokyotower.co.jp. Admission to main observatory ¥820 ($6.85) adults, ¥460 ($3.85) children; top observatory ¥1,420 ($12) adults, ¥860 ($7.15) children. Daily 9am–10pm. Station: Onarimon or Kamiyacho (6 min.).

7 Especially for Kids

Attractions listed earlier that are good for children include the Drum Museum, Edo-Tokyo Museum, Fukugawa Edo Museum, National Museum of Emerging Science and Innovation, Museum of Maritime Science, National Science Museum, Tepco Electric Energy Museum, Tokyo Tower, and the observatory of the Tokyo Metropolitan Government Office. Ueno and Shinjuku parks are good for getting rid of all that excess energy.

Hanayashiki Opened in 1853, this small and rather corny amusement park is Japan's oldest. It offers a small roller coaster, a kiddie Ferris wheel, a carousel, a haunted house, a 3-D theater, and other diversions that appeal to children. Note, however, that after paying admission, you must still buy tickets for each ride; tickets are ¥100 (85¢) each, and most rides require two or three.

2-28-1 Asakusa (northwest of Sensoji Temple), Taito-ku. ℂ 043/3842-8780. Admission ¥900 ($7.50) adults, ¥400 ($3.35) children 5–12 and seniors, free for children 4 and under. Wed–Mon 10am–6pm (to 5pm in winter). Station: Asakusa (5 min.).

Joypolis Sega   Bored teenagers in tow, grumbling at yet another temple or shrine? Bring them to life at Tokyo's most sophisticated virtual amusement arcade, outfitted with the latest in video games and high-tech virtual-reality attractions, courtesy of Sega. Video games include bobsledding and car races, in which participants maneuver curves utilizing virtual-reality equipment, as well as numerous aeronautical battle games. There's also a 3-D sightseeing tour with seats that move with the action on the screen, several virtual reality rides (sky-diving, anyone?), and much, much more. Most harmless are the Print Club machines, which will print your face on stickers with the background (Mt. Fuji, perhaps?) of your choice. If you think your kids will want to try everything, buy them a passport for ¥3,300 ($28).

There's a smaller Sega on Dogenzaka slope in Shibuya at 2–6–16 Dogenzaka (ℂ **03/5458-2201;** station: Shibuya, 2 min.), open daily 10am to midnight and offering arcade and virtual-reality games.

Tokyo Decks, 3rd floor, Odaiba. ℂ **03/5500-1801.** Admission ¥500 ($4.15) adults, ¥300 ($2.50) children; individual attractions an additional ¥200 – ¥700 ($1.65–$5.85) each. Daily 10am–11pm. Station: Odaiba Kai-hin Koen (2 min.). On Odaiba.

LaQua   Located in the center of town next to the Tokyo Dome is this newly renovated amusement park featuring a high-tech Ferris wheel called the Big O (hollow in the middle, with no spokes and no hub), the heart-stopping Thun-der Dolphin roller coaster which passes through the Big O and part of a build-ing at speeds reaching up to 130km (81 miles) per hour, the truly horrifying Thirteen Doors horror house with mutilated bodies, a water ride, and other amusements packed into cramped quarters.

Tokyo Dome City, 1–3–61 Koraku, Bunkyo-ku. ℂ **03/5800-9999.** www.laqua.jp. Free admission; individual rides cost ¥600 – ¥1,000 ($5–$8.35) each. Daily 10am–10pm. Station: Korakuen (1 min.), Kasuga (2 min.), or Suidobashi (7 min.).

National Children's Castle (Kodomo-no-Shiro) ✦   Here's a great place to bring the kids. Conceived by the Ministry of Health and Welfare to commemo-rate the International Year of the Child in 1979, the Children's Castle holds var-ious activity rooms for children of all ages. The third floor, designed for spontaneous and unstructured play, features a large climbing gym, a computer playroom, building blocks, a playhouse, dolls, books, and a teen corner with table tennis and other age-appropriate games; there's also an art room staffed with instructors to help children with projects suitable for their ages. On the fourth floor is a music room with instruments the kids are invited to play, as well as a video room with private cubicles where visitors can make selections from a library of English-language and Japanese videos. On the roof is an outdoor playground complete with tricycles and a small wading pool for toddlers (¥200/$1.65 extra), while in the basement is the family swimming pool (¥300/$2.50 for adults, ¥200/$1.65 for children). Various programs are offered throughout the week, including puppet shows, fairy tales, and origami presentations.

5-53-1 Jingumae, Shibuya-ku. ℂ **03/3797-5666.** Admission ¥500 ($4.15) adults, ¥400 ($3.35) children 3–17, free for children under 3. Tues–Fri 12:30–5:30pm; Sat–Sun and holidays (including school holidays)

10am–5:30pm. Station: Omotesando (exit B2, 8 min.) or Shibuya (10 min.). On Aoyama Dori between Omotesando and Shibuya stations.

Sunshine International Aquarium Claiming to be the world's highest aquarium, this Sunshine City complex is the unlikely home of more than 20,000 fish and animals, including dolphins, octopuses, eels, piranhas, sea horses, sea otters, seals, giant crabs, and rare—and rather weird—species of fish. There are also seal performances.

World Import Mart Building, 10th floor, Sunshine City, 3–1–3 Higashi Ikebukuro. © 03/3989-3466. Admission ¥1,600 ($13) adults, ¥800 ($6.65) children 4–15, free for children 4 and under. Mon–Sat 10am–6pm; Sun and holidays 10am–6:30pm. Station: Higashi Ikebukuro (3 min.) or Ikebukuro (7 min.).

Tokyo Disneyland and Tokyo DisneySea ★★★ If you (or your kids) have your heart set on visiting all the world's Disney parks, head to **Tokyo Disneyland.** Virtually a carbon copy of the back-home version, this one also boasts the Jungle Cruise, Pirates of the Caribbean, Haunted Mansion, and Space Mountain. Other hot attractions include Toontown, a wacky theme park where Mickey, Minnie, Donald, and other Disney characters work and play; MicroAdventure, which features 3-D glasses and special effects; and Star Tours, a thrill adventure created by Disney and George Lucas.

Opened in 2001 adjacent to Disneyland, **DisneySea,** a theme park based on ocean legends and myths, offers seven distinct "ports of call," including the futuristic Port Discovery marina with its StormRider which flies straight into the eye of a storm; the Lost River Delta with its Indiana Jones Adventure; Mermaid Lagoon based on the film *The Little Mermaid;* and the Arabian Coast, with its Sindbad's Seven Voyages boat ride.

1–1 Maihama, Urayasu-shi, Chiba. © 045/683-3777. www.tokyodisneyresort.co.jp. Tickets can be purchased in advance at the Tokyo Disneyland Reservation Center, Hibiya Mitsui Building, 1–1–2 Yurakucho (© 03/3595-1777; station: Hibiya). 1-day passport to either Disneyland or DisneySea, including entrance to and use of all attractions ¥5,500 ($46) adults, ¥4,800 ($40) seniors and junior high and high-school students, ¥3,700 ($31) children 4–11, free for children under 4. Starlight admission after 3pm on weekends to Disneyland, ¥4,500 ($38), ¥3,900 ($31), and ¥3,000 ($25), respectively. Disneyland, daily 8 or 9am to 9 or 10pm, with slightly shorter hours in winter. DisneySea, daily 8am–10pm in summer, 10am–7pm in winter. Station: Maihama Station on the JR Keiyo Line from Tokyo Station (1 min.).

Tokyo Metropolitan Children's Hall (Tokyo-To Jido Kaikan) *Finds* This is Tokyo's largest public facility for children—and it's absolutely free. There are toddler areas, indoor gyms, computers, a crafts corner, musical instruments, and a rooftop playground (open weekends and holidays), as well as a mini-theater with frequent showings of free films and monthly events and programs (in Japanese only). Although not as extensive or sophisticated as the National Children's Castle (above), the price is right and it's good for a rainy day.

1–18–24 Shibuya, Shibuya-ku. © 03/3409-6361. Free admission. Daily 9am–5pm. Closed 2nd and 4th Mon of every month. Station: Shibuya (7 min.) or Hanzomon (exit 11, 3 min.). Off Meiji Dori, on the side street beside Tower Records & Books.

Tokyo Sea Life Park ★ Located on the shore of Tokyo Bay in Kasai Rinkai Park, this public facility is Tokyo's largest—yet cheapest—aquarium, with tanks displaying marine life of Tokyo Bay and beyond, including the Pacific, Indian, and Atlantic oceans. Hammerhead sharks, bluefin tuna, the giant sunfish, penguins, a touch tide pool, and a 3-D movie are some of the highlights. The park also contains a beach, a small Japanese garden, a bird sanctuary, and what is claimed to be Japan's largest Ferris wheel (fare: ¥700/$5.85), making it a good family outing. I suggest coming by train and returning via boat to Hamatsucho.

6–2–3 Rinkai-cho, Edogawa-ku. © **03/3869-5152**. Admission ¥700 ($5.85) adults, ¥350 ($2.90) seniors, ¥250 ($2.10) children 12–14, free for children 11 and under. Thurs–Tues 9:30am–5pm (you must enter by 4pm). On weekdays, take the JR Keiyo Line rapid service from Tokyo Station to Shin-Kiba, change to the local Keiyo Line, and get off at the next station, Kasairinkai Koen, from which it's a 5-min. walk. On weekends and holidays, there's rapid service directly to Kasairinkai Koen. There are also boats departing 7 times daily from Hinode Pier near Hamamatsucho Station, costing ¥800 ($6.65) and taking 1 hr.

Ueno Zoo   Founded back in 1882, Japan's oldest zoo is small by today's standards but remains one of the most well-known zoos in Japan, due in part to its giant panda, donated by the Chinese government to mark the reestablishment of diplomatic relations between the two countries following World War II. A vivarium, opened in 1999, houses amphibians, fish, and reptiles, including Komodo dragons, green tree pythons, and dwarf crocodiles. Personally, I can't help but feel sorry for some of the animals in their small spaces, but children will enjoy the Japanese macaques, polar bears, California sea lions, penguins, gorillas, giraffes, zebras, elephants, deer, and tigers. Expect a minimum of 2 hours here.

Ueno Park, Taito-ku. © **03/3828-5171**. Admission ¥600 ($5) adults, ¥300 ($2.50) seniors, ¥200 ($1.65) children 12–14, free for children under 12. Tues–Sun 9:30am–5pm (enter by 4pm). Closed some holidays. Station: Ueno (4 min.).

8 Spectator Sports

For information on current sporting events taking place in Tokyo, ranging from kickboxing and pro wrestling to soccer, table tennis, and golf, check the quarterly magazine *Tokyo Journal* or contact the **Tourist Information Center.** Tickets for many events, including baseball and sumo, can be purchased at **Ticket Pia** (© **03/5237-9999**).

BASEBALL   Introduced into Japan from the United States in 1873, baseball is as popular among Japanese as it is among Americans. Even the annual high-school playoffs keep everyone glued to their television sets.

As with other imports, the Japanese have added their modifications. Some of the playing fields are smaller (new ones tend to have American dimensions) and, borrowing from American football, each team has its own cheerleaders. There are several American players who have proved very popular with local fans; but according to the rules, no more than four foreigners may play on any one team. In recent years, there's been a reverse exodus of top Japanese players defecting to American teams, including the hugely popular and successful Suzuki Ichiro, leadoff hitter and right fielder for the Seattle Mariners; and Matsui Hideki, a power-hitting right fielder with the New York Yankees. In fact, Japanese fans have been so mesmerized by the Mariners and Yankees (whose games are broadcast on Japanese TV), that television ratings for Japanese games have fallen.

While playing your hardest is at a premium in the United States, in Japan any attempt at excelling individually is frowned upon. As in other aspects of life, it is the group, the team, that counts. To what extent that is so may be illustrated by the case of an American player: When he missed opening day at training camp due to a life-or-death operation on his son at a hospital, his contract was immediately canceled. And rather than let a foreign player break the hitting record set by a Japanese, American Randy Bass was thrown only balls and walked.

There are two professional leagues, the Central and the Pacific, which play from April to October and meet in the final Japan Series playoffs. In Tokyo, the home teams are the **Yomiuri Giants** and the **Nippon Ham Fighters,** both of which play at the Tokyo Dome (© **03/3811-2111;** station: Suidobashi); and the

Yakult Swallows, which play at Jingu Stadium (station: Gaienmae). Other teams playing in the vicinity of Tokyo are the **Chiba Lotte Marines,** who play at Kawasaki Stadium, Kanagawa ((C) **044/244-1171;** station: Kawasaki on the JR Tokaido Line, then bus no. 16, 19, 21, 22, or 23); the **Seibu Lions,** Seibu Lions Stadium, Tokorozawa City ((C) **0429/24-1151;** station: JR to Seibu Kyujo-mae on the Seibu Sayama Line); and the **Yokohama Bay Stars,** Yokohama Stadium, Yokohama ((C) **045/661-1251;** station: Kannai on the JR Keihin Tohoku Line). Advance tickets go on sale Friday, 2 weeks prior to the game, and can be purchased at the stadium or, for Tokyo teams, at **Ticket Pia** ((C) **03/5237-9999**). Prices for the Tokyo Dome and Jingu Stadium range from ¥1,800 ($15) for an unreserved seat in the outfield to ¥6,000 ($50) for seats behind home plate. The Giants are so popular, however, that tickets are hard to come by.

SUMO ★★★ The Japanese form of wrestling known as sumo began perhaps as long as 1,500 years ago and is still the nation's most popular sport, with wrestlers—often taller than 6 feet and weighing well over 300 pounds—revered as national heroes. A sumo match takes place on a sandy-floored ring less than 4.5m (15 ft.) in diameter; the object is for a wrestler to either eject his opponent from the ring or cause him to touch the ground with any part of his body other than his feet. This is accomplished by shoving, slapping, tripping, throwing, and even carrying the opponent. Altogether, there are 48 holds and throws, and sumo fans know them all.

Sumo matches are held in Tokyo at the **Kokugikan,** 1-3–28 Yokoami, Sumida-ku ((C) **03/3623-5111;** station: Ryogoku, then a 1-min. walk). Matches are held in January, May, and September for 15 consecutive days, beginning at around 10am and lasting until 6pm; the top wrestlers compete after 3:30pm. The best seats are ringside box seats, but they're bought out by companies or by the friends and families of sumo wrestlers. Usually available are balcony seats, which can be purchased at **Ticket Pia** ((C) **03/5237-9999**). You can also purchase tickets directly at the Kokugikan ticket office beginning at 9am every morning of the tournament. Prices range from about ¥2,100 ($18) for an unreserved seat (sold on the day of the event) to ¥8,200 ($68) for a good reserved seat.

If you can't make it to a match, watching on TV is almost as good. Tournaments in Tokyo, as well as those that take place annually in Osaka, Nagoya, and Fukuoka, are broadcast on the NHK channel from 4 to 6pm daily during matches.

Tokyo Strolls

Because Tokyo is a jigsaw puzzle of distinct neighborhoods, it makes sense to explore the city section by section. Below are walking tours of four of Tokyo's most fascinating, diverse, and easily explored neighborhoods. For information on sightseeing and attractions outside these neighborhoods or for additional information on attractions described below, see chapter 6.

WALKING TOUR 1 ASAKUSA

Start:	Hama Rikyu Garden (Shiodome Station); or Asakusa Station (exit 1 or 3).
Finish:	Kappabashi Dori (station: Tawaramachi).
Time:	Allow approximately 5 hours, including the boat ride.
Best Times:	Tuesday through Friday, when the crowds aren't as big.
Worst Time:	Sunday, when Demboin Garden and the shops on Kappabashi Dori are closed.

If anything remains of old Tokyo, Asakusa is it. This is where you'll find narrow streets lined with small residential homes, women in kimono, Tokyo's oldest and most popular temple, and quaint shops selling boxwood combs, fans, sweet pastries, and other products of yore. With its temple market, old-fashioned amusement park, and traditional shops and restaurants, Asakusa preserves the charm of old downtown Edo better than anyplace else in Tokyo. For many older Japanese, a visit to Asakusa is like stepping back to the days of their childhood; for tourists, it provides a glimpse of the way things were.

Pleasure-seekers have been flocking to Asakusa for centuries. Originating as a temple town back in the 7th century, it grew in popularity during the Tokugawa regime, as merchants grew wealthy and whole new forms of popular entertainment arose to cater to them. Theaters for Kabuki and Bunraku flourished in Asakusa, as did restaurants and shops. By 1840, Asakusa had become Edo's main entertainment district. In stark contrast to the solemnity surrounding places of worship in the West, Asakusa's temple market had a carnival atmosphere reminiscent of medieval Europe, complete with street performers and exotic animals. It retains some of that festive atmosphere even today.

The most dramatic way to arrive in Asakusa is by boat from Hama Rikyu Garden (see stop no. 1, below), just as people used to arrive in the olden days. If you want to forgo the boat ride, take the subway directly to Asakusa Station and start your tour from stop no. 2. Otherwise, head to:

① Hama Rikyu Garden
Located at the south end of Tokyo (station: Shiodome, exit 5, then a 5-min. walk), this is considered by some to be Tokyo's finest garden. It was laid out during the Edo Period in a style

popular at the time, in which surrounding scenery was incorporated into its composition. It contains an inner tidal pool, bridges draped with wisteria, moon-viewing pavilions, and teahouses. (See "Parks & Gardens," in chapter 6, for more details.)

Boats depart the garden to make their way along the Sumida River hourly or more frequently between 10:20am and 3:50pm, with the fare to Asakusa costing ¥620 ($5.15). Although much of what you see along the working river today is only concrete embankments, I recommend the trip because it affords a different perspective of Tokyo—barges making their way down the river and high-rise apartment buildings with laundry fluttering from balconies, warehouses, and superhighways. The boat passes under approximately a dozen bridges during the 40-minute trip, each one completely different. During cherry blossom season, thousands of cherry trees lining the bank make the trip particularly memorable.

Upon your arrival in Asakusa, walk away from the boat pier a couple of blocks inland, where you'll soon see the colorful Kaminarimon Gate on your right. Across the street on your left is the:

❷ Asakusa Information Center
Located at 2–18–9 Kaminarimon (✆ **03/3842-5566**), the center is open daily from 9:30am to 8pm and is staffed by English-speaking volunteers from 10am to 5pm. Stop here to pick up a map of the area and to ask directions to restaurants and sights. In addition, note the huge Seiko clock on the center's facade—a music clock that performs every hour on the hour from 10am to 7pm. Mechanical dolls re-enact scenes from several of Asakusa's most famous festivals.

Then it's time to head across the street to the:

❸ Kaminarimon Gate
The gate is unmistakable with its bright red colors and 220-pound lantern hanging in the middle. The statues inside the gate are of the god of wind to the right and the god of thunder to the left, ready to protect the deity enshrined in the temple. The god of thunder is particularly fearsome—he has an insatiable appetite for navels.

To the left of the gate, on the corner, is:
❹ Tokiwado Kaminari Okoshi
This open-fronted confectionery has been selling rice-based sweets *(okoshi)* for 250 years and is popular with visiting Japanese buying gifts for the folks back home. It's open daily 9am to 9pm.

Once past Kaminarimon gate, you'll find yourself immediately on a pedestrian lane called:
❺ Nakamise Dori
This leads straight to the temple. Nakamise means "inside shops," and historical records show that vendors have sold wares here since the late 17th century. Today Nakamise Dori is lined on both sides with tiny stall after tiny stall, many owned by the same family for generations. If you're expecting austere religious artifacts, however, you're in for a surprise: Sweets, shoes, barking toy dogs, Japanese crackers (called *sembei*), bags, umbrellas, Japanese dolls, T-shirts, fans, masks, and traditional Japanese accessories are all sold. How about a brightly colored straight hairpin—and a black hairpiece to go with it? Or a temporary tattoo in the shape of a dragon? This is a great place to shop for souvenirs, gifts, and items you have no earthly need for—a little bit of unabashed consumerism on the way to spiritual purification.

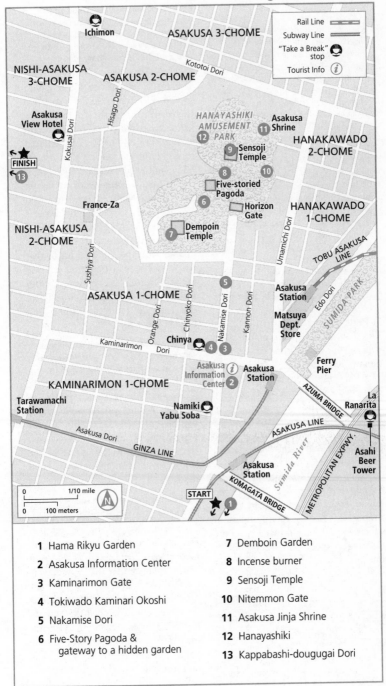

Rail Line
Subway Line
"Take a Break" stop
Tourist Info ⓘ

Ichimon

ASAKUSA 3-CHOME

NISHI-ASAKUSA 3-CHOME

Kototoi Dori

ASAKUSA 2-CHOME

Hisago Dori

Asakusa View Hotel

Kokusai Dori

HANAYASHIKI AMUSEMENT PARK

12

Asakusa Shrine

11

HANAKAWADO 2-CHOME

9 Sensoji Temple

FINISH

13

8

10

Five-storied Pagoda

6

France-Za

Horizon Gate

HANAKAWADO 1-CHOME

Umamichi Dori

7 Dempoin Temple

NISHI-ASAKUSA 2-CHOME

Sushiya Dori

TOBU ASAKUSA LINE

SUMIDA PARK

Edo Dori

5

ASAKUSA 1-CHOME

Orange Dori

Chinyoko Dori

Nakamise Dori

Kannon Dori

Asakusa Station

Matsuya Dept. Store

Kaminarimon Dori

Chinya

4 3

Asakusa Information Center ⓘ

2 Asakusa Station

Ferry Pier

KAMINARIMON 1-CHOME

Tarawamachi Station

Namiki Yabu Soba

La Ranarita

AZUMA BRIDGE

Asahi Beer Tower

Asakusa Dori GINZA LINE

ASAKUSA LINE

Sumida River

METROPOLITAN EXPWY.

0 — 1/10 mile
0 — 100 meters
N

START

Asakusa Station

KOMAGATA BRIDGE

1

1 Hama Rikyu Garden
2 Asakusa Information Center
3 Kaminarimon Gate
4 Tokiwado Kaminari Okoshi
5 Nakamise Dori
6 Five-Story Pagoda & gateway to a hidden garden

7 Demboin Garden
8 Incense burner
9 Sensoji Temple
10 Nitemmon Gate
11 Asakusa Jinja Shrine
12 Hanayashiki
13 Kappabashi-dougugai Dori

TAKE A BREAK
If you're hungry for lunch, there are a number of possibilities in the neighborhood. **Chinya,** 1–3–4 Asakusa, just west of Kaminarimon Gate on Kaminarimon Dori, has been serving sukiyaki and shabu-shabu since 1880. To the south of Kaminarimon Gate is **Namiki Yabu Soba,** 2–11–9 Kaminarimon, Asakusa's best-known noodle shop. For Western food, head to the other side of the Sumida River, where on the 22nd floor of the Asahi Beer Tower is **La Ranarita,** 1–23–1 Azumabashi, a moderately priced Italian restaurant with great views of Asakusa; and the utilitarian **Sky Lounge** with inexpensive beer, wine, and drinks.

Near the end of Nakamise Dori, as you head toward the temple, you'll pass a kindergarten on your left, followed by a five-story red-and-gold:

⑥ Pagoda

This is a 1970 remake of one constructed during the time of the third shogun, Iemitsu, in the 17th century.

A low-lying building connected to the pagoda is the gateway to the gem of this tour: a **hidden garden,** one of Asakusa's treasures, just a stone's throw from Nakamise Dori but barely visible on the other side of the kindergarten. Most visitors to Asakusa pass it by, unaware of its existence, primarily because it isn't open to the general public. However, anyone can visit it simply by asking for permission, which you can obtain by entering the building connected to the pagoda at the left. Go inside, turn right, and walk to the third door to the left; you'll be asked to sign your name and will be given a map showing the entrance to the garden, which is open Monday through Saturday from 9am to 3pm. However, because the garden is on private grounds belonging to the Demboin Monastery, it's often closed for functions (call ✆ **03/3842-0181** to see whether it's open, or trust to luck).

Once you've obtained permission, retrace your steps down Nakamise past the kindergarten, take the first right onto Demboin Dori, and then enter the second gate on your right. This is the entrance to:

⑦ Demboin Garden

The gate to Demboin Garden (also spelled Dempoin Garden) may be locked. If so, ring the doorbell to be let in. You'll find yourself in a peaceful oasis in the midst of bustling Asakusa, in a countryside setting that centers on a pond filled with carp and turtles. Enshu Kobori, a tea-ceremony master and famous landscape gardener who also designed a garden for the shogun's castle, designed the garden in the 17th century. Because most people are unaware that the garden exists or that it's accessible, you may find yourself the sole visitor. The best view is from the far side of the pond, where you can see the temple building and pagoda above the trees.

Return to Nakamise Dori and resume your walk north to the second gate, which opens onto a square filled with pigeons and a large:

⑧ Incense Burner

This is where worshippers "wash" themselves to ward off or help cure illness. If, for example, you have a sore throat, be sure to rub some of the smoke over your throat for good measure.

The building dominating the square is:

⑨ Sensoji Temple

Sensoji is Tokyo's oldest temple. Founded in the 7th century and therefore already well established long before Tokugawa settled in Edo, Sensoji Temple is dedicated to Kannon, the Buddhist goddess of mercy, and is therefore popularly called the Asakusa Kannon Temple. According to legend, the temple was founded after two fishermen pulled a golden statue of Kannon from the sea. The sacred statue is still housed in the temple, carefully preserved inside three boxes; even though it's never on display, people

The Floating World of Yoshiwara

During the Edo Period (1603–1867), prostitution in Japan was not only allowed, it was also—along with everything else in feudal Japan—regulated and strictly controlled by the Tokugawa shogunate. Licensed quarters arose in various parts of Edo (former Tokyo), but none was as famous or as long-standing as **Yoshiwara,** the "floating world of pleasure." Opened in 1657 in the midst of rice fields, far outside the city gates upriver from Asakusa, Yoshiwara rose to such prominence that, at its height, as many as 3,000 prostitutes, referred to as "courtesans," worked their trade here. The services they rendered depended on how much their customers were willing to spend. Some men, so they say, stayed for days. Stories abound of how more than a few lost their entire fortunes.

The top-ranked courtesan, known as Tayu, was distinguished by her gorgeous costume, which often weighed as much as 40 pounds and included a huge *obi* (sash) knotted in front. Many of the courtesans, however, had been sold into prostitution as young girls. To prevent their escape, a moat surrounded Yoshiwara, which could be entered or exited only through a guarded gate. The courtesans were allowed out of the compound once a year, during an autumn festival. Such virtual imprisonment was abolished only in 1900. Yoshiwara itself was closed down in 1957, when prostitution became illegal.

still flock to the temple to pay their respects.

Within the temple is a counter where you can buy your fortune by putting a 100-yen coin into a wooden box and shaking it until a long bamboo stick emerges from a small hole. The stick will have a Japanese number on it, which corresponds to one of the numbers on a set of drawers. Take the fortune, written in both English and Japanese, from the drawer that has your number. But don't expect the translation to clear things up; my fortune contained such cryptic messages as "Getting a beautiful lady at your home, you want to try all people know about this," and "Stop to start a trip." If you find that your fortune raises more questions than it answers or if you simply don't like what it has to say, you can conveniently negate it by tying it to one of the wires provided for this purpose just outside the main hall.

To the right (east) of the temple is the rather small:

⑩ Nitemmon Gate

Built in 1618, this is the only structure on temple grounds remaining from the Edo Period; all other buildings, including Sensoji Temple and the pagoda, were destroyed in a 1945 air raid.

On the northeast corner of the grounds is a small orange shrine, the:

⑪ Asakusa Jinja Shrine

The shrine was built in 1649 by Iemitsu Tokugawa, the third Tokugawa shogun, to commemorate the two fishermen who found the statue of Kannon and their village chief. Its architectural style, called Gongenzukuri, is the same as Toshogu Shrine's in Nikko. West of Sensoji Temple is a gardenlike area of lesser shrines and memorials, flowering bushes, and a stream of carp.

Farther west still is:

⑫ Hanayashiki

This is a small and corny amusement park that first opened in 1853 and still draws in the little ones. (See "Especially for Kids" in chapter 6 for details.)

Most of the area west of Sensoji Temple (the area to the left if you stand facing the front of the temple) is a small but interesting part of Asakusa popular among Tokyo's older working class. This is where several of Asakusa's old-fashioned pleasure houses remain, including bars, restaurants, strip shows, traditional Japanese vaudeville, and so-called "love hotels," which rent rooms by the hour.

If you keep walking west, past the Asakusa View Hotel, within 10 minutes you'll reach:

⑬ Kappabashi-dougugai Dori

Generally referred to as Kappabashi Dori, Tokyo's wholesale district for restaurant items has shop after shop selling pottery, chairs, tableware, cookware, lacquerware, rice cookers, noren, and everything else needed to run a restaurant. And yes, you can even buy those models of plastic food you've been drooling over in restaurant displays. Ice cream, pizza, sushi, mugs foaming with beer—they're all here, looking like the real thing. (Stores close about 5pm.)

WINDING DOWN
The **Asakusa View Hotel**, on Kokusai Dori Avenue between Sensoji Temple and Kappabashi Dori, has several restaurants and bars, including the clubby **Ice House** (the hotel's main bar), a coffee shop, and Japanese, Chinese, and French restaurants. Another good place to end a day of sightseeing in Asakusa is **Ichimon**, 3–12–6 Asakusa, near the intersection of Kokusai and Kototoi avenues. Decorated like a farmhouse, it specializes in different types of sake (see "The Bar Scene," in chapter 9, for more details). For inexpensive dining in a convivial, rustic setting, head to **Sometaro**, 2–2–2 Nishi-Asakusa, just off Kokusai Dori, where you cook your own okonomiyaki or fried noodles at your table.

WALKING TOUR 2 **HARAJUKU & AOYAMA**

Start:	Meiji Jingu Shrine (station: Harajuku).
Finish:	Nezu Institute of Fine Arts (station: Omotesando).
Time:	Allow approximately 5 hours, including stops along the way.
Best Times:	The 1st and 4th Sundays of every month, when there's an antiques flea market at Togo Shrine.
Worst Times:	Monday (when the Ota Memorial Museum of Art and the Nezu Institute of Fine Arts are closed), Thursday (when the Oriental Bazaar is closed), and from the 27th to the end of every month (when the Ota Memorial Museum of Art is closed for exhibit changes).

Harajuku is one of my favorite neighborhoods in Tokyo, though I'm too old to really fit in. In fact, anyone over 25 is apt to feel ancient here, since this is Tokyo's most popular hangout for Japanese high school and college students. The young come here to see and be seen; you're sure to spot Japanese punks, girls decked out in the fashions of the moment, and young couples looking their best. I like Harajuku for its vibrancy, its sidewalk cafes, its street hawkers, and its trendy clothing boutiques. It's also the home of Tokyo's most important Shinto shrine, as well as a woodblock-print museum and an excellent souvenir shop of traditional Japanese items.

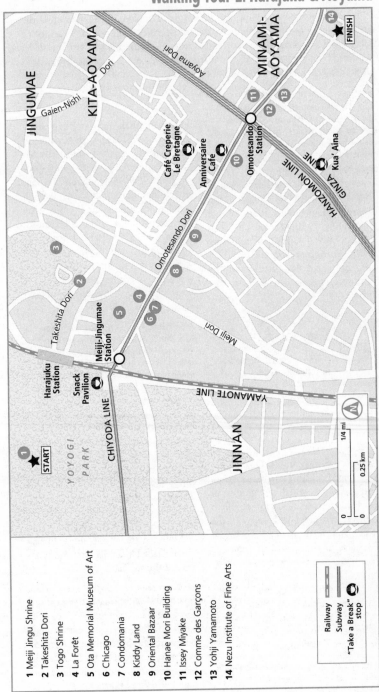

JINGUMAE

KITA-AOYAMA

MINAMI-AOYAMA

Aoyama Dori

Gaien-Nishi Dori

Café Creperie Le Bretagne

Anniversaire Cafe

Omotesando Station

GINZA LINE

HANZOMON LINE

Kua 'Aina

Omotesando Dori

Takeshita Dori

Meiji-Jingumae Station

Harajuku Station

Snack Pavilion

CHIYODA LINE

YOYOGI PARK

START

Meiji Dori

YAMANOTE LINE

JINNAN

N

0   1/4 mi
0   0.25 km

FINISH

1 Meiji Jingu Shrine
2 Takeshita Dori
3 Togo Shrine
4 La Forêt
5 Ota Memorial Museum of Art
6 Chicago
7 Condomania
8 Kiddy Land
9 Oriental Bazaar
10 Hanae Mori Building
11 Issey Miyake
12 Comme des Garçons
13 Yohji Yamamoto
14 Nezu Institute of Fine Arts

Railway
Subway
"Take a Break" stop

Nearby is **Aoyama,** a yuppified version of Harajuku, where the upwardly mobile shop and dine. It has a number of designer shops and a museum for Asian art. Connecting Harajuku and Aoyama is **Omotesando Dori,** a wide, tree-lined boulevard that forms the heart of this area and is a popular promenade for people-watching.

From Harajuku Station, take the south exit (the one closer to Shibuya) and turn right over the bridge, where you will immediately see the huge cypress torii marking the entrance to:

❶ Meiji Jingu Shrine

This is the most venerable shrine in Tokyo. Dedicated to Emperor and Empress Meiji, Meiji Jingu Shrine opened in 1920. (See "The Top Attractions," in chapter 6, for more details.) If it's June, stop off at the Iris Garden, located about halfway on the 10-minute tree-shaded path to the shrine.

TAKE A BREAK
If the hike to Meiji Shrine has made you thirsty, stop off at the rustic, outdoor snack pavilion just inside the entranceway to the shrine grounds. It offers coffee, beer, and ice cream, and is open daily from 9am to sunset.

After visiting the shrine, retrace your steps back to Harajuku Station. If it's Sunday, you'll see groups of teenaged Japanese—many of them bizarrely dressed—gathered on the bridge over the train tracks. They're all that's left of the masses of teenagers that used to congregate on nearby Yoyogi Dori back when it was closed to vehicular traffic on Sundays. Sadly, authorities decided to open Yoyogi and Omotesando Dori streets to traffic, thereby putting an end to Tokyo's most happening Sunday scene.

At Harajuku Station, continue walking north beside the station to its north exit. Across the street from Harajuku Station's north exit is:

❷ Takeshita Dori

This pedestrian-only street is lined nonstop with stores that cater to teenagers. It's packed—especially on Sunday afternoons—with young people hunting for bargains on inexpensive clothes, music, sunglasses, jewelry, watches, cosmetics, and more. One shop worth pointing out is **Harajuku Daiso** (✆ **5775-9641;** open daily 10am–9pm), one of many bargain variety stores to hit Japan since the recession. Everything in the store—cosmetics, kitchenware, household goods—costs ¥100 (85¢).

After inching your way along this narrow lane with its flow of humanity, you will eventually find yourself on a busy thoroughfare, Meiji Dori. If it's the 1st or 4th Sunday of the month, turn left (north) onto Meiji Dori, where in a couple of minutes on your left you'll see:

❸ Togo Shrine

Dedicated to Admiral Heihachiro Togo, who was in charge of the fleet that defeated the Russian navy in 1905 in the Russo-Japanese War, the shrine nowadays is most popular for its flea market held the first and fourth Sundays of every month, when everything from old chests, dolls, porcelain, and kimono are for sale, spread out on a tree-shaded sidewalk that meanders around the shrine.

Head back south on Meiji Dori where, to your right, just before the big intersection, is:

❹ La Forêt

This building is filled with trendy shoe and clothing boutiques. The less expensive boutiques tend to be on the lower floors, more exclusive boutiques higher up. (See chapter 8 for details on the shops and department stores listed in this walking tour.)

Behind La Forêt is one of my favorite museums, the:

5 Ota Memorial Museum of Art
Located at 1–10–10 Jingumae, this museum features the private *ukiyo-e* (woodblock prints) collection of the late Ota Seizo. Exhibitions of the museum's 12,000 prints change monthly and are always worth checking out. (See "More Museums" in chapter 6 for details.)

Across Omotesando Dori is:
6 Chicago
Specializing in used American clothing, Chicago also stocks hundreds of used and new kimono and yukata in a back corner of its basement.

Near La Forêt is Harajuku's major intersection, Meiji Dori and Omotesando Dori. Here, on the intersection near Chicago, is one of Harajuku's more unusual shops:
7 Condomania
Condoms are for sale here (at 6–30–1 Jingumae) in a wide range of sizes, colors, and styles, from glow-in-the-dark to scented. It's open daily 11am to 11pm.

Heading east on Omotesando Dori (away from Harajuku Station), you'll soon see, to your right:
8 Kiddy Land
This shop at 6–1–9 Jingumae sells gag gifts and a great deal more than just toys, including enough to amuse undiscerning adults. You could spend an hour browsing here, but the store is so crowded with teenagers that you may end up rushing for the door.

As you continue east on Omotesando Dori (where sidewalk vendors selling jewelry and ethnic accessories set up shop on weekends), to your right will soon be Harajuku's most famous store:
9 Oriental Bazaar
Located at 5–9–13 Jingumae, this is Tokyo's best one-stop shopping spot for Japanese souvenirs. Four floors offer antique chinaware, old kimono, Japanese paper products, fans, jewelry, woodblock prints, screens, chinaware,

and much more, all at reasonable prices. I always stock up on gifts here for the folks back home.

Continue walking east on Omotesando Dori, past the construction area on your left (being turned into a residential and commercial complex designed by Tadao Ando). Near the end of Omotesando Dori, to your right, is the:
10 Hanae Mori Building
This building was designed by Japanese architect Kenzo Tange (who also designed the Akasaka Prince Hotel and the TMG city hall in Shinjuku). It houses the entire collection of Hanae Mori, from casual wear to evening wear. In the basement is the Antique Market, where stalls sell china, jewelry, clothing, watches, swords, and items from the 1930s.

TAKE A BREAK
Harajuku and Aoyama have more sidewalk cafes than any other part of Tokyo. Most conspicuous is the fancy **Anniversaire Café**, 3–5–30 Kita-Aoyama, across from the Hanae Mori Building (see no. 10, below). If you backtrack a bit and take the small side street that runs beside McDonald's (underneath the HARAJUKU arch) and then turn left, you'll come to **Café Creperie Le Bretagne**, 4–9–8 Jingumae, selling buckwheat galettes and crepes filled with fruit and chocolate combinations.

At the end of Omotesando Dori, where it connects with Aoyama Dori, is Omotesando Station. You can board the subway here or, for more shopping, cross Aoyama Dori and continue heading east, where you'll pass a number of designer shops. First, on the left at 3–18–11 Minami-Aoyama, is:
11 Issey Miyake
The clothes here are known for their richness in texture and fabrics.

To the right, at 5–2–1 Minami-Aoyama, is:
12 Comme des Garçons
Rei Kawakubo's designs for both men and women are showcased here.

Farther down the street, on the right at 5–3–6 Minami-Aoyama, is:

⑬ Yohji Yamamoto

As with all Yamamoto shops, this store has an interesting avant-garde interior.

Continue walking in the same direction, curving to the left, until you come to a stop-light. Cross the street, turn right, and follow the sign that directs you to the:

⑭ Nezu Institute of Fine Arts

Located at 6–5–1 Minami-Aoyama, the institute houses a fine collection of Asian art and boasts a delightful small garden with a pond.

WINDING DOWN
The cafes on Omotesando Dori listed above are just a few minutes' walk away, but if you're dying for a burger, look no fur-ther than **Kua' Aina,** 5–10–21 Minami-Aoyama, on the corner of Aoyama Dori and Kotto Dori intersection. There are many other choices in Aoyama; see chapter 5 for details.

WALKING TOUR 3   UENO

Start:	South end of Ueno Park (station: Ueno).
Finish:	Ameya Yokocho flea market, along the tracks of the Yamanote Line (station: Ueno or Okachimachi).
Time:	Allow approximately 2 hours, not including stops along the way.
Best Times:	Weekdays, when museums and shops aren't as crowded.
Worst Time:	Monday, when the museums and zoo are closed.

Located on the northeast end of the Yamanote Line loop, Ueno is one of the most popular places in Tokyo for Japanese families on a day's outing. Unlike sophisticated Ginza, Ueno has always been favored by the working people of Tokyo and visitors from Tokyo's rural north. During the Edo Period, the area around Ueno was where merchants and craftspeople lived, worked, and played. Ueno was also the site of the enormous Kan'eiji Temple compound, which served as the private family temple and burial ground of the Tokugawa shoguns. Today, Ueno's main drawing card is Ueno Park, the largest park in Tokyo. It's famous throughout Japan for its cluster of historic monuments, zoo, and excel-lent museums, including the prestigious Tokyo National Museum.

You will probably arrive in Ueno by either subway or the JR Yamanote Line. Regardless, make your way to the main entrance of Kei-sei Ueno Station (terminus of the Skyliner train from Narita Airport and home to a Tokyo Tourist Information Center, open daily 9:30am to 6:30pm). If you wish, stop by one of the many obento counters that stretch along the road between the Keisei Ueno Sta-tion and JR Ueno Station. Sushi, sandwiches, and traditional obento can be purchased here for a picnic later in the park; there are few restaurants in the park itself. Outside Keisei Ueno Station's main entrance are two steep flights of stone stairs leading up to an area of trees. This is the south entrance to:

① Ueno Park

Located atop a broad hill, this was once part of the precincts of Kan'eiji Temple, a huge, 120-hectare (300-acre) complex consisting of a main temple and 36 subsidiary temples. Unfortunately, most of the complex was destroyed in 1868, when 2,000 die-hard shogun loyalists gathered on Ueno Hill for a last stand against the advancing forces of the imperial army. Ueno Park opened in 1873 as one of the nation's first public parks.

Although quite small compared to New York City's Central Park, this is

Walking Tour 3: Ueno

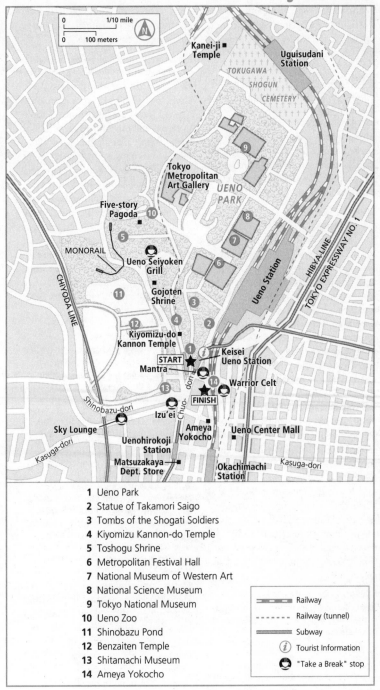

1 Ueno Park
2 Statue of Takamori Saigo
3 Tombs of the Shogati Soldiers
4 Kiyomizu Kannon-do Temple
5 Toshogu Shrine
6 Metropolitan Festival Hall
7 National Museum of Western Art
8 National Science Museum
9 Tokyo National Museum
10 Ueno Zoo
11 Shinobazu Pond
12 Benzaiten Temple
13 Shitamachi Museum
14 Ameya Yokocho

▬▬▬	Railway
----	Railway (tunnel)
▭▭▭	Subway
(i)	Tourist Information
◕	"Take a Break" stop

Japan's largest city park and Tokyo's most important museum district, making it a favorite destination for families and school groups in search of culture, relaxation, and fun. With its 1,000 cherry trees, it's one of the most famous cherry blossom–viewing spots in the country. By the way, it's also a popular hangout for Tokyo's homeless population, which has grown markedly since the recession. You'll see their makeshift cities—cardboard, blue tarp, and even clothes drying on lines—in amongst the trees.

A landmark near the south entrance to the park is a bronze:

❷ Statue of Takamori Saigo

This is the best-known monument in Tokyo, if not all of Japan. Born in 1827 near Kagoshima on Kyushu island, the samurai Takamori Saigo rose through the ranks as a soldier and statesman. He helped restore the emperor to power after the Tokugawa shogunate's downfall but later became disenchanted with the Meiji regime when rights enjoyed by the samurai class were suddenly rescinded. He led a revolt against the government that failed, and he ended up taking his own life in ritual suicide. The statue was erected in the 1890s but later became controversial when Gen. Douglas MacArthur, leader of the U.S. occupation forces in Japan after World War II, demanded its removal because of its nationalistic associations. Saved by public outcry, the statue today still depicts the stout Saigo dressed in a simple cotton kimono with his hand on his sword.

Ironically, behind the statue of Saigo and slightly to the left is a memorial dedicated to those very men Saigo originally opposed. Here lie the:

❸ Tombs of the Shogitai Soldiers

These were the die-hard Tokugawa loyalists who resisted imperial forces on Ueno Hill in 1868. Tended by

descendants of the soldiers, the grounds contain small paintings depicting the fierce battle.

Behind and to the left of the war memorial, on the other side of the pathway, is:

❹ Kiyomizu Kannon-do Temple

Completed in 1631 as a miniature copy of the famous Kiyomizu Temple in Kyoto and one of the few buildings left standing after the battle of 1868, this is one of the oldest temples in Tokyo. The temple houses the protectress of childbearing and child-raising, thereby attracting women hoping to become pregnant and those whose wishes have been fulfilled. To the right of the main altar is a room full of dolls, left by women to symbolize their children in a gesture they hope will further protect them. (See "Shrines & Temples" in chapter 6 for more information.)

TAKE A BREAK
Located between Kiyomizu Temple and Toshogu Shrine, **Ueno Seiyoken Grill** opened in 1876 as one of Japan's first restaurants serving Western food. It remains the best place for a meal in Ueno Park, serving pricey but quite good classic French cuisine.

Walking north from Kiyomizu Kannon-do Temple, you'll soon pass orange torii (made, horrendously enough, out of plastic) and Seiyoken restaurant on your left. Following signs that say Ueno Zoo, turn left at the Lions Club totem pole. Soon, to your left, you'll see the stone torii that marks the entrance to:

❺ Toshogu Shrine

Ueno Park's most famous religious structure—dedicated to Tokugawa Ieyasu, founder of the Tokugawa shogunate—was erected in 1651 by Ieyasu's grandson. Like Nikko's Toshogu Shrine (see chapter 10), it is ornately decorated with brilliant red, blue, green, and gold ornamentation. The pathway leading to the shrine is lined with massive stone lanterns, plus 50 copper lanterns donated by feudal lords from throughout Japan. To the right of the pathway is a five-storied pagoda (located on zoo grounds), covered entirely in lacquer and constructed in 1639. Also on the shrine grounds are the charred remains of a tree discovered in nearby Nishi-Nippori in 1991; it was burned during the bombing raids of 1945 and placed here in an appeal for peace. Nearby are photographs of the war's destruction in Hiroshima and Nagasaki. The shrine grounds are also famous for their peonies, which bloom both in spring and in winter.

But the most important thing to see here is the shrine, which contains murals by a famous Edo artist, Kano Tan-yu, and armor worn by Ieyasu. Note the lions decorating the arched, Chinese-style Karamon Gate—legend has it that when night falls, they sneak down to Shinobazu Pond for a drink. On a lighter note, you'll also see signs asking you to refrain from making a bonfire, just in case you are contemplating a cookout on these sacred grounds.

Across from Toshogu Shrine is a miniature amusement park for young children. Walk through it or around it to Ueno Park's main square, marked by an artificial pond with a spouting, dancing fountain. Keep walking straight, past the people feeding the pigeons and the koban police box. That building to your right is the:

6 Metropolitan Festival Hall
The hall opened in 1961 as a venue for classical music, ballet, and dance.

The building just beyond is the very good:

7 National Museum of Western Art (Kokuritsu Seiyo Bijutsukan)
Built in 1959 with a main building designed by French architect Le Corbusier, the museum features works by such Western artists as Renoir, Monet, Sisley, Manet, Delacroix, Cézanne, Degas, El Greco, and Goya; but it's probably most famous for its 50-some sculptures by Rodin.

Just north of this museum is the:

8 National Science Museum (Kokuritsu Kagaku Hakubutsukan)
This is a good attraction if you're traveling with children.

The most important museum in Ueno Park, however, is the one farthest to the north, the:

9 Tokyo National Museum (Tokyo Kokuritsu Hakubutsukan)
Japan's largest museum and the world's largest repository of Japanese art is the place to see antiques from Japan's past, including lacquerware, pottery, scrolls, screens, ukiyo-e (woodblock prints), samurai armor, swords, kimono, Buddhist statues, and much more. If you go to only one museum in Tokyo, this should be it.

Assuming you don't spend the entire day in museums, walk south from the National Museum past the dancing fountain, turn right, and follow signs for:

10 Ueno Zoo
Opened in 1882, this is Japan's oldest zoo. Although it seems rather small by today's standards (with miserably cramped quarters for its animals), it's famous for its giant panda, donated by the Chinese government. There are also Japanese macaques, polar bears, California sea lions, penguins, gorillas, giraffes, zebras, elephants, deer, and tigers. Be sure, too, to see the five-story pagoda mentioned earlier in the walk.

End your tour of the zoo at:

11 Shinobazu Pond
(You can also get to Shinobazu Pond without entering the zoo by retracing your steps to the orange plastic torii, or stairs to the left of the torii, then walking downhill toward the pond, passing the Gojoten Shrine along the way.) This marshy pond was constructed in the 17th century; teahouses once lined its banks. Now part of the pond has literally gone to the birds: It's a bird sanctuary. The pond is

filled with lotus plants, a lovely sight when they bloom in August.

There are small boats for rent, and on an island in the middle of the pond, connected to the bank with walkways, is the:

⑫ **Benzaiten Temple**
This temple is dedicated to the goddess of fortune.

At the southeastern edge of Shinobazu Pond is the:

⑬ **Shitamachi Museum (Shitamachi Fuzoku Shiryokan)**
Shitamachi means "downtown" and refers to the area of Tokyo where commoners used to live, mainly around Ueno and Asakusa. Displays here include a Shitamachi tenement house, as well as everyday objects used in work and play, all donated by people living in the area.

From the Shitamachi Museum, head south on Chuo Dori and turn left on Kasuga Dori, passing Matsuzakaya department store and Ueno Center Mall. Here, at Okachimachi Station, is:

⑭ **Ameya Yokocho**
This narrow shopping street is located under and along the west side of the elevated tracks of the Yamanote Line between Ueno and Okachimachi stations. Originally a wholesale market for candy and snacks, and after World War II a black market in U.S. Army goods, Ameya Yokocho (also referred to as Ameyacho or Ameyoko) today consists of hundreds of stalls and shops selling at a discount everything from fish and vegetables to handbags and clothes. Early evening is the most crowded time as workers rush through on their way home. Some shops close on Wednesday, but most are open from about 10am to 7pm.

WINDING DOWN
Across from the Shitamachi Museum, next to KFC, is **Izu'ei,** 2–12–22 Ueno, a modern restaurant that has served eel since the Edo Period. If spicy Indian food is more to your taste, head to nearby **Mantra,** 4–9–6 Ueno, located on the third floor of the Nagafuji Building Annex next to the Ameya Yokocho market. For a drink, the easiest place to find is the **Sky Lounge** on the 10th floor of the dated Hotel Park Side, located at the south end of Shinobazu Pond at 2–11–18 Ueno (✆ 03/3836-5711). It's open daily from 5 to 11:30pm with views of the pond, and a snack menu. Attracting a younger crowd is **Warrior Celt,** 6–9–2 Ueno, a friendly bar with a nightly happy hour and free live music; it's just a stone's throw from Ameya Yokocho.

WALKING TOUR 4   YANAKA

Start:	Tennoji Temple (station: Nippori, then the south exit).
Finish:	Nezu Temple (station: Nezu).
Time:	Allow approximately 4 hours, including stops along the way.
Best Times:	There is no "best" time, as such, for this walk, but head out early in the day.
Worst Times:	Monday and Friday, when museums, some shops, and restaurants are closed.

Yanaka has been famous for its large concentration of temples since the Edo Period, when most temples and shrines were removed from the inner city and relocated to the outskirts in an attempt to curb the frequent fires that ravaged the crowded shogunate capital. Not only did the religious structures' thatched roofs ignite like tinder, but the land they formerly occupied would subsequently be cleared and left empty, to act as fire breaks in the otherwise densely populated city. Furthermore, temples on the edge of town could double as forts to protect

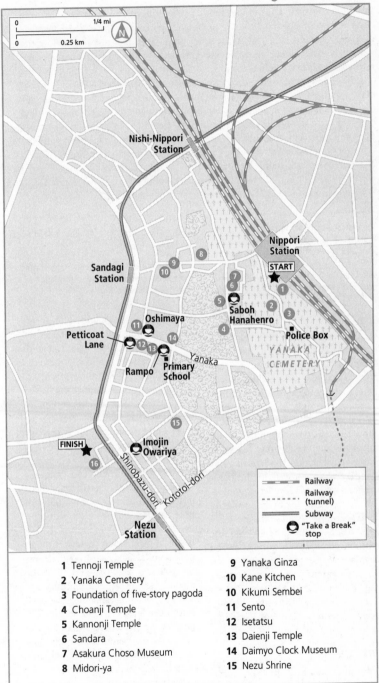

Nishi-Nippori Station

Nippori Station
START
1

Sandagi Station

8
9
10
7
6
5
Saboh Hanahenro
2
3
Police Box
4

YANAKA CEMETERY

11
Oshimaya
Petticoat Lane
12
13
14
Yanaka
Rampo
Primary School

15

FINISH
Imojin Owariya
16

Shinobazu-dori
Kototoi-dori

Nezu Station

		Railway
		Railway (tunnel)
		Subway
		"Take a Break" stop

0   1/4 mi
0   0.25 km
N

1 Tennoji Temple
2 Yanaka Cemetery
3 Foundation of five-story pagoda
4 Choanji Temple
5 Kannonji Temple
6 Sandara
7 Asakura Choso Museum
8 Midori-ya

9   Yanaka Ginza
10 Kane Kitchen
10 Kikumi Sembei
11 Sento
12 Isetatsu
13 Daienji Temple
14 Daimyo Clock Museum
15 Nezu Shrine

Edo from invasion. The only invasions Yanaka suffered, however, were friendly ones, as townspeople flocked here to enjoy its peacefulness, wooded hills, paddies, clear streams, and majestic temple compounds. It wasn't long before the wealthy began building country estates here, followed by artists and writers who favored Yanaka's picturesque setting and cool breezes.

One of Tokyo's few old quarters to have survived both the 1923 Kanto earthquake and firebombs of World War II, Yanaka is also largely residential, with narrow lanes, small houses, and a few unique museums and traditional shops tucked here and there among the gently sloping hills. Because there are no major attractions or department stores here, the atmosphere of this stroll is markedly different from the bustling liveliness of the previous walking tours—there are no crowds and there's very little traffic. Rather, a trip to Yanaka is like a visit to a small town, where the pace of life is slow and the people have time for one another. If Tokyo is starting to wear on your nerves, come here to refresh yourself.

The easiest way to get to Yanaka is on the Yamanote Line. Disembark at Nippori Station, take the south exit (the end closest to Ueno Station), and turn left for the west exit. Look for the flight of steps beside a map of the area. At the top of these stairs, to the left, is:

❶ Tennoji Temple

Founded more than 500 years ago, this used to be a grand and impressive complex, 10 times its present size and popular among townspeople as one of Edo's three temples authorized to hold lotteries. The lotteries, however, drew such huge crowds and got so out of hand that they were banned in the mid-19th century by the Tokugawa shogunate. Then, in 1868, most of the complex was destroyed in the battle between Tokugawa loyalists and imperial forces on nearby Ueno Hill. Today, Tennoji is quiet and peaceful, with neatly swept grounds and the soothing sounds of chirping birds and chanting monks. The first thing you see upon entering the compound is a seated bronze Buddha, which dates from 1690 and is one of the temple's dearest treasures. Nearby is a standing bronze *jizo,* guardian of children's spirits. It was erected by a grieving father more than 60 years ago, following the death of his son in a playground accident; a relief at the base depicts boys playing in school uniform. There's also a small stone statue of the Kannon, goddess of mercy.

Walk straight out of the temple compound's main entrance and continue walking on the paved road straight through:

❷ Yanaka Cemetery

Once the burial grounds of Kanei-ji and Tennoji temples and opened to the public in 1874, this is one of Tokyo's largest cemeteries. Among its more than 7,000 tombstones are graves belonging to famous public figures, artists, and writers, some of whom lived in the area. Among the most famous writers buried here are Soseki Natsume (1867–1916) and Ogai Mori (1862–1922), both novelists of the Meiji Era and longtime Yanaka residents. Natsume, whose portrait is featured on the 1,000-yen note, became famous after writing *I am a Cat,* a humorous look at the follies of human society as seen through the eyes of a cat. Ogai, who at 19 was the youngest graduate ever from the medical school at Tokyo University and who later became surgeon general, was a foremost figure of modern Japanese literature. His works tried to bridge the gap between the traditional and the modern, as Japan moved away from its feudal agrarian past.

Today the cemetery is quite peaceful and empty, but it wasn't always so. During the Edo Period, teahouses along its edge served more than tea, with monks among their frequent customers. One of the teahouse beauties, Osen Kasamori, achieved fame when ukiyo-e master Harunobu immortalized her in several of his works. Most poor girls were always looking for patrons, not necessarily one-night stands.

After a minute's walk, to your left you'll see two sights very strange for a cemetery—a police box and a children's playground. Here, between the two and surrounded by a low fence and hedge, is the:

❸ Foundation of Tennoji Temple's Five-story Pagoda

First built in 1644 but burned down in 1772, this was reconstructed as the tallest pagoda in Edo. It met its final demise in 1957, when it was burned down by two lovers who then committed suicide.

Take a right at the police box and continue through the cemetery into a residential street, following it 1 block until it ends at a T-intersection. Ahead is a plaque marking the tomb of Kano Hogai (1828–1888), a Japanese painter of the early Meiji Period who incorporated Western techniques into his work and who, along with Okakura Tenshin, is credited for "modernizing" Japanese art. Behind the plaque is:

❹ Choanji Temple

Established in 1669, it was dedicated to the god of longevity, one of Japan's seven lucky gods. During the Edo Period, a pilgrimage to all seven temples, each housing one of the seven gods of fortune, was thought to bring good luck. Now that such pilgrimages have lost their appeal, Choanji seems rather forgotten. In addition to Kano's tomb, located near the center of the temple's graveyard, the temple is notable for its three stone *stupas* dating from the 1200s, erected for the repose of departed souls. They are located straight ahead on the main path, by the statues and under the groomed cedars.

Turn left out of Choanji. At the next immediate left down a side street you'll see an old temple wall dating from the Edo Period. It's the only one in the area to have survived fires, earthquakes, and wars. Back on the main road, farther along on the left, is:

❺ Kannonji Temple

A small stone pagoda to the right of its front entrance is dedicated to the 47 ronin *(akoroshi)*, masterless samurai who avenged their master's death and then committed ritual suicide in 1702 (see the box in chapter 2, "The Masterless Samurai"). Their story captured the public's imagination and has become a popular Kabuki play. Two of the ronin were brothers of a head priest here, and several meetings plotting their revenge allegedly took place on this spot.

TAKE A BREAK

Just a stone's throw farther north, on the right, is **Saboh Hanahenro,** 7–17–11 Yanaka (✆ **03/3822-6387**), which translates as "Teahouse Flower Temple-pilgrimage." A modern, two-floor teahouse decorated with international folk crafts and open Tuesday through Sunday from 11am to 6pm, it offers a very tasty obento box lunch for ¥1,200 ($10); since it often runs out, you might wish to make an obento reservation (in which case it costs ¥1,500/$13). It also serves a teishoku set lunch for ¥1,000 ($8.35), Japanese green tea, coffee, beer, homemade cakes, and sweets.

Just past the teahouse, also on the right at 7–18–6 Yanaka, is:

❻ (53) Sandara

This small crafts shop sells pottery, baskets, and other crafts. It's open every day except Monday from 10:30am to 6pm. Its name comes from the sacks once used to hold rice.

Past this shop, also on the right at 7–18–10 Yanaka, is one of the highlights of this stroll, the:

Tips **A Note on Japanese Symbols**

Many hotels, restaurants, attractions, and shops in Japan do not have signs giving their names in Roman (English-language) letters. Appendix C lists the Japanese symbols for all such places described in this guide. Each set of characters representing an establishment name has a number in the appendix, which corresponds to the number that appears inside the oval preceding the establishment's name in the text. Thus, to find the Japanese symbol for, say, **Sandara,** refer to number 53 in appendix C.

❼ Asakura Choso Museum

With its modern black facade, it looks rather out of place in this traditional neighborhood, but its interior is a delightful mix of modern and traditional architecture. One of Tokyo's most intriguing homes open to the public, it was built in 1936 as the home and studio of Asakura Fumio, a Western-style sculptor known for his realistic statues of statesmen, women, and cats. After passing through his studio with its soaring ceilings, you'll find yourself in a traditional Japanese house wrapped around an inner courtyard pond, famous for its large stones arranged to reflect the Five Confucian Virtues. A rooftop garden offers views over the surrounding neighborhood. See chapter 6 for more information.

Take a right out of the museum, and turn left at the next street (if you take a right here, you will end up back at Nippori Station). Keep to the right and walk down the steps. Then take the first right, located just past the arched entryway marking the neighborhood's pedestrian-only shopping lane. Here, to your right, at 3–13–5 Nishi-Nippori, is:

❽ (54) Midori-ya

This exquisite basket shop with several samples on display outside its front door is the store and workshop of Suigetsu Buseki and his son Sui Koh, a charming father-and-son team who coax flexible strands of bamboo into beautifully crafted baskets, some of them signed. The shop is known for its use of smoked bamboo taken from the undersides of thatched farmhouses; the bamboo exhibits a beautiful gloss and subtle color gradation from years of exposure to indoor fire pits. Since such antique pieces of bamboo are increasingly hard to come by, some of the baskets here are rightfully expensive but are still less expensive than those at major department stores. You can linger here; the Busekis are happy to discuss their trade and their love with Japanese-speakers. The imperial family and visiting dignitaries, including a former U.S. ambassador to Japan, have been among their customers.

The shop is open daily 10am to 6:30pm (✆ **03/3828-1746**).

Retrace your steps to the corner and turn right onto:

❾ Yanaka Ginza

This is an ambitious name for an otherwise old-fashioned shopping lane. It's pleasant because it's free from cars and, unlike many shopping streets nowadays, isn't a covered arcade. One Japanese friend told me that it reminds her of neighborhood shopping streets from her childhood. Lining the lane are shops selling both modern and traditional toys, obento lunch boxes, sweets, household goods, tofu, rice, fish, and vegetables. One of my favorites is the tea shop:

❿ (55) Kane Kichien

Located about halfway down Yanaka Ginza on the left at 3–11–10 Yanaka (✆ **03/3823-0015**), it sells various kinds of tea at the counter toward the back of the store and usually gives a free glass of welcome green tea to customers. With all the reported benefits of green tea, you probably know someone who might appreciate a small gift from this store. It's open Monday to Saturday from 10am to 7:30pm.

At the end of the shopping street, turn left and walk for about 5 minutes, passing the Sendagi business hotel and Annex Katsutaro Ryokan on the way, until you come to a stoplight and a slightly larger road.

TAKE A BREAK
Immediately to the left of the stoplight, on the corner, is a noodle shop called ⑤⑥ **Oshimaya**, 3–2–5 Yanaka (✆ 03/3821-5052). It's located on the second floor of a modern building but has traditional bamboo screens at the window and an indoor pond with fish. It offers two different kinds of noodles—soba and udon—served in a variety of ways. Open every day except Thursday from 11am to 8pm (closed 3–5pm on weekdays).

If all you want is a drink, straight ahead at the stoplight is **Petticoat Lane**, 2–35–7 Sendagi (✆ 03/3821-8859), a tiny coffee shop open daily 11am to midnight. A minute's walk farther down the street on the right-hand side past Isetatsu (see below) is ⑤⑦ **Rampo**, 2–9–14 Yanaka (✆ 03/3828-9494), a cozy coffee shop packed with knickknacks, kitsch, and folk art. It offers soft drinks, coffee, tea, and beer; jazz plays softly in the background. Open every day except Monday from 10am to 8pm. Look for the wooden COFFEE SNACK sign above its door.

If you take a right at the stoplight mentioned above, to your right you will soon see:

⑪ ⑤⑧ **Kikumi Sembei**

You can't miss it—look for the beautiful, 110-year-old wooden building, with its traditional open-fronted shop selling Japanese crackers. It's definitely worth a photo. You might even want to buy some of its square-shaped sembei.

It's open every day except Monday from 10am to 7pm (3–37–16 Sendagi; ✆ 03/3821-1215).

Just beyond the cracker shop is Sendagi Station. Unless you're ready to call it quits, however, turn around and head back in the opposite direction, passing the stoplight and the noodle shop listed above. Almost immediately on your right will be a:

⑫ **Sento**

The *sento*, or public bathhouse, is easily recognizable by its shoe lockers in the entranceway and by the chimney rising in the back. Although on the decline, public bathhouses still serve as important gathering places, especially for those without private baths.

Farther along, on your right on a corner, is:

⑬ ⑤⑨ **Isetatsu**

This crafts store sells items made from Japanese paper, including paper fans, papier-mâché objects, and boxes. Founded in the mid-1800s and run by the Hirose family for four generations, it specializes in *chiyogami*, handmade decorative paper printed with wood blocks. Some of the designs are the family's own creations; others are taken from family crests used by samurai and members of the court and worn on kimono and armor. The store is open daily from 10am to 6pm (2–18–9 Yanaka; ✆ 03/3823-1453).

As you continue in the same direction (east), on the next block on the left side you'll find:

⑭ **Daienji**

Located at 3–1–2 Yanaka, opposite the grade school and recessed back from the street, this temple is famous for its chrysanthemum fair and honors ukiyo-e master Harunobu, one of Edo's most famous artists, and Osen Kasamori, who worked at one of the many teahouses near Tennoji in the 1760s and achieved fame when Harunobu singled her out as a model for many of his portraits. The larger stone marker is a monument to Harunobu; the smaller one to the left is Osen's.

Cross back to the other side of the street at the crosswalk, turn left to continue walking in the same direction you've been going, and then take the first right (beside the traditional-looking elementary school with an old-fashioned clock). Turn left at the end of the street, and presently, to your right, at 2–1–27 Yanaka (☎ 03/3821-6913), will be the:

ⓕ Daimyo Clock Museum (Daimyo Tokei Hakubutsukan)

This one-room display of clocks and watches from the Edo Period (1603–1867) features about 50 examples from the museum's extensive collection at any given time (displays change annually). On display are huge free-standing clocks, sundials, alarm clocks, pocket watches, and small watches that were attached to *obi* (the sash worn with a kimono); you can see them all in about 30 minutes. The first clock was brought to Japan by a missionary in the 16th century, and in typical Japanese fashion was quickly modified to suit local needs. Rather than measuring 24 hours a day, Edo clocks were based on the length of time between sunrise and sunset, so that time varied greatly with the seasons. Clocks had to be set once or twice a day, and were so expensive that only *daimyo*, or feudal lords, could afford them. Most daimyo had both a clockmaker and clock setter under their employ, since castles generally contained several huge clocks on their grounds. Apparently, time was of the essence in Japan even back then. Explanations in the museum are in Japanese only, but you can ask to see an English pamphlet. It's open Tuesday to Sunday 10am to 4pm (closed Dec 25–Jan 15 and July–Sept).

Take a right out of the museum to return to the street you were on, turn left and then left again (note the weirdly shaped pine tree on the corner), and walk down one of the many slopes for which Yanaka is famous and which still has some traditional wooden homes (including a beautiful one on your right). On the left-hand side of the slope, at the end of the street just before the stoplight, is Imojin Owariya, a Japanese sweet shop (see "Winding Down," below). Cross the busy street, Shinobazu-Dori Avenue, at the stoplight and continue straight (you'll pass another sento to your left). The road will begin to slope upward, and then, to your right, will be:

ⓖ Nezu Shrine

This is one of Tokyo's best-kept secrets. With its brightly colored orange torii, venerable cedars, and manicured azalea bushes, it's a welcome contrast to the austerity of the Buddhist temples that dominate Yanaka. It was built in 1706 by the fifth Tokugawa shogun and features a front courtyard gate of red lacquer with joists in gilt, green, blue, orange, and black. The shrine is most well-known, however, for its thousands of manicured azalea bushes. When they bloom in April, this place is heaven—but be prepared for crowds.

To reach Nezu Station, return to Shinobazu-Dori and turn right.

WINDING DOWN
On the slope upward from Shinobazu-Dori in the direction of the clock museum is ⑥⓪ **Imojin Owariya,** 2–30–4 Nezu (☎ 03/3821-5530), a tiny shop selling Japanese sweets and ice cream. Look for the small display case outside its front door. Inside it's very plain, with just a few tables, kind of like a Japanese version of a small-town ice-cream parlor. You can get homemade ice cream here, as well as shaved ice with flavorings of sweet-bean paste, lemon, strawberry, or melon. The shop is open Tuesday through Sunday from 11am to 7pm.

Shopping

I have never seen people shop as much as the Japanese do. Judging from the crowds that surge through Tokyo's department stores every day, I'm convinced it's the country's number-one pastime. Women, men, couples, and even whole families go on shopping expeditions in their free time, making Sunday the most crowded shopping day of the week.

1 The Shopping Scene

BEST BUYS   Tokyo is the country's showcase for everything from the latest in camera, computer, or stereo equipment to original woodblock prints. Traditional Japanese crafts and souvenirs that make good buys include toys (both traditional and the latest in technical wizardry), kites, Japanese dolls, carp banners, swords, lacquerware, bamboo baskets, ikebana accessories, ceramics, chopsticks, fans, masks, knives, scissors, sake, and silk and cotton kimono. And you don't have to spend a fortune: You can pick up handmade Japanese paper *(washi)* products, such as umbrellas, lanterns, boxes, stationery, and other souvenirs, for a fraction of what they would cost in import shops in the United States. In Harajuku, it's possible to buy a fully lined dress of the latest fashion craze for $75, and I can't even count the number of pairs of fun, casual shoes I've bought in Tokyo for a mere $40. Used cameras can be picked up for a song, reproductions of famous woodblock prints make great inexpensive gifts, and many items—from pearls to electronic video and audio equipment—can be bought tax-free (see "Taxes," below).

Japan is famous for its electronics, but if you're buying new you can probably find these products just as cheaply, or even more cheaply, in the United States. If you think you want to shop for electronic products while you're in Tokyo, it pays to do some comparison shopping before you leave home so that you can spot a deal when you see one. On the other hand, one of the joys of shopping for electronics in Japan is discovering new, advanced models; you might decide you want that new Sony MP3 player simply because it's the coolest thing you've ever seen, no matter what the price.

GREAT SHOPPING AREAS   Another enjoyable aspect of shopping in Tokyo is that specific areas are often devoted to certain goods, sold wholesale but also available to the individual shopper. **Kappabashi Dori** (station: Tawaramachi), for example, is where you'll find shops specializing in kitchenware, while **Kanda** (station: Jimbocho) is known for its bookstores. **Akihabara** (station: Akihabara) is packed with stores selling the latest in electronics. **Ginza** (station: Ginza) is the chic address for clothing boutiques as well as art galleries. **Aoyama** (station: Omotesando) boasts the city's largest concentration of designer-clothing stores, while nearby **Harajuku** (stations: Harajuku, Meiji-Jingu-mae, or Omotesando) and **Shibuya** (station: Shibuya) are the places to go for youthful, fun, and inexpensive fashions.

SALES   Department stores have sales throughout the year, during which you can pick up bargains on everything from electronic goods and men's suits to golf clubs, toys, kitchenware, food, and lingerie; there are even sales for used wedding kimono. The most popular sales are for **designer clothing,** usually held twice a year, in July and December or January. Here you can pick up fantastic clothing at cut-rate prices—but be prepared for the crowds. Sales are generally held on one of the top floors of the department store in what's usually labeled the "Exhibition Hall" or "Promotion Hall" in the store's English-language brochure. Stop by the department store's information desk, usually located near the main entrance, for the brochure as well as flyers listing sales promotions.

TAXES   Remember that a 5% consumption tax will be added on to the price marked, but all major department stores in Tokyo will refund the tax to foreign visitors if total purchases amount to more than ¥10,001 ($84) on that day. Exemptions include food, beverages, tobacco, pharmaceuticals, cosmetics, film, and batteries. When you've completed your shopping, take the purchased goods and receipts to the tax refund counter in the store. There are forms to fill out (you will need your passport). Upon completion, a record of your purchase is placed on the visa page of your passport and you are given the tax refund on the spot. When you leave Japan, make sure you have your purchases with you; you may be asked by Customs to show them (pack them in your carry-on).

SHIPPING IT HOME   Many first-class hotels in Tokyo provide a packing and shipping service. In addition, most large department stores, as well as tourist shops such as the Oriental Bazaar and antiques shops, will ship your purchases overseas.

　If you wish to ship packages yourself, the easiest method is to go to a post office and purchase an easy-to-assemble cardboard box, available in three sizes (along with the necessary tape and string). Keep in mind that packages mailed abroad cannot weigh more than 20 kilograms (about 44 lb.), and that only the larger international post offices accept packages to be mailed overseas. Remember, too, that mailing packages from Japan is expensive. Ask your hotel concierge for the closest international post office.

2 Shopping A to Z

ANTIQUES & CURIOS

In recent years, it has become a buyer-beware market in Japan, with fake antiques produced in China infiltrating the Japanese market. You shouldn't have any problems with the reputable dealers listed here; but if you're buying an expensive piece, be sure to ask whether there are any papers of authenticity.

　In addition to the listings here, other places to look for antiques include the **Oriental Bazaar** and Tokyo's **outdoor flea markets** (see later in this chapter).

Antique Mall Ginza   Japanese, European, and some American antiques, collectibles, and odds and ends crowd eight floors of Tokyo's largest antiques mall, where you could spend hours browsing among furniture, jewelry, watches, porcelain, pottery, dolls, scrolls, glassware, and much more, including a whole floor devoted to kimono and traditional clothing. Open Thursday to Tuesday 11am to 7pm. 1–20–15 Ginza, Chuo-ku. ☎ **03/3535-2115.** Station: Higashi-Ginza or Ginza-Itchome (4 min.). On Showa Dori.

Fuji-Torii   Open since 1948, this small, one-room shop in Harajuku specializes in traditional works of art and antiques, including screens, scrolls, woodblock prints, and ceramics. Open Wednesday to Monday from 11am to 6pm; closed third Monday of the month. 6–1–10 Jingumae, Shibuya-ku. © 03/3400-2777. Station: Meiji-jingumae (2 min.). On Omotesando Dori, next to Kiddy Land.

Ginza Antiques   While not nearly as extensive as the Antique Mall Ginza (above), the dozen or so shops here on the second floor of the Ginza Five Building (located under an expressway) offer a variety of high-end antiques, including porcelain, furniture, dolls, kimono, and other treasures from Japan and Europe. Daily 10am to 8pm. 5–1 Ginza © 03/5568-2650. Station: Ginza (exit C1, 1 min.). On Harumi Dori.

Kurofune *(Finds)*   Located in a large house in Roppongi, Kurofune is owned by an American, John Adair, who for more than 25 years has specialized in Japanese antique furniture in its original condition. The largest collection here is of mid- to top-quality pieces. Browsing is a delight even if you can't afford to buy; stock includes hibachi, fabrics, prints, maps, lanterns, screens, folk art, and the country's largest collection of Japanese baskets. Fax Adair (03/3479-0719) for a map of how to get here. Open Monday to Saturday from 10am to 6pm. 47–7–4 Roppongi. © 03/3479-1552. Station: Roppongi (5 min.). From Roppongi Crossing, walk away from Tokyo Tower on Gaien-Higashi Dori, take the diagonal street to the left, and then take a right at the 7-Eleven.

ARCADES & SHOPPING MALLS

ARCADES IN HOTELS   Shopping arcades are found in several of Tokyo's first-class hotels. Although they don't offer the excitement and challenge of rubbing elbows with the natives, they do offer convenience, English-speaking clerks, and consistently top-quality merchandise. The **Imperial Hotel Arcade** (station: Hibiya) is one of the best, with shops selling pearls, woodblock prints, porcelain, antiques, and expensive name-brand clothing like Hanae Mori. The **Okura** and **New Otani** hotels also have extensive shopping arcades.

UNDERGROUND ARCADES   Underground shopping arcades are found around several of Tokyo's train and subway stations; the biggest are at **Tokyo Station** (the Yaesu side) and **Shinjuku Station** (the east side). They often have great sales and bargains on clothing, accessories, and electronics. My only complaint is that once you're in them, it sometimes seems as if you'll never find your way out again.

DUTY-FREE ARCADES   Other good places to shop if you're short of time are duty-free stores. To qualify, you must present your passport, whereupon you'll be issued a piece of paper to surrender at the Customs desk when you depart Japan (the Customs desk at Narita Airport is well marked, so you can't miss it). At that time, you may also be requested to show your purchases to Customs officials, so be sure to put them in your carry-on.

The best-known tax-free arcade is the **International Arcade** near the Imperial Hotel under the elevated JR Yamamote train tracks (© 03/3571-1528; station: Hibiya). It features merchandise from pearls to antique kimono to electronics. Narita Airport's duty-free shops, located past the security machines and Customs, are also good places to shop for alcohol. Prices aren't cheaper and selections are limited, but I usually buy my sake here before boarding the plane just so I don't have to lug it around.

SHOPPING MALLS   **Sunshine City** (station: Higashi Ikebukuro or Ikebukuro) is one of Tokyo's oldest shopping malls, with more than 300 shops and restaurants spread through several adjoining buildings. Its popularity, however, is now challenged by newer and grander shopping malls. **Caretta Shiodome** (station: Shiodome), a 47-story monolith just southwest of the Ginza (and across from Hama Rikyu Garden), contains 58 shops and 33 restaurants. While there, stop by the Ad Museum Tokyo, Japan's first museum of advertising with cool posters from bygone eras; admission is free. Just across the harbor, on the man-made island of Odaiba (station: Odaiba Kaihin Koen), is **Palette Town,** an amusement/shopping center that contains the sophisticated Italian-themed **Venus Fort,** an indoor mall that evokes scenes from Italy with its store-fronted lanes, painted sky, fountains, plazas, and Italian name-brand boutiques. Nearby **Tokyo Decks** specializes in international household goods, including imports from the United States, Europe, China, and Hong Kong; I especially like its Daiba 1chome Syoutengai section on the fourth floor, a remake of mid-1900s Japan, with goods, food, songs, and TV shows of the period; and the sixth-floor Daiba Little Hong Kong department with its Chinese accessories, souvenirs, and restaurants.

ART GALLERIES

The Ginza has the highest concentration of art galleries in Tokyo, with more than 200 shops dealing in everything from old woodblock prints to silk-screens, lithographs, and contemporary paintings. In addition, Japanese department stores almost always contain art galleries, with changing exhibitions ranging from works by European masters to contemporary Japanese pottery. Check the free giveaway *Metropolis* for exhibition listings.

Complex   Unlike the other galleries listed here, this one has an unlikely home in the Roppongi nightlife district. Actually, it consists of five small galleries spread on several floors of two adjoining buildings, most of them dealing in cutting-edge, contemporary Japanese and international art. Among them, **Ota Fine Arts** (✆ 03/5786-2344) is probably the most well established and represents Yayoi Kusama, Tsuyoshi Ozawa, and other big names in contemporary Japanese art. And with the newly opened Mori Art Museum and the new National Gallery (slated to open in 2006), Roppongi may just be the future's art scene. Open Tuesday to Saturday 11am to 7pm. 6–8–14 Roppongi, Minato-ku ✆ 03/5411-7510. Station: Roppongi (4 min). From Roppongi Crossing, take the road downhill from the left side of Almond Coffee Shop; it will be on the right.

Nishimura Gallery   This gallery represents an even mix of established Japanese and foreign (mainly British) painters and sculptors, including David Hockney, Peter Blake, David Nash, and Funakoshi Katsura. Open Tuesday to Saturday 10:30am to 6:30pm. Nishi Ginza Building basement, 4–3–13 Ginza, Chuo-ku. ✆ 03/3567-3906. Station: Ginza (1 min.).

S. Watanabe   This long-established shop deals mostly in modern and some antique woodblock prints. Open Monday to Saturday 9:30am to 8pm. 8–6–19 Ginza, Chuo-ku. ✆ 03/3571-4684. Station: Shimbashi (2 min.). On Namiki Dori.

Sakai Kokodo Gallery   This gallery claims to be the oldest woodblock print shop in Japan. The first shop was opened back in 1870 in the Kanda area of Tokyo by the present owner's great-grandfather, and altogether four generations of the Sakai family have tended the store. It's a great place for original prints, as well as for reproductions of such great masters as Hiroshige. (If you're really a woodblock print fan, you'll want to visit the Sakai family's excellent museum, **Japan Ukiyo-e Museum,** in the small town of Matsumoto in the Japan Alps.) Open daily 11am to 6pm. 1–2–14 Yurakucho, Chiyoda-ku (across from the Imperial Hotel's Tower). ✆ 03/3591-4678. Station: Hibiya (1 min.).

Shiseido Gallery   Founded in 1919 by the Shiseido cosmetics company's first president, this is the Ginza's oldest gallery but it occupies very updated quarters in a basement with super-high ceilings (5m/15 ft.). It features contemporary art by young, promising talent, both Japanese and foreign. Open Tuesday to Saturday 11am to 7pm; Sunday and holidays 11am to 6pm. Tokyo Ginza Shiseido Building, B1, 8–8–3 Ginza, Chuo-ku. ☎ 03/3572-3901. Station: Ginza (3 min.). On Chuo Dori, south of Ginza 4-chome Crossing.

Tokyo Gallery   This tiny gallery specializes in one-person shows of avant-garde art, mostly by Japanese artists. Hours are Monday to Friday 11am to 7pm; Saturday 11am to 5pm. Dai-go Shuwa Building, 2nd floor, 8–6–18 Ginza, Chuo-ku. ☎ 03/3571-1808. Station: Shimbashi (2 min.). On Namiki Dori.

Yoseido Gallery   This shop deals in modern woodblock prints, etchings, silkscreens, copper plates, and lithographs. Open Monday to Saturday 11am to 7pm. 5–5–15 Ginza, Chuo-ku. ☎ 03/3571-1312. Station: Ginza (1 min.). On Namiki Dori near Harumi Dori.

BOOKS

Yasukuni Dori in Jimbocho, Kanda (station: Jimbocho), is lined with bookstores selling both new and used books, with several dealing in English-language books. Keep in mind, however, that English-language books are usually more expensive in Japan than back home. Still, no bibliophile should pass this street up, especially if your interest is in books related to Japan. **Oriental Bazaar** (see later in this chapter) also carries books on Japan.

Kinokuniya   This is one of Tokyo's best-known bookstores, with one of the city's largest selections of books and magazines in English—including books on Japan, dictionaries and textbooks for students of Japanese, and novels—on its sixth floor. Open daily 10am to 8pm; closed some Wednesdays. Takashimaya Annex, Takashimaya Times Sq. complex. ☎ 03/5361-3301. Station: Shinjuku (south exit, 2 min.).

Kitazawa   The largest of several English-language bookstores in Kanda, Kitazawa boasts an overwhelming selection of books, including the most recently published novels, American and English classic literature, topical books ranging from history to philosophy to politics, books on Japan, and antiquarian books (reservations needed to peruse the antique editions). Don't neglect the bargain-priced books on the trolleys outside the front door. Open Monday to Saturday 10am to 6pm; closed holidays. 2–5 Jimbocho, Kanda, Chiyoda-ku. ☎ 03/3263-0011. Station: Jimbocho (1A exit, then turn right, 1 min.). On Yasukuni Dori.

Maruzen   This is Japan's oldest bookstore, founded in 1869. Its English-language section is on the fourth floor, with everything from dictionaries to travel guides to special-interest books on Japan. It also carries books on science, politics, and history, as well as magazines and paperbacks. The basement contains an office-supply shop with printing and copying services, while the fourth-floor Craft Center sells traditional handmade products of Japan. Open Monday to Saturday 10am to 8pm; Sunday and holidays 10am to 7pm. 2–3–10 Nihombashi. ☎ 03/3272-7211. Station: Kyobashi (3 min.). On Chuo Dori across from Takashimaya department store, within walking distance of the Ginza and Tokyo stations.

Ohya Shobo   Established in 1882, this delightfully cramped shop in Kanda doesn't have any English-language books, but it does claim to have the world's largest stock of 18th- and 19th-century Japanese illustrated books, woodblock prints, and maps, including maps from the Edo Period. Note that credit cards

---

> **Tips　A Note on Japanese Symbols**
>
> Many hotels, restaurants, attractions, and shops in Japan do not have
> signs giving their names in Roman (English-language) letters. Appendix C
> lists the Japanese symbols for all such places described in this guide. Each
> set of characters representing an establishment name has a number in the
> appendix, which corresponds to the number that appears inside the oval
> preceding the establishment's name in the text.

---

are not accepted here. Open Monday to Saturday 10am to 6pm; closed some
holidays. 1–1 Jimbocho, Kanda, Chiyoda-ku. ⓒ 03/3291-0062. Station: Jimbocho (A7 exit, 3
min.). Turn right (east) onto Yasukuni Dori; it will be on your right, one of the last bookstores.

Tokyo Random Walk　This shop, the Tokyo branch of a Vermont firm, has a
wide selection of books on Japan and the Far East written in English, as well as
English translations of Japanese novels, guidebooks, paperback fiction, and
instructional books on the Japanese language. Open Monday to Saturday
10:30am to 8pm; Sunday and national holidays 11am to 7pm. 1–3 Jimbocho,
Kanda, Chiyoda-ku. ⓒ 03/3291-7071. Station: Jimbocho (A7 exit, 3 min.). Turn right (east) onto
Yasukuni Dori; it will be on your right.

Tower Records and Books　My friends in Tokyo don't shop anywhere else
for their books and magazines, as prices are usually lower here than elsewhere.
The seventh floor is devoted to imported publications, with a good selection of
English-language books, more than 3,000 different kinds of magazines, and the
Sunday editions of major newspapers. Open daily 10am to 10pm; closed some
Mondays. 1–22–14 Jinnan. ⓒ 03/3496-3661. Station: Shibuya (Hachiko exit, 5 min.).

DEPARTMENT STORES

Japanese department stores are institutions in themselves. Usually enormous,
well-designed, and chock-full of merchandise, they have about everything you
can imagine, including museums and art galleries, pet stores, rooftop play-
grounds or greenhouses, travel agencies, restaurants, grocery markets, and flower
shops. You could easily spend a whole day in a department store—eating,
attending cultural exhibitions, planning your next vacation, exchanging money,
purchasing tickets to local concerts and other events, and, well, shopping.

One of the most wonderful aspects of the Japanese department store is the
courteous service. If you arrive at a store as its doors open at 10 or 10:30am,
you'll witness a daily rite: Lined up at the entrance are staff who bow in welcome. Some Japanese shoppers arrive just before opening time so as not to miss
this favorite ritual. Sales clerks are everywhere, ready to help you. In some stores,
you don't even have to go to the cash register once you've made your choice; just
hand over the product, along with your money, to the sales clerk, who will
return with your change, your purchase neatly wrapped, and an *"Arigatoo goza-
imashita"* ("Thank you very much"). Many department stores will also ship your
purchases home for you. A day spent in a Japanese department store could spoil
you for the rest of your life.

The basement of the store is usually devoted to foodstuffs: fresh fish, produce,
and pre-prepared snacks and dinners. There are often free samples of food; if you're
hungry, walking through the food department could do nicely for a snack. Many
department stores include boutiques by such famous Japanese and international

fashion designers as Issey Miyake, Rei Kawakubo (creator of Comme des Garçons), Hanae Mori, Takeo Kikuchi, Vivienne Westwood, and Paul Smith, as well as a department devoted to the kimono. Near the kimono department may also be the section devoted to traditional crafts, including pottery and lacquerware. To find out what's where, stop by the store's information booth located on the ground floor near the front entrance and ask for the floor-by-floor pamphlet in English. Be sure, too, to ask about sales on the promotional floor—you never know what bargains you may chance upon.

IN GINZA & NIHOMBASHI

Matsuya   This is one of my favorite department stores in Tokyo; if I were buying a wedding gift, Matsuya is one of the first places I'd look. It has a good selection of Japanese folk crafts items, kitchenware, kimono, and beautifully designed contemporary household goods, in addition to the usual designer clothes and accessories. I always make a point of stopping by the seventh floor's Design Collection, which displays items from around the world selected by the Japan Design Committee as examples of fine design, from the Alessi teapot to Braun razors. Open daily 10am to 8pm. 3–6–1 Ginza, Chuo-ku. © 03/3567-1211. Station: Ginza (2 min.). On Chuo Dori Ave., just a long block north of Ginza 4–chome Crossing.

Matsuzakaya   Established almost 400 years ago, this was the first department store in Japan that did not require customers to take off their shoes at the entrance. It appeals mainly to Tokyo's older generation with its mostly men's and women's clothing, but it does have a pet shop, children's play area, and Shinto shrine on its roof. Hours are Monday to Thursday from 10:30am to 7:30pm; Friday to Saturday from 10:30am to 8pm; Sunday and holidays from 10:30am to 7pm. 6–10–1 Ginza, Chuo-ku. © 03/3572-1111. Station: Ginza (2 min.). 1 block from Ginza–4–chome Crossing on Chuo Dori in the direction of Shimbashi.

Mitsukoshi   This Nihombashi department store is one of Japan's oldest and grandest, founded in 1673 by the Mitsui family as a kimono store. In 1683, it became the first store in the world to deal only in cash sales; it was also one of the first stores in Japan to display goods on shelves rather than have merchants fetch bolts of cloth for each customer, as was the custom of the time. Yet another first: It was one of the first shops to employ female clerks. Today, housed in a building dating from 1914, it remains one of Tokyo's loveliest department stores, with a beautiful and stately Renaissance-style facade and an entrance guarded by two bronze lions, replicas of the lions in Trafalgar Square. For fortification, there's the Fortnum & Mason Tea Salon, Harrods Tea Salon, and Café Wien. The store carries many name-brand boutiques, including Givenchy, Dunhill, Chanel, Hanae Mori, Oscar de la Renta, Christian Dior, and Tiffany. Its

---

Tips **Department Store Hours**

Japanese department stores are generally open from 10 or 10:30am to 7:30 or 8pm. They used to close 1 day a week, but now they close irregularly, always on the same day of the week (say, on Tues), but in no apparent pattern. One month they may be closed the second and third Tuesday of the month, but the next month only the first or not at all. In any case, you can always find stores that are open, even on Sundays and holidays (major shopping days in Japan).

kimono, by the way, are still hot items. Open daily 10am to 7:30pm; closed some Mondays.

Another branch, located right on Ginza 4–chome Crossing (℃ 03/3562-1111; Mon–Sat 10am–8pm; Sun 10am–7:30pm), is popular with young shoppers. 1–4–1 Nihombashi Muromachi, Chuo-ku. ℃ **03/3241-3311.** Station: Mitsukoshimae (1 min.).

Takashimaya   This department store provides stiff competition for Mitsukoshi, with a history just as long. It was founded as a kimono shop in Kyoto during the Edo Period and opened in Tokyo in 1933. Today it's one of the city's most attractive department stores, with white-gloved elevator operators whisking customers to eight floors of shopping and dining. Naturally, it features boutiques by such famous designers as Chanel, Louis Vuitton, Gucci, Issey Miyake, and more. Daily 10am to 7:30pm; closed some Wednesdays. 2–4–1 Nihombashi (on Chuo Dori Ave.), Chuo-ku. ℃ **03/3211-4111.** Station: Nihombashi (1 min.).

Wako   This is one of Ginza's smallest department stores but also one of its classiest, housed in one of the few area buildings that survived World War II. It was erected in 1932 and is famous for its distinctive clock tower, graceful curved facade, and innovative window displays. The owners are the Hattori family, founders of the Seiko watch company. The store's ground floor carries a wide selection of Seiko watches and handbags, while the upper floors carry imported and domestic fashions and luxury items with prices to match. It caters to older, well-to-do customers; you won't find hordes of young Japanese girls shopping here. Open Monday to Saturday 10:30am to 6pm; closed holidays. 4–5–11 Ginza (at Ginza 4–chome Crossing), Chuo-ku. ℃ **03/3562-2111.** Station: Ginza (1 min.).

Yurakucho Hankyu   Connected to Seibu (below), this store carries mostly clothing and accessories. Nearby is the even newer H2 Sukiyabashi Hankyu annex, which attracts young shoppers with its Gap, Eddie Bauer, and Tommy Hilfiger outlets, as well as music stores. Open daily 11am to 8:30pm. 2–5–1 Yurakucho, Chiyoda-ku. ℃ **03/3575-2233.** Station: Yurakucho (1 min.) or Hibiya and Ginza (2 min.). In Yurakucho, just east of the elevated JR Yamanote Line tracks and between the Hibiya and Ginza subway stations.

Yurakucho Seibu   This Seibu branch, connected to Yurakucho Hankyu via covered square, contains clothing and accessories mostly for women, with a few floors devoted to men's fashions. Open Monday to Thursday 11:30am to 8:30pm; Friday 11:30am to 9pm; Saturday and Sunday and holidays 11am to 8pm. 2–5–1 Yurakucho, Chiyoda-ku. ℃ **03/3286-0111.** Station: Yurakucho (1 min.) or Hibiya and Ginza (2 min.). In Yurakucho near the elevated tracks of the JR Yamanote Line, between the Hibiya and Ginza stations.

IN IKEBUKURO

Seibu   Once the nation's largest department store—and still one of the biggest—Seibu has 47 entrances, thousands of sales clerks, dozens of restaurants, 12 floors, 31 elevators, and an average of 170,000 shoppers a day. Two basement floors are devoted to foodstuffs—you can buy everything from taco shells to octopus to seaweed. Dishes are set out so that you can sample the food as you move along, and hawkers yelling out their wares give the place a marketlike atmosphere. Fast-food counters sell salads, grilled eel, chicken, sushi, and other ready-to-eat dishes. The rest of the floors offer clothing, furniture, art galleries, jewelry, household goods, kitchenware, and a million other things. Loft, Seibu's department for household goods and interior design, and Wave, Seibu's CD department, occupy the top four floors of the main building. Many of the best Japanese and Western designers have boutiques here; Size World and Queen's Coordination, both on the fourth floor, specialize in large and petite women's sizes, respectively. Open Monday to Saturday from 10am to 9pm, Sunday and holidays from 10am to 8pm. Closed some Tuesdays. 1–28–1 Minami Ikebukuro, Toshima-ku. © 03/3981-0111. Station: Ikebukuro (underneath the store).

Tobu/Metropolitan Plaza   Once overshadowed by nearby Seibu, this flag-ship of the Tobu chain expanded and reopened in 1993 as Japan's largest depart-ment store, employing 3,000 clerks to serve the 180,000 customers who enter its doors daily. It consists of a main building, a connecting central building, and Metropolitan Plaza. It offers everything from luxury goods and the latest inter-national fashions to hardware, software, toys, daily necessities, and traditional Japanese products (good for souvenirs). Its basement food floor is massive—food accounts for nearly 20% of Tobu's total sales. Here, too, is the new home of the **Japan Traditional Craft Center,** a must for anyone shopping for tradi-tional and contemporary handmade Japanese crafts. Open daily 10am to 8pm; closed some Wednesdays. 1–1–25 Nishi-Ikebukuro, Toshima-ku. © 03/3981-2211. Station: Ikebukuro (west exit, 1 min.).

IN SHINJUKU

Isetan   Isetan is a favorite among foreigners living in Tokyo. It has a good line of conservative clothing appropriate for working situations, as well as contem-porary and fashionable styles, including designer clothes (Issey Miyake, Yohji Yamamoto, Tsumori Chisato, Comme des Garçons, Marc Jacobs, and Sonia Rykiel) and large dress sizes (on the 2nd floor). It also has a great kimono sec-tion along with all the traditional accessories (obi, shoes, purses). In the annex, which carries mostly men's clothing, is a New Creator's Space on the ground floor, unique among Japanese department stores (which are generally reluctant to carry anything but the tried and true), that showcases clothing by up-and-coming Japanese designers. Open daily 10am to 8pm; closed some Wednesdays. 3–14–1 Shinjuku, Shinjuku-ku. © 03/3352-1111. Station: Shinjuku Sanchome (1 min.) or Shin-juku (east exit, 6 min.). On Shinjuku Dori, east of Shinjuku Station.

Takashimaya Times Square   Since its opening in 1996, Takashimaya Times Square has been the number-one draw in Shinjuku and is packed on weekends. Much larger than Takashimaya's Nihombashi flagship, this huge complex is anchored by the Takashimaya department store, which boasts 10 floors of cloth-ing and restaurants (petite and "queen-size" clothing are on the 6th floor). There's also Tokyu Hands with everything imaginable for the home hobbyist, and Kinokuniya bookstore with English-language books on the sixth floor. Open daily 10am to 8pm; closed some Wednesdays. 5–24–2 Sendagaya, Shinjuku-ku. © 03/5361-1122. Station: Shinjuku (1 min.). Across the street from Shinjuku Station's south exit.

IN SHIBUYA

Shibuya is a shopping mecca for the fashionable young, with so many stores that there's a bona fide store war going on. Tokyu and Seibu are the two big names. In addition to the big stores here, see the "Fashions" section, below.

Seibu   Shibuya's largest department store consists of two buildings connected by pedestrian skywalks, with lots of designer boutiques like Issey Miyake, Comme des Garçons, and Yohji Yamamoto. Nearby are Loft, with household goods, and Movida, a fashion department store with fun young fashions for thin waifs. See the listing for the main store in Ikebukuro, above. Open Sunday to

Wednesday 10am to 8pm; Thursday to Saturday 10am to 9pm. Closed some Wednesdays. 21–1 Udagawacho. ℃ 03/3462-0111. Station: Shibuya (Hachiko exit, 3 min.).

Tokyu Honten (Main Store)   With its conservative styles in clothing and housewares, the Tokyu chain's flagship store appeals mainly to a 40s-and-older age group. Here you'll find women's fashions (including departments for larger sizes), men's fashions, children's clothing and toys, arts and crafts, and restaurants. It adjoins the ultramodern Bunkamura complex, the largest cultural center in Tokyo, with cinemas, theater and concert halls, a museum, a bookstore, and cafes. Open daily 10am to 8pm; closed some Tuesdays. 2–24–1 Dogenzaka. ℃ 03/3477-3111. Station: Shibuya (Hachiko exit, 7 min.).

ELECTRONICS

The largest concentration of electronics and electrical-appliance shops in Japan is in an area of Tokyo called **Akihabara Electric Town (Denkigai),** centered around Chuo Dori. Although you can find good deals on video and audio equipment elsewhere (especially just west of Shinjuku Station, where Yodobashi—see "Cameras" below—dominates with several stores devoted to electronics), Akihabara is special simply for its sheer volume. With more than 600 multilevel stores, shops, and stalls, Akihabara accounts for one-tenth of the nation's electronics and electrical-appliance sales. An estimated 50,000 shoppers come here on a weekday, 100,000 per day on a weekend. Even if you don't buy anything, it's great fun walking around. If you do intend to buy, make sure you know what the item would cost back home. Or you may be able to pick up something that's unavailable back home. Most of the stores and stalls are open-fronted, and many are painted neon green and pink. Inside, lights flash, fans blow, washing machines shimmy and shake, and stereos blast. Salespeople yell out their wares, trying to get customers to look at their rice cookers, refrigerators, computers, cellular phones, video equipment, digital cameras, CD and DVD players, TVs, calculators, and watches. This is the best place to see the latest models of everything electronic; it's an educational experience in itself.

If you are buying, be sure to bargain and don't buy at the first place you go to. One woman I know who was looking for a portable music device bought it at the third shop she went to for ¥4,000 ($33) less than what was quoted to her at the first shop. Make sure, too, that whatever you purchase is made for export—that is, with instructions in English, an international warranty, and the proper electrical connectors. All the larger stores have duty-free floors where products are made for export. Two of the largest are **Yamagiwa,** 3–13–10 Soto-Kanda (℃ 03/3253-2111); and **Laox,** 15–3 Soto-Kanda (℃ 03/3255-5301). If you're serious about buying, check these stores first.

The easiest way to get to Akihabara is via the Yamanote Line or Sobu Line to the JR Akihabara Station. You can also take the Hibiya subway line to Akihabara Station, but it's farther to walk. In any case, take the Akihabara Electric Town exit. Most shops are open daily from about 10:30am to 7 or 8pm.

CAMERAS

You can purchase cameras at many duty-free shops, including those in Akihabara, but if you're really serious about photographic equipment or want to stock up on film, make a trip to a shop dealing specifically in cameras. If a new camera is too formidable an expense, consider buying a used camera. New models come out so frequently in Japan that older models can be grabbed up for next to nothing.

Bic Camera   This huge, eight-floor store near the Ginza offers not only single-lens reflex, large and medium format, and digital cameras, but also computers, DVD players, video cameras, watches, toys, and much more. Note, however, that it caters primarily to Japanese; English-speaking sales clerks are scarce and export models are limited. Ask for the English-language brochure, and if you're buying sensitive equipment, make sure it will work outside Japan and comes with English-language instructions. Open daily 10am to 8pm. There's a branch in Shibuya at 1–24–12 Shibuya (C 03/5466-1111; open daily 10am–8pm; station: Shibuya, 2 min.). 1–11–1 Yurakucho, Chiyoda-ku. C 03/5221-1112. Station: Yurakucho (1 min.)

(61) **Lemon**   Its name doesn't inspire confidence, but this company specializes in used and new cameras from around the world, mostly Nikon but also Olympus, Leica, Canon, Pentax, Hasselblad, Rollei, and others. A camera buff's paradise. Open Monday to Saturday 11am to 8pm. 4–3–14 Ginza, Chuo-ku. C 03/3567-4582 for the ground floor of used models, C 03/3567-3131 for the 8th floor of new and used mostly foreign models. Station: Ginza (1 min.)

Yodobashi Camera   Shinjuku is the photographic equipment center for Tokyo, and this store, 1 block west of the station, is the biggest in the area. In fact, it ranks as one of the largest discount camera shops in the world, with around 30,000 items in stock, and it reputedly sells approximately 500 to 600 cameras daily. Although prices are marked, you can bargain here. This is the place to stock up on film; you can also have film developed here. In addition to cameras, it sells watches, calculators, computers, and other electronic equipment, though if you're interested specifically in watches, clocks, audio/video equipment, games, and other wares, nearby branches specialize in all of these (ask at the main shop for a map of the area). Open daily 9:30am to 9pm. 1–11–1 Nishi-Shinjuku, Shinjuku-ku. C 03/3346-1010. Station: Shinjuku (west exit, 3 min.).

FASHIONS

The **department stores** and **shopping malls** listed earlier are all good places to check out the latest trends. For inexpensive, basic clothing (think Japanese version of Gap), look for one of the 40 **Uniqlo** shops in Tokyo selling T-shirts, jeans, socks, shirts, and other clothing for the whole family. Two convenient locations are 6–10–8 Jingumae (C 03/5468-7313; station: Meiji-Jingumae, on Meiji Dori in the direction of Shibuya); and 16–17 Udagawacho (C 03/5728-8431; station: Shibuya).

Otherwise, Harajuku and Shibuya are the places to go for hundreds of small shops selling inexpensive designer knockoffs, as well as fashion department stores—multistoried buildings filled with concessions of various designers and labels. The stores below are two of the best known and largest.

La Forêt   This is not only the largest store in Harajuku but also one of the most fashionable, appealing mostly to teenage and 20-something shoppers. Young and upcoming Japanese designers are here as well as established names. You'll find the most reasonably priced fashions and accessories in the basement and on the fourth floor. There's also an annex. There's so much to see, you can easily kill a few hours here. Open daily 11am to 8pm. 1–11–6 Jingumae, Shibuya-ku. C 03/3475-0411. Station: Meiji-Jingumae (1 min.) or Harajuku (3 min.). Just off Harajuku's main intersection of Omotesando Dori and Meiji Dori.

Parco   A division of Seibu, Parco is actually three buildings clustered together and called Parco Part 1, Part 2, and Part 3. Parco Part 1 is the place to go for designer boutiques for men and women, with clothes by Japanese designers like Yohji Yamamoto and Tsumori Chisato. Part 2 has children's clothing, while Part 3 is devoted to sports clothes and casual clothing. Parco has two sales a year that you shouldn't miss if you're here—one in January and one in July. Open daily 10am to 8:30pm. 15–1 Udagawacho, Shibuya-ku. ℂ **03/3464-5111.** Station: Shibuya (Hachiko exit, 4 min.)

DESIGNER BOUTIQUES

The block between Omotesando Crossing and the Nezu Museum in **Aoyama** (station: Omotesando, 2 min.) has become the Rodeo Drive of Japan, the showcase of top designers. Even if you can't buy here (steep prices for most pocketbooks), a stroll is *de rigueur* for clothes hounds and those interested in design. Most shops are open daily from 11am to 8pm. **Comme des Garçons,** on the right side as you walk from Aoyama Dori (ℂ **03/3406-3951**), is Rei Kawakubo's showcase for her daring—and constantly evolving—men's and women's designs. The goddess of Japanese fashion and one of the few females in the business, Kawakubo has remained on the cutting edge of design for almost 2 decades. Across the street is **Issey Miyake** (ℂ **03/3423-1408**), with two floors of cool, spacious displays of Miyake's interestingly structured designs for men and women. (His very popular Pleats Please line is around the corner on Aoyama Dori, 3–13–21 Minami Aoyama; ℂ **03/5772-7750.**) One of Japan's newer designers, **Tsumori Chisato,** has a shop on the left side of the street (ℂ **03/3423-5170**). Also worth seeking out along this stretch is **Yohji Yamamoto** on the right (ℂ **03/3409-6006**), where Yamamoto's unique, classically wearable clothes are sparingly hung, flaunting the avant-garde interior space.

On the other side of Aoyama Dori, on Omotesando Dori, is **Hanae Mori** (ℂ **03/3400-3301**), the grande dame of Japanese design, with everything from separates and men's golf wear to haute couture and wedding gowns on display on three floors of a building designed by Japanese architect Kenzo Tange.

SECONDHAND SHOPS

Several secondhand consignment shops have been doing a thriving business of late near **Ebisu Station,** in the direction of Hiroo—most likely a result of Japan's recession. Prices here will be half—or maybe even a third or fourth—of what you'd pay in a designer boutique for this season's fashions, and you can expect the secondhand clothes to have little or no wear, even though they may be several seasons away from being the newest of the new.

Take the east exit from JR Ebisu Station (the one closest to Yebisu Garden Place) for Ebisu 1– and 4–chome and continue walking straight away (east) from the station 1 block to the busy street. Cross the street and turn right toward Mizuho Bank and Kinko's, cross the busy street that runs between them, and turn left (east) here. At the end of the block on a corner on your right is my favorite, **Garret** (ℂ **03/3446-6187;** open daily 11am–9pm), which stocks new and used clothing and accessories for men and women. I've seen men's sport coats by Paul Smith and Hugo Boss, Hermès and Chanel jewelry, Prada handbags, Rolex watches, and some women's tricot fashions from Comme des Garçons, as well as many other Japanese fashions, mostly for the under-30s crowd. Take a right out of Garret and continue walking east. On the left, before the next stoplight, is the more upscale **One Fifth** (ℂ **03/3442-7366;** open daily noon–8pm), which receives new inventory almost daily of mostly foreign designers. I've seen women's clothing by Alexander McQueen, Versace, Max

Mara, Fendi, and Chanel, as well as accessories by Louis Vuitton, Celine, Prada, Versace, and Fendi. It's a good place to look for serious work clothes.

For men, **Keymissbeemy,** several blocks behind One Fifth to the north at 1–26–17 Ebisu (C 03/3446-0094; open daily noon–8pm), carries new but discounted men's clothing, 50% of it by Paul Smith. From here, take a right out of the store and walk straight back to Ebisu Station in about 8 minutes.

Finally, there's one more used-clothing shop worth checking out on the west side of Ebisu Station. **Casablanca,** 1–10–10 Ebisu Nishi (C 03/5489-5861; open Mon–Sat 11am–8pm, Sun and holidays 11am–7pm), is owned by a former flight attendant and offers name-brand clothing, handbags, and shoes once worn by fellow attendants, as well as new clothing. Take the second right after Wendy's; it will be on the right.

FLEA MARKETS

Flea markets are good places to shop for antiques as well as for delightful junk. You can pick up secondhand kimono at very reasonable prices, as well as kitchenware, vases, cast-iron teapots, small chests, woodblock prints, dolls, household items, and odds and ends. (Don't expect to find any good buys in furniture.) The markets usually begin as early as dawn or 6am and last until 3 or 4pm or so, but go early if you want to pick up bargains. Bargaining is expected. Note that, since most markets are outdoors, they tend to be canceled if it rains. Tokyo also has huge antiques fairs several times a year, including the Heiwajima Antique Fair, held for several days in May, June, July, September, and December near Ryutsu Center Station on the Tokyo Monorail Line, and an antiques fair held at Ueno Shinobazu Pond for several weeks in April, July/August, and the month of October. Contact the Tourist Information Center for an update.

Togo Shrine, on Meiji Dori in Harajuku (near Meiji-Jingumae or Harajuku stations), has an antiques market on the first, fourth, and (when there is one) fifth Sunday of every month from 4am to 2pm. It's great for used kimono as well as small furniture and curios and is one of my favorites. For more information, see the walking tour of Harajuku and Aoyama in chapter 7.

Nogi Shrine, a 1-minute walk from Nogizaka Station, has an antiques flea market from dawn to about 2pm the second Sunday of each month except November. It has a lovely setting; the shrine commemorates General Nogi and his wife, both of whom committed suicide on September 13, 1912, to follow the Meiji emperor into the afterlife. Their simple home and stable are on shrine grounds.

Hanazono Shrine, near the Yasukuni Dori/Meiji Dori intersection east of Shinjuku Station (a 5-min. walk from Shinjuku Sanchome Station), has a flea market every Sunday from dawn to about 2pm (except in May and Nov due to festivals).

Finally, the closest thing Tokyo has to a permanent flea market is **Ameya Yokocho** (also referred to as Ameyokocho or Ameyacho), a narrow street near Ueno Park that runs along and underneath the elevated tracks of the JR Yamanote Line between Ueno and Okachimachi stations. There are about 400 stalls here selling discounted items ranging from fish, seaweed, and vegetables, to handbags, tennis shoes, cosmetics, watches, and casual clothes. The scene retains something of the *shitamachi* spirit of old Tokyo. Although housewives have been coming here for years, young Japanese recently discovered the market as a good bargain spot for fashions, accessories, and cosmetics. Some shops close on

Wednesdays, but hours are usually daily from 10am to 7pm; early evening is the most crowded time. Don't even think of coming here on a holiday—it's a stand-still pedestrian traffic jam.

INTERIOR DESIGN

The **department stores** listed earlier have furniture and interior-design sections: Ikebukuro's **Seibu** has an especially well-known and popular department, but my favorite is the Design Collection on the seventh floor of Ginza's **Matsuya.**

Loft   Loft is Seibu's store for the young homeowner and hobbyist, with table-ware, cookware, glassware, bathroom accessories, bed linens, office supplies, sta-tionery, and more. Don't miss the sixth-floor variety goods department, filled with an amazing amount of Japanese and American kitsch, party goods, cell-phone straps, and costumes. If you've yearned for a bank in the shape of a toilet or a clock that resembles a bag of french fries, this is the place for you. Open daily 10am to 8pm; closed some Wednesdays. 21–1 Udagawacho, Shibuya-ku. ℂ 03/ 3462-0111. Station: Shibuya (Hachiko exit, 4 min.). Behind Seibu B.

Three Minutes Happiness   Bargain yen shops have opened all over Japan the past few years, but this is one of the best I've seen. It carries tableware, house-hold goods, office supplies, cosmetics, watches, sunglasses, some basic clothing, and many other simple items, mostly in bright and happy colors like lime green and sky blue. Let's just hope most of the products give more than 3 minutes of happiness. Open daily 11am to 9pm. 3–5 Udagawacho, Shibuya-ku. ℂ 03/5459-1851. Station: Shibuya (Hachiko exit, 5 min.). On the left side of Koen Dori, just past Parco Part 2.

Tokyu Hands   Billing itself the "Creative Life Store," Tokyu Hands, part of the Tokyu chain, is a huge department store for the serious homeowner and hobbyist, with everything from travel accessories, *noren* (doorway curtains), chopsticks, and kitchen knives, to equipment and materials for do-it-yourselfers, including paper for shoji. If there's a practical Japanese product you've decided you can't live without (lunch box? bathroom slippers? hanging laundry rack?), this is a good place to look.

You'll also find Tokyu Hands in Higashi Ikebukuro near the Sunshine City Building (ℂ 03/3980-6111) and in the Takashimaya Times Square complex in Shinjuku (ℂ 03/5361-3111). Open daily 10am to 8pm; closed the second and third Mondays of each month. 12–18 Udagawacho, Shibuya-ku. ℂ 03/5489-5111. Sta-tion: Shibuya (Hachiko exit, 6 min.). Near the trio of Parco buildings.

JAPANESE CRAFTS & TRADITIONAL PRODUCTS

If you want to shop for traditional Japanese folk crafts in the right atmosphere, nothing beats **Nakamise Dori** (station: Akasaka), a pedestrian lane leading to Sensoji Temple in Asakusa. It's lined with stall after stall selling souvenirs galore, from wooden *geta* shoes (traditional wooden sandals)and hairpins worn by geisha to T-shirts, fans, umbrellas, toy swords, and dolls. Most stalls are open from 10am to 6pm; some close 1 day a week.

Another good place to search for traditional crafts is **department stores,** which usually have sections devoted to ceramics, pottery, bambooware, flower-arranging accessories, and fabrics.

Ando   Opened in 1880, this shop probably has Tokyo's largest selection of Japanese cloisonné, including jewelry, vases, and plates. Open Monday to Friday 9:30am to 6pm; Saturday to Sunday 11am to 7pm; closed holidays. 5–6–2 Ginza. ℂ 03/3572-2261. Station: Ginza (1 min.). On Harumi Dori, between Chuo Dori and Sotobori Dori.

⑥ **Bengara**   *Noren* are the doorway curtains hanging in front of Japanese restaurants, public bathhouses, and shops, signaling that the establishment is open. Bengara sells more than 100 different models of both traditional and modern noren of various sizes and colors, including those bearing *kanji* (Chinese characters) or scenes from famous woodblock prints. You can look through catalogs or have a noren custom-made with your own name. Open daily 10am to 6pm; closed third Thursday of every month. 1–35–6 Asakusa, Taito-ku. ℂ 03/3841-6613. Station: Asakusa (4 min.). 1 long block east of Nakamise Dori, on the corner of Yanagi Dori and Metoro Dori.

Blue & White   American Amy Katoh has been the driving force behind this small but unique 27-year-old shop specializing in Japanese modern and traditional crafts, including textiles, yukata, porcelain, candles, picture frames, notebooks, fans, and more, mostly in colors of indigo-dyed blue and white. Of note is the creative clothing made especially for this shop, and the crafts designed by artists with disabilities. Open Monday to Saturday 10am to 6pm; closed holidays. 2–9–2 Azabu Juban, Minato-ku. ℂ 03/3451-0537. Station: Azabu-Juban (exit 4, 3 min.) or Roppongi (exit 3, 12 min.).

Fujiya   *Tenugui* are cotton hand towels used since the Edo Period for everything from drying off after bathing to headgear. In this small shop they're elevated to works of art, designed by a father-and-son team and featuring traditional motifs, including Kabuki actors, festivals, masks, flowers, and much more. Inexpensive gifts, they can be fashioned into scarves, framed as pictures, or used in countless other ways. Open Friday to Wednesday 10am to 7pm. 2–2–15 Asakusa, Taito-ku. ℂ 03/3841-2283. Station: Asakusa (4 min.). East of Nakamise Dori, beside Hyakusuke (see below).

Fukumitsuya   A small cedar ball hanging above the door of this Ginza establishment signals that it's a sake shop, albeit with a sophisticated, coolly elegant interior. Established as sake brewers in Kanazawa in 1625, Fukumitsuya offers its own products here, along with sake flasks, glasses, snack bowls, and other accouterments. A tasting bar allows customers to sample brews for ¥300 ($2.50), while upstairs is a restaurant specializing in Japanese cuisine suited to sake. Open Monday to Saturday noon to 10pm; Sunday and holidays 11am to 7pm. Closed irregularly. 5–5–8 Ginza, Chuo-ku. ℂ 03/3569-2291. Station: Ginza (2 min.). West of Harumi Dori, on Ginza W. 5th St.

⑥ **Hyakusuke**   For traditional Japanese cosmetics *(kesho hin)*, come to Hyakusuke, a 200-year-old, family-owned shop that looks like it hasn't changed in decades. During the Edo Period, this shop did a brisk trade in teeth blackener (white teeth were considered ugly), but today it offers some rather mundane products, as well as such traditional treatments as *kombu to funori* (a seaweed hair treatment), *tsubaki* (camellia) oil for healthy hair, and—perhaps most interesting—*uguisu no hun,* nightingale droppings that are said to leave your skin soft and smooth. Simply mix it with a little soap to wash your face. A purchase of ¥1,000 ($8.35) will give you about a month of daily use. Make-up used by geisha and Kabuki actors is also sold here, attracting customers in these traditional professions, but I'm partial to face paper, used on humid days to blot away perspiration and grime. Open Wednesday to Monday from 11am to 5pm. 2–2–14 Asakusa, Taito-ku. ℂ 03/3841-7058. Station: Asakusa (3 min.). Just east of Nakamise Dori; walking toward Sensoji Temple, turn right after the last shop on Nakamise, pass the two Buddha statues, and turn right again at Benten-do Temple; the shop is on your right, across from the playground.

Ichy's   High-quality, hand-carved wooden Noh masks are sold here, as well as wood carvings of animals, religious figures, and other objects. They're crafted from yew, which turns darker and shinier with age. Open Monday to Friday from 10am to 6pm. 2–11–4 Minami Aoyama, Minato-ku. Station: Gaienmae or Aoyama Itchome (5 min.). On Aoyama Dori, between the two stations.

Japan Sword   Coming here is like visiting a museum. Japan Sword is the best-known sword shop in Tokyo, with a knowledgeable staff and an outstanding collection of fine swords, daggers, sword guards, fittings, and other sword accessories, as well as antique samurai armor. The place also sells copies and souvenir items of traditional swords at prices much lower than those of the very expensive historic swords. Open Monday to Friday 9:30am to 6pm; Saturday 9:30am to 5pm. Closed holidays. 3–8–1 Toranomon, Minato-ku. ✆ 03/3434-4321. Station: Toranomon (exit 2, 5 min.).

Japan Traditional Craft Center (Zenkoku Dentoteki Kogeihin Senta) _Finds_
This store is worth a trip even if you can't afford to buy anything. Established to publicize and distribute information on Japanese crafts and to promote the country's artisans, the center is a great introduction to both traditional and contemporary Japanese design. It sells various top-quality crafts from all over Japan on a rotating basis, so there are always new items on hand. Crafts for sale usually include lacquerware, ceramics, fabrics, paper products, bamboo items, writing brushes, ink stones, metalwork, furniture, and sometimes even stone lanterns or Buddhist family altars. Prices are high, but rightfully so. Unfortunately, its location in out-of-the-way Ikebukuro makes a trip here feasible only if you have time; otherwise, you're probably better off shopping in the crafts section of a department store. Open daily from 11am to 7pm. 1st floor of Metropolitan Plaza Building, 1–11–1 Nishi-Ikebukuro. ✆ 03/5954-6066. Station: Ikebukuro (1 min.).

Kanesoh   Knives and scissors (including gardening scissors) have been sold from this tiny shop since the 1870s, now in its fifth generation of knife makers. Open daily 11am to 7pm. 1–18–12 Asakusa. ✆ 03/3844-1379. Station: Asakusa (2 min.). 1 block west of Nakamise Dori; take the 1st left after passing under Kaminarimon Gate with its huge paper lantern.

Kotobukiya   This crowded shop specializes in vases and accessories for flower arranging, of mostly contemporary designs. It also features objects used in tea ceremonies, including cast-iron tea pots. Open daily 9:30am to 7:30pm; closed the first and third Tuesday of each month. 3–18–17 Minami-Aoyama, Minato-ku. ✆ 03/3408-4187. Station: Omotesando (1 min.). On Aoyama Dori, opposite Omotesando Dori.

Kurodaya   If you're visiting Asakusa, you might want to stop in at this shop. First opened back in 1856, it sells traditional Japanese paper and paper products, including kites, papier-mâché masks, boxes, and more. Open Tuesday to Sunday 11am to 7pm. 1–2–5 Asakusa, Taito-ku. ✆ 03/3844-7511. Station: Asakusa (1 min.). Next to Kaminarimon Gate, to the east.

Kyoto Kan   Kyoto—Japan's capital for more than 1,000 years—is known for the high quality of its craftsmanship. This small shop sells lacquerware, sake, jewelry, textiles, incense, confections, and other souvenirs and gifts produced in Kyoto. It also serves as an information center for tourists interested in Kyoto and even offers monthly classes in Japanese cooking, flower arranging, tea ceremony, and cultural pursuits. Open daily 10:30am to 7:30pm; closed second and third Sunday of every month. Ark Mori Building, 1–12–32 Akasaka, Minato-ku. ✆ 03/3560-3336. Station: Roppongi 1–chome (exit 3, 1 min) or Tameike-Sanno (exit 13, 1 min). On Roppongi Dori.

64 Kyugetsu   Asakusabashi is Tokyo's wholesale district for retailers of dolls, with several stores lining Edo Dori. This is one of the area's biggest stores, founded in 1830. It sells both modern and traditional dolls; its Japanese dolls range from elegant creatures with porcelain faces, delicate coiffures, and silk kimono to wooden dolls called *kokeshi*. Hours are Monday to Friday 9:15am to 6pm; Saturday to Sunday 9:15am to 5:15pm. Closed several days following Children's Day and in mid-August. 1–20–4 Yanagibashi, Taito-ku. ☏ **03/5687-5176.** Asakusabashi (1 min.). In front of the station.

Oriental Bazaar   If you have time for only one souvenir shop in Tokyo, this should be it. This is the city's best-known and largest souvenir/crafts store, selling products at reasonable prices and offering four floors of souvenir and gift items, including cotton yukata, kimono (new and used), woodblock prints, paper products, wind chimes, stationery, fans, chopsticks, lamps and vases, Imari chinaware, sake sets, Japanese dolls, pearls, and even books on Japan and a large selection of antique furniture. This store will also ship things home for you. There's a tiny branch on the fourth floor of Terminal 1 at Narita Airport (☏ **0476/32-9333**), open daily 7:30am to 8:30pm. Open Friday to Wednesday 10am to 7pm. 5–9–13 Jingumae, Shibuya-ku. ☏ **03/3400-3933.** Station: Meiji-Jingumae (3 min.), Harajuku (4 min.), or Omotesando (5 min.). On Omotesando Dori in Harajuku; look for an Asian-looking facade of orange and green.

65 Sukeroku *(Finds)*   This tiny, truly unique shop sells handmade figures of traditional Japanese characters, from mythological figures to priests, farmers, entertainers, and animals. Included are people of the many castes of the Edo Period, ranging from peasants to feudal lords. Most figures are in the ¥3,000 to ¥5,000 ($25–$42) price range, though some are much higher than that. Open daily 10am to 6pm. Nakamise Dori, Asakusa. ☏ **03/3844-0577.** Station: Asakusa (3 min.). It's the next-to-last shop on the right as you walk from Kaminarimon Gate toward Sensoji Temple.

Tsutaya   Tsutaya has everything you might need for *ikebana* (flower arranging) or the Japanese tea ceremony, including vases of unusual shapes and sizes, scissors, and tea whisks. Open daily 10am to 6:30pm; closed the first, fourth, and fifth Sunday of each month. 5–10–5 Minami-Aoyama, Minato-ku. ☏ **03/3400-3815.** Station: Omotesando (2 min.). On Kotto Dori, not far from the Kua' Aina hamburger joint.

66 Yamamoto Soroban Ten   You can still see older Japanese doing accounts with an abacus, although the sight is not as common as it was even a decade ago. This shop has been in business for over 65 years and is now in its third generation of owners. You wonder, however, how long it will survive in the world of computers and calculators (only two Japanese towns still produce the abacus, and Japanese children no longer learn how to use them in school). The founder's granddaughter speaks English, and English-language explanations of how an abacus works are available. Open Friday to Wednesday 10am to 6pm; closed third Wednesday of every month. 2–35–12 Asakusa, Taito-ku. ☏ **03/3841-7503.** Station: Asakusa (5 min.). 1 block east of Sensoji Temple's main building, on Umamichi Dori (also spelled Umamiti); look for the giant abacus outside the front door.

Yonoya   This unique shop sells its own handmade boxwood combs, crafted by a seventh-generation comb maker. Its history stretches back 300 years, to a time when women's hairstyles were elaborate and complicated, as many woodblock prints testify. Today such handcrafted combs are a dying art. The combs here range in price from about ¥3,000 to more than ¥25,000 ($25–$208). Open Thursday to Tuesday from 10am to 7pm. 1–37–10 Asakusa, Taito-ku. ☏ **03/3844-1755.** Station: Asakusa (3 min.). On Demboin Dori (also spelled Dempoin Dori), just off Nakamise Dori.

67 **Yoshitoku**   Yoshitoku has had a shop at this location since 1711, making it Tokyo's oldest wholesale doll and traditional crafts store. It carries a variety of Japanese dolls on its first floor, most traditionally dressed as samurai, geisha, Kabuki actors, sumo wrestlers, and other Japanese personalities. There are also fine—and expensive—dolls representing the imperial court, dressed in silk kimono that follow the originals down to the minutest detail. Obviously, these dolls are meant not for children's play but for display by collectors. Upstairs are more mundane modern dolls, including stuffed animals. Open daily 9:30am to 6pm; closed Sunday and holidays May 5 to November. 1–9–14 Asakusabashi, Taito-ku. ✆ **03/3863-4419**. Station: Asakusabashi (1 min.).

KIMONO

The **Oriental Bazaar** (see "Japanese Crafts & Traditional Products," earlier in this chapter) has a good selection of new and used kimono, including elaborate wedding kimono. In addition, the **Antique Mall Ginza** (see "Antiques & Curios," earlier in this chapter) has an entire floor devoted to used kimono and traditional clothing. Department stores also sell kimono, notably **Takashimaya** and **Mitsukoshi** in Nihombashi and **Isetan** in Shinjuku. They also have yearly sales of used, rental wedding kimono. Flea markets are another good option for used kimono and yukata, particularly the antiques market at **Togo Shrine** (see above).

Chicago   This is the place to go for used kimono. It stocks hundreds of affordable used kimono (including wedding kimono), cotton *yukata* (for sleeping), and *obi* (the sash worn around a kimono), all located in its Kimono Corner, in the very back left corner of the shop past the 1950s American clothing. Open daily 11am to 8pm. 6–31–21 Jingumae, Shibuya-ku. ✆ **03/3409-5017**. Station: Meiji-Jingu-mae (1 min.) or Harajuku (2 min.). On Omotesando Dori, between Meiji Dori and Harajuku Station.

Hayashi Kimono   Established in 1913, Hayashi sells all kinds of kimono, including wedding kimono, cotton yukata, and *tanzen* (the heavy winter overcoat that goes over the yukata), as well as used and antique kimono. If you're buying a gift for someone back home, this is the best place to start. Open Monday to Saturday 10am to 7pm; Sunday 10am to 6pm. 2 locations in the International Arcade (underneath the JR Yamanote Line's elevated tracks), 2–1–1 Yurakucho, Chiyoda-ku. ✆ **03/3501-4012**. Station: Yurakucho (2 min.).

KITCHENWARE & TABLEWARE

In addition to the department stores and interior design shops listed above, the best place to shop for items related to cooking and serving is **Kappabashi-dougugai Dori** (station: Tawaramachi), popularly known as Kappabashi and Japan's largest wholesale area for cookware. Here, approximately 150 specialty stores sell cookware, including sukiyaki pots, woks, lunch boxes, pots and pans, aprons, knives, china, lacquerware, rice cookers, plastic food (like the kind you see in restaurant display cases), and disposable wooden chopsticks in bulk. Although the stores are wholesalers selling mainly to restaurants, you're welcome to browse and purchase as well. Stores are closed on Sunday but otherwise open from about 10am to 5pm.

MUSIC

HMV   HMV offers five floors of music, from Japanese pop to dance, soul, reggae, rock, and New Age, to jazz, classical, and opera, with listening stages so you can hear before you buy. Open daily 10am to midnight. 24–1 Udagawacho, Shibuya-ku. ✆ **03/5458-3411**. Station: Shibuya (Hachiko exit, 3 min.). On the street between the two Seibu stores.

Tower Records and Books   From classical to new releases to Japanese pop to games to CD-ROMs, it's all here, on six floors. On the seventh floor are imported books and magazines. Open daily 10am to 11pm; closed some Mondays. 1–22–14 Jinnan, Shibuya-ku. ℂ 03/3496-3661. Station: Shibuya (Hachiko exit, 5 min.).

PEARLS

Mikimoto, on Chuo Dori not far from Ginza 4–chome Crossing, past Wako department store (ℂ 03/3535-4611), is Japan's most famous pearl shop. It was founded by Mikimoto Koichi, who in 1905 produced the world's first good cultured pearl. Open daily 11am to 7:30pm, closed occasionally on Wednesday. Otherwise, there's a Mikimoto branch (ℂ 03/3591-5001) in the Imperial Hotel Arcade of the Imperial Hotel (station: Hibiya), where you'll also find **Asahi Shoten** (ℂ 03/3503-2528), with a good selection in the modest-to-moderate price range; and **K. Uyeda Pearl Shop** (ℂ 03/3503-2587), with a wide selection of pearls in many different price ranges.

SHOES

Here are two shops where you may find shoes in your size.

Diana   Diana has long been a refuge for foreigners, with larger sizes in its basement. Still, don't count on finding anything larger than a women's size 8. The shop does, however, have all the latest styles. Open daily 10:30am to 8:30pm. There's another store at 6–9–6 Ginza (ℂ 03/3573-4001), open daily from 10:30am to 8pm. 1–8–6 Jingumae, Minato-ku. ℂ 03/3478-4001. Station: Omotesando (2 min.). Near La Forêt, on Meiji Dori in Harajuku.

Ginza Washington   This is one of Tokyo's largest shoe stores. You'll find the larger sizes on the fifth floor, but if none of these fit and you're desperate, you can have the shoes custom made. Open daily 10:30am to 8pm. 5–7–7 Ginza, Chuo-ku. ℂ 03/3572-5911. Station: Ginza (1 min.). On Chuo Dori, near the Ginza 4–chome Crossing.

TOYS

Hakuhinkan Toy Park   This is one of Tokyo's largest and best toy stores, with six floors. In addition to the usual dolls, puzzles, games, and other items, there's a large assortment of gag gifts, and a video arcade on the fourth floor. Open daily 11am–8pm. 8–8–11 Ginza. ℂ 03/3571-8008. Station: Shimbashi or Ginza (4 min.). On Chuo Dori, near the overhead expressway.

Kiddy Land   Toys, games, puzzles, dolls, action figures, Pokémon cards, and much more are packed into this immensely popular shop, usually so crowded with teenagers that it's impossible to get in the front door. It also has a large selection of gag gifts, including temporary tattoos and who knows what else. Open daily 10am to 8pm; closed the third Tuesday of each month. 6–1–9 Jingumae. ℂ 03/3409-3431. Station: Meiji-Jingumae (2 min.) or Harajuku and Omotesando (5 min.). On Omotesando Dori in Harajuku, near Oriental Bazaar.

9

Tokyo After Dark

By day, Tokyo is arguably one of the least attractive cities in the world. Come dusk, however, Tokyo comes into its own. The drabness fades, the city blossoms into a profusion of giant neon lights and paper lanterns, and its streets fill with millions of overworked Japanese out to have a good time. If you ask me, Tokyo at night is one of the craziest cities in the world, a city that never gives up and never seems to sleep. Entertainment districts are as crowded at 3am as they are at 10pm, and many places stay open until the first subways start running after 5am. Whether it's jazz, reggae, gay bars, sex shows, dance clubs, mania, or madness you're searching for, Tokyo has them all.

GETTING TO KNOW THE SCENE Tokyo has no one center of nighttime activity. There are many nightspots spread throughout the city, each with its own atmosphere, price range, and clientele. Most famous are probably **Ginza, Kabuki-cho** in Shinjuku, and **Roppongi.** Before visiting any of the locales listed in this chapter, be sure to walk around the neighborhoods and absorb the atmosphere. The streets will be crowded, the neon lights will be overwhelming, and you never know what you might discover on your own.

Although there are many bars, discos, and clubs packed with young Japanese of both sexes, nightlife in Japan for the older generations is still pretty much a man's domain, just as it has been for centuries. At the high end of this domain are the **geisha bars,** where highly trained women entertain

by playing traditional Japanese instruments, singing, and holding witty conversations—and nothing more risqué than that. Such places are located mainly in Kyoto and, generally speaking, are both outrageously expensive and closed to outsiders. As a foreigner, you'll have little opportunity to visit a geisha bar unless you're invited by a business associate.

All Japanese cities, however, have so-called **hostess bars;** in Tokyo these are concentrated in Ginza, Roppongi, Shinjuku, and Akasaka. A woman will sit at your table, talk to you, pour your drinks, listen to your problems, and boost your ego. You buy her drinks as well, which is one reason the tab can be so high. Hostess bars in various forms have been a part of Japanese society for centuries. Most of you will probably find the visit to one not worth the price, as the hostesses usually speak only Japanese, but such places provide Japanese males with sympathetic ears and the chance to escape the worlds of both work and family. Men usually have their favorite hostess bar, often a small place with just enough room for regular customers. In the more exclusive hostess bars, only those with an introduction are allowed entrance.

The most popular nightlife spots are **drinking establishments,** where most office workers, students, and expatriates go for an evening out. These places include Western-style bars, most commonly found in Roppongi, as well as Japanese-style watering holes, called *nomi-ya. Yakitori-ya,* bars that serve yakitori and other snacks, are included in this group.

Impressions
Then I saw for the first time the true beauty of Tokyo, and of all Japanese cities. They are only beautiful at night, when they become fairylands of gorgeous neon: towers and sheets and globes and rivers of neon, in stunning profusion, a wild razzle-dazzle of colors and shapes and movements, fierce and delicate, restrained and violent against the final afterglow of sunset.
—James Kirkup, *These Horned Islands* (1962)

Dancing and live-music venues are also hugely popular with young Tokyoites. At the low end of the spectrum are topless bars, sex shows, massage parlors, and porn shops, with the largest concentration of such places in Shinjuku's Kabuki-cho district.

In addition to the establishments listed in this chapter, be sure to check the restaurants listed in the inexpensive category in chapter 5 for a relatively cheap night out on the town. Many places serve as both eateries and watering holes, especially yakitori-ya.

EXTRA CHARGES & TAXES
One more thing you should be aware of is the "table charge" imposed on customers by some bars and many cocktail lounges. Included in the table charge is usually a small appetizer—maybe nuts, chips, or a vegetable; for this reason, some locales call it an *otsumami*, or snack charge. At any rate, the charge is usually between ¥300 and ¥500 ($2.70–$4.50) per person. Some establishments levy a table charge only after a certain time in the evening; others may add it only if you don't order food from the menu. If you're not sure and it matters to you, be sure to ask before you order anything. Remember, too, that a 5% consumption tax

will be added to your bill. Some higher-end establishments, especially nightclubs, hostess bars, and some dance clubs, will also add a 10% to 20% service charge.

FINDING OUT WHAT'S ON   To find out what's happening in the entertainment scene—contemporary and traditional music and theater, exhibitions in museums and galleries, films, and special events—keep an eye out for the free weekly *Metropolis,* which carries a nightlife section covering concerts and events and is available at bars, restaurants, and other venues around town. The *Japan Times* and *Daily Yomiuri* also carry entertainment sections.

GETTING TICKETS FOR EVENTS   If you're staying in one of the higher-class hotels, the concierge or guest-relations manager can usually get tickets for you. Otherwise, you can always head to the theater or hall itself. An easier way is to go through one of many ticket services available. **Ticket PIA** (© 03/5237-9999) is probably your best bet, as it has an English-language service. Another good service is provided by **CN Playguide** (© 03/5802-9999).

1 The Performing Arts

In addition to the performing-arts listings below, Tokyo has occasional shows of more avant-garde or lesser-known performing arts, including highly stylized Butoh dance performances by companies like Sankai Juku, and percussion demonstrations by Kodo drummers and other Japanese drum groups. See one of the publications listed above for complete listings.

TRADITIONAL PERFORMING ARTS

KABUKI   Probably Japan's best-known traditional theater art, Kabuki is also one of the country's most popular forms of entertainment. Visit a performance and it's easy to see why—in a word, Kabuki is fun! The plays are dramatic, the costumes are gorgeous, stage settings can be fantastic, and the themes are universal—love, revenge, and the conflict between duty and personal feelings. Probably one of the reasons Kabuki is so popular even today is that it originated centuries ago as a form of entertainment for the common people in feudal Japan, particularly the merchant class. One of Kabuki's interesting aspects is that all roles—even those depicting women—are portrayed by men.

Altogether, there are more than 300 Kabuki plays, all written before the 20th century. For a Westerner, one of the more arresting things about a Kabuki performance is the audience itself. Because this has always been entertainment for the masses, the spectators can get quite lively, adding yells of approval, guffaws, and laughter. Also contributing to the festive atmosphere are the box lunches and drinks available during intermission.

One of Japan's most prestigious theaters for Kabuki is **Kabukiza** ✸✸✸, 4-12-15 Ginza (© **03/5565-6000** for advance reservations; www.shochiku.co.jp/play/kabukiza/theater/index.html). Conveniently located within easy walking distance of the Ginza 4-chome Crossing (directly above the Higashi-Ginza Station), this impressive theater with a Momoyama-style facade (influenced by 16th-century castle architecture) is a remake of the 1924 original building. It seats almost 2,000 and features the usual Kabuki stage fittings, including a platform that can be raised above and lowered below the stage for dramatic appearances and disappearances of actors, a revolving stage, and a runway stage extending into the audience.

The Kabukiza stages about eight or nine Kabuki productions a year. Each production begins its run between the first and third of each month and runs about 25 days, with performances daily from 11 or 11:30am to about 9pm (there are no shows in Aug). Usually, two different programs are shown; matinees run from about 11 or 11:30am to 4pm, and evening performances run from about 4:30 or 5pm to about 9pm. It's considered perfectly okay to come for only part of a performance.

Of course, you won't be able to understand what's being said, but that doesn't matter; the productions themselves are great entertainment. For an outline of the plot, you can purchase an **English-language program,** which costs ¥1,000 ($8.35); you also can rent **English-language earphones** for ¥650 ($5.40), plus a ¥1,000 ($8.35) refundable deposit—these provide a running commentary on the story, music, actors, stage properties, and other aspects of Kabuki. Buying a program or renting earphones will add immensely to your enjoyment of the play.

Tickets generally range from ¥2,500 to ¥16,800 ($21–$140), depending on the program and seat location. Advance tickets can be purchased at the **Advance Ticket Office** to the right side of Kabukiza's main entrance from 10am to 6pm. You may also make advance reservations by phone (same-day bookings are not accepted). Otherwise, tickets for each day's performance are placed on sale 1 hour before the start of each performance.

If you don't have time for an entire performance or you wish to view Kabuki only for a short while, it's possible to watch only one act; tickets costing only ¥600 to ¥1,000 ($5–$8.35) are available depending on the time of day and length of the show. One-acts generally last about 1 or 1½ hours; note that English-language earphones are not available here, but you can buy an English-language program. Note also that seats are a bit far from the stage, on the very top two rows of the theater (on the 4th floor; there is no elevator). On the other hand, I have seen several acts this way, sometimes simply dropping by when I'm in the area; it's a marvelous mid-day break from the rigors of shopping. These tickets, sold at the smaller entrance to the left of the main entrance, are available on a first-come, first-served basis and go on sale 20 minutes prior to each act. If you liked the act so much that you wish to remain for the next one, it's possible to do so if the act is not sold out; tickets in these cases are usually available on the fourth floor.

If you're in Tokyo in August, you can usually see Kabuki at the **National Theater of Japan (Kokuritsu Gekijo)**, 4–1 Hayabusacho, Chiyoda-ku (© 03/3265-7411; station: Hanzomon, 6 min.). Kabuki is scheduled here throughout the year except during May, September, and December, when Bunraku (see below) is being staged instead. Matinees usually begin at noon, and evening performances at 5pm. Most tickets range from about ¥1,500 to ¥3,800 ($13–$32).

NOH   Whereas Kabuki developed as a form of entertainment for the masses, Noh was a much more traditional and aristocratic form of theater. In contrast to Kabuki's extroverted liveliness, Noh is very calculated and restrained. The oldest form of theater in Japan, it has changed very little in the past 600 years. The language is so archaic that today the Japanese cannot understand it at all, which explains in part why Noh does not have the popularity that Kabuki does.

As in Kabuki, all the performers are men. Altogether there are about 240 Noh plays, often concerned with supernatural beings, beautiful women, mentally confused and tormented people, or tragic-heroic epics.

Because the action is slow, sitting through an entire performance can be quite tedious unless you are particularly interested in Noh dance and music. In addition, most Noh plays do not have English translations. You may want to drop in for just a short while. Definitely worth seeing, however, are the short comic reliefs, called *kyogen,* that make fun of life in the 1600s and are performed between Noh dramas.

Noh is performed at a number of locations in Tokyo, with tickets ranging from about ¥2,300 to ¥6,000 ($19–$50). Performances are usually in the early afternoon at 1pm or in the late afternoon at 5 or 6:30pm; check the *Japan Times* or *Daily Yomiuri* for exact times. The **National Noh Theater (Kokuritsu Nohgakudo)**, 4–18–1 Sendagaya, Shibuya-ku (© 03/3423-1331; station: Sendagaya, 5 min.), is Tokyo's most famous. Other Noh theaters worth checking out are **Hosho Nohgakudo,** 1–5–9 Hongo, Bunkyo-ku (© 03/3811-4843; station: Suidobashi, 5 min.); **Kanze Nohgakudo,** 1–16–4 Shoto, Shibuya-ku (© 03/3469-5241; station: Shibuya, 10 min.); **Kita Nohgakudo,** 4–6–9 Kami-Osaki, Shinagawa-ku (© 03/3491-8813; station: JR Meguro, 10 min.); and **Tessenkai Nohgaku-do Kenshujo,** 4–21–29 Minami Aoyama, Minato-ku (© 03/3401-2285; station: Omotesando, exit A4, 5 min.).

BUNRAKU   Bunraku is traditional Japanese puppet theater, but contrary to what you might expect, the dramas are for adults, with themes centering on love, revenge, sacrifice, and suicide.

Popular in Japan since the 17th century, Bunraku is fascinating to watch because the puppeteers, dressed in black, are always right on stage with their puppets. They're wonderfully skilled at making the puppets seem like living beings. It usually takes three puppeteers to work one puppet, which is about three-quarters human size: One puppeteer is responsible for movement of the puppet's head, facial expressions, and right arm and hand; another operates the puppet's left arm and hand; the third moves its legs. A narrator recites the story and speaks all the parts, accompanied by the *samisen,* a traditional three-stringed Japanese instrument.

Although the main Bunraku theater in Japan is in Osaka, the **National Theatre of Japan (Kokuritsu Gekijo)** in Tokyo, 4–1 Hayabusacho, Chiyoda-ku (© 03/ 3265-7411; station: Hanzomon, 6 min.), stages about three Bunraku plays a year—in May, September, and December. There are usually two to three performances daily, at 11am, 2:30pm, and 6pm, with tickets averaging ¥5,000 to ¥6,000 ($42–$50). Earphones with English-language explanations are available for ¥650 ($5.40).

CONTEMPORARY PERFORMING ARTS

WESTERN CLASSICAL MUSIC   Among the best-known orchestras in Tokyo are the Tokyo Philharmonic Orchestra (Tokyo Phil Jimukyoku; © 03/ 3369-1661), Japan Philharmonic Symphony (Nihon Phil; © 03/5378-5911), Tokyo City Philharmonic Orchestra (Tokyo City Phil; © 03/3822-0727), and NHK Philharmonic Orchestra (NHK Phil; © 03/3465-1780), founded in 1926. They play in various theaters throughout Tokyo, with the majority of performances in Suntory Hall in Akasaka, Bunkamura Orchard Hall in Shibuya, or the Tokyo Geijutsu Gekijo in Ikebukuro. Since the schedule varies, it's best to call the orchestra directly or check the *Japan Times* or *Daily Yomiuri* to see whether there's a current performance. Tickets generally start at ¥3,000 or ¥4,000 ($25–$33).

TAKARAZUKA KAGEKIDAN   This world-famous, all-female troupe stages elaborate musical revues with dancing, singing, and gorgeous costumes. Performances range from Japanese versions of Broadway hits to original Japanese works based on local legends. The first Takarazuka troupe, formed in 1912 at a resort near Osaka, gained instant notoriety because all its performers were women, in contrast to the all-male Kabuki. When I went to see this troupe perform, I was surprised to find that the audience also consisted almost exclusively of women; indeed, the troupe has an almost cultlike following.

Performances, with story synopses available in English, are generally held in March, April, July, August, November, and December, and sometimes in June, at **Tokyo Takarazuka Gekijo,** 1–1–3 Yurakucho (© 03/5251-2001; station: Hibiya, 1 min.). Tickets, available at the box office or through **Ticket Pia** (© 03/ 5237-9999), generally range from about ¥3,500 to ¥10,000 ($29–$83).

KINGYO ✿   This sophisticated nightclub stages one of the most high-energy, visually charged acts I've ever seen—nonstop action of ascending and receding stages and stairs, fast-paced choreography, elaborate costumes, and loud music. There are a few female dancers, but most of the dancers are males assuming female parts, just like in Kabuki. In fact, many of the performances center on traditional Japanese themes with traditional dress and kimono, but the shows take place in a very technically sophisticated setting. There are also satires: One past performance included a piece on Microsoft vs. Apple; another featured aliens from outer space—great fun. It's located in the heart of the Roppongi nightlife district at 3–14–17 Roppongi (© 03/3478-3000; station: Roppongi, 4 min.), near the Roppongi cemetery (from Roppongi Crossing, walk toward Tokyo Tower on Gaien-Higashi Dori and turn left at Freshness Burger). Cover is ¥4,000 ($33) for daily shows at 7:30 and 10pm, with additional shows Friday and Saturday at 1:20am for only ¥2,000 ($17). Reservations are advised, as this is a very popular show.

2 The Club & Music Scene

THE MAJOR ENTERTAINMENT DISTRICTS

GINZA   A chic and expensive shopping area by day, Ginza transforms itself into a dazzling entertainment district of restaurants, bars, and first-grade hostess bars at night. It's the most sophisticated of Tokyo's nightlife districts and also one of the most expensive. Almost all the Japanese businessmen you see out carousing in Ginza are paying by expense account; the prices are ridiculously high.

Since I'm not wealthy, I prefer Shinjuku and Roppongi. However, because Ginza does have some fabulous restaurants and several hotels, I've included reasonably priced recommendations for a drink in the area if you happen to find yourself here after dinner. The cheapest way to absorb the atmosphere in Ginza is to wander through it, particularly around Namiki Dori, Suzuran Dori, and their side streets. The "Nightlife & Where to Stay & Dine in Ginza & Hibiya" map on p. 72 will help you locate the Ginza clubs and bars mentioned in this chapter.

SHINJUKU   Northeast of Shinjuku Station is an area called **Kabuki-cho,** which undoubtedly has the craziest nightlife in all of Tokyo, with block after block of strip joints, massage parlors, pornography shops, peep shows, bars, restaurants and, as the night wears on, lots of drunk revelers. A world of its own, it's sleazy, chaotic, crowded, vibrant, and fairly safe. Despite its name, Shinjuku's primary night hot spot has nothing to do with Kabuki, though at one time there was a plan to bring culture to the area by introducing a Kabuki theater. The plan never materialized, but the name stuck. Although Kabuki-cho was always the domain of salarymen out on the town, in recent years young Japanese, including college-age men and women, have claimed parts of it as their own and now outnumber the businessmen; the result is that there are a growing number of inexpensive drinking and live-music venues well worth a visit. The "Nightlife & Where to Stay & Dine in Shinjuku" map on p. 76 will help you locate the Shinjuku clubs and bars mentioned in this chapter.

To the east of Kabuki-cho, just west of Hanazono Shrine, is a smaller district called **Goruden Gai,** which is "Golden Guy" mispronounced. It's a warren of tiny alleyways leading past even tinier bars, each consisting of just a counter and a few chairs. Generally closed to outsiders, these closet-sized bars cater to regular customers. On hot summer evenings, the mama-san of these bars sit outside on stools and fan themselves, soft red light melting out of the open doorways. Things aren't as they appear, however. These aren't brothels—they're simply bars, and the "mama"-san are as likely to be men as women. Although many thought Goruden Gai would succumb to land-hungry developers in the 1980s, the economic recession has brought a stay of execution. In fact, in recent years Goruden Gai has experienced a revival, with approximately 200 tiny drinking dens lining the tiny streets. Still, it occupies such expensive land that I still fear for the life of this tiny enclave, one of Tokyo's most fascinating.

Even farther east is **Shinjuku 2–chome** (called Ni-chome; pronounced "knee-chomay"), officially recognized as the gay-bar district of Shinjuku. Its lively street scene of mostly gays and some straights of all ages (but mostly young) make this one of Tokyo's most vibrant nightlife districts. It's here that I was once taken to a host bar featuring young men in crotchless pants. The clientele included both gay men and groups of young, giggling office girls. That place has since closed down, but Shinjuku is riddled with other spots bordering on the absurd.

The best thing to do in Shinjuku is simply wander. In the glow of neon light, you'll pass everything from smoke-filled restaurants to hawkers trying to get you to step inside so they can part you from your money. If you're looking for strip joints, topless or bottomless coffee shops, peep shows, or porn, I leave you to your own devices, but you certainly won't have any problems finding them. In Kabuki-cho alone, there are an estimated 200 sex businesses in operation, including bathhouses where women are available for sex, usually at a cost of around ¥30,000 ($250). Although prostitution is illegal in Japan, everyone seems to ignore what goes on behind closed doors. Just be sure you know what you are getting into; your bill may add up to much more than you figured.

A word of **warning** for women traveling alone: Forgo the experience of Shinjuku. The streets are crowded and therefore relatively safe, but you may not feel comfortable with so many inebriated men stumbling around. If there are two of you, however, go for it. I took my mother to Kabuki-cho for a spin around the neon, and we escaped relatively unscathed. You're also fine walking alone to any of this guidebook's recommended restaurants.

ROPPONGI   To Tokyo's younger crowd, Roppongi is the city's most fashionable place to hang out. It's also a favorite with the foreign community, including models, business types, and English teachers. Roppongi has more than its fair share of live-music houses, restaurants, discos, expatriate bars, and pubs. Some Tokyoites complain that Roppongi is too crowded, too crass, and too commercialized (and has too many foreigners), but for the casual visitor I think Roppongi offers an excellent opportunity to see what's new and hot in the capital city and is easy to navigate because nightlife activity is so concentrated.

The center of Roppongi is **Roppongi Crossing** (the intersection of Roppongi Dori and Gaien-Higashi Dori), at the corner of which sits the garishly pink Almond Coffee Shop. The shop has mediocre coffee and desserts at inflated prices, but the sidewalk in front is the number-one meeting spot in Roppongi.

If you need directions, there's a conveniently located *koban* (police box) catty-corner from the Almond Coffee Shop and next to the Bank of Tokyo-Mitsubishi. It has a big outdoor map of the Roppongi area showing the address system, and someone is always there to help. The "Nightlife & Where to Stay & Dine in Roppongi" map on p. 143 will help you locate the Roppongi clubs and bars mentioned in this chapter.

If the buzz of Roppongi is too much, a quieter, saner alternative is neighboring **Nishi-Azabu,** which has restaurants and bars catering to both Japanese and foreigners. The center of Nishi-Azabu is the next big crossroads, Nishi-Azabu Crossing (the intersection of Roppongi Dori and Gaien-Nishi Dori). Nishi

A Guide to Tokyo Maps

Once you've chosen a nightlife spot that appeals to you, you can locate it using the following neighborhood maps:

- To locate bars and clubs in **Asakusa**, see map on p. 89.
- To locate bars and clubs in **Shinjuku**, see map on p. 76.
- To locate bars and clubs in **Harajuku**, see map on p. 133.
- To locate bars and clubs in **Roppongi**, see map on p. 143.
- To locate bars and clubs in **Akasaka**, see map on p. 83.

Azabu is about a 10-minute walk from Roppongi Station, past Roppongi Hills in the direction of Shibuya.

OTHER HOT SPOTS   Not quite as sophisticated as Ginza, **Akasaka** nonetheless has its share of exclusive geisha and hostess bars, hidden away behind forbidding walls and exquisite courtyards. More accessible are the many drinking bars, restaurants, and inexpensive holes-in-the-wall. Popular with both executive tycoons and ordinary office workers as well as foreigners staying in one of Akasaka's many hotels, this district stretches from the Akasaka-mitsuke subway station along three narrow streets, called Hitotsugi, Misuji, and Tamachi, all the way to the Akasaka station. In the past decade, many Koreans have opened restaurants in Akasaka, earning it the nickname "Little Korea." For orientation purposes, stop by the *koban* (police box) at the huge intersection of Aoyama Dori and Sotobori Dori at Akasaka-mitsuke station. The "Nightlife & Where to Stay & Dine in Akasaka" map on p. 83 will help you locate the Akasaka spots mentioned in this chapter.

One of the most popular districts for young Japanese by day, **Harajuku** doesn't have much of a nightlife district because of city zoning laws. A few places scattered through the area, however, are good alternatives if you don't like the crowds or the commercialism of Tokyo's more famous nightlife districts. There are also a fair number of sidewalk cafes open late into the night.

Shibuya's **Shibuya Center Gai,** a pedestrian lane just a minute's walk from the Hachiko exit of Shibuya Station (look for the pedestrian lane with the steel arch), is popular with young Japanese for its whirl of inexpensive restaurants, open-fronted shops, bars, fast-food joints, and pachinko parlors. **Ebisu** also has a few very popular expatriate bars.

LIVE MUSIC

The live-music scene exploded in the 1990s and is now spread throughout the metropolis. In addition to the dedicated venues below, several bars offer live music many nights of the week, including Warrior Celt, What the Dickens!, and Music Pub Gabi Gabi (see "The Bar Scene," later in this chapter).

Bauhaus   This small club has a great house band that plays mostly 1970s and 1980s British and American hard rock (Deep Purple, ZZ Top, Aerosmith, Queen, the Rolling Stones, Led Zeppelin), with five sets beginning at 8pm. The band puts on quite a show—a bit raunchy at times but very polished. Hours are Monday to Saturday 7pm to 1am. Reine Roppongi, 2nd floor, 5–3–4 Roppongi. © 03/3403-0092. Cover ¥2,700 ($23). Station: Roppongi (3 min.). From Roppongi Crossing, walk toward Tokyo Tower on Gaien-Higashi Dori and turn right at McDonald's.

Birdland   Down to earth and featuring good jazz (with an emphasis on 1940s swing) performed by Japanese musicians, Birdland has been a welcome refuge from Roppongi's madding crowd for more than a quarter of a century. It's small and cozy with candles and soft lighting and attracts an older, knowledgeable, and appreciative crowd. Incidentally, the official cover price is ¥3,500 ($29), but management told me if you show your *Frommer's* guide, you can get in for ¥1,500 ($13). Hours are Monday to Saturday 6pm to midnight (music begins at 7pm). Square Building (in the basement), 3–10–3 Roppongi. © 03/3478-3456. Cover ¥1,500 ($13) plus ¥900 ($7.50) drink minimum and 15% service charge. Station: Roppongi (2 min.). From Roppongi Crossing, walk toward Tokyo Tower on Gaien-Higashi Dori and take the 1st left.

Blue Note   Tokyo's most expensive, elegant jazz venue is cousin to the famous Blue Note in New York and has proven so popular it outgrew its original 1988 location and moved into this larger location 10 years later. Still, with 300 seats, it follows the frustrating practice of selling tickets good for only one set (there are two sets nightly). The musicians are top-notch; Oscar Peterson, Sarah Vaughan, Tony Bennett, David Sanborn, and the Milt Jackson Quartet have all performed here. Hours are Monday to Saturday 5:30pm to 1am, with shows at 7 and 9:30pm. 6–3–16 Minami Aoyama. ✆ **03/5485-0088.** Cover ¥7,000 – ¥8,000 ($58–$67) for most performances, more for top names. Station: Omotesando (8 min.). Off Kotto Dori.

Body & Soul   This low-ceilinged, tiny but cozy basement club with only a few tables and a long bar gives everyone a good view of its mostly jazz performances by Japanese and foreign musicians. Hours are Monday to Saturday 7pm to midnight. 6–13–9 Minami Aoyama. ✆ **03/5466-3348.** Cover ¥3,500 ($29) and up. Station: Omotesando (7 min.). Off Kotto Dori, near Nobu.

Cavern Club   If you know your Beatles history, you'll know Cavern is the name of the Liverpool club where the Fab Four got their start. The Tokyo club features Beatles memorabilia and house bands performing Beatles music exclusively and very convincingly at that. Close your eyes—and you'll swear you're listening to the real thing. Extremely popular with both Japanese and foreigners, it's packed on weekends—expect long lines. Reservations are taken but are good for only two sets—then you have to leave. Hours are Monday to Saturday 6pm to 2:30am; Sunday and holidays 6pm to midnight. 5–3–2 Roppongi. ✆ **03/3405-5207.** Cover ¥1,500 ($13), plus a 1 drink minimum and 10% service charge. Station: Roppongi (4 min.). Take the side street going downhill on the left side of Almond Coffee Shop and then take the 1st left; the club will be on the right.

Country House *(Value)*   This country-music spot is a fun place to spend an evening in Akasaka. The owner, Mr. Hirao, plays steel guitar in the house band and is always happy to see foreigners walk through the doors. There's a cover charge, but a better deal is the optional ¥4,000 ($33) charge (Japanese pay more), which includes cover; a choice of a main dish from a menu that includes pizza, Southern fried chicken, pasta, and salad; and all the beer or cocktails you can consume in a 2-hour period. And if seeing Tokyoites dressed as cowboys isn't a bit surreal, I don't know what is. Hours are Monday to Saturday 6pm to midnight; closed holidays. Live music 7:30 to 11pm. 5–1–4 Akasaka. ✆ **03/3583-9287.** Cover for foreigners ¥1,000 ($8.35). Station: Akasaka (TBS exit, 1 min.). On Hitotsugi Dori.

Crocodile   Popular with a young Japanese crowd, the eclectic Crocodile describes itself as a casual rock 'n roll club, with live bands ranging from rock and blues to jazz-fusion, reggae, soul, experimental, and even country and salsa; it's a good place to check out new Japanese bands. It has an interesting interior and a good, laid-back atmosphere; depending on the music, the clientele ranges from Japanese with bleached-blond hair and earrings to a grunge and even middle-aged crowd. Hours are daily 6pm to 2am; music starts at 8pm. 6–18–8 Jingumae, on Meiji Dori between Harajuku and Shibuya. ✆ **03/3499-5205.** Cover ¥2,000 – ¥3,000 ($17–$25), occasionally more for big acts. Station: Meiji-Jingumae or Shibuya (8 min.).

Liquid Room   This is one of Tokyo's longest-running live venues, home to some of the hottest Japanese and international bands; DJs hold court when there's no live music. As seating is very limited, most people come to keep moving, making this a good place to join the dancing crowd grooving to Tokyo's best sound system. Open most (but not all) nights from about 6pm. Humax Pavilion, 7th floor, 1–20–1 Kabuki-cho. ✆ **03/3200-6831.** Cover ¥3,000 – ¥5,000 ($25–$42) for most acts. Station: Shinjuku (east exit, 10 min.). Across from Koma Stadium's northwest side.

New York Bar   This is one of Tokyo's most sophisticated venues, boasting Manhattan-style jazz and breathtaking views of glittering west Shinjuku. Unfortunately, it's also one of the city's smallest. Consider coming for dinner in the adjacent **New York Grill** (p. 128); it costs a small fortune, but you'll save the cost of the cover. Hours are daily from 5pm, with live music 8pm to midnight. Park Hyatt Hotel, 52nd floor, 3–7–1–2 Nishi-Shinjuku. ✆ 03/5322-1234. Cover ¥2,000 ($17). Station: Shinjuku (13 min.), Hatsudai on the Keio Line (7 min.), or Tochomae (8 min.).

Roppongi Pit Inn   Another well-known music house, this no-frills joint has been catering to a younger crowd of jazz enthusiasts for 25 years. It boasts some of the finest in native and imported jazz, as well as fusion and jazz rock. Hours are daily from 6:30pm, with shows at about 7:30pm. 3–17–7 Roppongi (in the basement). ✆ 03/3585-1063. Cover ¥3,000 – ¥4,000 ($25–$33), including 1 drink. Station: Roppongi (7 min.).

Ruby Room   I've seen living rooms larger than this second-floor venue, home to local acts, open mike on Tuesdays, house and techno DJs, and other events. The crowd depends on the music, but since there's no room to move, people just dance where they are, and the band is close, close, close—any closer and you'd be in the drummer's lap. Hours are daily from 7pm to 5am. 2–25–17 Dogenzaka, Shibuya-ku. ✆ 03/3780-3022. Cover ¥1,000 ($8.35) Fri–Sat only, including 1 drink. Station: Shibuya (2 min.). Take the Hachiko exit to Dogenzaka and turn right at Mos.

Shinjuku Pit Inn   This is one of Tokyo's most famous and longest-running jazz, fusion, and blues clubs, featuring both Japanese and foreign musicians. There are two programs daily—at 2:30 and 7:30pm—making it a great place to stop for a bit of music in the middle of the day. Since only a few snacks (such as potato chips and sandwiches) are available, eat before you come. 2–12–4 Shinjuku, southeast of the Yasukuni Dori/Meiji Dori intersection. ✆ 03/3354-2024. Cover from ¥1,300 ($11), including 1 drink, for the 2:30pm show (¥2,500/$21 weekends and holidays), ¥3,000 – ¥4,000 ($25–$33) for the evening shows, including 1 drink. Station: Shinjuku Sanchome (4 min.).

STB 139   Popular with well-heeled Japanese, this classy venue in a modern brick building offers a wide range of musical entertainment, from jazz and classical to fusion, Latin, nostalgia, and Japanese pop, performed mostly by Japanese talent. Doors usually open at 6pm, and shows start at 7:30 or 8pm. Most people come here to dine as well, from a menu that includes seafood, pasta, and lighter fare. Hours are daily 6 to 11pm. 6–7–11 Roppongi. ✆ 03/5474-0139. Cover ¥4,000 – ¥6,000 ($33–$50). Station: Roppongi (3 min.). From Roppongi Crossing, take the road downhill from the left side of Almond Coffee Shop; it will be on the right.

DANCE CLUBS & DISCOS

Discos lost popularity after their 1980s heyday, but with the rise of almost cult-figure DJs, dance clubs have witnessed a resurgence in recent years, with Roppongi still boasting more dance clubs than anywhere else in the city. Sometimes the set cover charge includes drinks and occasionally even food, which makes for an inexpensive way to spend an evening. Keep in mind, however, that prices are usually higher on weekends and are sometimes higher for men than for women. Although discos are required by law to close at midnight, many of them ignore the rule and stay open until dawn.

Code   Known for its frequent trance and techno events, Kabuki-cho's largest club brings in both Japanese and foreign DJs to keep things hopping on its massive dance floor. Once a month (look for Code's leaflets distributed around town), it's for men only. Daily 8pm to midnight. Shinjuku Toho-Kaikan, 4th floor,

1–19–2 Kabuki-cho. ☎ 03/3209-0702. Depending on the event, cover is ¥3,000–¥3,500 ($25–$29), including 2 drinks. Station: Shinjuku (east exit, 10 min.). Beside Koma Stadium, a Shinjuku landmark.

Kento's   Kento's was one of the first places to open when the wave of 1950s nostalgia hit Japan in the 1980s; it has even been credited with creating the craze. This is the place to come to if you feel like dancing the night away to tunes of the 1950s and 1960s played by live bands. Although there's hardly room to dance, that doesn't stop the largely over-30 Japanese audience from twisting in the aisles to the tunes of Elvis, Little Richard, The Temptations, Chuck Berry, and others. Hours are Monday to Saturday from 6pm to 2:30am; Sunday and holidays from 6 to 11:30pm. Daini Reine Building, 5–3–1 Roppongi. ☎ 03/3401-5755. (Also at 6–7–12 Ginza; ☎ 03/3572-9161.) Cover ¥1,000 ($8.35) for females, ¥1,500 ($13) for males, plus 10% service charge and 1 drink minimum. Station: Roppongi (4 min.). Take the side street going downhill on the left side of Almond Coffee Shop and then take the 1st left; the club will be on the right.

Lexington Queen   Opened in 1980, Lexington Queen has been the reigning queen of disco in Tokyo for more than 2 decades. In fact, it's so much smaller than the newer, glitzier discos, it seems almost quaint. Its list of past guests reads like a Who's Who of foreign movie and rock stars to have visited Tokyo, from Rod Stewart to Stephen Dorff to Dustin Hoffman to Marilyn Manson; one night when I was there, Duran Duran walked in. This is the best place to be on Halloween and New Year's, if you can stand the crowds. Women are admitted free Monday and Thursday. Daily 8pm to 5am. Daisan Goto Bldg., 3–13–14 Roppongi. ☎ 03/3401-1661. Cover ¥3,000 ($25) for women, ¥4,000 ($33) for men, including free drinks. Station: Roppongi (3 min.). From Roppongi Crossing, walk toward Tokyo Tower on Gaien-Higashi Dori and take the 2nd left.

Maniac Love   This tiny basement venue has none of the glitz favored by some Tokyo discos; it relies instead on a great sound system to attract a vibrant young crowd. In fact, the music is so loud that you can feel the beat pulsing through your body, commanding you to dance. Founded more than 20 years ago—and older than many of its customers—this is a place with soul. If you get here before 11pm, cover is only ¥1,000 ($8.35). And if you come at 5am Saturday and Sunday morning, you pay a ¥1,000 ($8.35) cover, which includes free coffee (you'll probably need it by then). Hours are Sunday, Monday, and Thursday 10pm to 5am, Friday and Saturday 10pm to 10am. Closed some Sundays and Mondays. 5–10–6 Minami Aoyama. ☎ 03/3406-1166. Cover ¥2,000 ($17) weekdays, ¥2,500 ($21) Fri–Sat, including 1 drink. Station: Omotesando (2 min.). From Aoyama Dori, take the street opposite and leading away from Kinokuniya grocery store and turn right at the 1st alley; it's opposite the "Wood You Like Company" shop (there's no sign).

Milk   This split-level, psychedelic basement dance club packs 'em in with loud, loud, loud hard rock and alternative music. On Thursday, Friday, and Saturday nights, it features live bands from 10:30pm. In the same building is the very popular **What the Dickens!** expat bar (see later in this chapter). Open daily 8 or 9pm to 4 or 5am. 1–13–3 Ebisu Nishi. ☎ 03/5458-2826. Cover usually ¥2,500–¥3,000 ($21–$25), including 1 drink. Station: Ebisu (west exit, 2 min.). Take the side street between Wendy's and KFC; Milk will be on your left.

Velfarre   If you're looking for the disco scene, search no further. This huge, plush venue—run by a record group famous for its Eurobeat recordings—claims to be Japan's largest disco and has all the latest technical gadgetry to match. Tokyo's disco of the moment, it attracts young Japanese dressed to kill (there's even a dress code: smart casual). The staff is stylishly dressed, too. The dance floor is absolutely gigantic; stage dancers help set the pace. Leading DJs from Tokyo and abroad play everything from pop and retro to techno, hard house, and—what else?—Eurobeat. *Note:* Unlike other discos, this one closes promptly at 1am. Hours are Thursday to Sunday 7pm to 1am. 7–14–22 Roppongi. ℰ 03/3402-8000. Cover ¥3,000 ($25), including 2 drinks. Station: Roppongi (3 min.). From Roppongi Crossing, take the 1st left after Ibis Hotel.

Xanadu   This classy basement club in Shibuya attracts an international, 20-something crowd, with a young international staff to match. It offers a variety of DJ styles (house, trance, hip hop, progressive techno) and events. Ladies get in free on nights before holidays. On Fridays from 7 to 10pm, the music is 1970s and 1980s, with a special cover price of ¥2,000 ($17) that includes all the drinks you can consume. Hours are Sunday, Wednesday, and Thursday from 7pm to 2am; Friday and Saturday from 7pm to 5am. Fhontis Building, basement. 2–23–12 Dogenzaka. ℰ 03/5489-3750. Cover ¥500 ($4.15) Sun and Wed–Thurs; ¥1,000 ($8.35) Fri–Sat, including 1 drink for men and 2 drinks for women. Station: Shibuya (Hachiko exit, 5 min.). Across from Tokyu Honten department store.

Yellow   Closed on and off by the boys in blue during its infant rebellious years, this is the closest thing Tokyo has to a true underground disco, staging the city's most progressive events from Butoh performances (a modern minimalist form of dance) to gay nights. Guest DJs from abroad make appearances, playing a variety of music from salsa and reggae to hip-hop, soul, and techno. Only those in the know are supposed to come here, so there's no sign—just a blank, yellow neon square. Hours are daily 10pm to 2 or 4am; it's occasionally closed for private functions, so call ahead. 1–10–11 Nishi-Azabu. ℰ 03/3479-0690. Cover ¥3,000 – ¥3,500 ($25–$29) including 1 or 2 drinks, depending on the DJ and the event. Station: Roppongi (10 min.). From Roppongi Crossing, head toward Shibuya on Roppongi Dori. Turn right at the next-to-last street before Gaien-Nishi Dori; it's on the 2nd block on the right.

3 The Bar Scene

GINZA

See the map on p. 72 for the bars listed in this section.

Atariya   With its typical Japanese setting, this is a convivial place for an evening of yakitori and beer, made easy by an English-language menu. Hours are Monday to Saturday from 4:30 to 11pm. 3–5–17 Ginza. ℰ 03/3564-0045. Station: Ginza (3 min.). Near Ginza 4–chome Crossing; take the small side street that runs behind the Wako department store; it will be on the right in the 2nd block.

Ginza Sapporo Lion   Sapporo beer is the draw at this large beer hall with its mock Gothic ceiling and faux German decor. A large display of plastic foods and an English-language menu help you choose from snacks ranging from yakitori to sausage and spaghetti. The place is popular with older Japanese. Hours are Monday to Saturday from 11:30am to 11pm, Sunday and holidays from 11:30am to 10:30pm. 7–9–20 Ginza. ℰ 03/3571-2590. Station: Ginza (3 min.). On Chuo Dori not far from the Matsuzakaya department store.

68 **Lupin** *Finds*   You couldn't find a more subdued place than this tiny basement bar. First opened back in 1928 and little changed over the decades, it features a long wooden bar and booths. Even the staff looks like they've been here since it opened. Because no music is ever played here, it's a great place for conversation. Very civilized. There's a table charge of ¥500 ($4.50) per person, plus

a ¥200 ($1.65) snack charge. Hours are Tuesday to Saturday from 5 to 11pm. 5–5–11 Ginza. ℂ 03/3571-0750. Station: Ginza (2 min.). In a tiny alley behind Ketel, a German restaurant on Namiki Dori.

Nanbantei   Foreigners are cheerfully welcomed at this chain of yakitori-ya, which combines the modern with the traditional in its decor. Its English-language menu lists skewers of pork with asparagus, Japanese mushrooms, large shrimp, quail eggs, gingko nuts, chicken meatballs, and many other yakitori, including yakitori set courses starting at ¥3,000 ($25). A set course for ladies only costs ¥2,500 ($21). Open daily 5 to 10pm. 5–6–6 Ginza. ℂ 03/3571-5700. Station: Ginza (2 min.). On Suzuran Dor not far from Harumi Dori.

Old Imperial   This is the Imperial Hotel's tribute to its original architect, Frank Lloyd Wright, and is the only place in the hotel that contains Wright originals—the Art Deco terra-cotta wall behind the bar, the mural, and the small desk at the entrance. Its clubby atmosphere, low lighting, and comfortable chairs and tables (copies of Wright originals) make it perfect for a quiet drink. Try the Mount Fuji, the bar's own creation: dry gin, lemon juice, pineapple juice, egg white, and maraschino cherry. Hours are daily 11:30am to midnight. Imperial Hotel, 1–1–1 Uchisaiwai-cho. ℂ 03/3504-1111. Station: Hibiya (1 min.).

ASAKUSA
See the map on p. 89 for the bars listed in this section.

Ichimon   Ichimon takes its name from *mon*, which was the lowest piece of currency used by common people during the Edo Period. *Ichimon* means "one mon." This quirky place, specializing in sake, has a unique system whereby each customer purchases mon, issued here in wooden tokens at the rate of ¥100 (85¢) for each mon; the tokens are then used to pay for your sake, meal, and ¥500 ($4.15) snack charge. Plan on exchanging about ¥4,000 to ¥5,000 ($33–$42) into mon; mon you don't use can be exchanged for the real thing when you leave. An English-language menu lists sashimi, *gyoza* (fried dumplings), *shumai* (steamed dumplings), *nikujagu* (potato and beef stew), fugu (blowfish), fried fish, fried alligator, noodles, and other fare. This is a cozy place, decorated like an old farmhouse with wooden beams, shoji screens, and antiques. Hours are daily 6 to 11pm; closed on holidays. 3–12–6 Asakusa. ℂ 03/3875-6800. Station: Tawaramachi (10 min.) or Asakusa (15 min.). Just northeast of the Kokusai Dori/Kototoi Dori intersection; from the intersection, walk 1 block north on Kokusai Dori and turn right; it's almost immediately on your right, with a big sake barrel above its door.

Sky Room *(Value)*   This is a great—albeit simple—place for an inexpensive drink after an active day in historic Asakusa. The Asahi Beer Tower, which sits next to the distinctive building with the golden hops perched on top, belongs to the Asahi Beer company; it's thought to represent a mug of foaming beer. The plain, cafeteria-style bar, perched at the top of the building in the foam next to **La Ranarita** Azumabashi(see chapter 5), offers great views as well as different kinds of Asahi beer, wine, coffee, tea, and cider, all priced at only ¥500 ($4.15). With seating for only 26 at a window-side counter, it can be crowded on weekends. Open daily 10am to 9pm. Asahi Beer Tower, 22nd floor, 1–23–1 Azumabashi. ℂ 03/5608-5277. Station: Asakusa (4 min.). On the opposite side of the Sumida River from Sensoji Temple.

UENO
Hard Rock Cafe   Located in an old part of JR Ueno Station, this chain cafe has the usual rock 'n' roll memorabilia, American food, and loud music. Open daily 11am to 11pm. 7–1–1 Ueno. ℂ 03/5826-5821. Station: JR Ueno (1 min.).

Warrior Celt This third-floor pub is somewhat of a novelty in Ueno, especially for its nightly happy hour until 7pm (when all drinks are priced at just ¥500/$4.15) and for its (usually) free live music Tuesday, Friday, and Saturday nights. On Thursdays, beer costs just ¥500 ($4.15) for ladies. With its international, friendly mix, it's a good place to while away some hours if you find yourself in Ueno after the museums close. Open Tuesday to Saturday 5pm to 5am; Sunday to Monday 5pm to midnight. 6–9–22 Ueno. ✆ 03/3836-8588. Station: Ueno (Hirokoji exit, 5 min.). 1 block east of the Yamanote elevated train tracks, just a stone's throw from the Ameya Yokocho market. From Ueno Station, take the street to the right of OICity department store.

SHINJUKU

See the map on p. 76 for the bars listed in this section.

Christon Cafe This has to be one of the weirdest theme bars I've seen in Tokyo. Decorated like a church with its stained-glass windows, vaulted ceiling, organ music, crosses, and statue of Jesus, it's packed to the rafters despite the ¥300 ($2.50) cover charge. What to order? A Bloody Mary, of course. Hours are daily 5pm to 5am. Oriental Wave Building, 8th floor, 5–17–13 Shinjuku. ✆ 03/5287-2426. Station: Shinjuku Sanchome (5 min.). In east Shinjuku, on Yasukuni Dori just west of Hanazono Shrine.

Dubliners' Irish Pub Attracting expats and locals alike—mostly in their 30s and 40s—is this chain Irish bar, especially for its weekday happy hour until 7pm. A menu lists such perennial favorites as Irish stew, fish and chips, and beef-and-Guinness pie. Open Monday to Saturday noon to 1am; Sunday noon to 11pm. 3–28–9 Shinjuku. ✆ 03/3352-6606. Station: Shinjuku (east exit, 3 min). In east Shinjuku, behind Mitsukoshi department store above Sapporo Lion.

69 **Fukuriki Ichiza** *Finds* This tiny, funky bar, under the laid-back patronage of owner Dragon Shibata, attracts a young clientele with its Latin American music, Cuban beer and cigars, absinthe from France, pictures of Che Guevara, and kitsch. This is one of my favorite bars among the 200 or so nestled in Goruden Gai. Open daily 7pm to 2am. 1–1–10 Kabuki-cho. ✆ 03/5291-5139. Station: Shinjuku Sanchome (7 min.). In Goruden Gai.

New Sazae After other bars in this predominantly gay district close, those revelers who refuse to call it quits migrate around the corner to this dive, open since 1966. The diverse crowd is a bit rowdy, but if you get this far you're probably right where you belong. A ¥1,000 ($8.35) cover includes the first drink; drinks thereafter cost ¥700 ($5.85). Hours are Sunday to Thursday 9pm to 5am; Friday and Saturday 9pm to 7am. Ishikawa Building, 2nd floor, 2–18–5 Shinjuku. ✆ 03/3354-1745. Station: Shinjuku Sanchome (4 min.). Southeast of the Yasukuni Dori and Gyoen Dori intersection, behind Bygs, in Shinjuku Ni-chome.

Vagabond Although most of the night action in Shinjuku is east of the station, the west side also has an area of inexpensive restaurants and bars. This second-floor nightspot has been in operation for more than 25 years and is now managed by the original owner's son, Matsuoka Takahiko. It features a jazz pianist nightly, beginning at 7:30pm. Although there's no music charge per se, after 7:30pm there is an obligatory snack charge of ¥500 ($4.15) for the bowl of chips automatically brought to your table. Small and cozy, this place is popular with foreigners who live near Shinjuku Station and with Japanese who want to rub elbows with them; its Guinness brings in customers from the United Kingdom. Hours are daily 5:30 to 11:30pm. 1–4–20 Nishi Shinjuku. ✆ 03/3348-9109. Station: Shinjuku (west exit, 2 min.). In west Shinjuku, in the 2nd alley behind (north of) Odakyu Halc.

⑦ **Volga**   Volga, a yakitori-ya housed in an ivy-covered two-story brick building, features an open grill facing the street and a smoky and packed drinking hall typical of older establishments that once dotted the country. Its unrefined atmosphere has changed little since it opened here in the 1950s. Rooms are tiny and simply decorated with wooden tables and benches, and the clientele is middle-aged. Very Japanese. Get here soon after it opens to be assured a seat. Hours are Monday to Saturday from 5 to 10:30pm; closed holidays. 1–4–18 Nishi Shinjuku. ℂ 03/3342-4996. Station: Shinjuku (west exit, 2 min.). In west Shinjuku, on the corner down the street from Vagabond (see above).

HARAJUKU

See the map on p. 133 for the bars listed in this section.

Oh God   This mellow, dimly lit bar is a godsend for travelers on a budget looking for a casual place to hang out in Harajuku. It features a mural of a city at sunset and shows free foreign films every night at 9pm, midnight, and 3am (also at 6pm Fri–Sun and holidays). I've seen everything from James Bond to Fassbinder to grade-B movies here. Most of the "recent" releases are a couple years old. There are also two pool tables. Hours are daily from 6pm to 6am. 6–7–18 Jingumae. ℂ 03/3406-3206. Station: Meiji-Jingumae (3 min.) or Harajuku (5 min.). From the Meiji/Omotesando Dori intersection, walk on Omotesando Dori toward Aoyama and take the 3rd right (just before Kiddy Land); it's in the building at the end of the alley.

Music Pub Gabi Gabi   Harajuku's only bar with free live music every night of the week (but drinks are pricey, starting at ¥900/$7.50 for a beer), this smoky, scruffy-looking bar is a good place to check out up-and-coming local Japanese acts, including blues, jazz, rock, and pop, but you'll have to stay out past 10pm to hear it and the music can be hit-and-miss. If you want to have an actual conversation with the people you're with, come before the music starts. Open daily noon to 5am, with live music from 10pm. 6–5–6 Jingumae, Shibuya-ku. ℂ 03/ 3499-3145. Station: Meiji-Jingumae (1 min.) or Harajuku (3 min.). A stone's throw from the Meiji/Omotesando intersection, on Meiji Dori catty-corner from Condomania.

SHIBUYA

Dubliners' Irish Pub   This bar has several things going for it: It is open all day, is easy to find, has a covered balcony from which to observe the bustle of Tokyo, and offers free live Irish music every second Wednesday from 8pm. Hours are Monday to Saturday 11:30am to 1am, Sunday and holidays 11:30am to 11pm. 2–29–8 Dogenzaka. ℂ 03/5459-1736. Station: Shibuya (2 min.). Take the Hachiko exit and walk up Dozenzaka; it will be on the right side, on the 2nd floor.

Gaspanic Shibuya   Gaspanic has a well-earned reputation for hard-core partying, but patrons who prefer this Shibuya location over the original Roppongi bar (see below) say it's because the clientele (mostly Japanese and foreigners in their 20s) here tends to be mostly locals (as opposed to tourists and transients) and because DJs play what customers want to hear, which can range from the Beatles to rap. Happy hour—when all drinks are ¥400 ($3.35)—is until 9:30pm Friday through Wednesday and all night Thursday. Regular hours are daily 6pm to 5am. 21–7 Udagawa-cho. ℂ 03/3462-9099. Station: Shibuya (Hachiko exit, 1 min.). On Center Gai (Shibuya's nightlife street), on the right side past Starbucks.

EBISU

Beer Station   This attractive Sapporo Beer hall is a good imitation of a century-old Bavarian brewery—oompah music even greets you at the entrance. Among the several floors of dining and drinking—each with its own display of plastic

> **Tips** **A Note on Japanese Symbols**
>
> Many hotels, restaurants, attractions, and other establishments in Japan do not have signs giving their names in Roman (English-language) letters. Appendix C lists the Japanese symbols for all such places described in this guide. Each set of characters representing an establishment name has a number in the appendix, which corresponds to the number that appears inside the oval preceding the establishment's name in the text.

food—the most attractive is the huge basement beer hall, the Festbrau, with its vaulted ceiling and huge pillars. The outdoor terrace seating is good for people-watching. Hours are Monday to Saturday 11:30am to 11pm; Sunday and holidays 11:30am to 10pm. Yebisu Garden Place, 4–20 Ebisu. C 03/3442-5111. Station: Ebisu (7 min.). At the entrance to Yebisu Garden Place if you arrive via the moving walkway from Ebisu Station.

Enjoy House *(Finds* With its 1960s-style decor, efficient yet relaxed and funky staff, friendly atmosphere, and tiny dance floor, the inimitable Enjoy House is a great place to—well, enjoy yourself. Everyone here seems high and happy; the place is aptly named. Open Sunday and Tuesday to Thursday from 1pm to 2am; Friday and Saturday from 1pm to 4am. 2–9–9 Ebisu Nishi. C 03/5489-1591. Station: Ebisu (west exit, 3 min.). Take the road opposite Komazawa Dori from the koban police box (next to the J-Phone shop) and continue past Peacock grocery store to the juncture where 5 streets converge; it's on the other side of the intersection, on a diagonal street to the left.

What the Dickens!   One of Tokyo's most popular expat bars, What the Dickens! is undisputed proof that Ebisu is no longer the sleepy backwater it once was. This bar packs 'em in with live bands nightly from 8:30pm (everything from rock and pop to reggae, jazz, blues, Dixieland, and folk), no cover, British beer on tap, and hearty servings of pub grub, including lamb pie, steak and kidney, and beef Guinness. Hours are Tuesday and Wednesday 5pm to 1am; Thursday to Saturday 5pm to 2am, Sunday 3pm to midnight. 1–13–3 Ebisu Nishi, 4th floor. C 03/3780-2099. Station: Ebisu (west exit, 2 min.). Take the side street running between Wendy's and KFC; it's at the end of the 2nd block on the left, on the corner.

ROPPONGI

See the map on p. 143 for the bars listed in this section. Directions are from Roppongi Crossing, Roppongi's main intersection of Roppongi Dori and Gaien-Higashi Dori.

In addition to the listings below, you might try **Hobgoblin Roppongi**, on Gaien-Higashi Dori in the direction of Tokyo Tower at 3–16–33 Roppongi (C 03/3568-1280), open daily from noon and offering live Irish music the first and third Mondays of the month. See "Akasaka," below, for a review of this imported chain.

Agave   Tequila fans take note: This is Japan's largest tequila bar, with approximately 350 brands on offer. Margaritas, appetizers (nachos and the like), and cigars are also available. Yes, cigar smoking is allowed in this basement establishment, but an airy domed ceiling, Mexican decor and music, and a friendly staff—not to mention tequila—may make it sufferable for nonsmokers. Hours are Monday to Thursday from 6:30pm to 2am; Friday and Saturday from 6:30pm to 4am. 7–15–10 Roppongi. C 03/3497-0229. Station: Roppongi (2 min.). On Roppongi Dori, on the right side heading from Roppongi Crossing toward Roppongi Hills and Shibuya.

Bodeguita   This second-floor Cuban club features Latin music videos (that usually induce customers to dance), Cuban cocktails, and good food, including *arroz con frijoles* (the classic rice and beans) and *arroz saltado* (rice, fried potatoes, and meat). Quiet during most of the week, it fills up with Latinos on weekends and on Wednesdays for its live music from 8pm (for which there's a ¥1,000/$8.35 or more cover). If you're in town, don't miss the exuberant Cuban party thrown the last Saturday of most months, when this place rocks. Hours are Monday to Saturday 6pm to 2am; Sunday 6pm to midnight. 3–14–7 Roppongi. ✆ 03/3796-0232. Station: Roppongi (4 min.). From Roppongi Crossing, walk towards Tokyo Tower on Gaien-Higashi Dori, turning left at Hamburger Inn; it will be on the left.

Gaspanic Bar   This has long been *the* bar for foreign and Japanese 20-somethings. The music is loud, and after midnight the place gets so crowded that female patrons have been known to start dancing on the countertops. Thursdays are especially packed, since all drinks go for only ¥400 ($3.35). In the basement is Club 99, open only on Thursday, Friday, and Saturday for dancing. Large bouncers at the door serve as clues that this place can get rough. Hours are daily 6pm to 5am. 3–15–24 Roppongi. ✆ 03/3405-0633. Station: Roppongi (4 min.). From Roppongi Crossing, walk towards Tokyo Tower on Gaien-Higashi Dori, and turn left at Hamburger Inn.

Geronimo Shot Bar   People seem to either love or hate this place. It's tiny, dominated by a bar in the middle and people who come to drink, dance, and socialize. If the gong sounds, it means someone has bought a shot for everyone there, and this happens more than you might think. Hours are daily 7pm to 5am. 7–14–10 Roppongi. ✆ 03/3478-7449. Station: Roppongi (1 min.). On Roppongi Crossing, across from Almond Coffee Shop.

Hard Rock Cafe   If you like your music loud, the Hard Rock Cafe is the place for you. The outside is easily recognizable by King Kong scaling a wall; the inside looks like a modern yuppie version of the local hamburger joint, except, of course, there's the added attraction of all that rock 'n' roll paraphernalia. Hours are Monday to Thursday from 11:30am to 2am, Friday and Saturday from 11:30am to 4am, Sunday and holidays from 11:30am to 11:30pm. 5–4–20 Roppongi. ✆ 03/3408-7018. Station: Roppongi (3 min.). From Roppongi Crossing, walk toward Tokyo Tower on Gaien-Higashi Dori and turn right at McDonald's.

Hideout Bar   This small basement bar, owned and staffed by Nigerians, packs 'em in like the Yamanote Line during rush hour with its loud music and cheap drink prices until 11pm. By midnight, it's so crowded—mostly with 20-somethings and, on weekends, American military personnel—that everyone dances just where they are. Hours are daily 7pm to 7am. 3–14–9 Roppongi. ✆ 03/3497-5432. Station: Roppongi (3 min.). From Roppongi Crossing, head toward Tokyo Tower on Gaien-Higashi Dori; it's on the left, catty-corner from McDonald's and opposite the Roi Building.

Paddy Foley's   Easy to find, this lively Irish pub is popular with both Japanese and foreigners. Happy hour is until 8pm, several screens show live sports events (mainly soccer and rugby), and there's live music Friday (Irish), Sunday (ballads and folk), and Tuesday (blues). Hours are daily 5pm to 2am. Roi Building basement, 5–5–1 Roppongi. ✆ 03/3423-2250. Station: Roppongi (3 min.). On Gaien-Higashi Dori, on the right as you walk from Roppongi Crossing toward Tokyo Tower.

Quest   This sophisticated bar with blood-red walls and illuminated tables attracts a young, international (predominately Aussie) crowd with its Australian beers, daily happy hour (till 9:30pm), live sports coverage, and meat pies. Hours are Monday to Saturday 7pm to 5am; Sunday 9pm to 5am. 5–3–1 Roppongi.

C 03/5414-2225. Station: Roppongi (4 min.). Take the side street going downhill on the left side of Almond Coffee Shop and then take the 1st left; the club will be on the right.

Seventh Heaven Gentlemen's Club   One of several exotic dance clubs in Tokyo, this one features beauties mostly from Eastern Europe and is popular with both foreign business travelers and Japanese entertaining their clients. Admission is ¥5,000 to ¥7,000 ($42–$58), including two drinks, but discounts are offered on its website. Women are admitted free on Saturdays. Hours are Monday to Saturday from 7pm to 4am. 7–14–1 Roppongi. *C* 03/3401-3644. www. seventh-heaven.com. Station: Roppongi (3 min.). From Roppongi Crossing, it's on the left side of Gaien-Higashi Dori as you walk away from Tokyo Tower.

Tokyo Sports Café   If you think you'll die if can't see your alma mater's decisive game, you might have a chance of catching it live here. American football, baseball, and NBA basketball are aired, though U.K. sports like soccer, rugby, and even cricket may take precedence. If you can't see your game, work out your frustrations at the free pool table. Happy hour is until 9pm daily; Friday and Saturday feature guest DJs. Hours are Monday to Saturday 6pm to 6am. 7–15–31 Roppongi. *C* 03/3404-3675. Station: Roppongi (1 min.). From Roppongi Crossing, walk toward Shibuya and take the 1st right.

AKASAKA

See the map on p. 83 for the bars listed in this section.

Garden Lounge   If you prefer the view of a Japanese landscape garden to that of neon lights, get to this place before sunset, where you can look out over a 400-year-old garden complete with waterfall, pond, bridges, and manicured bushes. Cocktails begin at a pricey ¥1,300 ($11). There's live music from 7pm with a ¥300 ($2.50) cover charge. Hours are daily 7am–10pm. Hotel New Otani, 4–1 Kioi-cho. *C* 03/3265-1111. Station: Nagata-cho or Akasaka-mitsuke (3 min.).

Hobgoblin Tokyo   This U.K. chain import is a welcome addition to Akasaka's night scene. It offers a dozen brews on tap (the largest selection in town), satellite TVs broadcasting major sporting events, darts, hearty portions of typical pub fare, and happy hour from 5 to 7pm. Although it officially closes at 1am, a telephone call will let you in after hours. Hours are Monday to Friday 11:30am to 2pm; daily 5pm to 1am. Tamondo Building, basement. 2–13–19 Akasaka. *C* 03/6229-2636. Station: Akasaka (exit 2, 2 min.). From the station, turn right onto Akasaka Dori and right at Misuji Dori.

Sports Freak Aya   An English-speaking rugby fan is the owner of this small basement bar, with two TVs showing broadcasts of baseball, soccer, basketball, football, and, naturally, rugby games. Happy hour is until 8pm. Hours are Monday to Friday from 5:30pm to 2am; Saturday from 5:30pm to midnight. 3–8–17 Akasaka. *C* 03/3583-0080. Station: Akasaka-mitsuke (2 min.). On a small street nicknamed Esperanto Dori.

Top of Akasaka   I like to start out evenings in Akasaka with a quiet drink at this fancy and romantic cocktail lounge. With the city of Tokyo as a dramatic backdrop, I can watch the day fade into darkness as millions of lights and neon signs twinkle in the distance. Cocktails average ¥1,500 ($13), and after 5pm there's a cover charge of ¥800 ($6.65) for the piano music (no cover charge for hotel guests). *Note:* No children are allowed. Hours are Monday to Friday 5pm to 2am; Saturday noon to 2am; Sunday noon to 2pm. Akasaka Prince Hotel, 40th floor, 1–2 Kioi-cho. *C* 03/3234-1111. Station: Nagata-cho or Akasaka-mitsuke (2 min.).

SHINAGAWA

Top of Shinagawa   Occupying the whole top floor of the Shinagawa Prince Hotel's 39-story New Tower, the Top of Shinagawa boasts one of the best views of any hotel bar in Tokyo. It offers unparalleled panoramas of Tokyo Bay, Odaiba, the Rainbow Bridge, Mount Fuji, and the Tokyo cityscape. The bar is divided into sections; only the East Lounge (facing the bay) is open during the day, offering a dessert, fruit, and sandwich buffet for ¥1,650 ($14) from 11:30am to 4pm. An open restaurant called Prince Court at the center offers a fixed-price dinner for ¥5,000 ($42). Shinagawa Prince Hotel, 4–10–30 Takanawa. © 03/ 3440-1111. Daily 11:30am–4am. Station: Shinagawa (2 min.).

4 Gay & Lesbian Bars

Shinjuku Ni-chome (pronounced "knee-chomay"), southeast of the Yasukuni Dori and Gyoen Dori intersection, is Tokyo's gay and lesbian quarter, with numerous establishments catering to a variety of age groups and preferences and a lively street scene. Listed below are good places to start; you'll find a lot more in the immediate area by exploring on your own. Keep an eye out for the free *CIA* (short for Club Information Agency) with information on gay events and bars.

Ace   This basement disco, with a high-charged, energetic atmosphere, attracts young gays and lesbians, both Japanese and foreign, but heterosexuals are welcome. (*Note:* Occasional special events are restricted to either men or women.) On weekdays Ace has a relaxed atmosphere, but dancing and DJs Thursday through Saturday bring in the crowds. There's usually a ¥2,000 to ¥3,000 ($17–$25) cover charge, which includes one or two drinks. Hours are Tuesday to Sunday 8pm to 4:30am. 2–14–6 Shinjuku. © 03/3352-6297. Station: Shinjuku Sanchome (4 min.). In the 2nd block behind Bygs.

Advocates   Attracting both gays and straights, this small bar opens onto the street with a few sidewalk tables, making this a good vantage point for watching the street action. Hours are Monday to Saturday 6pm to 5am; Sunday 6pm to 1am. 2–18–1 Shinjuku. © 03/3358-3988. Station: Shinjuku Sanchome (4 min.). On the street behind Bygs, to the right.

Kinsmen   This long-standing second-floor gay bar welcomes customers of all persuasions. It's a pleasant oasis, small and civilized, with a huge flower arrangement dominating the center of the room. Occasionally there's live music. Hours are Wednesday to Monday 9pm to 3am (to 5am Sat). 2–18–5 Shinjuku. © 03/3354-4949. Station: Shinjuku Sanchome (4 min.). Down the street from Arty Farty, behind Bygs.

Kinswomyn   This casual, tiny, but welcoming women-only bar attracts a regular clientele of mainly Japanese lesbians. Weekends can get quite crowded, especially when some of the younger patrons start dancing, making weekdays preferable for those seeking a more relaxed, quiet setting. Hours are Wednesday to Monday 8pm to 4am. 2–15–10 Shinjuku. © 03/3354-8720. Station: Shinjuku Sanchome (4 min.). On a street behind Kinsmen.

5 Films

Going to the movies is an expensive pastime in Tokyo, with admission averaging about ¥1,800 ($15) for adults, ¥1,500 ($13) for senior-high and college students, and ¥1,000 ($8.35) for children and seniors over 60. If you want to see one of Hollywood's latest releases (which usually take a few months to reach

Japan), you may also have to contend with long lines and huge crowds. Movies are shown in the original language, with Japanese subtitles.

Although there are movie theaters spread throughout the metropolis, none is as sophisticated and upscale as **Virgin Cinemas,** located in the Roppongi Hills development at 6–10–2 Roppongi (© **03/5775-6090**). It offers seven screens at the usual movie-going price, plus a Premier Zone with its own bar, Japanese garden, and viewing room with armchair seating and side tables (admission here is a hefty ¥3,000/$25, including one drink). Like many other cinemas, it offers discounted tickets for ¥1,000 ($8.35) on the first day of each month and for ladies on Wednesday. Unlike other theaters, however, it shows movies Sunday to Wednesday from 10am to midnight, and Thursday, Friday, and Saturday from 10am to 5am.

If you're interested in seeing Japanese classics, your best bet is the **National Film Center,** 3–7–6 Kyobashi, Chuo-ku (© **03/5777-8600;** station: Take-bashi). Movies, shown Tuesday through Friday at 3 and 7pm and Saturday and Sunday at 1 and 4pm, include both Japanese and foreign films (some with English subtitles). Since programs change often, call to see what's playing and to check show times. A ticket here is ¥500 ($4.15) for adults, ¥300 ($2.50) for students and seniors, and ¥100 (85¢) for children.

Finally, remember that **Oh God** in Harajuku has free showings of older movies (see "The Bar Scene," above).

10

Side Trips from Tokyo

If your stay in Tokyo is 3 days or more, you should consider excursions in the vicinity. **Kamakura** and **Nikko** rank as two of the most important historical sites in Japan, each representing a completely different but equally exciting period of Japanese history. **Yokohama,** with its thriving port, waterfront development, museums, and great garden, makes an interesting day trip. **Fuji-Hakone-Izu National Park** serves as a huge recreational playground for the residents of Tokyo. For overnight stays, I recommend **Hakone,** both for its atmosphere and its Japanese-style inns *(ryokan),* where you'll be able to

experience a bit of old Japan. (For more information on ryokan, see chapter 4.) Active travelers may want to hike to the top of **Mount Fuji,** while shoppers may want to head for the pottery village of **Mashiko,** which can be toured on its own or in combination with an overnight trip to Nikko.

Before departing Tokyo, stop by the **Tourist Information Center (TIC)** for pamphlets about Kamakura, Nikko, Hakone, and the Mount Fuji area, some of which provide maps, train schedules, and other useful information (see "Visitor Information," in chapter 3, for the TIC location).

1 Kamakura ★★★

51km (32 miles) S of Tokyo

If you take only one day trip outside Tokyo, it should be to Kamakura, especially if you're unable to include the ancient capitals of Kyoto and Nara in your travels. (If you're going to Kyoto and Nara, I would probably choose Nikko, below.) Kamakura is a delightful hamlet with no fewer than 65 Buddhist temples and 19 Shinto shrines spread throughout the village and the surrounding wooded hills. Most of these were built centuries ago, when a warrior named Yoritomo Minamoto seized political power and established his shogunate government in Kamakura back in 1192. Wanting to set up his seat of government as far away as possible from what he considered to be the corrupt imperial court in Kyoto, Yoritomo selected Kamakura because it was easy to defend. The village is enclosed on three sides by wooded hills and on the fourth by the sea—a setting that lends a dramatic background to its many temples and shrines.

Although Kamakura remained the military and political center of the nation for a century and a half, the Minamoto clan was in power for only a short time. After Yoritomo's death, both of his sons were assassinated, one after the other, after taking up military rule. Power then passed to the family of Yoritomo's widow, the Hojo family, who ruled until 1333, when the emperor in Kyoto sent troops to crush the shogunate government. Unable to stop the invaders, 800 soldiers retired to the Hojo family temple at Toshoji, where they disemboweled themselves in ritualistic suicide known as *seppuku.*

Today a thriving seaside resort with a population of 175,000, Kamakura—with its old wooden homes, temples, shrines, and wooded hills—makes a pleasant

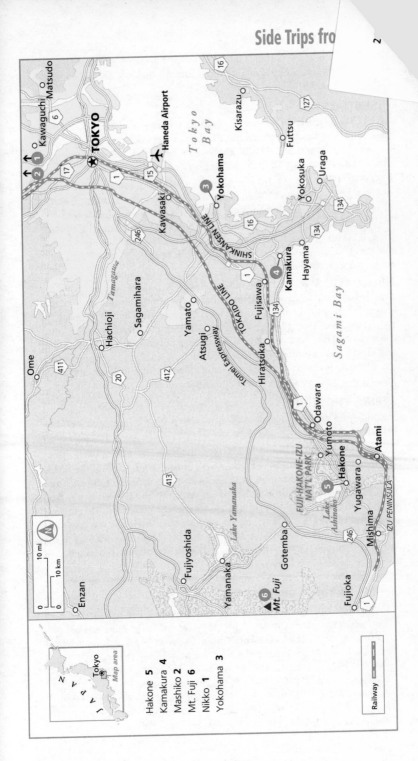

1-day trip from Tokyo. (There's also a beach in Kamakura called Yuigahama Beach, but I find it unappealing; it's often strewn with litter and unbelievably crowded in summer. Skip it.)

ESSENTIALS

GETTING THERE Take the **JR Yokosuka Line** bound for Zushi, Kurihama, or Yokosuka; it departs every 10 to 15 minutes from the Yokohama, Shinagawa, Shimbashi, and Tokyo JR stations. The trip takes almost 1 hour from Tokyo Station and costs ¥890 ($7.40) one-way to Kamakura Station.

VISITOR INFORMATION In Kamakura, there's a **tourist information window** (© 0467/22-3350; open daily 9am–5:30pm, to 5pm in winter) immediately to the right outside Kamakura Station's east exit in the direction of Tsurugaoka Hachimangu Shrine. It sells a color brochure with a map of Kamakura for ¥200 ($1.65); there's also a free map (in both English and Japanese), but it's not always in stock. Ask here for directions on how to get to the village's most important sights and restaurants.

ORIENTATION & GETTING AROUND Kamakura's major sights are clustered in two areas: **Kamakura Station,** the town's downtown with the tourist office, souvenir shops spread along Komachi Dori and Wakamiya Oji, restaurants, and Tsurugaoka Hachimangu Shrine; and **Hase,** with the Great Buddha and Hase Kannon Temple. You can travel between Kamakura Station and Hase Station via the **Enoden Line,** a wonderful small train, or you can walk the distance in about 15 minutes. Destinations in Kamakura are also easily reached by buses that depart from Kamakura Station.

SEEING THE SIGHTS

Keep in mind that most temples and shrines open at about 8 or 9am and close between 4 and 5pm.

AROUND KAMAKURA STATION About a 10-minute walk from Kamakura Station, **Tsurugaoka Hachimangu Shrine** ★★★ (© 0467/22-0315) is the spiritual heart of Kamakura and one of its most popular attractions. It was built by Yoritomo and dedicated to Hachiman, the Shinto god of war who served as the clan deity of the Minamoto family. The pathway to the shrine is along Wakamiya Oji, a cherry tree–lined pedestrian lane that was also constructed by Yoritomo back in the 1190s so that his oldest son's first visit to the family shrine could be accomplished in style with an elaborate procession. The

---

Tips **Touring Kamakura**

If you wish, an English-speaking **volunteer student guide** will escort you for free to Kamakura's major sights. They can be found most weekends outside the east exit of Kamakura Station between 10am to noon (try to arrive a little before 10am, before other visitors whisk them away). You can also reserve a guide at least a week prior to your visit by calling Tomoaki Saito at © 090/9845-1290; or by e-mail to tomoa-saito@jp-t.ne.jp or kamakuraguide@hotmail.com. You should provide your name, country, number in your party, time and date of your request, and contact telephone number. In return for the student's service, a nice gesture from you to him or her is reimbursement for transportation costs and payment for lunch and admission fees.

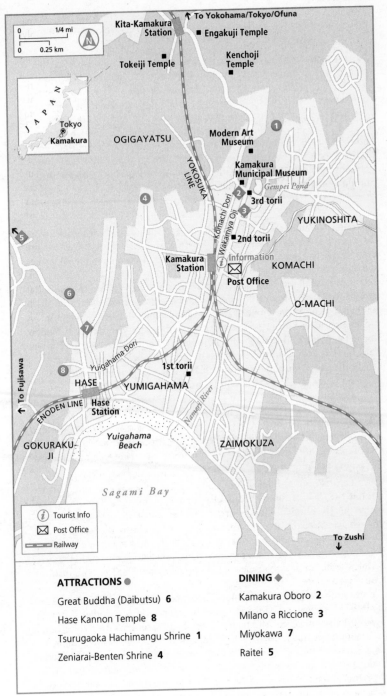

Kamakura

To Yokohama/Tokyo/Ofuna ↑

Kita-Kamakura Station

■ Engakuji Temple

Kenchoji Temple ■

■ Tokeiji Temple

0   1/4 mi
0   0.25 km

JAPAN
Tokyo ⊛
Kamakura ⊙

OGIGAYATSU

YOKOSUKA LINE

Modern Art Museum ■

Kamakura Municipal Museum ■

①

2 ■

3rd torii

Gempei Pond

③

YUKINOSHITA

④

■ 2nd torii

⑤

Komachi Dori

Wakamiya Oji

Kamakura Station

ⓘ Information
✉

Post Office

KOMACHI

O-MACHI

⑥

⑦

Yuigahama Dori

1st torii ■

⑧

HASE

YUMIGAHAMA

Nameri River

To Fujisawa ←

ENODEN LINE

Hase Station

GOKURAKU-JI

Yuigahama Beach

ZAIMOKUZA

Sagami Bay

ⓘ Tourist Info
✉ Post Office
▭▭ Railway

To Zushi ↓

ATTRACTIONS ●

Great Buddha (Daibutsu) **6**

Hase Kannon Temple **8**

Tsurugaoka Hachimangu Shrine **1**

Zeniarai-Benten Shrine **4**

DINING ◆

Kamakura Oboro **2**

Milano a Riccione **3**

Miyokawa **7**

Raitei **5**

> **Fun Fact Murder & Betrayal at Tsurugaoka Hachimangu Shrine**
>
> As you ascend the 62 steps to the vermilion-painted shrine, note the **gingko tree** to the left that's thought to be about 1,000 years old. This is supposedly the site where Yoritomo's second son was ambushed and murdered back in 1219; his head was never found. Such stories of murder and betrayal were common in feudal Japan. Fearful that his charismatic brother had designs on the shogunate, Yoritomo banished him and ordered him killed. Rather than face capture, the brother committed *seppuku*. When the brother's mistress gave birth to a boy, the baby was promptly killed. Today, the lotus ponds, arched bridge, pigeons, and bright vermilion sheen of the shrine give little clue to such violent history.

lane stretches from the shrine all the way to Yuigahama Beach, with three massive *torii* gates set at intervals along the route to signal the approach to the shrine. On both sides of the pathway are souvenir and antiques shops selling lacquerware, pottery, and folk art.

At the top of the stairs, which afford a panoramic view toward the sea, is the vermilion-colored shrine with its small shrine museum, not worth the ¥100 (85¢) admission. Shrine grounds are free to the public and are always open.

Although it's a bit out of the way, it might pay to visit **Zeniarai-Benten Shrine** (© **0467/25-1081**), about a 20-minute walk west of Kamakura Station. This shrine is dedicated to the goddess of good fortune. On the Asian zodiac's Day of the Snake, worshippers believe that if you take your money and wash it in spring water in a small cave on the shrine grounds, it will double or triple itself later on. This being modern Japan, don't be surprised if you see a bit of ingenuity; my Japanese landlady told me that when she visited the shrine she didn't have much cash on her, so she washed something that she thought would be equally as good—her credit card. Because the shrine is dedicated to the goddess of fortune, it's fitting that admission is free. Open daily 8am to 5pm.

AROUND HASE STATION   To get to these attractions, you can go by bus, which departs from in front of Kamakura Station (take any bus from platform 1 or 6 to the Daibutsuen-mae stop). Or, for a more romantic adventure, you can go by the **JR Enoden Line,** a tiny train that putt-putts its way seemingly through backyards on its way from Kamakura Station to Hase and beyond. Since it's mostly only one track, trains have to take turns going in either direction. I suggest that you take the bus from Kamakura Station directly to the Great Buddha, walk to Hase Shrine, and then take the Enoden train back to Kamakura Station.

Probably Kamakura's most famous attraction is the **Great Buddha** ★★★ (© **0467/22-0703**), called the Daibutsu in Japanese and located at **Kotokuin Temple.** Eleven meters (37 ft.) high and weighing 93 tons, it's the second-largest bronze image in Japan. The largest Buddha is in Nara, but in my opinion, the Kamakura Daibutsu is much more impressive. For one thing, the Kamakura Buddha sits outside against a dramatic backdrop of wooded hills. Cast in 1252, the Kamakura Buddha was indeed once housed in a temple like the Nara Buddha, but a huge tidal wave destroyed the wooden structure—and the statue has sat under sun, snow, and stars ever since. I also prefer the face of the Kamakura

Buddha; I find it more inspiring and divine, as though with its half-closed eyes and calm, serene face it's above the worries of the world. It seems to represent the plane above human suffering, the point at which birth and death, joy and sadness merge and become one. Open daily from 7am to 6pm (to 5:30pm in winter). Admission is ¥200 ($1.65) for adults and ¥150 ($1.25) for children, and your entry ticket is a bookmark, a nice souvenir. If you want, you can pay an extra ¥20 (15¢) to go inside the statue—it's hollow.

About a 10-minute walk from the Daibutsu is **Hase Kannon Temple** ★★★ or Hasedera (✆ **0467/22-6300**), located on a hill with a sweeping view of the sea. This is the home of an 11-headed gilt statue of Kannon, the goddess of mercy, housed in the Kannon-do (Kannon Hall). More than 9m (30 ft.) high and the tallest wooden image in Japan, it was made from a single piece of camphor wood back in the 8th century. The legend surrounding this Kannon is quite remarkable. Supposedly, two wooden images were made from the wood of a huge camphor tree. One of the images was kept in Hase, not far from Nara, while the second was given a short ceremony and then duly tossed into the sea to find a home of its own. The image drifted 483km (300 miles) eastward and washed up on shore but was thrown back in again because all who touched it became ill or incurred bad luck. Finally, the image reached Kamakura, where it gave the people no trouble. This was interpreted as a sign that the image was content with its surroundings, and Hase Kannon Temple was erected at its present site. Note how each face has a different expression, representing the Kannon's compassion for various kinds of human suffering. In the Kannon-do, you'll also find the **Treasure House** with relics from the Kamakura, Heian, Muromachi, and Edo periods.

Another statue housed here is of **Amida,** a Buddha who promised rebirth in the Pure Land to the West to all who chanted his name. It was created by order of Yoritomo Minamoto upon his 42nd birthday, which is considered an unlucky year for men. You'll find it housed in the Amida-do (Amida Hall) beside the Kannon-do.

As you climb the steps to the Kannon-do, you'll encounter statues of a different sort. All around you will be likenesses of **Jizo,** the guardian deity of children. Although parents originally came to Hase Temple to set up statues to represent their children in hopes the deity would protect and watch over them, through the years the purpose of the Jizo statues has changed. Now they represent miscarried, stillborn, or aborted children. More than 50,000 Jizo statues have been offered here since the war, but the thousand or so you see now will remain only a year before being burned or buried to make way for others. Some of the statues, which can be purchased on the temple grounds, are fitted with hand-knitted caps and sweaters. The effect is quite chilling.

Hase Temple is open daily 8am to 5:30pm (to 4:30pm in winter); admission is ¥300 ($2.50) for adults, ¥100 (85¢) for children.

WHERE TO DINE
MODERATE

⑦ **Miyokawa** MINI-KAISEKI/OBENTO   This modern, casual restaurant specializes in *kaiseki,* including beautifully prepared mini-kaiseki set meals that change with the seasons. It also offers a great obento lunch box, the least expensive of which is served in a container shaped like a gourd, as well as a set meal featuring steak prepared Japanese style. It also offers takeout obento, priced at ¥2,000 ($17) and under, which you can eat at the pavilion at Hase Temple.

1–16–17 Hase. ✆ **0467/25-5556.** Reservations recommended. Mini-kaiseki ¥5,500 – ¥10,000 ($46–$83); obento ¥2,000 – ¥5,000 ($17–$42); Japanese steak set meal ¥3,500 ($29). AE, MC, V. Daily 11am–9pm. Station: Hase (5 min.). On the main road leading from Hase Station to the Great Buddha (about a 5-min. walk from each).

INEXPENSIVE

In addition to the suggestions below, a pavilion at **Hase Temple,** described above, serves noodles, beer, and soft drinks, with both indoor and outdoor seating. It offers a great view, making it a good place for a snack on a fine day.

⑦² **Kamakura Oboro** TOFU/VEGETARIAN   Built in the traditional style of a *kura* (warehouse) with its whitewashed walls and dark wooden beams, this tofu restaurant offers simple but delicious vegetarian meals, including udon noodles with tofu, soba noodles with tofu and vegetables, and tofu kaiseki, as well as sweets made from red bean paste. You can watch tofu being made at the entranceway; the dining room is upstairs.

1–8–25 Yukinoshita. ✆ **0467/61-0570.** Main dishes ¥780 – ¥1,800 ($6.50–$15). No credit cards. Daily 11am–6pm. Station: Kamakura (8 min.). Between Komachi Dori and Wakamiya Oji streets, at the very end just before Tsurugaoka Hachimangu Shrine.

Milano a Riccione ITALIAN   This is the Japanese branch of a restaurant from Milan known for its handmade pasta, seafood, and good selection of wines. Although located in a basement, it opens onto a subterranean courtyard, making it brighter and more cheerful than you would expect. There's an English seasonal menu, but the best bargain is the daily set lunch for ¥1,300 ($12), which gives you a choice of pasta, an appetizer, and coffee, espresso, or tea. It's also the quickest meal you can order; otherwise, if you're in a hurry, you should dine elsewhere, as care and time are devoted to the preparation of such meals as grilled scallops with leeks and roast chicken with zucchini and ham.

2–12–30 Komachi. ✆ **0467/24-5491.** Pizza and pasta ¥950 – ¥1,700 ($7.90–$14); main dishes ¥1,800 – ¥2,400 ($15–$20); set dinner ¥3,800 ($32); set lunches ¥1,300 – ¥2,500 ($11–$21). AE, DC, MC, V. Thurs–Tues 11:30am–3pm and 5:30–9:30pm (last order). Station: Kamakura (6 min.). On the left side of Wakamiya Oji when walking from Kamakura Station to Tsurugaoka Hachimangu Shrine.

⑦³ **Raitei** ★★★ *Finds* NOODLES/OBENTO   Though it's a bit inconveniently located, this is the absolute winner for a meal in Kamakura. Visiting Raitei is as much fun as visiting the city's temples and shrines. The restaurant is situated in the hills on the edge of Kamakura, surrounded by verdant countryside, and the wonder is that it serves inexpensive *soba* (Japanese noodles) as well as priestly kaiseki feasts, which you must reserve in advance. If you're here for soba or one of the obento lunch boxes, go down the stone steps on the right to the back entry, where you'll be given an English-language menu with such

---

Tips **A Note on Japanese Symbols**

Many hotels, restaurants, attractions, and other establishments in Japan do not have signs giving their names in Roman (English-language) letters. Appendix C to this book lists the Japanese symbols for all such places described in this guide. Each set of characters representing an establishment name has a number in the appendix, which corresponds to the number that appears inside the oval preceding the establishment's name in the text. Thus, to find the Japanese symbol for, say, **Miyokawa,** refer to number 71 in appendix C.

offerings as noodles with chicken, mountain vegetables, tempura, and more. The pottery used here comes from the restaurant's own specially made kiln, and you'll dine while sitting on roughly hewn wood stools or on tatami.

When you've finished your meal, be sure to walk the path looping through the garden past a bamboo grove, stone images, and a miniature shrine. The stroll takes about 20 minutes, unless you stop for a beer at the refreshment house, which has outdoor seating and a view of the countryside.

Takasago. ℂ **0467/32-5656.** Reservations required for kaiseki. Noodles ¥700 – ¥1,200 ($5.85–$10); obento lunch boxes ¥3,500 – ¥4,500 ($29–$38); soba set meals ¥2,500 ($21); kaiseki feasts from ¥6,000 ($50). At the front gate, you must pay an entry fee of ¥500 ($4.15), which counts toward the price of your meal. AE, DC. Daily 11am–sundown (about 7pm in summer). Bus: 4 or 6 from platform 6 at Kamakura Station to Takasago stop (or a 15-min. taxi ride).

2 Nikko ✶✶✶

150km (30 miles) N of Tokyo

Since the publication of James Clavell's novel *Shogun,* many people have become familiar with Tokugawa Ieyasu, the powerful real-life shogun of the 1600s on whom Clavell's fictional shogun was based. Quashing all rebellions and unifying Japan under his leadership, Tokugawa established such a military stronghold that his heirs continued to rule Japan for the next 250 years without serious challenge.

If you'd like to join the millions of Japanese who through the centuries have paid homage to this great man, travel 140km (90 miles) north of Tokyo to Nikko, where **Toshogu Shrine** was constructed in his honor in the 17th century and where Tokugawa's remains were laid to rest in a mausoleum. Nikko means "sunlight"—an apt description of the way the sun's rays play upon this sumptuous shrine of wood and gold leaf. In fact, nothing else in Japan matches Toshogu Shrine for its opulence. Nearby is another mausoleum containing Tokugawa's grandson, as well as a temple, a shrine, and a garden. Surrounding the sacred grounds, known collectively as Nikko Sannai and designated a World Heritage Site by UNESCO in 1999, are thousands of majestic cedar trees in the 200,000-acre **Nikko National Park.** Another worthwhile sight is the **Nikko Tamozawa Imperial Villa,** built in 1899.

I've included a few recommendations for an overnight stay. Otherwise, you can see Nikko in a full day. Plan on 4 to 5 hours for transportation to Nikko and back to Tokyo, 2½ hours to see Toshogu Shrine and vicinity, and 1 hour to see the imperial villa.

ESSENTIALS
GETTING THERE   The easiest, fastest, and most luxurious way to get to Nikko is on the privately owned Tobu Line's Limited Express, called the **Spacia,** which departs every hour or more frequently from Asakusa Station and costs ¥2,740 ($23) one-way for the 2-hour trip (some trains require a transfer at Shimo-Imaichi Station). All seats are reserved, which means you are guaranteed a seat; if you're traveling on a holiday or a summer weekend, you may wish to purchase and reserve your ticket in advance. Another plus is that there's usually an English-speaking hostess on board who passes out pamphlets on the area and can answer sightseeing questions about Nikko.

Otherwise, you can reach Nikko on Tobu's slower **rapid train** from Asakusa, which costs ¥1,320 ($11) one-way and takes 2 hours and 10 minutes, with trains departing every hour or more frequently. There are no reserved seats, which means you might have to stand if trains are crowded.

You can also travel to Nikko via JR train. If you're visiting **Mashiko** (see later in this chapter), you can save yourself the hassle of buying train tickets from different rail companies by taking the JR Tohoku Honsen line from Ueno to JR Utsunomiya Station for the bus to Mashiko, and then continuing onward from JR Utsunomiya Station to Nikko (the Tobu line does not travel between Utsunomiya and Nikko). Slightly faster but more expensive is the Shinkansen bullet train from Ueno to Utsunomiya (there are departures every 15–30 min. and the trip takes about 47 min.), where you change to the train to Nikko (45 min.).

VISITOR INFORMATION Before leaving Tokyo, pick up the leaflet "Nikko" from the Tourist Information Center (TIC). It gives the train schedule for both the Tobu Line, which departs from Asakusa Station, and the JR trains that depart from Ueno Station. The TIC also has color brochures with maps of the Nikko area.

Nikko's Tobu and JR stations are located almost side by side in the village's downtown area. The **Nikko Tobu Station tourist information counter** (© **0288/53-4511**), located inside Tobu Station to the right after you pass through the wicket gate, is staffed by a friendly woman who speaks enough English to give you a map, answer basic questions, and point you in the right direction. You can also make hotel and ryokan reservations here for free. Open daily 8:30am to noon and 1 to 5pm.

Another tourist office, the **Nikko Information Center** (© **0288/54-2496**), is located on the left side of the main road leading from the train station to Toshogu Shrine (next to Eneos gas station). It has English-speaking staff and lots of information in English about Nikko, including information on public hot springs. Open daily from 8:30am to 5pm.

GETTING AROUND Toshogu Shrine and its mausoleum are on the edge of town, but you can walk from either the JR or Tobu train stations to the shrine in about half an hour. Head straight out the main exit, pass the bus stands, and then turn right. Signs in English point the way throughout town. Keep walking on this main road (you'll pass the Nikko Information Center about halfway down on the left side, as well as souvenir shops) until you come to a T intersection with a vermilion-colored bridge spanning a river (about a 15-min. walk from the train stations). The stone steps opposite lead up the hill into the woods and to Toshogu Shrine. You can also travel from Tobu Station by bus, getting off at either the Shinkyo (a 5-min. ride) or Nishi Sando (a 7-min. ride) bus stop.

SEEING THE SIGHTS

ON THE WAY TO THE SHRINE The first indication that you're nearing the shrine is the vermilion-painted **Sacred Bridge (Shinkyo)** arching over the rushing Daiyagawa River. It was built in 1636, and for more than 3 centuries only shoguns and their emissaries were allowed to cross it. Even today, mortals like us are prevented from completely crossing it because of a barrier at one end.

Across the road from the Sacred Bridge are some steps leading uphill into a forest of cedar where, after a 5-minute walk, you'll see a statue of **Shodo,** a priest who founded Nikko 1,200 years ago at a time when mountains were revered as gods. In the centuries that followed, Nikko became one of Japan's greatest mountain Buddhist retreats, with 500 sub-temples spread through the area. Behind Shodo is the first major temple, Rinnoji Temple, where you can buy a **combination ticket** for ¥1,000 ($8.35) that allows entry to Rinnoji Temple, Toshogu Shrine, neighboring Futarasan Shrine, and the other Tokugawa

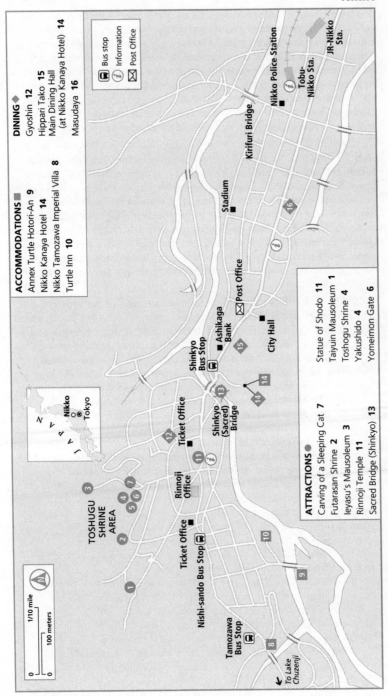

Nikko

ACCOMMODATIONS ■
Annex Turtle Hotori-An **9**
Nikko Kanaya Hotel **14**
Nikko Tamozawa Imperial Villa **8**
Turtle Inn **10**

DINING ◆
Gyoshin **12**
Hippari Tako **15**
Main Dining Hall
(at Nikko Kanaya Hotel) **14**
Masudaya **16**

ATTRACTIONS ●
Carving of a Sleeping Cat **7**
Futarasan Shrine **2**
Ieyasu's Mausoleum **3**
Rinnoji Temple **11**
Sacred Bridge (Shinkyo) **13**
Statue of Shodo **11**
Taiyuin Mausoleum **1**
Toshogu Shrine **4**
Yakushido **4**
Yomeimon Gate **6**

TOSHUGU
SHRINE
AREA

JAPAN
Nikko
Tokyo

Bus stop
Information
Post Office

Ticket Office
Rinnoji
Office
Ticket Office
Nishi-sando Bus Stop
Tamozawa
Bus Stop
To Lake
Chuzenji

Shinkyo
(Sacred)
Bridge
Shinkyo
Bus Stop
Ashikaga
Bank
Post Office
City Hall
Stadium
Kirifuri Bridge
Nikko Police Station
Tobu-
Nikko Sta.
JR-Nikko
Sta.

1/10 mile
100 meters

mauzoleum, Taiyuin. Once at Toshogu Shrine, you'll have to pay an extra ¥520 ($4.35) to see Ieyasu's tomb. Combination tickets sold at the entry to Toshogu Shrine already include Ieyasu's tomb. It doesn't really matter where you buy your combination ticket since you can always pay the extra fee to see sights not covered. A note for bus riders: If you take the bus to the Nishi Sando bus stop, the first place you'll come to is the Taiyuinb Mausoleum, where you can also purchase a combination ticket.

Toshogu Shrine and the other sights in Nikko Sannai are open daily April to October from 8am to 5pm (to 4pm the rest of the year); you must enter at least 30 minutes before closing time.

RINNOJI TEMPLE   Rinnoji Temple was founded by the priest Shodo in the 8th century, long before the Toshogu clan came onto the scene. Here you can visit the **Sanbutsudo Hall,** a large building that enshrines three 8.4m (28-ft.) high, gold-plated wooden images of Buddha, considered the "gods of Nikko"; today people pray here for world peace. Perhaps the best thing to see at Rinnoji Temple, however, is its **Shoyo-en Garden** (opposite Sanbutsudo Hall), which requires a separate ¥300 ($2.50) admission. Completed in 1815 and typical of Japanese landscaped gardens of the Edo Period, this small strolling garden provides a different vista with each turn of the path, making it seem much larger than it actually is.

TOSHOGU SHRINE ★★★   The most important and famous structure in Nikko is Toshogu Shrine, built by Tokugawa's grandson (and 3rd Tokugawa shogun), Tokugawa Iemitsu, as an act of devotion. It seems that no expense was too great in creating the monument: Some 15,000 artists and craftspeople were brought to Nikko from all over Japan, and after 2 years' work, they erected a group of buildings more elaborate and gorgeous than any other Japanese temple or shrine. Rich in colors and carvings, Toshogu Shrine is gilded with 2.4 million sheets of gold leaf (they could cover an area of almost 2.4ha/6 acres). The mausoleum was completed in 1636, almost 20 years after Ieyasu's death, and was most certainly meant to impress anyone who saw it as a demonstration of the Tokugawa shogunate's wealth and power.

Toshogu Shrine is set in a grove of magnificent ancient **Japanese cedars** planted over a 20-year period during the 1600s by a feudal lord named Matsudaira Masatsuna. Some 13,000 of the original trees are still standing, adding a sense of dignity to the mausoleum and the shrine.

You enter Toshogu Shrine via a flight of stairs that passes under a huge stone torii gateway, one of the largest in Japan. On your left is a five-story, 35m (115-ft.) high **pagoda.** Although normally pagodas are found only at temples, this pagoda is just one example of how both Buddhism and Shintoism are combined at Toshogu Shrine. After climbing a second flight of stairs, turn left and you'll see the **Sacred Stable,** which houses a sacred white horse. Horses have long been dedicated to Shinto gods and are kept at shrines. Shrines also kept monkeys as well, since they were thought to protect horses from disease; look for the three monkeys carved above the stable door, fixed in the poses of "see no evil, hear no evil, speak no evil"—they're considered guardians of the sacred horse. Across from the stable is **Kami-Jinko,** famous for its carving by Kano Tanyu, who painted the images of the two elephants after reading about them but without seeing what they actually looked like.

Up the next flight of stairs, to the left, is **Yakushido,** famous for its dragon painting on the ceiling. If you clap your hands under the painting, the echo supposedly resembles a dragon's roar. You also can visit the shrine's main sanctuary, the **Hai-den,** comprising three halls: One was reserved for the imperial family, one for the shogun, and one (the central hall) for conducting ceremonies. You can buy good-luck charms here that will guard against such misfortunes as traffic accidents, or that will insure good health, success in business, easy childbirth, or other achievements in daily life.

But the central showpiece of Nikko is **Yomeimon Gate,** popularly known as the Twilight Gate, implying that it could take you all day (until twilight) to see everything carved onto it. Painted in red, blue, and green and decorated with gilding and lacquerwork, this gate has about 400 carvings of flowers, dragons, birds, and other animals. It's almost too much to take in at once and is very un-Japanese in its opulence, having more in common with Chinese architecture than the usual austerity of most Japanese shrines.

To the right of the main hall is the entrance to **Tokugawa Ieyasu's mausoleum.** If it's not already included in your combination ticket, admission is ¥520 ($4.35). After the ticket counter, look for the carving of a sleeping cat above the door, dating from the Edo Period and famous today as a symbol of Nikko (you'll find many reproductions in area souvenir shops). Beyond that are 200 stone steps leading past cedars to Tokugawa's tomb. After the riotous colors of the shrine, the tomb seems surprisingly simple.

FUTARASAN SHRINE   Directly to the west of Toshogu Shrine is Futarasan Shrine, the oldest building in the district (from 1617), which has a pleasant garden and is dedicated to the gods of mountains surrounding Nikko. You'll find miniature shrines dedicated to the god of fortune, god of knowledge, god of health, and god of good marriages. On the shrine's grounds is the so-called **ghost lantern,** enclosed in a small wooden structure. According to legend, it used to come alive at night and sweep around Nikko in the form of a ghost. It apparently scared one of the guards so much that he struck it with his sword 70 times; the marks are still visible on the lamp's rim. Entrance to the miniature shrines and ghost lantern is ¥200 ($1.65) extra.

TAIYUIN MAUSOLEUM ⭐   Past Futarasan Shrine is **Taiyuin Mausoleum,** the final resting place of Iemitsu, the third Tokugawa shogun (look for his statue). Completed in 1653, it's not nearly as large nor as crowded as Toshogu Shrine, but is ornate and serenely elegant nevertheless, making it a pleasant last stop on your tour of Nikko Sannai.

NIKKO TAMOZAWA IMPERIAL VILLA (Tamozawa Goyoutei Kinen Koen) ⭐⭐   If you haven't seen the imperial villas of Kyoto (which require advance planning), the Nikko Tamozawa Imperial Villa, 8–27 Honcho (© **0288/ 53-6767**), is a great alternative. Though not as old (it was built in 1899 for Prince Yoshihito, who later became the Taisho emperor) and recently painstakingly restored so that it looks brand new, it has the distinction of being the largest wooden imperial villa of its era, with 106 rooms (37 of which are open to the public). The central core of the villa is actually much older, constructed in 1632 by a feudal lord and brought to Nikko from Edo (present-day Tokyo). A self-guided tour of the villa provides insight into traditional Japanese architectural methods—from its 11 layers of paper-plastered walls to its nail-less wood framing—as well as the lifestyle of Japan's aristocracy. Be sure to wander the small, outdoor garden. Admission is ¥500 ($4.15) for adults, half price for children. Open Wednesday to Monday 9am to 4:30pm. It's about a 20-minute walk from Toshogu Shrine; or take the bus to Tamozawa stop.

WHERE TO STAY

If it's peak season (May, Aug, and Oct) or a weekend, it's best to reserve a room in advance, which you can do by calling a lodging either directly or through a travel agency in Tokyo. Otherwise, if it's not peak season, you can make a reservation upon arrival at Nikko Tobu Station, either at the **tourist information counter**, where the service is free, or at the **accommodations-reservation window** (© **0288/54-0864;** open daily 9am–5pm), which charges a ¥200 to ¥500 ($1.65–$4.15) fee but is familiar with the accommodations in the area and will make all arrangements for you.

MODERATE

Nikko Kanaya Hotel ★★ *(Finds)* This distinguished-looking, old-fashioned place on a hill above the Sacred Bridge is the most famous hotel in Nikko, combining the rustic heartiness of a European country lodge with elements of old Japan. It was founded in 1873 by the Kanaya family, who wished to offer accommodations to foreigners, mainly missionaries and businessmen looking to escape the heat and humidity of Tokyo. The present complex, built in spurts over the past 100 years, has a rambling, delightfully old-fashioned atmosphere that fuses Western architecture with Japanese craftsmanship. Through the decades it has played host to a number of VIPs, from Charles Lindbergh to Indira Gandhi to Shirley MacLaine; Frank Lloyd Wright left a sketch for the bar fireplace, which was later built to his design. Even if you don't stay here, you might want to drop by for lunch (see review below). Pathways lead to the Daiyagawa River and several short hiking trails.

All rooms are Western-style twins, with the differences in price based on room size, view (river view is best), and facilities. They're simple but cozy and have character; some have antiques and claw-foot tubs. If you want to stay in the best room in the house, a corner room in the 70-year-old wing where the emperor once stayed, you'll pay the highest price below.

1300 Kami-Hatsuishi, Nikko City, Tochigi 321-1401. © **0288/54-0001.** Fax 0288/53-2487. www.kanaya hotel.co.jp. 70 units (68 with shower/tub and toilet, 2 with toilet only). ¥8,000 ($67) single with toilet only, ¥10,000 ($83) single with shower and toilet, ¥11,000–¥35,000 ($92–$292) single with bathroom; ¥10,000 ($83) twin with toilet only, ¥12,000 ($100) twin with shower and toilet, ¥13,000–¥40,000 ($108–$333) twin with bathroom. ¥3,000 ($25) extra on Sat and eve before national holidays; ¥5,000 ($42) extra in peak season. AE, DC, MC, V. Bus: From Nikko Tobu Station to the Shinkyo stop, a 5-min. ride. Station: On foot: 15 min. from Tobu Station. **Amenities:** 3 restaurants (shabu-shabu, Western, and coffee shop); bar; small outdoor heated pool (open only in summer and free for hotel guests); outdoor skating rink (in winter); souvenir shops; in-room massage. *In room:* A/C, TV, minibar.

INEXPENSIVE

Annex Turtle Hotori-An ★★ *(Kids)* Owned by the super-friendly family that runs Turtle Inn (see below), this is one of my favorite places to stay in Nikko. One dip in the hot-springs bath overlooking the Daiyagawa River (which you can lock for privacy) will tell you why; at night, you're lulled to sleep by the sound of the rushing waters. A simple but spotless modern structure (all nonsmoking), it's located in a nice rural setting on a quiet street with a few other houses; an adjoining park and playground provide plenty of space for kids to play. All its rooms except one are Japanese style. A plentiful Western-style breakfast costs ¥1,000 ($8.35) in the pleasant living area/dining room. For dinner, you can go to the nearby Turtle Inn (not available Sun and Thurs; reservations should be made by 10am), or buy a pizza from the freezer and microwave it yourself. There's also a communal refrigerator where you can store food.

8–28 Takumi-cho, Nikko City, Tochigi 321-1433. ☎ **0288/53-3663**. Fax 0288/53-3883. www.turtle-nikko. com. 11 units (all with bathroom). ¥5,800 ($48) per person. AE, MC, V. Bus: From Nikko Station to the Sogo Kaikan-mae stop, a 7-min. ride; then a 9-min. walk. **Amenities:** Computer with free Internet access at Turtle Inn; hot-spring baths; coin-op washer and dryer. In room: A/C, TV.

Turtle Inn ✿   This excellent, nonsmoking pension, a Japanese Inn Group member, is located within walking distance of Toshogu Shrine in a newer two-story house on a quiet side street beside the Daiyagawa River. It's run by the very friendly Fukuda family. Mr. Fukuda speaks English and is very helpful in planning a sightseeing itinerary for the area. Rooms are bright and cheerful in both Japanese and Western styles; the five tatami rooms are without bathroom. Excellent Japanese dinners are available for ¥2,000 ($17), as are Western breakfasts for ¥1,000 ($8.35). Be sure to order dinner by 10am and note that it's not available on Sunday and Thursday.

2–16 Takumi-cho, Nikko City, Tochigi 321-1433. ☎ **0288/53-3168**. Fax 0288/53-3883. www.turtle-nikko. com. 10 units (3 with bathroom). ¥4,200 ($35) single without bathroom, ¥5,000 ($42) single with bathroom; ¥8,400 ($70) double without bathroom, ¥10,000 ($83) double with bathroom. AE, MC, V. Bus: From Nikko Station to the Sogo Kaikan-mae stop, a 7-min. ride; then a 5-min. walk. **Amenities:** Computer with free Internet access; coin-op washer and dryer. In room: A/C, TV, no phone.

WHERE TO DINE
EXPENSIVE

Main Dining Hall at Nikko Kanaya Hotel ✿✿ *Finds* CONTINENTAL Even if you don't spend the night here, you might want to come for a meal in the hotel's quaint dining hall with its wood-carved pillars. It's one of the best places in town for lunch. Since it's beside the Sacred Bridge, only a 10-minute walk from Toshogu Shrine, you can easily combine it with your sightseeing tour of Nikko. I suggest Nikko's specialty, locally caught rainbow trout available in three different styles of cooking. I had mine cooked Kanaya style, covered with soy sauce, sugar, and sake, grilled and served whole. The best bargain is the set lunch for ¥2,800 ($23) available until 3pm, which comes with soup, salad, a main dish such as trout, bread or rice, and dessert. Steak, lobster, salmon, chicken, and other Western fare are also listed on the English-language menu.

Nikko Kanaya Hotel, 1300 Kami-Hatsuishi. ☎ **0288/54-0001**. Reservations recommended during peak season. Main dishes ¥2,500 – ¥8,000 ($21–$67); set lunches ¥2,800 – ¥10,000 ($23–$83); set dinners ¥7,000 ($58). AE, DC, MC, V. Daily noon–3pm and 6–8pm. A 15-min. walk from Nikko Tobu Station.

MODERATE

Gyoshin-Tei ✿✿ VEGETARIAN/KAISEKI This lovely Japanese restaurant, with a simple tatami room and a view of pines, moss, and bonsai, serves two kinds of set meals—kaiseki and Buddhist vegetarian cuisine—both of which change monthly and include the local specialty, *yuba* (see Masudaya, below). It's one of several restaurants in a parklike setting all under the same management and with the same open hours. Meiji-no-Yakata (closed Wed), occupying a stone house built 110 years ago as the private retreat of an American businessman, serves Western food such as grilled rainbow trout, veal cutlet, and steak, with set meals ranging from ¥3,800 to ¥8,000 ($32–$67). Fujimoto (closed Thurs), in a small stone cottage, serves French food created with Japanese ingredients and eaten with chopsticks. The drawback: This place is harder to find than this book's other recommendations, but it's only a 4-minute walk northeast of Rinnoji Temple.

2339-1 Sannai. ☎ **0288/53-3751**. Reservations recommended. Vegetarian/kaiseki meals ¥3,500 ($29) and ¥5,000 ($42). AE, DC, MC, V. Thurs–Tues 11am–7pm (from 11:30am in winter). A 25-min. walk from Nikko Tobu Station; or bus from Nikko Station to Seikoen (then a 1-min. walk).

Masudaya ⭐ YUBA   Only two fixed-price meals are served at this Japanese-style, 80-year-old restaurant, both featuring *yuba*. A high-protein food made from soybeans, yuba is a local specialty produced only in Kyoto and Nikko. Until 100 years ago, it could be eaten only by priests and members of the imperial family. Now you can enjoy it, too, along with such sides as rice, sashimi, soup, fried fish, and vegetables. Dining is either in a common dining hall (make reservations 2 days in advance) or, for the more expensive meals, in private tatami rooms upstairs, for which you should make a reservation 1 week in advance.

439 Ichiyamachi. ℂ **0288/54-2151.** Reservations required. Yuba kaiseki meals ¥3,900 ($33) and ¥5,200 ($43). No credit cards. Fri–Wed 11am–4pm (open Thurs if a holiday). A 5-min. walk from Nikko Tobu Station. On the left side of the main street leading from Tobu Station to Toshogu Shrine, just before the fire station.

INEXPENSIVE

㉗ **Hippari Tako** NOODLES   This tiny, three-table establishment is under the caring supervision of motherly Miki-san, who serves a limited selection of noodle dishes, including ramen and stir-fried noodles with vegetables as well as *onigiri* (rice balls) and yakitori. There's an English-language menu, and the walls, covered with business cards and messages left by appreciative guests from around the world, are testimony to both the tasty meals and Miki-san's warm hospitality.

1011 Kami-Hatsuishi. ℂ **0288/53-2933.** Main dishes ¥500 – ¥800 ($4.15–$6.65). No credit cards. Daily 11am–7pm (last order). A 15-min. walk from Nikko Tobu Station. On the left side of the main street leading from Toshogu Shrine, 1 min. before the Nikko Kanaya Hotel and the Sacred Bridge.

3 Mashiko

100km (62 miles) N of Tokyo

Mashiko is a small village known throughout Japan for its *Mashiko-yaki*, distinctive, heavy, country-style pottery. A visit to Mashiko can be combined with an overnight trip to Nikko (see earlier); both are not far from the town of Utsunomiya, north of Tokyo. Since the major attraction in Mashiko is its pottery shops and kilns and there's little in the way of restaurants and accommodations, I suggest that you come here just for the day, and return to Tokyo or travel on to Nikko before nightfall. Plan on spending about 3 hours in Mashiko, plus several hours for transportation.

Mashiko's history as a pottery town began in 1853, when a potter discovered ideal conditions in the nearby mountain clay and red pine wood for firing. It wasn't until 1930, however, that Mashiko gained national fame, when the late Hamada Shoji, designated a "Living National Treasure," built a kiln here and introduced Mashiko-ware throughout Japan. Other potters have since taken up his technique, producing ceramics for everyday use, including plates, cups, vases, and tableware. Altogether, there are about 50 pottery shops in Mashiko (along with about 300 kilns) into which you can wander and watch the craftspeople at work. Pottery fairs, held twice a year in late April/early May and late October/early November, attract visitors from throughout Japan.

ESSENTIALS

GETTING THERE   By Train   You must first take a train from Tokyo to Utsunomiya, and then transfer there for a bus that will take you to Mashiko. The fastest but most expensive way to reach Utsunomiya is aboard the **Tohoku Shinkansen,** which departs from Tokyo Station every 15 to 30 minutes and arrives in Utsunomiya approximately 50 minutes later (you can also catch the Shinkansen at Ueno Station); the one-way fare is ¥4,290 ($36) for an unreserved seat. Otherwise, take the **JR Tohoku Honsen** rapid train from Ueno Station, which departs approximately every hour, takes 90 minutes to reach Utsunomiya JR Station, and costs ¥1,890 ($16) one-way. If you're stopping off in Mashiko on your way to Nikko, note that only JR trains (not the Tobu line) travel between Utsunomiya and Nikko (see "Nikko," earlier).

Alternatively, you can take the Shonan Shinjuku Line from either Shibuya or Shinjuku to Utsunomiya; the trip from Shibuya takes 115 minutes and costs ¥1,890 ($16).

By Bus   Upon reaching Utsunomiya JR Station, take the west exit to the bus terminal just outside the station. Buses operated by the Toya Bus company (© 028/662-1080) depart from platform 14 approximately every hour, taking about 1 hour to reach Mashiko and costing ¥1,100 ($9.15) one-way.

VISITOR INFORMATION   There's a **tourist information counter** at JR Utsunomiya Station (© 028/636-2177), open daily 8:30am to 8pm, where you can obtain information on buses heading to Mashiko. In Mashiko, the **tourist information office** is inconveniently located at the tiny Mashiko train station, open daily 8:30am to 5pm (© 0285/70-1120).

WHAT TO SEE & DO

Upon reaching Mashiko, get off the bus at the **Sankokanmae bus stop.** Turn left at the stoplight just ahead for the **Mashiko Reference Collection Museum,** also called ⑦⑤ **Mashiko Sankokan** (© 0285/72-5300), a small compound of several thatch-roofed farmhouses and exhibition halls that served as Hamada Shoji's workshop and home from 1925 until his death in 1978 at the age of 83. Galleries here showcase about 30 of his works, as well as his private collection of Eastern and Western glass, ceramics, fabrics, furniture, and paintings, including pieces by Bernard Leach and Kanjiro Kawai. You can also see his "climbing kiln," built along the slope of a hill. Plan on at least a half-hour here. Admission is ¥800 ($6.65) for adults, half-price for children. It's open Tuesday through Sunday 9:30am to 4:30pm; closed New Year's and February.

A 7-minute walk from Mashiko Sankokan (reached by backtracking to the bus stop and then turning left at the first stoplight) is the **Ceramic Art Messe Mashiko,** or **Togei Messe Mashiko** (© 0285/72-7555), a visitor's complex devoted to pottery, woodblock prints, and changing art exhibits. Works by Hamada, as well as pieces by Mashiko potters and pottery from around Japan, are on display, along with a former thatched home that once belonged to Hamada. Admission is ¥600 ($5) for adults, half-price for children. The complex is open Thursday to Tuesday 9:30am to 5pm (to 4pm in winter).

SHOPPING

The main reason people come to Mashiko is to shop. Alongside the Togei Messe complex is one of the largest shops, the **Mashiko Pottery Center,** or ⑦⑥ **Mashikoyaki Kyohan Center** (© 0285/72-4444), open daily from 8:30am to 5:30pm. On the other side of the Kyohan Center is the **main street** of Mashiko, where you'll find dozens of shops offering a wide variety of pottery produced by the town's potters. Wander in and out—you're sure to find something that pleases you.

WHERE TO DINE

The **Jamu Lounge,** set back on Mashiko's main street just down from the Mashikoyaki Kyohan Center (© 0285/72-8634), occupies a yellow, adobe-style house decorated with a laid-back but artistic flair that fits the organic and vegetarian food the restaurant serves. The menu is limited to a few choices, like vegetable curry, *enak sayur* (four kinds of vegetables with *genmai* or unpolished brown rice), and Asian salad with *naan* (flat Indian bread) and spicy hot dressing, along with side dishes like fried tofu and *gyoza* (fried dumplings) with vegetable filling. Main dishes range from ¥1,000 ($8.35) to ¥1,200 ($10). No credit cards are accepted. The restaurant is open Friday to Wednesday noon to 8:30pm (last order).

4 Yokohama

29km (18 miles) S of Tokyo

Few attractions in Yokohama warrant a visit if you're just in Japan for a short time. If you find yourself in Tokyo for an extended period, however, Yokohama is a pleasant destination for an easy day trip. Be sure to make time for wonderful Sankei-en Garden; although a mere 90-some years old, it ranks on my long list as one of the top gardens in Japan.

A rather new city in Japan's history books, Yokohama was nothing more than a tiny fishing village when Commodore Perry arrived in the mid-1800s and demanded that Japan open its doors to the world. The village was selected by the shogun as one of several ports to be opened for international trade, transforming it from a backwater to Japan's most important gateway. Yokohama subsequently grew by leaps and bounds, and was a pioneer when it came to Western goods and services, boasting Japan's first bakery (1860), photo studio (1862), telephone (1869), beer brewery (1869), cinema (1870), daily newspaper (1870), public restroom (1871), and ice cream (1879).

Now Japan's second-largest city with a population of almost 3.5 million, Yokohama remains the nation's largest international port and supports a large international community, with many foreigners residing in the section called the Bluff. Yokohama has an especially large Chinese population and Japan's largest Chinatown, whose restaurants serve as a mecca for hungry Tokyoites. Befitting a city known for its firsts, for the past decade Yokohama has been developing Japan's largest urban development project to date, the **Minato-Mirai 21,** with a conference center, museums, hotels, and restaurants. In addition to Sankei-en Garden, Yokohama also boasts a handful of specialty museums. Hard to imagine that a mere 140-some years ago, Yokohama was a village of 100 houses.

ESSENTIALS

GETTING THERE   Because many Yokohama residents work in Tokyo, it's as easy to get to Yokohama as it is to get around Tokyo. Although Yokohama Station is the city's main train station, I suggest taking a train from Tokyo that will deposit you directly at Sakuragicho or Kannai stations in Yokohama, since most attractions are clustered here. (If you want to visit Sankei-en Garden, take the train to Yokohama Station and transfer there for bus no. 8.) Most convenient is probably the **JR Keihin-Tohoku Line,** which travels through Ueno, Tokyo, Yurakucho, Shimbashi, and Shinagawa stations before continuing on to Yokohama, Sakuragicho, and Kannai stations, with the journey from Tokyo Station to Sakuragicho Station taking approximately 43 minutes. From Shibuya, the express (not the local, which makes too many stops) **Tokyu-Toyoko Line** travels to Yokohama Station or Sakuragicho Station (but not Kannai) in about 30 minutes. Additionally, both the **JR Yokosuka Line** and **JR Tokaido Line** depart from Tokyo and Shinagawa stations, but they go only to Yokohama Station,

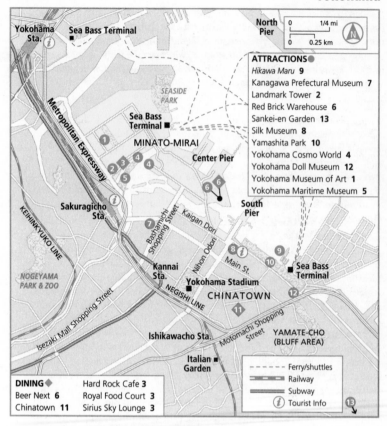

ATTRACTIONS

Hikawa Maru **9**
Kanagawa Prefectural Museum **7**
Landmark Tower **2**
Red Brick Warehouse **6**
Sankei-en Garden **13**
Silk Museum **8**
Yamashita Park **10**
Yokohama Cosmo World **4**
Yokohama Doll Museum **12**
Yokohama Museum of Art **1**
Yokohama Maritime Museum **5**

DINING
Beer Next **6**
Chinatown **11**
Hard Rock Cafe **3**
Royal Food Court **3**
Sirius Sky Lounge **3**

Ferry/shuttles
Railway
Subway
Tourist Info

where you'll have to transfer either to bus (for Sankei-en Garden) or subway (for Sakuragicho or Kannai). In any case, fares to Sakuragicho average ¥300 to ¥450 ($2.50–$4.15), depending on which line you take and which station you start from.

VISITOR INFORMATION   There are several tourist information centers in Yokohama, but probably the most convenient and easiest to find is the **Sakuragicho Station Tourist Information Center** (© 045/211-0111; open daily 9am–7), located in a kiosk outside Sakuragicho Station in the direction of Minato-Mirai 21 and its Landmark Tower. The main office, the **Yokohama Convention & Visitors Bureau,** is located in the Sangyo Boeki Center (nicknamed Sambo Center), 2 Yamashita-cho, Naka-ku (© 045/641-4759; open Mon–Fri 9am–5pm), an easy walk from Kannai Station and close to the Silk Center and Yamashita Park. Both have excellent city maps and brochures.

Next door to the Convention and Visitors Bureau, in the Silk Center, is the **Kanagawa Prefectural Tourist Office** (© 045/681-0007; open Mon–Fri 9am–5:30pm), where you can also get information on Hakone and Kamakura, both in Kanagawa Prefecture.

GETTING AROUND   Yokohama Station is connected to Sakuragicho and Kannai stations (which are close to most of Yokohama's attractions) by commuter train, subway, and bus. The **JR Keihin-Tohoku Line** from Tokyo passes through Yokohama Station and continues on to Sakuragicho and Kannai stations (the **Tokyu-Toyoko Line** goes only to Yokohama and Sakuragicho stations). Sakuragicho Station is the first stop from Yokohama Station by train (2nd by subway), Kannai the second. Bus no. 8, which travels from Yokohama Station to Sankei-en Garden, also passes Minato-Mirai 21, Chinatown, and Yamashita Park.

SEEING THE SIGHTS

A good plan for sightseeing would be to take the train to Sakuragicho to see the sights at Minato-Mirai 21; walk to Yamashita Park for the attractions there (about a 30-min. walk, stopping, perhaps with stops at the Kanagawa Prefectural Museum of Cultural History or Red Brick Warehouse on the way); and then board bus no. 8 for Sankei-en Garden (keeping in mind, of course, that most attractions close by 4:30 or 5pm). If you want to visit the garden first, board bus no. 8 at Yokohama Station.

AROUND SAKURAGICHO STATION   There's no mistaking the **Minato-Mirai 21** when you see it—it looks like a vision of the future with its dramatic monolithic buildings. Already boasting a huge state-of-the-art convention facility, three first-class hotels, Japan's tallest building, office buildings, two great museums, and an amusement park, the area is still under construction; upon completion, it will encompass 184 hectares (460 acres) housing 10,000 residents and employing 190,000. It's all a bit too sterile for my taste, but its two museums make a visit here worthwhile.

If you arrive by train or subway, take the moving walkway that connects Sakuragicho Station to the Landmark Tower in Minato-Mirai 21 in 5 minutes.

There are several shopping malls in Minato-Mirai 21, including Queen's Square, Yokohama World Porter's, Landmark Plaza, Jack Mall, and the restored Red Brick Warehouse, but the area's most conspicuous building is the **Landmark Tower,** Japan's tallest building. The fastest elevator in the world will whisk you up 270m (900 ft.) in about 40 seconds to the 69th floor, where there's an observation room called **Sky Garden** (✆ **045/222-5030**), open daily from 10am to 9pm (to 10pm Sat). From here you can see the harbor with its container port and Yokohama Bay Bridge, as well as almost the entire city and even, on clear days in winter, Mount Fuji. However, its admission fees—¥1,000 ($8.35) for adults, ¥800 ($6.65) for seniors and high-school students, ¥500 ($4.15) for elementary and junior-high students, and ¥200 ($1.65) for children—make it too expensive in my book. Better is the Landmark Tower's 70th-floor **Sirius Sky Lounge;** although there's a cover charge, its atmosphere is more relaxing. (See below.)

It would be hard to miss **Yokohama Cosmo World** (✆ **045/641-6591**), an amusement park spread along both sides of a canal: It boasts one of the largest Ferris wheels in the world. Other diversions include a roller coaster that looks like it dives right into a pond (but vanishes instead into a tunnel), a haunted house, a simulation theater with seats that move with the action, kiddie rides, a games arcade, and much more. Admission is free but rides cost extra, usually ¥300 to ¥700 ($2.50–$5.85) each. The park is open 11am to 8pm (to 10pm July 20–Aug); closed most Thursdays and weekdays in February.

The most important thing to see at Minato-Mirai 21 is the **Yokohama Museum of Art** ✮, 3–4–1 Minato-Mirai (✆ **045/221-0300**), which emphasizes works by Western and Japanese artists since the 1850s. The museum's ambitious goal is to collect and display works reflecting the mutual influence between the modern art of Europe and that of Japan since the opening of Yokohama's port in 1859. The light and airy building, designed by Kenzo Tange and Urtec Inc., features exhibits from its permanent collection—which includes works by Cézanne, Picasso, Matisse, Leger, Max Ernst, Dalí, and Japanese artists—that change three times a year (you can tour its four rooms in about 30 min.), as well as special exhibits on loan from other museums. Open Friday through Wednesday from 10am to 6pm (closed the day following a national holiday). Admission for the permanent collection is ¥500 ($4.15) for adults, ¥300 ($2.50) for high-school and college students, and ¥100 (85¢) for children. Special exhibitions cost more. You'll spend at least an hour here.

Maritime buffs should check out the **Yokohama Maritime Museum,** 2–1–1 Minato-Mirai (© **045/221-0280**), which concentrates on Yokohama's history as a port, beginning with the arrival of Perry's "Black Ships." Other displays chart the evolution of ships from Japan and around the world from the 19th century to the present, with lots of models of everything from passenger ships to oil tankers. Kids like the three telescopes connected to cameras placed around Yokohama and the captain's bridge with a steering wheel; sailing fans enjoy touring the 96m (320-ft.), four-masted *Nippon-Maru* moored nearby, built in 1930 as a sail-training ship for students of the merchant marines. Admission is ¥600 ($5) for adults and ¥300 ($2.50) for children. Open 10am to 5pm (to 6:30pm in July–Aug, to 4:30pm Nov–Feb). The museum is closed the fourth Monday of every month; the *Maru* is closed every Monday. It takes more than an hour to see everything.

History buffs should wander over to the **Kanagawa Prefectural Museum of Cultural History,** or Kanagawa Kenritsu Rekishi Hakubutsukan, 5–60 Minaminaka-dori (© **045/201-0926**), located between Sakuragicho Station and Yamashita Park (see below), or about a 7-minute walk from either Sakuragicho or Kannai Station. It's housed in a Renaissance-style building constructed in 1904 as the nation's first modern foreign-exchange bank, but the interior has been completely renovated. Start by taking the escalator up to the third floor, where you'll begin a chronological odyssey through Kanagawa Prefecture's history from the Paleolithic Period 30,000 years ago to the opening of Yokohama Port and the modernization of Japan. I found the villages modeled after various periods especially fascinating. Check out the four large-scale drawings of foreigners dating from the 19th century—they have distinct Japanese features despite the blue eyes. (The one on the left is Commodore Perry.) There are also models of both Perry's ships and Japan's first train, which ran between Tokyo and Yokohama. Open Tuesday through Sunday from 9:30am to 5pm; admission is ¥300 ($2.50) for adults, ¥200 ($1.65) for students, and free for seniors and children. Plan on about 45 minutes here.

Shoppers, meanwhile, might want to swing by the **Red Brick Warehouse (Aka Renga),** located in the Shinko-cho District of Minato-Mirai 21 (© **045/227-2002;** station: Sakuragicho or Kannai, about a 15-min. walk from both), located about halfway between Minato-Mirai 21 and Yamashita Park. This restored waterfront warehouse is home to dozens of shops selling crafts, furniture, housewares, clothing, and jewelry, as well as restaurants, with most shops open daily 11am to 8pm.

IN & AROUND YAMASHITA PARK   You can walk to Yamashita Park from Minato-Mirai 21 in less than 30 minutes. Otherwise, it's about a 10-minute walk from Kannai Station, which is three stops by subway (two by commuter train) from Yokohama Station.

Laid out after the huge 1923 earthquake that destroyed much of Tokyo and Yokohama, Yamashita Park is Japan's first seaside park, a pleasant place for a stroll along the waterfront where you have a view of the city's mighty harbor and Bay Bridge. Moored alongside the park is the *Hikawa-Maru* (© **045/641-4361**), a 1930 ocean liner that transported 25,000 passengers between Yokohama and North America before being called to military service during World War II. One of the few Japanese ships to survive the war, it now serves as a museum, with its engine room, bridge, sleeping quarters (including the captain's room and a stateroom once occupied by Charlie Chaplin), deck, and more, on display. In summer from 5 to 9pm daily, the city's most unique beer garden sprawls on a top deck. *Hikawa-Maru* is open daily 9:30am to 9:30pm in summer and 9:30am to 6:30pm in winter. Admission is ¥800 ($6.65) for adults, ¥400 ($3.35) for children 6 to 15 years old, and ¥300 ($2.50) for children 3 to 5. It takes about 30 minutes to walk through the ship.

Across the gingko-lined street from Yamashita Park are two worthwhile special-interest museums. At the west end (closest to Minato-Mirai 21) is the Silk Center, where you'll find both the prefectural tourist office and the excellent **Silk Museum** ★★, 1 Yamashita-cho, Naka-ku (© **045/641-0841**). For many years after Japan opened its doors, silk was its major export, and most of it was shipped to the rest of the world from Yokohama, the nation's largest raw-silk market. In tribute to the role silk has played in Yokohama's history, this museum has displays showing the metamorphosis of the silkworm and the process by which silk is obtained from cocoons, all well documented in English; from April to October you can even observe live cocoons and silkworms at work (compared to the beauty they produce, silkworms are amazingly ugly). The museum also displays various kinds of silk fabrics, as well as gorgeous kimono and reproduction Japanese costumes from the Nara, Heian, and Edo periods. Don't miss this museum, which takes about 30 minutes to see; surprisingly, it's never crowded. Open Tuesday through Sunday from 9am to 4:30pm; admission is ¥500 ($4.15) for adults, ¥300 ($2.50) for seniors, ¥200 ($1.65) for students, and ¥100 (85¢) for children 6 to 11.

At the opposite end of Yamashita Park is the **Yokohama Doll Museum,** 18 Yamashita-cho (© **045/671-9361**), which houses approximately 9,000 dolls from 139 countries around the world. Its main floor displays antique dolls, including those produced by such famous doll makers as Lenci and Jumeau, as well as dolls from around the world dressed in native costume. The upstairs floor is devoted to Japanese dolls, including folk dolls traditionally sold at shrines and temples, classical Edo-Period dolls, *hina* (elaborate dolls representing the empress and emperor, used for the March Hina Festival), and *kokeshi* (simple wooden dolls). Open 10am to 6:30pm; closed third Monday of every month. Admission is ¥300 ($2.50) for adults and ¥150 ($1.25) for children. Plan on spending about 30 to 45 minutes here.

Not far from Yamashita Park is **Chukagai,** Japan's largest Chinatown with hundreds of souvenir shops and restaurants; see "Where to Dine," below.

SANKEI-EN GARDEN ★★★   In my opinion, **Sankei-en Garden** (© **045/621-0634**) is the best reason to visit Yokohama. Although not old itself, this lovely park contains more than a dozen historical buildings that were brought here from other parts of Japan, including Kyoto and Nara, all situated around streams and ponds and surrounded by Japanese-style landscape gardens. The park, which is divided into an Inner Garden and Outer Garden, was laid out in 1906 by Tomitaro Hara, a local millionaire who made his fortune exporting silk.

As you wander along the gently winding pathways, you'll see a villa built in 1649 by the Tokugawa shogunate clan, tea arbors, a 500-year-old three-story pagoda, and a farmhouse built in 1750 without the use of nails. The gardens are well known for their blossoms of plums, cherries, wisteria, azaleas, irises, and water lilies, but no matter what the season, the views here are beautiful.

Plan on at least 2 hours to see both gardens. Sankei-en is open daily from 9am to 5pm (you must enter the Inner Garden by 4pm, the Outer Garden by 4:30pm); admission is ¥300 ($2.50) for the Outer Garden and another ¥300 ($2.50) for the Inner Garden (¥60/50¢ and ¥120/$1 respectively for children). The easiest way to reach Sankei-en Garden is by bus no. 8, which departs from platform no. 2 at Yokohama Station's east exit (near Sogo department store) and winds its way past Sakuragicho Station, past Chinatown, and through Kannai before it reaches the Honmoku-Sankeien-mae bus stop 30 minutes later (the bus stop is announced in English).

GREAT FOR KIDS   If you have children, you may wish to get on their good side by taking them to **Hakkeijima Sea Paradise,** Hakkeijima (© **045/788-8888**), a combination seaside amusement park and aquarium. Among the dozen thrill rides are a roller coaster that juts over the sea, a fiberglass boat that shoots the currents, a tower ride that lets you "fall" 105m (350 ft.) at bloodcurdling speed, and a carousel. The aquarium features such popular animals as sea otters, Atlantic puffins, polar bears, penguins, and belugas; an underwater tunnel moves visitors past stingrays, moray eels, and exotic tropical fish. There are also marine mammal shows featuring dolphins, belugas, and seals. Admission is free, with separate charges for activities. Admission to the aquarium and its shows costs ¥2,450 ($20) for adults, ¥1,400 ($12) for children 6 to 15, and ¥700 ($5.85) for children 4 and 5. Individual thrill rides range from ¥300 to ¥1,000 ($2.50–$8.35). Otherwise, a combination "free" pass good for everything (available only Apr–Nov) costs ¥4,900 ($41), ¥3,500 ($29), and ¥2,000 ($17), respectively.

The aquarium is open mid-March through September, Monday through Friday from 10:30am to 7pm and weekends 9am to 8pm, with slightly longer hours in summer. It takes approximately 1 hour to reach Hakkeijima Sea Paradise from Yokohama Station. Take the Keihin Tohoku Line from Tokyo, Yokohama, Sakuragi-cho, or Kannai stations to Shin-sugita, and then transfer to the Seaside Line to Hakkeijima Station.

WHERE TO DINE

MINATO-MIRAI 21   For casual, inexpensive, and fast dining with a view, head to the Landmark Plaza shopping mall at the base of Landmark Tower, where on the fifth floor you'll find the large, American-style **Royal Food Court** (© **045/222-5566**) with a half-dozen self-serve counters offering different kinds of food. You can dine here for less than ¥1,200 ($10). Among the options are ramen noodles, curry rice, a salad bar, and Chinese dishes. Some seats have a view of the harbor and Yokohama Bay Bridge. Open daily from 11am to 9pm.

For more sophisticated surroundings or just a romantic evening cocktail (no children allowed after 5pm), take the elevator up to the 70th floor of Landmark Tower, where you'll find the Yokohama Royal Park Hotel Nikko's **Sirius Sky Lounge** ✦ (© **045/221-1111**) with stunning seaside views. It serves a buffet lunch for ¥3,500 ($29) daily from 11:30am to 2:30pm, with choices of Asian and Continental dishes that may range from sautéed chili shrimp to pizza. After lunch, you can come for a drink during teatime until 5pm. From 5pm to 1am daily, Sirius is a cocktail lounge and levies a cover charge: ¥1,000 ($6.65) per person from 5 to 7pm and again from 11pm to 1am; ¥2,000 ($17) for live music from 7 to 11pm.

The 1911 renovated Red Brick Warehouse (see above) also has fast-food outlets, but for something more substantial, head to the third floor for **Beer Next** (**© 045/226-1961**), which admirably strives to create an international cuisine that goes down well with beer. Pizza, pasta, rotisserie roast chicken, and a pickled cabbage, sausage, and corned pork stew are just some of the dishes offered, with prices ranging from ¥1,200 to ¥2,200 ($10–$18). Beer Next is open daily 11am to 11pm.

Finally, another good place for a drink or a hamburger is the local branch of the **Hard Rock Cafe,** located on the first floor of Queen's Square Yokohama Tower A (**© 045/682-5626**; open daily 11am–11pm).

CHUKAGAI (CHINATOWN)   Located in Yamashita-cho, a couple blocks inland from Yamashita Park, Chinatown has more than 500 restaurants and shops lining one main street and dozens of offshoots. Tokyoites have long been coming to Yokohama just to dine here; many of the restaurants have been owned by the same families for generations. Most serve Cantonese food and have plastic-food displays, English-language menus, or pictures of their dishes, so your best bet is to wander around and let your budget be your guide. Most dishes run ¥800 to ¥3,000 ($6.65–$25), and set lunches go for ¥800 to ¥1,200 ($6.65–$10). Larger restaurants accept credit cards; those that do display them on the front door. Most Chinatown restaurants are open from 11 or 11:30am to 9:30pm or later; some close Tuesday or Wednesday, but there are always restaurants open. Chinatown is about a 15-minute walk from Kannai Station or a 10-minute walk from Ishikawacho Station.

5 Hakone ★★★

97km (60 miles) SW of Tokyo

Part of the **Fuji-Hakone-Izu National Park,** Hakone is one of the closest and most popular destinations for residents of Tokyo. Beautiful Hakone has about everything a vacationer could wish for—hot-spring resorts, mountains, lakes, breathtaking views of Mount Fuji, and interesting historical sites. You can tour Hakone as a day trip if you leave early in the morning and limit your sightseeing to a few key attractions, but adding an overnight stay—complete with a soak in a hot-spring tub—is much more pleasant. If you plan to return to Tokyo, I suggest leaving your luggage in storage at your Tokyo hotel or Shinjuku Station and traveling to Hakone with only an overnight bag. If you're traveling onward, say, to Kyoto, leave your bags at a check-in counter at Hakone Yumoto Station.

ESSENTIALS
GETTING THERE & GETTING AROUND   Getting to and around Hakone is half the fun! An easy loop tour you can follow through Hakone includes various forms of unique transportation: Starting out by train from Tokyo, you switch to a small two-car tram that zigzags up the mountain, change to a cable car and then to a smaller ropeway, and end your trip with a boat ride across Lake Ashi, stopping to see major attractions along the way. From Lake Ashi (that is, from the villages of Togendai, Hakone-machi, or Moto-Hakone), you can then board a bus bound for Odawara Station (an hour's ride), where you board the train back to Tokyo. These same buses also pass by all the recommendations listed below, which is useful if you wish to complete most of your

Hakone

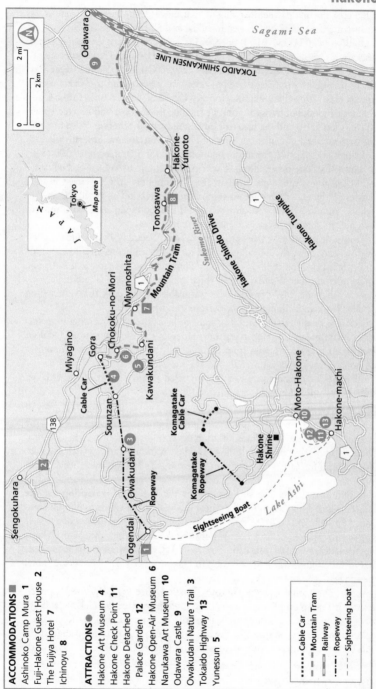

ACCOMMODATIONS ■

Ashinoko Camp Mura **1**
Fuji-Hakone Guest House **2**
The Fujiya Hotel **7**
Ichinoyu **8**

ATTRACTIONS ●

Hakone Art Museum **4**
Hakone Check Point **11**
Hakone Detached
  Palace Garden **12**
Hakone Open-Air Museum **6**
Narukawa Art Museum **10**
Odawara Castle **9**
Owakudani Nature Trail **3**
Tokaido Highway **13**
Yunessun **5**

····· Cable Car
– – – Mountain Tram
      Railway
–·–·– Ropeway
– – – Sightseeing boat

Sagami Sea

TOKAIDO SHINKANSEN LINE

Odawara **9**

Hakone-Yumoto

Tonosawa **8**

Miyanoshita

Chokoku-no-Mori

Miyagino

Gora

Cable Car

Sounzan

Kawakundani

6
5
4

7

Mountain Tram

Sukomo River

Hakone Shinpo Drive

Hakone Turnpike

1

1

138

Sengokuhara **2**

Owakudani **3**

Ropeway

Togendai **1**

Komagatake
Cable Car

Komagatake
Ropeway

Hakone
Shrine

Moto-Hakone **10**

12 **11** **13**

Hakone-machi

1

Lake Ashi

Sightseeing Boat

JAPAN
Tokyo
Map area

N

0   2 km
0   2 mi

265

sightseeing the first day before going to your hotel for the evening. There is also a bus that travels directly between Togendai and Shinjuku.

Odakyu (© 03/3481-0103) operates the most convenient network of trains, buses, trams, cable cars, and boats to and around Hakone. The most economical and by far easiest way to see Hakone is with Odakyu's **Hakone Free Pass** which, despite its name, isn't free but does give you a round-trip ticket on the express train from Shinjuku Station to Odawara or Hakone Yumoto and includes all modes of transportation in Hakone listed above and covered below. The pass lets you avoid the hassle of buying individual tickets and also provides you with nominal discounts on most of Hakone's attractions. Several variations of the pass are available; the most common, valid for 3 days, costs ¥5,500 ($46) for adults (half fare for children). The trip from Shinjuku to Odawara takes 1½ hours, and trains run approximately every 30 minutes. In Odawara, you then transfer to the electric mountain tram. Some express trains go all the way to Hakone Yumoto, where you can then board the mountain tram, with the trip from Shinjuku taking 2 hours.

If you can, travel on a weekday. The **Hakone Weekday Pass,** which is good only Monday through Thursday, is valid for 2 days and costs ¥4,700 ($39) for adults, half-price for children. Not only are weekdays less crowded, but some hotels offer cheaper weekday rates, which means you'll save all around. Note, however, that the Weekday Pass is not available during peak times, including Golden Week and summer school vacation (mid-July to Aug).

If time is of the essence or if you want to be assured a seat during peak season, I recommend reserving a seat on the faster and more luxurious **Odakyu Romance Car,** which travels from Shinjuku all the way to Hakone Yumoto in 1½ hours and costs an extra ¥870 ($7.25) one-way.

All passes described above can be purchased at any station of the Odakyu Railway, including Shinjuku Station and Odawara.

VISITOR INFORMATION   Before leaving Tokyo, pick up the "Hakone and Kamakura" leaflet available from the Tourist Information Center; it lists the schedules for the extensive transportation network throughout the Hakone area. There's also a color brochure called "Hakone National Park," which includes sightseeing information and contains a map of the Hakone area. See "Visitor Information" in chapter 3 for TIC locations.

In Shinjuku Station, be sure to stop by the **Odakyu Sightseeing Service Center** (located on the ground floor near the west exit of Odakyu Shinjuku Station; © 03/5321-7887; www.odakyu-group.co.jp/english; open daily 8am–6pm), where you can obtain sightseeing information, purchase Hakone Free Pass tickets and, if you wish, buy 1- or 2-day do-it-yourself package tours that include round-trip transportation to Hakone, meals, sightseeing, and hotel stays.

In Hakone Yumoto, at the **Yumoto Tourist Office** (© 0460/5-8911; open daily 9:30am–5:30pm), you can pick up more pamphlets on Hakone and ask for directions. It's a 2-minute walk from the Hakone Yumoto Station. Take a right out of the station onto the town's main street; the office is on the left. In Odawara, the **Odawara Tourist Information Center** (© 0465/22-2339; open daily 9am–5pm) is located to the left of the east exit of Odawara Station.

WHAT TO SEE & DO

If you plan on spending only a day in Hakone, you should leave Tokyo very early in the morning and plan on visiting only a few key attractions—I recommend the **Hakone Open-Air Museum, Owakudani Nature Trail,** and, if time permits, **Hakone Check Point** and/or **Narukawa Art Museum.**

If you're spending the night—and I strongly urge that you do—you can arrange your itinerary in a more leisurely fashion and devote more time to Hakone's attractions. You may wish to travel only as far as your hotel the first day, stopping at sights along the way and in the vicinity. The next day you could continue with the rest of the circuit through Hakone. Or, you can opt to complete most of your sightseeing the first day, and then backtrack to your accommodations or reach it by bus from Togendai, Hakone-machi, or Moto-Hakone.

SCENIC RAILWAY TO GORA

Regardless of whether you travel via the Odakyu Romance Car or the ordinary Odakyu express, you'll end up at either Odawara Station, considered the gateway to Hakone, or a bit farther at Hakone Yumoto Station, located in Hakone. At either station, you can transfer to the **Hakone Tozan Railway,** a delightful, mountain-climbing, two-car electric tram that winds its way through forests and over streams and ravines as it travels upward to Gora, making several switchbacks along the way. The entire trip from Hakone Yumoto Station to Gora takes only 45 minutes, but it's a beautiful ride on a narrow track through the mountains. This is my favorite part of the whole journey. The trains, which run every 10 to 15 minutes, make about a half-dozen stops before reaching Gora, including **Tonosawa** and **Miyanoshita,** two hot-spring spa resorts with a number of old ryokan and hotels. Some of these ryokan date back several centuries, to the days when they were on the main thoroughfare to Edo, called the old Tokaido Highway. Miyanoshita is also the best place for lunch. See "Where to Dine," and "Where to Stay," below.

As for things to do along the way, if you're changing from the Odakyu train to the electric tram in Odawara, consider making a short excursion to **Odawara Castle,** Odawara Joshi-koen (✆ **0465/23-1373**), especially if you won't have the opportunity to see any of Japan's more famous castles. A 10-minute walk from Odawara Station (take the east exit out of the station and turn right), this three-tiered, four-story castle dates from 1416 but was rebuilt in 1960. Its keep contains a small historical museum relating to the castle, including models of castles, a palanquin used to transport people up and down mountains during the Edo Period, mirrors, Noh masks, lacquerware, and samurai armor and weapons, while the tower affords a panoramic view of the surrounding park. You can see it all in less than 30 minutes. Admission is ¥400 ($3.35) for adults and ¥150 ($1.25) for children. It's open daily from 9am to 5pm.

For some relaxing hot-springs bathing en route, stop at the thoroughly modern, sophisticated public bath called **Yunessun** ★★ (✆ **0460/2-4126**). About a 15-minute taxi or bus ride from the Kowakudani stop on the Hakone Tozan Railway, this self-described "Mediterranean Style Spa Resort" offers a variety of both indoor and outdoor family baths, which means you wear your bathing suit. In addition to indoor Turkish, Roman, and salt baths, there's also a small children's play area with slides and a large outdoor area with a variety of small baths, including those mixed with coffee, sake, rose petals, or healthy minerals. For those who desire more traditional bathing, there's the Mori No Yu, with both indoor and outdoor baths separated for men and women (you don't wear your suit here). Most people who come stay 2 to 3 hours. Admission is ¥3,500 ($29) to Yunessun, ¥1,800 ($15) to Mori No Yu, and ¥4,000 ($33) to both; children pay half fare. Upon admission, you'll be given a towel, robe, and wristband to pay for drinks and extras (rental suits are available), so you can leave all valuables in your assigned locker. It's open daily 9am to 7pm (Mori No Yu is open to 8pm).

The most important stop on the Hakone Tozan Railway is the next-to-the-last stop, Chokoku-no-Mori, where you'll find the famous **Hakone Open-Air Museum (Chokoku-no-Mori Bijutsukan)** ✿✿✿, (© **0460/2-1161;** www.hakone-oam.or.jp), a minute's walk from the station. With the possible exception of views of Mount Fuji, this museum is, in my opinion, Hakone's number one attraction. Using nature itself as a dramatic backdrop, it showcases sculpture primarily of the 20th century in a spectacular setting of glens, formal gardens, ponds, and meadows. There are 700 sculptures on display, both outdoors and in several buildings, with works by Carl Milles, Manzu Giacomo, Jean Dubuffet, Willem de Kooning, Barbara Hepworth, Joan Miró, and more than 20 pieces by Henry Moore. The Picasso Pavilion contains more than 200 works by Picasso from pastels to ceramics (it's one of the world's largest collections), while the Picture Gallery displays paintings by Miró, Renoir, Kandinsky, Vlaminck, Utrillo, and Takeshi Hayashi. Several installations geared toward children allow them to climb and play. I could spend all day here; barring that, count on staying at least 2 hours. When you're done, an informal cafe provides a peaceful view. It's open daily from 9am to 5pm (to 4pm Dec–Feb); admission is ¥1,600 ($13) for adults, ¥1,100 ($9.15) for university and high-school students and seniors, and ¥800 ($6.65) for children. Your Hakone Free Pass gives you a ¥200 ($1.65) discount.

BY CABLE CAR TO SOUNZAN

Cable cars leave Gora every 20 minutes or so and arrive 9 minutes later at the end station of Sounzan, making several stops along the way as they travel steeply uphill. One of the stops is Koen-Kami, from which it's only a minute's walk to the **Hakone Art Museum** (© **0460/2-2623**). This five-room museum displays Japanese pottery and ceramics from the Jomon Period (around 4000–2000 B.C.) to the Edo Period, including terra-cotta *haniwa* burial figures, huge 16th-century Bizen jars, and Imari ware. What makes this place particularly rewarding are the bamboo grove and small but lovely moss garden with a teahouse where you can sample Japanese tea for ¥630 ($5.25). It is most beautiful in autumn. Open Friday through Wednesday from 9am to 4:30pm (to 4pm in winter); admission is ¥900 ($7.50) for adults, ¥400 ($4.15) for university and high-school students and seniors, and free for children. The Hakone Free Pass gives you a ¥200 ($1.65) discount. Plan on spending about a half-hour here, more if you opt for tea.

BY ROPEWAY TO TOGENDAI

From Sounzan, you board a ropeway with gondolas for a long, 30-minute haul over a mountain to Togendai on the other side, which lies beside Lake Ashi, known as Lake Ashinoko in Japanese. Note that the ropeway stops running at 5 or 5:30pm in summer and 4pm in winter.

Before reaching Togendai, however, get off at the first stop, Owakudani, the ropeway's highest point, to hike the 30-minute **Owakudani Nature Trail** ✿. Owakudani means "Great Boiling Valley," and you'll soon understand how it got its name when you see (and smell) the sulfurous steam escaping from fissures in the rock, testimony to the volcanic activity still present here. Most Japanese commemorate their trip here by buying boiled eggs cooked in the boiling waters, available at the small hut midway along the trail.

ACROSS LAKE ASHI BY BOAT

From Togendai you can take a pleasure boat across Lake Ashi, also referred to as
"Lake Hakone" in some English-language brochures. Believe it or not, one of the
boats plying the waters is a replica of a man-of-war pirate ship. It takes about half
an hour to cross the lake to Hakone-machi (also called simply Hakone; *machi*
means city) and Moto-Hakone, two resort towns right next to each other on the
southern edge of the lake. This end of the lake affords the best view of Mount
Fuji, one often depicted in tourist publications. Boats are in operation year-round
(though they run less frequently in winter and not at all in stormy weather); the
last boat departs around 5pm from the end of March to the end of November.
Buses connect Togendai with Moto-Hakone, Odawara, and Shinjuku.

If you're heading back to Tokyo, buses depart for Odawara near the boat piers
in both Hakone-machi and Moto-Hakone. Otherwise, for more sightseeing, get
off the boat in Hakone-machi, turn left, and walk about 5 minutes on the town's
main road, following the signs and turning left to the **Hakone Check Point** ⋆
(**Hakone Seki-sho;** ✆ **0460/3-6635**), on a road lined with souvenir shops. This
is a reconstructed guardhouse originally built in 1619 to serve as a checkpoint
along the famous Tokaido Highway, which connected Edo (present-day Tokyo)
with Kyoto. In feudal days, local lords, called *daimyo,* were required to spend
alternate years in Edo; their wives were kept on in Edo as virtual hostages to dis-
courage the lords from planning rebellions while in their homelands. This was
one of several points along the highway to guard against the transport of guns,
spies, and female travelers trying to flee Edo. Passes were necessary for travel, and
although it was possible to sneak around it, male violators who were caught were
promptly executed, while women suffered the indignity of having their heads
shaven and then being given away to anyone who wanted them. Inside the
reconstructed guardhouse, you'll see life-size models re-enacting scenes inside a
checkpoint. Your ticket also allows admission to a small museum with displays
relating to the Edo Period, including items used for travel, samurai armor, and
gruesome articles of torture. Open daily from 9am to 5pm (until 4:30pm in
winter); admission is ¥300 ($2.50) for adults and ¥150 ($1.25) for children. It
shouldn't take more than 30 minutes to see everything.

Just beyond the Hakone Check Point, at the big parking lot with the traditional gate, is the **Hakone Detached Palace Garden (Onshi-Hakone-Koen),**
which lies on a small promontory on Lake Ashi and has spectacular views of the
lake and, sometimes, Mount Fuji. Originally part of an imperial summer villa
built in 1886, the garden is open free to the public 24 hours daily. It's a great
place for wandering. On its grounds is the **Lakeside Observation Building**
(open daily 9am–4:30pm), with displays relating to the Hakone Palace, which
was destroyed by earthquakes.

If you take the northernmost exit from the garden, crossing a bridge, you'll
see the neighboring resort town, **Moto-Hakone.** Across the highway and lined
with ancient and mighty cedars is part of the old **Tokaido Highway** itself. During the Edo Period, more than 400 cedars were planted along this important
road, which today stretches 1½ miles along the curve of Lake Ashi and makes
for a pleasant stroll (unfortunately, though, a modern road has been built right
beside the original one). Moto-Hakone is a 5-minute walk from the Detached
Palace Garden.

In Moto-Hakone, the **Narukawa Art Museum** ⋆⋆ (✆ **0460/3-6828**) is
very worthwhile and located just after you enter town, up the hill to the right
when you reach the orange torii gate. It specializes in modern works of the

Nihonga style of painting, developed during the Heian period (794–1185) and sparser than Western paintings (which tend to fill in backgrounds and every inch of canvas). Large paintings and screens by contemporary Nihonga artists are on display, including works by Yamamoto Kyujin, Maki Susumu, Kayama Matazo, Hirayama Ikuo, and Hori Fumiko. Changing exhibitions feature younger up-and-coming artists, as well as glassware. I wouldn't miss it; views of Lake Ashi and Mount Fuji are a bonus. Open daily 9am to 5pm; admission is ¥1,200 ($10) for adults and ¥600 ($5) for children.

WHEN YOU'RE DONE SIGHTSEEING FOR THE DAY

Buses depart for Hakone Yumoto and Odawara from both Hakone-machi and Moto-Hakone two to four times an hour. Be sure to check the time of the last departure; generally it's around 8pm, but this can change with the season and the day of the week. (The bus also passes two of the accommodations recommended below, The Fujiya Hotel and Ichinoyu, as well as Yunessun hot-springs baths; another bus will take you to Fuji-Hakone Guest House.) Otherwise, the trip from Moto-Hakone takes approximately 30 minutes to Hakone Yumoto, where you can catch the Romance Car bound for Shinjuku, or 50 minutes to Odawara, where you can then catch the Odakyu express train or Romance Car back to Shinjuku.

WHERE TO STAY

Japan's ryokan sprang into existence to accommodate the stately processions of daimyo and shogun as they traversed the roads between Edo and the rest of Japan. Many of these ryokan were built along the Tokaido Highway, and some of the oldest are found in Hakone.

EXPENSIVE

The Fujiya Hotel ★★★ *(Finds)* The Fujiya, which was established in 1878, is quite simply the grandest, most majestic old hotel in Hakone; indeed, it might be the loveliest historic hotel in Japan. I love this hotel for its comfortably old-fashioned atmosphere, including such Asian touches as a Japanese-style roof, lots of windows, and long wooden corridors with photographs of famous guests. Staying here transports me to a gentler, and more genteel, past. There are five separate buildings, all different and added on at various times in the hotel's long history, but management has been meticulous in retaining its historic traditions. A landscaped garden out back, with a waterfall, a pond, a greenhouse, and stunning views over the valley, is great for strolls and meditation. An outdoor pool, fed by river water, occupies a corner of the garden, and there's also an indoor thermal pool and hot-spring public baths. Even the private bathroom in each room has piped in hot-spring water.

Except for rooms in the Forest Lodge (built in 1960 and rather ordinary), rooms are old-fashioned and spacious with high ceilings and antique furnishings; some even have claw-foot tubs. The most expensive rooms are the largest, but my favorites are those in the Flower Palace, which has an architectural style that reminds me of a Japanese temple and seems unchanged since its 1936 construction. Even if you don't stay here, do come for a meal or tea. Highly recommended.

Note: The special rate for foreigners, below, is higher on weekends and is not available during Golden Week, the month of August, or New Year's; if you want to stay in the Flower Palace, you'll pay $30 extra.

359 Miyanoshita, Hakone-machi, Ashigarashimo-gun 250-0404. ℂ **0460/2-2211.** Fax 0460/2-2210. www. fujiyahotel.co.jp. 146 units. Special foreigners' rate, $125 single or double; $50 extra Sat or night before

> **Tips   A Note on Japanese Symbols**
>
> Many hotels, restaurants, attractions, and other establishments in Japan
> do not have signs giving their names in Roman (English-language) letters.
> Appendix C lists the Japanese symbols for all such places described in this
> guide. Each set of characters representing an establishment name has a
> number in the appendix, which corresponds to the number that appears
> inside the oval preceding the establishment's name in the text. Thus, to
> find the Japanese symbol for, say, **Ichinoyu,** refer to number 77 in appen-
> dix C.

holiday. Regular rates, ¥18,000 – ¥25,000 ($150–$208) single or double; ¥5,000 ($42) extra on Sat or night before holiday; ¥10,000 ($83) extra mid-Aug and New Year's. AE, DC, MC, V. Station: Miyanoshita, Hakone Tozan Railway (5 min.). Bus: From Odawara or Moto-Hakone to Miyanoshita Onsen stop (1 min.). **Amenities:** 3 restaurants (see "Where to Dine," below); bar; indoor and outdoor pools (free for hotel guests); hot-spring baths; Jacuzzi; sauna; souvenir shops; game room; golf course; room service (9am–10pm); in-room massage; same-day laundry service; landscaped garden. *In room:* A/C, TV, minibar, hair dryer.

(77) **Ichinoyu** ★★   Located near Tonosawa Station (on the Hakone Tozan Line) next to a roaring river, this delightful, rambling, wooden building stands on a tree-shaded winding road that follows the track of the old Tokaido High-way. First opened more than 370 years ago, Ichinoyu is now in its 15th genera-tion of owners. It claims to be the oldest ryokan in the area and was once honored by the visit of a shogun during the Edo Period. Old artwork, wall hang-ings, and paintings decorate the place.

The ryokan has only tatami rooms. The oldest date from the Meiji Period, more than 100 years ago. My favorite is the Take, old-fashioned and consisting mainly of seasoned and weathered wood; it faces the river and even has its own private outdoor bath, also with views of the river. Ditto for the Kotobuki room (rooms with private *rotenburo,* or outdoor hot-spring bath, cost ¥5,000/$42 extra). Both the communal tubs and the tubs in the rooms are supplied with hot water from a natural spring. The price you pay depends on your room, the meals you select, and the time of year.

90 Tonosawa, Hakone-machi, Ashigarashimo-gun 250-0315. ✆ **0460/5-5331.** Fax 0460/5-5335. www.ichinoyu. co.jp. 24 units (12 with bathroom). ¥8,800 – ¥14,800 ($73–$123) per person including 2 meals. ¥3,000 ($25) extra per person in Aug and on Sat and holidays. AE, DC, MC, V. Station: Tonosawa, Hakone Tozan Railway (6 min.). Bus: From Odawara or Moto-Hakone to Tonosawa bus stop (2 min.). **Amenities:** Indoor and outdoor hot-spring baths. *In room:* A/C, TV, fridge, safe.

INEXPENSIVE

Ashinoko Camp Mura *Kids*   Since you're in a national park, you might be inclined to enjoy nature by roughing it in a cabin beside Lake Ashi, just a 10-minute walk from the ropeway to Sounzan and the boat to Hakone-machi. Operated by Kanagawa Prefecture and also with tent camping, it offers row and detached (more expensive and closer to the lake) cabins that sleep up to six per-sons, each with two bedrooms, a bathroom, a living room with cooking facili-ties and tableware, and a deck with picnic table. However, there is no supermarket in nearby Togendai, so you'll either want to bring your own food or dine on Japanese breakfast and dinner in the camp restaurant (reservations required). There's a hiking trail around the lake. A great place for kids.

164 Hakone-machi, Moto-Hakone, Ashigarashimo-gun, Kanagawa 250-0522. ✆ **0460/4-8279.** Fax 0460/4-6489. 36 units. Peak season ¥26,250 ($218) row cabin; ¥31,500 ($262) detached cabin. Off season ¥15,750

($131) row cabin; ¥21,000 ($175) detached cabin. No credit cards. Bus: Togendai, from Odawara (1 hr.) or Shinjuku (2 hr.), then a 10-min. walk. **Amenities:** Restaurant; rental bikes; barbecue grills. *In room:* Kitchenette, fridge.

Fuji-Hakone Guest House   It's a bit isolated, but this Japanese Inn Group member offers inexpensive, spotlessly clean lodging in tatami rooms, all non-smoking. A newer house, situated in tranquil surroundings set back from a tree-shaded road, is run by a man who speaks very good English and is happy to provide sightseeing information, including a map of the area with local restaurants. Some of the rooms face the Hakone mountain range. Pluses are the communal lounge area with TV and even a piano and a guitar; and the outdoor hot-spring bath (for which there's an extra ¥500/$4.15 charge).

912 Sengokuhara, Hakone, Kanagawa 250-0631. ℂ 0460/4-6577. Fax 0460/4-6578. www.fujihakone.com. 14 units (none with bathroom). ¥5,000–¥6,000 ($42–$50) single; ¥10,000–¥12,000 ($83–$100) double; ¥15,000–¥16,000 ($125–$133) triple. Plus ¥150 ($1.25) local tax per person. Peak season and weekends ¥1,000–¥2,000 ($8.35–$17) extra. Minimum 2-night stay preferred. Western breakfast ¥800 ($6.65) extra. AE, MC, V. Bus: Hakone Tozan (included in the Hakone Free Pass) from Togendai (15 min.) or from Odawara Station (50 min.) to the Senkyoro-mae stop (announced in English), then a 1-min. walk. **Amenities:** Hot-spring bath; coin-op laundry and dryer; communal fridge and microwave. *In room:* A/C, TV.

WHERE TO DINE

For casual dining while sightseeing, the Hakone Open-Air Museum has a pleasant cafe overlooking the park's fantastic scenery. Also sporting a view is the even less formal restaurant at the Owakudani Ropeway Station, serving spaghetti, curry rice, noodles, and other inexpensive fare.

Main Dining Room ★★ CONTINENTAL   Hakone's grandest, oldest hotel, conveniently located near a stop on the two-car Hakone Tozan Railway, is a memorable place for a good Western meal. The main dining hall, dating from 1930, is very bright and cheerful, with a high and intricately detailed ceiling, large windows with Japanese screens, a wooden floor, and white tablecloths. The views of the Hakone Hills are impressive, and the service by the bow-tied wait-staff is attentive. For lunch you can have such dishes as spaghetti, sandwiches, fried chicken, rainbow trout, and sirloin steak. The excellent dinners feature elaborate set courses or a la carte dishes ranging from scallops and sole to grilled lamb, chicken, rainbow trout, and steaks. Afterward, be sure to tour the landscaped garden.

In The Fujiya Hotel, 359 Miyanoshita. ℂ 0460/2-2211. Reservations required for dinner. Main dishes ¥2,200–¥6,800 ($18–$57); set dinners ¥10,000–¥15,000 ($83–$125); lunch main dishes ¥1,500–¥5,800 ($13–$48). AE, DC, MC, V. Daily noon–2pm and 6–8:30pm. Station: Miyanoshita on the Hakone Tozan Railway (5 min.).

6 Mount Fuji

100km (62 miles) SW of Tokyo

Mount Fuji, affectionately called "Fuji-san" by the Japanese, has been revered since ancient times. Throughout the centuries Japanese poets have written about it, painters have painted it, pilgrims have flocked to it, and more than a few people have died on it. Without a doubt, this mountain has been photographed more than anything else in Japan.

Mount Fuji is stunningly impressive. At 3,716m (12,388 ft.) the tallest mountain in Japan, it towers far above anything else around it, a cone of almost perfectly symmetrical proportions. It is majestic, grand, and awe-inspiring. To the Japanese it symbolizes the very spirit of their country. Though it's visible on clear days (mostly in winter) from as far as 161km (100 miles) away, Fuji-san is, unfortunately, almost always cloaked in clouds. If you catch a glimpse of this mighty mountain, consider yourself extremely lucky. One of the best spots for views of Mount Fuji is **Hakone** (see above).

ESSENTIALS

There are six ascending trails to the summit of Mount Fuji (and six descending trails), each divided into 10 stages of unequal length, with most climbs starting at the Go-go-me, or the Fifth Stage. From Tokyo, **Kawaguchiko Trail** is the most popular and most easily accessible, as well as the least steep. Although the "official" climbing season is from mid-July to the end of August, you can climb Mount Fuji April through October, weather permitting.

GETTING THERE   The easiest way to reach Kawaguchiko Trail's Fifth Stage is by **bus** from Shinjuku Station, and most trips require a change of buses at Kawaguchiko Station. There are some 15 buses a day in operation between Shinjuku and Kawaguchiko Station from mid-July to the end of August, with less frequent service April through mid-July and September through October. The bus ride from Shinjuku Station, with departures a 2-minute walk from the west side of the station in front of the Yasuda Seimi no. 2 Building at bus platform no. 50, takes about 1 hour and 45 minutes and costs ¥1,700 ($14) one-way to Kawaguchiko Station. Note that you must make a reservation for this bus through **Keio Kosoku Bus Yoyaku Center** (© **03/5376-2222**) or a travel agency such as JTB. Less frequent buses also depart from Tokyo Station's Yaesu south exit for the same price.

From Kawaguchiko Station there are buses onward to the Fifth Stage, with the trip taking approximately 45 minutes and costing another ¥1,700 ($14). During the official climbing season, a handful of buses travel directly from Shinjuku Station to Kawaguchiko Trail's Fifth Stage, costing ¥2,600 ($22) one-way and taking almost 2½ hours. Note that bus service is suspended in winter, when Mount Fuji is blanketed in snow and is considered too dangerous for novice climbers. Otherwise, buses generally run April through October to the Fifth Stage unless there is inclement weather (including snow), though they run far less frequently than during the official season.

If you want to use your Japan Rail Pass, you can leave from Tokyo's Shinjuku Station via the **JR Chuo Line** to Otsuki, where you change to the **Fuji Kyuko Line** for Kawaguchiko Station (note, however, that you must pay an extra ¥1,100/$9.15 for the last leg of the journey). The entire trip takes about 2 hours. From Kawaguchiko Station, you can then take the 45-minute bus ride onward to the Fifth Stage.

VISITOR INFORMATION   More information and train and bus schedules can be obtained from the **Tokyo Tourist Information Center,** including a leaflet called "Mount Fuji and Fuji Five Lakes." See "Visitor Information," in chapter 3.

CLIMBING MOUNT FUJI

Mount Fuji is part of a larger national park called **Fuji-Hakone-Izu National Park.** Of the handful of trails leading to the top, most popular for Tokyoites is the **Kawaguchiko Trail,** which is divided into 10 different stages; the Fifth Stage, located about 2,475m (8,250 ft.) up and served by bus, is the usual starting point. From here it takes about 6 hours to reach the summit and 3 hours for the descent.

PREPARING FOR YOUR CLIMB   You don't need climbing experience to ascend Mount Fuji (you'll see everyone from grandmothers to children making the pilgrimage), but you do need stamina and a good pair of walking shoes. The climb is possible in tennis shoes, but if the rocks are wet, they can get awfully slippery. You should also bring a light plastic raincoat (which you can buy at souvenir shops at the Fifth Stage) since it often rains on the mountain, a sun hat, a bottle of water, a sweater for the evening, and a flashlight if you plan on hiking at night. It gets very chilly on Mount Fuji at night. Even in August, the average temperature on the summit is 42.5°F (5.8°C).

Because of snow and inclement weather from fall through late spring, the best time to make an ascent is during the "official" climbing season from mid-July to August 31. This is also when buses run most frequently. However, it's the most crowded time of the year. Consider the fact that there are more than 120 million Japanese, most of whom wouldn't dream of climbing the mountain outside the "official" 1½ months it's open, and you begin to get the picture. About 600,000 people climb Fuji-san every year, mostly in July and August and mostly on weekends—so if you plan on climbing Mount Fuji on a Saturday or a Sunday in summer, go to the end of the line, please.

Don't be disappointed when your bus deposits you at **Kawaguchiko Fifth Stage,** where you'll be bombarded with souvenir shops, restaurants, and busloads of tourists; most of these tourists aren't climbing to the top. As soon as you get past them and the blaring loudspeakers, you'll find yourself on a steep rocky path, surrounded only by scrub brush and the hikers on the path below and above you. After a couple hours, you'll probably find yourself above the roily clouds, which stretch in all directions. It will be as if you are on an island, barren and rocky, in the middle of an ocean.

STRATEGIES FOR CLIMBING TO THE TOP   The usual procedure for climbing Mount Fuji is to take a morning bus, start climbing in early afternoon, spend the night near the summit, get up early in the morning to climb the rest of the way to the top, and then watch the sun rise (about 4:30am) from atop Mount Fuji (you can, of course, also wake up in time to see the sun rise and then continue climbing). At the top is a 1-hour hiking trail that circles the crater. Hikers then begin the descent, reaching the Fifth Stage about noon.

There are about 20 **mountain huts** along the Kawaguchiko Trail above the Fifth Stage, but they're very primitive, providing only a futon and toilet facilities, and some with a capacity to house 500 hikers. The cost is ¥5,000 ($42) per person without meals, ¥7,000 ($58) with meals. When I stayed in one of these huts, dinner consisted of dried fish, rice, bean-paste soup, and pickled vegetables; breakfast was exactly the same. Still, unless you want to carry your own food, I'd opt for the meals. Note that huts are open only in July and August; book as early as you can to assure a place. I recommend the **Toyokan Hut** at the Seventh Stage (© **0555/22-1040**) or the **Taishikan Hut** at the Eighth Stage

---

(Fun Fact   **Mount Fuji or Bust**

The first documented case of someone scaling Mount Fuji is from the early 8th century. During the Edo Period, pilgrimages to the top were considered a purifying ritual, with strict rules governing dress and route. Women, thought to defile sacred places, were prohibited from climbing mountains until 1871.

(© 0555/22-1947). Call the **Japanese Inn Union of Mount Fuji** at © 0555/22-1944 for more information.

In the past few decades, there's been a trend in which climbers arrive at the Fifth Stage late in the evening and then climb to the top during the night with the aid of flashlights. After watching the sunrise, they then make their descent. That way, they don't have to spend the night in one of the huts.

Climbing Mount Fuji is definitely a unique experience, but there's a saying in Japan: "Everyone should climb Mount Fuji once; only a fool would climb it twice."

Appendix A:
Tokyo in Depth

With a population of about 12 million, Tokyo is one of the largest cities in the world—and one of the most intriguing, exciting, and invigorating. As the nation's capital and financial nerve center, Tokyo is where it's happening in Asia. In a nation of overachievers, Tokyo has more than its fair share of intelligentsia, academics, politicians, businesspeople, artists, and writers, and it's the country's showcase for technology, fashion, art, music, and advertising. People rush around here with such purpose and determination, it's hard not to feel that you're in the midst of something important, that you're witnessing history in the making.

As for innovation, Tokyo has long been recognized as a leader. Indeed, Japan, once dismissed as merely an imitator with no imagination of its own, has long been at the forefront of all things technological, from computers and cars to audiovisual equipment and kitchen and office gadgetry. Walking through the stores of Akihabara, Tokyo's electronics center, provokes an uneasiness few visitors can shake, for it's here that the latest goods are sold long before they reach Western markets.

Yet despite outward appearances, all is not rosy in the land of the rising sun. Its unparalleled economic growth, considered invincible in the 1980s and generating both admiration and envy worldwide, came to an abrupt halt in 1992 with the burst of the economic bubble and the onset of the country's worst recession since World War II. On its heels came political scandal, rising unemployment, Kobe's catastrophic 1995 earthquake, the release of nerve gas on a Tokyo subway, a nuclear power accident only 113km (70 miles) from the capital, a schoolyard massacre in Osaka Prefecture, and a declining birth rate coupled with an aging population, all of which conspired to create a sense of anxiety and uncertainty.

Today, the economy is still stagnant, growing at a rate of less than 1% a year compared to the 6% annual growth it enjoyed in the 1980s. In April 2003, the Nikkei (the Japanese version of the American Dow) plunged to a 20-year low. Unemployment hovers around 5.3%. Homelessness is now so common that it no longer draws stares, even in the swank Ginza district. Moreover, crime, once almost unheard of, is a major topic of concern. My former Tokyo landlady fears burglary so much that she no longer opens her door to strangers. The car of my friend's boyfriend was stolen from a parking lot, one of 119 luxury cars reported stolen in Tokyo in 2000. In 2001, 2.34 million thefts were reported to police nationwide, almost triple the number reported a decade earlier.

For the short-term visitor to Tokyo, however, problems that loom in the public psyche are not readily apparent—unless you go to Ueno or Yoyogi parks, where the growing number of homeless is nothing short of astounding. Crime, though undeniably on the increase, is still negligible when compared to levels in the United States, and Tokyo remains one of the safest cities in the world. Although it's true that I am more careful than I was 15 years ago—I guard my purse in crowded subways and I avoid parks after dark—for Americans such precautions seem merely self-evident. But while I'm cautious about theft and

Impressions

*The Japanese are in general intelligent and provident, free and uncon-
strained, obedient and courteous, curious and inquisitive, industrious
and ingenious, frugal and sober, cleanly, good-natured and friendly,
upright and just, trusty and honest, mistrustful, superstitious, proud, and
haughty, unforgiving, brave, and invincible.*
  —Charles Peter Thunberg, *Travels in Europe, Africa, and Asia* (1795)

purse-snatching, I never worry about personal safety when I'm walking the
streets of Tokyo. In fact, it never even crosses my mind. Violent crime—especially against strangers—remains virtually unheard of in Japan.

Moreover, while Tokyo remains one of the most expensive cities in the world,
it now offers something that would have been unthinkable during the spending-
happy 1980s: bargains. Tony French restaurants serve value-conscious fixed-
price lunches, secondhand clothing stores sell last year's designer wear, 100-Yen
discount shops do a brisk business, and some hotels—particularly those at the
lower end—haven't raised their rates in years.

But for the first time since the economic bubble burst, I've noticed currents
of change in Tokyo. After years of no new attractions, few new hotels, deflated
prices, and only a scattered handful of new developments, Tokyo is experiencing something of a development boom, spurred by auctions of massive land
tracts once owned by Japan Railways near train stations. Former railway switch-
ing yards near Tokyo Bay have blossomed into skyscrapers containing offices,
restaurants, shops, and a hotel, known collectively as Shiodome. Land beside
Tokyo Station now boasts the new Four Seasons Hotel Tokyo at Marunouchi,
with rooms costing more than $500 a night. In fact, Tokyo will see a blitz of
new, foreign-owned luxury hotels opening in the coming years, including the St.
Regis Tokyo in 2004, the Mandarin Oriental Tokyo in 2006, the Peninsula
Tokyo in 2006, and a Ritz-Carlton in 2007.

But the biggest land development to hit Tokyo is Roppongi Hills, which
stretches over 11.6 hectares (28 acres) and contains more than 120 high-end
boutiques, more than 60 restaurants, the new Grand Hyatt Tokyo, offices, luxury apartments, an art museum, an observation deck, and a multiplex cinema.
My favorite part of the story: It took developer Mori Minoru 18 years of nego-
tiation with 500 property owners to secure the land for development.

Of course, the influx of new hotels and office buildings is giving some Tokyoites the jitters. A glut of new office space may translate into empty buildings;
an onslaught of new hotels may launch a battle for survival.

Yet despite what the future may bring, I'm convinced Tokyo at street level will
remain as it's always been—humming with energy, crowded beyond belief, and
filled with acts of human kindness.

2 A Look at the Past

EARLY HISTORY Archaeological
finds show that the region was inhab-
ited as early as 30,000 B.C., but it was-
n't until the 6th century that Japan
began spreading its cultural wings.
Taking its cues from China, its great

Dateline

- 794 Kyoto becomes Japan's capital.
- 1192 Minamoto Yoritomo becomes
  shogun and establishes his shogunate
  government in Kamakura.

continues

neighbor to the west, Japan adopted Buddhism, the character system of writing, and Chinese art forms and architecture, and molded them into a style of its own.

In A.D. 794 the Japanese imperial family established a new capital in Heiankyo (present-day Kyoto), where it remained for more than 1,000 years. The arts flourished, and extravagant temples and pavilions were erected. Noh drama, the tea ceremony, flower arranging, and landscape gardening developed. But even though Kyoto served as the cultural heart of the nation, it was often the nation's capital in name only. Preoccupied by their own luxurious lifestyle, the nobles and royal court of Kyoto were little match for rebellious military clans in the provinces.

THE FEUDAL PERIOD   The first successful clan uprising took place at the end of the 12th century, when a young warrior named Minamoto Yoritomo won a bloody civil war that brought him supremacy over the land. Wishing to set up his rule far away from the imperial family in Kyoto, he made his capital in a remote and easily defended fishing village called Kamakura, not far from today's Tokyo. He created a military government, a shogunate, ushering in a new era in Japan's history in which the power of the country passed from the aristocratic court into the hands of the warrior class. In becoming the nation's first shogun, or military dictator, Yoritomo laid the groundwork for the military governments that lasted for another 700 years in Japan—until the imperial court was restored in 1868.

The Kamakura Period, from 1192 to 1333, is perhaps best known for the unrivaled ascendancy of the warrior caste, called samurai. Ruled by a rigid code of honor, the samurai were bound in loyalty to their feudal lord and would defend him to the death. If they failed in their duties, they could

- 1333 The Kamakura shogunate falls and the imperial system is restored.
- 1603 Tokugawa Ieyasu becomes shogun and establishes his shogunate in Edo (present-day Tokyo), marking the beginning of a 264-year rule by the Tokugawa clan.
- 1612 Silver mint opens in the Ginza.
- 1633 Japan closes its doors to foreign trade and subsequently forbids all foreigners from landing in Japan and all Japanese from leaving.
- 1787 The population of Tokyo reaches 1.3 million.
- 1853 Commodore Matthew C. Perry of the U.S. Navy persuades the Japanese to sign a trade agreement with the United States.
- 1867 Tokugawa regime is overthrown, bringing Japan's feudal era to a close.
- 1868 Emperor Meiji assumes power, moves his imperial capital from Kyoto to Tokyo, and begins the industrialization of Japan.
- 1873 Ueno Park opens to the public as Tokyo's first city park.
- 1878 Establishment of the Tokyo Stock Exchange.
- 1922 The Imperial Hotel, designed by Frank Lloyd Wright, opens in Hibiya, opposite the Imperial Palace.
- 1923 Tokyo and Yokohama are devastated by a major earthquake in which more than 100,000 people lose their lives.
- 1937 Japan goes to war with China and conquers Nanking.
- 1940 Japan forms a military alliance with Germany and Italy.
- 1941 The Pacific War begins as Japan bombs Pearl Harbor.
- 1945 Hiroshima and Nagasaki suffer atomic bomb attacks; Japan agrees to surrender.
- 1946 The emperor renounces his claim to divinity; Japan adopts a new, democratic constitution; women gain the right to vote.
- 1952 The Allied occupation of Japan ends; Japan regains its independence.
- 1956 Japan is admitted to the United Nations.
- 1964 The XVIII Summer Olympic Games are held in Tokyo.
- 1989 Emperor Hirohito dies after a 63-year reign.

redeem their honor by committing ritualistic suicide, or *seppuku*. Spurning
the soft life led by the noble court
in Kyoto, the samurai embraced a
harsher and simpler set of ideals and a
spartan lifestyle, embodied in the
tenets of Zen Buddhism's mental and
physical disciplines.

The Kamakura Period was followed
by 200 years of vicious civil wars and
confusion as *daimyo* (feudal lords)
staked out their fiefdoms throughout
the land and strove for supremacy.
Not unlike a baron in medieval
Europe, a daimyo had absolute rule
over the people who lived in his fief-
dom and was aided in battles by his
samurai retainers.

THE RISE OF TOKUGAWA In
the second half of the 16th century,
several brilliant military strategists rose
to power, but none proved as shrewd
as Tokugawa Ieyasu, a statesman so
skillful in eliminating his enemies that
his heirs would continue to rule Japan
for the next 250 years. It was with him
that Tokyo's history began.

For centuries, present-day Tokyo
was nothing more than a rather
obscure village called Edo, which
means simply "mouth of the estuary."
Then, in 1590, Tokugawa acquired
eight provinces surrounding Edo,
much of it marsh and wilderness, with
little fresh water available. Undaunted,
Tokugawa chose Edo as his base and
immediately set to work correcting the
area's shortcomings by reclaiming land,
building a conduit for fresh water, and
constructing a castle surrounded by
moats.

In 1603, Tokugawa succeeded in
defeating all his rivals in a series of

1990 Hirohito's son, Akihito, formally ascends the throne and proclaims the new "Era of Peace" (Heisei).

1991 Tokyo's new city hall, the Tokyo Metropolitan Government Office, designed by Kenzo Tange, opens in Shinjuku.

1992 The worst recession since World War II hits Japan. The Diet approves use of military forces for United Nations peacekeeping efforts.

1993 Liberal Democratic party loses election for the first time since 1955. Akebono, a Hawaiian, becomes first non-Japanese to reach sumo's highest rank of yokozuna.

1995 Japan's sense of security is shaken by the Great Hanshin Earth-quake (and the subsequent mishan-dling of rescue aid), which flattens the city of Kobe; and by the sarin-gas attack upon Tokyo's crowded com-muter trains.

1997 New Shinkansen bullet train connects Tokyo with Nagano in the Japan Alps, site of the 1998 Winter Olympics.

1998 The XVIII Winter Olympic Games are held in Nagano.

1999 A nuclear plant 113km (70 miles) northeast of Tokyo suffers Japan's worst nuclear accident, expos-ing dozens to radiation.

2001 A man storms into an elemen-tary school in Osaka Prefecture, fatally stabbing eight children. Public spirits rise with the birth of a baby girl to the crown prince and princess.

2002 North Korea admits that it kid-napped 13 young Japanese in the 1970s and 1980s to teach Japanese language and customs to North Korean spies.

2003 Shinagawa Station becomes a stop on the Tokaido-Sanyo line with connections to Kyoto, Hiroshima, and other points west.

brilliant battles, becoming shogun over all of Japan. He declared the sleepy village of Edo the seat of his shogunate government, leaving the emperor intact but
virtually powerless in Kyoto. He then set about expanding Edo Castle to make
it the most impressive castle in the land, surrounding it with an ingenious system of moats that radiated from the castle in a great swirl, giving him access to
the sea and thwarting enemy attack.

THE EDO PERIOD   Edo grew quickly as the shogunate capital. For greater protection, and to ensure that no daimyo in the distant provinces could grow strong enough to usurp the shogun's power, the Tokugawa government ordered every daimyo to reside in Edo for a prescribed number of months every other year, thus keeping the feudal lords under the watchful eye of the shogunate. Furthermore, all daimyo were required to leave their families in Edo as permanent residents, to serve as virtual hostages. There were as many as 270 daimyo in Japan in the 17th century, with each maintaining several mansions in Edo for family members and retainers, complete with elaborate compounds and expansive landscaped gardens. Together with their samurai, who made up almost half of Edo's population in the 17th century, the daimyo and their entourage must have created quite a colorful sight on the dusty streets of old Edo. By expending so much time and money traveling back and forth and maintaining residences in both the provinces and Edo, a daimyo would have been hard put to wage war against the shogun.

To cater to the needs of the shogun, daimyo, and their samurai retainers, merchants and craftsmen from throughout Japan swarmed to Edo. To accommodate them, hills were leveled and marshes filled in, creating what is now the Ginza, Shimbashi, and Nihombashi. By 1787 the population had swelled to 1.3 million, making Edo one of the largest cities in the world. It was a city few outsiders were ever permitted to see, however. Fearing the spread of Western influence and Christianity in Japan, not to mention daimyo growing rich through international trade, the Tokugawa shogunate adopted a policy of complete isolation in 1633, slamming Japan's doors to the outside world for more than 200 years. The shogunate forbade foreigners to enter Japan and forbade the Japanese to leave. Those who defied the strict decrees paid with their lives. The only exception to this policy of isolation was a colony of tightly controlled Chinese merchants in Nagasaki, and a handful of Dutch confined to a small trading post on a tiny island in Nagasaki.

The Edo Period (1603–1867) was a time of political stability, with all policy dictated by the shogunate government. Japanese society was divided into four distinct classes: samurai, farmers, craftsmen, and merchants. After daimyo and nobles, samurai occupied the most exalted social position and were the only ones allowed to carry two swords. At the bottom of the social ladder were the merchants. They occupied squalid tenements, which were typically long row houses constructed of wood and facing narrow meter-wide alleys, with open sewers running down the middle. Family homes were unimaginably small, consisting of a tiny entryway that also doubled as the kitchen and a single room about 9.2 sq. m (100 sq. ft.) in size. Since most of Edo was built of wood, it goes without saying that fires were a constant threat. In fact, rare indeed was the person who didn't lose his house at least several times during his lifetime. Between 1603 and 1868, almost 100 major fires swept through Edo, along with countless smaller fires. One of the most tragic fires occurred in 1657, after a severe drought had plagued the city for almost 3 months. Buffeted by strong winds, the flames ignited wooden homes and thatched roofs like tinder, raging for 3 days and reducing three-fourths of the city to smoldering ruins. More than 100,000 people lost their lives.

Despite such setbacks, the merchants of Tokyo grew in number and became so wealthy that new forms of luxury and entertainment arose to occupy their time. Kabuki drama and woodblock prints became the rage, while stone and porcelain ware, silk brocade for elaborate and gorgeous kimono, and lacquerware were elevated to wondrous works of art. Japan's most famous pleasure district was an area in northeast Edo called Yoshiwara, the "floating world of pleasure," where rich merchants spent fortunes to cavort with beautiful courtesans.

THE OPENING OF JAPAN   By the mid–19th century it was clear that the feudal system was outdated. With economic power in the hands of the merchants, money rather than rice became the primary means of exchange. Many samurai families found themselves on the brink of poverty, and discontent with the shogunate grew widespread.

In 1854, Commodore Matthew C. Perry of the U.S. Navy succeeded in forcing the shogun to sign an agreement granting America trading rights, thus ending 2 centuries of isolation. In 1868, the Tokugawas were overthrown, and Emperor Meiji was restored as ruler. The feudal era drew to an end.

THE MEIJI RESTORATION   Rather than remain in Kyoto, Emperor Meiji decided to take Edo for his own and moved his imperial capital to its new home in 1868. Renaming Edo Tokyo, or "Eastern Capital" (to distinguish it from the "western" capital of Kyoto), the emperor was quick to welcome ideas and technology from the West. The ensuing years, known as the Meiji Period (1868–1911), were nothing short of amazing, as Japan progressed rapidly from a feudal agricultural society of samurai and peasants to an industrial nation. The samurai were stripped of their power and were no longer permitted to carry swords; a prime minister and cabinet were appointed; a constitution was drafted; and a parliament, called the Diet, was elected. The railway, postal system, and even specialists and advisers were imported from the West. Between 1881 and 1898, 6,177 British, 2,764 Americans, 913 Germans, and 619 French were retained by the Japanese government to help transform Japan into a modern society.

As the nation's capital, Tokyo was hardest hit by this craze for modernization. Ideas for fashion, architecture, food, and department stores were imported from the West—West was best, and things Japanese were forgotten or pushed aside. It didn't help that Tokyo was almost totally destroyed *twice* in the first half of the 20th century: In 1923 a huge earthquake, measuring 7.9 on the Richter scale and known as the Great Kanto Earthquake, struck the city, followed by tsunami (tidal waves). More than 100,000 people died and a third of Tokyo was in ruins. Disaster struck again during World War II, when incendiary bombs laid more than half the city to waste and killed another 100,000 people.

WORLD WAR II & ITS AFTERMATH   Japan's expansionist policies in Asia during the 1930s and early 1940s spread the flag of the rising sun over Hong Kong, China, Singapore, Burma, Malaysia, the Philippines, the Dutch East Indies, and Guam. World War II, however, halted Japan's advance. Shortly after the United States dropped the world's first atomic bombs—over Hiroshima on August 6, 1945, and over Nagasaki 3 days later—surrender came, on August 14, 1945.

The end of the war brought American occupation forces to Japan, where they remained until 1952. It was the first time in Japan's history that the island nation had suffered defeat and occupation by a foreign power. The experience had a profound effect on the Japanese people. Emerging from their defeat, they began the long effort to rebuild their cities and economy. In 1946, under the guidance of the Allied military authority, headed by U.S. Gen. Douglas MacArthur, they adopted a new, democratic constitution that renounced war and divested the emperor of his claim to divinity. A parliamentary system of government was set up, and in 1947 the first general elections were held. The following year, the militarists and generals who had carried out the Pacific War were tried, and many of them were convicted. To the younger generation of Japanese, the occupation was less a painful burden that had to be suffered than an opportunity to remake their country, with American encouragement, into a modern, peace-loving, and democratic state.

A special relationship developed between the Japanese and their American occupiers. In the early 1950s, as the cold war between the United States and the Communist world erupted into hostilities in Korea, that relationship grew into a firm alliance, strengthened by a security treaty between Tokyo and Washington. In 1952, the occupation ended, and in 1956 Japan joined the United Nations as an independent country.

POSTWAR JAPAN   Perhaps unsurprising in a city trained in natural calamities, Tokyo was so adept at rebuilding that a decade later not a trace of wartime destruction remained. Avoiding involvement in foreign conflicts, the Japanese concentrated on economic recovery. Through a series of policies that favored domestic industries and shielded Japan from foreign competition, the country achieved rapid economic growth. By the mid-1960s—only a century after Japan had opened its doors to the rest of the world and embraced modernization—the Japanese had transformed their nation into a major industrial power, with Tokyo riding the crest of the economic wave. In 1964, in recognition of Japan's increasing importance, the Summer Olympic Games were held in Tokyo, thrusting the city into the international limelight.

As their economy continued to expand, the Japanese sought new markets abroad; by the early 1970s, they had attained a trade surplus, as Japanese products—cars and electronic goods—attracted more and more foreign buyers. By the 1980s, Japan Inc. seemed on the economic brink of ruling the world, as Japanese companies bought prime real estate around the globe, books flooded the Western market expounding Japanese business principles, and Japan enjoyed unprecedented financial growth.

In 1992, recession hit Japan, bursting the economic bubble and plunging the country into its worst recession since World War II. Bankruptcies reached an all-time high, Tokyo real-estate prices plummeted 70% from what they were in 1990, the Nikkei (Japan's version of the American Dow) fell a gut-churning 63% from its 1989 peak, and the country was rocked by one political scandal after another. Public confidence was further eroded in 1995, first by a major earthquake in Kobe that killed more than 6,000 people and proved that Japan's cities were not as safe as the government had maintained, and then by an attack by an obscure religious sect that released the deadly nerve gas sarin on Tokyo's subway system during rush hour, killing 12 people and sickening thousands. The nation had another scare in 1999 when an accident at a nuclear power plant only 113km (70 miles) from Tokyo exposed dozens to radiation; two workers subsequently died from the radiation. But the worst blow of all was in 2001, when a knife-wielding man stormed into an elementary school in Osaka Prefecture, fatally stabbing eight children and wounding 15 others. For many Japanese, it seemed that the very core of their society had begun to crumble.

Since 1999, Tokyo has been led by outspoken governor Ishihara Shintaro, a nationalist writer who, together with former Sony chairman Morita Akio, penned the 1989 best-selling *The Japan That Can Say No*. His election was regarded as a clear rejection of the status quo and a belief that change in Japan must come from within, with Tokyo clearly at the forefront. In 2001, that desire for change ushered in long-haired, 59-year-old Koizumi Junichiro as the new prime minister, long considered a maverick for his battles against the established power brokers and his cries for reform. The wished-for reforms, however, have been slow to materialize, and even though Tokyo has seen a spurt of urban development projects the past 2 years, worries abound that the recession is not yet over.

3 Dealing with the Language Barrier

Without a doubt, the hardest part of being in Tokyo is the language barrier. Suddenly you find yourself transported to a crowded city of 12 million people, where you can neither speak nor read the language. To make matters worse, many Japanese cannot speak English, and signs, menus, and shop names are often in Japanese only.

Realizing the difficulties foreigners have with the language, the **Japan National Tourist Organization (JNTO)** puts out a nifty booklet called *The Tourist's Language Handbook,* with sentences in English and their Japanese equivalents for almost every activity, from asking directions and shopping to ordering in a restaurant and staying in a Japanese inn. In addition, a glossary of common phrases and words appears in appendix B of this book.

If you need to ask directions in Tokyo, your best bet is to **ask younger people.** They have all studied English in school and are most likely to be able to help you. Japanese businessmen also often know some English. And as strange as it sounds, if you're having problems communicating with someone, try writing your question instead of speaking it. The emphasis in schools is on written rather than oral English (even many English-language teachers can't speak English very well), so Japanese who can't understand a word you say may know all the subtleties of syntax and English grammar. If you still have problems communicating, you can always call the **Tourist Information Center** (© **03/3201-3331**). And if you're heading out for a particular restaurant or shop, have your destination written out in Japanese by someone at your hotel to show to taxi drivers or passersby. If you get lost along the way, look for one of the police boxes, called *koban,* found in virtually every neighborhood. They have maps of their district and can pinpoint exactly where you want to go if you have the address with you.

THE WRITTEN LANGUAGE No one knows the exact origins of the Japanese language, but we do know that it existed only in spoken form until the 6th century. It was then that the Japanese borrowed Chinese characters, called **kanji,** and used them to develop their own form of written language. Later, two phonetic alphabet systems, **hiragana** and **katakana,** were added to kanji to form the existing Japanese writing system. Thus, Chinese and Japanese use some of the same pictographs, but otherwise there's no similarity between the languages; while they may be able to recognize some of each other's written language, the Chinese and Japanese cannot communicate verbally.

The Japanese written language—a combination of kanji, hiragana, and katakana—is probably one of the most difficult systems of written communication in the modern world. As for the spoken language, there are many levels of speech and forms of expression relating to a person's social status, age, and sex. Even nonverbal communication is vital to understanding Japanese, since what isn't said is often more important than what is. It's little wonder that Saint Francis Xavier, a Jesuit missionary who came to Japan in the 16th century, wrote that

Japanese was an invention of the devil designed to thwart the spread of Christianity. And yet, astoundingly, adult literacy in Japan is estimated to be 99%.

A note on establishment names: Many hotels, restaurants, and sightseeing attractions in Tokyo now have signs in **romaji** (Roman, or English-language, characters); many others do not. For places mentioned in this book that have only Japanese signs, I've included an appendix of the Japanese character names so you'll be able to recognize them. When you see a number in an oval preceding the name of a restaurant, Japanese-style inn, or other establishment, turn to appendix C, "A Japanese-Character Index of Establishment Names," and look for the corresponding number to find the Japanese character name of that establishment.

PRONUNCIATION   If you're having difficulty communicating with a Japanese-speaker, it may help to pronounce an English word in a Japanese way. Foreign words, especially English, have penetrated the Japanese language to such an extent that they're now estimated to make up 20% of everyday vocabulary. The problem is that these words change in Japanese pronunciation, because words always end in either a vowel or an n, and because two consonants in a single syllable are usually separated by a vowel. Would you recognize *terebi* as "television," *koohi* as "coffee," or *rajio* as "radio"?

OTHER HELPFUL TIPS   It's worth noting that Japanese nouns do not have plural forms; thus, for example, *ryokan*, a Japanese-style inn, can be both singular and plural. Plural sense is indicated by context. In addition, the Japanese custom is to list the family name first, followed by the given name. That is the format followed in this book, but note that many things published in English—business cards, city brochures, and so on—may follow the Western custom of listing family name last.

And finally, you may find yourself confused because of suffixes attached to Japanese place names. For example, *dori* can mean street, avenue, or road, and sometimes it's attached to the proper noun with a hyphen while at other times it stands alone. Thus, you may see Chuo-dori, Chuo Dori, or even Chuo-dori Avenue on English-language maps and street signs, but they are all one and the same street. Likewise, *dera* means "temple" and is often included at the end of the name, as in Kiyomizudera; *ji* means shrine.

WRITTEN ENGLISH IN JAPAN   You'll see English on shop signs, billboards, posters, shopping bags, and T-shirts. The words are often wonderfully misspelled, however, or used in such unusual contexts that you can only guess at the original intent. My days have been brightened innumerable times by the discovery of zany or unfathomable English. What, for example, could possibly be the meaning behind "Today birds, tomorrow men," which appeared under a picture of birds on a shopping bag? I have treasured ashtrays that read "The young boy grasped her heart firmly" and "Let's Trip in Hokkaido." In Matsue a "Beauty Saloon" conjures up images of beauties chugging mugs of beer, while in Gifu you can only surmise at the pleasures to be had at the Hotel Joybox. I appreciated the honesty of a Hokkaido Tourist Association employee whose business card identified him as working for the "Propagana Section." But imagine my consternation upon stepping on a bathroom scale that called itself the "Beauty-Checker."

The best sign I saw was at Narita Airport. At all check-in counters was a sign telling passengers they would be required to pay a departure tax at "the time of check in for your fright." I explained the cause of my amusement to the person behind the counter, and when I came back 2 weeks later, I was almost disappointed to find that all signs had been corrected. That's Japanese efficiency.

4 Shrines & Temples: Religion in Japan

The main religions in Japan are Shintoism and Buddhism, and many Japanese consider themselves believers in both. Most Japanese, for example, will marry in a Shinto ceremony, but when they die, they'll have a Buddhist funeral.

A native religion of Japan, **Shintoism** is the worship of ancestors and national heroes, as well as of all natural things, both animate and inanimate. These natural things are thought to embody gods and can be anyone or anything—mountains, trees, the moon, stars, rivers, seas, fires, animals, rocks, even vegetables. Shintoism also embraces much of Confucianism, which entered Japan in the 5th century and stressed the importance of family and loyalty. There are no scriptures in Shintoism, nor any ordained code of morals or ethics.

The place of worship in Shintoism is called a *jinja,* or shrine. The most obvious sign of a shrine is its *torii,* an entrance gate, usually of wood, consisting of two tall poles topped with either one or two crossbeams. Another feature common to shrines is a water trough with communal cups, where the Japanese will rinse out their mouths and wash their hands. Purification and cleanliness are important in Shintoism because they show respect to the gods. At the shrine, worshippers will throw a few coins into a money box, clap their hands twice to get the gods' attention, and then bow their heads and pray for whatever they wish—good health, protection, the safe delivery of a child, or a prosperous year. The most famous shrine in Tokyo is **Meiji Shrine.**

Founded in India in the 5th century, **Buddhism** came to Japan in the 6th century via China and Korea, bringing with it the concept of eternal life, and by the end of the 6th century it had gained such popularity that it was declared the state religion. Of the various Buddhist sects in Japan today, Zen Buddhism is probably the most well known in the West. Considered the most Japanese form of Buddhism, Zen is the practice of meditation and a strictly disciplined lifestyle to rid yourself of desire so that you can achieve enlightenment. There are no rites in Zen Buddhism, no dogmas, no theological conceptions of divinity. You do not analyze rationally, but rather know things intuitively. The strict and simple lifestyle of Zen appealed greatly to Japan's samurai warrior class, and many of Japan's arts, including the tea ceremony, arose from the practice of Zen.

Whereas Shintoists have shrines, Buddhists have temples, called *otera.* Instead of torii, temples will often have an entrance gate with a raised doorsill and heavy doors. Temples may also have a cemetery on their grounds (which Shinto shrines never have) as well as a pagoda. Tokyo's most famous temple is **Sensoji Temple** in Asakusa.

Appendix B: Glossary of Japanese Terms

Needless to say, it takes years to become fluent in Japanese, particularly in written Japanese, with its thousands of *kanji,* or Chinese characters, and many hiragana and katakana characters. Knowing just a few words of Japanese, however, is not only useful but will delight the Japanese people you meet in the course of your trip.

PRONUNCIATION

In pronouncing the following vocabulary, keep in mind that there's very little stress on individual syllables (pronunciation of Japanese is often compared to Italian). Here's an approximation of some of the sounds of Japanese:

a	*as in* father	**u**	*as in* boo
e	*as in* pen	**g**	*as in* gift at the beginning of
i	*as in* see		words; like ng in sing in the middle
o	*as in* oh		or at the end of words
oo	*as in* oooh		

Vowel sounds are almost always short unless they are pronounced double, in which case you hold the vowel a bit longer. *Okashi,* for example, means "a sweet," whereas *okashii* means "strange." As you can see, even slight mispronunciation of a word can result in confusion or hilarity. (Incidentally, jokes in Japanese are nearly always plays on words.) Similarly, double consonants are given more emphasis than only one consonant by itself.

USEFUL WORDS & PHRASES

BASIC TERMS

Yes   **Hai**
No   **Iie**
Hello   **Haro (or Konnichiwa)**
How are you?   **Ogenki desu ka?**
Thank you.   **Domo arigatoo.**
Please (go ahead)   **Doozo**
You're welcome.   **Doo-itashimashite.**
Good morning.   **Ohayo gozaimasu.**
Good afternoon.   **Konnichiwa.**
Good evening.   **Konbanwa.**
Good night.   **Oyasuminasai.**
How do you do?   **Hajimemashite?**
Good-bye.   **Sayonara (or Bye-bye!).**
Excuse me/Pardon me/I'm sorry.   **Sumimasen.**
Please (when offering something)   **Dozo**
Please (when requesting something)   **Kudasai**

BASIC QUESTIONS & EXPRESSIONS

I'm American.   **Amerikajin desu.**
I'm Canadian.   **Canadajin desu.**

I'm English. **Eikokujin desu.**
It's expensive. **Takai desu.**
It's cheap. **Yasui desu.**
How much is it? **Ikura desu ka?**
Where is it? **Doko desu ka?**
When is it? **Itsu desu ka?**
What is it? **Kore-wa, nan-desu-ka?**
Sorry, I don't speak Japanese. **Sumimasen, Nihongo was wakarimasen.**
Do you understand English? **Eigo wa wakarimasu ka?**
Do you understand? **Wakarimasu ka?**
I understand. **Wakarimasu.**
I don't understand. **Wakarimasen.**
Can I ask you a question? **Otazune shitaino desu ka?**
Just a minute, please. **Chotto matte kudasai.**
I like it. **Suki desu** (pronounced "ski").
Where is the toilet? **Toire wa, doko desu ka?**
My name is . . . [Your name] **to mo shimasu.**
What is your name? **O-namae wa, nan desu ka?**

TRAVEL EXPRESSIONS & DIRECTIONALS
Train station **Eki**
Airport **Kuukoo**
Subway **Chika-tetsu**
Bus **Bus-u**
Taxi **Takushi**
Airplane **Hikooki**
Train **Densha**
Bullet train **Shinkansen**
Where is . . . ? **Doko desu ka . . . ?**
Where is the train station? **Eki wa, doko desu ka?**
Limited express train (long distance) **Tokkyu**
Ordinary express train (doesn't stop at every station) **Kyuko**
Rapid train **Kaisoku densha**
Local train (one that stops at every station) **Kakueki teisha** (or **futsu**)
I would like a reserved seat, please. **Shiteiseki o kudasai.**
I would like a seat in the nonsmoking car, please. **Kinensha no shiteiski o kudasai.**
Unreserved seat **Jiyuseki**
Platform **Platt-homu**
Ticket **Kippu**
Destination **Ikisaki**
One-way ticket **Katamichi-kippu** (or **katamichiken**)
Round-trip ticket **Ofuku-kippu** (or **ofukuken**)
I would like to buy a ticket. **Kippu ichimai o kaitai no desu kedo.**
I would like to buy two tickets. **Kippu nimai o kaitai no desu kedo.**
Exit **Deguchi**
Entrance **Iriguchi**
North **Kita**
South **Minami**
East **Higashi**
West **Nishi**

Left   **Hidari**
Right   **Migi**
Straight ahead   **Massugu** (or **zutto**)
Is it far?   **Toi desu ka?**
Is it near?   **Chikai desu ka?**
Can I walk there?   **Aruite ikemasu ka?**
Street   **Dori** (or **michi**)
Tourist Information Office   **Kanko annaijo** (or **kanko kyokai**)
Where is the tourist office?   **Kanko annaijo, doko desu ka?**
May I have a map, please?   **Chizu o kudasai?**
Police   **Keisatsu**
Police box   **Koban**
Post office   **Yubin-kyoku**
I'd like to buy a stamp.   **Kitte o kaitai no desu kedo.**
Bank   **Ginko**
Hospital   **Byooin**
Drugstore   **Yakkyoku**
Convenience store   **Konbiniensu stoa**
Embassy   **Taishkan**
Department store   **Depaato**
Downtown area   **Hanka-gai**

LODGING TERMS

Hotel   **Hoteru**
Japanese-style inn   **Ryokan**
Youth hostel   **Yusu hosuteru**
Cotton kimono   **Yukata**
Room   **Heya**
Do you have a room available?   **Heya ga arimasu ka?**
Does that include meals?   **Shokuji wa tsuite imasu ka?**
Tax   **Zei**
Service charge   **Saavice**
Key   **Kagi**
Balcony   **Baranda**
Hot-spring spa   **Onsen**
Outdoor hot-spring bath   **Rotenburo**
Bath   **Ofuro**
Public bath   **Sento**
Where is the nearest public bath?   **Ichiban chikai sento wa, doko desu ka?**

DINING TERMS & PHRASES

Restaurant   **Resutoran** (serves Western-style food)
Dining hall   **Shokudo** (usually serves Japanese food)
Coffee shop   **Kissaten**
Japanese pub   **Izakaya** or **Nomiya**
Western food   **Yoshoku**
Japanese food   **Washoku**
Breakfast   **Chosoku**
Dinner   **Yushoku**
I'd like to make a reservation.   **Yoyaku oneigai shimasu.**
Menu   **Menyu**

Japanese green tea   **Ocha**
Black (Indian) tea   **Kocha**
Coffee   **Koohi**
Water   **Mizu**
Lunch or daily special, set menu   **Teishoku** (Japanese food)
Lunch or daily special, set menu   **Cosu,** or **seto** (usually Western food)
This is delicious.   **Oishii desu.**
Thank you for the meal.   **Gochisoo-sama deshita.**
I would like a fork, please.   **Foku o kudasai.**
I would like a spoon, please.   **Saji o kudasai.**
I would like a knife, please.   **Naifu o kudasai.**
May I have some more, please? (if you're asking for liquid, such as more coffee, or food)   **Mo skoshi o kudasai?**
May I have some more, please? (if you're asking for another bottle—say, of soda or sake)   **Mo ipon o kudasai?**
May I have some more, please? (if you asking for another cup—say, of coffee or tea)   **Mo ippai o kudasai?**
I would like sake, please.   **Osake o kudasai.**
I would like a cup of coffee.   **Koohii o ippai o kudasai.**
I would like the set meal, please.   **Seto o kudasai** or **Teishoku o kudasai.**

FOOD TERMS

Ayu   A small river fish; a delicacy of western Japan.
Anago   Conger eel.
Chu-hai Shochu   Shochu mixed with soda water and flavored with syrup and lemon (see below).
Dengaku   Lightly grilled tofu (see below) coated with a bean paste.
Dojo   A small, eel-like river fish.
Fugu   Pufferfish (also known as blowfish or globefish).
"Genghis Khan"   Mutton and vegetables grilled at your table.
Gohan   Rice.
Gyoza   Chinese fried pork dumplings.
Kaiseki   A formal Japanese meal consisting of many courses and served originally during the tea ceremony.
Kamameshi   A rice casserole topped with seafood, meat, or vegetables.
Kushiage (also **kushikatsu** or **kushiyaki**)   Deep-fried skewers of chicken, beef, seafood, and vegetables.
Maguro   Tuna.
Makizushi   Sushi (see below), vegetables, and rice rolled inside dried seaweed.
Miso   A soybean paste, used as a seasoning in soups and sauces.
Miso-shiru   Miso soup.
Mochi   Japanese rice cake.
Nabemono   A single-pot dish of chicken, beef, pork, or seafood, stewed with vegetables.
Natto   Fermented soybeans.
Nikujaga   A beef, potato, and carrot stew, flavored with sake (see below) and soy sauce; popular in winter.
Oden   Fish cakes, hard-boiled eggs, and vegetables, simmered in a light broth.

Okonomiyaki   A thick pancake filled with meat, fish, shredded cabbage, and vegetables or noodles, often cooked by diners at their table.

Ramen   Thick, yellow Chinese noodles, served in a hot soup.

Sake (also **Nihon-shu**)   Rice wine.

Sansai   Mountain vegetables, including bracken and flowering fern.

Sashimi   Raw seafood.

Shabu-shabu   Thinly sliced beef quickly dipped in boiling water and then dipped in a sauce.

Shochu   Japanese whiskey, made from rice, wheat, or potatoes.

Shojin-ryori   Japanese vegetarian food, served at Buddhist temples.

Shoyu   Soy sauce.

Shumai   Steamed Chinese pork dumplings.

Soba   Buckwheat noodles.

Somen   Fine white wheat vermicelli, eaten cold in summer.

Sukiyaki   A Japanese fondue of thinly sliced beef cooked in a sweetened soy sauce with vegetables.

Sushi (also **nigiri-zushi**)   Raw seafood placed on top of vinegared rice.

Tempura   Deep-fried food coated in a batter of egg, water, and wheat flour.

Teppanyaki   Japanese-style steak, seafood, and vegetables cooked by a chef on a smooth, hot tableside grill.

Tofu   Soft bean curd.

Tonkatsu   Deep-fried pork cutlets.

Udon   Thick white wheat noodles.

Unagi   Grilled eel.

Wasabi   Japanese horseradish, served with sushi.

Yakisoba   Chinese fried noodles, served with sautéed vegetables.

Yakitori   Charcoal-grilled chicken, vegetables, and other specialties, served on bamboo skewers.

Yudofu   Tofu simmered in a pot at your table.

MATTERS OF TIME

Now **Ima**		What time is it? **Nan-ji desu ka?**	
Later **Sto de**		Daytime **Hiruma**	
Today **Kyoo**		Morning **Asa**	
Tomorrow **Ashita**		Night **Yoru**	
Day after tomorrow **Asatte**		Afternoon **Gogo**	
Yesterday **Kinoo**		Holiday **Yasumi** (or **kyujitsu**)	
Which day? **Nan-nichi desu ka?**		Weekdays **Heijitsu**	

DAYS OF THE WEEK

Sunday **Nichiyoobi**	Thursday **Mokuyoobi**
Monday **Getsuyoobi**	Friday **Kinyoobi**
Tuesday **Kayoobi**	Saturday **Doyoobi**
Wednesday **Suiyoobi**	

MONTHS OF THE YEAR

January **Ichi-gatsu**	July **Shichi-gatsu**
February **Ni-gatsu**	August **Hachi-gatsu**
March **San-gatsu**	September **Kyuu-gatsu**
April **Shi-gatsu**	October **Juu-gatsu**
May **Go-gatsu**	November **Juuichi-gatsu**
June **Roku-gatsu**	December **Juuni-gatsu**

NUMBERS

01	Ichi	20	Nijuu
02	Ni	30	Sanjuu
03	San	40	Shijuu (or yonjuu)
04	Shi	50	Gojuu
05	Go	60	Rokujuu
06	Roku	70	Nanajuu
07	Shichi (or nana)	80	Hachijuu
08	Hachi	90	Kyuujuu
09	Kyuu	100	Hyaku
10	Juu	1,000	Sen
11	Juuichi	10,000	Ichiman
12	Juuni		

OTHER GENERAL NOUNS

Fusuma   Sliding paper doors.

Gaijin   Foreigner.

Geta   Wooden sandals.

Haori   A short coat worn over a kimono.

Irori   Open-hearth fireplace.

Izakaya (or Nomiya)   Japanese pub

Jinja   Shinto shrine.

Kotatsu   A heating element placed under a low table (which is covered with a blanket) for keeping your legs warm; used in place of a heater in traditional Japanese homes.

Minshuku   Inexpensive lodging in a private home; the Japanese equivalent of a European pension.

Nihonjin   Japanese person.

Shoji   White paper sliding windows.

Tatami   Rice mats.

Tera (or **dera**)   Temple.

Tokonoma   A small, recessed alcove in a Japanese room used to display a flower arrangement, scroll, or art object.

Torii   Entrance gate of a Shinto shrine, consisting usually of two poles topped with one or two crossbeams.

Washlet   Bidet toilet.

Yukata   A cotton kimono worn for sleeping.

Zabuton   Floor cushions.

Appendix C:
A Japanese-Character Index

Index

See also Accommodations and Restaurant indexes, below.

Frommer's Complete Guides

Frommer's
Southeast Asia
With Coverage of the Best Temples and Beaches

The only guide independent travelers need to make smart choices, avoid rip-offs, get the most for their money, and travel like a pro.

Frommer's Alaska
Frommer's Alaska Cruises & Ports of Call
Frommer's Amsterdam
Frommer's Argentina & Chile
Frommer's Arizona
Frommer's Atlanta
Frommer's Australia
Frommer's Austria
Frommer's Bahamas
Frommer's Barcelona, Madrid & Seville
Frommer's Beijing
Frommer's Belgium, Holland & Luxembourg
Frommer's Bermuda
Frommer's Boston
Frommer's Brazil
Frommer's British Columbia & the Canadian Rockies
Frommer's Brussels & Bruges with Ghent & Antwerp
Frommer's Budapest & the Best of Hungary
Frommer's California
Frommer's Canada
Frommer's Cancun, Cozumel & the Yucatan
Frommer's Cape Cod, Nantucket & Martha's Vineyard
Frommer's Caribbean
Frommer's Caribbean Cruises & Ports of Call
Frommer's Caribbean Ports of Call
Frommer's Carolinas & Georgia
Frommer's Chicago
Frommer's China
Frommer's Colorado
Frommer's Costa Rica
Frommer's Cuba

Frommer's Denmark
Frommer's Denver, Boulder & Colorado Springs
Frommer's England
Frommer's Europe
Frommer's European Cruises & Ports of Call
Frommer's Florence, Tuscany & Umbria
Frommer's Florida
Frommer's France
Frommer's Germany
Frommer's Great Britain
Frommer's Greece
Frommer's Greek Islands
Frommer's Hawaii
Frommer's Hong Kong
Frommer's Honolulu, Waikiki & Oahu
Frommer's Ireland
Frommer's Israel
Frommer's Italy
Frommer's Jamaica
Frommer's Japan
Frommer's Las Vegas
Frommer's London
Frommer's Los Angeles with Disneyland® & Palm Springs
Frommer's Maryland & Delaware
Frommer's Maui
Frommer's Mexico
Frommer's Montana & Wyoming
Frommer's Montreal & Quebec City
Frommer's Munich & the Bavarian Alps
Frommer's Nashville & Memphis
Frommer's Nepal
Frommer's New England
Frommer's Newfoundland & Labrador
Frommer's New Mexico
Frommer's New Orleans
Frommer's New York City
Frommer's New Zealand
Frommer's Northern Italy
Frommer's Norway
Frommer's Nova Scotia, New Brunswick & Prince Edward Island
Frommer's Oregon

Frommer's Ottawa
Frommer's Paris
Frommer's Peru
Frommer's Philadelphia & the Amish Cou
Frommer's Portugal
Frommer's Prague & the Best of the Czech Republic
Frommer's Provence & the Riviera
Frommer's Puerto Rico
Frommer's Rome
Frommer's San Antonio & Austin
Frommer's San Diego
Frommer's San Francisco
Frommer's Santa Fe, Taos & Albuquerque
Frommer's Scandinavia
Frommer's Scotland
Frommer's Seattle
Frommer's Shanghai
Frommer's Sicily
Frommer's Singapore & Malaysia
Frommer's South Africa
Frommer's South America
Frommer's Southeast Asia
Frommer's South Florida
Frommer's South Pacific
Frommer's Spain
Frommer's Sweden
Frommer's Switzerland
Frommer's Texas
Frommer's Thailand
Frommer's Tokyo
Frommer's Toronto
Frommer's Turkey
Frommer's USA
Frommer's Utah
Frommer's Vancouver & Victoria
Frommer's Vermont, New Hampshire & Maine
Frommer's Vienna & the Danube Valley
Frommer's Virginia
Frommer's Virgin Islands
Frommer's Walt Disney World® & Orland
Frommer's Washington, D.C.
Frommer's Washington State

Frommer's

(W) WILE

erywhere.

FROMMER'S® COMPLETE TRAVEL GUIDES

Alaska
Alaska Cruises & Ports of Call
American Southwest
Amsterdam
Argentina & Chile
Arizona
Atlanta
Australia
Austria
Bahamas
Barcelona, Madrid & Seville
Beijing
Belgium, Holland & Luxembourg
Bermuda
Boston
Brazil
British Columbia & the Canadian
  Rockies
Brussels & Bruges
Budapest & the Best of Hungary
Calgary
California
Canada
Cancún, Cozumel & the Yucatán
Cape Cod, Nantucket & Martha's
  Vineyard
Caribbean
Caribbean Cruises & Ports of Call
Caribbean Ports of Call
Carolinas & Georgia
Chicago
China
Colorado
Costa Rica
Cuba
Denmark
Denver, Boulder & Colorado
  Springs
England
Europe
Europe by Rail
European Cruises & Ports of Call

Florence, Tuscany & Umbria
Florida
France
Germany
Great Britain
Greece
Greek Islands
Halifax
Hawaii
Hong Kong
Honolulu, Waikiki & Oahu
India
Ireland
Israel
Italy
Jamaica
Japan
Kauai
Las Vegas
London
Los Angeles
Maryland & Delaware
Maui
Mexico
Montana & Wyoming
Montréal & Québec City
Munich & the Bavarian Alps
Nashville & Memphis
Newfoundland & Labrador
New England
New Mexico
New Orleans
New York City
New York State
New Zealand
Northern Italy
Norway
Nova Scotia, New Brunswick &
  Prince Edward Island
Oregon
Ottawa
Paris

Peru
Philadelphia & the Amish
  Country
Portugal
Prague & the Best of the Czech
  Republic
Provence & the Riviera
Puerto Rico
Rome
San Antonio & Austin
San Diego
San Francisco
Santa Fe, Taos & Albuquerque
Scandinavia
Scotland
Seattle
Shanghai
Sicily
Singapore & Malaysia
South Africa
South America
South Florida
South Pacific
Southeast Asia
Spain
Sweden
Switzerland
Texas
Thailand
Tokyo
Toronto
USA
Utah
Vancouver & Victoria
Vermont, New Hampshire &
  Maine
Vienna & the Danube Valley
Virgin Islands
Virginia
Walt Disney World® & Orlando
Washington, D.C.
Washington State

FROMMER'S® DOLLAR-A-DAY GUIDES

Australia from $50 a Day
California from $70 a Day
England from $75 a Day
Europe from $70 a Day
Florida from $70 a Day
Hawaii from $80 a Day

Ireland from $80 a Day
Italy from $70 a Day
London from $90 a Day
New York from $90 a Day
Paris from $90 a Day
San Francisco from $70 a Day

Washington, D.C. from $80 a
  Day
Portable London from $90 a Day
Portable New York City from $90
  a Day
Portable Paris from $90 a Day

FROMMER'S® PORTABLE GUIDES

Acapulco, Ixtapa & Zihuatanejo
Amsterdam
Aruba
Australia's Great Barrier Reef
Bahamas
Berlin
Big Island of Hawaii
Boston
California Wine Country
Cancún
Cayman Islands
Charleston
Chicago
Disneyland®
Dominican Republic
Dublin

Florence
Frankfurt
Hong Kong
Las Vegas
Las Vegas for Non-Gamblers
London
Los Angeles
Los Cabos & Baja
Maine Coast
Maui
Miami
Nantucket & Martha's Vineyard
New Orleans
New York City
Paris

Phoenix & Scottsdale
Portland
Puerto Rico
Puerto Vallarta, Manzanillo &
  Guadalajara
Rio de Janeiro
San Diego
San Francisco
Savannah
Vancouver
Vancouver Island
Venice
Virgin Islands
Washington, D.C.
Whistler

FROMMER'S® NATIONAL PARK GUIDES

Algonquin Provincial Park
Banff & Jasper
Family Vacations in the National
  Parks

Grand Canyon
National Parks of the American
  West
Rocky Mountain

Yellowstone & Grand Teton
Yosemite & Sequoia/Kings
  Canyon
Zion & Bryce Canyon

FROMMER'S® MEMORABLE WALKS

Chicago
London

New York
Paris

San Francisco

FROMMER'S® WITH KIDS GUIDES

Chicago
Las Vegas
New York City

Ottawa
San Francisco
Toronto

Vancouver
Walt Disney World® & Orlando
Washington, D.C.

SUZY GERSHMAN'S BORN TO SHOP GUIDES

Born to Shop: France
Born to Shop: Hong Kong,
  Shanghai & Beijing

Born to Shop: Italy
Born to Shop: London

Born to Shop: New York
Born to Shop: Paris

FROMMER'S® IRREVERENT GUIDES

Amsterdam
Boston
Chicago
Las Vegas
London

Los Angeles
Manhattan
New Orleans
Paris
Rome

San Francisco
Seattle & Portland
Vancouver
Walt Disney World®
Washington, D.C.

FROMMER'S® BEST-LOVED DRIVING TOURS

Austria
Britain
California
France

Germany
Ireland
Italy
New England

Northern Italy
Scotland
Spain
Tuscany & Umbria

THE UNOFFICIAL GUIDES®

Beyond Disney
Central Italy
Chicago
Cruises
Disneyland®
England
Florida
Florida with Kids
Inside Disney

Hawaii
Las Vegas
London
Maui
Mexico's Best Beach Resorts
Mini Las Vegas
Mini-Mickey
New Orleans
New York City

Paris
San Francisco
Skiing & Snowboarding in the
  West
Walt Disney World®
Walt Disney World® for
  Grown-ups
Walt Disney World® with Kids
Washington, D.C.

SPECIAL-INTEREST TITLES

Athens Past & Present
Cities Ranked & Rated
Frommer's Best Day Trips from London
Frommer's Caribbean Hideaways
Frommer's China: The 50 Most Memorable Trips
Frommer's Exploring America by RV
Frommer's Gay & Lesbian Europe
Frommer's Best RV and Tent Campgrounds
  in the U.S.A.

Frommer's Road Atlas Europe
Frommer's Road Atlas France
Frommer's Road Atlas Ireland
Frommer's Wonderful Weekends from
  New York City
The New York Times' Guide to Unforgettable
  Weekends
Retirement Places Rated
Rome Past & Present

Booked aisle seat.

Reserved room with a view.

With a queen – no, make that a king-size bed.

Fly.
Sleep.
Save.

Now you can book your flights and
hotels together, so you can get even better deals
than if you booked them separately.

Travelocity
Visit www.travelocity.com
or call 1-888-TRAVELOCITY